South Vietnam

Volume 2

U.S.-Communist
Confrontation in
Southeast Asia

1966-1967

South Vietnam

Volume 2

U.S.-Communist Confrontation in Southeast Asia

1966-1967

Edited by Lester A. Sobel
Contributing editor: Hal Kosut

FACTS ON FILE, INC.   NEW YORK, N.Y.

South Vietnam

Volume 2
U.S.-Communist Confrontation in Southeast Asia

1966-67

Published by Facts on File, Inc.,
119 West 57th Street, New York, N.Y. 10019.

Originally published as an Interim History paperback by Facts On File, Inc.

Library of Congress Card Catalog No. 66-23943
ISBN 0-87196-162-8

9 8 7 6 5 4 3 2
PRINTED IN
THE UNITED STATES OF AMERICA

CONTENTS

1967

Preface

THE FIGHTING IN VIETNAM increased in intensity—and so did the confusion and controversy about the issues involved—since the events recorded in *South Vietnam: U.S.-Communist Confrontation in Southeast Asia (Volume I) 1961-1965*.

Like most of the other volumes in the FACTS ON FILE series, these books on Vietnam are largely a journalistic narration of events in the field they cover. They attempt to set down the facts of a particularly confusing conflict, and they try to present fairly the different arguments about these facts. Great pains are taken to avoid bias. The principal objective of this series is to bring together the information needed for an adequate understanding of one of the most troubling periods of American history.

The material in these books is based largely on FACTS ON FILE's weekly reports. Of necessity, the greatest source of information used has been the press—American and foreign. Reports and statements of all governments involved, Communist as well as non-Communist, have also been used in an effort to fill any gaps in information and to provide a balanced and accurate reference work.

1

1966

The tempo of the Vietnamese war accelerated in 1966, mainly because of the commitment of large numbers of U.S. troops to combat. During the year the U.S. more than doubled its forces in South Vietnam, and the Viet Cong and North Vietnamese forces were reported to have substantially increased their combat strength despite attacks of American bombers against North Vietnam and against the Ho Chi Minh Trail, the Communist supply route through Laos. Peace seemed as far away at the end of the year as it did at the beginning. Although the year began and ended with short holiday battlefield truces, the 2d series of truces was not complemented—as had been the first—by a prolonged cessation of American bombing attacks against North Vietnam. The combatants failed to find an acceptable formula for going to the peace table despite "peace missions" and "peace feelers" that were reported throughout the year.

PEACE EFFORTS CONTINUE

U.S. Envoys Seek Peace Talks

The U.S. diplomatic drive for peace talks that had begun in the closing weeks of 1965 continued into the first weeks of 1966. U.S. Amb.-to-UN Arthur J. Goldberg and Vice Pres. Hubert H. Humphrey were among a number of high-ranking diplomatic envoys sent by Pres. Lyndon B. Johnson to world capitals to restate and seek support for U.S. policy while sounding out the possibilities of a negotiated settlement of the Vietnamese war. Goldberg and Humphrey returned to the U.S. in the first week of January, but Amb.-at-Large W. Averell Harriman and Asst. State Secy. (for African Affairs) G. Mennen Williams continued the diplomatic drive through mid-January. Harriman conferred with Eastern European and Asian leaders, Williams with African leaders.

An extended suspension of American bombing raids against North Vietnam accompanied the peace drive.

Discussing the U.S. peace campaign, Mr. Johnson said in his State-of-the-Union message Jan. 12: "So far we have received no response to prove either success or failure." "In 1965 alone we had 300 private talks for peace in Vietnam with friends and adversaries throughout the world." The U.S.' position had been made "abundantly clear" to 113 nations "that we have relations with and some that we don't." "I am hopeful, and I will try as best I can with everything I've got to end this battle and to return our sons to their desires." "There may be some who do not want peace, whose ambitions stretch so far that war in Vietnam is but a welcome and convenient episode in an immense design to subdue history to their will. But for others it must now be clear. The choice is not between peace and victory. It lies between peace and the ravages of a conflict from which they can only lose."

Principal developments of the U.S. peace drive:

Goldberg mission — Goldberg returned to Washington Jan. 2 following a European tour that included meetings with Pope Paul VI, French Pres. Charles de Gaulle and British Prime Min. Harold Wilson. Goldberg reported informally to Pres. Johnson Jan. 4. After the meeting, Goldberg said at a news conference that during his meetings with the European leaders he had informed them of the U.S. decision to suspend air strikes against North Vietnam. "Many people and some governments had said" that these bombings "stood in the way of a peaceful settlement," Goldberg reported. He said he had urged the European leaders to judge America in the light of the raid suspension on the assumption that "actions speak louder than words." Goldberg thus became the first U.S. official to acknowledge publicly the U.S. raid suspension that had been in effect since Dec. 24, 1965. (North Vietnam officially acknowledged the suspension the same day but accused the U.S. in a Foreign Ministry statement of halting the bombings as a trick to obtain concessions for ending illegal acts.)

Goldberg returned to UN headquarters in New York Jan. 5 and circulated a letter (dated Jan. 4) appealing to UN Secy. Gen. U Thant and UN members to employ "any appropriate measure" to "advance the cause of a peaceful settlement." Goldberg said that the purpose of the current American peace mission was to "make sure that the channels of communications are open, that there is no misunderstanding about positions, so that it is crystal clear what the attitudes are, at least on the part of the [U.S.] government." Goldberg's letter said that the U.S. position, as presented to foreign capitals by Washington's envoys, included these points: The U.S. was "prepared for discussions or negotiations without prior conditions whatsoever or on the basis of the Geneva accords"; the U.S. was ready to withdraw its forces from South Vietnam as soon as the Saigon government was "in a position to determine its own future"; the U.S. sought no permanent military base in South Vietnam; South Vietnam's political future should be determined by the South Vietnamese people, and "the question of the reunification of the 2 Vietnams should be decided by the free decision of their 2 peoples." The letter said the U.S. was prepared to "collaborate unconditionally" with the UN Security Council in the search for peace in Southeast Asia.

Goldberg had reviewed the Vietnam situation in talks with Prime Min. Wilson in London Jan. 1. Goldberg said later that Wilson was pursuing his "constructive efforts to

NORTH
& SOUTH
VIETNAM
& THEIR
NEIGHBORS

- - - International boundary
⊛ National capital
—— Road
+—+ Railroad

0 20 40   80   120 Miles
0 20 40   80   120 Kilometers

bring about an honorable and peaceful solution" and that the U.S. welcomed his efforts.

Humphrey mission—On his return to Washington Jan. 3 from a 5-day tour of Japan, Nationalist China, South Korea and the Philippines, Vice Pres. Humphrey reported to Pres. Johnson and his chief military and foreign policy advisers. Mr. Johnson said the mission was "very successful." Humphrey said at a news conference later that he had submitted to the officials he had visited copies of a document titled "The Heart of the Matter." The 3-page paper, drawn up by Humphrey and State Secy. Dean Rusk, summarized U.S. efforts to promote an international conference on Vietnam and restated Washington's conditions for peace. "We have put everything into the basket of peace except the surrender of South Vietnam," the document said. White House Press Secy. Bill D. Moyers said the pamphlet contained the essence of the U.S. peace message that had been delivered to foreign leaders by the other U.S. emissaries.

On disembarking from his plane earlier Jan. 3, Humphrey had said he had found no evidence on his tour that the Communists were willing to sit down at the conference table. After visiting the Philippines Dec. 31, 1965, Humphrey had flown to Taipei, where he conferred Jan. 1 with Chinese Nationalist Pres. Chiang Kai-shek. Humphrey left later Jan. 1 for Seoul. He said on arriving at the South Korean capital that the purpose of his visits to Tokyo (Dec. 28-29), Manila, Taipei and Seoul was to convey "to our friends . . . our solidarity with them" and "to have an exchange" of views on world problems, particularly Southeast Asia. Humphrey met Jan. 2 with South Korean Foreign Min. Lee Tong Won, Premier Chung Il Kwon and Pres. Chung Hee Park. Premier Chung was quoted as having told Humphrey that "South Vietnam should not become another Panmunjom." Before returning to the U.S., Humphrey stopped off in Honolulu Jan. 2. In an address after receiving an honorary degree at the University of Hawaii, Humphrey said he had learned on his tour that non-Communist Asia was "not willing to have peace at the sacrifice of a neighbor."

Harriman mission—Amb.-at-Large Harriman who had started his peace mission with a visit to Warsaw Dec. 29, 1965, met with Yugoslav Pres. Tito in Slovenia Jan. 1. Other leaders with whom Harriman conferred during his trip to explain U.S. policy on Vietnam: Jan. 3—Indian Prime Min. Lal Bahadur Shastri in New Delhi; Pakistani Pres. Mohammed Ayub Khan in Peshawar, West Pakistan; Iranian Shah Mohammed Riza Pahlevi in Teheran. Jan. 4—UAR Pres. Gamal Abdel Nasser in Cairo. Jan. 6—Thai Foreign Min. Thanat Khoman in Bangkok. Jan. 7—Japanese Premier Eisaku Sato in Tokyo.

Harriman said in Tokyo Jan. 7 that "all the men I have talked to" on the mission "accept the President's sincerity in urging peace." Sato was reported Jan. 8 to have stressed in his talks with Harriman that the U.S. should continue the suspension of air strikes against North Vietnam for at least 2 weeks. Harriman was said to have replied that extension of the bombing pause depended on the reaction of Hanoi to the U.S.' current peace drive and the extent of the Viet Cong's aggressive actions in South Vietnam. Harriman arrived in Canberra Jan. 9 and said in an airport statement: "Peiping [Peking] does not want peace, but let's hope sanity prevails in Hanoi and ends this struggle the honorable way." He conferred with Australian officials Jan. 12, then flew to Vientiane, where he conferred Jan. 13 with Laotian Premier Souvanna Phouma and other Laotian officials.

Harriman then continued on to Bangkok, Thailand, where he met with U.S. State Secy. Dean Rusk. Harriman and Rusk flew to Saigon Jan. 15 and held immediate discussions with South Vietnamese Premier Nguyen Cao Ky, Foreign Min. Tran Van Do and Chief of State Nguyen Van Thieu. They also met with U.S. Amb. Henry Cabot Lodge and Gen. William C. Westmoreland, commander of U.S. forces in South Vietnam. The Saigon mission reportedly was aimed at allaying South Vietnamese fears that the U.S. peace drive would be detrimental to the Saigon government. (Maj. Gen. Pham Xuan Chieu, secretary of South Vietnam's 11-general National Leadership Council, had declared at an armed forces congress Jan. 14 that victory over the Viet Cong was the only means of achieving peace and that any peace terms must guarantee South Vietnam's territory and sovereignty. Ky told the congress Jan. 15 that Vietnam insisted on "a peace that will guarantee its freedom, independence, sovereignty and territorial integrity.") A communiqué issued Jan. 16 at the conclusion of the U.S.-South Vietnamese talks said: Ky and Rusk had "agreed that the Vietnamese government and its allies must continue to take all necessary measures while remaining alert to all proposals and initiatives that might lead to peace." "The basic positions of the 2 governments were consistent in all fundamental respects" in the efforts to attain a peaceful settlement of the war and at the same time protect South Vietnam from a Communist take-over; the U.S. would continue to support South Vietnam in the war against the Viet Cong and North Vietnamese troops; the U.S. would "do all in its power" to provide South Vietnam with economic assistance. The communiqué restated Saigon's demands that "all aggression" in South Vietnam must stop before Ky's regime would attend a peace conference.

Rusk and Harriman, accompanied by Sen. John Sherman Cooper (R., Ky.), flew to Manila Jan. 16 and conferred with Philippine Pres. Ferdinand E. Marcos. The 3 Americans departed for Washington Jan. 17.

Williams mission—Asst. State Secy. Williams confined his Vietnam peace mission to African states Jan. 3-6. He met with leaders in Tunisia, Ethiopia, Morocco, Algeria, Kenya, Tanzania, Uganda, Nigeria, Ghana, the Ivory Coast, Liberia, Guinea and Senegal.

Communists Reject U.S. Overtures

The U.S. diplomatic drive was uniformly condemned by the Communist side—especially by Communist China and North Vietnam.

The Chinese Communist Party newspaper *Jenmin Jih Pao (People's Daily),* in an editorial Jan. 1, described the U.S. emissaries visiting world capitals as "monsters and freaks" who were "raising a lot of dust with their sinister activities." The newspaper said: "Paralleled with its frenzied preparation for expanding its war of aggression against Vietnam," the U.S.

"has lately been chanting its worn-out tune of 'peace' more loudly than ever before"; the U.S. was the "common enemy of the people of the whole world"; Soviet policies were "Khrushchev revisionism." In a further comment on the U.S. peace efforts, *Jenmin Jih Pao* Jan. 5 urged "the well-intentioned people" visited by the American emissaries not to be taken in by Washington's "peace-talks hoax." The newspaper said the U.S.' peace overtures were a prelude to expansion of the war and the eventual permanent occupation by the U.S. of South Vietnam.

The Communist Chinese news agency, Hsinhua, said Jan. 1 that North Vietnam had rejected Washington's latest peace overtures. Quoting Hanoi radio and *Nhan Dan*, North Vietnam's Communist Party newspaper, Hsinhua said North Vietnam had "scuttled the conspiratorial schemes of United States imperialists and reiterated the solemn stand for the withdrawal of United States aggressors from South Vietnam." The U.S.' Vietnam peace missions were denounced by *Nhan Dan* Jan. 3 as "a noisy propaganda campaign" and "a trick aimed at screening their plans of war intensification and expansion."

A more detailed response to the U.S.' peace drive and Hanoi's first reaction to the pause in air strikes against North Vietnam were made in a statement issued Jan. 4 by the North Vietnamese Foreign Ministry. The Hanoi statement said: The U.S. moves were "a largescale deceptive peace campaign coupled with the trick of 'temporary suspension of air attacks' on North Vietnam." The "new 'peace proposals'" carried by Washington's emissaries were "actually a mere repetition of old themes." Despite the halt in the raids, the U.S. "still brazenly gives itself the right to launch air attacks" on North Vietnam. The U.S. "has no right to impose" on North Vietnam "any condition whatsoever in exchange for stopping its air raids on North Vietnam." The U.S.' "real purpose" in calling for "unconditional discussions" was "to carry out the plot of conducting negotiations from a position of strength and attempting to force on the Vietnamese people acceptance of United States terms." Hanoi's 4-point peace formula for Vietnam remained the "concentrated expression of the essential military and political provisions" of the Geneva agreements on Vietnam. The U.S., "with the puppet regime rigged up by itself in Saigon," was "clinging to South Vietnam and perpetuating the partition of Vietnam." "While making a noise about its 'peace efforts,' the United States is making feverish preparations to double the United States strength in South Vietnam." The U.S. had "intensified its air attacks on the liberated areas in Laos and impudently authorized United States troops to intrude into central Laos and into Cambodian territory, thus extending the war from South Vietnam to these 2 countries."

The U.S.' peace offensive was described Jan. 5 by the National Liberation Front (NLF), political arm of the Communist Viet Cong, as a "smokescreen" designed to "cover up" a "crazy and adventurous policy of military build-up and to hoodwink public opinion." The NLF statement, broadcast Jan. 7 by North Vietnam radio, said U.S. diplomats were being sent to world capitals to "stage buffoonery of U.S. 'peace efforts,' to advertise the 'suspension' of bombing raids on North Vietnam as a gesture of goodwill."

The Soviet Union had charged Jan. 2 that the U.S. planned to extend the Vietnamese war to Laos and Cambodia. The accusation was made by the Communist Party newspaper *Pravda,* which asked: "How can this be reconciled with Washington's notorious attempts to achieve peace in Vietnam about which American propaganda has now raised such an outcry?"

A 5-man Soviet mission led by Communist Party (CP) Central Committee Secy. Aleksandr N. Shelepin visited Hanoi Jan. 7-12 and paved the way for a Soviet pledge of increased military aid to North Vietnam. The military assistance pledge was made in a communiqué issued in Moscow Jan. 14, one day after Shelepin had returned to the Soviet capital. The amount and type of the military aid was not disclosed. Citing Soviet support of North Vietnam's 4-point peace formula and the NLF's prerequisites for negotiations, the communiqué asserted that "these positions are the only correct basis for solving the Vietnamese problem."

The 5 Soviet officials accompanying Shelepin were: Col. Gen. Vladimir F. Tolubko, first deputy commander-in-chief of the Strategic Rocket Command; Dmitri Ustinov, a CP secretary and leading Soviet arms production expert; Konstantin Rusakov, deputy chief of the department handling relations between the Soviet CP and foreign Communist parties; Anatoly S. Chistyakov, head of the Soviet Foreign Ministry's Southeast Asia Department; Ilya Shcherbakov, Soviet ambassador to North Vietnam.

During his 6-day visit, Shelepin conferred with Pres. Ho, Premier Pham Van Dong and other North Vietnamese officials. At a reception in Hanoi Jan. 8, Shelepin declared that Moscow fully supported North Vietnam and the NLF "on the settlement of the Vietnam problem." At a public meeting in Hanoi Jan. 9 Shelepin assailed the U.S. peace drive. He said that "while advertising for its so-called 'peace-initiative,' the United States simultaneously continues to increase its troops in South Vietnam and to introduce more military and technical equipment." Shelepin appealed to all Communist states "to pool their efforts to render all assistance to Vietnam" in its "struggle against the [U.S.'] aggressive policy." Speaking at a Soviet embassy reception honoring Shelepin and his party, Premier Dong Jan. 11 thanked the USSR and other Communist countries for giving North Vietnam "great and valuable" economic and military assistance. He said the Vietnamese had "always enjoyed the support" of the Soviet Union "and also that of other fraternal Socialist countries."

Before returning to Moscow the Soviet mission flew to Peking Jan. 13 for an overnight stay. A Communist Chinese government reception was given by Le Hsien-nien, a vice premier. (Shelepin and his group had stopped over briefly in Peking Jan. 7 for refueling en route to Hanoi.) Communist China had charged Jan. 6 that the Soviet mission to Hanoi was linked to the U.S.' peace campaign. Hsinhua said: "Notable is the fact" that the USSR had announced the Shelepin visit to Hanoi the day before the U.S. had started its "peace offensive."

Polish United Workers' (Communist) Party First Secy. Wladyslaw Gomulka, who had discussed the Vietnam situation in Warsaw with U.S. Amb.-at-Large W. Averell Harriman in Dec. 1965, said in a New Year's message Jan. 1: The question of whether peace or war would prevail "depends on whether common sense will win the U.S.A. and point out the necessity to return from the . . . road of aggression against the Vietnamese people, or whether political blindness to the contemporary realities of the world will continue to lead."

North Vietnamese and U.S. Terms

Both North Vietnam and the U.S. had placed on the record their conditions for a peaceful settlement in Vietnam. The Communist terms, generally referred to as "the 4 points," were stated by North Vietnamese Premier Pham Van Dong in a speech to the North Vietnamese National Assembly Apr. 8, 1965 and repeated Apr. 20, 1965 in the North Vietnamese reply to a peace plea made by 17 non-aligned nations.* The U.S. position was stated by various U.S. spokesmen on different occasions; a 14-point list based on statements made by these spokesmen was made public by U.S. Vice Pres. Humphrey Jan. 3, 1966 as "elements which the U.S. believes can go into peace in Southeast Asia."

The North Vietnamese "4 points":

1. Recognition of the basic national rights of the Vietnamese people—peace, independence, sovereignty, unity, and territorial integrity. In accordance with the Geneva Agreements, the U.S. government must withdraw from South Vietnam U.S. troops, military personnel, and weapons of all kinds, dismantle all U.S. military bases there, and cancel its military alliance with South Vietnam. It must end its policy of intervention and aggression in South Vietnam. In accordance with the Geneva Agreements, the U.S. government must stop its acts of war against North Vietnam, and completely cease all encroachments on the territory and sovereignty of the Democratic Republic of Vietnam.

2. Pending the peaceful reunification of Vietnam, while Vietnam is still temporarily divided into two zones, the military provisions of the 1954 Geneva Agreements on Vietnam must be strictly respected. The two zones must refrain from joining any military alliance with foreign countries. There must be no foreign military bases, troops or military personnel in the respective territories.

---

*The U.S. and other parties to the Vietnamese dispute had received an appeal Apr. 1, 1965 from these 17 non-aligned nations seeking peaceful solution of the war: Afghanistan, Algeria, Cyprus, Ceylon, Ethiopia, Ghana, Guinea, India, Iraq, Kenya, Nepal, Syria, Tunisia, UAR, Uganda, Yugoslavia and Zambia.

3. The internal affairs of South Vietnam must be settled by the South Vietnamese people themselves, in accordance with the program of the National Front for the Liberation of South Vietnam, without any foreign interference.

4. The peaceful reunification of Vietnam is to be settled by the Vietnamese people in both zones, without any foreign interference. . . .

The U.S.' 14 points :

1. The Geneva Agreements of 1954 and 1962 are an adequate basis for peace in Southeast Asia;

2. We would welcome a conference on Southeast Asia or on any part thereof;

3. We would welcome "negotiations without preconditions" as the 17 nations put it;

4. We would welcome unconditional discussions as Pres. Johnson put it;

5. A cessation of hostilities could be the first order of business at a conference or could be the subject of preliminary discussions;

6. Hanoi's 4 points could be discussed along with other points which others might wish to propose;

7. We want no U.S. bases in Southeast Asia;

8. We do not desire to retain U.S. troops in South Vietnam after peace is assured;

9. We support free elections in South Vietnam to give the South Vietnamese a government of their own choice;

10. The question of reunification of Vietnam should be determined by the Vietnamese through their own free decision;

11. The countries of Southeast Asia can be non-aligned or neutral if that be their option;

12. We would much prefer to use our resources for the economic reconstruction of Southeast Asia than in war. If there is peace, North Vietnam could participate in a regional effort to which we would be prepared to contribute at least $1 billion;

13. The President has said: "The Viet Cong would not have difficulty being represented and having their views represented if for a moment Hanoi decided she wanted to cease aggression. I don't think that would be an insurmountable problem."

14. We have said publicly and privately that we could stop the bombing of North Vietnam as a step toward peace although there has not been the slightest hint or suggestion from the other side as to what they would do if the bombing stopped.

U.S. Note to North Vietnam

White House Press Secy. Bill D. Moyers acknowledged Jan. 10 that a U.S. official had met with a North Vietnamese representative and had handed him an Administration note. This was the first direct contact between Hanoi and Washington representatives. Moyers would not say when or where the meeting had taken place nor disclose the note's contents. Rep. Cornelius Gallagher (D., N.J.), a member of the House Foreign Affairs Committee, said in Washington Jan. 11 that the U.S. note had been handed to the Hanoi representative shortly after the 1965 Christmas Eve truce had gone into effect, when the U.S. had suspended air strikes against North Vietnam. The letter reportedly informed Hanoi of the raid pause and suggested peace negotiations. It was reported in Washington Feb. 5 that U.S. Amb.-to-Burma Henry A. Byroade had made the contact with North Vietnam. Byroade was said to have handed a note Dec. 29, 1965 to the North Vietnamese consulate in Rangoon. The message was said to have contained the 14-point U.S. summation of American policy on Vietnam.

Hanoi's receipt of the U.S. note had been confirmed in Paris Jan. 15 by Sanford Gottlieb of the National Committee for a Sane Nuclear Policy (SANE), a private U.S. peace organization. Gottlieb said he had met with North Vietnamese and Viet Cong officials in Paris and Algiers and had received the impression that Hanoi's silence did not mean rejection of the U.S. message. He said the Communists were analyzing it and had not decided how to answer it.

Pres. Johnson called on North Vietnam Jan. 20 to respond positively to the U.S. peace drive and the bombing pause by agreeing to enter negotiations to end the war. The President made the plea one day prior to a 3-day battlefield truce that was to go into effect Jan. 20 to mark the Vietnamese Lunar New Year, *Tet*. The Viet Cong had initiated the truce Jan. 15 with an order to their forces to cease fighting between Jan. 20 and 24. The U.S. and allied commands announced later that they would comply with a South Vietnamese decision to honor the truce from noon Jan. 20 to 6 p.m. Jan. 23. The truce was observed despite reports of sporadic clashes. The President's statement was made at ceremonies in Independence, Mo. in observance of the establishment in Israel of the Harry S. Truman Center for the Advancement of Peace. The President said: "What is holding up peace is the mistaken view on the part of the aggressors that the United

States is going to give up our principles, that we will yield to pressure, or abandon our allies, or finally get tired and get out." "If the aggressors are ready for peace, . . . let them come to the meeting place and we will meet with them there."

Ho Chi Minh Jan. 24 assailed U.S. peace overtures and demanded that Washington instead accept Hanoi's 4-point peace formula as the basis for ending the war. Ho's statement, made in messages to the leaders of Communist and non-Communist nations, was made public Jan. 28. He charged that Pres. Johnson's State-of-the-Union Message (in which the President Jan. 12 had said the U.S. would not pull out of South Vietnam and he "hoped the Vietnamese people would choose between peace" and war) was an "impudent . . . attempt to impose on the Vietnamese people the conditions of the so-called U.S. unconditional discussion." Ho said that if Washington "really wants peace it must recognize" the National Liberation Front "as the sole genuine representative of the people of South Vietnam," and "it must end unconditionally and for good all bombing raids and other acts of war" against North Vietnam.

Reviewing the American peace drive, State Secy. Dean Rusk had said at a news conference in Washington Jan. 21 that U.S. diplomatic efforts had evoked "an overwhelming favorable response" "except from those who could, in fact, sit down and make peace." He said: The U.S. suspension of air strikes against North Vietnam, in its 29th day, provided North Vietnamese officials with "every opportunity" "to make some serious response"; but "I regret that I cannot report . . . any positive and encouraging response to the hopes of the overwhelming majority of mankind." U.S. reconnaissance flights had shown that the North Vietnamese had taken advantage of the bombing lull by repairing many of their bombed-out installations; "this is a matter that was taken fully into account" when the decision had been made in Dec. 1965 to suspend the raids.

On the matter of whether the U.S. would favor the inclusion of the National Liberation Front (NLF) in future peace talks as a political entity, Rusk said: the NLF was "only a fraction of the South Vietnamese people"; although

Pres. Johnson did not oppose considering the NLF's views, "that does not mean that they are the representatives of the South Vietnamese people"; "the overwhelming majority" of South Vietnamese "want something other than what the Liberation Front has been offering." "The central issue" in Vietnam was: "Is Hanoi going to . . . refrain from trying to impose a political solution on South Vietnam by force? If the answer is 'Yes, . . .' then peace can be brought about very quickly. If their answer is 'No,' then we will have to do what is required."

Sen. George McGovern (D., S.D.) had said Jan. 4 that any negotiation of the Vietnamese war should "be primarily between the 2 competing groups in South Vietnam"—the South Vietnamese government and the NLF. McGovern, who had recently returned from a visit to South Vietnam, held that the exclusion of these 2 parties remained the "basic flaw" in U.S. peace proposals. McGovern said: "This war began as a local conflict in South Vietnam, and that is still the primary battle ground, no matter how many major powers feel called upon to gamble their national honor" on South Vietnamese Premier Nguyen Cao Ky and North Vietnamese Pres. Ho Chi Minh. Sen. Frank Church (D., Ida.), supporting McGovern's views, said Jan. 4 that the U.S. "can back Saigon at the negotiating table as Hanoi can back the Viet Cong, but neither the American government nor the government of North Vietnam can end the revolution in South Vietnam without the participation and consent of those engaged in it." (Although the U.S. had not advocated direct NLF participation in future peace talks, Pres. Johnson had stated that the NLF "would not have difficulty being represented and having their views represented.")

In a letter made public Jan. 22, Pres. Johnson assured 76 U.S. House members (who had told him of their concern about a possible expansion of the war) that there would be "no abandonment of our peace efforts" despite "continuing hostility and aggressiveness in Hanoi and an insistence on the abandonment of South Vietnam to Communist take-over." Despite the American bombing pause, Mr. Johnson pointed out, "the infiltration of the aggressors' forces has continued, and so have his attacks on our allies and on our own men. I am sure you will agree that we have a heavy obligation not to add lightly to the dangers our troops must face. We must give them the support they need."

Senate minority leader Everett M. Dirksen (R., Ill.) Jan. 8 had expressed open opposition for the first time to Pres. Johnson's repeated offer of "negotiations without prior conditions." Dirksen asserted that there must be total "victory" over the Viet Cong "before negotiations." Dirksen urged extension of the war by blockading North Vietnam, particularly the country's major port of Haiphong. Dirksen criticized Britain, France and Turkey for having failed to join the U.S. military effort. He assailed what he called the continued allied trade with North Vietnam. (The U.S. State Department had reported Jan. 4 that non-Communist countries' shipments to North Vietnam had decreased under U.S. pressure. Department spokesman Robert J. McCloskey said that in the period Aug.-Nov. 1965, 13 non-Communist ships a month had put in at North Vietnamese ports, compared with a 1964 monthly average of 34 vessels.)

Japanese Premier Eisaku Sato said Jan. 25 that the U.S. halt in air strikes against North Vietnam and the American peace missions had not produced "the desired result." He reported that Japanese Foreign Min. Etsusaburo Shiina had unsuccessfully supported the U.S. "peace offensive" while conferring with Soviet leaders in Moscow the previous week. At a meeting Jan. 21 with U.S. Amb.-to-Japan Edwin O. Reischauer, Sato had urged that the U.S. not resume its bombing raids while Japan pressed its own diplomatic peace efforts. Sato said Japan strongly favored a settlement of the war and supported the U.S.' peace drive. (Takechiyo Matsuda of Japan's ruling Liberation Democratic Party said Apr. 19 that Ho Chi Minh had rejected his offer to meet him in Hanoi to discuss the war. Matsuda said he had received from Ho a cable stating that the time was not propitious.)

Staughton Lynd's Trip to Hanoi

Harvard Prof. Staughton Lynd, accompanied by Dr. Herbert Aptheker and Thomas Hayden, returned to New York Jan. 9 after a 10-day visit to North Vietnam. At an airport news conference Lynd reported on a 90-minute interview the trio had held with North Vietnamese Premier Pham Van Dong. He quoted Dong as saying: A "political settlement of the Vietnam problem" could be attained "only when the United States has accepted the 4-point stand of the government of the Democratic Republic of Vietnam [North Vietnam], has proved this by actual deeds and . . . has stopped unconditionally and for good its air raid and all other acts of war" against North Vietnam; then "it will be possible to consider the reconvening of an international conference of the type of the 1954 Geneva Conference on Vietnam."

Lynd added that both North Vietnam and the NLF demanded as a prerequisite for negotiations "an unambiguous decision" by the U.S. to withdraw its military forces from Vietnam. But, Lynd said, "there is no explicit requirement of the physical withdrawal of all United States troops prior to negotiations." He called the North Vietnamese suspicious of the U.S. "peace offensive" because of what they regarded as "a deep inconsistency between a peace posture looking toward a negotiated settlement and an interventionist posture which has in view the permanent partition of Vietnam and an expanded war."

Lynd had told newsmen in Moscow during an overnight stopover Jan. 8: He and his companions had asked Premier Dong whether the U.S. "had made direct contact" with North Vietnam "since Pres. Johnson stated on Dec. 20 that his Administration would knock on all doors in quest of peace. The premier answered 'No.' "

Pope Repeats Peace Pleas

Pope Paul VI Jan. 1 had made public messages he had sent Dec. 31, 1965 to Moscow, Peking, Hanoi and Saigon urging their leaders to seek an end to the Vietnamese war. The pope also disclosed that he had handed U.S. Amb.-to-UN Goldberg a message for Pres. Johnson during their meeting in Rome Dec. 31. In his note to Soviet Pres. Nikolai V. Podgorny, the pope said that "an intervention of your government" in the Vietnam crisis "could weigh greatly in leading the belligerents to a cessation of hostilities as a prelude to a final pacification" of the country. Paul's message to Chinese

Communist Party Chrmn. Mao Tse-tung expressed hope that the Peking leader "will want in this painful crisis to help favor a just solution safeguarding the independence of the country." In his messages to North Vietnamese Pres. Ho Chi Minh and South Vietnamese Chief of State Nguyen Van Thieu, the pope lauded the suspension of air strikes against North Vietnam.

The Vatican newspaper *L'Osservatore Romano* Jan. 3 disclosed the contents of the message to Pres. Johnson. The newspaper said the pope had urged Mr. Johnson to "neglect nothing which might produce a meeting of minds, to overlook no favorable occasion . . . to reach a fair and pacific solution of the Southeast Asia crisis."

The Roman Catholic Church's role as an independent force for peace free of political alignments was stressed by Pope Paul Jan. 8, in an address at a reception for diplomats accredited to the Holy See. The pope said: "We are ready, for our part, to attempt all steps—even outside the generally accepted protocol forms— every time we believe that the church can usefully bring to world leaders the weight of its moral authority for the maintenance and progress of a just peace among men and peoples."

An encyclical letter issued by Pope Paul Sept. 19 repeated the Vatican's call to world leaders to end the war in Vietnam. In it, the pope urged "those who have charge of the public welfare to strive with every means available to prevent the further spread of this conflagration and even to extinguish it entirely." The letter said that a peace settlement "should be reached now, even at the expense of some inconvenience or loss." But the pope insisted that "this peace must rest on justice . . . and take into account the rights of individuals and communities, otherwise it will be shifting and unstable." The pope designated Oct. 4 as a special day of prayer for peace.

In a speech marking the first anniversary of his 1965 peace appeal to the UN General Assembly, Pope Paul called again Oct. 4 for an end to the war in Vietnam through negotiations. Addressing 150,000 persons in St. Peter's Square in Rome, the pope repeated the statement he had made to the UN General Assembly: "Let peace reign in the world. Never again war, never again." Pope Paul said: "We will pray for peace, especially in the Far East."

A 3-member Vatican delegation representing Pope Paul visited Saigon Sept. 28-Oct. 7. The ostensible purpose of the mission was to discuss church problems with South Vietnamese Roman Catholic bishops, but the group also discussed the prospects for peace.

Mansfield Doubts Early Peace

Senate majority leader Mike Mansfield (D., Mont.) Jan. 8 expressed the view that "a rapid solution to the conflict in Vietnam is not in immediate prospect," either through military victory or through negotiations. This observation was made in a report Mansfield and 4 other Senators filed with the Senate Foreign Relations Committee. The report was based on the Senator's trip to South Vietnam and other countries Nov. 18-Dec. 18, 1965.

Despite the efforts of 3d parties to bring about peace talks, "any prospects for effective negotiations at this time are slim," the report said. Even if negotiations, accompanied by a truce, were to be held, Mansfield said, they "would serve to stabilize a situation in which a majority of the population remains under nominal government control but in which dominance of the countryside rests largely in the hands of the Viet Cong."

Mansfield warned that all of the Southeast Asian mainland "cannot be ruled out as a potential battlefield." He noted that "the war already has expanded significantly into Laos and is beginning to lap over into Cambodia while pressures increase in the northeast of Thailand." Mansfield expressed fear that if the U.S. peace offensive failed, a general Southeast Asian war would ensue.

Except for South Korea, which had provided 20,000 troops, Mansfield said there was little likelihood that other nations would join the U.S. in military action in Vietnam.

Despite the U.S.' expanded military efforts in Vietnam, the report went on, the Viet Cong offensive had only been "blunted," not "driven back". The report said: The guerrillas had responded to the U.S.' increased drive with "a further strengthening of their forces by local recruitment in the South and reinforcements from the North and a general stepping up of military activity." As a result, the military situation remained "substantially the same" as it had been "at the outset of the increased U.S. military commitment."

Mansfield noted that both sides were taking advantage of the suspension of U.S. air strikes against North Vietnam by increasing forces and supplies. He said the U.S. would have to further expand its military forces in South Vietnam if the infiltration from the North continued at the current pace.

(A warning about the possible consequences of bombing Hanoi and Haiphong was delivered by Senate minority leader Everett M. Dirksen [R., Ill.] at a meeting of the Senate Republican Conference Jan. 11. He read this sentence from Mansfield's Vietnam report: "It is considered by some that Saigon, with its many vulnerabilities to sabotage and terrorism, and Hanoi, with its exposure to air attack, are mutual hostages, one for the other.")

U.S. Debates Bombing Halt

Gen. Earle G. Wheeler, chairman of the Joint Chiefs of Staff, cautioned against a permanent halt in air raids on North Vietnam. His warning came in testimony Jan. 20 before a joint session of the Senate Armed Services and Appropriations subcommittees for defense; it was made public Jan. 22. Wheeler said the U.S. had "3 blue chips" in possible negotiations: (1) the bombing of North Vietnam, (2) the presence of U.S. troops in South Vietnam and (3) the time of an ultimate American withdrawal. Wheeler challenged retired Lt. Gen. James M. Gavin's suggestion that the U.S. permanently halt air strikes against North Vietnam and withdraw its forces to enclaves along the South Vietnamese coast. Wheeler said the proposals had been "considered at a pretty high level" but had been rejected. If the U.S. had adopted Gavin's suggestions, Wheeler said, "there would be very little point in negotiation." South Vietnam "would be going down the drain before you ever got a negotiation going."

Gen. Maxwell D. Taylor, a special adviser to Pres. Johnson, said Jan. 26 that the reasons for suspending the air raids had been "exhausted" and that, therefore, the bombings should be resumed. Speaking in New York at the annual luncheon of

the Pilgrims of the United States, Taylor said that by halting
the air attacks "we have shown friends and foes the sincerity
of our peaceful purposes."

A continuation of the pause in the bombing of North
Vietnam was strongly urged Jan. 22 by a group of experts at a
meeting in Washington sponsored by 8 Democratic House
members. Arthur Larson, director of the U.S. Information
Agency in Pres. Eisenhower's Administration, was chairman
of the meeting (which had opened Jan. 21). The conferees,
including professors and former U.S. government officials,
examined Washington's Vietnam policy with the view toward
achieving a negotiated settlement of the war. They favored
political contacts between the South Vietnamese government
and the NLF. The conference had been initiated by Rep. Benjamin Rosenthal (D., N.Y.). The 7 other sponsors were Reps.
Charles C. Diggs Jr. (Mich.), Don Edwards (Calif.), Leonard
Farbstein (N.Y.), Donald M. Fraser (Minn.), Robert W. Kas-
tenmeier (Wis.), Henry S. Reuss (Wis.) and William F. Ryan
(N.Y.).

Key members of the Senate Foreign Relations Committee
Jan. 24 voiced strong support for a continuance of the bombing
pause. They expressed their views during 3 hours of closed-
door testimony by Rusk. Chrmn. J. W. Fulbright (D., Ark.)
and other committee members sought assurances from Rusk
that the committee would be consulted before the U.S. decided
to resume the bombing of North Vietnam. Fulbright said
after the meeting that Rusk had refused to make such a pledge
but promised to refer the question to Pres. Johnson. Fulbright
said: A renewal of the U.S. raids "would mean that we had
given up any hope for the present of negotiation"; it would
"stop any efforts to get a conference" and result in "ever
increasing escalation" of the conflict; the U.S.' refusal to
recognize the Viet Cong "as a party to the conference may be
very significant to the question of whether a conference may
be set up"; Rusk had opposed Fulbright's suggestion that the
Viet Cong be invited to peace talks before the bombings were
resumed.

Senate majority leader Mike Mansfield (D., Mont.), who
had attended the Foreign Relations Committee meeting, said

he was "doubtful . . . at this moment" about U.S. recognition of the Viet Cong. Mansfield called for an "indefinite" suspension of U.S. air strikes against North Vietnam. Another committee member, Sen. Richard B. Russell (D., Ga.), chairman of the Senate Armed Services Committee, urged that the bombings be resumed.

In testimony before the House Foreign Affairs Committee Jan. 26, State Secy. Rusk said that since the U.S. had stopped bombing North Vietnam Washington had extended its peace efforts "from A to Z and almost through Z." Rusk described the clamor for continuation of the bombing pause a "curious double standard." While the U.S. raids remained suspended, the Viet Cong terrorists were carrying out bombings and assassinations in South Vietnam, Rusk said. Rusk restated Administration opposition to including the Viet Cong's NLF (National Liberation Front) in peace talks. Asserting that this matter was "directly related to what the fighting is all about," Rusk said: The NLF was "organized in Hanoi in 1960, specifically for the purpose of taking over South Vietnam by force. Now, if the Viet Cong come to the conference table as full partners, they will in a sense have been victorious in the very aims that South Vietnam and the United States are pledged to prevent."

An Associated Press poll of 50 (of 100) Senators willing to express their views showed Jan. 26 that 25 favored and 25 opposed a resumption of bombing of North Vietnam. Among those listed as against the renewed raids were Sens. Mansfield, Fulbright, George D. Aiken (R., Vt.), John Sherman Cooper (R., Ky.), Thruston Morton (R., Ky.) and Robert F. Kennedy (D., N.Y.). Among the 25 for resuming the air strikes were Sens. Russell, (D., Ga.), Henry Jackson (D., Wash.) and John Stennis (D., Miss.).

A letter calling for continued suspension of the air strikes was signed by 15 Democratic Senators and presented to Pres. Johnson Jan. 27. The message said: "We believe we understand in some small degree the agony you must suffer when called upon by our Constitutional system to make judgements which may involve war or peace. We believe you should have our collective judgement before you when you make your decision." The letter had been drafted by Sens. Vance Hartke (Ind.), Eugene McCarthy (Minn.), George McGovern (S.D.), Quentin Burdick (N.D.), Lee Metcalf (Mont.), Frank E. Moss (Utah). (Moss was in London and was unable to sign the letter.) The other signers were Sens. Edward L. Bartlett (Alaska), Maurine Neuberger (Ore.), Frank Church (Ida.), William Proxmire (Wis.), Stephen M. Young (O.), Joseph S. Clark (Pa.), Ernest Gruening (Alaska) and Harrison A. Williams Jr. (N.J.).

The Senators' appeal was answered by Pres. Johnson Jan. 28 in a letter to Hartke. Mr. Johnson reminded Hartke that he, the President, was being "guided" in his actions on Vietnam in accordance with the joint Congressional resolution of Aug. 10, 1964, which gave the President broad powers to make decisions on the Vietnam situation. Mr. Johnson said his "views of the present situation remain as stated in my recent reply" to 76 House Democrats who had urged him Jan. 21 not to renew the air strikes.

Many Congress members had commented on Vietnam as Congress convened Jan. 10. Among remarks made in interviews or in statements: Sen. Cooper—"Negotiation, not escalation, should be the dominant theme of our activity now"; the President should "make clear, without reservation, that negotiations could include the Viet Cong, because it is obvious that neither negotiations nor a settlement are possible without their inclusion." . . . Sen. Joseph S. Clark (D., Pa.)—The President should have "complete freedom to play out the string for peace"; the people did not want "the reckless and impatient bomb throwers to force the President's hand or limit his flexibility of action." . . . Sen. Bourke B. Hickenlooper (R., Ia.)—"I don't see that the [U.S.] suspension [of the bombing] has accomplished anything"; "I think it is a mistake to stop the pressure." . . . Rep. Leslie C. Arends (Ill.), assistant GOP House leader—"There's a limit how long we can keep this [suspension] up"; "something" would have to be done unless North Vietnam indicated agreement "to talk things over." . . . Rep. L. Mendel Rivers (D., S.C.), chairman of the House Armed Services Committee—Resumption of the bombing "should start yesterday—no, make it the day before yesterday"; he was in favor of "unleashing" the military in Vietnam.

U.S. Resumes Air Raids on North

For the first time in 37 days, U.S. bombers struck Jan. 31 at North Vietnamese targets. Navy carrier-based planes and Air Force jets attacked ferries, bridges, roads and trucks. North Vietnam claimed 5 American planes were downed; the U.S. conceded the loss of 3. The resumption of the bombing was announced by Pres. Johnson in a radio-TV address broadcast several hours after the raids had been resumed. The President simultaneously instructed Amb. Goldberg to ask the UN Security Council to intervene in the crisis and seek an international conference to end the war and establish peace in Southeast Asia. The Council began deliberations Feb. 1.

The President's Jan. 31 statement:

. . . For 37 days no bombs fell on North Vietnam. During that time we have made a most intense and determined effort to enlist the help and support of all the world in order to persuade the government in Hanoi that peace is better than war, that talking is better than fighting and that the road to peace is open. Our effort has met with understanding and support throughout most of the world, but not in Hanoi and Peiping. From those 2 capitals have come only denunciation and rejection.

In these 37 days the efforts of our allies have been rebuffed. The efforts of neutral nations have come to nothing. We have sought without success to learn of any response to efforts made by the governments of Eastern Europe. There has been no answer to the enlightened efforts of the Vatican. Our own direct private approaches have all been in vain.

The answer of Hanoi to all is the answer that was published 3 days ago; they persist in aggression, they insist on the surrender of South Vietnam to communism. It is therefore very plain that there is no readiness or willingness to talk. No readiness for peace in that regime today.

And what is plain in words is also plain in acts.

Throughout these 37 days, even at moments of truce, there has been continued violence against the people of South Vietnam. Against their government, against their soldiers and against our American forces.

We do not regret the pause in the bombing. We yield to none in our determination to seek peace. We have given a full and decent respect to the opinions of those who thought that such a pause might give new hope for peace in the world. Some said that 10 days might do it. Others said 20. Now we have paused for twice the time suggested by some of those who urged it. And now, the world knows more clearly than it's ever known before who it is that insists on aggression, and who it is that works for peace.

The Vietnamese, American and allied troops that are engaged in South Vietnam with increasing strength and increasing success want peace, I am sure, as much as any of us here at home.

But while there is no peace, those men are entitled to the full support of American strength and American determination. And we will give them both.

As Constitutional commander in chief, I have, as I must, given proper weight to the judgment of those, all of those, who have any responsibility for counselling with me or sharing with me the burdensome decisions I am called upon to make.

The distinguished secretary of state, the secretary of defense, our national security adviser and America's professional military men represented by the Joint Chiefs of Staff, these advisers tell me that if continued immunity is given to all that supports North Vietnam aggression, the cost in lives—Vietnamese lives and American lives and allied lives—will only be greatly increased. In the light of the words and actions of the government in Hanoi, for more than 37 days now, it is our clear duty to do what we can to limit these costs. So on this Monday morning in Vietnam, at my direction, after complete and thorough consultation and agreement with the government of South Vietnam, United States aircraft have resumed action in North Vietnam.

They struck the lines of supply which support the continuing movement of men and arms against the people and the government of South Vietnam. Our air strikes on North Vietnam, from the beginning, have been aimed at military targets and have been controlled with the greatest of care.

Those who direct and supply the aggression really have no claim to immunity from military reply. The end of the pause does not mean the end of our own pursuit of peace.

That pursuit will be as determined and as unremitting as the pressure of our military strength on the field of battle.

In our continuing pursuit of peace I have instructed Amb. Goldberg at the United Nations to ask for an immediate meeting of the United Nations Security Council. He will present a full report on the situation in Vietnam and a resolution which can open the way to the conference table.

This report and this resolution will be responsive to the spirit of the renewed appeal of Pope Paul, and that appeal has our full sympathy.

I have asked Secy. Rusk to meet with the representatives of the press later this morning to give to the country and to the entire world a thorough and a comprehensive account of all of the diplomatic efforts conducted in these last 5 weeks in our continuing policy of peace and freedom for South Vietnam.

The Presidential order to resume the raids had been sent
to the U.S. command in South Vietnam Jan. 29. Earlier Jan.
29 Mr. Johnson had met with Vice Pres. Hubert H. Humphrey, State Secy. Dean Rusk, Defense Secy. Robert S.
McNamara, Goldberg and other advisers. The Jan. 29 talks
were the culmination of intensive consultations Mr. Johnson
had held with his top aides during the previous 9 days. The
Administration was believed to have first started consideration of ending the raid suspension after Rusk Jan. 20 had
delivered a pessimistic report on the U.S. peace drive. (Rusk
had returned to Washington Jan. 19 from a trip to South
Vietnam and India, where he had conferred in New Delhi with
Soviet Premier Aleksei N. Kosygin.)

Following Pres. Johnson's speech, Rusk summarized at a
news conference later Jan. 31 "the unprecedented effort of the
past 40 days, an effort aimed at peace, and the tragically negative responses from Hanoi": "We were in touch with all the
governments of the world, more than 115 of them, as well as
with . . . the pope, the Secretary General of the United
Nations, the North Atlantic Council of NATO, the Organization of American States, the Organization of African Unity
and the International Committee of the Red Cross. 6 special
Presidential envoys visited 34 capitals, and personal communications from the President went to the chiefs of government of
many more." "At an early stage of the suspension of the
bombing," North Vietnamese officials were told "that no decision had been made regarding a resumption of bombing, and
that if Hanoi would reciprocate by making a serious contribution toward peace, it would obviously have a favorable
effect on the possibility of further extending the suspension."
Rusk emphasized that "one of the obstacles to peace has been
a failure on the part of Hanoi to understand that the United
States will in fact meet its commitment" to South Vietnam.
Rusk said the U.S. had decided to submit the Vietnamese controversy to the UN Security Council because Washington's
peace efforts "have not yielded any results." Nevertheless,
Rusk insisted, the U.S.' "quiet diplomacy" "will not be abandoned." Rusk denied reports that there had been a diminution
of North Vietnamese regular troop activity in South Vietnam.

He said allied soldiers had had "some contact in December" with North Vietnamese forces, and "there are indications at the present time that there is very active contact with North Vietnamese forces."

President Johnson Jan. 25 had strongly indicated his decision to resume the bombing. He did so at a joint White House meeting of the National Security Council and a bi-partisan group of Congressional leaders. The meeting was described as a briefing, and the lawmakers reportedly were given intelligence accounts of North Vietnamese military activity during the bombing pause.

The intelligence report was simultaneously released to the press. It said: According to aerial reconnaissance photos and reports from Laotian refugees, North Vietnam had increased its shipments of war supplies to the Viet Cong in South Vietnam via the Ho Chi Minh Trail through Laos. U.S. reconnaissance planes had taken pictures of more than 200 trucks in southern North Vietnam between Dec. 31, 1965 and Jan. 13. Most of these vehicles had been sighted on Routes 1A and 15, which ran west to Laos and were principal connecting routes to the Ho Chi Minh Trail. The infiltration of men from North Vietnam to South Vietnam was increasing, and about 1,000 infiltrators had moved into South Vietnam's northernmost Quangtri Province Dec. 24, 1965, the day the bombing lull had started. North Vietnam was repairing bridges and other installations damaged by U.S. bombings, and ferry traffic across rivers, presumably carrying supplies, was increasing.

Among those attending the White House conference were Vice Pres. Humphrey, Amb.-at-Large W. Averell Harriman, Gen. Earle G. Wheeler, chairman of the Joint Chiefs of Staff, Senate majority leader Mike Mansfield (D., Mont.), Senate Foreign Relations Committee Chrmn. J. W. Fulbright (D., Ark.), Senate minority leader Everett M. Dirksen (R., Ill.) and House minority leader Gerald Ford (R., Mich.).

The U.S. decision to resume air attacks on North Vietnam precipitated debate Jan. 31 in the U.S. Senate and House of Representatives. The Congress members, however, were nearly unanimous in their approval of Mr. Johnson's decision to submit the Vietnamese crisis to the UN. Among statements made: Senate majority leader Mike Mansfield—"I will do my best to support him [Pres. Johnson]. . . . I fully appreciate the difficulty and the agony of the decision which was his—and his alone—to make." . . . Sen. George D. Aiken—Mr. Johnson had "erred in taking new steps which may lead to a cataclysmic world conflict." Communism would be defeated "on the battlefield of men's minds," not in military combat. . . . Sen. Russell B. Long (D., La.)—Pres. Johnson had "no other choice." The decision to submit the Vietnamese crisis to the UN Security Council was "an exercise in futility." . . . Sen. Robert F. Kennedy—"If we regard bombing as the answer to Vietnam we are heading straight for disaster." . . . Sen. Fulbright—While "the wisdom" of Pres. Johnson's decision "may be questioned, we must back our men in the fight." (Fulbright said he had received 300 letters and 300 telegrams expressing opposition to the renewed raids; many other Senators reported their mail running 10-1 against the bombings.) . . . Rep. Wayne L. Hays (D., O.)—Peking must be warned that if even one Chinese Communist soldier "gets into the fighting, China's A-bomb apparatus will disappear."

Vice Pres. Humphrey said Jan. 31 that the resumption of the raids was necessary "to restore military pressure on North Vietnam" because Hanoi had rejected all U.S. peace overtures.

Ex-Presidents Harry S. Truman and Dwight D. Eisenhower Jan. 31 supported Mr. Johnson's decision. Eisenhower said that to have acted otherwise would have "given sanctuary to those responsible for sending guerrilla forces and supplies in South Vietnam."

The Western reaction to the U.S. resumption of air raids on North Vietnam was largely one of regret. But Communist nations uniformly assailed the American move.

A protest note sent by the North Vietnamese government to the International Control Commission on Vietnam Jan. 31 charged that the new raids "had brought about a very serious crisis to peace and security of all countries in Indochina and Southeast Asia." The note said the U.S. raids "showed that the [U.S.] 'search-for-peace' . . . was actually aimed at . . .

covering up . . . moves to intensify and expand the war of aggression in Vietnam."

An official Soviet government statement questioned Jan. 31 whether the resumption of the raids "creates an atmosphere favoring a political settlement in Vietnam." No matter how the U.S. government "assesses the position of North Vietnam, nothing can justify the new acts of aggression," the statement said.

Peking radio charged that the U.S. had "recklessly resumed its bombings" "after the utter failure of its peace hoax." The Chinese Communist statement called the renewal of the air strikes a "flagrant" violation of the Geneva agreements.

The British government announced Jan. 31 that it "understands and supports" Pres. Johnson's decision to resume the raids. A Foreign Office statement expressed regret that Hanoi had not taken "advantage of the suspension of bombing to respond to repeated American offers to negotiate." But the resumption of the raids was protested in a cablegram sent to U.S. Sen. J. W. Fulbright by about 90 Labor Party MPs and 4 Liberals. Prime Min. Harold Wilson declared in House of Commons debate on Asian policy Feb. 8 that his government opposed the bombing of Hanoi and the North Vietnamese port of Haiphong. Asserting that London "deprecates pressures for a wider war," Wilson said: "As long as this fighting lasts there is danger of its escalation to the scale of a major war in Asia and possibly something worse."

A French cabinet statement reputedly edited by Pres. Charles de Gaulle said Feb. 2 that Paris "can only regret and disapprove of the resumption of bombing" of North Vietnam. The renewed raids, the statement said, were "jeopardizing the cause of peace." The statement criticized the U.S.' action in taking the Vietnam case to the UN. It said that since North and South Vietnam and Communist China were not UN members, the UN was "not qualified to intervene." France suggested instead that the matter be taken up again at a reconvened Geneva conference. (De Gaulle was reported Feb. 17 to have let Pres. Johnson know of France's opposition to the U.S.' resumption of the air strikes. The French leader was said to have called military intervention self-defeating. De

Gaulle's remarks were made in a message sent to Pres. Johnson Feb. 9 in response to a letter de Gaulle had received from Mr. Johnson during U.S. Amb.-to-UN Arthur Goldberg's visit to Paris Dec. 31, 1965. The Johnson letter was delivered in conjunction with the start of the U.S. peace drive.)

Canadian Prime Min. Lester B. Pearson had said Jan. 31 that he "regretted" the U.S. action. He spoke only when pressed in the House of Commons by opposition members to condemn the American raids or appeal to Washington to stop them.

The Japanese government Jan. 31 voiced "extreme regret" over the resumption of the raids, but it called the action an "unavoidable military necessity."

120 persons participated in an overnight vigil at United Nations Plaza in New York Feb. 1-2 in protest against the air-raid resumption. The demonstration was sponsored by the Committe for Non-Violent Action. The vigil was joined Feb. 2 by 200 members of Women Strike for Peace. Later Feb. 2 1,000 demonstrators marched from the UN to Times Square, where 32 were arrested on disorderly conduct charges after they sat down in the street. The march had been organized by the Times Square Demonstration Committee and the N.Y. Workshop in Nonviolence.

UN Gets U.S. Proposal

The UN Security Council met Feb. 1 to consider a U.S. draft resolution calling for Council action to arrange an international conference to bring peace to Vietnam and Southeast Asia. But after 3 weeks of private consultations, Akira Matsui of Japan, the Council president for February, reported failure to agree on the U.S. proposal or on any other Vietnam peace plan.

The Council had agreed Feb. 2 by 9-2 vote (the USSR and Bulgaria opposed; France, Mali, Nigeria and Uganda abstaining) to put the matter on its agenda. Several hours before the Council had convened, however, the North Vietnamese Foreign Ministry had formally rejected any UN action on the Vietnamese war.

The Council meeting had been called Jan. 31 by French Amb.-to-UN Roger Seydoux, January president of the Council. He acted in response to a letter the same day from U.S. Amb.-to-UN Arthur J. Goldberg, who had requested a Council meeting to debate the draft U.S. resolution. This was the first time the U.S. had formally asked for UN action on Vietnam, and the Feb. 1 Council meeting was the first formal consideration of the issue by a UN body.

The Feb. 1 Hanoi statement declared that any Council resolution "intervening in the Vietnam question would be null and void." The statement said that the Hanoi government "reaffirms that, on the international plane, consideration of the United States war acts in Vietnam falls within the competence of the 1954 Geneva Conference... and not of the United Nations Security Council." The Hanoi statement was distributed first by Hsinhua, the Chinese Communist news agency, and then by Tass, the Soviet press agency. Chrmn. J. W. Fulbright of the U.S. Senate Foreign Relations Committee said Feb. 1, following Hanoi's rejection of UN action: "If that is their attitude, why not take them up on it? If the effort in the United Nations fails, why not try to get the Geneva conference reconvened?" (In a separate statement, also issued Feb. 1, Hanoi called for international action to end "definitely and unconditionally" the U.S. bombing of North Vietnam. It declared that the renewal of the bombing had "laid bare the hypocritical character of the Johnson Administration's talks about peace." The Viet Cong and Communist China Feb. 2 denounced any UN effort to deal with the Vietnamese war. A representative of the Central Committee of the NLF said in a radio broadcast that any UN action on Vietnam would be "null and void." *Jenmin Jih Pao,* the Chinese Communist Party newspaper, said Feb. 2 that the U.S. "had better stop dreaming of using the United Nations to serve its aggressive war in Vietnam.")

Goldberg's Jan. 31 letter to Seydoux had stressed the U.S.' continued efforts to achieve "a peaceful settlement of this conflict on the basis of unconditional negotiations and the Geneva accords of 1954." Repeating the text of his Jan. 4 letter to UN Secy. Gen. U Thant, Goldberg said the U.S. had "transmitted" its peace proposals to North Vietnam but had received "no affirmative response from Hanoi." Therefore, he declared, the U.S. "has concluded it should now bring this problem ... formally before the Security Council." Goldberg referred to a "renewed appeal of . . . the pope only 2 days ago." (Pope Paul VI, speaking Jan. 29 to a group of Catholic journalists, had said: "Who knows whether finally an arbitration by the United Nations, entrusted to neutral nations, might tomorrow—we could hope for such a thing even today—be able to resolve the terrible question?" Referring to the U.S. "peace offensive," the pope deplored the fact that no "positive reception" had been made. He added that it was "a most grave responsibility" to reject negotiations. Thant had said Jan. 20 that "at this stage," no "useful purpose" would be served by a Security Council debate on Vietnam.)

The U.S. draft resolution was appended to Goldberg's request for a Council meeting. The draft called on the Council to "arrange a conference" to secure "application of the Geneva accords of 1954 and 1962." The conference would include "appropriate interested governments" and would aim at establishing "durable peace in Southeast Asia." The resolution's full text:

The Security Council,

Deeply concerned at the continuation of hostilities in Vietnam,

Mindful of its responsibilities for the maintenance of international peace and security,

Noting that the provisions of the Geneva accords of 1954 and 1962 have not been implemented,

Desirous of contributing to a peaceful and honorable settlement of the conflict in Vietnam,

Recognizing the right of all peoples, including those in Vietnam, to self-determination,

1. Calls for immediate discussions without preconditions at — on — date, among the appropriate interested governments to arrange a conference looking toward the application of the Geneva accords of 1954 and 1962 and the establishment of a durable peace in Southeast Asia,

2. Recommends that the first order of business of such a conference be arrangements for a cessation of hostilities under effective supervision,

3. Offers to assist in achieving the purposes of this resolution by all appropriate means, including the provision of arbitrators or mediators,

4. Calls on all concerned to cooperate fully in the implementation of this resolution,

5. Requests the secretary general to assist as appropriate in the implementation of this resolution.

Council debate Feb. 1 was marked by a sharp exchange between Goldberg and Soviet delegate Nikolai T. Fedorenko. Goldberg, after summarizing U.S. peace efforts in Vietnam, said the U.S. had brought the matter to the Security Council because it would "not accept as final and immutable" Ho Chi Minh's Jan. 29 rejection of the U.S.' efforts to settle the conflict peacefully. Goldberg charged that Ho's rejection had cast on him "full responsibility for the [U.S.] decision" to resume bombing of North Vietnam. Fedorenko, opposing the U.S. request to place Vietnam on the Council agenda, said the request was designed to mask a further U.S. extension of the war.

Seydoux argued Feb. 1 that the UN was "not the proper forum for achieving a peaceful settlement" because North Vietnam and Communist China "are not represented in our organization." The Nigerian ambassador, Chief S. O. Adebo, described the U.S., resumption of bombing as "unfortunate" and said he would support debate of the question in the Council if Communist China, North Vietnam and the National Liberation Front (Viet Cong) were invited to participate.

Goldberg, in his 2d speech of the day, replied to Seydoux that he could not "understand how those states [France and the USSR] which repeatedly insist that the Security Council . . . has responsibility for maintenance of peace and security can now deny its competence." Replying to assertions that the Geneva conference, and not the UN, was the proper place to negotiate a Vietnam settlement, Goldberg said the U.S. had supported the Geneva agreements repeatedly as "an adequate basis for peace in Southeast Asia." "Let the joint chairmen [of the Geneva conference—the USSR and Britain] issue the call today, and we will be in Geneva tomorrow," he pledged. "The door to Geneva is, at least for the time being, closed and the question we have to decide is a plain and simple one: Do we wish to close the door to the United Nations."

The discussion Feb. 1 centered on the procedural issue of placing the Vietnam question on the Council's agenda for debate. 7 new Council members—Argentina, Bulgaria, Japan, Mali, New Zealand, Nigeria and Uganda—participated as membership in the Council rose from 11 to 15 Feb. 1. 9 votes were needed in the newly enlarged Council to place the issue on the agenda. (No veto applied to a procedural vote.) The discussion Feb. 1 revealed that the U.S. could count on these 8 votes in favor of placing Vietnam on the agenda: Argentina, Britain, Nationalist China, Japan, New Zealand, the Netherlands, Uruguay and the U.S. The Jordanian delegate, Waleed M. Sadi, whose vote was needed if the U.S. were to get the required 9th vote, requested that the Council postpone the procedural vote to give him time to receive instructions from his government. Nigeria and Uganda supported Jordan's request, and the Council adjourned.

The 15 Council members consulted privately for the next 3 weeks. Council Pres. Akira Matsui finally reported Feb. 26 that no progress had been made towards negotiating a settlement. In a letter to UN Secy. Gen. Thant and to the Council members, Matsui said: "The differences of views have made it impossible for me to report at this stage agreement on the precise course of action." But he "could detect a certain degree of common feeling among many members" on 2 issues: (1) There was "general grave concern and . . . anxiety over the continuation of hostilities and a strong desire for . . . a peaceful solution to the problem"; (2) there was a desire to end the conflict through negotiations to "work out implementation of the Geneva accords." The Council, he concluded, "remains seized of the Vietnam problem."

Goldberg said Feb. 26 that he "welcomed" Matsui's letter and believed it would "help continue to inspire and intensify a peaceful settlement." The U.S., he said, had not "put to sleep" its request for Council debate and action on the U.S. resolution, "both of which may be brought up again in the Council at an appropriate time." Fedorenko said Mar. 2 that Matsui's letter to the members of the Council was an "illegal action" exceeding the Council president's powers. The USSR and Bulgaria refused to accept Matsui's letter. 11 of the remaining 13 Council members indorsed Matsui's statement, but Mali and France refused to do so. The replies of the 15 Council members were made in letters to Council Pres.-for-March Muhammed H. el-Farra of Jordan.

UN Secy. Gen. U Thant, addressing the convention of the AFL-CIO Amalgamated Clothing Workers of America in Atlantic City May 24, said that "unfortunately, the United Nations is not, at present, so constituted" that it could bring "the parties together to negotiate." He asserted that most UN members were "convinced that military methods will not restore peace in Vietnam," and he reiterated his view that "peace can only be restored by a return to the Geneva agreements." He expressed hope that a reduction of military activities and an agreement to negotiations that would include the National Liberation Front would make possible "an agreement between all powers concerned and, among them, the 5 major powers, including the People's Republic of China."

Thant called on the parties to the war to "start scaling down military operations and to agree to discussions which include the actual combatants"—specifically the Viet Cong. Tracing the development and effects of the war's escalation, Thant said "an anguished and perplexed world has suddenly found that a limited and local conflict is threatening to turn into a major confrontation." He warned that "though the fear of a much larger conflict may still have a restraining influence upon the demands of military strategy, the temptation to win a military success may still prove stronger than the more prudent call to reason."

Thant held that the war's "justification in terms of a confrontation of ideologies" was "becoming more and more misleading." He said the events of the past 20 years had "so profoundly affected Vietnamese political life" that "the passion for national identity, perhaps one should say national survival, is the only ideology that may be left to a growing number of Vietnamese." Thus, "what is really at stake" in Vietnam, he added, "is the independence, the identity and the survival of the country itself."

Thant concluded by asking those "genuinely troubled" by the "problem of war and peace" not to "delude themselves" into believing that he or the UN could "resolve the problem."

"The solution lies in the hands of those who have the power, and the responsibility, to decide," he said.

Churchmen Urge Truce

The 100-member Central Committee of the World Council of Churches Feb. 16 unanimously adopted a resolution calling for a ceasefire in Vietnam "of sufficient duration to serve as a cooling-off period and as an opportunity for testing possibilities of negotiations." The resolution, adopted during a meeting at the council's Ecumenical Center in Geneva, also proposed:

(1) "That the United States and South Vietnam stop bombing of the North and North Vietnam stop military infiltration of the South."

(2) That the U.S. commit itself to a phased troop withdrawal under international auspices.

(3) That the NLF be accorded "a place in negotiations."

(4) "That all parties recognize the extent to which what is happening in Vietnam is part of a social revolution" and "the futility of military action" in solving Vietnam's underlying problems.

(5) That the U.S. "review and modify its policy of 'containment' of communism and Communist countries supporting 'wars of liberation' review and modify their policy."

(6) That Communist China be brought into "the world community of nations."

The resolution had been drafted by delegates representing the U.S., the USSR, Czechoslovakia, India and Cameroon. The Council's Commission of the Churches on International Affairs had submitted to the Central Committee Feb. 12 a report advocating support by the council of efforts to "move from the battlefield to the conference table by way of a reconvened 1954 Geneva conference on Vietnam." The Rev. Dr. Eugene Carson Blake of the U.S., who had been elected secretary general of the council Feb. 11, had said at the Feb. 12 meeting that "the more successful present American policy is now, the more difficulties the nation will face later on." He warned that victory in Vietnam would "be the case of a predominantly white power killing an Asian nation."

France, Canada & UK Contact Hanoi

France, Canada and Britain all made direct contact with North Vietnam during February in attempts to bring about a negotiated settlement of the war. None of the contacts were fruitful.

French Pres. de Gaulle informed Ho Chi Minh that France was ready to "actively take part" "in exerting her influence" to end the Vietnamese war "as soon as this appears possible." De Gaulle's offer was made in a letter to Ho released to the press Feb. 15. The message was in response to a note de Gaulle had received from Ho Jan. 24. In his note Ho had appealed to de Gaulle to use his influence to "prevent perfidious new maneuvers" by the U.S. in Indochina. De Gaulle said that France adhered to the principles that the Geneva agreements on Vietnam should be implemented, that Vietnam's independence should be "guaranted by the non-intervention of any outside power" and that the Vietnamese government should follow "a policy of strict neutrality." De Gaulle emphasized that France "exclude[d] every military solution" of the Vietnamese controversy and did "not approve of the prolongation of the fighting." He expressed sympathy for "the Vietnamese tragedy" and cited France's ties with Vietnam, which, he said, "still exist." De Gaulle told Ho that France was "ready to maintain with your government all contacts that may be useful" during the current crisis.

(A former French cabinet minister, Jean Sainteny, reported to de Gaulle July 20 on a personal mission to Hanoi carried out at de Gaulle's request. Sainteny, who had arrived in the North Vietnamese capital July 4 and had returned to Paris July 12, handed de Gaulle a message in which Ho Chi Minh said "we are glad that France, signer of the 1954 Geneva accords on Vietnam, is trying to make an active contribution towards the reestablishment of peace in this region on the basis of the correct execution of these accords." The French Foreign Ministry said Sainteny had found the North Vietnamese adamant in their demands that peace negotiations be held on their terms.)

Canadian Foreign Min. Paul Martin announced in the House of Commons in Ottawa Feb. 21 that Victor Moore, senior Canadian representative on the International Control Commission for Vietnam, had had a "very fruitful discussion"

"in the last 10 days" with high North Vietnamese officials
in Hanoi on "matters which would interest all who wanted to
see a cease-fire and an end to the war in Vietnam." Moore
accompanied Chester Ronning, a personal representative of
Prime Min. Lester B. Pearson, to Hanoi Mar. 7 and to Saigon
Mar. 11. On his return to Canada Mar. 15, Ronning said the
ICC could help bring about negotiations. But he said he
believed the other ICC members—Poland and India—felt
that the time was not yet right. It had been reported Feb.
8 that Ho Chi Minh had asked Indian Pres. Sarvepalli
Radhakrishnan (in a letter sent 2 weeks previously) to use
New Delhi's good offices to seek an end to the war in Vietnam. But U.S. officials denied that the message was a peace
feeler. They said the note was similar to a Jan. 24 one to the
leaders of other nations in which Ho had denounced the U.S.'
peace moves and had restated Hanoi's terms for ending the
conflict. A report from UN headquarters in New York Feb.
8 said that the message to India and a message to Canada
had been sent by Ho to remind those nations of their responsibilities as members (along with Poland) of the ICC. In his
message to Prime Min. Pearson, Ho was quoted as having
said: "In the face of the extremely serious situation brought
about by the United States in Vietnam I hope that your
government will fulfill its obligations under the Geneva
agreements."

Lord Chalfont, British minister of state, conferred in
Moscow Feb. 23 with North Vietnamese Chargé d'Affaires
Li Chang in a search for clarification of Hanoi's conditions
for ending the war. Chalfont had participated in high-level
talks in Moscow Feb. 22-24 with British Prime Min. Harold
Wilson and Soviet Premier Aleksei Kosygin, Communist
Party Chrmn. Leonid Brezhnev and other Soviet officials.
Wilson reported Feb. 23 on Chalfont's meeting with Li. In
a TV broadcast to Britain from Moscow, Wilson said that
as a result of the talks Britain had succeeded in "getting a
line open" to Hanoi on possible peace talks.

In speeches at a meeting of North Vietnam's National
Assembly (held Apr. 16-22), Pres. Ho and Premier Pham
Van Dong reiterated that U.S. acceptance of North Vietnam's

4-point peace formula remained the only basis for ending the Vietnamese war. It was reported Apr. 26 that Ho had said in his address: "Our people are resolved to fight until final victory. Again we say to Pres. Johnson: If the United States really wants peace it must withdraw all United States and satellite troops from South Vietnam and stop the aggressive war there." The U.S. must halt its air strikes against North Vietnam "at once and unconditionally," and the Vietnamese must be permitted to reunify their country without foreign interference. Dong assailed the Johnson Administration for "turning a blind eye and a deaf ear" to the 4-point plan, particularly to the 3d point, which called for settlement of South Vietnam's internal affairs on the basis of the National Liberation Front's political program. "To object to the 3d point," Dong declared, "is to object to the whole 4-point stand."

North Vietnam was reported June 21 to have rejected a new U.S. offer for talks on ending the war. The American proposal called for the opening of negotiations while both sides reduced military activities. North Vietnamese officials were reported to have assailed the plan as another "peace offensive fraud" and to have insisted that an unconditional halt in the U.S. air strikes against North Vietnam remained Hanoi's prerequisite for peace talks. The U.S. proposal was said to have been forwarded to Hanoi through the U.S.-Chinese Communist ambassadorial talks in Warsaw and through Eastern European diplomatic sources. The State Department confirmed June 22 that "Hanoi's attitude continues to be that expressed last Jan. 24 [the demand for a stoppage of U.S. air raids]. We have not seen any change in this position." The department statement was issued after Asst. State Secy. (for Far Eastern affairs) William P. Bundy had reported earlier in the day to State Secy. Rusk on a meeting in Ottawa June 21 with Canadian Amb. Ronning. Ronning had briefed Bundy on his talks in Hanoi earlier in June with North Vietnamese Foreign Min. Nguyen Duy Trinh on the possible basis for peace talks. The essence of Ronning's report was that Hanoi's position remained unchanged.

In a speech in Des Moines June 30, Pres. Johnson again expressed his determination to seek peace in Vietnam. Referring to North Vietnam's leaders, he said: "If they will only let me know when and where they would like to bring peace to South Vietnam, I will have my closest and most trusted associates there in a matter of hours." "There need be no agenda," he said, "there need be no previous understanding of what will and will not be discussed. There need be no commitments on either side. There need only be a room and a table and people willing to talk respectfully." Repeating this offer at a news conference July 20, the President added: "We have stated again and again our desire to engage in unconditional discussion and I repeat them again today. But we can't talk about just half the war. We should talk about all the war. We have not the slightest indication that the other side is willing to make any concession, to take any action that would lead to the peace table. Until there is some indication on their part, we, of course, would not expect to tie the hands of our men in Vietnam."

Mansfield Urges International Talks

Senate majority leader Mike Mansfield proposed Apr. 18 "a direct confrontation across a peace table" of the U.S., North Vietnam, Communist China "and such elements in South Vietnam as may be essential to the making and keeping of a peaceful settlement" of the Vietnamese war. In a speech to the Senate, Mansfield suggested that his proposed peace conference be held in Japan or Burma "or some other proximate and appropriate Asian setting." Citing as "most unfortunate" the failure of the UN or Britain and the Soviet Union (as co-chairmen of the Geneva conference) to convene an international parley, Mansfield expressed the belief "that efforts to bring about peace negotiations may be pressed more usefully elsewhere."

Mansfield said: The need for such talks was made more urgent by a political crisis in South Vietnam. This political instability furnished "added emphasis to the validity of the President's [Johnson's] policy. He has designed that policy to serve United States interests by an active and continuing search for negotiations in an effort to end the war and so contain our involvement in Vietnam within reasonable limits." The U.S.' military objective and Mr. Johnson's policy remained the "establishment of conditions, through nego- tiations, which will assure and safeguard an authentic and free choice to the people of South Vietnam as to their political future and as to their ultimate relationship with North Vietnam."

Communist China Apr. 21 rejected Mansfield's peace proposals. A statement issued by the Chinese news agency Hsinhua said: "The Johnson Administration and Congress notables resort to the 'peace talks' hoax again in an attempt to force the Vietnamese people into submission by the dual tactics of increasing 'military pressure' and making peace gestures."

Mrs. Gandhi, Wilson & Thant Visit Moscow

Indian Prime Min. Indira Gandhi, British Prime Min. Harold Wilson, and UN Secy. Gen. Thant visited Moscow during July for talks with Soviet leaders on the Vietnamese war and other subjects.

Before leaving New Delhi, Mrs. Gandhi July 7 had delivered a radio speech in which she urged the USSR and Great Britain, as co-chairmen of the Geneva Conference, to call an immediate meeting of the conference to get negotiations under way "instead of debating how this might be done." She called for an end to U.S. bombings of North Vietnam to be followed by a cessation of hostilities "on all sides throughout Vietnam" and eventually by a withdrawal of "all foreign forces." (Communist Chinese Premier Chou En-lai's rejection of Mrs. Gandhi's proposals was announced by Peking radio July 9.) She expressed India's willingness, as chairman of the International Control Commission on Viet- nam, to take on additional responsibilities in the implemen- tation of a peace plan. (Briefings on Mrs. Gandhi's proposals had been given by the Indian External Affairs Ministry earlier July 7 to diplomatic representatives of the U.S., the USSR, North and South Vietnam, Great Britain, France, Poland, Canada and the UAR.)

En route to Moscow Mrs. Gandhi conferred with Yugoslav Pres. Tito July 10-11 at Tito's vacation home on the island of Brioni. In a speech July 10, Mrs. Gandhi cited the "special responsibility" of "nonaligned nations, and all other countries, . . . to find ways and means to a just solution which would satisfy the legitimate rights and hopes of the Vietnamese people." A joint communiqué issued July 12 in Belgrade expressed the 2 leaders' concern over the use of force and armed intervention and urged peace-loving nations to move to prevent any broadened conflict.

Mrs. Gandhi arrived July 12 in Moscow, where she had 3 formal discussion sessions and a number of informal ones with Premier Aleksei N. Kosygin before her departure July 16. The talks covered a variety of issues, including Vietnam. At a July 14 Soviet-Indian friendship meeting at the Kremlin honoring Mrs. Gandhi and attended by 2,000 guests, Kosygin delivered a speech attacking the U.S. for "vandalism and barbarism on an international scale" in Vietnam. He accused the Johnson Administration of having "passed the brink" and of seeking "to achieve the impossible—to break the resistance of the Vietnamese people." Mrs. Gandhi's speech urged restraint by both sides in Vietnam. She reiterated her proposal for a 2d Geneva conference but added that "there might be more suitable or acceptable alternatives." In a speech recorded for TV July 15, Mrs. Gandhi said that "the bombing of North Vietnam must stop."

A joint communiqué issued in Moscow before Mrs. Gandhi's departure July 16 called on the U.S. to end its bombing of North Vietnam and said that settlement of the Vietnam conflict could "only be found within the framework of the Geneva Agreements of 1954." At a news conference Mrs. Gandhi said the Soviet stand on negotiations was "that any proposals should first have the approval of North Vietnam before they are able to commit themselves." "A precondition for anything," she added, "must be the stopping of the bombing of North Vietnam." (Kosygin had told newsmen at an Indian reception earlier in the day that "the only possible solution" to the Vietnam conflict required that "military

aggression . . . be stopped immediately and foreign troops
. . . be withdrawn.")

At a July 19 news conference in New Delhi, Mrs. Gandhi
was asked to clarify her position on Vietnam in the light of
her talks with foreign leaders. She replied: "It will be very
difficult to call a conference while the bombing is going on.
Nobody is really willing to discuss anything until the bombing is stopped." She added that she had found this position
"not only in the Socialist or the Communist countries but
even in a country like Great Britain and many of the European countries."

Wilson arrived in Moscow July 16 within an hour of the
departure of Mrs. Gandhi. After 7 hours of formal and
informal discussion between the 2 government heads July 18,
a spokesman for the Soviet Foreign Ministry called an
unusual press briefing and told reporters that the USSR and
Great Britain "hold absolutely different positions" on Vietnam.
He said Kosygin had responded to an expression of concern
by Wilson over the fate of captured U.S. pilots in North
Vietnam by saying that the issue "remains fully within the
competence of the government of North Vietnam, which will
settle it as it finds fit." Kosygin's position on the British
role in bringing peace to Vietnam was said to be that "if
Britain really wanted to facilitate a settlement of the situation
in Vietnam, she would . . . demand of the United States
an immediate and unconditional ending of the aggression in
Vietnam, the withdrawal of American troops and the troops
of its satellites from South Vietnam, an end to the interference
in the Vietnamese people's domestic affairs and the liquidation
of the military bases in South Vietnam." Wilson returned
to London July 19 and told the House of Commons that
"there was no change at all in the general position of the
Soviet Union . . . and no signs of an early move toward
a conference or other forms of negotiation" on Vietnam.

Thant visited Moscow July 25-30 at the invitation of the
Soviet government. In a news conference on his departure
July 30, Thant said he was "convinced that the Vietnam war
will develop into a major war if the present trend continues."
At UN headquarters in New York, Thant said July 30 the

Soviet leaders had told him that they were "prepared to render all possible assistance to North Vietnam." The "general feeling in Moscow," he said, was that any peace initiatives would have to come from those "doing the fighting." "There is nothing the United Nations can do at this moment," he concluded.

U.S. State Secy. Rusk told Thant at UN headquarters in New York Aug. 22 that the U.S. wished to reduce its military effort in Vietnam but could not because North Vietnam and its allies were not interested in de-escalation. Rusk said he had assured Thant that the U.S. was interested in reducing the fighting. In a speech delivered later Aug. 22 at the annual convention of the Veterans of Foreign Wars in New York, Rusk warned that if the U.S. withdrew from Vietnam prematurely, "we can . . . await the great catastrophe that surely awaits at the end of the trail." Current U.S. policy, Rusk explained, was the reverse of what it had been between World Wars I and II, when the U.S. regarded Japan's aggression in Manchuria as no threat to American security. It was "that neglect that led to World War II," Rusk said. Currently, Rusk pointed out, the Southeast Asia Treaty Organization and other defensive alliances were "the backbone of peace" and were designed to prevent World War III. As for peace prospects in Vietnam, Rusk said: The U.S.' goal was a "peace that permits an independent people in any area to live in peace with the institutions of their own choice"; U.S. troops would withdraw from Vietnam "tomorrow if the [North Vietnamese] infiltration stopped and those who have no business in South Vietnam would go home."

(An AP dispatch from Washington Aug. 27 said the Johnson Administration had renewed its appeal to North Vietnam through an undisclosed 3d country to agree to peace talks or to de-escalate its military activities in South Vietnam.)

South Vietnamese Terms

A formal statement issued by the South Vietnamese government July 20 said allied forces would "stop all military action" against Communists in South Vietnam if they "would agree to put an end to their ambition of forced expansion."

The statement said that the bombing of North Vietnam would "immediately stop" if North Vietnam: (a) withdrew "to the North all of its soldiers and political cadres"; (b) "dissolve[d] the so-called South Vietnam Liberation Front and end[ed] all military, sabotage and terrorist actions in South Vietnam"; (c) observed the Geneva agreements "so that the South Vietnamese people can decide about their lives by themselves . . . and without any interference from any source."

South Vietnamese Premier Nguyen Cao Ky Aug. 9 expressed willingness to negotiate an end to the war with North Vietnam "if they would be willing to compromise." Ky said: "We would go to the conference table to tell them we draw the line at the 17th Parallel. We're not sitting down to give them a couple of provinces south of the 17th Parallel. They would have to withdraw their agents and soldiers from South Vietnam."

Ky said at a meeting of the Philippines-Vietnamese Society in Manila Aug. 12 that the determination of non-Communist Asian countries, "coupled with the strength of the allies fighting in Vietnam, will discourage Communist China from pushing plans for political disintegration and military conquest of the Asian countries." Ky said allied forces could withdraw from South Vietnam "the day they [the Communists] stop infiltration and aggression." Ky expressed the belief that the South Vietnamese forces would be in a position to conduct the war by themselves in 2 years and that some U.S. forces and most other allied troops could be pulled out. On returning to Saigon Aug. 13, Ky explained at an airport news conference that he had not advocated nor would his government request a withdrawal of American troops. But he reiterated the view that "within 2 years South Vietnam will be strong enough in many fields to defend ourselves."

Asians Propose All-Asian Peace Conference

Appeals for an end to the Vietnamese war were sounded at a conference of the 3-nation (Thailand, Malaysia and the Philippines) Association of Southeast Asia held in Bangkok, Thailand Aug. 3-6.

The peace plea was first voiced by Thai Foreign Min. Thanat Khoman at the meeting Aug. 3. Khoman proposed that a "peace for Asia committee" be formed, composed solely of "interested nations in the area" and of "all the principals in the war in Vietnam." The committee, he said, would "attempt to hold a conference, this time not in Geneva, but somewhere in Asia." Khoman asserted that it was vital that Asians "take our destiny into our own hands instead of letting others from far away mold it at their whim."

Khoman"s proposal was incorporated into a joint statement issued by the association at the conclusion of its talks Aug. 6. The statement said that the 3 ministers (Khoman, Foreign Affairs Min. Narciso Ramos of the Philippines and Deputy Premier Tun Abdul Razak of Malaysia) had "agreed to request all those nations interested in bringing about peace in Vietnam to join together in an appeal to leaders of all the countries involved in the Vietnam conflict to come to the conference table." The nations invited to attend the proposed all-Asian conference were Communist China, Iran, Afghanistan, North and South Korea, Cambodia, Pakistan, India, Nepal, Ceylon, Burma, Singapore, Indonesia, Laos, Japan and Nationalist China.

Communist China Aug. 7 rejected an invitation to attend the proposed conference. A Peking statement called the proposal another move in "the United States peace talk fraud." The North Vietnamese Communist Party newspaper *Nhan Dan* Aug. 8 assailed the projected meeting. The newspaper asked: Since the U.S.' "peace-negotiation fraud" "has fallen flat, how can the cheap farce by 3d-class henchmen such as Khoman have any chance of working?"

The proposed meeting was endorsed by South Vietnamese Premier Ky at a Manila news conference held Aug. 10 shortly after his arrival for a 4-day visit to the Philippines. Speaking in Baguio Aug. 11, Ky suggested that the non-Communist nations of Asia first meet to "get a better understanding and decide one common policy." The Communist states then would be invited to the conference to "let them know what we decided," Ky said.

The U.S.' acceptance of the plan was announced by Pres. Johnson Aug. 24. Speaking at a news conference in Washington, the President said that although his Administration favored such a parley, "we do not want to make it appear that we are trying to direct it or force it . . . because it would have an opposite effect." Expressing continued U.S. interest in the reconvening of the Geneva conference, Mr. Johnson reiterated his willingness "to go to a conference anywhere I think it would be helpful." The President denied that the U.S. planned to build permanent bases in South Vietnam and Thailand: "We have no desire to keep our men there and we are ready to stop the moment they [the Communists] are willing to stop."

A position paper of the U.S. Republican Congressional leadership, released Aug. 25, endorsed the proposal for an all-Asian peace conference. The GOP statement said the reconvening of the former Geneva conference on Indochina (involving non-Asian countries) was "no longer viable nor valid, because the approach must come from the Asian nations themselves." The GOP Congressional leaders foresaw "genuine hope of success" of a peace meeting held "only under Asian skies, under Asian auspices, [and] under Asian responsibilities." Ex-Vice Pres. Richard M. Nixon, who attended the Republican leadership meeting that adopted the position paper, had voiced approval of an all-Asia conference and opposition to reconvening of the Geneva conference. At a news conference in Washington Aug. 23, Nixon said: "Geneva is a dead-end street. I think the Adminstration ought to get off that wicket. An Asian settlement rather than a Geneva settlement is the best way to end the war in Vietnam." Washington should "welcome the initiative of free Asian countries without domination by the United States." Nixon said he favored inclusion of Communist China and North Vietnam in an all-Asia conference.

NLF Outlines Peace Terms

Pres. Nguyen Huu Tho of the Viet Cong's National Liberation Front invited other political groups Aug. 28 to join the NLF in a coalition government for South Vietnam. The Tho statement, which contained a 3-point summary of the NLF's conditions for a Vietnamese settlement, was made in an interview granted to Australian correspondent Wilfred Burchett. The interview was broadcast by the NLF's clandestine transmitter Sept. 13 and was rebroadcast by Hanoi radio Sept. 28.

Tho declared that the NLF's goal was "a broad and democratic coalition government consisting of representatives of all social strata, nationalities, religious communities and patriotic personalities." Tho said former members of the Ngo Dinh Diem regime would be acceptable in the coalition, but he ruled out the inclusion of Premier Ky, Chief-of-State Thieu and "a handful of tratiors." Tho listed these 3 points as "the basis for the only correct political solution for the South Vietnam problem:

"1. The United States must end the aggressive war in South Vietnam, withdraw the troops and weapons of the United States and its satellites from South Vietnam, and dissolve all U.S. military bases there.

"2. The United States must respect the national rights of the South Vietnamese people, which are independence, democracy, peace and neutrality. The internal affairs of South Vietnam must be settled by the South Vietnamese people themselves without foreign interference. The reunification of Vietnam must be decided by the people in both zones of Vietnam.

"3. The South Vietnam National Liberation Front, the sole genuine representative of the South Vietnamese people, must have its decisive place and voice in any political solution concerning South Vietnam."

Tran Hoai Nam, NLF representative in Algeria, had reiterated in an NBC-TV interview in Algiers Aug. 27 (rebroadcast in the U.S. Aug. 31) that the U.S. must withdraw its forces from South Vietnam before peace talks could begin. Nam said: "For our people, peace means that there is no longer any aggressor on Vietnamese soil. As long as the American troops still hang on to our country, the South Vietnamese people will fight them until the achievement of independence, democracy and peace."

Nam said NLF policy had not changed since the front's central committee had pledged Mar. 22, 1965 to continue the war until U.S. forces were withdrawn and the NLF won a "decisive" voice in the South Vietnamese government. Describing the NLF as "the only genuine representative of the South Vietnamese people," Nam said the front's goals were the overthrow of South Vietnam's "disguised colonial regime," the establishment of a broadly-based and "progressive" coalition government and a foreign policy based on "peace and neutrality." Nam said the front favored the "gradual" reunification of North and South Vietnam "on the

principal of negotiations and discussions between the 2 zones."
He said it was "absolutely impossible to talk about free election" while U.S. and other foreign troops remained in Vietnam.

De Gaulle Calls for U.S. Withdrawal

French Pres. de Gaulle called on the U.S. Sept. 1 to withdraw its forces from South Vietnam as a prelude to genuine
peace negotiations. De Gaulle, addressing an audience of 100,-
000 in Pnompenh, Cambodia, strongly condemned U.S. policy
in Southeast Asia and argued that a withdrawal would bring
the U.S. greater world influence than it could achieve by continuing its military commitment. He cited France's withdrawal from Algeria as proof that a nation gained by abandonment of an unwise position. De Gaulle had arrived in Cambodia Aug. 30 on the 2d stop in an 18-day world tour.

De Gaulle said the war was expanding because "illusions
about the use of force [had] led to the continual reinforcement
of the expeditionary corps and to increasingly extensive
escalation in Asia, increasingly closer to China, increasingly
provoking in the eye of the Soviet Union, increasingly cen-
sured by numerous peoples of Europe, Africa and Latin
America and, in the final analysis, increasingly menacing for
the peace of the world." He declared that France was determined "not to be . . . automatically implicated in the eventual
extension of the drama and, in any event, to keep her hands
free." While France believed it "unthinkable that the American war apparatus will be annihilated on the spot," de Gaulle
said, "there is . . . no chance that the peoples of Asia will subject themselves to the law of the foreigner who comes from
the other shores of the Pacific, whatever his intentions, however powerful his weapons. In short, as long and cruel as the
ordeal must be, France holds for certain that it will have no
military solution."

To end the war, de Gaulle proposed an "agreement, just
like the [Geneva] one of 1954, . . . [with] the goal of establishing and guaranteeing the neutrality of the peoples of Indochina, . . . leaving each of them full responsibility for its
affairs. The contracting parties would therefore be the real

powers being exercised there and among the other powers, at least the 5 world powers." (The U.S., Britain, USSR, Communist China and France had participated in the 1954 Geneva agreements.)

De Gaulle said: Negotiations toward such an agreement "would depend, obviously," on a prior "commitment" by the U.S. "to repatriate its forces within a suitable and determined period of time." France "is saying this" as a result of the colonial experience in Algeria and Southeast Asia, its "disinterestedness," "because of the exceptional and 2-century-old friendship . . . she has for America," and because France believed that the U.S., like France, was a "country championing the concept that we must allow people to determine their own destiny in their own way." The U.S., by "renouncing . . . a distant expedition once it appears unprofitable and . . . [by] substituting for it an international arrangement organizing the peace and development of an important region of the world, will not . . . involve anything that could injure its pride, interfere with its ideals and jeopardize its interests. On the contrary, . . . what an audience would the United States recapture from one end of the world to the other, and what an opportunity would peace find on the scene and everywhere else. In any event, lacking this outcome, no mediation will offer a prospect of success, and that is why France, for her part, has never thought and does not think of proposing one."

De Gaulle praised Cambodia for its "policy of neutrality" and its "effort" to remain "outside the conflict." France would "continue to lend it her help and support toward this goal," he said. De Gaulle argued that a policy of neutrality "alone could have spared" the other Indochina states "from becoming a field of confrontation for rival dominations and ideologies and an attraction for American intervention. That is why, while your country [Cambodia] succeeded in safeguarding its body and its soul because it remained its own master, the political and military authority of the United States was seen installed in its turn in South Vietnam and, simultaneously, the war gained new strength there in the form of national resistance."

Cambodian Prince Norodom Sihanouk, who introduced de Gaulle, charged that the U.S. and South Vietnam had joined in an attempt to destroy "our liberty, our independence, our territorial integrity and, finally, our peace." (The U.S. and South Vietnam had charged that Viet Cong and North Vietnamese forces used Cambodian territory as a sanctuary from which to attack targets in South Vietnam.)

In a declaration signed Sept. 2 at the royal palace, Sihanouk and de Gaulle declared: "Despite the disputes that have divided and still divide Vietnamese, it is essentially foreign intervention that, by turning a civil war into an international war, has given the hostilities their present dimensions. In order to end them, it is above all necessary for the powers whose interests and ideologies are confronting one another in Indochina . . . , in conjunction with all the countries concerned, . . . to observe strictly the clauses of the 1954 Geneva agreements, namely respect for the independence and sovereignty of Vietnam and non-interference in its internal affairs." Subject to the "agreement by all the Vietnamese, a status of guaranteed controlled neutrality should be conferred on Vietnam by international agreement." The agreement "should be applied to the entire Indochinese peninsula. . . ."

De Gaulle's Sept. 1 suggestion that negotiations toward a settlement of the war could begin if the U.S. committed itself to withdrawing its troops by a certain date was apparently rejected the same day by North Vietnam's Premier Pham Van Dong. The North Vietnamese news agency reported Sept. 2 that Dong had said in a Hanoi speech Sept. 1 that the U.S. would have to complete its troop withdrawal from South Vietnam before peace negotiations could begin. In a report on de Gaulle's speech, however, the news agency said Sept. 2 that Hanoi welcomed it with "intense satisfaction" and that the speech "went far beyond what one might have expected."

U.S. Asst. State Secy. William P. Bundy Sept. 4 rejected de Gaulle's proposal that the U.S. make the initial step toward peace negotiations by announcing a timetable for the departure of its troops. In an interview on NBC-TV's "Meet the Press" he said: "it is up to them [North Vietnam] to make the first move because it is their aggression and interference that is the central violation of the Geneva accords and the principles of the United Nations Charter that has started this whole thing"; the U.S. was "prepared to withdraw, and categorically we intend to withdraw as and when the North Vietnamese get out." Referring to the U.S.' role in Thailand, Bundy said that U.S. strength there was "about 25,000 . . . principally Air Force units." This figure, he said, "has been widely reported and is understood, I think, in Congress. . . . There is really no secret about this." (Bundy's statement was thought to be the Administration's first official acknowledgement of U.S. military strength in Thailand.) Bundy rejected the suggestion that Pres. Johnson meet de Gaulle to discuss Vietnam. Sen. Mike Mansfield (D., Mont.) had suggested in a Senate speech Aug. 29 that Johnson meet de Gaulle after the French leader's visit to Cambodia. Presidential Press Secy. Bill D. Moyers said Aug. 30 that Mr. Johnson had, "in the past, spoken" of a meeting with de Gaulle and "would be glad to meet with the general . . . when they felt that something fruitful might be the result of such a meeting."

At a Washington news conference Sept. 8, Pres. Johnson rejected de Gaulle's withdrawal suggestions. He said that the U.S. had no evidence that a timetable for the withdrawal of American troops would lead to peace negotiations. In speeches in Detroit, Mich. and Lancaster, O. Sept. 5, the President said the U.S. troops in Vietnam would "come home" and the U.S. bases there would "be turned over or constructed for peacetime purposes as soon as . . . vicious aggression stops." He added that "if anyone will show me the time schedule when aggression and infiltration and 'might makes right' will be halted, then I . . . will lay on the table the schedule for the withdrawal of all of our forces from Vietnam."

It was revealed later that U.S. State Secy. Dean Rusk had sent to French Foreign Min. Maurice Couve de Murville Aug. 24 a letter outlining U.S. proposals for ending the war. U.S. officials had hoped that the message, approved by Pres. Johnson, would go to de Gaulle and that he would use the proposals as a basis for his own peace plans in discussion with Cambodian and North Vietnamese officials in Cambodia. But it was reported that de Gaulle apparently did not raise the American proposals at his meetings with Hanoi representatives during his visit to Pnompenh. The U.S. State Department Sept. 9 confirmed the Rusk letter to Couve de Murville but refused to disclose its contents. According to a *N.Y. Times* report Sept. 10: (a) one of the Rusk proposals was for the U.S. and North Vietnam to negotiate a military "withdrawal by phases" from South Vietnam and for the troop pullback to be verified by international observers; (b) Rusk suggested that if North Vietnam rejected this idea the U.S. and North Vietnam could undertake "unilateral" withdrawals, arranged beforehand in secret talks. A French Foreign Ministry source Sept. 10 acknowledged receipt of the Rusk letter but dismissed it as containing nothing new, only the "often-stated American position." Therefore, the ministry source explained, there was no need for de Gaulle to have forwarded American views on Vietnam during his visit to Cambodia.

De Gaulle Aug. 31 had met Nguyen Thuong, 45, newly appointed head of North Vietnam's diplomatic mission in Pnompenh. Thuong told newsmen after his 35-minute meeting with de Gaulle that he had conveyed a message of greeting from Pres. Ho Chi Minh. He described the meeting as a "courtesy visit." Nguyen Van Hieu, a foreign affairs specialist of the Viet Cong's National Liberation Front, conferred in Pnompenh Aug. 31 with a member of de Gaulle's entourage.

U.S. Proposes Reciprocal De-Escalation

An American offer to halt the bombing of North Vietnam and begin a reciprocal de-escalation of the Vietnamese war was advanced Sept. 22 at the beginning of a new session of the UN General Assembly in New York. The U.S. bid was denounced by North Vietnam and other Communist powers, but the bid and the responses to it both were considered to have been couched in terms slightly less rigid than in previous exchanges.

The peace offer was made by Amb.-to-UN Arthur J. Goldberg in an address to the Assembly outlining U.S. positions on the major problems facing the current session. Goldberg declared that the U.S. was prepared to halt the bombings and begin de-escalation of all military activity in Vietnam "the moment we are assured, privately or otherwise," that the moves would be matched by a reduction of North Vietnam's war effort. Goldberg said that

the 2d step toward de-escalation of the war would be a reciprocal withdrawal of all foreign troops from South Vietnam.
Supervision of the "phased withdrawal," he said, could be
carried out by the UN or other "international machinery."

Taking up the issue of proposed Viet Cong participation in
peace negotiations, he said that Pres. Johnson had "made
clear that . . . this question would not be 'an insurmountable
problem.' " Goldberg criticized those who appealed only "to
one side to stop [the war] while encouraging the other." He
denied that the U.S. was involved in a "holy war" against
communism or that it sought to win an empire in Southeast
Asia. The U.S., he declared, did not intend to harm "mainland China nor threaten any off its legitimate interests." The
U.S., he said, would "welcome discussion" of the Vietnam
question by either the Assembly or the Security Council.

Goldberg said:

"My government remains determined to exercise every restraint to
limit the war and to exert every effort to bring the conflict to the earliest possible end."

"Our aims . . . are strictly limited. We are not engaged in a 'holy
war' against communism. We do not seek . . . an American empire . . .
in Asia. We seek no permanent military bases, . . . no permanent
American 'presence' of any kind in South Vietnam. We do not seek to
impose a policy of alignment on South Vietnam. We do not seek the
overthrow . . . of North Vietnam. We do not seek to do any injury to
mainland China nor to threaten any of its legitimate interests. We do
not ask of North Vietnam an unconditional surrender . . . ; nor do we
seek to exclude any segment of the South Vietnamese people from
peaceful participation in their country's future."

The U.S. desired a "political solution" that would "assure for the
people of South Vietnam the right . . . of self-determination. . . ." The
"reunification of Vietnam should be decided upon through a free choice
by the peoples of both North and South without outside interference,
the results of which we are fully prepared to support."

". . . It is said that one obstacle is the United States bombing of
North Vietnam. Let it be recalled that there was no bombing of North
Vietnam for years during which there was steadily increasing infiltration from North Vietnam; during which there were no United States
combat forces in Vietnam. . . . And let it further be recalled that twice
before we have suspended our bombing, once for 37 days, without any
reciprocal act of de-escalation from the other side, and without any sign
from them of a willingness to negotiate.

"Nevertheless, let me say that, in this matter, the United States is
willing once again to take the first step. We are prepared to order a

cessation of all bombing of North Vietnam—the moment we are assured, privately or otherwise, that this step will be answered promptly by a corresponding and appropriate de-escalation on the other side. We therefore urge before this Assembly that the government in Hanoi be asked the following question, to which we would be prepared to receive either a private or a public response: Would it, in the interest of peace, and in response to a prior cessation by the United States of the bombing in North Vietnam, take corresponding and timely steps to reduce or bring to an end its own military activities against South Vietnam?

"Another obstacle is said to be North Vietnam's conviction or fear that the United States intends to establish a permanent military presence in Vietnam. . . . The United States stands ready to withdraw its forces as others withdraw theirs . . . and favors international machinery—either of the United Nations or other machinery—to insure effective supervision of the withdrawal. We therefore urge that Hanoi be asked the following question also: Would North Vietnam be willing to agree to a time schedule for supervised, phased withdrawal from South Vietnam of all external forces—those of North Vietnam as well as those from the United States and other countries aiding South Vietnam?

"A further obstacle is said to be disagreement over the place of the Viet Cong in the negotiations. Some argue that, regardless of different views on who controls the Viet Cong, it is a combatant force and, as such, should take part in the negotiations. . . . Some time ago our view on this matter was stated by Pres. Johnson, who made clear that, as far as we are concerned, this question would not be 'an insurmountable problem.' We therefore invite the authorities in Hanoi to consider whether this obstacle to negotiation may not be more imaginary than real."

Goldberg's speech was believed to indicate acceptance of the major provisions of UN Secy. Gen. Thant's 3-point plan for negotiations on Vietnam. It differed from previous U.S. statements on Vietnam only in its announcement of willingness to accept "assurances" rather than insist on "evidence" of a North Vietnamese military cutback and in its emphasis on U.S. readiness to accept the Viet Cong at the bargaining table.

Questioned at his news conference Sept. 22 as to whether the Goldberg address constituted a new U.S. peace initiative, Pres. Johnson would say only that the speech was important and had "my full approval and the Secretary of State's full approval." Sen. J. William Fulbright (D., Ark.), chairman of the Senate Foreign Relations Committee and a leading critic of the President's Vietnam policies, said Sept. 22 that the speech was "in the right direction" and "in the spirit of compromise."

The quotation cited by Goldberg on Pres. Johnson's readiness to accept the presence of Viet Cong envoys in peace talks was drawn from Mr. Johnson's July 28, 1965 White House press conference. The text of the newsman's question and the President's reply:

Q: "Mr. President, would you be willing to permit direct negotiations with the Viet Cong forces that are in South Vietnam?"

The President: "We have stated time and time again that we would negotiate with any government, any place, any time. The Viet Cong would have no difficulty in being represented and having their views presented if Hanoi for a moment decides she wants to cease aggression. And I would not think that would be an insurmountable problem at all. I think that could be worked out."

Soviet Foreign Min. Andrei A. Gromyko rejected the U.S. proposals Sept. 23 in a speech to the UN General Assembly. Gromyko charged that Goldberg's offer gave "no signs testifying to the seriousness of the intention of Washington to seek for a settlement of this problem and to stop the aggression against the Vietnamese people." Gromyko said that the only basis for peace was the Hanoi-NLF program: "unconditional cessation" of the U.S. bombing of North Vietnam, "withdrawal of all armed forces" of the U.S. and its allies from South Vietnam, "removal of foreign armaments" and "granting to the Vietnamese people . . . a chance to settle their internal problems themselves." Gromyko said that "the indisputable fact is that each so-called 'peaceful offensive' of Washington is followed by a further escalation of aggressive actions." The Soviet Union, he warned, had "rendered and will render all necessary assistance" to North Vietnam.

Goldberg addressed the Assembly immediately following Gromyko's speech to defend the U.S. proposals on Vietnam as "serious and genuine offers to break out of the tragic impasse." The U.S., he said, would continue its peace efforts and was awaiting "a considered reply" to its "affirmative proposals." Japanese Foreign Min. Etsusaburo Shiina told the Assembly that Goldberg's statement was "very important and constructive." Canadian External Affairs Min. Paul Martin said that peace efforts "should not and must not be abandoned."

The U.S. de-escalation proposal was denounced in Hanoi and Peking radio broadcasts Sept. 23-24 and by North Vietnamese Premier Pham Van Dong Sept. 25.

A North Vietnamese broadcast monitored Sept. 23 in Tokyo said the U.S. proposals were an attempt "to cover up its scheme to expand and prolong aggression in South Vietnam and to stay and maintain American troops in Vietnam." Goldberg had tried "to get the UN to interfere in the . . . issue so that the U.S. will be able to continue its aggression," Hanoi declared. Peking radio Sept. 24 said the Goldberg proposals were "another peace swindle in collaboration with Soviet revisionism." "The United Nations had no right to deal with the Vietnam problem," the Chinese broadcast said.

Premier Dong's rejection was delivered in a speech Sept. 25 at a Hanoi reception for visiting Czech premier Josef Lenárt. In an apparent reference to Goldberg's speech to the UN, Dong accused the U.S. of "trying again to use the United Nations as an instrument for their aggressive policy in Vietnam." Dong said if U.S. government leaders were interested in a peaceful solution of the conflict "they must recognize" North Vietnam's 4-point peace formula "and show their good will by acts, that is, to put a definitive and unconditional end to their air strikes." The U.S. also "must recognize the National Liberation Front of South Vietnam as their interlocutor to solve all questions in South Vietnam," Dong said. Dong said North Vietnam adhered to its previously stated view that the UN had "absolutely no right whatsoever to intervene in the Vietnam issue."

Goldberg said Sept. 30 in Washington that he did not regard the Communist broadcasts or the Dong statement as a rejection of the U.S. proposals. Goldberg, who had conferred earlier with Pres. Johnson, said that it was "natural" that the initial Communist responses would be "largely propagandistic in nature." He told newsmen that the U.S. had examined "with great interest" press reports from Hanoi describing the statements by Dong and Pres. Nguyen Huu Tho of the National Liberation Front as an easing of the Communist side's terms for peace. One of these reports, written by Jean Raffaelli, the Agence France-Presse correspondent in Hanoi, said that their significance lay in the fact that they softened emphasis on demands for a U.S. military withdrawal and recognition of the Viet Cong as the only legitimate representative of the South Vietnamese people.

A renewed appeal for joint Asian action to settle the Vietnam problem had been voiced by Philippine Pres. Ferdinand E. Marcos in a speech to the UN Assembly Sept. 21. Marcos, on a state visit to the U.S., told the Assembly that the Tashkent conference, called by the Soviet Union in 1965 to end fighting between India and Pakistan, was a precedent that should be repeated for Vietnam. "Malaysia, Thailand and the Philippines, the members of the Association of Southeast Asia, hereby renew their appeal to all Asian nations and the Soviet Union to act with equal boldness of imagination by calling a new Tashkent for Southeast Asia to end the brutal war in South Vietnam," he declared. Marcos also urged the Assembly to create a new political grouping of Asian states, paralleling the UN's Economic Commission for Asia and the Far East, to provide a forum for discussion of pressing issues such as the Vietnam crisis. He declared that the principle of "Asian solutions to Asian problems is at once so just and so indisputably right that Hanoi and Peking will be under strong moral obligation to relax their hostile attitude."

French Foreign Min. Maurice Couve de Murville called on the U.S. Sept. 28 to make a "new move" toward a political solution of the Vietnamese war. Addressing the UN Assembly, Couve de Murville declared that responsibility for a genuine peace overture rested with the U.S. U.S. intervention, he said, had been one of the "basic elements" in the "escalation," and the U.S. "alone" was in a position to "render everything possible, and first of all, peace. . . ." Couve de Murville echoed Charles de Gaulle's Sept. 1 speech by arguing that, as France had done in Algeria, the U.S. could relinquish its military position in Vietnam without losing world stature. Couve called for a return to the Geneva agreements of 1954 and 1962 on Indochina and Laos. He said that this would mean a withdrawal of all foreign troops from Vietnam, a prohibition against their return and a ban on foreign interference embodied in an "international treaty . . . binding upon all the great powers and the other countries directly involved." The Vietnamese, he declared, should be left to settle their own affairs "in full freedom" with reunification becoming "exclusively" a Vietnamese problem "regardless of the regime they might think fit to adopt." He repeated de Gaulle's proposal that the first step toward peace negotiations would have to be a prior commitment by the U.S. to "repatriate its forces within a suitable and determined period of time."

Swedish Foreign Min. Torsten Nilsson told the UN Assembly Oct. 10 that "a veritable poll of international opinion" advocated unilateral U.S. action to initiate Vietnam peace talks. As an inducement to starting negotiations, Nilsson said, the U.S. should not only stop bombing North Vietnam but should also reduce its ground operations.

(In a letter made public Nov. 11, U Thant called for a final and unconditional halt in U.S. air attacks on the North. The letter had been sent Oct. 19 to Lord Brockway of the British Council for Peace in Vietnam. It was made public at the opening of a Council peace seminar in London. Thant took issue with the proposal advanced by Goldberg at the UN Sept. 22. "If the bombing is to cease, there should be no conditions, no time limit," Thant insisted. There was no other way to achieve peace negotiations, he said.)

Thant's 3-Point Plan

UN Secy. Gen. Thant had taken various occasions during 1966 to propose a 3-point peace plan for Vietnam. He called for (1) cessation of U.S. bombing of North Vietnam; (2) de-escalation of the ground war in South Vietnam; (3) inclusion of the NLF in peace talks. Announcing Sept. 19 his willingness to continue in office after the expiration of his current 5-year term Nov. 3, Thant again repeated his 3-point formula. Speaking at a luncheon given him by the UN Correspondents' Association June 20, Thant had said that his plan "alone can create conditions conducive to the holding of a conference and conducive to the creation of conditions for a peaceful settlement of the problem of Vietnam." Thant said that "people are being killed in the hundreds every day" in "one of the most barbarous wars in history." Thant held that "without the spirit of give and take on the part of the parties primarily concerned there will be no negotiations leading to the return to the Geneva agreements on which everybody now seems to agree." He warned that "the more we wait the worse will be the war situation."

North Vietnam's first authoritative response to Thant's 3-point plan appeared in an article in the North Vietnamese Communist Party organ, *Nhan Dan* (reported Oct. 6 and discussed at UN headquarters Oct. 10). The article rejected de-escalation by both sides, but lauded the call for a halt in U.S. raids on North Vietnam. *Nhan Dan* called Thant's de-escalation proposal "passive and contradictory." It said: "Thant has not made the necessary distinction, namely that American imperialism is the aggressor and the Vietnamese people is the victim of aggression. He demands that this people should curb its struggle for independence and freedom." *Nhan Dan* praised Thant's 3d point—Viet Cong representation at future peace talks.

(In a letter delivered to Thant Oct. 5, South Vietnamese Premier Nguyen Cao Ky had thanked Thant for his efforts to bring peace to Vietnam. Ky said South Vietnam was prepared "to consider any initiative for a settlement which would preserve the independence of the Republic of Vietnam and the right of its people to choose their own way of life.")

During UN Assembly debate Sept. 27, Thailand Foreign Min. Thanat Khoman criticized U Thant's 3-point proposal. He said the UN and its officials had no right to barter South Vietnam's freedom and sovereignty. He opposed peace proposals that rewarded aggression and failed to force concessions from North Vietnam.

Among other statements made during the Assembly's general debate:

Sept. 29—Danish Foreign Min. Per Haekkerup called on Hanoi to respond favorably to the U.S.' peace offers. Others supporting the U.S.' proposals were Kenyan Vice Pres. Joseph Murumbi and Turkish Foreign Min. Ihsan Sabri Caglayangil. Albanian Foreign Min. Nesti Nase rejected any UN role in the solution of the Vietnamese problem. Bulgarian Foreign Min. Ivan Bashev also denounced the U.S.' proposals.

Sept. 30—Foreign Min. Joseph M. A. H. Luns of the Netherlands denounced those who asked "primarily or even exclusively" for military de-escalation on the U.S. side alone. He said that in the past year the U.S. had made "several serious peace proposals" that had been "spurned and turned down with contempt" by the Communists.

Oct. 4—Israeli Foreign Min. Abba Eban said North Vietnam would earn respect if it submitted the U.S.' peace proposals to "the challenge of negotiation." Eban called on Secy. General Thant to bring the U.S. and North Vietnam together to discuss peace proposals in detail. The UN's ultimate aim, he said, would be to rebuild the structure set forth in the 1954 Geneva agreements—with Cambodia, Laos and North and South Vietnam "independent, sovereign, safe from external interference and able to fashion their government and society according to their own will and choice."

Oct. 7—Indian External Affairs Min. Swaran Singh said he was "confident" that if the U.S. bombing of North Vietnam ended, both sides would find their way to the conference table. Yugoslav Foreign Min. Marko Nikezic said the U.S. would have to make the first move to end the Vietnamese war. He said the U.S. would have to end the bombing, recognize the NLF as a party to negotiations and then "undertake to withdraw its military forces from South Vietnam within a fixed period of time."

Oct. 12—Nationalist Chinese Amb.-to-UN Liu Chieh said that North Vietnam and Communist China had "nothing but contempt" for U.S. peace moves. He said peace would come only if the "Communist aggressors are convinced that they cannot win by force and violence and that aggression does not pay." UAR Foreign Min. Mahmoud Riad called for the "cessation of air raids over North Vietnam, without conditions or reservations," as "an essential step conducive to any progress toward restoration of peace in Vietnam." He said the next steps to peace would be withdrawal of "all foreign troops" and recognition of the NLF as "an essential party to the existing conflict."

Oct. 17—Cambodian Amb.-to-UN Huot Sambath said the UN could not be a peace mediator for Vietnam but could call on the U.S. to end its aggression. He said the withdrawal of U.S. troops should be arranged with the "genuine representatives of the Vietnamese people," *i.e.*, the NLF and the Hanoi government of North Vietnam. Sambath said the U.S. would not commit against whites "atrocities such as those of which it is guilty every day in Vietnam." "The only people responsible for the martyrdom of the Vietnamese people are the United States, who will have to answer to history for their actions," he declared.

6 clergymen of the Inter-Religious Conference on Peace urged Oct. 21 that the U.S. "act in conscience upon U Thant's first peace proposal—a cessation of the bombing of North Vietnam." The message, sent to Thant and to Arthur J. Goldberg, proposed that the U.S. "and its allies agree

explicitly to state and restate their willingness to enter into negotiations with all parties actually engaged in the war." The statement was signed by Rabbi Maurice N. Eisendrath, president of the Union of American Hebrew Congregations; Dr. Dana McLean Greeley, president of the Unitarian Universalist Association; Archbishop Iakavos, head of the Greek Orthodox Church of North & South America; Bishop John Wesley Lord of the Washington area of the Methodist Church; Bishop John J. Wright of the Roman Catholic Diocese of Pittsburgh; Episcopal Bishop William Crittenden of Erie, Pa.

LBJ Bars Air-Strike Halt

Suggestions that the U.S. unilaterally suspend air attacks on North Vietnam were rejected Oct. 13 by Pres. Johnson. Speaking to newsmen in Washington, the President ruled out any cessation of the bombings in connection with a planned forthcoming Manila conference on Vietnam. Mr. Johnson said that during the 2 U.S. bombing pauses that had already taken place (5 days in May 1965 and 37 days ending in 1966), American troops had "sat there and watched the enemy" while "he kept up his bombing" and killed American soldiers. Mr. Johnson expressed interest in a fresh halt in the air strikes only "if I could have assurance that it would be reciprocated and the other people would pause."

Mr. Johnson said it was generally understood that it was not the U.S. "who refuses to come to the conference table" and that "there are only 2 governments ,in the world [presumably North Vietnam and Communist China] that now appear opposed to ending the war and achieving the peace." He expressed hope that pleaders for peace "will direct their efforts to those 2 governments." The President said the U.S. would "withdraw immediately" from South Vietnam if the Communist forces also pulled out. Mr. Johnson reiterated his previous assertion that the U.S. was ready to submit "tomorrow" "a schedule to move out of South Vietnam, . . . provided they [the Communists] will lay on the table their schedule for withdrawal."

(Pres. Johnson Nov. 4 again opposed halting the U.S. air strikes without a reciprocal move by the Communists. Speaking at his news conference, the President said: "I can't conceive of anyone feeling that one side ought to stop the bombing and the other side to continue it"; the U.S. was "willing to do anything we can to get peace, except surrender"; but the U.S. was determined to prove militarily to the Communists "the utter futility of continuing this confrontation.")

LBJ Meets Allied Leaders in Manila

Pres. Johnson left Washington Oct. 17 for a 17-day trip to 7 Asian and Pacific nations and the planned Manila conference with the leaders of the other countries fighting as U.S. allies in Vietnam. En route to Manila the President visited Hawaii, American Samoa, New Zealand and Australia and delivered addresses in which he reiterated his pleas for peace. He conferred Oct. 20 in Wellington, N.Z. with Prime Min. Keith J. Holyoake and delivered an address in which he defended the U.S. role in South Vietnam as in accordance with "reason and conscience." Mr. Johnson received a tumultuous welcome during his Oct. 20-23 tour of Australia, but he met with 2 outbursts of anti-Vietnamese war demonstrations—in Melbourne Oct. 21 and in Sydney Oct. 22. In the Melbourne incident, the President's car was struck by 2 plastic bags of paint thrown by anti-war demonstrators. The car and 3 Presidential bodyguards near it were splattered with paint. The President and Mrs. Johnson were not touched.

Mr. Johnson and the other allied leaders conferred in Manila Oct. 24-25. They pledged at the conclusion of their meeting to withdraw their troops from the country within 6 months if North Vietnam "withdraws its forces to the North" and "ceases infiltration" of South Vietnam. The proposal was made in a communiqué signed by the leaders of the 7 participating nations: Mr. Johnson, Australian Prime Min. Harold E. Holt, New Zealand Prime Min. Keith J. Holyoake, South Korean Pres. Chung Hee Park, Philippine Pres. Ferdinand E. Marcos, Thai Prime Min. Thanom Kittikachorn and South Vietnamese Premier Ky and Chief-of-State Thieu. The communiqué, signed Oct. 25 after the 4th formal session of the conference, said: The allied forces were in South Vietnam "because that country is the object of aggression and its government requested support in the resistance of its people to aggression. They shall be withdrawn, after close consultation, as the other side withdraws its forces to the North. Those forces will be withdrawn as soon as possible and not later than 6 months after the above conditions have been fulfilled."

A 4-point "Declaration of Peace" contained in the statement stressed the need for a "peaceful settlement of the war in Vietnam" and for "future peace and progress" in the rest of the Asian and Pacific area. The declaration said: (1) "Aggression must not succeed"; (2) " the bonds of poverty, illiteracy and disease" must be broken; (3) "economic, social and cultural cooperation with the Asian and Pacific region" must be strengthened; (4) the allies must seek peace in Asia.

North Vietnamese Pres. Ho Chi Minh charged that the Manila conference was an allied attempt to "peddle their sham peace while actually stepping up the war." Ho's statement (quoted in a North Vietnamese news agency report broadcast by Hanoi radio Nov. 2) was made in a speech to a visiting Cuban delegation. Ho said there could be no peace in Vietnam until the U.S. ceased "for good and unconditionally the bombing raids and all other acts of war" against North Vietnam "and withdraws all troops of the U.S. and its satellites from South Vietnam."

The call for the conference had been issued in Honolulu Sept. 26 by the press secretary for Philippine Pres. Ferdinand E. Marcos, who was returning home from a visit with Mr. Johnson. The idea of the conference was criticized Sept. 27 by Chrmn. J. W. Fulbright (D., Ark.) of the Senate Foreign Relations Committee. He expressed doubt that a conference of "such a cozy little group" of "our boys" would be constructive. Fulbright said such Asian nations as India, Japan and Pakistan should have been invited if such a conference was expected to be useful. He indicated suspicion that an attempt to convey "a great earnestness and desire for peace" just prior to the Nov. 8 Congressional and gubernatorial elections in the U.S. could have been a motivation for the trip. White House Press Secy. Bill D. Moyers retorted that "we could not turn down the invitation just because a political campaign is going on." Asked about the criticism at his news conference Oct. 6, Mr. Johnson said: "I just think you have to evaluate the critics and judge the circumstances and draw your own conclusions." The President said the Administration's policy in Vietnam was to provide enough strength "to prevent the aggressor from succeeding without attempting either to conquer or to invade or to destroy North Vietnam."

Pres. Johnson flew from the Philippines to South Vietnam Oct. 26 for a surprise 2½-hour visit with U.S. troops stationed at Camranh Bay, about 180 miles northeast of Saigon. The visit, confined to the military base at Camranh Bay, was prepared in total secrecy and carried out under conditions of maximum security. Welcomed by Chief-of-State Thieu, who had preceded him from Manila, the President reviewed troops at the base and then addressed them. He said: Americans were proud of "what you are doing" and "the way you are doing it." "No American army in all of our long history has ever been so compassionate." "We shall never let you down . . . , not the 15 million people of South Vietnam, nor the hundreds of millions of Asians who are counting on us to show here in Vietnam that aggression does not pay . . . and cannot succeed." When the war ends "this wonderful harbor built here by you will become a source of strength to the economic life of Vietnam and of Asia. . . ." The President returned to Manila Oct. 26 before starting on the remainder of his Asian tour. He visited Thailand Oct. 27-30, Malaysia Oct. 30-31, South Korea Oct. 31-Nov. 2, and returned to Washington via Alaska Nov. 2. His Malaysian visit was marked by widespread anti-American rioting, but elsewhere his welcome was warm and enthusiastic.

The decisions reached at the Manila conference were assailed by Communist China, North Vietnam and the Soviet Union. The Chinese Communist news agency Hsinhua Oct. 27 called the allies' troop withdrawal proposal "out-and-out blackmail and shameless humbug." The North Vietnamese Communist Party newspaper *Nhan Dan* Oct. 27 described the suggestion for the simultaneous withdrawal of allied and North

Vietnamese troops from South Vietnam as "a demand for the Vietnamese people to lay down their arms and surrender to U.S. aggressors." The Soviet government newspaper *Izvestia* Oct. 26 interpreted the Manila conference communiqué as a "demand that North Vietnam capitulate before American conditions."

(At a New Delhi conference, the leaders of India, Yugoslavia, and the United Arab Republic Oct. 23 had issued a plea urging an immediate cessation of American air raids, "without any preconditions," as the first step toward peace. The report was signed by Indian Prime Min. Gandhi, Yugoslav Pres. Tito and UAR Pres. Gamal Abdel Nasser.)

Ex-Vice Pres. Richard M. Nixon Nov. 3 criticized the Manila conference decisions. In a speech in Johnson City, Tenn. and in a statement issued from his New York law office, Nixon questioned the pledge to withdraw military forces from Vietnam if North Vietnam withdrew its forces. "If we kept our Manila pledge to withdraw," Nixon said, "we would leave the South Vietnamese people to the mercy of the Viet Cong. But if we decided to stay in South Vietnam until the Viet Cong were pacified, we would be breaking our Manila pledge of mutual withdrawal and suffer a world-wide crisis of credibility." "Let us be thankful," he said, "that Hanoi has not been diplomatically alert enough to catch us off base." In reply Nov. 3, Mr. Johnson emphasized the communiqué's condition that withdrawal would occur only "if the violence ceased."

British Restate Peace Plan

A British government plan to end the war in Vietnam was outlined at a Labor Party conference in Brighton Oct. 6 by Foreign Secy. George Brown. The plan, largely a restatement of previous British proposals on Vietnam, called for: (a) peace negotiations that would include Viet Cong representation; (b) a simultaneous halt of U.S. raids on North Vietnam and of Communist infiltration into South Vietnam; (c) a cessation of the U.S. military buildup in South Vietnam; (d) orders by both sides, "as soon as is practicable," barring their forces from initiating any new aggressive actions; (e) the strengthening of the ICC and the establishment of a UN peace-keeping force, if necessary. Brown renewed London's previous suggestions that the Soviet Union, as co-chairman of the 1954 Geneva Conference, join Britain in reconvening the conference to seek an end to the war. (The British peace plan was denounced Oct. 7-10 by South Vietnam, the Viet Cong, North Vietnam and Communist China. But U.S. Amb.-to-UN Goldberg assured Brown Oct. 10 that the U.S. would give "sober consideration" to the British plan.)

In a subsequent vote at the Labor Party conference, a majority of party delegates, defying Prime Min. Wilson's policy on Vietnam, approved a resolution calling on the British government "to bring all pressures on the United States" to end the conflict and to cease air strikes against North Vietnam.

Brown Oct. 11 called on the Soviet Union to join with Britain in reconvening the Geneva conference to end the war in Vietnam. "I am convinced," he said in an address to the UN General Assembly, that "there is now common ground in the 1954 Geneva agreements, which both the North Vietnamese and the United States have said can be a basis for a settlement. . . . I repeat to . . . [Soviet Foreign Min. Andrei A.] Gromyko from this world rostrum the invitation which I made to him from the Labor Party conference in Brighton. I invite him to join with me in reconvening the Geneva conference, and to join with me today." Brown had conferred with Gromyko in New York Oct. 8 and 11 and discussed Vietnam on both occasions. Following the Oct. 11 meeting, he said he would go to Moscow "very early next year" at the invitation of the USSR to continue Britain's Vietnam peace offensive.

Renewing British efforts to promote a settlement, Brown Dec. 30 announced a plan for an immediate conference of the U.S., South Vietnam and North Vietnam to "arrange a cessation of hostilities." In messages sent to State Secy. Rusk, North Vietnamese Foreign Secy. Nguyen Duy Trinh and South Vietnamese Foreign Min. Tran Van Do, Brown offered to furnish facilities "in any suitable British territory and to help with transmitting any messages about arranging a meeting." Brown informed Soviet Foreign Min. Gromyko and UN Secy. Gen. U Thant of the plan in notes sent Dec. 31. The Soviet Union denounced the British proposal Dec. 31. An article appearing in the government newspaper *Izvestia* charged that the plan was a political move designed to still criticism of Prime Min. Harold Wilson's support of U.S. policy on Vietnam and of the British government's failure to speak out against U.S. air strikes on Hanoi and other North Vietnamese cities. Alluding to a report that Pres. Johnson had urged Wilson not to take a stand against the American bombing, *Izvestia* said: "Evidently the voice of Washington was heard quickly." Moscow radio earlier Dec. 31 had complained that Brown "puts the aggressor, the United States, and the victim, North Vietnam, in the same boat." The British plan, the broadcast protested, "does not even mention the South Vietnam National Liberation Front, which controls ⅘ of the country and is a lawful representative of its people."

Envoys Seek Path to Peace

U.S. Amb.-at-Large Harriman and Canadian State Secy. for External Affairs Paul Martin carried out diplomatic missions connected with the Vietnam situation in early November. Harriman visited 10 nations Oct. 27-Nov. 9 to explain the results of the Manila conference and the current U.S. evaluation of the situation in Southeast Asia. Harriman, acting as Pres. Johnson's personal emissary, visited the leaders of Ceylon, Indonesia, India, Pakistan, Iran, Italy, France, West Germany, Britain and Morocco. Harriman reported to the President Nov. 11 at his ranch in Johnson City, Tex. Harriman said at a news conference later that his trip had confirmed that "every country in the world, with the exception of Red China and Hanoi, wants to see peace." He said there were indications "that Hanoi is willing to talk, provided we do certain things." Martin conferred in Moscow Nov. 9-11 to ascertain Soviet views on possible negotiations to end the war. At the meetings, Martin stressed the need for strengthening the ICC. But at the conclusion of the talks Nov. 11 Martin said at a news conference that the Soviet leaders were "not so enthusiastic" about the idea. Before arriving in Moscow, Martin had discussed the Vietnam situation with Polish offiicials in Warsaw Nov. 7-8. The Polish leaders reportedly were cool to Martin's suggestion that the ICC should exert greater influence to bring about talks on ending the war.

Algerian efforts to secure a settlement of the war were suggested by Harriman at a meeting with Algerian Pres. Houari Boumedienne in Algiers Dec. 9 during a new tour. It was reported that Algerian Foreign Min. Abdelaziz Bouteflika forwarded Harriman's views Dec. 10 to the North Vietnamese and Chinese Communist ambassadors to Algeria. Harriman met with Tunisian Pres. Habib Bourguiba in Tunis Dec. 8 and with Gen. Francisco Franco, the Spanish premier, in Madrid Dec. 13. Harriman also visited Britain and France. On returning to the U.S. Dec. 14, Harriman said in an airport statement in New York that he had found "general support" for Pres. Johnson's policies on Vietnam. Despite some criticism of American conduct of the war, Harriman said, the leaders he had met "recognize and understand that we are fighting against Communist aggression and for Vietnamese self-determination."

Holiday Truces

The Vietnamese battlefield was temporarily stilled Jan. 20-23 by a truce in observance of *Tet,* the Vietnamese Lunar New Year. The Viet Cong Jan. 15 had first ordered their forces to cease fighting between Jan. 20 and 24. But the U.S. and allied commands complied with a South Vietnamese decision to honor the truce from noon Jan. 20 to 6 p.m. Jan. 23. The truce was largely observed despite reports of sporadic clashes. A U.S. military spokesman said Jan. 24 that the Viet Cong had initiated 82 incidents between 1 a.m. Jan. 20 and 5 p.m. Jan. 23. He reported these fatalities during the cease-fire period: 56 guerrillas, 5 Americans, 6 South Koreans (8 missing), 3 South Vietnamese soldiers and 4 South Vietnamese civilians.

At the expiration of the allied-decreed truce Jan. 23, U.S. B-52s bombed suspected Viet Cong concentrations in Phuoctuy and Tayninh Provinces in the south, and allied forces were ordered to resume offensive operations.

A Lunar New Year message broadcast by Hanoi radio Jan. 21 had appealed to the North Vietnamese and the Viet Cong to "march forward to strike deadly blows at the United States aggressors, annihilate and disintegrate many puppet troops" after the cease-fire ended. 23 hours before the truce had gone into effect a Viet Cong platoon Jan. 19 stormed a Vietnamese refugee camp at Tuhiep, 350 miles north of Saigon, and killed 33 civilians, wounded 54 and kidnapped 9 men. Before fleeing, the guerrillas burned the camps' huts.

Christmas and New Year's truces of 48 hours each were proposed by the Viet Cong Nov. 26 and agreed to by South Vietnam, the U.S. and other allies Nov. 30. Saigon also proposed a Feb. 8-12, 1967 ceasefire during *Tet*. The Viet Cong proposal, announced Nov. 26 by the NLF's clandestine radio, said the guerrilla forces would suspend military operations for Christmas from 7 a.m. Dec. 24 to 7 a.m. Dec. 26 and for New Year's from 7 a.m. Dec. 31 to 7 a.m. Jan. 2, 1967. The broadcast said the Viet Cong would honor the truce as long as no military action was initiated against the guerrilla forces, "including the enemy air strikes or the spraying of poisonous chemicals, as well as artillery bombardment of any area in South Vietnam."

Discussing the proposed suspension of fighting, U.S. State Secy. Rusk Nov. 18 had ruled out "any expectation that there will be a long pause" in the American air strikes against North Vietnam.

Speaking in St. Peter's Basilica Dec. 8 Pope Paul expressed the hope that the 2 seperate 48-hour cease-fires could be merged "into a single continuous period of time" to bring about an "armistice" that would be followed by "sincere negotiations which will lead to peace." A Vatican spokesman explained Dec. 9 that the pope actually had in mind a 51-day truce from Dec. 24 to Feb. 12, 1967, the expiration of the proposed *Tet* truce. The pope's suggestion was supported Dec. 13 by U.S. Senate majority leader Mike Mansfield, who urged the Administration to accept it. White House Press Secy. Bill D. Moyers said Dec. 14 that the U.S. would be willing to discuss the pope's proposal if the Communists showed interest in it.

An NLF broadcast Dec. 19 reiterated the Communist view that "the only solution for negotiations . . . is for the Americans to go home and to recognize the Liberation Front as the only representative of South Vietnam's population."

The U.S. called on UN Secy. Gen. U Thant Dec. 19 to "take whatever steps you consider necessary to bring about the necessary discussions which could lead to . . . a cease-fire" in Vietnam. U.S. officials explained that the U.S. action did not represent the start of a fresh American peace drive. They said it was designed only to spur new efforts by Thant to get the Communists interested in negotiations. The request, made in a letter submitted to Thant by Amb. Goldberg, said the U.S. government would "cooperate fully . . . in getting such discussions started promptly and in bringing them to a successful completion." This proposal, Goldberg said, was in line with Pope Paul's call for an extension of the holiday truce.

In a New Year's message Dec. 30, Thant called "once again for an early end to the war." Thant renewed his plea to the U.S. for an unconditional cessation of the bombing of North Vietnam. His statement was made in a letter to Goldberg in a reply to Goldberg's request that Thant use his good offices to obtain a cease-fire. Thant's note (made public Dec. 31) said that a halt in the bombing of North Vietnam was "the first and essential part" of his 3-point formula for peace in Vietnam. Thant also urged extension of the New Year's truce to "provide a welcome respite for private contacts and diplomatic explorations so that, in time, formal discussions can take place." In reply to Thant Dec. 31, Goldberg wrote that the U.S. favored an extended truce and was "ready to order a prior end to all bombing of North Vietnam the moment there is an assurance, private or otherwise, that there would be a reciprocal response toward peace from North Vietnam."

Pres. Johnson declared at a news conference in Johnson City, Tex. Dec. 31 that the U.S. would "be very glad to do more than our part in meeting Hanoi half-way in any possible cease-fire, or truce, or peace conference negotiations." But the President said he would have to await the response of North

Vietnamese officials to U.S. overtures "before irrevocably committing this country."

The Chinese Communist Party newspaper *Jenmin Jih Pao* Dec. 20 had called on North Vietnam and the Viet Cong to spurn negotiations with the U.S. and to continue the war. The newspaper charged that the Soviet Union, "in collusion" with the U.S., was "resorting to the dirty tricks of forcing peace talks by coercion, inducement or persuasion . . . with the aim of compelling the Vietnamese people to lay down their arms and give up the struggle." The Communist Party organ urged the Vietnamese to continue the war until "all the U.S. aggressors" were driven "out of their national soil."

The Christmas and New Year's truces were in effect Dec. 24-26 and beginning Dec. 31. Each side accused the other of repeated violations, however, the U.S. reporting more than 60 minor skirmishes with Communist forces during the Dec. 24-26 period. Heavy fighting occurred in the period between the 2 truces.

(Francis Cardinal Spellman, Roman Catholic archbishop of New York and military vicar of the U.S. armed forces for Roman Catholics, visited U.S. servicemen in South Vietnam Dec. 23-28. While there he evoked criticism from the Vatican and other sources by endorsing the U.S.' participation in the Vietnamese war. In an address at an open-air mass in Saigon, Spellman said: The Vietnamese conflict was "a war for civilization—certainly it is not a war of our seeking. It is a war thrust on us—we cannot yield to tyranny." Anything "less than victory is inconceivable." In a sermon at Camranh Bay Dec. 25 Spellman prayed for the acceptance of Pope Paul's plea for an extension of the Christmas-New Year's truces. "There is nothing honorable about war as such," he said, "but it is an honorable and an heroic thing to fight for those ideals and principles we account worthy of preservation. War, in fact, has brought out the noblest instincts and the best traits of human courage and endurance in the annals of history." In a speech at an open-air mass in Saigon Dec. 26, Spellman said American soldiers were in Vietnam for the "defense, protection and salvation not only of our country but . . . of civilization itself."

(Moscow radio charged Dec. 25 that Spellman "openly contradicts the pope's appeal for peace in Vietnam." The Soviet government newspaper *Izvestia* Dec. 26 asserted that Spellman's "militant sermons" were "in sharp dissonance with" Pope Paul's appeals "for an end to the bloody killing."

(Vatican sources Dec. 27 expressed displeasure with Spellman's statements in Vietnam. One source said the cardinal "did not speak for the pope or the church." The Rev. Pierre Wenger, 88, editor of the French Roman Catholic newspaper *Le Croix,* said in an editorial Dec. 27 that Spellman's views had "scandalized pacific men" and "appeared in contradiction with" the pope's "position on peace through negotiation.")

MILITARY ACTION

Fighting Intensified; Forces Increased

The fighting was intensified in Vietnam during 1966, and the opposing allied and Communist military forces in Vietnam were greatly augmented both in manpower and matériel. By the year's end, allied forces totaled approximately 1,138,000 men. Communist strength in South Vietnam was variously estimated at from 180,000 to 280,000 men.

The U.S. began the year with approximately 180,000 men in South Vietnam and ended it with 380,000 there. American forces supporting the war effort but not based physically in Vietnam included nearly 60,000 men aboard warships operating off Vietnam and an estimated 35,000 U.S. servicemen in neighboring Thailand. South Vietnamese forces (as of mid-August) numbered 705,000 men, about equally divided between regular army units and police, irregular and regional defense units. South Korean forces in Vietnam were increased by 25,000 men during 1966 to a total of 46,000 men. Other nations with troops in South Vietnam: Australia, 5,500; Philippines, 1,000 (support units); Thailand, 180; New Zealand, 150.

Estimates of the size and composition of the Communist force varied widely. A U.S. Senate report issued Jan. 8 put the total Communist force at 230,000 men, comprising 59,000 "main force" guerrillas, 14,000 North Vietnamese regulars, 100,000 militiamen, 40,000 political cadres and 17,000 support troops. A U.S. military spokesman in Saigon estimated the number of North Vietnamese regulars at 36,000 Feb. 18. Gen. William C. Westmoreland, U.S. commander in Vietnam, estimated the enemy at 282,000 troops (110,000 North Vietnamese regulars). A U.S. estimate Dec. 1 put the Communist force at 180,000. (Defense Secy. Robert S. McNamara in Senate testimony Jan. 23, 1967 said there were 275,000 Communist troops in South Vietnam, including 45,000 North Vietnamese regulars.) The South Vietnamese Foreign Ministry estimated that 73,900 North Vietnamese troops and political workers had infiltrated into South Vietnam in 1966; this was twice the number of North Vietnamese who had infiltrated in 1965.

According to Westmoreland, the major change in Communist tactics in 1966 was the stationing of North Vietnamese troops in the demilitarized zone between North and South Vietnam and along the Cambodian border in the Central Highlands.

Casualties & Desertions Increase

The greatly extended scope of the fighting in Vietnam was reflected in the year's casualty figures, especially in the increased number of American dead, and in the unusually high rate of desertions from both South Vietnamese and Communist forces.

The U.S. Defense Department reported Jan. 5, 1967 that 5,008 American soldiers had been killed and 30,093 wounded in fighting in Vietnam in 1966. This brought total U.S. losses in Vietnam since Jan. 1, 1961 to 6,664 killed and 37,738 wounded. U.S. Negro soldiers suffered proportionately higher combat fatalities than white American soldiers in Vietnam in 1966. Negro troops during Jan.-Sept. 1966 comprised 10.2% of the American force; but the Negro battle death rate for the period Jan.-Nov. 1966 constituted 16.3% of the 4,557 fatalities suffered by U.S. troops. Of the 4 services (Army, Marine Corps, Air Force, Navy), Negroes suffered the highest proportionate death rate in the Army during the 11-month period. Of the 2,801 Army men slain, 578 (20.6% of the total) were Negroes. (Negroes comprised 14.5% of the Army force.) According to a U.S. Defense Department spokesman, South

Vietnamese government combat fatalities totaled 10,110 during 1966 (43,582 since 1961). Viet Cong combat deaths in 1966, he said, numbered 61,631 (168,631 since 1961). (The North Vietnamese, in an article published in the Hanoi newspaper *Nhan Dan* Jan. 1, 1967, claimed that 240,000 allied troops, including 100,000 Americans, had been killed in Vietnam in 1966.)

Desertions from the South Vietnamese and Viet Cong ranks were up sharply, according to estimates of U.S. and South Vietnamese authorities. A U.S. spokesman reported Jan. 3, 1967, that 20,242 Viet Cong had defected in 1966, compared with 11,124 in 1965. The 1966 desertions raised to more than 48,000 the number of Viet Cong who had responded to Saigon's *Chieu Hoi* ("Open Arms") program, which had started in 1963. The Saigon government reported Jan. 9, 1967 that a record 116,858 South Vietnamese soldiers had deserted in 1966, compared with 113,000 the previous year.

U.S. Aircraft Losses Exceed 1,800

The increased use of American air power over Vietnam during 1966 was reflected in the higher number of U.S. planes and helicopters lost to both enemy gunners and "other causes." According to the Defense Department, 1,804 American aircraft of all types had been lost in Vietnam since 1961. This figure included 255 'copters lost in air combat (153 of them in 1966), 427 'copters lost due to other causes, 597 fixed-wing aircraft lost in air combat (451 over the North, 146 over the South) and approximately 525 planes* lost from other causes, primarily in crashes and due to Viet Cong ground action.

Of the 451 U.S. planes lost over the North, 10 were downed by MiGs, 30 by surface-to-air missiles and the rest by conventional anti-aircraft fire, according to a U.S. report issued Jan. 2, 1967. The North Vietnamese claimed Jan. 2 that 1,621 U.S. planes had been shot down over the North.

Civilians Die in Cross-Fire

South Vietnam's civilian population suffered heavy casualties and material losses in 1966, as Communist guerrillas and

---

* All other figures are as reported by the Defense Department through Dec. 31, 1966. The figures of 525 is an approximation based on a Defense Department report that 550 fixed-wing aircraft had been lost through Jan. 31, 1967.

American and allied troops fought throughout the country. The civilians were the victims of air strikes and artillery bombardments by allied forces, of booby traps and mines set by the Viet Cong, and of the increasingly indiscriminate weapons employed by both sides.

The number of civilian casualties could only be approximated. The *N.Y. Times* of Feb. 1, 1967 reported the results of a survey conducted by a U.S. study team showing that South Vietnamese hospitals had admitted 2,510 war-wounded civilians in the month of Dec. 1966. The report said that if the usual ratio of wounded to killed of 2:1 were used, civilian deaths might number about 1,250 a month, or nearly 15,000 a year. The report held that the real number probably was much higher because many wounded civilians could not reach a hospital. Maj. Gen. James W. Humphreys Jr., head of the U.S. medical aid program in South Vietnam, had said in Washington Jan. 5, 1966, that "many thousands" of Vietnamese civilians in heavily populated areas had been killed in military actions. He said civilian casualties generally were higher than those suffered by the military.

The frequency of Viet Cong terrorist attacks in the Saigon area led to the assignment of several battalions of U.S. troops to patrol duties in and around the capital district in December. Viet Cong attacks in all areas of Vietnam generally followed the same pattern: a mine or a bomb, presumably intended for soldiers or government officials, caused more civilian than military casualties when it exploded. In some typical incidents: 56 South Vietnamese peasants were killed Feb. 14 within a 3-hour period by Viet Cong mine blasts on a road near Tuyhoa, 225 miles northeast of Saigon; 3 days later a Viet Cong mine explosion killed 12 Vietnamese and injured 60 outside South Vietnamese Armed Forces headquarters in Saigon. Within 4 days in mid-October 11 persons were killed and 54 wounded when a mine exploded in the market place of the Mekong delta town of Traon, 75 miles southwest of Saigon, and a bus carrying Vietnamese civilians detonated a mine on a road 18 miles north of Hué; the explosion killed 15 civilians and injured 19.

The increasing number of accidental deaths among both civilians and allied soldiers resulting from war action was cited in a statement of concern issued Aug. 24 by Gen. Westmoreland. He reported that in 12 incidents since July 1 at least 143 civilians and soldiers had been killed and 234 wounded by allied air and artillery strikes. In the worst of a series of August incidents, 63 persons had been killed and nearly 100 wounded Aug. 9 when 2 Air Force jets attacked the villages of Truongtrung and Truongtay about 80 miles south of Saigon. 2 U.S. Marine jets mistakenly bombed the village of Hombe (5 miles from Quangngai) Sept. 27 and killed at least 35 civilians. Airplane crashes in populated areas also took a toll. A U.S. Marine jet crashed into a village near Danang Aug. 17, killing 26 civilians. A U.S. cargo plane, en route from Japan, crashed Dec. 24 in the village of Hoavang near the Danang airbase while coming in for a landing; 103-125 civilians and all 4 crewmen aboard the plane were killed.

Hanoi Foresees Victory

Gen. Vo Nguyen Giap, North Vietnamese defense minister, predicted Feb. 1 that the Viet Cong and North Vietnam would defeat the South Vietnamese and the U.S. despite the growing American war effort. Giap's prediction was in an article in the January issue of the North Vietnamese Lao Dong (Communist) party journal Hoc Tap. Giap said the U.S. was stepping up its military efforts because its ground operations in South Vietnam and air raids against North Vietnam had failed "to stabilize the very critical position of the puppet army and administration" of the South Vietnamese government. Giap said the purpose of the current U.S. drive was: (a) to "control important strategic areas and set up firm bases as springboards" in order to attack "liberated areas" and "to decimate our forces"; (b) to "prevent the collapse of the puppet army and administration" of South Vietnam; (c) to "intensify the war against the North"; (d) to "carry on their deceptive peace negotiations campaign." Giap said: The Communist forces had grown up, and the liberated areas have included the major part of the southern population and territory"; despite the dispatch of "hundreds of thousands of troops, [the Americans] cannot avoid being driven into passivity in strategy, compelled to scatter their forces . . . , and cannot easily wrest back the initiative they wish but instead face increasing failure"; the U.S. had "directly invaded the South of our country at a moment when the puppet army and administration are seriously weakening"; "the more direct the Americans' aggression, the more isolated and differentiated" South Vietnam's army and government became; the U.S. was "meeting with increasingly energetic opposition from the peoples of the Socialist countries and the world's progressive people, including the American people"; the U.S. was in no position to send an unlimited number of troops to Vietnam because America had to defend its other interests elsewhere.

The presence in the Lao Dong party of a faction not in complete agreement with Hanoi's war policy was indicated in an article appearing in the Feb. 3 issue of the party newspaper *Nhan Dan* and the February issue of *Hoc Tap*. The article was written by Le Duc Tho, a party leader in charge of organization affairs. Tho warned that there was a long struggle ahead and that Hanoi must be on the alert for "all plots and tricks of the enemy." He added: "Faced with great changes in the situation and with the revolutionary tasks, a small number of comrades have developed erroneous thoughts and views." "They have made an incorrect assessment of the balance of power between the enemy and us and of the enemy ruses. Now they entertain subjectivism and pacifism, slacken their vigilance and fail to get ideologically ready for combat." They "display pessimism . . . and a reluctance to protracted resistance, fail to realize clearly the deceptive peace negotiation plot of the enemy and rely on outside aid."

An assessment that North Vietnam could defeat any full-scale U.S. invasion of its soil was made by Maj. Gen. Nguyen Van Vinh, deputy chief of the North Vietnamese army's general staff. In a military analysis written in *Hoc Tap* (made public Feb. 22), Vinh said a projected U.S. invasion force of 400,000-500,000 men would not even be sufficient to overcome the unremitting Viet Cong attacks in South Vietnam. Vinh asked: "How could the Yankees envisage a massive concentration of forces on the front aimed at North Vietnam and

Laos and try to encircle and isolate the patriotic war of our compatriots in the south?" North Vietnamese Communist Party Politburo member Truong Chinh, reportedly a leader of the party's pro-Peking faction, warned Mar. 16 that the war would probably be a long one. His warning was delivered in a speech at the closing session in Hanoi of the current meeting of the Central Committee of the Fatherland Front. (The front coordinated all political groups in North Vietnam and maintained close contact with the National Liberation Front in South Vietnam.) Chinh said: "The North Vietnamese people must enhance solidarity to defeat the U.S. war of destruction, defend North Vietnam, continue Socialist construction and actively support the liberation war of the South Vietnamese people." Chinh scoffed at U.S. peace overtures as an "extremely crafty trick aimed at covering their acts of intensifying the war and continuing their escalation against North Vietnam."

(In anticipation of a long war and an expected intensification of U.S. aerial bombing, the North Vietnamese reportedly were decentralizing industry and government offices to minimize the loss that could be anticipated in a concentrated attack.)

U.S. Resumes Air Attacks on North

After a 37-day pause in U.S. air raids on North Vietnam, the American strikes were resumed Jan. 31 with attacks by land-based Air Force jet planes and Navy aircraft from the carriers *Ranger* and *Kitty Hawk* in the Gulf of Tonkin. Bad weather marred the effectiveness of the raids. A military communiqué said bridges, roads, ferry points, supply depots and a truck convoy were hit in the 23-mission attack in the southern part of North Vietnam, well south of Hanoi. The targets were near the cities of Donghoi, Vinh and Thanhhoa. The U.S. report said that 3 U.S. planes were downed and that 3 crewmen of 2 of the aircraft were rescued at sea. Another crewman was missing. North Vietnam claimed that its anti-aircraft had shot down 5 U.S. planes.

It was reported that all raids beginning Jan. 31 were ordered limited to south of the 21st Parallel. U.S. pilots were forbidden to strike targets in North Vietnam's Tonkin delta, in the Hanoi area or near the Chinese Communist border. Under a revised policy, neither the number of planes nor bomb loads were disclosed.

Among air developments following the resumption of the raids:

■ U.S. planes Feb. 1 struck at North Vietnamese port facilities and communications lines in the same area. One of the targets bombed was the port of Benthuy, about 5 miles southeast of Vinh.

■ U.S. Air Force planes Feb. 2 bombed 2 bridges 70 and 75 miles south of Vinh and a storage area 5 miles south of the coastal city. Other North Vietnamese bridges and storage areas were hit by Navy planes.

■ 2 U.S. Navy planes were lost in missions in the Vinh area Feb. 3. One of the planes, an A-4 from the carrier *Ranger,* was brought down by North Vietnamese antiaircraft fire. The 2d plane, an R-5 Vigilante from the carrier *Kitty Hawk,* was badly damaged by ground fire and crashed into the sea 35 miles northeast of Vinh.

■ Roads, bridges, rail lines and ferry points were struck Feb. 4 and other targets were hit Feb. 6 near Vinh, Dongh and Thanhhoa.

■ U.S. Air Force planes Feb. 7 struck Dienbienphu, site of a North Vietnamese training center. Although Dienbienphu was north of the 21st Parallel, a U.S. source said that the attack represented "no change in orders or in policy."

■ U.S. planes Feb. 4-8 dropped a record number of propaganda leaflets over North Vietnam. The leaflets were dropped in the Red River delta area, which included the Hanoi and Haiphong areas and the heavily populated coastal region between the delta and the demilitarized zone. The leaflets urged the North Vietnamese to "help end this cruel and senseless war." They said: "Your rulers foolishly rejected efforts to restore peace . . . , completely disregarding the disastrous consequences for you."

■ U.S. Navy and Air Force pilots Feb. 17 carried out a 27-mission attack on North Vietnam, striking bridges and storage centers in the areas of Dienbienphu, Donghoi and Vinh.

■ U.S. Navy planes flew 6 missions over North Vietnam Feb. 23 despite heavy rain and overcast. One of the targets struck was a highway 36 miles southwest of Vinh. In another mission flown by U.S. Air Force jets, the pilots reported striking North Vietnamese barracks 3 miles south of Dienbienphu and destroying 2 buildings.

(The U.S. Air Force announced in Washington Apr. 11 a new policy [which had gone into effect in January] limiting pilots and crews assigned to the Vietnamese war to a 12-month period or to 100 combat missions over North Vietnam. No limit was placed on missions against targets in South Vietnam. The Marine Corps and Navy said they would retain a policy of no limit on the number of missions their pilots fly over North or South Vietnam.)

Air Strikes Extended & Intensified

U.S. Air Force jets Mar. 3 bombed targets in North Vietnam's Red River Valley within 40 miles of the Chinese Communist border. A U.S. military communiqué said that the 30-mission attack had destroyed a bridge 100 miles northwest of Hanoi, had "possibly cut" a railroad bridge at Langbun, 120 miles northwest of Hanoi, and had cut another rail track from China about 105 miles from the capital. The raid was the first in the area since the bombing of North Vietnam had been resumed Jan. 31. The strikes against the Red River Valley reportedly had been authorized following a report that the North Vietnamese were concentrating supplies at Yenbay and Phutho, northwest of Hanoi.

In another operation Mar. 3, F-4 Phantom jets from the aircraft carrier *Ranger* attacked 2 motorized junks in the Gulf of Tonkin 24 miles southeast of the port city of Haiphong. Pilots reported one vessel sunk and the other badly damaged. Other carrier-based planes struck targets in the southern part of North Vietnam.

U.S. Air Force and Navy planes Mar. 4 carried out the heaviest attack on North Vietnam since the raids had started in Feb. 1965. 61 raids were directed against transportation lines, truck convoys, coastal junks and supply and ammunition depots over a widespread area. In one attack, Air Force Sabre and Thunderchief jets hit a battery of Soviet-made surface-to-air missiles 34 miles west of Hanoi, setting off explosives and fires on the ground. Pilots reported intense conventional anti-aircraft fire. The raiders clashed briefly twice with North Vietnamese MiG-17 jet fighters. In one incident 3 MiGs made single firing passes at Phantom jets protecting other planes pounding rail and highway bridges 80 miles northwest of Hanoi. The MiGs then fled. In the 2d MiG incident, Thunderchief jets chased 2 North Vietnamese planes that were spotted on the return from a raid on a bridge 120 miles north of Hanoi; the MiGs fled.

U.S. planes Mar. 5 again struck at Hanoi-Communist China rail lines in the Red River Valley, but heavy clouds marred the effectiveness of the attack. The raids on the valley were intensified Mar. 6 as the weather cleared. 71 bombing missions were flown against the Communist transportation system in the area. Highways and railroads were struck in the vicinity of Vinh and Donghoi.

U.S. Air Force and Navy planes flew an estimated 200 sorties against North Vietnamese targets Mar. 7 in the heaviest bombardment of the war. Among the targets hit were an oil storage area 60 miles southeast of Dienbienphu, a missile site 22 miles west of Thanhhoa and a staging area 60 miles northwest of Vinh. 4 planes were lost.

U.S. F-4C Phantom bombers Apr. 4 attacked the main supply link between North Vietnam and Nanning, China. The targets struck were the Phulangthuong railroad bridge and ferry, 25 miles northeast of Hanoi, and a road bridge 33 miles northeast of Hanoi. Other planes bombed a railroad yard 52 miles northeast of Hanoi. The pilots reported the yard had been made completely unusable. A less important North Vietnam-China rail link also was bombed—the Phutho railroad bridge northwest of Hanoi. The span was said to have been completely destroyed. The raid against the Nanning-Hanoi rail link was said to have been ordered by U.S. Amb. Henry Cabot Lodge in retaliation for a Viet Cong attack Apr. 1 on a U.S. military billet in Saigon.

Air Attacks Mounted from Guam

B-52 bombers from the U.S. Strategic Air Command base in Guam bombed North Vietnam for the first time Apr. 12. A U.S. military spokesman in Saigon said the aircraft had raided the approaches to Mugia Pass, the main road used by North Vietnam to ship supplies and infiltrators into South Vietnam via Laos. The pass was about 70 miles northwest of the 17th Parallel and about 200 miles south of Hanoi. U.S. sources said that U.S. fighter-bombers had been attacking the pass area repeatedly in recent weeks in response to an increase in North Vietnamese infiltration. The bombers dropped more than a million tons of bombs on Mugia Pass, causing a landslide that completely blocked strategic Route 15, which ran through the pass. Route 15 connected with the Ho Chi Minh Trail, which ran through Laos and into South Vietnam.

5 days later U.S. bombers began hitting targets closer to Hanoi, the North Vietnamese capital, and to Haiphong, the country's main port, than had ever before been attacked in the American air campaign. 5 U.S. planes Apr. 17 struck 2 missile sites 15 and 17 miles from Hanoi, a U.S. Air Force spokesman reported Apr. 18. The spokesman said that the targets were left engulfed in flames and that the sites' radar equipment apparently had been destroyed. The 5 planes had accompanied other U.S. Air Force aircraft in an attack mission against a railroad bridge linking Hanoi with Haiphong (33 miles south of Hanoi) when the North Vietnamese missiles opened fire. The anti-aircraft fire was heavy, but no attacking plane was shot down. The bridge and its approaches were reported heavily damaged. The North Vietnamese press agency reported that the Apr. 17 U.S. air attack had been directed at a Hanoi suburb and that the North Vietnamese army had protested to the International Control Commission on Vietnam.

2 U.S. Navy intruder bombers from the carrier *Enterprise* Apr. 18 bombed the 24,000-kilowatt Uongbi power plant, 14 miles northeast of Haiphong. A U.S. military spokesman said Apr. 19 that the planes' 2 pilots had reported that all the lights in the target area and in the Hanoi-Haiphong complex served by the power plant were "sharply extinguished" after they dropped their 1,000-pound bombs. The Uongbi plant had been reported destroyed after a previous raid by about 50 Navy planes Dec. 20, 1965. The plant apparently had been rebuilt since.

2 flights of Navy A-4 Skyhawk jets from the carrier *Ticonderoga* Apr. 19 bombed a bridge on the Haiphong highway, 10 miles north of the port city. Pilots reported having knocked out at least one span. The raiders were fired on by surface-to-air missiles, but none was hit. Hanoi claimed that one of the jets had been brought down by anti-aircraft fire "over Haiphong city." Hanoi said 3 more U.S. aircraft had been shot down and many others damaged in other attacks that day against North Vietnamese targets.

U.S. jet planes downed 2 Communist MiG-17 jet planes in one of 2 encounters over North Vietnam Apr. 23. It was the first time Communist aircraft had appeared in strength over North Vietnam to challenge American raiders. At least 16 MiGs clashed with 14 American planes. In the first aerial duel, 2 supersonic MiG-21s— the most advanced Soviet-made fighter planes—attacked 4 F-4C Phantom jets accompanying an Air Force RB-66, designed to jam North Vietnamese radar and anti-aircraft missile-guidance systems. The MiGs fled after the Phantoms fired Sidewinder missiles. In the 2d incident, 4 other Phantoms shot down 2 of 6-8 slower MiG-17s about 65 miles north of Hanoi. The Phantoms were accompanying 16 Thunderchief jets on a bombing mission against the Bacgiang railroad bridge 25 miles north of Hanoi. The Thunderchiefs went on to bomb the span (2 of the planes were downed by anti-aircraft fire) while the dog-fight was in progress.

A North Vietnamese Foreign Ministry statement (quoted Apr. 25 by Tass, the Soviet news agency) said: U.S. planes had bombed and strafed Vandinh, Vinh, Phouli, Ninhbinh, the Wangbi power station, Thakbak Dam and industrial targets in Kampha.

After North Vietnamese workers cleared Mugia Pass Apr. 20, B-52s from the U.S. SAC base on Guam attacked it again Apr. 27 and blocked it once again.

A U.S. military spokesman in Saigon reported May 8 that U.S. air strikes had severed 4 major railroad links serving Hanoi and at least 2 main highways that shared bridges with 2 of the rail lines. Most of the aerial attacks had occurred during mid-April. Reconnaissance reports of a May 4 attack (made public May 7) by U.S. Air Force Thunderchief jets said that a vital link between Hanoi and Nanning, China had been severed. The planes destroyed 2 of 4 spans of the Bacgiang highway and railroad bridge, 25 miles northeast of Hanoi. The other North Vietnamese arteries reportedly made impassable by the U.S. air attacks: (1) The railroad running 154 miles northwest to Kunming, China. It was cut 70 and 120 miles from Hanoi. U.S. bombers also attacked highways paralleling the rail line. (2) A highway-railroad bridge between Hanoi and Haiphong. It was destroyed. (3) A railroad bridge at Phuly (about 50 miles south of Hanoi). It was destroyed, but a highway bridge was still in use. The bridge was on the principal route from Namdinh, Thanhhoa and Vinh.

A U.S. military spokesman said that although North Vietnam's principal arterial supply routes had been wrecked, "a lot of other routes from China" remained open. Despite the fact that these routes were "longer and in worse condition," he said, "they were usable. Hanoi can still get supplies. It's just going to take much work and more time." The U.S. official said American success in putting out of action North Vietnam's land routes was indicated by reconnaissance reports of an increase in river and coastal shipping.

U.S. Navy A-4 Skyhawk fighter-bombers from the carrier *Enterprise* May 11 bombed and strafed a surface-to-air missile site 10 miles northeast of Haiphong. It was the closest U.S. air strike to the port city. The pilots reported scoring a direct hit on the site, which had 3 missile launchers. During the attack 3 missiles were fired at the raiders, but they missed.

LBJ Vs. Widening Air War

U.S. Air Force Secy. Harold Brown said May 22 that Pres. Johnson opposed widening the air war against North Vietnam by bombing Hanoi, Haiphong and other major cities. Speaking on the NBC-TV program "Meet the Press," Brown conceded that current U.S. air strikes against North Vietnam had reduced but not cut off the flow of men and supplies to Viet Cong forces in the south. A step-up in the American air raids might further reduce the North-South movement but "still would not cut off that infiltration," he said. Expansion of the air attacks, however, "might well carry with it the likelihood of a wider war, and no responsible government can lightly step into such a situation," Brown declared. He emphasized that Pres. Johnson's "decision . . . is not to expand the targets. . . . It doesn't do very much good to win one war and find yourself in a much bigger one," possibly with Communist China.

An extension of the bombing in North Vietnam had been urged by Chrmn. Richard B. Russell (D., Ga.) of the Senate Armed Services Committee in a speech in Atlanta Apr. 26. "I think we should bomb any and all military and strategic targets in North Vietnam that contribute to the Communist campaign of tyranny and aggression against the South," he declared. Ex-Sen. Barry M. Goldwater, in an interview published Apr. 18 in *U.S. News & World Report,* advocated the bombing of "the petroleum depots around Hanoi" and the closing of the port of Haiphong by "sinking light ships in its very shallow and narrow channel."

Sen. Robert F. Kennedy Apr. 27 assailed the Administration's stated policy of permitting "no sanctuary" in Communist China or elsewhere for planes attacking U.S. aircraft over North Vietnam. Speaking in the Senate, Kennedy said: "What is occurring in North Vietnam is escalation of the war by them or by us—the fact is that we are both inexorably involved. . . . What will be the Chinese response if her territory is bombed or her airspace invaded? Will the Chinese seek to strike at our bases—in Vietnam, or Thailand, or aboard our aircraft carriers? And if they do, what then will our response be?—further bombing? And if the scale of bombing increases, will China confine herself to air fighting?—or will it send its troops to engage ours on the ground in South Vietnam?" There must be "a viable political structure" in South Vietnam, and this could be achieved not by any military action in North Vietnam or China but only by "a unified effort" of the South Vietnamese "to organize their society and the government to continue the fight." Kennedy said it would be "neither prudent nor wise to undertake risks of a still wider war until some progress has been made toward achieving the stability that is essential for the successful prosecution of our efforts in Vietnam."

Despite the U.S. Administration's declared opposition to expanding the air war, U.S. planes carried out record air attacks on North Vietnam May 30 and 31. In the May 30 operation, Air Force and Navy jets flew 83 missions (estimated plane total: 249-332), striking at bridges and roads. The number of attacking planes was described as the largest since the U.S. raids on North Vietnam had begun Feb. 7, 1965. The heaviest strikes were centered in the Vinh-Thanhhoa area, where 5 bridges, 17 railroad cars and 20 buildings were destroyed. The planes also hit Highway 12 in 4 places north of Mugia Pass. A U.S. spokesman attributed the heavy attack largely to an improvement in weather conditions, not to escalation of the air war. The May 31 raid reportedly inflicted heavy damage on the Yenbay arsenal and munitions storage area, about 75 miles northwest of Hanoi. A U.S. Air Force officer said June 1 that in the 1½-hour raid 71 of the arsenal's estimated 120 buildings had been destroyed and 44 damaged and 25 of the 30 anti-aircraft batteries protecting the installation silenced. Pilots said the square-mile area had been enveloped in flames. North Vietnamese anti-aircraft fire downed 2 of the attacking planes.

U.S. planes carried out devastating raids against North Vietnamese petroleum storage areas June 21-27. In one 11-strike mission June 21-22, U.S. Air Force planes struck oil storage tanks 30-45 miles from Hanoi. A reconnaissance photo released June 27 showed that extensive damage had been caused by the explosions that followed the dropping of 1,000- and 3,000-pound bombs. U.S. Navy planes from the carrier *Constellation* struck June 26 at the Yenhau petroleum area, 35 miles northeast of Vinh. A-6 Intruder planes dropped 24 500-pound bombs on the target and left it in flames. Sailors aboard the *Constellation,* 150 miles offshore, reported seeing the smoke from the target site. 4 U.S. A-4 Skyhawk planes June 27 bombed a fuel dump 12 miles south of Vinh. 2 large explosions were reported following the dropping of 500-pound and 1,000-pound bombs. U.S. State Undersecy. George W. Ball said June 26 that the U.S. had made "no decision to bomb Haiphong or to bomb the [fuel] installations" in the Haiphong-Hanoi area. Speaking on NBC-TV's "Meet the Press," Ball said he was "departing from the practice of not talking about operational matters because of the amount of discussion there has been in the press on this subject." Ball, however, had said he did not rule out an attack on the oil depots in the future.

U.S. Bombs Hanoi-Haiphong Area

American bombers began attacking fuel storage installations near the North Vietnamese cities of Hanoi and Haiphong June 29. The attacks, repeated on successive days, were reported to have destroyed a substantial portion of North Vietnam's fuel handling and storage facilities. The raids were the first in the immediate vicinity of the North Vietnamese capital and the country's major port city. They were considered a major escalation of the U.S. air war against North Vietnam. All prior attacks had been directed at objectives away from the 2 North Vietnamese population centers. U.S. military authorities in Saigon reported that the raids had destroyed more than 50% of North Vietnam's supply of fuel and the facilities needed to handle it.

The first air attack on the Hanoi area was carried out by Air Force F-105 fighter-bombers that struck a fuel dump 3½ miles from the center of the city. The pilots reported that they had destroyed 90% of the target, described as the main North Vietnamese transshipment point for petroleum products. The Hanoi tank farm, at the edge of the Red River, had a capacity of 34,000 metric tons, 20% of the country's fuel storage capacity. North Vietnam claimed that 4 attacking planes were shot down over the capital, but the U.S. reported that only one had been lost.

The initial raid on the Haiphong area was made June 29 by Navy A-4 and A-6 fighter-bombers that attacked fuel storage and handling facilities on the banks of the Cuacam River, 2 miles from the center of the city. Preliminary reports said that the installation, which represented 40% of North Vietnam's storage capacity and 95% of its tanker-unloading capacity, was 80% destroyed. The Haiphong complex was said to have had tanks capable of holding 72,000 metric tons of fuel. North Vietnam claimed to have shot down 3 of the Haiphong raiders; the U.S. reported that all had returned safely.

The Chinese news agency Hsinhua reported July 4 that North Vietnamese authorities had decided July 1 to evacuate all persons from Hanoi "except those who had tasks of production or fighting to assure the defeat of the U.S. war escalation." An Agence France-Presse dispatch from Hanoi July 2 said the evacuation already had begun. According to an AFP follow-up report July 15, 10,000 persons a day were being evacuated from Hanoi.

Defense Secy. Robert S. McNamara said at a press conference in Washington June 29 that the U.S. had begun bombing oil facilities in the previously immune Hanoi-Haiphong area "to counter a mounting reliance by North Vietnam on the use of trucks and powered junks to facilitate the infiltration of men and arms into South Vietnam." McNamara said that the fuel facilities had become "increasingly important" and that the targets were acquiring a "perishable nature" because "in recent weeks the North Vietnamese have been carrying on a program to disperse and redistribute their petroleum storage facilities" to less-vulnerable excavated sites.

McNamara said that the new air strikes, "made after consultation with the government of South Vietnam, are intended to achieve the following military objectives: (1) Neutralize at Haiphong the only existing North Vietnamese shore facility for offloading petroleum from ocean-going tankers. . . . Haipong is estimated to have handled 95% of all petroleum imports. (2) Destroy the contents of the major central storage facilities; Hanoi is estimated at over 20% and Haiphong at over 40% of the remaining national capacity. (3) Cripple the major transshipment facility at Hanoi. (4) Require North Vietnam to devote men, matériel, time and effort to establish new storage and distribution facilities. (5) Force a high competition for the reduced petroleum assets, thereby requiring more stringent rationing and imposing a lower ceiling on the number of men that can be supported for aggression in the South."

McNamara restated the 3 principal objectives "of our bombing campaign in the North": (1) to raise the morale of the South Vietnamese, (2) "to reduce the level of infiltration or substantially increase the cost of infiltration . . . from the North to the South" and (3) "to show the North that as long as they continued their attempts to subvert and destroy the political institutions of the South, they would pay a price not only in the South but in the North as well."

McNamara reported that: "North Vietnamese units in South Vietnam are estimated to have increased by more than 100% since the end of 1965 . . . despite heavy battle losses. . . ." "Enemy truck movement to South Vietnam has doubled during the first 5 months of 1966, compared with the same period in 1965. . . . The daily tonnage of supplies moved overland has increased 150%, and personnel infiltration has increased 120% in the same period. "The rate of infiltration today we estimate to be about 4,500 men a month." Average monthly petroleum imports by North Vietnam "have increased 50-70% over 1965. Stocks on hand are estimated to represent a 2-4-month supply." "A result of the greatly increased movement of men and supplies by truck and powered junk has been a shift from a small-arms guerrilla action against South Vietnam to a quasi-conventional military operation involving major supplies, weapons and heavier equipment."

Pres. Johnson warned in a speech in Omaha June 30 that the U.S. air attacks on military targets in North Vietnam "will continue to impose a growing burden and a high price on those who wage war against the freedom of their neighbors." Mr. Johnson said: "The American purpose [in Vietnam] is to convince North Vietnam that . . . aggression is too costly, that this kind of power cannot succeed. And we have learned from their prisoners and their defectors and their captured documents that the Hanoi government really thought a few months ago that conquest was in its grasp. But the free men have rallied to prevent this conquest from succeeding. In the past 15 months our actions and those of our fighting allies . . . have already begun to turn the tide." "The Communists are not happy about the military defeat they are taking in South Vietnam. But sometimes they do get encouraged . . . about the dissension" in the U.S. "They believe that the [U.S.'] political disagreements . . ., confusion and doubt . . . will hand them a victory on a silver platter in Southeast Asia. Well, . . . they are wrong. . . . There can be only one decision in Vietnam, and that is this: We will see this through; we shall persist; we shall succeed.

Other Presidents have made the commitment. I have reaffirmed it."

North Vietnamese Pres. Ho Chi Minh July 17 ordered a "partial mobilization" throughout North Vietnam. Ho's directive was made in a radio address on the 12th anniversary of the Geneva accords on Indochina. Ho assailed the U.S. for "madly intensifying air raids in the Hanoi and Haiphong area." He declared that negotiations to end the war were "out of the question." Ho assured his people that "although some cities may be destroyed [by the U.S. raids], we will eventually score a victory and will start reconstructing the destroyed cities." Ho vowed that North Vietnam would wage war for "20 years or longer" until it achieved victory. He repeated the demand for acceptance of Hanoi's 4-point peace formula for ending the war, asserting that "there is no alternative." Hanoi radio reported later July 17 that in response to Ho's mobilization order many North Vietnamese military reservists had presented themselves to rejoin the armed forces.

Red Nations Pledge Aid to Hanoi

The expansion of the U.S. air attacks on North Vietnam evoked pledges from Communist countries of unstinting aid to Hanoi and of possible military intervention.

The USSR's response took the form of warnings that all possible support would be given Hanoi. A Soviet government statement issued June 30 charged that by its "criminal air raids" the U.S. had aggravated the Vietnam war and the "entire international situation." It said the new bombings proved that the U.S. had "set a course for a further escalation of the disgraceful war against the Democratic Republic of Vietnam and the entire Vietnamese people." It said that the USSR would continue to give Hanoi "political, economic and military" support for its "just cause."

Addressing a Kremlin reception for visiting French Pres. Charles de Gaulle, Soviet Premier Aleksei N. Kosygin declared June 30 that the U.S. had shown "once again that it is not at all interested in a peaceful settlement which it so often mentions." (Kosygin told the Supreme Soviet Aug. 3: "The Soviet government will do everything in its power to help . . . drive the American invaders from Vietnamese soil at the earliest possible date.")

Soviet Communist Party Gen. Secy. Leonid I. Brezhnev, in a Moscow speech July 1 to graduates of Soviet military academies, warned: "We are drawing the proper conclusion from the latest crimes of American imperialism. Our assistance to Vietnam will keep growing. The Soviet Union will never leave the Vietnam people in trouble."

(A note transmitted to the U.S. embassy in Moscow July 9 charged that the U.S. air strikes on the port of Haiphong had endangered 4 Soviet ships in the harbor. It said that U.S. planes had strafed to within 100 yards of the Russian vessels and that the threat to their safety constituted a violation of international principles of free navigation. The U.S. rejected the Soviet protest July 23 in a note that said great care had been taken to assure the safety of shipping in Haiphong during the raid, which the U.S. had been forced to carry out to curb North Vietnam's "aggression" against the South. It expressed regret "that the Soviet Union has been supplying petroleum products used by North Vietnam to pursue its armed attack against South Vietnam." A 2d Soviet note, charging that "large-caliber bullets" had struck a Russian vessel during a U.S. air attack on Haiphong Aug. 2, was rejected by the U.S. embassy in Moscow Aug. 5. The new note, refused because of its "abusive" language, said that U.S. ships and planes were harassing Soviet vessels bound for Haiphong.)

In its first reaction to the Hanoi-Haiphong raids, the Communist Chinese government declared July 3 that "this barbarous, wanton and criminal act of aggression and war" by the U.S. had "further freed us from any bounds or restrictions in rendering" more aid to Hanoi. The statement warned that Peking would "at any time take such actions as we deem necessary" to fulfill "the interests and demands of the Vietnamese people." The possible use of Chinese soil as a haven for North Vietnamese military forces was suggested by Peking in a new aid offer to Hanoi July 18. The Chinese Communist Party newspaper *Jenmin Jih Pao* said: "The vast expanse of our country is in the rear area of the Vietnamese people." The Chinese army newspaper *Chiehfang Chun Pao* warned July

19 that China was "ready at any time to join the Vietnamese people in wiping out U.S. aggressors." The newspaper quoted CP Chrmn. Mao Tse-tung as having said that the Chinese army, "confronted with the U.S. imperialist war threat," "should . . . thoroughly strengthen war preparedness . . . so as to be ready at all times for combat action . . . with the Vietnamese people to wipe out the murderous American bandits completely." Chinese Communist Chief of State Liu Shao-chi warned the U.S. July 22 not to "miscalculate" Peking's intentions "to support the Vietnamese people in winning a thorough victory." Speaking at a Peking rally in support of North Vietnam and the Viet Cong, Liu said: "If you think you can unscrupulously escalate the war of aggression without meeting due punishment, then you will find it too late to repent." Liu renewed Peking's offer of "the vast expanse of China territory" as "the reliable rear area of the Vietnamese people."

The 7 active member governments of the Communist bloc's Warsaw Treaty military alliance declared their readiness July 6 to send "volunteers" to aid North Vietnam in its fight against American "aggression." The pledge was contained in a declaration signed by the 7 nations' delegations to a Bucharest meeting of the Warsaw Treaty's Political Consultative Committee. The declaration, signed July 6 and made public the following day, specified that volunteers would be sent to Vietnam only at Hanoi's request. The declaration was signed by Todor Zhivkov, Bulgarian premier and CP first secretary; Hungarian Premier Gyula Kallai and CP First Secy. János Kádár; East German Premier Willi Stoph and CP First Secy. Walter Ulbricht; Polish Premier Josef Cyrankiewicz and CP First Secy. Wladyslaw Gomulka; Rumanian Premier Ion Gheorghe Maurer and CP Gen. Secy. Nicolae Ceausescu; Soviet Premier Aleksei Kosygin and CP Gen. Secy. Leonid I. Brezhnev; Czech Premier Josef Lenart and CP First Secy. Antonin Novotny. A joint statement issued in Moscow July 11 by the Soviet government and Communist Party announced that Soviet government agencies had been instructed to take "all necessary measures" to carry out the Warsaw Treaty pledge.

(State Secy. Dean Rusk warned the Communist bloc nations July 17 that "it would be very unwise for them to get involved" in the Vietnamese war by sending volunteers to North Vietnam.)

Bombing Attacked and Defended

The expansion of the air attacks on North Vietnam was attacked by domestic and foreign critics of the Johnson Administration and was defended by Administration spokesmen.

In response to June 29 criticism by Secy. Gen. U Thant, U.S. Amb.-to-UN Arthur J. Goldberg made public June 30 a letter to the Security Council in which he said that the bombings had been "made necessary by a substantial increase in the level of infiltration of armed men and war supplies from North Vietnam into South Vietnam—an increase in which petroleum products have been a key factor." Rejecting Thant's repeated pleas for a halt in the bombing of North Vietnam, Goldberg argued that the 2 suspensions of air raids previously attempted by the U.S. had shown "that it is not enough to stop the bombing over North Vietnam while the war in all its other manifestations continues." "It is the war, not just the bombing," Goldberg said, "that should come to an end."

Reacting to criticism from abroad, Pres. Johnson July 5 expressed his disappointment at the reaction of "a few" of the U.S.' allies, presumably Britain and France. Speaking at a televised press conference at his Texas ranch, the President said: "I cannot understand the thinking of any country or any people, or any person, that says we should sit by with our hands tied behind us while these men bring their mortars, their hand grenades and their bombs into our barracks, killing our Marines, attacking our camps, murdering the village chiefs, and that we should not do anything about it. We have tried to make this difficult for them to continue at their present rate. We do not say it will stop the infiltration. We do not say that it will even reduce it. But we do think it will make it more difficult for them. . . . We have a policy of measured response and gradually increasing our strength from time to time. We plan to continue that. . . ." "It is difficult for me to understand the response of some nation that is not involved, when a few years ago when their own security was at stake they needed American men and they wanted us to furnish American troops, not to be understanding of what we are trying to do to help others maintain their independence now."

A statement issued by British Prime Min. Harold Wilson June 29 had expressed his government's regret at the extension of U.S. air attacks and dissociated Britain from them. Wilson, however, pledged Britain's continued support for the Johnson Administration's Vietnamese war policy in general. Wilson disclosed that Pres. Johnson had informed him of the impending raids on the Hanoi-Haiphong area and that he (Wilson) had responded by expressing hope "that everything possible would be done to avoid harm to the civilian population." Nevertheless, Wilson said, he had told Mr. Johnson that Britain felt "bound to reaffirm that we must dissociate ourselves from any action of this kind." He said that his government refused to "support an extension of the bombing to such [populated] areas," "even though we were confident that the U.S. forces would take every precaution . . . to avoid civilian casualties." Wilson said, however, that the U.S. was fully justified in providing South Vietnam with massive military support until North Vietnam gave up its "attempt to gain control of South Vietnam" and agreed to enter unconditional peace talks. Wilson charged that it was North Vietnam's "refusal alone that prevents these negotiations, and we deplore Hanoi's constant rejection of the path of peace." In a personal report to the House of Commons later June 29, Wilson declared that the U.S. air strike "in a military sense . . . was a justifiable action." British opposition to it, he explained, "was for quite other reasons." Conservative Party leader Edward Heath replied that Wilson's attempt to give backing to U.S. policy in Vietnam generally and yet "dissociate himself from the implementation of that policy" was "completely untenable." Dissatisfaction with Wilson's Vietnam policies was further evidenced by a motion signed in Commons June 30 by 100 Laborites and 8 Liberals calling on the government to "dissociate itself completely" from the "misguided policies" of the U.S. as well as the bombing of the Hanoi-Haiphong installations. A counter-motion filed by 50 Laborites of the party's center and rightwing factions lauded Wilson's opposition to the expanded air war and urged Wilson to make new efforts to bring "both sides in the conflict unconditionally round the conference table."

Commons July 7, by 331-230 vote, defeated a Conservative motion that would have committed Britain to support U.S. policy on Vietnam without reservations. A government motion upholding Wilson's support of American policy but dissociating Britain from the U.S. raids on the Hanoi-Haiphong area was adopted by 299-230 vote. The reduced government margin in the latter vote resulted from the abstention of 32 leftwing Laborites who favored a complete break with U.S. policy on Vietnam.

2 demonstrations were held in London July 3 in protest against the bombing. About 4,000 demonstrators took part in a march to the U.S. embassy organized by the London district of the Communist Party; 31 persons were arrested in a melee in which a policeman was knocked off his motorcycle. The Youth for Peace in Vietnam Movement sponsored a march by about 2,000 to 10 Downing Street, where a delegation delivered a letter to Prime Min. Wilson calling on his government to disavow U.S. policies in Vietnam. 250 demonstrators July 3 conducted a protest rally near the U.S. Air Force base at Alconbury.

(U.S. air strikes against targets in the Vietnam demilitarized zone July 30 received British government support in a statement released by the British Foreign Office July 31. Charging that Communist military activity in the zone was "in violation of the Geneva agreement," the statement said that such action "must inevitably lead to countermeasures by the South Vietnamese and their American allies.")

French government criticism of the U.S. raids on the Hanoi-Haiphong oil depots was expressed in a statement released after a cabinet meeting July 2. Recalling that Paris had "made known its disapproval of what is called the escalation into which the United States had been drawn in Vietnam," the statement said France "even more strongly" condemns the recent bombing of Hanoi and Haiphong, which can only make any solution of this problem more difficult." French Pres. Charles de Gaulle presided over the cabinet session and was reported to have delivered a strong personal criticism of the latest American raids.

Canadian Prime Min. Lester B. Pearson said June 29 that his government "regretted" the U.S. bombings. Addressing the House of Commons, Pearson said Canada had "always held a let-up in the pattern of air strikes is one of the major elements constituting a prelude to peaceful negotiations."

Australian Prime Min. Harold E. Holt declared in New York July 5 that he agreed with Pres. Johnson that the bombing of the Hanoi-Haiphong area had been "a military necessity." Holt had reaffirmed Australian support of the allied war effort in Vietnam in talks held with Pres. Johnson in Washington June 29-30 and again July 13-14.

Indian mobs protested the raids on the Hanoi-Haiphong area with violent anti-American demonstrations in several cities beginning July 1. The worst outbreak occurred in Calcutta, where the U.S. Information Service building was stoned and invaded by youths who burned magazines and other literature. The building was closed but came under further attack July 5 by about 500 students. The mob burned an effigy of Pres. Johnson and tore down the American flag. (Indian officials reported July 20 that India's consul general in Saigon, P. S. Kotda Sanghani, was being recalled for defending the U.S. raids on the North Vietnamese oil installations. Prime Min. Indira Gandhi, who had condemned the air strikes, had explained July 19 that Sanghani had expressed "his personal opinion and not the views of the government.")

A cable sent to Pres. Johnson from the World Council of Churches in Geneva July 1 said that the latest bombing of North Vietnam was causing a "widespread reaction" of "resentment and alarm" among many Christians. The cable was signed by Dr. W. A. Visser 't Hooft, the council's outgoing general secretary, and Dr. O. Frederick Nolde, director of its Commission of the Churches on International Affairs.

Although an overwhelming majority of Congress members of both parties were known to support the Administration's new action in Vietnam, many prominent members, particularly in the Senate, voiced fears that the expanded air raids would lead to a wider war and not to the conference table.

The strongest Congressional criticism of the Administration came from Chrmn. J. W. Fullbright (D. Ark.) of the Senate Foreign Relations Committee. Speaking on the Senate floor July 22, Fulbright charged that Pres. Johnson was following a policy in which the U.S. was "taking on the role of policeman and provider for all of non-Communist Asia." The U.S. "on its own," Fulbright asserted, "has undertaken to win a victory for its protégés in the Vietnam civil war and thereon to build a 'Great Society' in Asia, whatever that may turn out to mean." "One wonders," Fullbright continued, "whether anyone ever thought of asking the Asians if they really want to join the Great Society."

Among statements made by Congress members June 30, immediately after the U.S. attacks on the Hanoi-Haiphong area:

Sen. Mike Mansfield (D., Mont.) said "the destruction of petrol facilities won't deter infiltration" but may "make the road to the negotiating table that much more difficult." (Mansfield had proposed June 16 a meeting between the foreign ministers of the U.S. and Communist China to seek "a curb on the expansion of the [Vietnamese] war" and "a prompt and durable termination of the tragic bloodletting.")

Sen. Richard B. Russell (D., Ga.) said he approved of the raids because the U.S. had "exhausted every effort to arrive at negotiations." "Any further delay in drying up the sources of supply" for Communist troops in South Vietnam, Russell said, "could only increase" American casualties.

Asserting that Pres. Johnson had acted "in the best interest of accomplishing our objective in Vietnam," Sen. Leverett Saltonstall (R., Mass.) said the raids were worth the risk of Chinese intervention.

Sen. George D. Aiken (R., Vt.) said the new raids would expand the war, not "shorten it." Aiken said Pres. Johnson was "apparently taking the advice of the same people who assured him 18 months ago that a few days bombing of North Vietnam" would bring the Communists to the negotiating table." "They were wrong then," Aiken said.

Sen. Robert F. Kennedy (D., N.Y.) questioned whether the bombing would "effectively prevent" North Vietnam from supplying the Viet Cong in South Vietnam.

A joint statement signed by 16 Democratic Representatives declared that extending the air strikes "further commits this country to a profoundly dangerous policy of brinkmanship" and openly challenged Communist China "to raise the level of its commitment in Vietnam."

Rep. Gerald Ford (R., Mich.) said the U.S. should have bombed the Hanoi-Haiphong oil installations "months ago." Praising the latest raids, Ford said the Administration should act to prevent use of Haiphong harbor. (In a speech in Dallas, Tex. June 17, Ford had called the war "Pres. Johnson's war" because "it is an undeclared war" and "because the President plays everything too close to the vest . . . [and] has an unhealthy passion for secrecy.")

Testifying before the Senate Foreign Relations Committee June 30, State Undersecy. George W. Ball had declared that the fuel-depot bombings "should speed the move to the conference table," that there was "great basis for real encouragement" in the military aspects of the war and that there were signs of "weakening morale" in North Vietnam. He said the Administration considered that there was no "serious possibility" that the new bombings would bring Chinese intervention in the war.

A warning was voiced by State Secy. Rusk July 22 that bombing the port of Haiphong could lead to "a larger war very quickly" and an eventual nuclear conflict. Speaking to the International Platform Association in Washington, Rusk said the U.S. was determined to continue its policy of "firmness with prudence," which, he said, was aimed at keeping open the possibility of a peaceful settlement without widening the fighting. The American bombing of the Hanoi-Haiphong fuel dumps was part of the U.S. strategy of restricting Hanoi's ability to infiltrate men and supplies into South Vietnam, Rusk said.

(Results of a Harris Survey taken shortly after the Hanoi-Haiphong raids and published July 11 showed that 62% of those interviewed favored the raids, 11% were opposed and 27% were undecided. 86% of those polled felt the raids would hasten the end of the war; 43% felt that the escalation had increased the likelihood of intervention by Communist China.

(In testimony released July 24 by a House Appropriations subcommittee, Defense Secy. McNamara was quoted as having testified Mar. 30 that good reasons existed for not mining Haiphong harbor. McNamara asserted that there was "no assurance" that such an operation "would stop the flow, or even significantly reduce the flow of supplies from North Vietnam into South Vietnam." Even if Haiphong harbor were to be blocked, he said, the Communists could still move material "over the beaches or they could move it along the roads from south China into North Vietnam."

(U.S. officials in Washington were quoted as saying Aug. 25 that no large tanker had unloaded in North Vietnam since the U.S. air strikes against the Hanoi-Haiphong oil installations began June 29. As a result, North Vietnam's fuel supplies were said to have dropped substantially. The officials stressed, however, that there was no evidence that the fuel shortage had inhibited the flow of armed men from North to South Vietnam.)

U.S. Bombers Hit Northern Targets

Among details of intensifying U.S. air attacks on North Vietnamese targets:

June 30—3 fuel installations in the Hanoi area were raided by U.S. Air Force and Navy jets. The Air Force planes attacked the Nguyenkhe fuel dump, 7½ miles north of Hanoi, and the Viettri storage area, 28 miles northwest of the capital. The Navy jets raided the Bacgiang fuel complex, 25 miles northeast of Hanoi. The Bacgiang facility, with tanks able to hold 6,000 metric tons of fuel, represented 4% of North Vietnam's petroleum storage capacity. (Saigon dispatches June 30 said that the Bacgiang depot had been destroyed.) An air strike by Navy jets near Kep, 38 miles northeast of Hanoi, destroyed a radar interception center.

July 1—Navy jets from the carrier *Constellation* attacked the Dongnham fuel dump, 15 miles northwest of Hanoi. A-4, A-6 and F-4C Phantom jets struck the depot area. The Dongnham facility had a fuel storage capacity of 14,000 metric tons, or 9% of North Vietnam's total storage capacity.

July 3—The Doson petroleum installation, 12 miles southeast of Haiphong, was attacked for the 2d time. The fuel dump's capacity was 14,000 metric tons. U.S. briefing officers in Saigon reported July 4 that several large tanks and other oil equipment in the Doson complex had escaped damage in the first raid. Communist China's Hsinhua news agency broadcast North Vietnamese reports that 2 U.S. planes had been shot down during raids on the outskirts of Hanoi and Haiphong; no planes were listed missing by the U.S. military command in Saigon.

(Rear Adm. James R. Reedy, commander of the 7th Fleet task force operating off Vietnam, said July 4 that half of the Hanoi-Haiphong area's petroleum installations had already been levelled by the U.S. raids.)

July 4—Petroleum facilities near Haiphong, Thanhhoa and Vinh were attacked by carrier-based Navy jets. The target in the Haiphong area was identified only as an underground fuel dump 19 miles southeast of the city. The Thanhhoa area target, the Baiphuong fuel storage depot, was said to have been saturated with bombs.

July 5—Fuel tanks in the Hanoi area were hit again by U.S. jets. The 2 objectives were located 28 miles north of Hanoi and 33 miles northwest of the city. The day's major attacks concentrated on missile-launching sites northwest of Hanoi, along the Red River road and rail routes from Communist China. Pilots reported that 26 to 29 surface-to-air missiles—a record number—had been fired at them during the attacks but that none had hit a plane. (Military spokesmen in Saigon said July 6 that the July 5 raids had demonstrated the effectiveness of new countermeasures against anti-aircraft missiles. An Air Force spokesman said that "we've found a way to nullify the SAM [surface-to-air missile] system." He described it as "a combination of technique, tactics and electronics." None of the missiles fired at the attacking U.S. planes were reported to have come closer that 700 feet.)

July 6—U.S. jets flew 80 missions—some involving several aircraft —against North Vietnamese targets. They attacked 2 fuel dumps, a petroleum tank factory and an anti-aircraft missile site, all within 65 miles of Hanoi. Hanoi broadcasts charged that several attacks had been aimed at river dams for the purpose of causing floods and endangering rural populations.

July 7—Navy jets from the carrier *Hancock* struck at fuel storage tanks and pumping installations 2 miles northwest of Haiphong. (The Haiphong complex, accounting for an estimated 40% of North Vietnam's fuel supply, had been bombed and reported 80% destroyed in the first raid on the port city June 29, but Pentagon officials July 7 said reconnaissance photos later had shown 70% of the installation still in operation. The officials said that by July 7, 80%-90% of North Vietnam's fuel facilities and reserves had come under air attack and 55% of its facilities had been destroyed.)

July 15—121 missions—each flown by several planes—were launched against North Vietnam; this was a record number for any one day since the U.S. began bombing North Vietnam in 1965. Missile launching sites in the Hanoi area were attacked; 2 of them, located 18 and 25 miles from the city, were destroyed. Navy jets struck at a fuel dump 2 miles from the port city of Vinh. 10 Soviet-built surface-to-air missiles were fired ineffectively at other Navy jets southeast of Hanoi.

Aug. 2—U.S. bombers returned to the Haiphong area for the 3d time to attack the port city's fuel intallations. The raid was disclosed in Washington by the Defense Department after North Vietnam protested the attack to the International Control Coommission. North Vietnam charged the U.S. with "indiscriminately bombing residential quarters and factories" in the Haiphong raid. Defense Department officials asserted that there were no homes or factories in the vicinity of the target and that precision bombing techniques had been used by the pilots. The Haiphong area mission was one of a dozen mounted against North Vietnamese oil facilities.

Aug. 3—U.S. planes bombed near Haiphong again, hitting a military headquarters 25 miles northeast of the port and barges and trucks elsewhere.

Aug. 8—North Vietnamese ground fire shot down 3 F-105 Thunderchief jets, including one piloted by Maj. James H. Kasler, regarded as the leading flyer of the war. He bailed out over the Red River Valley, and his capture was confirmed by North Vietnam Aug. 12.

Aug. 11—U.S. jets flew 118 missions against North Vietnam Aug. 11, blasting the Uongbi power plant, about 15 miles northeast of Haiphong, and pounding 14 oil depots and storage areas.

Aug. 12—U.S. Navy, Air Force and Marine planes hit 4 petroleum and oil dumps within a 14-mile radius of Haiphong. Other planes struck 4 missile sites 12-15 miles from Hanoi. The day's 121 multi-plane bombing missions also resulted in the destruction and damage of barges, trucks and bridges. Some of the raids were carried out 2-8 miles north of the demilitarized zone.

Aug. 13—A North Vietnamese broadcast charged that U.S. planes had "intruded into the airspace of Hanoi," hitting Red River Valley dikes and causing "many losses in lives and property." North Vietnam protested to the International Control Commission.

Aug. 24—U.S. Navy, Air Force and Marine Corps planes flew a record 146 missions. As many as 400 planes were believed to have taken part. Among the 195 targets struck were 47 railroad and highway bridges, 20 petroleum depots and 11 munitions storage areas around the cities of Donghoi, Vinh and Thanhhoa along the coastal strip south of Hanoi. No U.S. planes were lost despite heavy anti-aircraft fire encountered over most of the targets.

Aug. 26—A record 156 missions were flown by U.S. pilots. Nearly 400 planes reportedly were involved in strikes against North Vietnam's southern coast and panhandle regions. Among the reported results of the day's raids: 11 ground explosions were touched off in a raid 36 miles south of Donghoi; more than 300 boats, trucks and cars were hit; a railroad yard 17 miles northeast of Thanhhoa was heavily damaged.

Sept. 11—U.S. planes flew a record 171 missions, destroying or damaging 107 cargo barges, 11 junks, 19 bridges, 38 supply buildings and one surface-to-air missile. 3 North Vietnamese torpedo boats were struck in the Gulf of Tonkin off Haiphong.

Sept. 12—U.S. planes carried out the heaviest raid of the war on North Vietnam to date. It was believed that 500 planes participated in attacks on coastal cities, transportation lines, supply areas and missile sites. 2 of the sites were reported destroyed.

Oct. 13—U.S. planes flew a record 173 multi-plane missions against radar sites, storage areas, transportation facilities and missile centers in North Vietnam's panhandle region.

Oct. 14—A record 175 missions were flown against North Vietnamese targets, and about 450-500 individual plane strikes were made.

Dec. 2—U.S. aircraft bombed a target 5 miles south of Hanoi in one of a series of air strikes. The raid was the closest to the North Vietnamese capital since June 29. 8 U.S. planes were downed (a record number for a single day). Their loss brought to 435 the number of American aircraft lost over North Vietnam. The target 5 miles south of Hanoi was a truck park, which was pounded by 15-20 Navy jets. 50-60 other U.S. F-4C Phantom jets dropped bombs on the Hagia fuel storage depot 14½ miles north of Hanoi. F-105 Thunderchiefs, escorting the Phantoms, destroyed 4 radar-missile sites and an anti-aircraft emplacement. A 2d fuel dump was hit by other Navy pilots about 40 miles northeast of Hanoi. (A North Vietnamese Foreign Ministry statement broadcast Dec. 3 by the North Vietnamese press agency charged that in the Dec. 2 raids U.S. planes had "attacked densely populated areas in the southern suburb of Hanoi and other densely populated areas inside the city." The statement claimed that other U.S. planes that day had "bombed and strafed the provincial capital of Ninhbinh and many densely populated areas in Habac, Bacthai, Langson, Vinhphue, Tuyenquang and other provinces." The ministry said "many American planes were shot down, many others destroyed and many American air pirates captured." North Vietnam said it had filed a protest with the International Control Commission.)

Dec. 4—U.S. fighter-bombers struck the Yenvien railway yard 6 miles northeast of Hanoi. The Hagia fuel storage depot, 14½ miles north of the city, was hit again.

Thailand had been growing in importance as a U.S. base for raids against the Communists. A U.S.-built airbase was opened Aug. 10 in Sattihip, on the Gulf of Siam. During dedication ceremonies, U.S.-Thai cooperation in the war in Vietnam was publicly acknowledged for the first time in statements made by Thai Premier Thanom Kittikachorn and U.S. Amb. Graham A. Martin. Kittikachorn declared that Thailand was cooperating with the U.S. "because we realize that our intentions are the same." Martin replied that the new base, called the U-Tapao Airfield (to be used jointly by the U.S. and Thailand), was an example of the "added responsibilities and added obligations" that the U.S. and Thailand were assuming "toward each other and toward their common cause." The U-Tapao Airfield was part of the U.S.-assisted development program for building a major supply port at Sattihip Bay. The airbase was the 6th to be built or expanded by the U.S. in Thailand since 1960. About 2/3 of the 25,000 U.S. military personnel in Thailand were stationed at the 6 fields.

Bombing of Hanoi Homes Charged

Reports from North Vietnam, the Soviet Union and East Germany Dec. 13 claimed that U.S. planes had bombed the city of Hanoi for the first time Dec. 12, inflicting civilian casualties in residential areas. U.S. officials did not specifically deny the Communist charges. Stating that U.S. "policy is to attack military targets only," the Defense Department said Dec. 13 that "the only targets scheduled for attack during the past 24 hours were military targets which have been previously struck." The State Department did not rule out the possibility that a residential section (which a Soviet dispatch claimed had been struck) might have been hit accidentally.

The Soviet news agency Tass said Dec. 13 that U.S. planes Dec. 12 had bombed "workers' districts situated along the Red River embankment" in Hanoi. "Scores of buildings were destroyed" and many persons were taken to hospitals, Tass said. According to the Tass report, other U.S. planes had "bombed the Hanoi suburb of Dhatram and the southwestern outskirts of the capital." In its report of the raid, the East German news agency ADN said explosions had killed "numerous residents" and destroyed many houses. A Hanoi broadcast, confirming the Tass and ADN reports, said residential centers in the Hanoi area had been bombed. Hanoi radio claimed 4 U.S. planes had been shot down and their pilots captured. North Vietnam had filed a protest with the International Control Commission.

U.S. air raids in the Hanoi area Dec. 13-14 prompted Communist charges that the air strikes had been carried out against civilians in the city. Washington at first insisted that the targets struck were just outside Hanoi but later conceded that civilian sections might have been hit. The U.S. statements did not acknowledge that the damage had been caused by U.S. action. The U.S. had announced officially that the North Vietnamese targets struck in the Dec. 13-14 raids were the Yenvien railway yard, 6 miles northeast of Hanoi, and a truck depot at Vandien, 2 miles south of the city. A spokesman at the U.S. embassy in Saigon said Dec. 14 that "if by some remote chance Hanoi was struck by bombs, it was an accident."

The initial U.S. reaction to the Communist charges was given by State Department spokesman Robert J. McCloskey at a meeting with newsmen Dec. 14. McCloskey at first denied that U.S. planes had bombed Hanoi. But he quickly added that "I took the question to mean that these are civilian targets or population centers, . . . which one generally associates when talking about a city." McCloskey said U.S. "policy, so far as targets is concerned, is directed against military and military associated targets." U.S. policy was "to avoid populated areas and civilian targets," he declared. When asked whether these targets were inside Hanoi's limits, McCloskey said "I don't know . . . how one defines what the city limits are." At the close of the news conference McCloskey said the State Department "could not confirm or deny reports which have appeared in various capitals over the past few days about targets, or other places, which allegedly have been struck by American aircraft."

In a statement released Dec. 15, the State Department reaffirmed its position that "there is no fixed geographical definition which would be called the city limits" of Hanoi. But Administration officials later Dec. 15 stated definitely that Hanoi had not been bombed. They produced a map, reportedly based on a North Vietnamese map, to support their contention that the targets bombed were more than at least 2 miles outside the city limits. Other U.S. officials conceded that civilian areas might have been struck during the U.S. attacks but did not admit publicly that U.S. planes were responsible for the damage. (The State Department said in a statement Dec. 22: An investigation, based partially on interviews with pilots, indicated that the only targets struck, were "military ones well outside the city proper. However, we cannot rule out completely the possibility of an accident." If civilian casualties were inflicted, "we regret it.")

A statement issued Dec. 16 by the Saigon headquarters of Gen. William C. Westmoreland, U.S. commander in Vietnam, said: "A complete review of pilot reports of the Dec. 13-14 air strikes" on Vandien and Yenvien "showed that all ordnance expended by U.S. air strike aircraft was in the military target areas. None fell in the city of Hanoi." In reporting the Dec. 14 attack on Yenvien and Vandien, the U.S. command in Saigon said Dec. 15 that U.S. Air Force and Navy planes had heavily bombed both targets despite strong ground fire and resistance by Communist MiG-17s and MiG-21s. Damage to the Yenvien railroad yard and the Vandien truck park was described as extensive.

The Hanoi correspondent of the French press agency, Jacques Maolic, reported Dec. 14 that a residential area near the approach to a bridge across the Red River had been "devastated" in the Dec. 13 raid. Maolic speculated that the damage might have been caused by North Vietnamese rockets. Maolic said the village of Caudat outside Hanoi had been "completely destroyed by bombs and fire." The *N.Y. Times* reported Dec. 15 that an unidentified Western traveler in Hanoi who had witnessed the Dec. 13 U.S. air raid "near Hanoi" had said one section of the city proper had been heavily damaged. The witness did not definitely know that the damage had been inflicted by the American planes.

Y. Kobelev, Hanoi correspondent for the Soviet news agency Tass, reported Dec. 14 that U.S. aircraft that day had "violated again the air space of Hanoi." "As yesterday, they bombed the right and left banks of the Red River, the embankment and the area of the bridge linking Hanoi with its suburb of Gialam," he said. In a more detailed report filed Dec. 15, Kobelev said: "The working class district of Phucthan, on the right bank of the Red River," had been bombed and "tens of houses" had been destroyed by fire. "The victims included children." 15 homes were destroyed after "6 demolition bombs were dropped onto a street near the bridge linking Hanoi with . . . Gialam." "An American F-105 fighter-bomber fired a guided missile on the diplomatic district" during the Dec. 14 raid.

The Italian Communist newspaper *L'Unità* Dec. 14 published a report of its correspondent in Hanoi, Antonello Trombadori, that 6 U.S. planes Dec. 13 had bombed the center of Hanoi, "hitting deliberately 2 quarters inhabited by 500 workers' families."

Hanoi claimed Dec. 15 that 100 persons had been killed or wounded in the Dec. 13-14 raids on Hanoi and that many official buildings and homes had been damaged in the city's foreign diplomatic sector.

The Chinese Communist news agency Hsinhua reported Dec. 17 that 4 U.S. planes had "repeatedly dive-bombed" the Chinese Communist embassy in Hanoi Dec. 14. The agency said that the embassy was "seriously damaged" and that the adjacent Hsinhua office also was struck and completely destroyed. Hsinhua quoted North Vietnamese Supreme Court Pres. Pham Van Back as having said that the Dec. 13 raids on Hanoi had killed or wounded 15 persons and that the Dec. 14 air strike had "brought to over 100 the total number of victims of the 2 raids." (The French Communist newspaper *L'Humanité* Dec. 15 had reported an air attack on the Chinese embassy in Hanoi. The report said the building had been "hit by a projectile Wednesday [Dec. 14], according to a good source.")

A Bucharest announcement charged Dec. 17 that the Rumanian embassy in Hanoi had been bombed in the Dec. 13-14 raids.

The Hanoi area bombing was protested Dec. 18 at a Peking rally attended by 100,000 persons. A resolution adopted at the gathering said Communist China "will march to the front" "to deal devastating blows at U.S. aggressors till final victory" "whenever the Vietnamese people" call for such assistance.

Bombing Controversy over Salisbury Report

The U.S. Defense Department conceded Dec. 26 that North Vietnamese civilians had been bombed accidentally by American pilots during missions against military targets. But the department insisted that there was no change in U.S. policy to confine air raids to strictly military targets and to take "all possible care" "to avoid civilian casualties." "It was impossible," however, "to avoid all damage to civilian areas," the department said. The statement was issued in response to a report filed from Hanoi Dec. 25 by Harrison Salisbury, assistant managing editor of the *N.Y. Times*, who had gone to North Vietnam with the authorization of both Hanoi and Washington. Salisbury had reported that Namdinh, about 50 miles southeast of Hanoi, had been bombed repeatedly by U.S.

planes since June 28, 1965, that 13% of its homes had been destroyed and that 89 civilians had been killed and 405 wounded. According to Salisbury, an American raid on Namdinh Apr. 14 had resulted in the killing of 49 persons and the wounding of 135.

Salisbury had reported that another North Vietnamese city, Phuly, about 35 miles south of Hanoi, had been attacked by U.S. planes Oct. 1, 2 and 9 and that all its homes and buildings were destroyed. About 40 civilians were killed or wounded. Salisbury said Phuly (population 20,000) had no industry. He speculated that the air strikes were directed against the city's highway and railroad line.

The Defense Department's Dec. 26 statement explained that the targets in Phuly and Namdinh had been "limited to highway bridges, railroad bridges and junctions, POL [petroleum, oil and lubricants] storage areas and air defense sites." (Anti-aircraft guns and missile-firing equipment were stationed in populated sections around both cities, American officials said.) The department statement added: "It is impossible to avoid all damage to civilian areas, especially when the North Vietnamese deliberately emplace their air defense sites, their dispersed POL sites, their radar and other military facilities in populated areas and, indeed, sometimes on the roofs of government buildings."

Salisbury's reports on the Namdinh air raids were denounced by Asst. Defense Secy. (for public affairs) Arthur Sylvester Dec. 29 as "misstatements of facts." Taking issue with Salisbury's observation that "there are no military targets in the city," Sylvester said "it is difficult to understand why the Communists defend it so heavily, as testified by pilots who attacked the military targets." Sylvester cited anti-aircraft installations in the center of Namdinh and around the city's edge. Sylvester reiterated that the U.S. air strikes were directed against military targets in Namdinh: railroad yards, a warehouse, petroleum storage depots and a thermal power plant. But he would not say that civilian areas had been accidentally bombed. Sylvester said Namdinh had been hit by U.S. planes 64 times since mid-1965. If Salisbury's report that 89 civilians had been killed in the city during that period were correct, it would indicate "rather precise, careful bombing," Sylvester said. He added: "I would say it's a pretty low figure. That's 1½ persons per raid." Sylvester said Namdinh had been mentioned 3 times as a target in communiqués issued from Saigon. The latest communiqué, released Dec. 29, had said its freight yards were bombed.

Salisbury, writing from Hanoi Dec. 30, quoted North Vietnamese officials as saying that as far as they knew the Dec. 29 U.S. communiqué was the first to report Namdinh as a target. Salisbury said Hanoi authorities had insisted that there was nothing of military value in Namdinh, that the city was largely a cotton and silk textile center. Salisbury said bomb damage to civilian and business areas in Namdinh was extensive and that whole blocks had been abandoned. Black River dikes outside Namdinh had been bombed and breached by U.S. planes May 31 and July 14, 20 and 31. Salisbury said city officials suspected the dikes were hit deliberately. U.S. officials denied that the dikes were on the list of American aerial targets, although they conceded they may have been struck accidentally.

The *Washington Post* reported Dec. 31 that the Namdinh casualty figures cited by Salisbury were similar to the totals that had appeared in a North Vietnamese pamphlet that had been distributed to foreign correspondents in Moscow in November. The *Post* said U.S. officials were "furious" when they noted the similarity between the figures mentioned by Salisbury and the North Vietnamese document, called "Report on United States War Crimes in Namdinh City." The *Post* noted that Salisbury had given no attribution for the Namdinh casualty toll in his first dispatch filed from Hanoi Dec. 25. But the *Post* recalled that in a Dec. 29 report Salisbury had written that "all casualty estimates and statistics in these dispatches are those of North Vietnamese officials." Clifton Daniel, managing editor of the *N.Y. Times,* said Dec. 31 that it was "not surprising that the casualty figures reported by Harrison Salisbury and those given out by a North Vietnamese official in Moscow should be identical. They came from the same source—the North Vietnamese government."

Discussing the controversy over North Vietnamese civilian casualties, Pres. Johnson asserted Dec. 31 that there had been no change in orders "to bomb only military targets." Expressing the belief that "our men have carried out those orders to the best of their ability," the President added: "There will be civilian casualties in connection with the bombing of military targets and there are civilian casualties taking place every day—some this morning in South Vietnam. And I am concerned with casualties in both South Vietnam and North Vietnam, and I wish that all of our people would be equally as concerned."

(Leonard C. Meeker, the U.S. State Department's legal adviser, had declared in a statement released Dec. 13 that the U.S. was justified under international law in bombing North Vietnam. Meeker made the statement in an address to the University of Pittsburgh Law School. Accusing North Vietnam of an "armed attack" on South Vietnam, Meeker asserted that "legitimate defense includes military action against the aggressor whenever such action is needed to halt the attack."

(Meeker's remarks were in answer to American critics of the U.S. bombing policy. The New York-based Lawyers Committee on American Policy Towards Vietnam had charged in a statement Dec. 8 that U.S. military action in Vietnam "constitutes a series of violations of fundamental rules of international law governing the use of force in international relations," including the UN Charter. The group's statement called on the UN General Assembly's Legal Committee to seek an International Court of Justice opinion on whether the UN Charter had been violated.)

Raids on North Assessed

In one of the most detailed assessments of the American air war over North Vietnam yet provided by the Johnson Administration, U.S. Air Force Secy. Harold Brown had reported Dec. 8 that the aerial strikes had caused "serious manpower, supply and morale problems" for North Vietnam. But despite the devastating effects of the raids, they were still not severe enough to persuade Hanoi to enter peace talks, Brown said. Speaking at a meeting of the Aviation-Space Writers Association in Washington, Brown provided these statistics:

■ The U.S. raids had so disrupted Communist supply routes that North Vietnamese troops in South Vietnam were receiving only about ½ of their daily requirements of weapons and ammunition; battalion-size attacks by Communist units had decreased from 7 in one month in 1965 to an average of 2 a month in the previous 5 months of 1966.

■ Since the start of the U.S. air raids on North Vietnam in Feb. 1965, American planes had destroyed or damaged more than 7,000 trucks, 3,000 railway cars, 5,000 bridges and 5,000 barges and boats.

■ During Sept. 1966 alone, 700 trucks, 700 freight cars and 1,400 barges had been hit; during the same period, 450 bridges had been destroyed or damaged and roads had been cut or damaged at about 600 points.

■ U.S. planes had destroyed more than ⅔ of North Vietnam's oil storage supplies, most of its ammunition storage and explosive plants and "nearly all bridges" outside the Hanoi-Haiphong area.

■ Hanoi had been forced to form a work force totaling an estimated 200,000-300,000 civilians, accompanied by large numbers of troops to protect them from air attacks, to repair bridges, roads and railroads. The cost, feeding and supplying of this work detail added to North Vietnam's war burdens.

■ In American air activity over South Vietnam, individual B-52 attacks had increased from an average of 150 a month in June 1965 to an average of 450 a month during 1966; tactical strikes by individual American planes during June-Nov. 1966 had averaged more than 10,000 a month.

■ South Vietnamese air force planes during the June-Nov. 1966 period had flown an average of 2,500 strikes a month.

Defending what he called American restraint in its air offensive, Brown said: "There is no doubt that airpower could destroy North Vietnam—and without nuclear weapons —if it were in our interests, the interests of South Vietnam and the interests of the free world to do so." But the nuclear age precluded the American military principle of applying "maximum power" "in the shortest possible time" to bring about the defeat and surrender of an opposing force, Brown declared. Brown warned North Vietnam, however, that the bombing "can be increased to a much higher level if it is concluded, on balance, that this will contribute to the attainment of our objectives."

Reporting on the effects of the air war against the North, Lt. Gen. William W. Momyer, commander of the 7th Air Force, disclosed in Saigon Jan. 6, 1967 that U.S. Air Force planes had flown 13,000 missions over North Vietnam during Jan.-Nov. 1966. The report said the raids had destroyed or damaged 1,893 barges, 3,227 buildings, 32 surface-to-air missile sites, 319 railroad cars and 1,809 trucks. The report did not include the thousands of missions that had been flown by U.S. Navy and Marine pilots during the 11-month period.

The North Vietnam news agency had reported Oct. 30 that in an interview with Emmanuel d'Astier de la Vigerie, editor of the French review *Evenement*, North Vietnamese Pres. Ho Chi Minh had conceded that the bombing of North Vietnam had resulted in "some losses" but had denied that the country's economy had been disrupted. He said North Vietnam's cost of living had not gone up because "we have adapted our economy to the present situation."

War in 'Demilitarized Zone'

The U.S. bombing offensive against North Vietnam was extended July 30 to the demilitarized zone (DMZ) separating North and South Vietnam. The 6-mile wide zone along the 17th Parallel, established by the 1954 Geneva agreements, had been designated as an area in which the forces of both sides would be forbidden. U.S. officials had been charging for years, however, that North Vietnam had been sending troops through the DMZ to infiltrate South Vietnam and that Hanoi had set up supply dumps and armed strongpoints in the zone.

The July 30 bombing of the demilitarized zone was disclosed by U.S. military officers in Saigon after newsmen had pressed them for the precise location of the raid, initially described only as an attack on targets in South Vietnam's northernmost Quangtri Province. Responding to reporters' questions, the briefing officers confirmed that the target area was situated on the South Vietnamese side of the demarcation line. The target was described as a Communist camp and supply area located one mile south of the Benhai River, the physical border betwen North and South Vietnam. The raid was carried out by 15 B-52 Strato-fortress jets flying 2,500 miles from Andersen Air Force Base on Guam. The B-52s returned to attack targets in the zone again July 31 and August 4 and 5. The demilitarized zone previously had been bombed 3 times by U.S. aircraft—Sept. 16, 17 and Nov. 13, 1965—but each of these attacks was described as unintentional.

Washington officials insisted July 30 that the attack on the zone did not constitute "escalation" of the conflict and was not a prelude to ground action in the area by U.S. troops. They said the raid was intended as a warning to North Vietnam that the zone could not be used as a sanctuary for troops operating in South Vietnam.

Saigon sources said July 30 that the North Vietnamese 324-B Division, an 8,000-10,000-man force reportedly operating in Quangtri Province, had been sent into South Vietnam through the zone after monsoon rains had closed the Ho Chi Minh Trail infiltration route through Laos. The South Vietnamese government had lodged a formal protest July 22 with the International Control Commission for Vietnam, charging North Vietnam with using the zone to infiltrate troops into Quangtri Province. The protest warned that South Vietnam would take whatever measures were necessary unless its borders were protected against incursions.

North Vietnam protested to the ICC July 31 against the B-52 attack on the demilitarized zone. (Other Hanoi protests to the ICC during the previous month had charged the U.S. with violating the zone by sending warplanes across its borders to bomb targets on North Vietnamese territory.)

ICC Chrmn. M. A. Rahman of India declared August 1 that the commission "views with concern the most recent developments in the demilitarized zone." He said that the ICC would exert every effort to enforce the 1954 Geneva accord provisions concerning the zone.

India was reported August 4 to have proposed expansion of ICC observation in the DMZ to prevent a further spread of fighting in the area. A small ICC team currently was stationed in the zone at a bridge over the Benhai River, but it was confined to its base. Under the Indian plan (a) several teams of ICC observers would move about the zone to investigate alleged violations of its neutrality and (b) the zone's joint military committee would be revived. The 1954 Geneva agreements had provided for joint French-North Vietnamese inspection teams to clear the zone of troops, but the committee had not functioned in 10 years. Under the Indian plan, South Vietnam would replace France on the committee. The

U.S. and Canada supported the Indian proposals August 5. American acceptance was expressed by State Secy. Dean Rusk at a news conference in Washington. Rusk said the U.S. would be willing to give the ICC observers "more of a role to play and help them clear out this demilitarized zone, and at least consolidate one step that might have to do with the possible escalation of this situation." Rusk did not rule out American penetration of the zone. When questioned as to whether U.S. troops would be sent into the zone if the North Vietnamese continued to make us of it, Rusk replied: "We have not wanted to go into the zone or cross the 17th Parallel. Our attitude has been that we don't want any shooting by anybody at anyone. . . . We have no desire to destroy the regime in North Vietnam; we have no desire to drop any bombs on North Vietnam."

South Vietnamese Foreign Min. Tran Van Do said August 6 that his government favored bolstering the ICC force in the demilitarized zone. But Saigon's acceptance of reactivation of the joint committee, Do said, was conditioned on Hanoi's agreement to rejoin the group.

U.S. approval of the Indian proposal was reiterated in a State Department statement issued August 12. Department spokesman Marshall Wright said the U.S. "favor[ed] any arrangement that will insure that the demilitarized zone is not used for military purposes, and, especially, that would deny the use of the zone by North Vietnam" to infiltrate the south with troops and supplies.

The southern section of the DMZ was struck twice Sept. 6 by B-52 bombers. U.S. spokesmen said that an infiltration route and a Communist base camp had been bombed. U.S. B-52s carried out their 8th raid against suspected North Vietnamese troop concentrations in the zone Sept. 15. Guam-based U.S. B-52 bombers Sept. 19-23 carried out heavy raids against North Vietnamese targets in the demilitarized zone that divided North and South Vietnam and in the area just north of the zone. The purpose of the bombing was to prevent supplies from reaching North Vietnamese forces battling U.S. Marines near the southern sector of the buffer area. The targets included infiltration trails, troop concentrations, supply areas and base camps. U.S. Air Force Phantom jets Sept. 19 bombed the zone in 3 separate raids, setting off at least 4 large secondary explosions and several fires. Smaller U.S. planes also pounded targets in and near the DMZ while other American aircraft ranged further north Sept. 19-25 in the continued aerial drive against Commuist roads, supply depots and missile sites. The Hanoi regime protested to the ICC Sept. 21.

The U.S. halted its air strikes against the southeastern corner of the zone Sept. 27. The suspension of air strikes was confirmed by State Secy. Rusk at a UN news conference Oct. 5. He said that its purpose was to allow the ICC to resume patrols in the area. An ICC statement Oct. 7 said "conditions have not been considered sufficiently secure" for commission observers to patrol the buffer zone despite the suspension of the air attacks on the sector. The area, 4 miles wide, 6 miles deep and heavily populated, was the only part of the demilitarized zone that had been patrolled by the ICC. It was disclosed that the raid pause had followed an ICC request to the U.S. and South Vietnamese August 19 for a suspension of military activity in the entire zone. A similar appeal to North Vietnam to cease military movements in the zone was rejected.

The bombings were resumed Oct. 17 on an increased scale. The target struck Oct. 17 was a suspected North Vietnamese storage area. The U.S. military mission in Saigon had warned Oct. 14 that American planes would resume bombing the southeastern sector of the zone "if there is North Vietnamese army or Viet Cong military action in the area."

The mission expressed regret that the Hanoi regime had "consistently rebuffed" "repeated efforts" by ICC observers to enter and patrol North Vietnam's northern sector of the buffer zone. The U.S. mission disclosed that no American military activity had taken place in the eastern sector of the zone for more than a month prior to the start of the raid pause Sept. 27. The mission's Oct. 14 announcement said that U.S. planes had bombed North Vietnam's sector of the zone near the coast 3 times in early August and that the area had not been struck since then.

It had been disclosed in New Delhi Oct. 14 that India, as ICC chairman, had appealed to the U.S. and North Vietnam earlier in the week not to carry the ground fighting into the demilitarized zone. Y. N. Kaul, secretary to India's External Affairs Ministry, was reported to have told U.S. Chargé d'Affaires Joseph Greene Jr. and Nguyen Hoa, North Vietnamese consul general in New Delhi, that India feared that the current fighting just south of the zone might spill over into the buffer area itself.

It had been reported in Saigon Oct. 11 that military authorities were considering placing mines and other obstacles just south of the demilitarized zone to prevent the infiltration of North Vietnamese forces into South Vietnam. U.S. Air Force and Marine pilots had conducted at least 12 separate strikes Oct. 2 against North Vietnamese supply and staging areas in the DMZ. B-57 bombers pounded the zone Oct. 4; pilots reported destroying 25 structures.

U.S. Defense Department officials in Washington disclosed Oct. 11 that U.S. planes had struck the eastern sector of the demilitarized zone in July during fighting between North Vietnamese and U.S. forces.

U.S. B-52s from Guam bombed the zone Dec. 18-20. The strikes were against North Vietnamese supply bases and staging areas just south of the buffer area, where the reorganized North Vietnamese 324-B Division was believed massing for a new drive.

U.S. Attacks Ho Trail in Laos

It had been reported in Saigon Jan. 8 that up to 300 U.S. planes were carrying out daily raids against North Vietnam's Ho Chi Minh Trail in eastern Laos. The Ho Chi Minh Trail was a network of roads that served as the main infiltration and supply route from North Vietnam to the Viet Cong and North Vietnamese units in South Vietnam. The U.S. attacks were said to have been stepped up to counter an increase in supply shipments along the trail. Hanoi was said to have taken advantage of the U.S. pause in air strikes against North Vietnam by making increasing use of the supply trail.

It was reported in Vientiane, Laos Feb. 15 that North Vietnamese military units were expanding the Ho Chi Minh Trail. Communist forces were said to have secured territory west of the current routes to build 4 additional roads. The purpose of the expansion was to provide greater protection against U.S.-Laotian air strikes by dispersing supplies and infiltrators over additional roads. The new roads, running south and west from the Mugia Pass in Laos, carried trucks from Vinh, North Vietnam's principal staging area on the coast. Increased U.S. air attacks to interdict North Vietnamese infiltration in Laos were reported in Saigon July 11. More than 100 air strikes a day were being carried out against the Communist supply lines; this contrasted with less than 50 a day 6 months previously. The report said that U.S. air attacks on Communist targets in Laos originated from aircraft carriers in the South China Sea and from airfields in South Vietnam and Thailand. It was reported from Bangkok, Thailand Aug. 20 that, according to American sources, in the previous 18 months North Vietnam had enlarged and improved the Ho Chi Minh Trail despite the increased U.S. air strikes. The North Vietnamese were said to have succeeded since mid-1965 in building new routes and in using them to supply Communist forces in South Vietnam.

(The U.S. Defense Department reported August 4 that it was revising the American casualty lists in the Vietnamese fighting to include U.S. military personnel killed in Laos. According to the department's new summary form, during the period Jan. 1, 1961-July 30, 1966, 30 Americans had been killed in Laos, more than 30 were missing, 2 were captured and 4 died of non-combat causes.)

North Vietnamese Aid Pathet Lao

It was also reported that North Vietnamese troops were increasing their support of the pro-Communist Pathet Lao rebels against Laotian government soldiers. A Laotian government communiqué said Jan. 29 that North Vietnamese troops were headed for Thateng to support a Pathet Lao attack there. The government said North Vietnamese troops were also reinforcing Pathet Lao forces in the 4th Military Region in southern Laos. A communiqué issued Feb. 6 by the Laotian neutralist army of Gen. Kong Le said that government forces Feb. 4 had launched a "purely defensive" operation against North Vietnamese and Pathet Lao troops at Ban Ban, Khang Khay and the Plaine des Jarres. Another neutralist report Feb. 9 said that at least 40 Pathet Lao and North Vietnamese had been killed in Laotian air attacks in fighting around Mt. Phoukout in northern Laos. The report said that fighting had started there Feb. 4 and that some Soviet-made equipment had been destroyed, including 4 amphibious tanks; 7 Soviet-manufactured anti-aircraft machineguns were said to have been captured.

A Laotian Defense Ministry official, Col. Thongpunh Knoksy, asserted Feb. 11 that 2 North Vietnamese regiments plus other elements had blocked off the Ho Chi Minh Trail's approaches from western Laos and Thailand. Thongpunh said "the North Vietnamese were forced to move there because the Pathet Lao commanders in the area are bickering, and the area is too important to have anything go wrong."

Gen. Oudone Sananikone, Laotian armed forces chief of staff, reported Feb. 19 that government troops attacked by combined North Vietnamese/Pathet Lao forces had retreated 3 miles Feb. 18 from Ban Nakhang, the government's strongest position in Northern Samneua Province. The government's last remaining airstrip for heavy transport planes was captured in the fighting. A Laotian government spokesman, Phagna Bouasy, asserted in a statement Feb. 23 that the Vientiane government held North Vietnam "responsible for all the aggression, all the dead, all the bad things that have happened to our kindom since" Hanoi "took the decision to aid the Neo Lao Hak Sat [the Pathet Lao's political arm] in nourishing, adding to and spreading disorder in this country." Phagna estimated North Vietnamese troop strength in Laos at 20,000 men.

Government troops were reported Feb. 25 in new positions near Attopeu, capital of Attopeu Province in southern Laos, after a heavy attack by Pathet Lao units and several North Vietnamese battalions. (The Ho Chi Minh Trail ran through Attopeu Province at the edge of Cambodia into South Vietnam.)

A government-held airstrip at Muong Hiem in Samneua Province was captured by the Pathet Lao March 11. It was the government's last important airfield in the area. Neutralist forces under Gen. Kong Le's command recaptured Mont Phoukout from Pathet Lao troops March 14 and then were driven from the strategic height March 19.

The British Foreign Office August 22 released a 16-month-old report, prepared by the Indian and Canadian members of the International Control Commission for Laos, that, according to the office, "provides convincing evidence of operations of North Vietnamese troops in Laos contrary to the 1962 Geneva agreements." Britain had asked the Soviet Union, as co-chairman of the Geneva accords, to circulate the report jointly. But Moscow rejected the British invitation on the ground that Poland, the 3d member of the commission, had refused to participate in the ICC probe. Polish objection had delayed circulation of the report. India had decided in July to side with the Canadian member in releasing it, and Britain had submitted the report to the Geneva conference members August 12. The ICC report was based largely on evidence provided by 9 prisoners, allegedly North Vietnamese army regulars, who had been captured during an attack on a Laotian army officer cadet school at Dong Heng March 8-9, 1965. The report said the attack on Dong Heng had been carried out by North Vietnamese troops with the possible assistance of Pathet Lao forces. (Hanoi and the Pathet Lao had denied allegations earlier in 1966 that 20,000 North Vietnamese troops were fighting in Laos.)

Cambodian Border Clashes

The neutral Kingdom of Cambodia became increasingly involved in border disputes with neighboring Thailand and South Vietnam during 1966. On its eastern border, the intense fighting in South Vietnam spilled over into Cambodian territory several times. On its western border, clashes with Thailand, an ally of South Vietnam, were reported.

Cambodia informed the UN Jan. 3 that it would use force to repel any violation of its territory by U.S. and South Vietnamese troops. It was also disclosed that the Pnompenh government had sent a letter to UN Secy. Gen. U Thant Dec. 30, 1965 suggesting that the International Control Commission (ICC) for Cambodia be reinforced to investigate the Cambodian charges. U.S. Amb.-to-UN Arthur J. Goldberg Jan. 8 accepted Cambodia's ICC proposal. In a letter sent to Thant, Goldberg simultaneously indicated continued U.S. suspicion that North Vietnamese/Viet Cong troops were using Cambodian territory.

A U.S. military spokesman in Saigon reported May 3 that a battalion of U.S. First Infantry Division troops had fired May 1 into Cambodia 70 miles northwest of Saigon during a clash with Viet Cong. It was the first deliberate attack on a target in Cambodian territory that had been officially confirmed. According to the spokesman's account: The U.S. battalion was carrying out a search mission (as part of Operation Birmingham) along the east bank of the Caibac River, which separates South Vietnam's Tayninh Province from Cambodia. The U.S. force overran the Vietnamese village of Logo and killed 8 Viet Cong after being subjected to guerrilla fire. During this operation, the American troops came under heavy automatic-weapon and mortar attack from the Cambodian side of the river. On orders of the battalion commander, division artillery pounded the target in Cambodia, and the enemy was silenced.

A. U.S. government protest to Cambodia charged that 2 American soldiers had been killed by Viet Cong fire from Cambodia Apr. 29 and 30. The note was sent to Cambodia May 17 through the Australian embassy in Pnompenh. It was disclosed by the U.S. State Department May 18. The note said the U.S. soldiers had been slain by small-arms and machinegun fire during the U.S. First Division's sweep of Tayninh Province, near the Cambodian border northwest of Saigon. Expressing "no desire to see the war in Asia widened," the note hinted that U.S. forces would take military action against Cambodia if it did not prevent the use of its territory by Communist forces. The Cambodian government said that Cambodian border guards repelling aggression had fired on U.S. troops.

Maj. Gen. Stanley R. Larsen, commander of U.S. forces in central South Vietnam, said May 27 that about 10,000

North Vietnamese troops were massed in Cambodia for a possible drive into South Vietnam. State Secy. Rusk and the Defense Department immediately denied knowledge of any Communist build-up in Cambodia. Larsen, who had just returned from Vietnam, said at a Pentagon news conference that there was "enough evidence to satisfy us that at least 4 and probably 6 North Vietnamese regiments" were in Cambodia. He reported that these troops were concentrated near the Central Highlands' Chuprong mountain area, scene of some of the heaviest fighting in Vietnam. In his statement of denial, Rusk said: "I do not have the information that Gen. Larsen gave." A Defense Department statement issued after Rusk's news conference conceded that "there have been unconfirmed reports of North Vietnamese activity in Cambodia." But the department said "there exists no evidence strong enough for the U.S. military command in Vietnam to validate the presence of any North Vietnamese regiment in Cambodia at this time." A Cambodian government statement May 29 said that "no foreign troops are stationed in the region in question nor in any other part of Cambodian territory." It charged that the U.S. had decided to start operations against Cambodia and was using claims of a North Vietnamese build-up on its territory as a pretext.

Cambodia accused the U.S. of carrying out air attacks against Cambodian border villages July 31 and Aug. 2 and killing several of the villagers. A U.S. spokesman held at first that the villages were not in Cambodian territory, but after further investigation, the U.S. admitted that they were.

The official Cambodian news agency said Aug. 3 that 2 U.S. F-105 Thunderchief fighter-bombers had attacked the frontier village of Thlok Trach Aug. 2, killing at least 3 persons and wounding 9. The agency said the village was inside Cambodia and the bombings occurred as ICC representatives were on their way to the area to inspect damage inflicted in previous alleged U.S. air attacks July 31 on Thlok Trach and on another village, Anlong Trach. The agency said the ICC observers were accompanied by foreign correspondents and military attachés of several embassies in Pnompenh and that all had witnessed the Aug. 2 incident. The Cambodian account of the Aug. 2 raid was supported by the Polish government Aug. 6. The ICC's Canadian observers partially supported the Polish government's version of the Aug. 2 attack, according to a report of the incident released by the Canadian External Affairs Department Aug. 8. The department said the ICC observers had witnessed the strafing by planes.

A spokesman at the U.S. embassy in Saigon acknowledged Aug. 12 that U.S. air attacks had occurred July 31 "in the vicinity of" the village of Thlok Trach and Aug. 2 at another point more than 900 yards east of the village. The spokesman said that all "maps available to us show that the 2 targets are in South Vietnam." But in a statement issued Aug. 16 the U.S. State Department conceded that a visit by ICC officials and other diplomatic observers to the village Aug. 2 had "clearly indicated that the area in question is under the administration" of the Cambodian government. The statement reiterated the previous U.S. contention that "the maps available to us show the area in question to be on the Vietnamese side of the border, and these maps include a Cambodian map of recent date." The statement expressed "regrets" at "any loss of Cambodian life and property and any intrusion into Cambodian territory which may have occurred in connection with these incidents." The South Vietnamese government Aug. 17 said it regretted the attack on Thlok Trach, but it said that a 1964 Cambodian map supported South Vietnam's claim to the village.

Prince Norodom Sihanouk, Cambodian chief of state, Aug. 13 had assailed the U.S.' initial claim that Thlok Trach was in South Vietnam. Sihanouk complained that U.S. maps also falsely placed other Cambodian border villages and islands inside South Vietnam. Sihanouk declared that as a result of the U.S. position on the latest border incidents, he would refuse to meet in Pnompenh with U.S. Amb.-at-Large W. Averell Harriman. (The U.S. State Department had announced Aug. 2 that Harriman would go to Pnompenh in September to confer with Sihanouk on U.S.-Cambodian diplomatic relations, severed by Cambodia in May 1965.) Sihanouk said that in order for him to meet with Harriman, the U.S. "must first recognize that Cambodia is a country that has a border." Sihanouk said Aug. 19 that he had called off the Harriman visit because U.S. air raids against Cambodian territory would have continued during his stay and this "would have provoked grave reaction among the people, which the government would have had to put down." Sihanouk said that the South Vietnamese government had repeatedly rejected his proposals for clear demarcation of the border and that he was instead working out a frontier accord with the NLF. Sihanouk said the NLF and North Vietnam supported Cambodia against South Vietnam in a further dispute over several coastal islands.

Cambodia's version of the U.S. air attacks had been supported in a statement issued in New York Aug. 13 by a private U.S. organization called Americans Want to Know. 9 members of the group had visited Cambodian border areas July 29-Aug. 8 at Sihanouk's request to investigate U.S. charges that Cambodia was permitting the use of its territory as a haven and supply base for Viet Cong forces. The mission's statement, made by Marc Stone, said his group had been in Thlok Trach Aug. 1 and 8 and was convinced that the residents "were unquestionably Cambodian." Stone said that the village had come under air attack 3 times, not twice, that all 12 of its thatched homes had been destroyed and that 3 persons had been killed. In a meeting with the U.S. group July 30, Sihanouk had said that he was "willing to discard" one of 3 conditions he had set as a prerequisite for the restoration of U.S.-Cambodian relations. Cambodia, Sihanouk said, no longer would insist on "compensation for our casualties suffered as a result of U.S. aggression." Sihanouk said Cambodia's 2 other conditions for resumption of ties remained fixed: formal U.S. recognition of Cambodia's boundary claims and the halting of "aggression or armed incursion into our territory." (Among the members of Americans Want to Know who had toured Cambodia were novelist Kay Boyle and Floyd McKissick, national director of the Congress of Racial Equality.)

Sihanouk had suggested that a solution to the Vietnamese war rested with peace negotiations with the NLF rather than with North Vietnam or Communist China. Sihanouk's statement was one of several answers to questions on Cambodia's role in Southeast Asia, which *N.Y. Times* correspondent Harrison E. Salisbury had submitted during a recent trip to Pnompenh. In his reply, received by the *Times* Aug. 3, Sihanouk said that since the Viet Cong had the greatest popular support among the Vietnamese people, the U.S. pursuit of a peaceful solution to the conflict was "perhaps within your hand's reach, not far from Saigon itself." He asked: "Why look for a solution in Hanoi or even in Peking?" In another reply to Salisbury, Sihanouk denied the existence of a Cambodian link to North Vietnam's Ho Chi Minh Trail to South Vietnam or that the Viet Cong were using Cambodian territory as a privileged sanctuary. Sihanouk acknowledged the existence of the Sihanouk Trail, but he said it was used only to supply Cambodian forces maintaining surveillance on the northern frontier with Laos.

Cambodia charged Sept. 9 and 22 that U.S. helicopters had raided Cambodian border areas Sept. 7 and 21. Cambodian government statements said that: 2 helicopters bearing U.S. markings had machinegunned the Cambodian border village of Sramar Sept. 7, killing one person and wounding 2; 2 U.S. helicopters had fired 8 rockets Sept. 21 at a Cambodian army post near Snoul, about 20 miles west of the Cambodian-South Vietnamese frontier, killing one soldier and wounding 4. The U.S. State Department Sept. 23 expressed regret for "any violation of Cambodian territory or any loss of life or property that might have occurred." A department statement Oct. 14 acknowledged that "due to a pilot error," 2 U.S. helicopters had "strayed across the border and fired on Cambodian territory." The department note said that "compensation . . . is being offered" by the South Vietnamese government. U.S. officials explained that Saigon would pay for the loss of life or property because U.S. forces involved in the Sept. 21 attack had been acting on South Vietnamese request. The department promised that in the future "much more care would be exercised by pilots when they know they are near the Cambodian border."

Southern Leaders for Invasion of North

As the U.S. maintained its aerial pressure against the North, South Vietnam's Premier Ky and Chief of State Thieu called for sterner military measures, including a land invasion of North Vietnam. In a speech at the graduation of officers at a military academy near Saigon July 8, Thieu said that since South Vietnam had been "invaded" by North Vietnam, "we must demolish . . . all military, economic and manufacturing zones without distinction throughout the North. . . . This should include the movement of troops into . . . North Vietnam . . . if it is necessary to end the war." In an interview appearing in the Aug. 1 issue of *U.S. News & World Report* (published July 25), Ky urged an allied invasion of North Vietnam, even at the risk of a military confrontation with Communist China. "As long as we have no right to invade North Vietnam," Ky said, "you cannot say we definitely are going to win the war."

The U.S. government responded to Ky's remarks in a statement July 26 by State Department press officer Robert J. McCloskey. He said: "I would say our position of not seeking any wider war has been repeatedly made clear and remains our position. We do not threaten any regime." The statement was issued after Senate majority leader Mike Mansfield (D., Mont.) had insisted earlier July 26 that the Johnson Administration dissociate itself from Ky's proposal for an invasion.

The South Vietnamese Advisory Council of the People & the Armed Forces Aug. 31 also recommended a South Vietnamese land invasion of North Vietnam. Asserting that South Vietnam was "in danger as a result of the invasion from the north," a council statement suggested that the South Vietnamese armed forces "retaliate and make counter offensives over the 17th Parallel."

Naval Activity

An increase in U.S. Navy attacks against North Vietnamese coastal shipping and shore installations began Oct. 25, and by Nov. 23 more than 230 Communist vessels were reported sunk in the attacks on coastal ships. All the operations took place in the Donghoi area. The series of naval attacks started when 2 U.S. destroyers shelled the North Vietnamese coast north of Donghoi Oct. 25 after coming under fire from Communist coastal guns. It was the first exchange between U.S. ships and North Vietnamese shore batteries. The North Vietnamese coast came under naval shelling again Nov. 4 when 2 U.S. destroyers pounded Communist batteries that had opened fire on them. 3 flights of U.S. F-4C Phantom jets, responding to a call from the destroyers, bombed the North Vietnamese guns. 2 U.S. destroyers shelled a North Vietnamese radar site and 12 nearby cargo boats 2 miles north of the demilitarized zone Nov. 18. The 200-shell barrage was believed to have been the first U.S. naval attack not carried out in retaliation against fire from Communist batteries. 2 U.S. destroyers Nov. 23 sank or damaged 47 of 60 Communist military supply barges off the southern panhandle of North Vietnam. The U.S. destroyer *Ingersoll* was slightly damaged in an exchange of gunfire with a North Vietnamese coastal battery 11 miles northeast of Donghoi Dec. 5.

A fire Oct. 26 swept the 42,000-ton U.S. aircraft carrier *Oriskany* in the Gulf of Tonkin 60-100 miles off the coast of North Vietnam. It killed 43 men (35 officers and 8 enlisted men) and injured 16. 4 jet fighter-bombers and 2 helicopters were destroyed. The blaze caused extensive damage and put the 21-year-old *Oriskany* out of action for months. A Navy spokesman said the fire had started on the hangar deck when a locker filled with night-illumination magnesium flares burst into flame. All of the dead were pilots trapped in their staterooms adjoining both sides of the deck. The fire quickly spread through most of the ship and was brought under control only after 3 hours. Smaller flash fires continued for several hours thereafter. Crewmen threw about 300 bombs overboard as a safety measure. Medical aid was flown to the *Oriskany* from 2 other carriers in the gulf—the *Constellation* and the *Franklin D. Roosevelt*. Some of the *Oriskany's* injured were transferred to the 2 carriers while others were flown to a U.S. naval hospital at Subic Bay in the Philippines. The *Oriskany* arrived in Subic Bay Oct. 28 for repairs. Its position off Vietnam was taken by the carrier *Coral Sea*.

8 enlisted men were killed and 14 injured Nov. 4 by a flash fire aboard the carrier *Franklin D. Roosevelt* in the Gulf of Ton-

kin off North Vietnam. The blaze broke out 5 decks below the flight deck in a storage compartment containing paint and oil. The fire was extinguished in 15 minutes, and the ship remained on duty.

The U.S. Navy announced Dec. 29 that all 3 of its nuclear-powered surface ships comprising Task Force 1 in the Gulf of Tonkin off North Vietnam were currently on duty. The ships were the cruiser *Long Beach,* the carrier *Enterprise* and the frigate *Bainbridge.*

The 8,500-ton U.S. freighter *Baton Rouge Victory* had been disabled and 7 of its crew-members had been killed and one injured when it struck a Viet Cong mine Aug. 23 in the Longtao River, 22 miles south of Saigon. The vessel, carrying general cargo to Saigon, partially sank and blocked traffic in the vital channel linking Saigon with the sea. Traffic was resumed Aug. 24. The sinking of the *Baton Rouge Victory* was followed by a series of other mine blasts in the channel. A South Vietnamese minesweeper struck a mine Aug. 28, 19 miles southeast of Saigon, and reportedly was totally destroyed. One Vietnamese sailor was killed and 2 others and a U.S. adviser were wounded. A mine exploded Aug. 29 off the bow of a U.S. Navy minesweeper in the river, 18 miles southeast of Saigon, but the ship was undamaged. Another U.S. minesweeper sank Nov. 1 after detonating a mine in the river. As the vessel struck the mine, guerrillas on the river bank poured heavy small-arms fire into it. American casualties were reported.

Major Military Operations in the South

Most of the fighting in South Vietnam was guerrilla warfare carried on anonymously at the squad or company level. The only military operations able to be reported meaningfully were the larger search-and-destroy offensive carried out by American and allied troops. Among the most important allied military operations of 1966:

New Year's Operations—U.S. and allied military forces in South Vietnam started the New Year Jan. 1 with 2 major assaults against the Viet Cong—(a) near Tuyhoa, 240 miles north of Saigon, and (b) in Haunghia Province, in the Mekong Delta, 35 miles northeast of Saigon. Tear gas dropped by planes in both engagements led to the capture of guerrillas.

In the Tuyhoa operation, a joint South Vietnamese-South Korean force killed 218 guerrillas and captured 19 Jan. 1-4. The Koreans, a unit of marines, accounted for 188 of the enemy dead. (The marines were among the 20,000 South Korean troops that had arrived in South Vietnam Oct. 8, 1965.) Tear gas dropped by the Koreans in the early part of the operation forced 27 Viet Cong suspects from a tunnel. The Koreans flushed 20 more guerrillas out of cave positions after a 2d tear-gas drop Jan. 3. Fighting was particularly savage Jan. 4, and the Koreans killed 38 guerrillas. The South Vietnamese and South Koreans were fighting to protect the vital rice harvest in Phuyen Province.

In the Haunghia Province battle, U.S. and Australian infantrymen, supported by New Zealand artillery units, were flown into the area by helicopter Jan. 1 to join South Vietnamese units that had been fighting a 600-man Viet Cong force on the Vaico River near the Cambodian border since the previous day. A U.S. military spokesman said Jan. 2 that it was the first time American combat units (850 paratroops of the 173d Airborne Brigade) had participated in fighting in the Mekong Delta; heretofore, only U.S. advisers attached to Vietnamese units had operated in the area. After the fighting of Dec. 31, 1965–Jan. 1, 1966, South Vietnamese soldiers counted the bodies of 134 guerrillas. The U.S. paratroopers were reported to have killed 111 guerrillas Jan. 2 on the northeast bank of the Vaico River. The allied force was assisted by U.S. fighter-bombers that pounded enemy positions. Some of the planes dropped tear gas on the Viet Cong concentrations Jan. 2. Although the non-lethal gas (CN-type) was described as ineffective because of erratic winds, the drops were believed responsible for the high number of guerrillas captured (more than 500). A U.S. military spokesman said that this was not the first time American forces had used gas in this manner, that it had been employed several times since its use had been authorized in Oct. 1965 by Gen. William C. Westmoreland, commander of U.S. forces in Vietnam. Several U.S. soldiers were killed and wounded Jan. 3 when they were accidentally struck by American artillery shells in the Haunghia operation.

Operation Crimp—A joint U.S.-Australian drive against the Viet Cong Iron Triangle stronghold 25 miles north of Saigon Jan. 8-14 failed to flush out a suspected large guerrilla concentration in the area. The offensive involved about 8,000 troops of the U.S. First Infantry Division, the U.S. 173d Airborne Brigade and an Australian infantry battalion. The force killed 107 guerrillas through Jan. 26 and captured 683 suspected guerrillas. During the operation the Australians Jan. 8 discovered a vast 3-level network of abandoned Viet Cong tunnels capable of housing 10,000-15,000 troops.

Operations Masher & Double Eagle—About 20,000 U.S. and allied soldiers launched 2 separate but coordinated drives Jan. 25 and 28 against an estimated 8,000 North Vietnamese and Viet Cong troops in Quangngai and Binhdinh Provinces. Targets of the drive were the 18th and 98th North Vietnamese Regiments and the First and 2d Viet Cong Regiments. The first prong of the offensive—Operation Masher —started Jan. 25 when the allied force moved into northern Binhdinh Province. The 2d phase of the offensive—Operation Double Eagle —was launched Jan. 28 when 4,000 U.S. Marines landed on the coast of the Ducpho district in Quangngai Province. The landing was the largest since the Inchon operation of the Korean War. The fiercest fighting occurred Jan. 28 when 2 companies of First Cavalry troops were pinned down by heavy fire as they landed by helicopter near Anthai, Binhdinh Province. The Americans suffered heavy losses but were rescued Jan. 29. Operation Masher—retitled White Wing—resulted in the killing of 1,130 Communist troops by Feb. 22. The burden of the fighting had been carried by the U.S. First Cavalry Division.

Anlao Valley Battle—U.S. troops moved into the Anlao Valley in the Central Highlands Feb. 7 in an effort to find and destroy the major elements of a 2,000-man combined force of 2 North Vietnamese and 2 Viet Cong regiments. Most of the Communist troops had fled to the valley after the force had been severely mauled in the offensive in the coastal regions of Binhdinh and Quangngai Provinces. Enemy deaths since the U.S.-South Vietnamese-South Korean drive started Jan. 25 totaled 1,295 by Feb. 14.

Operation Utah—About 7,000 U.S. and South Vietnamese troops inflicted heavy casualties in a battle with 2,000 North Vietnamese regular army troops and an undisclosed number of Viet Cong Mar. 4-6 in Quangngai Province. The battle was centered on the North Vietnamese regiment's headquarters in the village of Sonchau, about 7 miles northwest of the town of Quangngai. The battle ended Mar. 6 when U.S. Marines and South Vietnamese paratroopers swept into the village and met only slight resistance. Col. Oscar F. Peatross, chief of staff of the Marine task force, said in Saigon Mar. 7 that at least ½ of the 2,000-man North Vietnamese regiment had been killed or wounded. Col. Bruce Jones, senior adviser to the South Vietnamese Army 2d Division, said the presence of the North Vietnamese headquarters at Sonchau had been discovered Mar. 3 as the result of interrogation of a prisoner.

Ashau Camp Battle—American and Vietnamese troops were forced to abandon a U.S. Special Forces camp at Ashau Mar. 10 as a result of a fierce attack by a North Vietnamese regular army force of about 2,000 men. The camp, located 60 miles southwest of Danang, was astride a section of the Ho Chi Minh Trail, 2 miles from the Laotian border. The camp's defenders, 17 U.S. Special Forces advisers and 400 *montagnard* and Nung (ethnic Chinese) tribesmen, suffered overwhelming losses in fighting that had started when the North Vietnamese surrounded the outpost Mar. 9. About 200 of the camp's defenders were evacuated by plane. Capt. John D. Blair, the post's U.S. commander, charged that many of his men had secretly been Viet Cong sympathizers.

Operation Hawthorne—In one of the biggest battles of the Vietnamese war, troops of the U.S. Army's 101st Airborne Division fought the North Vietnamese army's 24th Regiment in Kontum Province in the Central Highlands June 3-13. Sporadic clashes continued through June 17. The number of North Vietnamese bodies found since the start of the battle totaled 565, but only 20 Communist troops were captured. The brigade had started a search-and-destroy offensive June 3 but did not encounter many of the Communist troops until June 7. During June 9 fighting, Capt. William S. Carpenter Jr., a company commander, radioed for U.S. planes to strike his own position. The bombings temporarily stopped the North Vietnamese attack and enabled most of Carpenter's men to escape (the number of Carpenter's men killed or wounded in the bombing was not disclosed). He was awarded the Silver Star medal June 12 for his action.

Operation Nathan Hale—U.S. and allied forces launched a search-and-destroy operation June 20 against Communist troops 15 miles north of the Phuyen Province coastal city of Tuyhoa (240 miles north of Saigon). The allied offensive started when a battalion of the First Brigade of the U.S. 101st Airborne Division (which shared the brunt of the fighting with the U.S. First Cavalry Division) made contact with the Communist forces near the U.S. Special Forces camp at Dongtri. An estimated 392 enemy troops were reported to have been slain by June 26. The Communists, estimated at 500-700, were entrenched in foxholes and bunkers near Dongtri.

Operation Hastings—A force of more than 8,500 U.S. Marines and 2,500 South Vietnamese troops launched a massive drive July 14 in Quangtri Province. Their target was a Communist force estimated at 8,000-10,000 soldiers, identified by U.S. intelligence sources as North Vietnam's 324-B Division. The fighting raged near the demilitarized zone (DMZ), which the Communist troops reportedly had crossed to pass into Quangtri, South Vietnam's northernmost province. The allied operation was officially described as completed by U.S. authorities Aug. 4, and prisoners reported that the North Vietnamese had fled back into the DMZ. An estimated 818 North Vietnamese were reported to have been killed through July 29. Captured enemy troops were said to have told U.S. interrogators that the division's mission was to take control of Quangtri Province by destroying the South Vietnamese First Infantry Division, assigned to protect the area. Brig. Gen. Lowell English, commander of the operation, said July 17 that Operation Hastings had thwarted the North Vietnamese division's plan to start an offensive against the northern provinces at the beginning of the monsoon season.

Operation Prairie—Several regiments of U.S. Marines began a sweep Aug. 3 just south of the demilitarized zone against 3 battalions of North Vietnam's 324-B Division. 1,500 U.S. Marines Sept. 15 landed from ships of the 7th Fleet on the shores of Quangtri Province, 3 miles south of the demilitarized zone dividing North and South Vietnam. The landing coincided with Operation Prairie, some 20 miles inland. In other action near the zone, 2 companies of the 4th Marine Regiment encountered a large North Vietnamese force 3 miles south of the zone Sept. 16. The outnumbered American troops were trapped and did not break out until Sept. 18. A U.S. military spokesman reported Oct. 14 that 1,099 North Vietnamese troops had been slain in Operation Prairie.

Operation Irving—U.S. First Cavalry (Airmobile) Division troops, assisted by South Vietnamese and South Korean soldiers, launched a drive Oct. 2 against a combined Viet Cong-North Vietnamese force in the central coastal area 28 miles northwest of Quinhon (about 305 miles northwest of Saigon). The allied troops killed 902 Communists by Oct. 25. (A South Korean force had killed 1,071 Communists in the same area in September.) B-52s bombed enemy positions behind the lines in support of the operation. The battle had started when U.S. helicopter observers spotted an estimated 300 Communist troops marching west through a valley. 2 First Cavalry Division companies were sent in pursuit, and they killed more than 170 enemy troops. The Communist forces then fled east toward the South China Sea coast, where they came under further allied attack. The allied troops surrounded the Viet Cong-North Vietnamese force, and U.S. and South Vietnamese patrol boats were stationed offshore to prevent escape by sea.

Operation Attleboro—U.S. troops sweeping Tayninh Province near the Cambodian border (40-60 miles north of Saigon) in search of enemy soldiers since Oct. 15 came upon a major Communist force Nov. 3 and fought one of the biggest battles of the war. The engagements continued through Nov. 12, and the American force, assisted by South Vietnamese troops, inflicted heavy casualties on the Communists. Several thousand Communist troops were involved in the battle. The Communists were identified as major elements of the 9th Viet Cong Division (the 271st, 272d and 273d Regiments), the guerrillas' best trained and equipped unit, and the 101st North Vietnamese Regiment. The allied force was made up of the U.S. First and 25th Infantry Divisions, the 196th Light Infantry Brigade, the 173d Airborne Brigade and at least 2 South Vietnamese battalions. At the height of the fighting 20,000 U.S. and South Vietnamese troops—a record number —were committed. 1,101 Viet Cong and North Vietnamese were reported slain by the end of the offensive Nov. 26. Maj. Gen. William E. DePuy, First Division commander, who assumed direction of Operation Attleboro Nov. 5, said Nov. 9 that he believed the operation had thwarted a major Communist attack on an isolated U.S. Special Forces camp at Suoida, near the Cambodian border. Stationed at the camp were several hundred South Vietnamese troops and several American advisers. DePuy said a captured Communist document indicated that the project assault against the camp was to be the start of a major winter offensive in the area. DePuy said it appeared that Communist troops had attempted to keep a battalion of U.S. troops from overrunning a regimental headquarters. According to U.S. intelligence sources, the Communists had put up stiff resistance because the Tayninh Province sector, part of the Communists' War Zone C stronghold, was the site of the Viet Cong's principal command center for all guerrilla operations in South Vietnam and of the National Liberation Front's "central office for South Vietnam."

U Minh Forest Drive—About 6,000 South Vietnamese troops launched a major drive Dec. 27 against the Viet Cong in the Mekong Delta's U Minh Forest, more than 125 miles southwest of Saigon. 104 Viet Cong were reported killed and 18 captured by Dec. 31. Participating in the offensive were an estimated 1,200 South Vietnamese paratroopers dropped from 13 U.S. Air Force and 20 South Vietnamese air force planes. Just before the air-drop, U.S. planes had saturated the eastern fringe of the forest area with hundreds of tons of bombs and napalm. The U.S. destroyer *Herbert J. Thomas* Dec. 29 shelled suspected Viet Cong positions in the area for 7 hours. The U Minh Forest was considered one of the most fortified Viet Cong strongholds in South Vietnam. According to intelligence reports, the Viet Cong's 10th, 303d and 306th battalions were operating in or near the forest. (Troops of the U.S. 25th Infantry Division had begun combat operations with South Vietnamese forces in the Mekong Delta in mid-September, and additional U.S. combat troops entered the area in late December. Heretofore the delta had been under the sole jurisdiction of the 40,000 regular troops and 100,000 militiamen of the South Vietnamese army's IV Corps area. The only U.S. military personnel in the delta were 5,000 U.S. advisers and American helicopter and river patrol boat crews. U.S. Navy patrol boats and Navy helicopters had prevented a Viet Cong battalion from crossing the Mekong River near Mytho Oct. 31 in a flotilla of junks and sampans. The patrol boats sank 35 vessels, while the 'copters accounted for another 15.)

Tansonnhut Airbase Attacked

A Viet Cong unit estimated at 25-30 men carried out a damaging 20-minute mortar-and-rifle attack Apr. 13 against the U.S. airbase at Saigon's Tansonnhut Airport. 7 U.S. servicemen and a South Vietnamese civilian engineer were killed. 109 U.S. and 14 South Vietnamese military personnel were injured. 5 Vietnamese and one U.S. civilian also were wounded. The attackers destroyed about 12 helicopters, and 9 transports and jets. The guerrillas also attacked an aviation fuel dump; the fire destroyed several thousand gallons of gasoline. The base's main runway was slightly damaged, and the control tower was knocked out.

Guerrillas attacked Tansonnhut again Dec. 4 in 2 assaults. In the first, a Viet Cong unit penetrated the 13-mile defense perimeter, reached the main runway and shelled the field. The guerrillas broke off the attack 4½ hours later after clashing with U.S. and South Vietnamese security guards. U.S.

spokesmen said 18 Viet Cong guerrillas had been killed; 4 were wounded and captured. 3 U.S. Air Force policemen were killed and 5 USAF policemen and 2 South Vietnamese security guards were injured. One U.S. RF-101 reconnaissance jet was heavily damaged. The guerrillas resumed their attack against Tansonnhut during the night of Dec. 4; 11 of them were killed by security guards who again repulsed the raid. The defenders were assisted by armed helicopters providing air support and by flares dropped by other aircraft. Sporadic fighting continued past midnight. A Viet Cong broadcast Dec. 5 called the Tansonnhut attack a "great victory for the National Liberation Front." The broadcast said the raids were in retaliation for an American air strike in the Hanoi area Dec. 2.

Americans Burn Village

The U.S. military command in Saigon disclosed Sept. 16 that U.S. troops Sept. 14 had burned down the South Vietnamese village of Lienhoa (43 miles northwest of Quinhon) after warning the inhabitants to leave. There were no reports of civilian casualties. The U.S. spokesman said troops of the U.S. First Cavalry Division had set fire to the village because it was regarded as "definitely hostile." He said that 2 U.S. helicopters and a jet had been shot down in the area Sept. 13 and that First Cavalry troops had come under fire from bunkers in the village complex. 70 Viet Cong suspects were seized after Lienhoa was razed, and 62 of them were turned over to the South Vietnamese as prisoners. In an initial report on the incident, a U.S. spokesman had said Sept. 15 that the village had been destroyed by air strikes and artillery fire. But newsmen who had been at the village said that some U.S. troops had set fire to the thatched-roof houses with matches.

Westmoreland Reports Progress

A personal assessment of allied progress in the war was delivered to Pres. Johnson by Gen. William C. Westmoreland, commander of U.S. forces in Vietnam, at a meeting Aug. 13-14 at the LBJ Ranch in Johnson City, Tex. In a statement to newsmen after the conclusion of the talks Aug. 14, Pres. Johnson said that his meeting with Westmoreland had "confirmed the conviction" that " a Communist military take-over in South Vietnam is no longer just improbable . . . it is impossible." But Mr. Johnson warned that there "will be no quick victory." "The single most important factor now is our will to prosecute the war until the Communists . . . either end the fighting or seek a peaceful settlement," the President said.

Westmoreland told newsmen that despite the increased air attacks against North Vietnam there was "no indication that the resolve of the leadership in Hanoi has been reduced." To the contrary, Westmoreland asserted, there was "every indication that the leadership has planned to continue the conflict in accordance with the present pattern that prevails." U.S. air attack on North Vietnam's communications arteries and oil depots "has had an impact," but "this has not reflected itself yet in large measure," Westmoreland said. The general conceded that U.S. air losses in the war the previous week "were unusually high." But Westmoreland said the average weekly loss of aircraft was "not out of line and is not far different from expectations."

Westmoreland said there were 282,000 Communist troops in South Vietnam. He said the force comprised 110,000 main-force North Vietnamese regular army troops, 112,000 in "guerrilla forces," 40,000 "political cadre" personnel and 20,000 "support troops."

Westmoreland was questioned by newsmen about "apparently inspired reports from Saigon" that the war in Vietnam could be "considerably shortened if the number of American troops in the field were increased to 750,000." He replied that he understood "there is an alleged study coming to such a conclusion." But he said that he had not seen the study and that his staff had not prepared it.

A report from Saigon Aug. 7 had said that some military men in Washington favored increasing the current 286,000-man U.S. force in Vietnam to 750,000 men on the basis of 2 recent assessments of the military situation—one prepared by the U.S. Marine Corps, the other by the Defense Department. The Marine Corps report, which was said to have been originated by Gen. Wallace M. Greene Jr., Marine commandant, was said to have predicted that North Vietnam could continue indefinitely to absorb casualties in South Vietnam at the current rate. A Defense Department research paper was quoted as saying that North Vietnam could maintain its force in South Vietnam for another 8 years.

Pres. Johnson had said at a news conference Aug. 9 that "we have been unable to find any of those reports in the government here." Defense Secy. Robert S. McNamara had told him that he "was not aware that there was any Defense Department report" on the matter and that McNamara did not agree with its reputed conclusions.

Gen. Greene denied Aug. 15 that he had been the source of the reports that 750,000 American troops would be needed in Vietnam. Greene said he had provided background information for some news media in Saigon, but he said he had made no reference to Defense Department or Joint Chiefs of Staff studies on the question of the length of the war and the number of troops required to fight it.

McNamara's 8th Vietnam Mission

U.S. Defense Secy. Robert S. McNamara spent 4 days in South Vietnam Oct. 10-13 on his 8th fact-finding mission to the war-torn country. Returning to the U.S. Oct. 14, McNamara declared that he anticipated no great boost in U.S. military activity in Vietnam. In a statement made on landing at Andrews Air Force Base, McNamara said: "I see no reason to expect any significant increase in the level or tempo of operations in South Vietnam, nor do I see any reason to believe that deployments of U.S. forces to that country will change significantly in the future." McNamara then went to the White House, where he reported to Pres. Johnson. Contents of the McNamara report were not disclosed, but the President said afterward that "I now have a clearer picture of the cost of the war." McNamara said after the meeting that he saw no necessity to call up the Reserves or National Guard.

During his meetings with U.S. commanders in Saigon Oct. 10, McNamara reportedly had been asked to send a substantially larger number of U.S. troops to South Vietnam. McNamara received briefings Oct. 10 from Gen. William C. Westmoreland, commander of U.S. forces, and Amb. Henry

Cabot Lodge. A spokesman for Lodge said later that "it was probably fair to say" that in his talks with McNamara the ambassador had been "more optimistic on the military progress than on progress in pacification and the civilian side."

McNamara conferred Oct. 11 with South Vietnamese Premier Nguyen Cao Ky and Chief-of-State Nguyen Van Thieu.

McNamara flew Oct. 12 to Phucat, where he was briefed by Maj. Gen. John Norton, commander of the First Cavalry Division (Airmobile), on the division's drive against Communist forces in the coastal plain just north of Quinhon. McNamara went on to Danang and met with officers of the 3d Marine Amphibious Force. He received more military briefings after flying to the aircraft carrier *Oriskany* in the South China Sea. McNamara assured military officials aboard the carrier that "under no circumstances" would American soldiers in South Vietnam be required to serve longer than their normal 12-month tour of duty. McNamara's statement appeared to contradict a Defense Department announcement the previous weekend that some key U.S. officers and field advisers would have to serve in South Vietnam an additional 6-12 months.

In a news conference statement before leaving Saigon Oct. 13, McNamara said that he had found that military operations had "progressed very satisfactorily" since 1965 and that "the rate of progress had exceeded our expectations." As for South Vietnam's economy, McNamara said progress was "likewise more than we would have forecast a year ago," and the Saigon government's decision to devalue the piaster had "stemmed" inflation. Although South Vietnamese officials were pursuing the pacification program in a "vigorous" manner, McNamara conceded that "progress is very slow indeed." He said "this is one area which requires vigorous action during the next year."

McNamara had been accompanied to South Vietnam by State Undersecy. Nicholas deB. Katzenbach, Adm. U. S. Grant Sharp, commander-in-chief of Pacific Forces, Gen. Earle G. Wheeler, chairman of the Joint Chiefs of Staff, and Robert W. Komer, special Presidential assistant for rural pacification in South Vietnam.

McNamara conferred with Pres. Johnson at the latter's ranch Nov. 5 and then announced plans to slow the U.S. military build-up in Vietnam. Speaking at the President's press conference Nov. 5, 3 days before the 1966 Congressional elections, McNamara said: The build-up of U.S. troops in Vietnam would continue in 1967 but "will be nothing on . . . [the] order" of the 1966 increase of 200,000 troops (to a total of 385,000); the number of men drafted in the 4-month period ending Mar. 1967 would be "significantly smaller" (80,000-100,000) than in the 4-month period ending in Nov. 1966 (estimated at 161,000); no "sharp increases" were planned in the number of air attacks in Vietnam (current monthly average: 25,000 sorties).

Terrorism

Among the numerous incidents of terrorism reported during 1966:

■ A South Vietnamese civilian rice convoy was ambushed by Viet Cong Jan. 8 at Conson, between Danang and Hué. A British missionary and 3 civilians were machinegunned to death. The missionary was identified as John Haywood, 31, of the World Wide Evangelization Crusade. He had been in charge of a leper colony in Danang.

■ The floating My Canh restaurant in Saigon was the target of a terrorist bomb explosion Jan. 8. 2 South Vietnamese civilians and a policeman were injured on the street, but no one in the restaurant was hurt. (The My Canh had been blasted by a Viet Cong bomb Jan. 25, 1965, and 42 persons had been killed.)

■ A U.S. aid mission representative, Douglas Ramsey, 28, was kidnaped by the Viet Cong Jan. 17 near the Haunghia Province village of Trunglap, 35 miles northwest of Saigon. The guerrillas seized Ramsey after ambushing his car. The vehicle's driver, a Vietnamese civilian, was shot in the leg but was released.

■ A U.S. sergeant was killed and 2 other American soldiers wounded when a bomb exploded Jan. 22 outsides their billet in the Gia Dinh suburb of Saigon. 4 South Vietnamese civilians in a nearby building were seriously wounded.

■ 6 Vietnamese civilians were shot to death in a 10-man Viet Cong ambush Feb. 2 while riding in a station wagon on a road near Phuocan, about 25 miles northwest of Saigon. The victims included Nguyen Van Thuy, an employe of the Psychological Warfare Branch of the U.S. Information Service, Pham Van Thuan, chief of the provincial branch of the Vietnamese Information Service, and 4 of his employes. A 7th occupant of the vehicle, a woman, escaped.

■ Viet Cong terrorists Feb. 5 exploded mines and grenades in a restaurant in Vinhlong, about 65 miles southwest of Saigon, killing

2 U.S. servicemen and 5 Vietnamese civilians. 6 Americans and 10 Vietnamese were wounded. Police shot and killed one of the terrorists. ■ 2 Viet Cong terrorists Feb. 5 machinegunned to death 3 persons in the town of Apquangnam. One of the victims was Ngo Tuong, 45, mayor of the nearby village of Lemy, 7 miles from Danang. Tuong had gone to Apquangnam for Buddhist ceremonies. Enraged villagers later killed the man who had invited Tuong in the belief that he had set a trap for the mayor.

■ 56 South Vietnamese peasants were killed within a 3-hour period by Viet Cong mine blasts Feb. 14 on a road near Tuyhoa, 225 miles northeast of Saigon. In the first incident, 29 farmers were killed and 5 injured when their bus detonated a mine. Later, a 2d bus detonated another mine 800 yards away and 20 persons were killed; most of them were civilians watching a crane lift the wreckage of the first bus from a nearby canal. The 3d mine explosion killed 7 bus passengers. (2 Viet Cong were ambushed Mar. 22 while attempting to plant a mine in the same road. One of the guerrillas was killed. The 2d said he and his companion had planted 16 mines in the road since mid-February.)

■ A Viet Cong mine explosion Feb. 17 killed 12 Vietnamese and injured 60 outside South Vietnamese Armed Forces headquarters in Saigon.

■ A Viet Cong mine exploded on a road 240 miles northeast of Saigon Mar. 18; it killed 15 South Vietnamese peasants and wounded 4 others. A U.S. military spokesman said most of the victims had been riding in a scooter bus.

■ Viet Cong terrorists Apr. 1 set off 200 pounds of explosives at a U.S. military billet (the Victoria Hotel) in Saigon. The explosion heavily damaged the 9-story structure and killed 3 Americans and 4 South Vietnamese. 6 of the victims were killed outright. The 7th— a Vietnamese woman—died of her wounds Apr. 2. Military authorities described her as a Viet Cong agent working in the building. 127 persons were injured—110 Americans, 14 Vietnamese and 3 Australians. 3 U.S. MPs and 2 South Vietnamese soldiers guarding the building were killed in an exchange of gunfire with approaching Viet Cong terrorists, firing automatic weapons. Under cover of the attack, other terrorists drove a bomb-laden panel truck to the entrance of the hotel, where it was blown up. 2 Vietnamese suspects were arrested. South Vietnamese police said that one of them had confessed that an 18-man Viet Cong commando unit had carried out the raid against the U.S. billet.

■ A mine explosion killed 11 South Korean and South Vietnamese civilian construction workers and wounded 23 at a Saigon bus stop Apr. 27.

■ Following a pre-dawn explosion of a terrorist bomb near a U.S. Army officers' quarters (the Brink) in Saigon May 10, U.S. soldiers shot 5 South Vietnamese civilians to death. The Vietnamese were mistaken for Viet Cong. 26 other Vietnamese and 8 Americans were wounded in the wild shooting. U.S. Deputy Amb. William J. Porter met with Premier Nguyen Cao Ky May 11 and expressed "sympathy and regret" over the incident. Porter said the U.S. would consider compensating the victims and their families.

Immediately after the bomb explosion (which injured 3 persons), U.S. MPs guarding the Brink and several MPs 4 blocks away had started shooting at no apparent target. Officers in the building also fired from the windows of their rooms. Most of the Vietnamese casualties resulted from the machinegunning of a truck that appeared on the scene. The vehicle carried men, women and children going to the Saigon docks. A nurse at a nearby hospital said MPs fired into the building, killing a 17-year-old boy who was visiting his brother. 7 Vietnamese were arrested as suspected terrorists but were later released.

In an initial account of the shooting, Brig. Gen. Robert L. Ashworth, Saigon area commander, said the MPs had engaged a group of well-armed Viet Cong. But other U.S. Army officials later acknowledged the error. A witness, U.S. Vice Consul Ralph Cadeaux, who had watched from his 4th floor apartment, said he had seen no one shoot back at the MPs.

■ A Viet Cong unit May 22 abducted 35 Vietnamese civilian laborers in the village of Hogiang, 110 miles southwest of Saigon. The guerrillas killed 19 of them and wounded the 16 others when a government force sought to rescue the captives.

■ 11 persons were killed and 54 wounded Oct. 21 when a terrorist mine exploded in the market place of the Mekong delta town of Traon, 75 miles southwest of Saigon. The dead included 4 South Vietnamese soldiers.

■ A bus carrying Vietnamese civilians detonated a Viet Cong mine on a road 18 miles north of Hué Oct. 24. 15 persons were killed and 19 injured.

■ At least 8 persons were killed and 26 injured in 2 separate Viet Cong terror attacks in the center of Saigon Nov. 1. In the first incident, 24 shells were fired from a 75-mm. recoiless rifle at a throng of civilians waiting at a reviewing stand for the start of a parade in celebration of South Vietnam's National Day. (The week-long celebration marked the 3d anniversary of the overthrow of the Ngo Dinh Diem regime in 1963.) Military officials speculated that the shelling, which lasted 7 minutes, had been directed from Thuthiem, a mile away on the east bank of the Saigon River. In the 2d incident, a Viet Cong grenade was thrown at a crowded bus terminal in the city's central market. Of the 8 persons killed in the 2 attacks, 7 were Vietnamese civilians. The 8th was a U.S. naval commander.

(The Viet Cong attacks followed a South Vietnamese government announcement Oct. 30 that the National Police had smashed a guerrilla plot to blow up U.S. and Vietnamese buildings in Saigon during National Day celebrations. Maj. Nguyen Thien, National Police director, said that 10 "leaders and liaison men" of a sabotage ring had been seized in Saigon Oct. 29 and had admitted planning the bombings. Thien said the police had also recovered nearly 900 tons of Viet Cong explosives and assorted weapons in 3 caches along the Saigon River. 7 Viet Cong suspects were arrested.)

■Tran Van Van, 58, a prominent member of the South Vietnamese Constituent Assembly, was shot to death Dec. 7 while driving to an Assembly meeting in Saigon. 2 alleged Viet Cong terrorists, riding a motorbike, were believed responsible for the assassination, and one suspect was arrested. He was identified as Vo Van Em, 20. Police charged that Em had fired the 3 shots at Van; Em insisted that he was driving the motorbike and that his accomplice, who escaped, had fired the gun. Em said he had been recruited for the assassination by the National Liberation Front. He said he had been serving with the Viet Cong Capital Liberation Regiment (which operated in the Saigon area) until he was assigned to Saigon the previous week. Van was a former chairman of the 80-member civilian-military advisory council to the government. He had expressed interest in running for the presidency of a civilian-ruled South Vietnam. Van had belonged to the government's "Southern faction," aligned against South Vietnamese political leaders of North Vietnamese origin.

It was reported Dec. 23 that U.S. troops had been assigned to guard Saigon for the first time in the wake of Viet Cong terrorist attacks on the outskirts of the city. The American force, consisting of several battalions of 800 men each, had started the patrol operations Dec. 1 in several districts of Giadinh Province, outside the Saigon capital district. Also assigned to the patrol was a battalion of South Vietnamese rangers. U.S. Amb. Henry Cabot Lodge had estimated Dec. 5 that civilian-clad terrorists in South Vietnam totaled 150,000, 20,000 of them in Saigon.

Crop Destruction & Defoliation

The U.S. State Department disclosed Mar. 9 that U.S. and Vietnamese authorities had destroyed about 20,000 acres of crops in South Vietnam (⅓ of 1% of land under cultivation) in a military move whose purpose was to deny food to the Viet Cong guerrillas. The department said this figure did not include the defoliation of jungle and underbrush to prevent the insurgents from taking cover. According to the department, the crop destruction and defoliation programs were initiated by the South Vietnamese with the use of U.S. planes and equipment. The department said the crop destruction was confined to remote, sparsely populated areas "known to be used to produce food for Viet Cong military units." The acreage was sprayed with herbicides, which were "nontoxic and not dangerous to man or animal life" and left the land unaffected for future growth, the statement said. The department added: "The Viet Cong and any innocent persons in the area are warned of the planned action. They are asked to leave the area. They are promised food and good treatment when they move out." The department's statement was prompted by a letter written to Pres. Johnson by Robert Brayton Nichols, 46, of New York, a landscape architect and former consultant to a Presidential task force on natural beauty. Nichols had asked why the U.S. was helping South Vietnam grow more food while destroying crops. (After writing the letter, Nichols had gone on a hunger strike Feb. 28 in protest against the crop destruction; he ended the fast Mar. 10.)

The North Vietnam press agency had said Jan. 5 that U.S. planes had destroyed more than 20,000 acres of fields and gardens in the Chauthanh and Omon districts of South Vietnam's Cantho Province by spraying the farmland with "toxic chemicals." The report, quoting the Viet Cong's National Liberation Front, said the incident had been protested by 30,000 provincial civilians, who had marched on the district capitals demanding U.S. compensation for crop losses. (It had been reported in Dec. 1965 that U.S. planes had launched a drive to destroy rice crops in some Viet Cong-held areas by spraying them with what was described as a non-toxic commercial weed killer.)

16 Harvard University professors and 13 other scientists Jan. 16 released a statement attacking the use of chemicals by U.S. troops in Vietnam to destroy crops. "Even if it can be shown the chemicals are not toxic to man, such tactics are barbarous because they are indiscriminate," the statement charged.

It was reported from Saigon Sept. 9 that the U.S. was planning to increase by 3-fold its aerial crop-destruction campaign (Operation Ranch Hand) against Viet Cong-held territory. According to the report, C-123 planes had sprayed 1,324,430 gallons of poisonous plant-killer over 530,872 acres of Viet Cong-occupied areas of South Vietnam thus far in 1966. The crop-destroying aerial force (currently averaging 6 planes) had recently been designated as the 12th Air Commando Squadron (Defoliation).

The U.S. military command disclosed Sept. 23 that U.S. planes were defoliating dense jungle areas just south of the demilitarized zone "to deny cover and concealment to the 324B Division and any other North Vietnamese army units that might be using that area." The spokesman denied published reports that the U.S. planes had sprayed chemicals within the zone itself.

U.S.-Chinese 'Clashes'

Occasional "clashes" involving U.S. and Communist Chinese planes and ships took place during 1966.

A Peking broadcast Apr. 12 said 4 U.S. planes had killed 2 Chinese fishermen and wounded 15 in attacks in the Gulf of Tonkin Apr. 7.

Communist China Apr. 12 claimed the downing of a U.S. "A-3B heavy attack plane" over China's Luichow Peninsula, north of Hainan Island. In broadcasting news of the incident, the Chinese news agency Hsinhua said: A Chinese air force plane had taken off and pursued the U.S. aircraft after it had been observed "engaging in military provocation" over Luichow Peninsula; the Chinese aircraft "shot down the enemy plane" after the U.S. aircraft, "disregarding warnings," had flown "deeper and deeper into China's territorial airspace." Peking then had delivered "the strongest possible protest" "against this cut-throat behavior of United States imperialism." The only U.S. comment on the incident came from the Defense Department later Apr. 12. The statement quoted Adm. U. S. Grant Sharp, head of U.S. naval forces in the Pacific, as having said that a KA-B3 tanker plane, flying from Subic Point in the Philippines to rejoin the carrier *Kitty Hawk* off South Vietnam, was "overdue."

Communist China charged May 13 that 5 U.S. planes had "flagrantly intruded" over Yunnan Province May 12 and "shot down a Chinese plane in training flight." "When Chinese planes counterattacked, the U.S. pirates fled southwestward," according to Peking's account. The Chinese statement claimed that the alleged action took place near Makwan, 20 miles north of the North Vietnamese border. Chinese MiGs from the nearby base at Mengtsz frequently flew over the Makwan area in patrolling the North Vietnamese frontier, but there was no other case known of a Chinese plane downed by U.S. planes in the Vietnamese war. The statement called the incident a "systematic act of war provocation by the Johnson Administration." It said "it took place after the U.S. had openly declared China as its main enemy and [State Secy.] Dean Rusk had clamored that there are of course risks of war with China, and followed the repeated intrusions by U.S. military aircraft into China's territorial airspace for provocations." The statement said that "the debt in blood owed by U.S. imperialism to the Chinese people must be cleared." It recalled a warning that had been voiced by Premier Chou En-lai in an interview with the Pakistani newspaper *Dawn* Apr. 10. Chou had said: "China will not take the initiative to provoke a war with the United States," but "once the war breaks out, it will have no boundaries." The U.S. government made no direct comment on the incident. But State Department spokesman Robert J. McCloskey May 13 cited a U.S. military report that a U.S. Air Force jet had shot down a Communist MiG-17 May 12 over North Vietnam 25-30 miles south of the Chinese border. McCloskey told newsmen that he called attention to this incident because it was the only U.S.-Communist aerial clash that had occurred in the time period of the incident. Communist China said May 17 that it had photographic evidence to support its claim that U.S. fighter planes had downed a Chinese plane over China May 12. The Chinese news agency Hsinhua said: "Today we make public photographs showing the remains of guided missiles and auxiliary fuel tanks jettisoned by the U.S. aircraft" allegedly involved in the incident.

The Chinese Defense Ministry charged May 30 that U.S. planes had attacked Chinese fishing boats north of the Gulf of Tonkin in international waters May 29, killing 3 persons and wounding 18. The ministry statement said: In the first attack, 2 U.S. planes had machinegunned and dropped 7 bombs on 2 fishing boats; one boat was sunk and the other damaged; one fisherman was killed and 6 wounded. 4 Chinese fishing boats were hit 20 minutes later by 2 U.S. planes; 2 of them were damaged; a Chinese fisherwoman and her small daughter were killed; 12 others were wounded.

Hsinhua claimed Sept. 5 that U.S. planes Aug. 29 had sunk a Communist Chinese merchant ship and damaged another in the Gulf of Tonkin, killing 9 Chinese seamen and wounding 7. The Chinese statement said the 2 ships had been bombed and strafed "for as long as 3 hours." Asserting that this "open war provocation against China by U.S. imperialism" was "by no means an isolated incident," Peking charged that Red Chinese merchant and fishing vessels had been attacked by U.S. planes recently "on many occasions." In response to the charge, a U.S. State Department statement said Sept. 5 that U.S. planes Aug. 29 had attacked and sunk at least one presumed North Vietnamese patrol boat in the Gulf of Tonkin. "It is by no means clear that the incident is related to the Chinese Communist charge," the statement said.

Communist China charged Sept. 16 and 18 that U.S. planes had attacked points in Chinese territory at least twice during 3 intrusions Sept. 5, 9 and 17. The U.S. conceded Sept. 19 that its planes might have strayed over China. The Communist Chinese Defense Ministry said Sept. 16 that U.S. planes had bombed Chinese territory Sept. 5 near Munankwan Pass, a main border-crossing point on the North Vietnamese frontier. In the 2d incident, the Peking statement said that U.S. F-105 jets had "intruded into China's territorial airspace over the Tunghing multinational county of the Kwangsi-Chuang autonomous region [bordering northeastern North Vietnam]" Sept. 9 and had "strafed Chinese villages and commune members," wounding 3 persons. The statement claimed Chinese planes had intercepted the U.S. aircraft, damaging one and driving off the others. State Secy. Dean Rusk said Sept. 16 that U.S. planes had encountered some MiG fighters Sept. 9, about 30 miles south of the Chinese border. (The U.S. military command had reported Sept. 10 that 2 U.S. jets had been attacked by 3 MiG-21s during a mission in the area mentioned by Rusk.) Hsinhua reported Sept. 18 that American planes Sept. 17 again had flown over the Kwangsi-Chuang Autonomous Region (in the Lungchow and Tsungtso areas). Chinese planes clashed with the intruders and damaged one American plane, the statement said. A U.S. State Department statement Sept. 19 conceded that there was "a possibility that some inadvertent intrusions of Communist China may have taken place during the breakoff from air engagements over North Vietnam." The department regretted "any such inadvertent intrusions." But it denied Peking's charges that U.S. planes had bombed Chinese Communist territory.

Communist China charged Dec. 6 that U.S. planes had bombed Chinese fishing boats in international waters in the Gulf of Tonkin off North Vietnam Nov. 30 and Dec. 1. 17 persons were killed and 29 wounded in the attack, Peking charged. A Peking broadcast said that in the first attack, Nov. 30, 2 U.S. planes had dropped 20 bombs on a fleet of Chinese fishing boats. 5 boats were sunk and 14 Chinese were killed and 20 wounded, the broadcast said. One Chinese boat was sunk and 3 crewmen were killed and 9 wounded in the 2d air strike, Dec. 1, Peking claimed. The U.S. State Department denied Dec. 14 that U.S. planes had attacked the Chinese vessels. Department spokesman Robert J. McCloskey said that American "naval aircraft were involved in actions against motorized cargo junks and barges close to the North Vietnamese coast" Nov. 30 and Dec. 1, but "we have found no evidence that United States aircraft attacked Chinese fishing boats as charged."

PRISONERS OF WAR

Trial of U.S. Captives Feared

The intensified air war over North Vietnam resulted in the capture of a number of American airmen and in Communist threats to try the captives as war criminals. The Communist threats brought U.S. warnings that the pilots were prisoners of war and that North Vietnam would be held responsible for their safety. Following the U.S. warnings and international appeals to spare the lives of the U.S. pilots, North Vietnamese Pres. Ho Chi Minh issued statements indicating that the prisoners would not be tried but would be treated humanely.

The first public indication that North Vietnam might put the pilots on trial came in commentaries on the display in Hanoi of U.S. airmen shot down in the bombing offensive against the capital and the port city of Haiphong. A North Vietnamese report June 29 on the display to Hanoi crowds of Capt. Murphy Neal Jones, shot down earlier that day, charged that U.S. pilots "indiscriminately bombed and strafed residential and economic areas." Hanoi radio reported July 6 that several captured U.S. pilots had been paraded in Hanoi and that angered mobs had demanded punishment of the "American air pirates." Hanoi July 7 broadcast the texts of statements in which 2 captive pilots, Air Force Capt. David B. Hatcher and Navy Cmndr. James Muligan, allegedly confessed their "crimes" against the North Vietnamese. The North Vietnamese news agency reported July 9 that at least 2 more U.S. pilots had "admitted their crimes" and had asked "forgiveness."

Parallel statements issued July 19 by the North Vietnamese ambassadors in Peking and Prague asserted that the captured Americans would go on trial. Pres. Ho said July 19 that North Vietnam's policy "with regard to the enemies captured in war is a humanitarian policy." Ho's reassurance was in response to appeals he had received July 12 and 13 from the National Committee for a Sane Nuclear Policy (SANE), a U.S. peace group, and from U.S. Socialist leader Norman Thomas. Thomas said that the "execution of captured American fliers would have disastrous effects upon the American public in our efforts to win it for peace and justice in Vietnam."

In response to a cablegram, received July 21 from CBS, asking whether North Vietnam planned to try the American pilots, Ho said July 23 that there was "no trial in view" for the U.S. prisoners. A White House spokesman said Ho's statement "confirms information we had" about North Vietnam's intentions. This remark was in reference to a dispatch from Hanoi July 22 by the French press agency, Agence France-Presse. The dispatch quoted diplomats in Hanoi as having been told the trials would be "postponed." White House Press Secy. Bill D. Moyers said July 25 that information relayed to Pres. Johnson through diplomatic channels that North Vietnam had no plans to put captured Americans on trial was "consistent" with what CBS was told.

In his first public comment on the prisoner controversy,

Pres. Johnson had said at his news conference in Washington July 20: "We feel strongly that these men are military men who are carrying out military assignments in line of duty, are not war criminals and should not be treated as such." Mr. Johnson said the American people would regard war-crime trials of American prisoners as "very revolting and repulsive" and would "react accordingly."

18 U.S. Senators generally opposed to Pres. Johnson's Vietnam policy had signed a statement July 15 calling on North Vietnam "to refrain from any act of vengeance against American airmen." The statement warned that the execution of the Americans "would incite a public demand for retaliation swift and sure, inflicting new levels of suffering . . . and fixing more firmly still the seal of an implacable war." Among the signers of the statement: Sens. Frank Church (D., Ida.), J. William Fulbright (D., Ark.), Wayne Morse (D., Ore.) and Ernest Gruening (D., Alaska).

UN Secy. Gen. U Thant July 16 urged North Vietnam "to exercise restraint in its treatment of American prisoners." He warned that "the possible trial of American prisoners is certain to generate still more intense escalation of the war" and possibly lead to World War III.

Pope Paul called on North Vietnam July 20 to afford American prisoners "the safety and the treatment provided for by international norms." Mistreatment of the U.S. captives, the pope warned, would result in "very grave consequences."

(Hanoi radio reported July 23 the establishment of an official 11-member committee to investigate U.S. "war crimes" in Vietnam.)

Hanoi Rejects PW Talks

The International Red Cross Committee (IRC) announced in Geneva Dec. 8 that North Vietnam had rejected a proposal by Pres. Johnson for joint discussion of fair treatment and possible exchange of the war captives held by both sides. The IRC had submitted the proposal to Hanoi in July after Pres. Johnson had first broached the plan at a news conference July 20. The IRC had privately informed the U.S. of North Vietnam's rejection in November. U.S. State Department spokesman Robert J. McCloskey confirmed Dec. 9 that the IRC had acted as Washington's intermediary.

U.S. Amb.-at-Large W. Averell Harriman and Sen. Edward M. Kennedy (D., Mass.) had conferred separately with IRC officials in Geneva May 6 and May 9-10 on the possible exchange of prisoners. At his meeting May 6 with IRC Pres. Samuel A. Gonard and other IRC officials, Harriman expressed Washington's concern over North Vietnam's refusal to grant U.S. prisoners "the treatment provided for in the Geneva convention." Although Hanoi had signed the convention, it had refused to give the American captives prisoner-of-war status on the grounds that they were "criminals." Such status would entitle the prisoners to the right to visits by Red Cross representatives and the receipt of correspondence and gift parcels.

An aide of Harriman's had said May 5 that 30-40 Americans were held captive by the Viet Cong in South Vietnam and that 60 others were imprisoned in North Vietnam. 100-150 other Americans were reported missing in South Vietnam. U.S. military authorities turned over Communist prisoners to the South Vietnamese. As a result of U.S. pressure, South Vietnam had been permitting IRC officials to visit those captives since Dec. 1965.

Reporting on his talks with the IRC officials, Sen. Kennedy said in Rome May 11 that he had been unsuccessful in his efforts to arrange a prisoner exchange.

(Sanford Gottlieb of SANE had said in Paris Jan. 15 that the Viet Cong had authorized him to announce that the guerrillas had opened "a new channel of communication" between U.S. prisoners of the Viet Cong and their families. A SANE official in New York Jan. 16 made public a postal address in Algiers [18 Rue Langevin, Quartier de Redoute] where packages and mail could be sent to captive Americans. An NLF spokesman disclosed May 4 that the mission's office [at 18 Rue Langevin] had been established as a relay point for sending letters [but not packages] to the captives. The spokesman said some letters already had been received by the American prisoners.)

PW Torture Charges

In an article published Feb. 11 in the magazine *Ramparts,* ex-M/Sgt. Donald Duncan, 34, charged that U.S. Special Forces in Vietnam were taught to torture prisoners. Duncan had received an honorable discharge from the Army in Sept. 1965 after 10 years of service, including 6 years in the Special Forces and 18 months with the forces in Vietnam. He said in the article: Members of the Special Forces who had asked whether they were expected to use the methods of torture they had been taught were told, "We can't tell you that. The mothers of America wouldn't approve." "I was later to witness first-hand the practice of turning prisoners over to ARVN [Army of the Republic of Vietnam] for 'interrogation' and the atrocities which ensued." Duncan questioned official assertions that most South Vietnamese supported the Saigon government; on the basis of his experience, he said, "I had to accept the fact that Communist or not, the vast majority of the people were pro-Viet Cong and anti-Saigon."

At a Washington news conference Feb. 10 Duncan reiterated the charges made in his article.

The Defense Department Feb. 10 released statements by the past and current commanders of the Special Forces denying Duncan's charges. Maj. Gen. William P. Yarborough, the ex-commander, was quoted as saying: "I am shocked . . . at the distortions, misstatements and disclosures of sensitive information in Duncan's statements." Yarborough and Brig. Gen. Joseph W. Stillwell, the forces' current commander, were said by the department to have "emphatically denied that methods of torture are taught to Special Forces personnel."

German-born U.S. Navy pilot, Lt. Dieter Dengler, was rescued by a U.S. helicopter in North Vietnam July 20 after escaping Communist captivity. Dengler said at a news conference Sept. 13 that the North Vietnamese mistreated American prisoners. He said some captives had been beaten, shot at and hung upside down on trees. Dengler had been captured by Pathet Lao troops near the Laotian-Vietnamese frontier.

South Vietnam Frees Some PWs

The South Vietnamese government Jan. 30 released 21 North Vietnamese soldiers held captive during the past year.

The captives crossed the Benhai River into North Vietnamese territory. The group had originally included 24 men, but 3 North Vietnamese accepted a Saigon government invitation to remain in South Vietnam. The released men had either served in Viet Cong units or in regular North Vietnamese battalions.

South Vietnam released 13 more North Vietnamese prisoners of war July 20. The repatriates crossed into North Vietnam over the Benhai River bridge. Originally 16 North Vietnamese soldiers had been offered their liberty, but 3 elected to remain in South Vietnam. South Vietnam released the latest captives to mark the 12th anniversary of the 1954 Geneva accords, which had partitioned Vietnam. (Dinh Trinh Chinh, secretary of state in Premier Nguyen Cao Ky's office, said in ceremonies at the border bridge that because of Vietnam's division July 20, the date had been officially designated as "National Shame Day.")

U.S. POLICY & DISSENT

Issue Debated

With the possible exception of the civil rights issue, no problem was debated more widely or with more heat during 1966 than the issue of the war in Vietnam. The subject opened deep divisions in both political parties and in groups as varied as church organizations and labor unions. The extremes ranged from (a) the "hawks," who called for the U.S. to pour more men and matériel into Vietnam in an all-out drive to win a military victory, to (b) the "doves," whose varied proposals included demands that the U.S. stop bombing North Vietnam, that the U.S. stop fighting in Vietnam altogether and either pull out of the country completely or withdraw to defensible "enclaves," that the U.S. negotiate peace and/or that the U.S. bring the National Liberation Front (NLF), the Viet Cong's political arm, into a South Vietnamese coalition government.

In his State-of-the-Union message Jan. 12, Pres. Johnson pledged that the U.S. would stay in Vietnam "until aggression has stopped." He promised to "give our fighting men [in Vietnam] what they must have." But "we will strive to limit conflict," he declared, "for we wish neither increased destruction nor increased danger." He asserted that "there are no arbitrary limits to our search for peace." Mr. Johnson said: "We may have to face long, hard combat or a long hard conference, or even both at once. . . . The days may become months and the months may become years, but we will stay as long as aggression commands us to battle." "We stand by the Geneva agreements of 1954 and 1962. We will meet at any conference table, we will discuss any proposals . . . we will consider the views of any group. We will work for a ceasefire now or once discussions have begun. We'll respond if others reduce their use of force; and we will withdraw our soldiers once South Vietnam is securely guaranteed the right to shape its own future."

A Republican rebuttal to Pres. Johnson's State-of-the-Union message was televised by the 3 major networks Jan. 17. The GOP views on Vietnam were presented by Senate minority leader Everett McKinley Dirksen (Ill.), who indorsed the Administration's Vietnam policy. He said the war, "a grim, bloody and costly business," was "not of our making" but should be pursued. "To retreat and get out would be deemed a confession that we are a paper tiger," he said. "To forsake our pledges would shatter confidence in us and further diminish our prestige." He said: "Let the peace efforts continue. . . . Let the military effort continue. . . . Let it be intensified if necessary as sound military judgment dictates. There is, after all, no substitute for victory."

Johnson and Ky Confer in Honolulu

Pres. Johnson, accompanied by his leading military and political advisers, conferred in Honolulu Feb. 6–8 with South Vietnamese Premier Nguyen Cao Ky and other Saigon government officials. The conference was concluded Feb. 8 with the issuance of a joint communiqué and a "Declaration of Honolulu" outlining future U.S.-South Vietnamese political and military policy.

The declaration was a 3-part document that stated the "purpose of the U.S. and South Vietnam and the common commitments of both governments." Stress was placed on an expansion of civic reforms as well as military efforts in winning the war. South Vietnam cited as its aims the defeat of the Viet Cong and "those illegally fighting with them on our soil," "the eradication of social injustice among our people" and the establishment of a "true democracy for our land and for our people." The U.S. section of the declaration said America pledged to help South Vietnam to (a) "prevent aggression," (b) establish "the principles of the self-determination of peoples and of government by the consent of the governed" and (c) "stabilize" its economy. "The Common Commitment," a section of the declaration, stated that the U.S. and South Vietnam would continue to pool their efforts to fight "aggression," to work for "social revolution," to seek "free self-government," to "attack" "hunger, ignorance and disease," and to carry on "the unending quest for peace."

The joint communiqué said that Mr. Johnson, Ky and South Vietnamese Chief of State Nguyen Van Thieu and their advisers had thoroughly reviewed the economic and military aspects of the Vietnamese situation. The 2 governments, the statement said, had "reached full agreement on a policy of growing military effectiveness and of still closer cooperation between [their] military forces." The conferees had "noted with regret the total absence of a present interest in peace on the part" of North Vietnam. Despite Hanoi's negative reaction, the U.S. and South Vietnam had "agreed upon continued diplomatic efforts for peace," the communiqué said.

Among major economic and social goals outlined in the communiqué: The U.S. and South Vietnam would "take further concrete steps to combat inflation in Vietnam"; Pres. Johnson pledged full support for Saigon's "intensified program of rural construction"; the U.S. would help Vietnam develop "enlarged programs of agriculture cooperation"; U.S. assistance in the fields of health and education "would be intensified"; Vietnamese refugees who "come over from the enemy side must be adequately cared for and prepared to resume a useful role in society."

South Vietnamese refusal to participate in any peace talks with the Viet Cong's National Liberation Front was stressed by Ky and Thieu at a news conference Feb. 8. Ky also said that he would refuse to enter a coalition government with the

NLF. Ky predicted "that by the end of 1967 . . . we will eliminate the influence of the Communists in South Vietnam." He conceded there would be some Viet Cong guerrillas left by then, but he said they would "have no support from the population." Ky and Thieu said they believed that the North Vietnamese port of Haiphong should be bombed. But they said they had not pressed this view in their talks with Pres. Johnson.

Ky's optimism contrasted with the views expressed Feb. 7 by another South Vietnamese participant in the Honolulu conference, Rural Pacification Min. Nguyen Duc Thang. Thang said that Saigon's 1966 pacification program involved only 1,900 of the country's 15,000 hamlets and that it might take 5-6 years to bring a typical province under complete government control.

Pres. Johnson and his aides had arrived in Honolulu Feb. 5. The trip marked his first departure from continental North America since assuming office and his first meeting with top South Vietnamese officials. The South Vietnamese leaders had arrived in the Hawaiian capital Feb. 6. In a welcoming speech, Mr. Johnson lauded Ky and Thieu as "2 brave leaders of the Vietnamese republic." Mr. Johnson restated the U.S.' determination to defeat the Communists, and he lashed out at domestic critics of his policy: "There are special pleaders who counsel retreat in Vietnam. They belong to a group that has always been blind to experience and deaf to hope. We cannot accept their logic that tyranny 10,000 miles away is not tyranny to concern us—or that subjugation by an armed minority in Asia is different from subjugation by an armed minority in Europe."

(In a Senate speech Feb. 7 Sen. Wayne L. Morse, one of the most vocal of U.S. critics of Pres. Johnson's Vietnam policies, assailed the President's welcoming address to South Vietnam's leaders. Referring to Mr. Johnson's criticism of "special pleaders who counsel retreat in Vietnam," Morse asked: "Do you mean Pope Paul? Do you mean Senators who believe communism in Asia will not fall before weapons? Do you mean the millions of Americans who voted for you in 1964 when you counseled them against expanding the war into North Vietnam?")

Among U.S. officials attending the Honolulu talks were State Secy. Dean Rusk, Defense Secy. Robert S. McNamara, Gen. Earle G. Wheeler, chairman of the Joint Chiefs of Staff, HEW Secy. John W. Gardner, Agriculture Secy. Orville L. Freeman, Adm. U. S. Grant Sharp Jr. (commander of U.S. naval forces in the Pacific), U.S. Amb.-to-South Vietnam Henry Cabot Lodge, Gen. William C. Westmoreland (commander of U.S. forces in South Vietnam), Amb.-at-Large W. Averell Harriman, Agency for International Development Director David E. Bell, Presidential Asst. McGeorge Bundy, State Undersecy. (for political affairs) U. Alexis Johnson, White House Press Secy. Bill D. Moyers and Gen. Maxwell D. Taylor (Presidential adviser).

In addition to Ky and Thieu, the South Vietnamese leaders who attended the Honolulu conference included: Foreign Min. Tran Van Do, Lt. Gen. Nguyen Huu Co (defense minister) and Economy & Finance Min. Truong Thai Ton.

Pres. Johnson Feb. 8 gave an optimistic report on the Honolulu conference. The President delivered his statement in Los Angeles, where he stopped briefly on his way back to Washington. With Mr. Johnson was Vice Pres. Humphrey, who left later for South Vietnam and other Asian countries. Mr. Johnson said that U.S. and South Vietnamese leaders, at their meeting in Honolulu, had reached an understanding that "the war we are helping them fight must be won on 2 fronts." "One front is military," he said. "The other front is the struggle against social injustice: against hunger, disease, and ignorance, against political apathy and indifference."

The President said the conferees had discussed ways of improving South Vietnam's agriculture, education and medical programs and of fighting its inflation. The conference also dealt with the problems "of how to build the basis for a democratic constitution and free elections; of how to seek the peace; of how to conduct the war." Asserting that the solutions to these problems "will not be easy," Mr. Johnson said U.S. and South Vietnamese leaders "would meet again in the months ahead to measure that progress." "This revolutionary transformation cannot wait until the guns grow silent and the terrorism stops," the President declared. Mr. Johnson said Agriculture Secy. Orville L. Freeman was going to Saigon with Humphrey "to see how we can help with food and rural development." Health, Education & Welfare Secy. John W. Gardner also would go to Saigon to advise the Vietnamese on education and health, the President said. Mr. Johnson said the Vice President was going "to carry forward the mission we defined at Honolulu." Humphrey's assignment in Saigon, Mr. Johnson said, would be "to assure that our representatives there get to work rapidly and effectively on the tasks we laid out at Honolulu."

The President returned to Washington Feb. 9 and said at his news conference Feb. 11 that U.S. military forces in South Vietnam would be expanded; but he indicated that the build-up would be gradual. Mr. Johnson said "there will be additional men needed and they will be supplied as Gen. [William C.] Westmoreland is able to use them and as he may require them." (The current U.S. force in South Vietnam totaled about 205,000 men.)

The President indicated a desire to correct what he considered the widely held but inaccurate view that U.S. activity in Vietnam "is just a military effort." He pointed out that "we distributed 8 million textbooks" and "doubled the rice production" in South Vietnam. He said he "thought it was good that we could go" to Honolulu and "try to expose to the world . . . what this country is trying to do to feed the hungry, and to educate the people, and to improve the life span for people who just live to be 35 now. . . ."

Humphrey Tours Asian Capitals

Vice Pres. Humphrey flew to Saigon Feb. 10 for a 3-day inspection of South Vietnam's rural pacification programs and U.S. troop installations. Saigon was the first stop on a 14-day tour of 9 Asian nations. Arriving in the same plane with the Vice President were Premier Ky and Lt. Gen. Thieu. They had boarded Humphrey's plane Feb. 9 in Honolulu. Also accompanying Humphrey were Amb.-at-Large Harriman, Presidential Asst. McGeorge Bundy, Agriculture Secy. Orville Freeman and HEW Secy. John Gardner.

Humphrey, accompanied Feb. 11 by Ky and U.S. Amb.

Henry Cabot Lodge, visited a slum clearance and civic reform
project in Saigon and the Tansonnhut Agricultural Experi-
ment Station. Humphrey toured allied military installations
near Saigon Feb. 12. He said later at a news conference
that "every free country in the world should be making a
contribution to the strengthening of the Vietnamese people."
He promised to ask the leaders of 6 other Asian nations he
was to visit to contribute such assistance. Humphrey said
he believed that great progress had been made in the allied
military effort against the Viet Cong. But he said the campaign for social, political and economic reforms had only
begun.

Other stops on Humphrey's tour were Thailand, Laos,
Pakistan, India, Australia, New Zealand, the Philippines and
South Korea. At a press conference in Wellington, New Zealand Feb. 21, Humphrey denounced a suggestion by Sen.
Robert F. Kennedy (D., N.Y.) that the NLF (the Viet Cong's
National Liberation Front) be included in a future coalition
government in South Vietnam. Humphrey described the
proposal as "a prescription for the ills of South Vietnam which
includes a dose of arsenic." Bringing the NLF into a Saigon
regime would be like putting "a fox in a chickencoop," Humphrey warned; "soon there wouldn't be any chickens left"; it
would be like putting "an arsonist in a fire department."
Establishing a coalition government would "impose" on the
South Vietnamese people "the very forces that have been
destroying them," Humphrey declared. Humphrey insisted
that recognition of the Viet Cong "would not bring about a
settlement that would result in establishment or continuity
of a democratic government."

Humphrey flew back to Washington Feb. 23. He declared
that he had returned from his trip "with renewed confidence
and . . . encouragement . . . because the tide of battle in
Vietnam has turned in our favor." Humphrey Feb. 24 delivered
briefings on his trip at 2 separate White House meetings with
Congressional leaders of both parties and with 200 members
of the House and Senate Foreign Relations, Armed Services
and Appropriations Committees.

Kennedy for Coalition with NLF

Sen. Robert Kennedy's suggestion of a coalition including the NLF had been made at a press conference in Washington Feb. 19. He recommended that the NLF be "admit[ted] to a share of power and responsibility" in a future coalition South Vietnamese government as part of a negotiated settlement of the Vietnamese war. Kennedy said that "whatever the exact status" of the NLF—"puppet or partly independent —any negotiated settlement must accept the fact that there are discontented elements in South Vietnam, Communist and non-Communist, who desire to change the existing political and economic system of the country."

The inclusion of the NLF in a future coalition government, Kennedy said, "may come about through a single conference or many meetings, or by a slow undramatic process of gradual accommodation. . . . It may mean a compromise government acceptable to neither side. It certainly means that we must take considerable risks in the expectation that social and economic success will weaken the appeal of communism.   .   ." "It will require enormous skill and political wisdom," he emphasized, "to find the point at which [NLF] participation does not bring domination or internal conquest." But the only alternative, he warned, would be to solve the problem "through force of arms"—"kill or repress them [the Viet Cong]," or "turn the country over to them."

Kennedy held that "it is always necessary to understand what an opponent can accept and what he cannot retreat from." He said: "Both sides must come to any discussion with at least one basic condition; one irreducible demand; one point they will not yield. For the United States it must be that we will not turn South Vietnam over to the North. For North Vietnam it must be that they will not accept a settlement which leaves in the South a hostile government, dedicated to the final physical destruction of all Communist elements, refusing any economic cooperation with the North, dependent upon the continued presence of American military power. These conditions, these minimum terms, can be breached only at sword's point; only by driving the adversary's force from the field. For either side to yield its minimum conditions would be in fact to accept defeat."

Kennedy said: The U.S. also must "face the uncertainties of election and the possibility of an eventual vote on reunification" of North and South Vietnam into a single nation. Any political agreement on Vietnam must be supported by "international guarantees." "Foreign forces must be withdrawn, by balanced and verified stages," and "a trusted international body" must supervise the new nation's political transformation. The U.S. "must make clear" that it would not tolerate action by "an outside power" to seize the country or the government.

Kennedy urged the Johnson Administration to clearly outline its position to North Vietnam on negotiations "to eliminate any reasonable fear that we ask them to talk now, only to demand their surrender." He said Hanoi must likewise be told that its prerequisites for talks were "in fact a bid for us to surrender a vital national interest," "an objective which cannot be achieved" by them.

Kennedy conceded that his "middle way of negotiation" involved the risks that "an adversary who lives may perhaps fight another day, and a government which is not continuously sheltered by American military power may be again attacked or subverted or overthrown." But he noted that the U.S. already had taken such risks in countries "which might be the target of Communist aggression or subversion." To do otherwise, he pointed out, the U.S. might have to occupy "all" of these countries to prevent a Communist take-over.

Kennedy's proposals were criticized Feb. 20 by 2 leading Johnson Administration officials—State Undersecretary George W. Ball and Presidential Asst. McGeorge Bundy.

_ Ball said Kennedy's suggestion "would mean creating a coalition government in which the Communists, who are the hardcore elements trained in subversion, would move in with people politically who played no part in the present government, and what we would have would be only, in a very short time, a Communist government in Saigon." (Ball, who spoke on ABC-TV's "Issues and Answers" program, said he would not "rule out the possibility of a Chinese involvement [in the Vietnamese conflict] just as it occurred in Korea.")

Bundy, who spoke on NBC-TV's "Meet the Press" program, attacked Kennedy's suggestion by quoting this statement made by the late Pres. John F. Kennedy in a speech in Berlin in 1963: "I am not impressed by the opportunities open to popular front throughout the world. I do not believe that any democrat can successfully ride that tiger."

In a clarifying statement, Kennedy said Feb. 22 on NBC-TV's "Today" program that he had not proposed that the NLF be "automatically" included in a coalition government prior to elections. Kennedy said he had meant that the NLF should not be "automatically excluded" from a share of power. The question of the make-up of an interim government prior to elections, Kennedy suggested, should be settled at the negotiating table. Kennedy said he had gotten the impression from Administration leaders' statements that Washington's offer of "unconditional negotiations" actually contained the "preconditions" that the U.S. would not "abide by free elections" in Vietnam if the NLF won representation in a government. Kennedy said a refusal to grant the NLF representation won in balloting would lead to "a bloody, bloody war" because the current South Vietnamese government controlled only "25% of the population." Kennedy said he thought the Administration displayed "confusion" in its stated positions.

The Johnson Administration's first official reaction to Kennedy's proposals was voiced Feb. 22 by White House Press Secy. Bill D. Moyers. Moyers said the Administration and Kennedy were in no disagreement "if Sen. Kennedy did not propose a coalition government with Communist participation before elections were held." Moyers said the Administration also agreed with Kennedy that the composition of a South Vietnamese government prior to elections "should be left to the negotiating parties." Moyers, however, denied Kennedy's contention of Administration "confusion" and the setting of preconditions. Citing testimony by State Secy. Rusk before the Senate Foreign Relations Committee Feb. 18, Moyers said: The Administration was willing "to accept the decision of the people of Vietnam as expressed in a free election. We are for free elections with all of us abiding by the consequences of those elections, whatever they may be."

Kennedy said Feb. 22 that he had phoned Moyers and that they agreed that their views coincided.

Gen. Maxwell D. Taylor, adviser to Pres. Johnson, had said Feb. 21 that Kennedy's position was "very, very close to what I consider my position." In an interview with the *N.Y. Herald Tribune,* Taylor emphasized, however, that he opposed the presence of Communists in a coalition government before elections. Taylor sought Feb. 22 to clarify this remark in view of his assertion to the Senate Foreign Relations Committee the previous week that he favored a settlement of the war along the 17th Parallel "if all the Viet Cong would go home and go north." In his clarification statement, Taylor said he favored "unconditional negotiations followed by free elections, with all of us abiding by the results. . . . The way to get there is through negotiations without setting any preconditions whatsoever."

Senate Foreign Relations Committee Chrmn. Fulbright Feb. 21 supported Kennedy's proposal and stated that he favored giving the NLF "a share of power and responsibility" in a coalition government. He said he also backed Kennedy's view that the NLF should attend future peace talks as "an independent entity," not only as part of the North Vietnamese delegation.

Sen. Jacob K. Javits (R., N.Y.) Feb. 21 characterized Kennedy's proposal for inclusion of the NLF in a coalition regime as "a way-out suggestion" that would not lead to peace talks since North Vietnam had insisted that the NLF be given "a decisive role" in any new Saigon government. Javits came out for the NLF as an "independent negotiating party" at a peace conference. The composition of a future coalition government, Javits said, should be decided during negotiations and "should not be prejudged by any prior concessions."

(A coalition with the NLF had been suggested inferentially by UN Secy. Gen. U Thant Jan. 20. Speaking at a news conference at UN headquarters in New York, Thant said he wondered "whether the time has come to raise such practical questions as to what type of government in South Vietnam—representative of all sections of the South Vietnamese people—should take over the responsibility of organizing the exercise by the people of their right to decide their own affairs." Thant added: "If the parties were to make concrete proposals on this issue, I think a refusal to negotiate would be difficult to justify, particularly if . . . discussions to bring about an end to the fighting must be held with those who are fighting."

(Thant said he thought there would be peace talks if the "present psychological climate" [resulting from the air raid suspension then in effect] could be improved "by all possible measures." Thant said there was "an undeniable *rapprochement* between the positions of the parties" on a negotiated settlement of the war. He cited agreement on all sides that the Geneva conference of 1954 was the proper basis for any future settlement.

(The inclusion of the NLF in peace negotiation and a halt in U.S. air strikes against North Vietnam were recommended in a report made public Feb. 15 on behalf of 8 Democratic House members who had sponsored a conference on Vietnam in Washington Jan. 21-22. The report, issued by Arthur Larson, who had been chairman of the Washington meeting, also proposed that political elements not opposed to negotiations be brought into the South Vietnamese government, that the U.S. accept Hanoi's 4 points as one interpretation of the 1954 Geneva agreements [and thus as a basis for negotiations] and that the U.S. do nothing further to escalate the war.)

Vice Pres. Humphrey Feb. 27 again expressed opposition to a South Vietnamese coalition with the NLF. Appearing on the ABC-TV "Issues & Answers" program, Humphrey said: The Viet Cong "engage in assassination, murder, pillage, conquest, and I can't for the life of me see why the United States of America would want to propose that such an outfit be made part of any government." "If the people of South Vietnam wish to make that choice themselves," that would be a different matter, but he did not think it likely to happen.

Kennedy said Feb. 27 on the CBS-TV "Face the Nation"

program: If U.S. policy was "realistic" and "candid," it would concede that the Communists "are going to end up, in some way or another, within the governmental structure of South Vietnam." Such a development would occur either in an interim government, prior to a general peace settlement, or in an elected government, dependent on the election results. If the Communists were barred in advance from the government, "then we really can't expect that they will come to the negotiating table." "I think that statements . . . that we will never deal with assassins or murderers make it difficult for them to believe that they are being asked to come to the negotiating table for anything other than to surrender."

Humphrey reiterated in a speech at the National Press Club in Washington Mar. 11 that the U.S. would not try to keep the Communists out of the South Vietnamese government if they won their place fairly in free elections. "If the Viet Cong, in those elections, gain honestly a voice in government by the expressed will of the electorate, so be it," he said. "But prior to elections, the American government will not be a party to any settlement which amounts to a pre-election victory for the Communists which cannot be won at the ballot box." Humphrey said the Viet Cong sought a place in a coalition government, without an election, as a 3d "declared route to power, to victory," and he promised that the U.S. would not force the South Vietnamese to accept such a Communist victory. He said the first 2 routes the Viet Cong had chosen were (1) a general revolt in South Vietnam, which "didn't work," and (2) guerrilla war, such as they were currently conducting. Humphrey said that U.S. forces would remain in Vietnam "until genuinely free elections can be held." He said the Administration had rejected both withdrawal and "massive escalation" in Vietnam in favor of "measured use of strength and perseverance."

'Enclave' Controversy

Retired Lt. Gen. James M. Gavin's suggestion that U.S. troops in South Vietnam limit their operations to coastal enclaves generated heated comment among U.S. officials. Defense Secy. Robert S. McNamara disclosed Feb. 2 that the proposal had been considered by senior officers at the

Pentagon and that all had rejected it. Some Defence Department officials reportedy had discussed the matter prior to Gavin's public advocacy of the plan in the February issue of *Harper's* magazine (published Jan. 16). The officials were said to have opposed pulling U.S. troops back to coastal positions on the ground that this would permit Communist troops to consolidate their grip over wide areas of South Vietnam and leave South Vietnamese government forces at the mercy of superior Communist troops.

Gen. Maxwell D. Taylor, special adviser to Pres. Johnson, said in a speech in New York Feb. 3 that "the impulse to withdraw our troops into safe enclaves in South Vietnam has much in common with the yearning for safety behind defenses at our coast lines, and is equally illusory." Adoption of such strategy, Taylor warned, would result in "a crushing defeat of international proportions" for the U.S. and a victory for North Vietnam and Communist China.

Gavin said at a Boston news conference Feb. 3 that his views had been misinterpreted. Gavin asserted: "I did not suggest we withdraw to the enclaves, I said that where we are now, we have these enclaves, and if we stay with what we have until we weigh the alternatives, we can neither hold on or consolidate in several large areas or one large area."

In the *Harper's* article, Gavin had recalled that in the 1950s, when the U.S. was considering sending a military force to Vietnam to help fight Ho Chi Minh's Viet Minh forces, "we realized that we were in fact considering going to war with China, since she was supplying all the arms, ammunition and medical and other supplies to Ho Chi Minh." Fighting Communist China in Southeast Asia currently, Gavin wrote, would be fighting "in the wrong place, on terms entirely to her advantage." China "should be engaged, if at all," in Manchuria, with its tremendous industrial "war-making capacity," Gavin held. Gavin questioned the feasibility of bombing Hanoi or Peking. He predicted that such a move would "add to our problems rather than detract from them, and it will not stop the penetrations of North Vietnamese troops into the South." Gavin also warned that if the U.S. were to "quadruple" its military force in South Vietnam, Chinese military intervention could be anticipated and Peking might reopen the Korean front.

Gavin's enclave proposals were supported by Gen. Matthew B. Ridgway in an article in *Harper's* March issue (published Feb. 6). Ridgway had commanded UN forces in the Korean war and later commanded NATO forces.

McNamara's opposition to the enclave proposal had been expressed when McNamara and the Joint Chiefs of Staff appeared at closed hearings Jan. 20-25 and Feb. 2 of the Senate Armed Services Committee and the Defense Subcommittee of the Appropriations Committee. The hearings were on the $12.3 billion supplemental fund request for financing the Vietnamese war. A censored version of the testimony was released by the committees Feb. 15.

According to the transcript, McNamara said: (a) "I know of no military expert in the Department of Defense who supports such a policy" as the "enclaves" proposal. (b) He opposed the expansion of bombing raids on North Vietnam. "There is every likelihood" that the U.S. could destroy all of North Vietnam's power systems, oil, harbors, dams, "and they could still carry on the infiltration of the men and equipment necessary to support some level of operations in the South." The Viet Cong had increased their strength since the summer of 1965 despite heavy losses, and "they have raised the number of men that they are moving from North Vietnam to South Vietnam with every passing month, and I can look forward to nothing more than continuing actions of the kind we have had in the past 6 months." (c) The U.S. had no desire to invade North Vietnam on the ground or to destroy the North Vietnamese military forces. He and other officials "did not at present conceive of any circumstances in which he would use nuclear weapons in Vietnam." (d) The military funds request was based on the assumption that the war would continue "through the end of June 1967." The funds would finance "a massive application of fire power" and the addition of 112,843 men to the armed forces, including a new Marine division. "We must be prepared to deploy even more forces if the Communists choose to expand their operations in Vietnam." In air actions over North and South Vietnam the

U.S. had lost 38 fixed-wing aircraft and 24 helicopters in 1964 and 275 fixed-wing aircraft and 76 helicopters in 1965. Ammunition for air and ground forces was being consumed at the rate of $210 million a month, "and we are preparing to support a much higher rate."

The transcript disclosed that Sen. Stuart Symington (D., Mo.) had criticized limited bombing as ineffective and had said that unless bombing operations were expanded, the bombing should be stopped. Symington termed it "incredible" that the U.S. refrained from bombing the Haiphong harbor area.

Senate Hearings

Public, televised hearings on the Administration's Vietnam policy were held by the Senate Foreign Relations Committee in Washington Feb. 8, 10, 17 and 18. Retired Lt. Gen. James M. Gavin testified Feb. 8, George F. Kennan of the Institute for Advanced Study in Princeton, N.J. testified Feb. 10, Gen. Maxwell D. Taylor testified Feb. 17, and State Secy. Rusk testified Feb. 18. Committee Chrmn. J. W. Fulbright (D., Ark.) reported Feb. 8 that State Undersecy. George Ball had declined, as had Defense Secy. McNamara and Gen. Earle G. Wheeler, chairman of the Joint Chiefs of Staff, to appear at the inquiry in public session.

McNamara had told the committee Feb. 4 that "it is not in the public interest to appear in a public session" on U.S. Vietnam policy. But he expressed willingness to testify in secret. Fulbright, who had announced Feb. 3 the committee's decision to hold public hearings on Vietnam policy, said that "something civilized" could be worked out. "There's no war on with the White House," he said. But an immediate objection to McNamara's view was expressed by Sen. Wayne Morse (D., Ore.). Morse charged that "the people of the Pentagon and the State Department have already led the American people down the road toward government by secrecy." He said he would not attend a closed hearing. (Morse Jan. 29 had introduced a resolution directing the Senate Foreign Relations Committee to conduct "a full and complete investigation of all aspects of United States policies in Vietnam." He also introduced a resolution to rescind the Aug.

10, 1964 joint Congressional resolution giving the President power to take "all necessary measures" to repel aggression in Southeast Asia. Morse had been one of only 2 Congress members [Sen. Ernest Gruening (D., Alaska) was the other] to vote against the 1964 resolution.)

At a suddenly-called news conference Feb. 4, Pres. Johnson said that he did not consider the matter of informing Senators "any great problem" but that "it is not a matter that you want to have a show about." The President announced at the conference his decision to go to Hawaii for a conference on Vietnam.

In an open session held Feb. 4, the committee heard testimony from David E. Bell, administrator of foreign aid. Bell testified on behalf of Pres. Johnson's request for $415 million in fiscal 1966 in supplemental aid funds, of which $275 million was for South Vietnam. During questioning, Bell conceded the possibility of Red Chinese intervention with troops and airpower in an escalating war situation. (Bell and State Secy. Rusk, testifying before the House Foreign Affairs Committee Jan. 26 on the aid request, had admitted that some Americans and South Vietnamese were misappropriating U.S. aid to South Vietnam. Bell said his agency was "trying to track down and prevent it as best we can," but he indicated that prevention was difficult in such a "fast-moving operation.")

The possibility of Chinese intervention in the war was cited by Fulbright Feb. 7. Fulbright told newsmen he was "fearful that if the war in Vietnam is not handled extremely well, the Chinese Communists will come in." Fulbright said that in his committee's hearings on Vietnam, the Administration's "policies beyond Vietnam" were involved: "Communist China overshadowed the whole thing. There are rumors of very drastic action." Fulbright said his latter statement referred to statements that had been made publicly by some Congress members and privately by some military officials on possible actions the U.S. would take if Communist China intervened in the war in response to an extension of air strikes against North Vietnam.

During his appearance before the committee Feb. 8,

Gavin favored keeping U.S. troops in South Vietnam but opposed escalation of the war. He said: The U.S. had become "mesmerized" with Vietnam, and its policy there had become "alarmingly out of balance." "We have been escalating at the will of our opponents rather than on our own judgment." Additional large increases in U.S. troop strength in Vietnam would bring the U.S. "into another kind of confrontation" and raise the likelihood of intervention by the Chinese Communists, which would further raise the possibility of Soviet involvement and of a reopening of the Korean front. The U.S. was "slowly creeping" toward "urban bombing," which had only dubious military value but evoked adverse "world opinion." Concerning his previously expressed opinion that the U.S. should limit its Vietnam military operations to defensible "enclaves" along Vietnam's coast, the use of the word "coast" was unfortunate, and he would include any enclave currently held by U.S. forces. These positions should be maintained while the U.S. took stock of the entire situation.

Kennan told the committee Feb. 10: The U.S. should "restrict" its Vietnam military operations "to the minimum necessary to assure the security of our forces and to maintain our military presence there until we can achieve a satisfactory peaceful resolution of the conflict. . . . [We should] continue to pursue vigorously and consistently the quest for such a resolution of it, even if this involves some moderation of our stated objectives and if the resulting settlement appears to us as something less than ideal." The U.S. "commitment" in South Vietnam seemingly involved an obligation "to assure the internal security of its government in circumstances where that government is unable to assure that security by its own means." Such an obligation "obviously" went "considerably further than the normal obligations of a military alliance," and "if we did not really incur it in any formal way, then we should not be inventing it . . . and assuring ourselves that we are bound by it today." "Our military involvement in Vietnam has to be recognized as unfortunate"; "it should be our . . . aim to liquidate this involvement just as soon as this can be done without inordinate damage to our own prestige or to the stability of conditions in that area."

He opposed both "a precipitate and disorderly withdrawal" or "any deliberate expansion of hostilities on our part directed to the achievement of something called 'victory'—if, by the use of that term, we envisage the complete disappearance" of opposition, "the formal submission by the adversary to our will, and the complete realization of our present stated political aims. I doubt that these things can be achieved even by the most formidable military successes." A "total rooting out of the Viet Cong" from South Vietnam could be achieved, if at all, only at a prohibitive cost in civilian suffering, and an attempt to crush North Vietnamese support for the Viet Cong "would almost certainly have the effect of bringing in Chinese forces." Because of "our preoccupation with Vietnam," the more important problems of Germany, proliferation of nuclear weapons and disarmament were not receiving "the attention they should be receiving." Pursuit of the war had damaged U.S.-Soviet relations and the Japanese people's feelings towards the U.S. "There is no success we could have in Vietnam that could conceivably warrant the sacrifice by us of the confidence and goodwill of the Japanese people." The first goal of U.S. foreign policy should be to maintain a *détente* with the Soviet Union. The USSR might reconvene the Geneva conference under continued pressure from Western and neutralist countries, but further escalation of the war would force the Soviet Union "to come down on the side of the Viet Cong."

Commenting on the hearings, Pres. Johnson said at his press conference in Washington Feb. 11: "There is no great deal of difference between" the testimony of Gavin and Kennan and "what the government is doing." "I don't see any real program that anyone has presented that offers a clear alternative to recommend itself in preference to what we are doing." "No one wants to escalate the war and no one wants to lose any more men than is necessary. No one wants to surrender and get out." The President was not opposed to the committee hearings "as long as they are conducted in an atmosphere of objectivity. . . . I have not observed that these have been conducted in any other manner."

In his testimony Feb. 17, Taylor, ex-chairman of the

Joint Chiefs of Staff and ex-ambassador to South Vietnam, quoted Pres. Johnson's statement that "our objective [in Vietnam] is the independence of South Vietnam and its freedom from attack." Taylor, a consultant to the President, said the U.S. also had a "secondary" objective: "We intend to show that the 'war of liberation' . . . is costly, dangerous and doomed to failure. We must destroy the myth of its invincibility in order to protect the independence of many weak nations which are vulnerable targets for subversive aggression." Taylor also said: He was aware of "the concern . . . over the growing requirement for American troops in South Vietnam. Is this an endless requirement in an open-ended war? I do not believe that anyone can give a completely satisfactory reply to this question, but I can suggest the consideration of certain limiting factors. . . . We are not setting as an objective for our ground forces the occupation of all South Vietnam or the hunting down of the last armed guerrilla." "In a very real sense, the objective of our air campaign is to change the will of the enemy leadership." The Communist leaders "have not forgotten that the Viet Minh won more in Paris than in [the 1954 battle of] Dienbienphu and believe that the Viet Cong might be as fortunate in Washington. They doubt the will of the American public to continue the conflict indefinitely."

In an angry exchange with Taylor, Sen. Morse predicted that "it isn't going to be too long before the American people as a people will repudiate our war in Southeast Asia." "That, of course, is good news to Hanoi, Senator," Taylor replied. "I know," Morse said, "that that is the smear artist that you militarists give to those of us who have honest differences of opinion with you, but I don't intend to get down in the gutter with you and engage in that kind of debate, general. I am simply saying that . . . [the President] is already losing the people of the country by the millions in connection with this war. . . . All I am asking is if the people decide that this war should be stopped . . . , are you going to take the position that is weakness on the home front in a democracy?" Taylor replied: "I would feel that our people were badly misguided and did not understand the consequences of such a disaster." Morse then said: "We agree on one thing, that they can be badly misguided, and you and the President in my judgment have been misguiding them for a long time in this war."

Sen. George D. Aiken (R., Vt.) asked Taylor if he thought the French would have won in Vietnam "had it not been for the weakening will in Paris." "I doubt it," Taylor said. ". . . Colonialism was doomed in Vietnam, but I think they could have lasted longer and could have had better terms." Fulbright questioned Taylor about the implication in Taylor's testimony on the French defeat that the "war may be lost in Washington" and that this might be a "possible reflection upon the validity or the value of these hearings." Taylor called it "only my personal feeling . . . that the leaders in Hanoi will hope that the same kind of situation will arise here."

Taylor agreed with Sen. Karl Mundt (R., S.D.) that the tide of battle seemed "to be moving in our favor." Taylor said Viet Cong losses were running at 17,000 a month—3,800 killed, 11,000 wounded, 2,400 defections. At that rate, he said "they will theoretically run out of troops by the end of 1966." But he conceded that "data on Viet Cong logistics are too uncertain to permit precision" and that it was difficult to estimate how many troops North Vietnam could supply under air and ground attacks. Questioning also evoked Taylor's opinion that Chinese intervention, "always the risk," was a "relatively small possibility" and that it was the Chinese who "should feel nervous" about a war with the U.S. because "it would be disastrous for them."

State Secy. Rusk said during a 7-hour appearance before the committee Feb. 18: The U.S. was in the Vietnamese war "to check the extension of Communist power in order to maintain a reasonable stability in a precarious world." U.S. soldiers were fighting there because "South Vietnam had, under the language of the SEATO treaty, been the victim of 'aggression by means of armed attack.'" "These are moments when toughness is absolutely essential for peace. If we don't make clear where we stand, then the prospect for peace disappears." "If there is doubt in Congress about the policy, let us vote, let us find out, let's have that decision considered in 1966." But before the vote, members of Congress should ponder "on what basis we have any chance to organize peace in the world."

Fulbright said the failure of most of the Asian members of SEATO to supply forces for the war indicated their belief that the war was a civil war and not "truly an example of Communist aggression." Fulbright also questioned Rusk's contention that the National Liberation Front (NLF) was an "agent" of Hanoi. He said the U.S.' pledge to leave Vietnam after peace was attained was contradicted by the seemingly permanent U.S. military installations in Vietnam. Rusk replied that the bases were necessary to sustain the current effort and that the U.S. had built and left such bases before.

Fulbright said the Vietnamese conflict was not the kind "that warrants escalation" because it did not involve the vital security of the U.S., yet it could be a "trigger for world war." He said the U.S. had not stressed that it would accept the results of free supervised elections in which the NLF would be permitted to participate and that he had the impression "that we are in an unlimited war and the only kind of settlement is unconditional surrender." "Unconditional surrender of what?" Rusk asked. "That they give up and . . . come to the conference at your mercy, and we have total victory," Fulbright answered. "I see no occasion of any disposition to compromise."

Denying that the U.S. was asking for "unconditional surrender," Rusk said: "We are not asking anything from Hanoi except to stop shooting their neighbors in Laos and South Vietnam. We are not asking them to give up an acre of territory. We are not asking them to surrender a single individual, nor to change the form of government. . . . We are not asking them to surrender a thing except their appetite to take over South Vietnam by force."

Fulbright contended that the Communists should be given convincing assurances "that if an election is held in Vietnam, that we will abide by it regardless of the outcome." Rusk replied: "The only convincing way in which you could say that to the other side apparently is to let them have the government to start with that would conduct the elections." Asked by Sen. Albert Gore (D., Tenn.) if the U.S. would agree to elections and abide by their results, Rusk said, "Yes."

Congress Debates U.S. Policy

A 2-week Senate debate on U.S. policy in Vietnam pre-ceeded the Senate's passage Mar. 1 of a bill to authorize $4,-807,750,000 in emergency funds in fiscal 1966 to finance the war. The vote was 93-2; Sens. Wayne L. Morse (D., Ore.) and Ernest Gruening (D., Alaska) cast the opposition votes. The House also passed the bill Mar. 1, by 392-4 vote; the opposition votes were cast by Reps. Philip Burton (D., Calif.), George Brown (D., Calif.), William F. Ryan (D., N.Y.) and John Conyers (D., Mich.).

Prior to its final vote, the Senate had voted 92-5 to reject (by tabling) Sen. Morse's amendment to repeal the 1964 "Gulf-of-Tonkin resolution" authorizing Presidential action to repel aggression in Southeast Asia. Just before this vote, White House Press Secy. Bill D. Moyers told newsmen of the President's view that Senators who wanted to "reverse" the Tonkin resolution because of "a change of heart" should vote for the Morse amendment. But Pres. Johnson also felt, Moyers said, that if there were no change of heart and the Senators wanted the resolution to stand, "they ought to vote" to table the Morse amendment. The President's position on the action was reinforced as soon as debate opened Mar. 1 when about a dozen pro-Johnson Senators, joined by Senate minority leader Everett M. Dirksen (R., Ill.), rose to declare that the vote was a test of support for the President's policy.

Sen. J. W. Fulbright (D., Ark.) voted against tabling the Morse amendment. He told reporters later that he did not "want to reaffirm" the resolution. Fulbright, who had helped win passage of the original Tonkin resolution, said: "This thing [the Vietnamese war] has got so big now that it ought to be pursued under a declaration of war as the Constitution requires." Also voting against tabling were Sens. Morse, Gruening, Eugene J. McCarthy (D., Minn.) and Stephen M. Young (D., O.).

The decision to seek to table the impending Morse amend-ment and get a quick vote on the authorization had been made at a conference Feb. 28 by Fulbright, majority leader Mike Mansfield (D., Mont.) and Chrmn. Richard B. Russell (D., Ga.) of the Senate Armed Services Committee. As a result of the meeting, Russell agreed not to offer an amendment re-affirming the Tonkin resolution, and 17 Democratic critics of Administration policy in Vietnam agreed not to offer an amendment specifying that their support of the money measure did not constitute advance approval of expansion of the war. Both amendments were considered capable of evoking more divisive debate on Vietnam than the Morse amendment, which was known to be backed by only 2 Senators.

When the debate opened, however, the Administration made its moves to transform the vote on the Morse amend-ment more or less into an expression of support for or opposi-tion to Administration policy.

Fulbright made a major speech on Southeast Asia on the last day of debate Mar. 1. He said that unless the U.S. was prepared to fight a general war in Asia over South Vietnam, it had "no alternative but to seek a general accommodation" with Communist China for the "neutralization" of all Southeast Asia. "If the issue between Chinese and American power in Southeast Asia can be resolved," he said, "the future of Viet-nam should not be too difficult to arrange; but if the issue of Chinese and American power is left unresolved, even a total victory in South Vietnam is unlikely to solve very much."

Fulbright said: "It would seem to be highly advisable that . . . we indicate to the Chinese that we are prepared to re-move American military power not only from Vietnam but from all of Southeast Asia in return for a similar withdrawal on her part." A "general neutralization agreement for South-east Asia could be enforced" (1) by "the prospect that the re-introduction of Chinese power would be followed by the rein-troduction of American power," and (2) by placing the neutra-lization agreement "under the guarantee of the major powers with interests in Southeast Asia, notably the United States, China, the Soviet Union, Great Britain, France, India and Japan."

To get China's consent to the neutralization pact, Ful-bright proposed "entrench[ing] ourselves in powerful bases on the coast of Vietnam" and thus confronting the Chinese "with a perfectly credible threat of permanent American bases on their periphery." "History . . . suggests," Fulbright said, "that the military solution that seems so promising today is likely to result in disaster tomorrow, whereas the course of accommodation, which always seems so difficult, is the only course with demonstrated promise of being able to bring about a lasting and honorable peace."

The Senate debate on Vietnam had been opened Feb. 16 by Senate Democratic whip Russell B. Long (D., La.), acting as majority leader in the absence of Mansfield. Long attacked critics of Pres. Johnson's Vietnam policy and said they "do nothing but encourage the Communists to prolong the war." He said: "These advocates of retreat, defeat and surrender and national dishonor have not been doing the country any good when they went before a television network suggesting that this nation was not committed to fighting aggression in [Vietnam]"; if the U.S. forces were beaten "it will be in Washington" not in Vietnam.

Sen. Albert Gore (D., Tenn.) replied: "The issue is between a limited war or a global war. Such an issue deserves the deliberate consideration which the Congress is giving it." The war should be kept "within bounds which appear manageable, with limited goals and limited commitments." The U.S.' main goal should be "a tolerable political arrangement that would permit honorable disengagement of United States combat forces at the earliest feasible time."

Sen. George McGovern (D., S.D.) Feb. 16 also criticized the suggestion "here that some people who are concerned about [the] worry about a major war in Asia are somehow lacking in patriotism and willingness to defend our country's interest."

Morse said Feb. 16 that he wanted to "support the boys in Vietnam though they shouldn't be there." He predicted that the Viet Cong and North Vietnam would surrender "in a matter of not too many weeks from now." Later he amended his remark to "may" surrender and added: "At least their capacity to fight conventional warfare may be destroyed." "But that is not going to produce peace, for guerrilla warfare can still be carried on indefinitely. That will only bog us down in Asia for decades."

Sen. John Stennis (D., Miss.) said during the debate Feb.

17: "Bringing an end to the war . . . is the first order of business. If this cannot be accomplished through diplomatic channels, then we must be prepared to face up to the situation and take other necessary steps. . . ." Such steps included more combat troops, increased draft calls, a probable partial call-up of National Guardsmen and reservists, more money and, "if the war continues, increased taxes." "We may ultimately be forced to a choice between guns and butter."

Sen. Frank Church (D., Ida.) said Feb. 21: "However difficult it may be to achieve a satisfactory settlement in Southeast Asia, we must not permit South Vietnam to become another Asian garrison for American forces. Our country has no need for fixed footholds . . . so close to China. These enclaves mire us down, inhibit our mobility and exacerbate against whatever prospect there may be for an eventual accommodation with Peking."

Sen. Stephen M. Young (D., O.) Feb. 23 proposed replacing Dean Rusk, "this warhawk Secretary of State," with Amb. W. Averell Harriman, Amb.-to-UN Arthur Goldberg or Sen. Richard B. Russell (D., Ga.).

Sen. Jacob K. Javits (R., N.Y.) Feb. 23 backed Administration policy "to date" and the policy of "limited objectives and limited military force." He said U.S. forces in Vietnam should be held to 400,000 men. He did not oppose a seat at the negotiations for the Viet Cong.

Sen. Gruening said Feb. 23: "Involving ourselves militarily in Vietnam" was a "great folly." "Nothing that happens in Vietnam affects our national security. . . . We are fighting there for people who do not fight effectively for themselves. We have had very little support from our allies, with whom we have pleaded for it." U.S. bombing of North Vietnam was "illegal."

Sen. Morse Feb. 25 denounced the use of tear gas against the Viet Cong by U.S. forces.

Similar debate took place during consideration of a bill appropriating $13,135,719,000 in fiscal 1966 for supplemental defense and foreign aid funds, primarily for U.S. operations in Vietnam. The appropriation was passed by 87-2 Senate vote Mar. 22 and House voice vote Mar. 23 and was signed by Pres.

Johnson Mar. 25. The 2 opposing votes were cast by Sens. Morse and Gruening.

Sen. Russell warned Mar. 21 that Americans would not accept the Vietnamese war as it was being fought currently for the 10 or 12 years it might take to defeat the Viet Cong. He said a policy change "in some direction" was necessary or the war would "assume political proportions that will absolutely force it [a policy change] upon any man who has to go before the electorate . . . and seek public office."

During House debate Mar. 15, minority leader Gerald R. Ford (R., Mich.) had said: "The uncertainty as to the course of the war and our policy and the underestimation of expenditures by the Defense Department has created to a very significant degree the inflationary pressures which we face in the United States at the present time." Majority leader Carl Albert (D., Okla.) replied that "appropriations should be requested when needs are known and not when we do not know how much might be needed."

The supplemental appropriations had required the enactment of new authorizations for all the foreign aid funds in the bill and for $4,807,750,000 of the bill's defense funds. The authorization bill was passed by voice votes of the House and Senate Mar. 10. In signing the bill Mar. 15, Pres. Johnson said: "By its overwhelming vote on this measure, I believe the Congress has repeated its declaration to the American people that they stand behind our fighting men in Vietnam." During a 2½-hour House debate on the bill, however, Rep. Jeffrey Cohelan (D., Calif.) presented a statement signed by 78 Democratic members of the House who stated specifically that their vote for the bill did not "constitute a mandate for unrestrained or indiscriminate enlargement of the military effort in Vietnam." House Speaker John W. McCormack (D., Mass.) told the House during the debate that he considered a vote for the bill an indorsement of the President's Southeast Asian policy. Rep. Melvin R. Laird (R., Wis.) warned that "unless the United States is prepared to oppose a coalition interim government at a peace conference, South Vietnam will go the way of the satellite nations of Eastern Europe and of Laos."

A bill authorizing $415 million in fiscal 1966 supplemental

foreign aid was passed by voice votes of the Senate Mar. 15 and House Mar. 16 and was signed by Pres. Johnson Mar. 18. The bill barred the use of the $100 million in contingency funds for aiding nations that permitted shipment under their registries of goods to or from North Vietnam unless the President determined such restriction would be contrary to the national interest. (Pres. Johnson had authorized a blacklist of non-Communist and Polish ships that traded with North Vietnam, the U.S. State Department confirmed Feb. 12. A department spokesman said that under an order issued earlier Feb. 12 by the Maritime Administration's Federal Register, such vessels would be barred from picking up American foreign aid cargoes at U.S. ports. Poland was affected by the ruling because it received U.S. foreign aid. The department spokesman said that U.S. diplomatic pressure had reduced the flow of non-Communist trade with Hanoi by about 60% in the past year and that the minimal flow of non-Communist goods to North Vietnam was of no strategic value.)

54 Senators and 259 Representatives (58½% of Congress' members) favored the basic course being followed by the U.S. in Vietnam, according to a *Congressional Quarterly* poll released Oct. 26. Another 121 Representatives and 20 Senators (26.4%) favored more decisive military action toward quick victory; 55 Representatives and 26 Senators (15.1%) favored increased emphasis on peace talks and deescalation of the war.

U.S. Military Weakness Denied

Defense Secy. McNamara denied at a press conference Mar. 2 that Vietnam requirements had weakened U.S. military strength by overextension and supply shortages. U.S. military forces in Vietnam currently totaled 215,000 men, and another 20,000 were being sent there, he reported. "It can be stated categorically that no shortages have impeded our combat operations in Southeast Asia," McNamara declared. He said the U.S. could sustain a major buildup in Vietnam and remain "fully capable of meeting our commitments elsewhere in the world." The U.S. 7th Army in Germany, he said, was the most combat-ready military force in the world. In the event of a new threat anywhere in the world, McNamara declared, a combat-ready U.S. force of 350,000 men, including 9 divisions

(5 from the reserves), could be ready for deployment within 90 days.

In addition to the 43 combat battalions currently in Vietnam, McNamara said, the U.S. could field 21 more combat battalions there or have them *en route* to Vietnam by June 30 if it were required. Such an addition (including the 20,000-man increase he had just announced), plus additional Air Force units, would bring U.S. forces in Vietnam to 350,000 men. Noting that the peak number of U.S. troops in Korea during the Korean War had been 350,000 (305,000 ground troops), McNamara said the U.S. could put more men into Vietnam than the Korean peak number without calling up reserves, extending duty tours, imposing "direct economic controls" or weakening U.S. forces in Europe.

Charges of overextension of U.S. forces had been made by Hanson W. Baldwin in the Feb. 21 *N.Y. Times* and by Sen. John C. Stennis (D., Miss.) in a speech Feb. 25 before the Reserve Officers Association. Baldwin's article said U.S. armed services "have almost exhausted their trained and ready military units, with all available forces spread dangerously thin. . . . " Stennis said: "This heavy drain of Vietnam has brought on serious problems in personnel, equipment, repair parts and other materials."

House Republican leader Gerald R. Ford (Mich.) charged at a press conference Apr. 14 that U.S. airmen in South Vietnam were hampered by a "shortage of bombs" and that the Administration was trying to cover up "shocking mismanagement [of the Vietnamese war] in the name of national unity." The "shortage of bombs and the back-up of ships in Vietnam is a national scandal," he said. The Defense Department Apr. 11 had acknowledged a "temporary problem" in the unloading of bombs because of civil disorders in the port of Danang. McNamara, however, denied Apr. 14 that the U.S. had a shortage of bombs, and he assured newsmen that the unloading of military supplies in Vietnam was "normal."

Deputy Defense Secy. Cyrus R. Vance denied on the ABC-TV "Issues and Answers" program Apr. 24 that shortages had interfered with combat operations in Vietnam. He read a statement in which Gen. Earle G. Wheeler, Joint Chiefs of Staff chairman, said: "There have been no shortages in supplies for the troops in Vietnam which have adversely affected combat operations or the health or welfare of our troops. No required air sorties have been canceled. As a matter of fact, the air support given our forces is without parallel in our history."

U.S. Calls Its Intervention Legal

The State Department Mar. 9 made available copies of a 52-page statement holding that U.S. intervention in Vietnam was legally justified under international law, the UN Charter and the U.S. Constitution. This legal brief, which had been submitted to the Senate Foreign Relations Committee, was entitled "The Legality of United States Participation in the Defense of Vietnam."

The statement asserted that "the infiltration of thousands of armed men" from North Vietnam into South Vietnam "clearly constitutes an 'armed attack' under any reasonable definition." While acknowledging that "there may be some question as to the exact date at which North Vietnam's aggression grew into an 'armed attack,'" the document argued that "there can be no doubt that it had occurred before Feb. 1965," when the U.S. began bombing raids on North Vietnam and a large-scale build-up of forces in South Vietnam.

Since South Vietnam had been subjected to armed attack, the document said, U.S. intervention was justified under "the right of individual and collective defense" recognized by international law and the UN Charter; the fact that South Vietnam was not a UN member and was a zone of a temporarily divided state did not diminish the right of collective defense; the 1954 Southeast Asia Collective Defense Treaty obligated the U.S. "to defend South Vietnam against Communist armed aggression" without requiring a "collective decision" including other signatories.

The U.S. policy declaration given at the close of the 1954 Geneva conference on Indochina was cited as a commitment to South Vietnam. According to the brief, the U.S. had not violated the Geneva agreements, which prohibited the introduction of outside troops or armaments into Vietnam, because "the substantial breach of an international agreement by one side permits the other side to suspend performance of corresponding obligations."

The legality of the U.S.' military involvement in South Vietnam had been challenged by members of the Senate Foreign Relations Committee Jan. 28 as they subjected State Secy. Rusk to 4 hours of questioning on Vietnam. (Rusk appeared before the committee in support of the Administration's request for a $12.7 billion supplemental appropriation for economic and military activities in South Vietnam.) Chrmn. Fulbright told Rusk that neither the Aug. 1964 resolution on Vietnam nor the Southeast Asia Collective Defense Treaty was a legal justification for Washington's military actions. Fulbright said the Congressional resolution was a response only to the North Vietnamese attack on U.S. destroyers in the Gulf of Tonkin. The Southeast Asian Defense Treaty, Fulbright insisted, required its signatories only to consult in the event of aggression against any member, and, he said, it specifically excluded Vietnam.

The House of Delegates of the American Bar Association, holding its mid-year meeting in Chicago, unanimously passed without debate Feb. 21 a resolution affirming that "the position of the United States in Vietnam is legal under international law, and is in accordance with the Charter of the United Nations and the Southeast Asia Treaty." At hearings of the Senate Foreign Relations Committee on Vietnam, Sen. Russell B. Long (D., La.) had suggested that the ABA reply to a remark by Sen. Wayne Morse (D., Ore) that some international lawyers regarded U.S. participation in the Vietnam war as illegal. The ABA resolution was sent to Sen. J. W. Fulbright (D., Ark.), chairman of the committee. Morse commented in the Senate Feb. 21 in reply to the resolution: "Apparently what the ABA needs is a freshman refresher course in constitutional law."

The Lawyers Committee on American Policy Towards Vietnam, with a claimed membership of 4,100, attacked the ABA resolution Mar. 14 as a "disservice to the bar." A letter to ABA Pres. Edward W. Kuhn from Chrmn. William L. Standard and Secy. Joseph H. Crown of the lawyers committee said the ABA position was based on "a minuscule analysis consisting of a distorted excerpting of a few phrases, out of context, from Articles 51 and 52 of the United Nations Charter." It pointed out that Article 51 of the UN Charter applied only "if an armed attack occurs against a member of the United Nations."

President Explains Policy

Faced with persistent, angry criticism of his policy in Vietnam, Pres. Johnson found frequent occasions to answer his critics, to explain what the U.S. hoped to accomplish in Vietnam and to appeal for support.

Mr. Johnson said Apr. 21: "It must never be said that when the freedom and the independence of a new and a struggling people were at stake that this mighty, powerful nation . . . would ever turn aside because we had the harassments that always go with conflict and because some thought the outcome was uncertain or the course too steep, or the cost too high." The President made this remark while presenting a Medal of Honor that had been awarded posthumously to Pfc. Milton L. Olive 3d, 19, of Chicago. Olive had been killed when he had thrown himself on a Viet Cong grenade to save the lives of 4 others in his platoon. He was the 8th Negro to win a Medal of Honor.

Pres. Johnson appealed May 17 for national unity on Vietnam. Speaking at a Democratic Party fund-raising dinner in Chicago, Mr. Johnson said: "There will be some Nervous Nellies and some who will . . . break ranks under the strain" and "some" who "will turn on their leaders and on their country and on our own fighting men." The U.S. soldiers "out there somewhere in Southeast Asia . . . , fighting to quarantine another aggressor," were "trying to find a way to peace," and "they know, and I don't understand why we don't all recognize, that we can't get peace just for wishing for it. We must get on with the job. . . . " "As commander in chief, I am neither a Democrat nor a Republican. The men fighting in Vietnam are simply Americans. Our policy in Vietnam is a national policy." "I ask every American to put our country first. Put it above parties, if you want it to seize the larger victories of freedom, peace and prosperity. . . . I ask you to read the statements of every public official and of every candidate for every office. . . . Ask yourselves, 'Is he helping the cause of his country, or is he advancing the cause of himself? Is he trying to draw us together and unite our land, or is he trying to pull us apart to promote himself?' . . ." Mr. Johnson desired peace and "did not seek to enlarge this war." But the war involved "not just that one little country of 14 million people but more than 100 other little countries [that] stand tonight and watch and wait. If America's commitment is dishonored in South Vietnam, it is dishonored in 40 other alliances or more that we have made."

Mr. Johnson was asked at his news conference May 21 whether he was "indicating" in his May 17 speech "that some people were less patriotic than others and that you might be interested in purging some members of your own party." His reply: "No. . . . We just want to be sure that others understand that because we have dissent does not mean that we have been dissected, and because we do have differences does not mean that we are torn to pieces. . . ."

Mr. Johnson declared in a speech June 16: ". . . We say to any . . . would-be conqueror: When and if you attempt by force to subjugate people, you will meet the United States of America." "An essential basic part of our policy . . . is to serve notice on those who live in this world with us that gangsterism and aggression and force are not to be rewarded." "We must continue to fight until men are convinced that it is better to talk than to fight. . . . We are ready to talk any time, anywhere, with any government. . . . But you can't have a unilateral contract. The other side has to want to talk, too." (The speech was made before leaders of state legislatures at a national conference sponsored by the Administration. The conferees earlier June 16 had adopted a resolution indorsing Administration policy on Vietnam.)

In an opening statement at his news conference June 18, Pres. Johnson declared his intention to "persist in our present [Vietnamese] policy . . . to bring to bear the ground, naval and air strength required to achieve our objectives." He said: "I must observe that this does not mean that we shall not increase our forces or our operations. It is not good national policy publicly to declare to those conducting aggression that there are particular limits on how we shall act to defeat that aggression." "Our attacks on military targets in North Vietnam have imposed a growing burden on those who support the insurgency in the South. We must continue to raise the cost of aggression at its source, and that is the sole purpose of our use of air strength against selected military targets." "Our intelligence indicates that the aggressor presently bases his hopes . . . more on political differences in Saigon and Washington than on his military capacity in South Vietnam. While we have differences and divisions, I want our men in the field and our people at home to know that our course is resolute, that our conviction is firm and we shall not be diverted from doing what is necessary in the nation's interest and the cause of freedom." "I am encouraged that the Vietnamese are carrying forward the first steps in building a constitutional process. . . . Rival political forces are now contending for power, and this is natural and inevitable. . . . We shall continue to back the Vietnamese effort to achieve government by the consent of the people even as they fight the war." "Here in the United States, I believe that our people are really determined to see this thing through. In recent primary elections not one single candidate was able to make opposition to the resistance of aggression in South Vietnam a successful position that led him to victory. A minority of our people, it is true, are willing now to pull out. Another minority are prepared to see us use our total power. The rest of us . . . are determined that this nation honor its responsibility and its commitment to help Vietnam turn back aggression from the North. . . ."

Humphrey Backs LBJ Policy

Vice Pres. Humphrey continued his defense of Johnson Administration policy in Vietnam.

Speaking Apr. 23 before the Americans for Democratic Action (ADA) convention in Washington, Humphrey quoted the late Adlai E. Stevenson's assertion that retreat in Asia would not make "any contribution whatsoever to the idea that violence shall not be the final arbiter in world affairs." Humphrey reiterated the Administration's willingness "to talk to anyone" at a Vietnam peace conference and said the U.S.

would "cooperate willingly and gladly with any government the people of South Vietnam freely choose" in the promised elections. He denied suggestions that the NLF represented a majority of South Vietnamese. The NLF had so little public support, Humphrey declared, that its 2 attempts at general strikes were "total failures." He pointed out that some 800,000 South Vietnamese had fled from Viet Cong-controlled areas to government-controlled parts of South Vietnam in the past 18 months and that "not one single recognized nationalist, religious, labor or student leader in South Vietnam had identified himself with the front."

Before Humphrey's speech, the ADA Apr. 23 had adopted a resolution deploring Administration policy in Vietnam and "the continuing intensification" of the war by the U.S. It called for de-escalation and an end to the bombing of North Vietnam. The resolution supported participation by the Viet Cong in negotiations for a cease-fire and their inclusion in a provisional government until free elections were held. It called for eventual neutralization of Southeast Asia under UN or other international guarantees. The convention voted to retain disputed language asserting that the U.S. "has only a marginal national interest in Vietnam, or at most a self-created interest," and rejecting "the unthinking application in Asia of our containment policy in Europe or the false analogy of Munich." (A speech critical of Administration foreign policy had been delivered before the convention Apr. 22 by Harvard economist John K. Galbraith. Galbraith said Pres. Johnson, whom he praised as a "force for restraint and for change in the old [Vietnam] policy," needed "more and better help" in formulating policy. Galbraith favored confining military action to "small" areas held as havens for pro-U.S. South Vietnamese.)

Speaking Apr. 25 at the annual AP luncheon meeting in New York, Humphrey said the situation in Vietnam would be "frustrating and at times heartbreaking" but: "We must stay and see it through. And the free nations of the world need to know that we have the vision and the endurance to do so." As for recent political unrest in South Vietnam, "I would rather have the disorder of a vital vigorous people, such as is in [South] Vietnam, than the easy silence of a people that have been subdued by communism in Hanoi." There were 2 things agreed to by the contending groups in South Vietnam—the Buddhists, Catholics, students, laborers, peasants: "They do not want the Communists to control them. And they do not want us to abandon them." The National Liberation Front "is a front of Ho Chi Minh from Hanoi. And he says so. The only ones that seem to misunderstand that are some folks here in America, where communism becomes a matter of academic discussion rather than a matter of life and death."

Humphrey, addressing the 168th graduating class at the U.S. Military Academy at West Point, N.Y., predicted June 8 that "peace and development of Asia will be high on our national agenda for the rest of the century." He said: "We seek and will continue to seek to build bridges, to keep open the doors of communication to the Communist states of Asia and, in particular, Communist China." Commenting on the dispute between the "so-called hawks" and "so-called doves" over policy in Vietnam, Humphrey said: The hawks "must learn that military power is not enough" and "can be wholly unavailing if not accompanied by political effort and by the credible promise to ordinary people of a better life"; "doves must learn that there are times when power must be used, . . . that there is no substitute for force in the face of a determined enemy who resorts to terror, subversion, aggression, whether concealed or open." In Vietnam the "war against the aggressor and the war against misery and despair are fused as never before"; "if we can succeed there—if we can help sustain an independent South Vietnam, free to determine its own future even in its rather disruptive and confusing way—then our prospects and the prospects for free men throughout Asia will be bright indeed."

Governors Support Administration

38 state governors, receiving a White House orientation on Vietnam Mar. 12, "wholeheartedly" backed the Administration's Vietnam policy. They stated their support in a unanimously approved resolution offered by Gov. James Rhodes (R.) of Ohio. Gov. John Reed (R.) of Maine, chairman of the executive committee of the National Governors Conference, said: "We are completely united behind the President and we

believe the vast majority of Americans are, too." He said the 12 governors who did not attend the meeting would be given an opportunity to sign the resolution. The absentees included Govs. George Romney (R.) of Michigan and Mark Hatfield (R.) of Oregon. Among the 24 Democratic and 14 Republican signers of the resolution were Govs. Nelson Rockefeller (R.) of New York and William Scranton (R.) of Pennsylvania. The governors of Puerto Rico, Guam and the Virgin Islands also attended the meeting and supported the resolution. The 3-hour briefing was presented by Pres. Johnson, Vice Pres. Humphrey, State Secy. Dean Rusk, Defense Secy. McNamara and other top officials. Mr. Johnson told reporters after the meeting that he had had no advance notice that the resolution would be offered.

State and territorial governors at the 58th National Governors Conference, held in Los Angeles July 5-7, adopted by 49-1 vote July 7 a resolution expressing the conference's "resolute support of our global commitments, including our support of the military defense of South Vietnam against aggression." The dissenting vote was cast by Oregon Gov. Mark O. Hatfield (R.). (The governors of New York, Maryland and Tennessee were not present at the conference.) The resolution's specific reference to Vietnam was added on a motion by New Jersey Gov. Richard J. Hughes (D.) ; a motion by Hatfield to restrict the resolution to an expression of support for U.S. servicemen in Vietnam was defeated by voice vote.

But Michigan Gov. George Romney (R.) June 12 had criticized U.S. policy in Vietnam as not "adequate in terms of military results nor . . . in terms of negotiated settlement." Speaking on the CBS-TV "Face the Nation" program, Romney said: The North Vietnamese could not be brought to the bargaining table "by simply saying that you are going to demonstrate to them that they can't win. Now, I think they have to be confronted with the fact that they are going to lose." It was "ridiculous" to bomb trucks carrying gasoline and "ignore the fact that 65% of the petroleum oil and lubrication products used by the Viet Cong and the North Vietnamese military are located in a half-mile-by-a-half-mile area in the port of Haiphong." The U.S. should never have become involved in a land war in South Vietnam in the first place and should be ready to withdraw if the planned elections in South Vietnam resulted in a government that wanted the U.S. to leave. The only valid reason for the U.S. presence was "to support the South Vietnamese in their struggle to resist aggression."

In a press conference at the Republican Governors Association meeting in Colorado Springs Dec. 10, Gov.-elect Ronald Reagan (R.) of California declared that he, like ex-Pres. Dwight D. Eisenhower, favored "an all-out, total effort" in Vietnam. "I just don't recognize that a nation of our size can choose to be in a little war or a big war," he said. "When you consider the size of our country and of Vietnam, how can we talk with a straight face about spending 10 years on this war? I think we should go in and get it over with." Asked whether such a policy would involve nuclear weapons, Reagan said it would be an error to inform the enemy that such weapons were never going to be used against them. As for the potential involvement of Red China, he said the Chinese Communists would fight the U.S. "in their own time in their own way if they decide to." (Eisenhower had told newsmen in Chicago Sept. 30 that he was in favor of using "as much force as we need to win" the war in Vietnam. Asked about specific measures concerning more force, Eisenhower replied: "I'm not sure—I'm not on the ground. I'm not familiar with all the political considerations. If they gave me the problem, I'd take any action to win." He said that winning the war should have priority over "the war on poverty, or getting to the moon, or anything else." At a news conference in Washington, where he was attending a meeting of the Republican Coordinating Committee, Eisenhower was asked Oct. 3 if he would preclude the use of atomic weapons in Vietnam. "I would not automatically preclude anything," he responded. "I would do anything that would bring the war to an honorable and successful conclusion as rapidly as I could.")

Republican Views

In a statement issued Sept. 19, Republican House leaders warned that the U.S. was becoming a "full-fledged combatant" in a war that was becoming "bigger than the Korean War."

The statement, an updating of a 1965 GOP white paper on Vietnam, was issued by House Republican leader Gerald R. Ford (Mich.), Rep. Melvin R. Laird (Wis.), chairman of the Republican Conference, and Rep. Charles E. Goodell (N.Y.), chairman of the GOP Committee on Planning & Research. The statement said the U.S. must end the war "more speedily and at a smaller cost while safeguarding the independence and freedom of South Vietnam."

In amplification of the white paper, Laird said at a news conference Sept. 20 that the paper "clearly sets forth the deception practiced by the Democratic spokesmen during the 1964 campaign" and that "the same approach is being followed in the 1966 election period by withholding information concerning the costs of the war and the planned escalation of the war within the next year."

Laird said Sept. 24 that an additional $1 billion for Vietnam had been requested by the Administration for fiscal 1967, that the monthly spending for the war would reach $2½ billion by Jan. 1967 and that "deception is being used on the amount of money being expended in Vietnam." The Johnson Administration is not telling the people about it," he said, "but the manpower commitment has been made, and it is a major escalation of ground operations. The decision has been made to go forward in the [Mekong] Delta area."

Ex-Vice Pres. Richard M. Nixon had called Aug. 8 for a substantial increase in U.S. military strength in Vietnam since he believed there was "no reasonable possibility of a negotiated settlement." Nixon made the suggestion in Saigon at the end of a 3-day visit to South Vietnam. Proposing a 25% rise in the number of troops, which would bring the total to 500,000 men, Nixon said he was "convinced" that the massive build-up would reduce American and South Vietnamese casualties. In a further move to bring the war "to a conclusion," Nixon urged additional pressure on North Vietnam by extension of U.S. air strikes against targets in the Hanoi area. But Nixon rejected South Vietnamese Premier Nguyen Cao Ky's call for an invasion of North Vietnam. As for peace talks, Nixon emphasized that "further discussion of a negotiated settlement delays the end of the war by simply encouraging the enemy that we are begging for peace."

In a speech before the American Legion convention in Washington Aug. 31, Nixon said that with current policy commitments, the war must be expected to last for at least 5 more years. He advocated the cutting of North Vietnam's oil and other supplies. He warned that "if Vietnam falls, the Pacific will be transformed into a Red ocean, and the road will be open to a 3d world war."

On the CBS-TV "Face the Nation" program Sept. 11, Nixon said: "There is grave danger . . . that the Administration will go overboard in increasing American forces in Vietnam. We might be able to win the war, but by doing so we would have on our hands a dependency for a generation to come. That's the wrong way to handle it."

Nixon Sept. 28 ridiculed the Johnson Administration's diplomatic efforts to end the war in Vietnam as a "pathetic exercise in instant diplomacy." He urged a firm commitment by the Administration "to an Asian conference to solve this Asian war." He called for the withdrawal of (1) U.S. offers "to return to Geneva to settle" the war and (2) Amb.-to-UN Arthur J. Goldberg's recent offer to halt the bombing of North Vietnam in return for assurances of de-escalation "from the other side." Nixon said the latter offer would grant "immunity" from aerial attack in return for a potentially "worthless pledge" from Hanoi.

Nixon Nov. 2 urged the U.S. to undertake an "economic offensive" of aid and trade curbs against nations trading with North Vietnam.

Fulbright Charges 'Arrogance of Power'

Chrmn. Fulbright of the Senate Foreign Relations Committee warned in a speech in New York Apr. 28 before the Bureau of Advertising of the American Newspaper Publishers Association that "America is showing some signs of that fatal presumption, that overextension of power and mission, which brought ruin to ancient Athens, to Napoleonic France and to Nazi Germany." "Gradually but unmistakably," he said, "America is succumbing to that arrogance of power which has afflicted, weakened and in some cases destroyed great nations in the past." Fulbright deplored the "facile assumption" that the U.S. could spend billions on "great society" programs at home as well as tens of billions on an Asian war. Congress had become, politically and psychologically, a "war Congress," he said, and "the President simply cannot think about implementing the great society at home while he is supervising bombing missions over North Vietnam." "But even if the material resources can somehow be drawn from an expanding economy," he continued, "I do not think that the spiritual resources will long be forthcoming from an angry and disappointed people."

The warning that the U.S. was "succumbing to the arrogance of power" had been delivered previously by Fulbright in a lecture Apr. 21 to students of the Johns Hopkins University School of Advanced International Studies. He said then that "in a democracy, dissent is an act of faith" and criticism "an act of patriotism." But he opposed such "direct-action" dissent as the burning of draft cards and called instead for protest through "conservative" channels like Congress. In a 2d lecture at the school Apr. 27, Fulbright said: "The evil of communism, it seems to me, is not its doctrinal content, which at worst is Utopian, but its fanatical certainty of itself, its messianic zeal and its brutal intolerance of dissent." He said he hoped "that one day soon we will moderate our hostility and offer to China the hand of friendship, knowing full well that it is almost certain to be rejected but knowing as well that honest and repeated offers of friendship may weaken the Chinese image of a hostile America and hasten the day" of normality in Peking. In his 3d lecture, delivered May 5, Fulbright expressed doubt that the U.S. could "go into a small, alien, undeveloped Asian nation and create stability where there is chaos, the will to fight where there is defeatism, democracy where there is no tradition of it and honest government where corruption is almost a way of life." He declared that in Vietnam "we are still acting like boy scouts dragging reluctant old ladies across streets they do not want to cross."

Pres. Johnson replied to Fulbright May 11 in an address at dedication ceremonies for Princeton University's Woodrow Wilson School of Public and International Affairs. Rebutting Fulbright's charge without mentioning his name, Mr. Johnson urged "responsible" intellectuals, "in the language of the current generation, to 'cool it'—to bring what my generation called 'not heat but light' to public affairs." "The exercise of power in this century," he said, "has meant for all of us in the United States not arrogance but agony. We have used our power not willingly and recklessly, ever, but always reluctantly and with restraint." Referring to Vietnam, Mr. Johnson asked: "What nation has announced such limited objectives or such willingness to remove its military presence once those objectives are secured and achieved?" The President said America was "a nation whose might is not her master but her servant," "a nation conscious of lessons so recently learned that security and aggression as well as peace and war must be the concerns of our foreign policy; that a great power influences the world just as surely when it withdraws its strength as when it exercises its strength; that aggression must be deterred where possible and met early when undertaken; that the application of military force when it becomes necessary must be for limited purposes and must be tightly controlled."

Sen. Jacob Javits (R., N.Y.) said in a Senate speech May 5 that the U.S. had been motivated by "an acceptance of power" rather than "an arrogance of power" in its foreign policy since World War II. Fulbright was attacked May 5 by ex-Sen. Barry Goldwater, who said he should resign as chairman of the Senate Foreign Relations Committee for giving "aid and comfort to the enemy."

Fulbright May 17 expressed regret that he had used the words "arrogance of power" because they lent themselves to misinterpretation. He stressed that he "did not charge any American official with arrogance in the exercise of power" but rather was critical of the tendency of powerful nations, "of which the United States is the current example, to get puffed up about all the terrific things they think they ought to be doing with their power." (Fulbright also said he regretted his statement May 5 that "Saigon had become an American brothel." "I had not thought I was maligning the brave young Americans in Vietnam," he said. "What I was referring to was the inevitable impact on a fragile Asian society of Western soldiers" with money to spend "behaving in the way that is to be expected of men of war.")

U.S. Achievements Claimed

Sen. Wayne L. Morse questioned Defense Secy. McNamara May 11 about whether the loss of 3,234 U.S. troops killed and 15,000 wounded had brought the Vietnamese war closer to victory or negotiated settlement. The confrontation occurred at a Senate Foreign Relations Committee hearing on foreign aid. McNamara replied: "The first step in a negotiated peace is the avoidance of a loss, and that step has been taken as a direct result of the introduction of United States forces." "Had the men [U.S. troops] not been introduced, the Viet Cong and North Vietnam would have won. They would have slaughtered thousands and probably tens of thousands of South Vietnamese, and all of Southeast Asia would be in turmoil."

Asserting that he "disagree[d] completely," Morse said: "We must find some way to get some other forces to come in and try to settle the thing" or put a resolution for a cease-fire before the UN Security Council; "I would put France and Russia right on the spot, and if that didn't work I would push for the resolution before the General Assembly." McNamara replied that "even the UN Secretary General," U Thant, "seems to have despaired of the ability of the UN to act in this situation." Morse replied: "That's why we should have a new Secretary General."

McNamara told the committee that: (a) The U.S. bombing had had a "noticeably adverse effect on Viet Cong morale and expectation of victory" (the observation was based on intelligence reports of increases in desertions and defections among Communists and of Communist drafting of youths 15-17 years old); (b) "it appears that the Viet Cong is losing what support it had from the rural population"; (c) these comments should not lead to undue optimism since the dominant theme was the "deliberate decision" of the North Vietnamese to continue and intensify the war; (d) political upheaval in South Vietnam had reduced the level of military operations.

(Harvard economist John Kenneth Galbraith had told the

Senate Foreign Relations Committee Apr. 25: "I don't think Vietnam is a testing place of American democracy or that it is strategically or otherwise important to United States interests. If we were not in Vietnam, all that part of the world would be enjoying the obscurity it so richly deserves.")

Turmoil at House Hearings

At least 50 persons were arrested for disorderly conduct at hearings held in Washington Aug. 16-19 by the House Un-American Activities Committee. The committee was investigating Americans who aided the Viet Cong in Vietnam. The purpose of the inquiry was to provide data for legislation to outlaw such aid. Those arrested included several of 12 subpoenaed witnesses, a lawyer for a witness and many student spectators. The hearings were marked by outbursts against the committee and against the U.S.' participation in the Vietnamese war. Some witnesses admitted being Communists. Among the highlights of the hearings:

Aug. 16. About 400 persons attended the hearing, and 200 more stood in the halls outside the hearing room. Uproar began before the hearing started: photographers, lawyers, bearded youths, U.S. marshals and policemen milled around; several lawyers tried to make motions to halt the hearing; Jerry Clyde Rubin, in a Revolutionary War uniform, passed out pamphlets saying he was trying to "symbolize . . . that America was born in revolution" but was "denying the right of others to revolution."

Rep. Joe Richard Pool (D., Tex.), chairman of the subcommittee holding the hearing, instructed the police to remove demonstrators. He said that the subject of the hearing was a bill to make it a crime to aid anyone engaged in hostilities against the U.S. The hearings, he said, were "concerned largely with overt acts" such as "sending aid to an enemy" of the U.S. and "obstructing the movement of armed forces, personnel and supplies."

Philip M. Luce, 28, a friendly witness, was the first to testify. He said he had been a member of the Progressive Labor Party (PLP) July 1964-Jan. 1965 but had severed all ties with it. He described the party as a "Marxist-Leninist Communist organization" sympathetic to the "Chinese-Albanian faction." He said it had formed several front groups, including the May 2d Movement (later disbanded). During Luce's testimony, Jeffrey Gordon, 23, of New York, was forcibly ejected by officers after shouting: "Let's stop this fink testimony and get the United States out of Vietnam." Shortly thereafter Richard Mark Rhodes, 22, was also ejected for shouting. Similar evictions followed periodically.

During the afternoon session, Gordon returned from the police station and testified that he was a member of the PLP and formerly of the May 2d Movement.

During the course of the day's hearing, 17 persons were arrested, 9 of them outside the hearing room.

Aug. 17. An attorney for subpoenaed witnesses, Arthur Kinoy, 45, of New York, was forcibly ejected and arrested by 3 U.S. marshals for arguing a legal point after being overruled by Pool. Kinoy and his law partner had protested when Philip A. McCombs, a friendly witness, had mentioned the name of Walter D. Teague 3d, one of their subpoenaed clients. 7 other lawyers walked out of the hearing in protest against the Kinoy ouster. They later submitted a statement saying "attorneys cannot function in an atmosphere of terror and intimidation." (Kinoy, a law professor at Rutgers University, was found guilty Aug. 19 of disorderly conduct.)

Rhodes, who had been ejected Aug. 16, testified that he was a Communist and a member of the PLP. He accused the Johnson Administration of a "war of genocide" and said the initials "USA" had "replaced the crooked cross of Nazi Germany as a symbol of death."

Other witnesses included Edwin Meese, 30, a deputy district attorney of Alameda County, Calif., who told how the Vietnam Day Committee of California had tried to delay troop trains Aug. 5, 6 and 12, 1965.

McCombs named Teague as a collector of money for the Viet Cong during the Assembly of Unrepresented People in Washington in Aug. 1965. He said Teague had "said he could put me in contact with underground agents to help me" if "I wanted to fight and help the Viet Cong." Teague and another subpoenaed witness, Dr. Allen M. Krebs, 31, director of the Free University of New York, denounced the hearing as a "grotesque inquisition" and walked out with their lawyers despite their subpoenas.

16 persons were arrested for disturbances in the hearing room or in the halls during the course of the day's hearing.

Aug. 18. Pool called Krebs and Teague as witnesses, but both were absent. Stanley Nadel and Anatole Ben Anton, 2 other subpoenaed witnesses, were called but agreed to withdraw at the subcommittee's suggestion because of the absence of their lawyers.

A 3d subpoenaed witness, Stuart McRae, 22, of Stanford University, insisted on testifying. He said he had helped set up the Stanford Medical Aid Committee for Vietnam, which had raised $300 to aid persons wounded by Americans. He refused to answer the subcommittee's question about Anton's involvement in the movement.

Aug. 19. Pool announced that the Aug. 19 session would end the investigative stage of the hearings. He said the hearings had revealed "that the key leadership" of groups in the U.S. that aided the Viet Cong "is made up of revolutionary, hard-core Communists."

2 of 3 hostile witnesses were removed forcibly from the stand, and a dozen other persons were ejected from the hearing room and arrested.

Steven Cherkoss, 22, of Berkeley, Calif. testified that he was a West

Coast organizer for the PLP, that "we are Communists and . . . proud of it," that "your government's days are numbered" and that the committee was composed of "coward yellow-bellied racists." Steven C. Hamilton, 22, said that he was PLP chairman at Berkeley, had been president of the May 2d Movement and had worked in the Medical Aid Committee for Vietnam. Cherkoss and Hamilton refused to be excused from testifying and were carried away by marshals.

George Ewart Jr., of Berkeley, who had been carried out of the Aug. 17 hearing by marshals after refusing to remove a button saying "Advance the Cause of Socialism," also testified. He identified himself as a West Coast coordinator for the May 2d Movement, a Communist and a member of the Progressive Labor Movement (an early name for the PLP).

Retired Marine Corps Brig. Gen. James Hittle testified in favor of legislation to control aid sent to the enemy from the U.S. 6 persons were ejected from the hearing for shouting "murderer" at Hittle, who had served in Vietnam. Among others arrested during the day was Jerry Rubin, still wearing his Revolutionary War uniform; Rubin objected to not being called as a witness.

Before the hearings had started, the American Civil Liberties Union had sued to bar the hearings on the ground that they would unconstitutionally impair witnesses' rights to freedom of speech. The suit was brought on behalf of Krebs and Teague. U.S. District Judge Howard F. Corcoran Aug. 15 issued an order "restraining and enjoining" the subcommittee from holding the hearing and from enforcing subpoenas for witnesses. The Justice Department asked the U.S. Court of Appeals later Aug. 15 to disolve the Corcoran order. A 3-judge panel of the court dissolved it Apr. 16 shortly before the committee met.

Churchmen Divided on Policy

Although religious leaders were prominent among the opponents of U.S. policy in Vietnam, a deep division on the issue was evident in church groups:

■ The formation of a National Emergency Committee of Clergy Concerned About Vietnam was announced at a New York press conference Jan. 18. The group's 41 members included Richard Cardinal Cushing, archbishop of Boston; the Rev. Dr. Martin Luther King Jr.; the Rev. Dr. Eugene Carson Blake, stated clerk of the United Presbyterian Church, and Rabbi Jacob Weinstein, president of the Central Conference of American Rabbis. The acting executive secretary was the Rev. William Sloane Coffin of Yale University. The organization was formed to coordinate local Clergy Concerned About Vietnam Committees; Coffin said 150 such groups existed in 43 states. Their purpose, he said, was to make Pres. Johnson aware of "a growing consensus across the country against the war and in support of his peace offensive."

■ The Synagogue Council of America, a coordinating agency for the 3 branches of American Judaism, issued a statement in New York Jan. 15 urging Pres. Johnson to refrain from escalating the war. The statement warned that a resumption of bombing raids on North Vietnam would create "discouragement and frustration" leading to "pressures for unlimited escalation." It called for negotiations through the UN and including NLF representatives.

■ The International Committee of Conscience on Vietnam announced in New York Jan. 22 that it had sent messages urging an end to the Vietnamese war to Pres. Johnson, the National Liberation Front and the governments of South Vietnam, North Vietnam and Communist China. The committee, composed of Catholic, Protestant and Jewish clergymen, had been formed under the auspices of the Fellowship of Reconciliation, a pacifist organization. Its appeal to Pres. Johnson held that "the horrors that your planes and massive fire power are inflicting on the people of Vietnam are beyond any moral or political justification."

■ The national executive committee of the American Jewish Congress (AJC) issued a statement in New York Feb. 26 calling on Pres. Johnson to suspend bombing raids on North Vietnam, offer a cease-fire of unlimited duration and offer to negotiate with "all states, governments and groups that are engaged in or have a direct interest in the hostilities in Vietnam." The AJC, at its national biennial convention at Grossinger, N.Y., passed a resolution Apr. 30 reaffirming this call and urging the U.S. Administration to declare its willingness to negotiate "without prior conditions all points now outstanding between the adversaries in Vietnam."

■ The American Baptist Association, at its convention in Houston, unanimously passed a resolution June 23 deploring "the rash of protests and demonstrations" against U.S. Vietnam policies for "tend[ing] to destroy the respect of the American people for their flag and country." The resolution added that its position against demonstrations should not be "interpreted in any way as an effort to support or condemn the current action in Vietnam."

■ The National Council of Churches July 1 sent a telegram to Pres. Johnson warning of "the dangers and deadends of unilateral action and escalation" and asking for continued efforts "to move the conflict to the conference table." The council statement added that "increasing reliance upon military methods cannot produce a victory that can compensate for distrust and hatred because we are seen as a predominantly white nation using our overwhelming strength to kill more and more Asians." At a meeting in Miami Beach Dec. 9, the Council's General Assembly approved a statement urging the Administration to consider a halt in air strikes on North Vietnam "even though there may be no advance assurance of reciprocal action" by North Vietnam. The council called on its members Dec. 23 to "take extraordinary steps at this Christmas season" to support Pres. Johnson's offer of "cease-fire negotiations in Vietnam."

■ 600 delegates at the biennial congress in Montreal of the Greek Orthodox Church of North and South America July 1 adopted a resolution expressing "whole-hearted" support for the U.S.' stand against "all aggression, particularly in Vietnam." The resolution urged the Administration "to continue its efforts to bring about a speedy and honorable settlement of the conflict."

■ A pastoral letter by Lawrence Cardinal Shehan, read July 3 in Roman Catholic churches in his Baltimore archdiocese, urged American Catholics to "exert whatever moral, civic influences" they could to keep the Vietnamese war "within moral bounds." The letter cited "harsh voices" that "argue against restraint" and attempt "to pressure leaders into decisions which the Christian conscience could not endorse."

■ Richard Cardinal Cushing of Boston, in a speech delivered July 17 to the convention of the Catholic Daughters of America, called the war a struggle against "evil men and evil ways" that "can prove to the aggressors of the world that wars of oppression will not be won."

■ Pres. Johnson's efforts to end the war in Vietnam were indorsed in a joint statement issued in New York Oct. 24 by 2 major Jewish groups— the Rabbinical Council of America and the Union of Orthodox Jewish Congregations of America. The statement warned North Vietnam and "its supporters not to misunderstand the American will for peace."

■ A "statement of peace" approved by the National Conference of Catholic Bishops in Washington Nov. 18 (released Nov. 21) declared that the U.S. "presence in Vietnam is justified." The declaration, however, warned of "a grave danger that the circumstances of the present war in Vietnam may, in time, diminish our moral sensitivity to its evils." "Every means at our disposal, therefore, must be used to create a climate of peace," the bishops said. "We must clearly protest whenever there is a danger that the conflict will be escalated beyond morally accepted limits." The statement added: "While we can conscientiously support the position of our country in the present circumstance, it is the duty of everyone to search for alternatives. And everyone . . . must be prepared to change our course whenever a change in circumstances warrants it." The pastoral letter expressed support for the Johnson Administration's "efforts to negotiate a workable formula for disarmament."

■ In an open letter addressed to Pres. Johnson Dec. 26, the Central Board of Christian Social Concerns of the Methodist Church questioned how his Administration's call "for negotiations and a peaceful settlement [could] be taken seriously when the United States forces escalate their actions at a time like this." The letter said "the world looks upon this as an act of bad faith."

■ Pres. Johnson was reported to have complained to Jewish War Veterans (JWV) officials visiting the White House Sept. 6 that he could not understand why so many American Jewish leaders and rabbis opposed his policies on Vietnam. The President was said to have expressed disappointment with this alleged lack of support in view of the Jews' concern about Communist rule in other nations and their interest in American backing of other small nations, such as Israel. 2 officials of the Jewish organization B'nai B'rith conferred with Pres. Johnson at the White House Sept. 10. The officials—Dr. William A. Wexler, president, and Rabbi Jay Kaufman, executive vice president—reported Sept. 12 "that the views attributed to the President conveyed neither his attitude nor his convictions."

Widespread Dissent

Opposition to Administration policy in Vietnam was widespread throughout the U.S. and was expressed in forms ranging from orderly demonstrations and the adoption of resolutions to draft-card burnings and the shouting-down of Administration speakers. Among developments involving this dissent during 1966:

■ Chrmn. John Lewis of the Student Nonviolent Coordinating Committee (SNCC) Jan. 6 issued an SNCC policy statement assailing U.S. policy in Vietnam and declaring SNCC's support of "the men in this country who are unwilling to respond to a military draft." The statement, issued at SNCC's headquarters in Atlanta, added: "We believe that work in the civil rights movement and with other human relations organizations is a valid alternative to the draft. We urge all Americans to seek this alternative. . . ." Lewis explained that SNCC was not advocating illegal means of avoiding the draft. He said the statement had been drafted by SNCC's 23-member executive committee and approved by its 130-member staff. Roy Wilkins, executive director of the National Association for the Advancement of Colored People (NAACP), said Jan. 8 that the NAACP "disassociates itself" from the SNCC statement and cautioned the public that the SNCC statement "is not the statement . . . of what is loosely called the civil rights movement." The Rev. Dr. Martin Luther King Jr., president of the Southern Christian Leadership Conference, commented Jan. 8: "I would be the last person to condemn one who on the basis of conscience is a conscientious objector. It would be a fine thing for such persons to devote their lives to our domestic problems."

■ "Read-ins" for peace in Vietnam were held in New York Feb. 20, in Portland, Ore. Mar. 4 and 5, in Seattle, Wash. Mar. 6, and in Cambridge, Mass. May 3. 1,500 persons attended the New York event at Town Hall to hear readings by 30 writers and actors, including Robert Lowell, Lillian Hellman, Norman Mailer, Arthur Miller, Dwight MacDonald, Ossie Davis, Ruby Dee and Jules Feiffer. The performance was sponsored by the Committee of the Professions to End the War in Vietnam. The Portland, Seattle and Cambridge read-ins were sponsored by American Writers Against the Vietnam War; the participating authors included Lawrence Ferlinghetti, Louis Simpson, Susan Sontag, Robert Bly and David Ray. The groups read their own and others' works before 500 students and teachers at Portland State College Mar. 4, before an audience of 700 at Reed College Mar. 5, before 200 persons at the University of Washington Mar. 6 and before a Harvard audience May 3.

■ In New York Mar. 25 a Union Square rally sponsored by Veterans & Reservists to End the War in Vietnam featured the burning of discharge and separation papers by 15 veterans of both world wars and the Korean War.

A Mar. 26 parade of 20,000-25,000 persons down New York's 5th Avenue was followed by a rally of 10,000 persons in Central Park. Several arrests were made when marchers carrying National Liberation Front flags were attacked by onlookers. Other spectators jeered and threw eggs at marchers. Speakers at the rally included ex-Special Forces member Donald Duncan, author Norman Mailer and the Rev. A. J. Muste, chairman of the sponsoring 5th Avenue Peace Parade Committee.

4,400 anti-war demonstrators organized by the 5th Avenue Peace Parade Committee marched for 2 hours Apr. 16 in New York's Times Square while members of Women Strike for Peace conducted a silent vigil on a traffic island. 400 policemen separated the demonstrators from angry spectators and from 40 counter-demonstrators of American Patriots for Freedom.

■ About 3,500 anti-war demonstrators marched in San Francisco Mar. 26, wearing black armbands and carrying cardboard coffins.

■ About 2,000 persons marched Mar. 26 through downtown Chicago. Later, a rally at the Coliseum was addressed by Prof. Staughton Lynd of Yale and Julian Bond of the SNCC. Several prospective participants in the Chicago demonstrations had withdrawn because of the leftist and pro-Hanoi tone of some of the sponsors.

■ At a meeting in Miami Apr. 13, the Southern Christian Leadership Conference adopted a resolution calling on the Johnson Administration to consider pulling U.S. forces out of South Vietnam. The resolution, read by SCLC leader Martin Luther King Jr., stated: "We call on our government to desist from aiding the military junta against the Buddhists, Catholics and students of Vietnam, whose efforts to democratize their government are more in consonance with our traditions than the policy of the military oligarchy. . . . We believe the moment is now opportune . . . to reassess our position and seriously examine the wisdom of prompt withdrawal." In a statement of his own, King said: The U.S. war effort in South Vietnam was "rapidly degenerating into a sordid military adventure. It is imperative to end a war that has played havoc with our domestic destinies." At its annual convention, held in Jackson, Miss., the Southern Christian Leadership Conference Aug. 11 adopted a resolution assailing U.S. involvement in the Vietnamese war. The resolution stated that "the war is corrupting society from within and degrading it from without." It contended that "Negroes suffer double the unemployment rate of whites, double the poverty and double the combat responsibility to fight for the society that inflicts this discrimination on them."

■ 350 persons announced in an advertisement in the *Washington Post* Apr. 14 that they would express their disapproval of the Vietnamese war by refusing to pay federal income taxes voluntarily. "We prefer to risk violating the Internal Revenue Code rather than to participate, by voluntarily paying our taxes, in the serious crimes against humanity being committed by our government," the ad said. Signatories included Prof. Staughton Lynd of Yale, folk singer Joan Baez and the Rev. A. J. Muste.

■ 6 U.S. pacifists were expelled from South Vietnam Apr. 21 for attempting to stage anti-war demonstrations. The group was led by A. J. Muste, 81, chairman of the New York-based National Committee for Non-Violent Action, which had sponsored the trip. The pacifists, who had arrived in Saigon Apr. 14, had held a news conference at Saigon City Hall Apr. 20, but the conference was disrupted by 50-60 South Vietnamese students, who shouted anti-Communist slogans and hurled eggs and tomatoes at the speakers. Later in the day the pacifists sought to march on the U.S. embassy but were blocked by police. Muste returned to New York Apr. 25. The pacifists who had accompanied Muste: Bradford Lyttle, 38, of Voluntown, Conn., chairman of the New England Committee for Non-Violetn Action; Prof. William Davidson, 39, a Haverford (Pa.) College physics professor; Karl Meyer, 28, of Chicago, an editor of the *Catholic Worker*; Barbara Deming of Cape Cod, Mass., an editor of *Liberation* magazine; Charlotte Elizabeth (Sherri) Thurber, 22, of Greenwich, Conn., a Sarah Lawrence College student.

■ At a Washington news conference Apr. 26, 24 prominent writers issued a statement urging a 5-point program to end the Vietnamese war and criticizing Vice Pres. Humphrey for his defense of Administration policy. The group then met with Humphrey in his office. The writers' recommendations for achieving peace in Vietnam: an immediate halt to bombing raids on North Vietnam and announcement by the Administration of its willingness (1) to negotiate with "all interested parties, including the National Liberation Front"; (2) to support authorization of an international agency to supervise an immediate cease-fire and a transition to free elections; (3) to accept the results of such elections; (4) to withdraw U.S. troops and bases "upon the signing of appropriate agreements." The writers included Lillian Hellman, John Hersey, Elmer Rice, Alfred Kazin, Louis Untermeyer, Edmund Wilson, Maxwell Geismar and Harvey Swados. Their statement had been drafted by ex-Sarah Lawrence Pres. Harold Taylor, *Dissent* editor Irving Howe, poet Lenore Marshall and Kazin.

■ A demonstration in support of Congressional candidates pledged to work for peace in Vietnam brought 8,000-11,000 demonstrators to Washington May 15. The participants, who picketed the White House for 2 hours and then attended a rally at the Washington Monument, brought with them about 63,000 "voters pledges," whose signatories promised to campaign for candidates "who agree to work vigorously for U.S. steps to scale down the fighting and achieve a cease-fire; for

U.S. initiatives to encourage negotiations with all concerned parties, including the Viet Cong." The demonstration and signature-gathering campaign were sponsored by the National Committee for a Sane Nuclear Policy (SANE), in cooperation with the American Friends Service Committee, Women Strike for Peace, the Women's International League for Peace & Freedom and the Universities Committee on the Problems of War & Peace. Sanford Gottlieb of SANE, demonstration coordinator, acknowledged May 14 that several leftwing pacifist groups and other radical organizations had declined to support the march because they viewed the pledge as too moderate. Speakers at the rally included Dr. Benjamin Spock (who had led the White House picketing), Norman Thomas (co-chairman of the SANE campaign, with Yale chaplain William Sloane Coffin), *Dissent* editor Irving Howe, Harvard history Prof. H. Stuart Hughes, SNCC staff member Julian Bond and 2 Senatorial candidates—Dr. David Frost of New Jersey and Thomas Boylston Adams of Boston.

■ Various incidents involved the destruction of draft cards or refusal to register or be inducted. Among the incidents:

James E. Wilson, 21, pleaded guilty in New York Jan. 11 and was sentenced Mar. 4 to a 2-year suspended sentence and 2 years' probation for burning his draft card at a Union Square rally in Nov. 1965. (Maximum penalty under the federal law forbidding the destruction of a draft card was 5 years in prison and a $10,000 fine.) One of the conditions of Wilson's probation was that he obtain and carry a new draft card.

David J. Miller was convicted in New York Feb. 10 of burning his draft card. He was sentenced Mar. 15 to a 3-year suspended term and was put on probation for 2 years. Under the conditions of his probation, Miller was required to carry a draft card "at all times" and to cooperate with his draft board. Miller refused Mar. 15 to sign an agreement to abide by the conditions of his probation.

3 Roman Catholic pacifists—Terry Sullivan, 27, John Baehler, 22, and Peter Kiger, 27—destroyed their draft cards in New York Mar. 24 at the office of the Committee for Non-Violent Action. Sullivan tore his card in half and placed it in an envelope addressed to Atty. Gen. Nicholas deB. Katzenbach. Baehler and Kiger burned theirs before TV cameras. Sullivan was convicted and sentenced July 29 to a year's imprisonment.

A group of 50-75 high school boys attacked 7 anti-war demonstrators Mar. 31 on the steps of the South Boston District Court House. Of the 7, David P. O'Brien, 19, and John A. Phillips, 22, had just burned their draft cards; David C. Benson, 18, and David A. Reed, 18, who had burned their draft cards several days previously, had just burned their reclassification notices. The 4 were among 11 appearing in court to face charges stemming from a Mar. 25 demonstration at the Boston Army Base. The 11 demonstrators were found guilty of loitering and blocking traffic and were fined $20 each; 2 paid the fine, and the remainder elected to work off their fines at $1 a day.

O'Brien was convicted June 2 on a draft-card-burning charge and was sentenced July 1 to an indefinite term not to exceed 4 years.

Thomas Rodd, 19, was sentenced in Pittsburgh Jan. 7 to a 4-year prison term for failure to register for the draft. Rodd had been sentenced to 5 years' probation on the draft charge in Sept. 1964; U.S. Judge Louis Rosenberg ruled before imposing the prison sentence that Rodd had violated probation by participating in a peace demonstration Dec. 30, 1965 at the Boeing Vertol Helicopter Co. in Morton, Pa.

David H. Mitchell 3d, 23, was convicted in Hartford, Conn. Mar. 16 of "knowingly and willfully" failing to report for Army induction. A previous conviction on the same charge had been overturned Jan. 13 by the 2d Circuit Court of Appeals. Mitchell's attorney, Mark Lane, had been denied permission by Judge T. Emmett Clarie to call witnesses to testify to alleged U.S. atrocities in Vietnam in violation of international agreements and particularly of the Nuremberg judgments. Clarie sentenced Mitchell Apr. 1 to up to 5 years in prison; Mitchell remained free on bond pending appeal.

■ Student protests against draft procedures broke out at several universities prior to the administration of draft-deferment examinations May 14, May 21 and June 3.

A group of University of Chicago students took over the school's administration building with a sit-in May 12-16 in protest against the Selective Service System's policy of basing deferment on a student's scholastic rank in his class and against the school's cooperation with the system. School policy was to release a student's ranking to the local draft board if the student requested it. School officials remained away from the administration building to prevent incidents during the sit-in. The protest stemmed from a rally the week before by the Students for a Democratic Society. It was indorsed by the National Coordinating Committee to End the War in Vietnam (in Madison, Wis.). The protesters banded together in a group called Students Against Rank. About 350 students began the sit-in, which was carried on later by a "token force" of about 25 students. It was ended May 16, and an outdoor rally May 18 attracted about 250 students.

About 150 students conducted a sit-in at the administration building of the City College of New York May 13-14, then left to picket the campus site where the draft-deferment test was being given. The sit-in followed a confrontation May 12 of protesting students and City College Pres. Dr. Buell G. Gallagher; Gallagher conceded that the test was unfairly biased toward science and mathematical skills but asked the students to help the school in its effort to "maintain, in what is essentially an unfair and inequitable situation, as much fairness and freedom as possible."

About 75 Brooklyn (N.Y.) College students staged a 24-hour anti-draft sit-in May 19-20 at the school's administration building. About 80 students and faculty members held an anti-Vietnamese war demonstration on the Cornell University campus in Ithaca, N.Y. May 17. There was also an anti-draft demonstration at Hunter College (N.Y.)

May 24-25. During the administration of the draft-deferment test May 14, test sites were picketed by 30 students at the University of Wisconsin, by 30 students and faculty members at Cornell and by a handful of students at Columbia University in New York and at Princeton (N.J.) University. 250 students held a sit-in at Oberlin (Ohio) College. During the draft-deferment test May 21 the demonstrations dwindled to protests at Roosevelt University in Chicago and at Stanford (Calif.) University. At Roosevelt University, anti-draft protests May 19-25 resulted in the arrest of 39 students who refused to leave administration offices at closing time.

University of Wisconsin students staged a sit-in at the school administration building in Madison May 16-20. Participation ranged from 25 to 700 students. An anti-draft rally on the campus May 18 was attended by about 10,000 students. A faculty meeting, urged by the demonstrators, was held May 23, and about 750 participants voted (a) to call for a re-evaluation of national draft deferment policy and (b) to ask the university to give class rankings directly to the students. The faculty rejected the students' demand for the cancellation of draft-deferment tests on the Wisconsin campus.

■ Several war protesters in the armed forces refused to fight in Vietnam:

Pvt. Robert Luftig sued Mar. 18, for the 2d time, in a futile challenge of the government's right to send him to Vietnam. The suit was filed in Washington, D.C. Defense Secy. McNamara and Army Secy. Stanley Resor were named as defendants. It charged that U.S. intervention in Vietnam violated the UN Charter, the Southeast Asia Collective Defense Treaty, the 1954 Geneva agreements, the Nuremberg judgments and the 1928 Kellogg-Briand Pact. Luftig's original suit had been dismissed Feb. 15 on technical grounds. His Mar. 18 suit was dismissed by Judge Alexander Holtzoff Apr. 5; Holtzoff ruled that "the courts may not substitute themselves in the position of commander-in-chief of the armed forces."

Pvt. Adam R. Weber Jr., 24, a New Orleans Negro stationed near Cuchi, South Vietnam with the 25th Infantry Division, was convicted by a court-martial June 11 of "wilful disobedience" of an Apr. 30 order to carry a rifle and join an infantry battalion. He was sentenced to one year's imprisonment at hard labor, forfeiture of $45 of his $101.90 monthly pay and reduction in rank from Private E-2 to Private E-1. Weber told the court before sentencing that he hoped to remain in the Army in "some job more involved in saving lives than in taking them." His attorney, Capt. Sanford V. Lavine of Syracuse, N.Y., had argued that Weber had been entrapped into disobedience inasmuch as Army authorities had been aware of his unwillingness to kill. Following his induction in Nov. 1965, Weber had submitted a statement in which he said he could not "in all conscience take the life of another human being, especially in reference to the war in Vietnam." He had been ineligible for conscientious objector status because he would not certify that his convictions were based on "religious training and belief" and had been ineligible for non-combatant jobs requiring security clearance because of his refusal to sign an oath that he would "obey . . . the orders of the officers appointed over me."

3 Army privates on furlough were arrested by military police in New York July 7, one week after they had announced their intention of refusing shipment to Vietnam when they reported to the Oakland, Calif. Army Terminal at the end of their leave. They were convicted by an Army court martial in Ft. Dix, N.J. Sept. 6 and 9 of disobeying orders by refusing to go to Vietnam. In the first trial Sept. 6, Pvt. Dennis Mora, 25, of N.Y. City received a sentence of 3 years in prison at hard labor. In the Sept. 9 trials, Pfc. James A. Johnson Jr., 20, of N.Y. City and Pvt. David A. Samas, 20, of Modesto, Calif. were sentenced to 5 years in prison at hard labor. All 3 were sentenced to dishonorable discharges and forfeiture of pay. The court rejected defense argument that the Vietnamese war was "illegal and immoral." (N.Y. City attorney Stanley Faulkner had failed in legal maneuvers to prevent their shipment to Vietnam. U.S. District Judge Edward M. Curran, ruling in Washington, D.C. July 11, had dismissed Faulkner's request, filed June 30, for a preliminary injunction against their deployment to Vietnam on the ground that Congress had not declared war.)

■ A 3-page advertisement in the June 4 *N.Y. Times,* costing $20,880 and bearing more than 6,400 signatures, urged the Administration "to cease all bombing, North and South, and all other offensive military operations immediately" and "to evaluate seriously whether self-determination for the Vietnamese as well as our own national interest would not be best served by termination of our military presence in Vietnam." The signers included 3,938 faculty members and administrators from 180 colleges and universities in 39 states, 351 teachers, 324 artists, 272 psychologists, 259 physicians, 203 writers, 142 clergymen and church representatives and 105 scientists and technologists. The ad was sponsored by the Ad Hoc Universities Committee for the Statement on Vietnam and the Committee of the Professions to End the War in Vietnam.

■ College and university graduation ceremonies were seized on as forums for demonstrations against U.S. policy in Vietnam. The protests were directed at high Administration officials receiving honorary degrees:

20 of the 270 graduating seniors at Amherst College in Amherst, Mass. walked out of commencement exercises June 3 as an honorary LLD was about to be presented to Defense Secy. McNamara. 38 seniors wore white armbands on their academic robes as a token of protest against the granting of the degree. The commencement was picketed by anti-war demonstrators. (McNamara had submitted to questions on U.S. foreign policies at a gathering of Amherst students preceding the ceremonies.)

McNamara was the target of a student demonstration June 8 as 130-200 NYU seniors and faculty members staged a commencement walk-out in protest against the university's granting of an honorary LLD to McNamara. The demonstration had been organized by an Ad Hoc Student-Faculty Committee on Vietnam, which asserted that conferring an honorary degree on McNamara "represents approval of his deeds." Amb.-to-UN Arthur J. Goldberg, principal commencement speaker and himself the recipient of an honorary LLD, chided the protesters for not remaining to "hear what I have to say" and defended McNamara by saying that "no man has more by his actions demonstrated an abiding attachment to the peace and freedom that we earnestly pursue."

Goldberg became directly involved in a commencement protest at Brandeis University in Waltham, Mass. June 12. About 165 graduates and 65 faculty members at the ceremonies wore white ribbons pinned to their gowns as a symbolic protest against the granting to Goldberg of an honorary LLD; most of the protesting students, about 10 faculty members and about 100 of the 4,000 spectators stood up during the first 5 minutes of the ambassador's commencement address. Goldberg said he welcomed "the freedom of expression . . . being manifested by students in the colleges and universities," but he warned that "if freedom of speech is to be protected, the rules of the game must be preserved."

■ 3 University of California (Berkeley) professors released in Washington June 25 a "Citizens' White Paper" charging that "movements toward a political settlement" of the Vietnamese war "have been retarded or broken off by American . . . military escalation." The 3 professors had drafted the document and sent it to Pres. Johnson June 22 with a covering letter signed by 29 professors, clergymen, attorneys and business and union leaders. The 3 were Franz Schurmann, director of Berkeley's Center for Chinese Studies, Peter Dale Scott of the speech department and Reginald Zelnik of the history department. Signatories of the covering letter included the Rev. Dr. Eugene Carson Blake, general secretary-elect of the World Council of Churches, the Rev. Dr. Martin Luther King Jr., president of the Southern Christian Leadership Conference, and Robert M. Hutchins, president of the Fund for the Republic. (Blake had said in Pittsburgh Mar. 6 that "Pres. Johnson is following a policy of restraint in Vietnam, and the Christian church supports this restraint." Urging negotiations with the Viet Cong, Blake said: "When you fight somebody, you'd better get whomever you're fighting with to the conference table.")

■ The national convention of the Congress of Racial Equality, held in Baltimore, voted July 4 to adopt 2 resolutions dealing with the Vietnamese war. One called for the withdrawal of U.S. troops from Vietnam; the other attacked the draft as placing "a heavy discriminatory burden" on minority groups and the poor and supported persons refusing to serve in the armed forces because of their objection to the Vietnamese war.

■ The 21st anniversary (Aug. 6) of the dropping of a U.S. atomic bomb on Hiroshima was the occasion for anti-Vietnam protests staged across the country. The demonstrations were coordinated by the National Coordinating Committee to End the War in Vietnam, a peace-movement clearing house in Madison, Wis.

5,000 persons marched in N.Y. City's Times Square in a protest sponsored by the 5th Ave. Peace Parade Committee. A midtown rally following the march was addressed by A. J. Muste, the committee's chairman, Lincoln Lynch, associate national director of CORE, and Marine Corps Cpl. John M. Morgan of Martin, Tenn., who said that he had been AWOL since July 15 from Camp LeJeune, N.C. In other N.Y. City protests, demonstrators picketed the offices of the Dow Chemical Co. to protest the firm's manufacture of napalm, and 250 persons took part in a silent vigil at the UN sponsored by the American Friends Service Committee. (A Nagasaki Day protest was staged in N.Y. City Aug. 9 by 200 demonstrators who picketed the Dow Chemical Co.'s offices; 20 were arrested on disorderly conduct charges.)

About 1,000 persons gathered at Philadelphia's Independence Hall for a 3-hour anti-war rally. In San Francisco, about 4,000 war protesters staged a mile-long parade. At the University of Wisconsin in Madison, demonstrators held a silent vigil and distributed anti-war leaflets to Army reservists stationed on the campus. U.S. and Canadian peace groups demonstrated on the Rainbow Bridge at Niagara Falls. Demonstrations in Washington, D.C. included a rally and march to the White House, with protesters also picketing both the National Shrine of the Immaculate Conception and the White House in connection with the wedding of Pres. Johnson's daughter Luci. (The wedding protests were organized by the Student Nonviolent Coordinating Committee; SNCC had rejected a telegram, objecting to the "extremely poor taste" of the planned demonstrations, sent Aug. 4 by 4 Negro leaders—the Rev. Dr. Martin Luther King Jr., A. Philip Randolph, Roy Wilkins and Whitney Young Jr.)

Other cities in which demonstrations took place Aug. 6 included Cleveland, Denver, Minneapolis, Los Angeles, Pittsburgh, Boston and Atlanta.

■ About 100 anti-Administration students, supporters of the Students for a Democratic Society, shouted at Defense Secy. McNamara at Harvard University Nov. 7 and demanded that he debate with them. But they shouted him down whenever he tried to speak. The incident took place as he emerged from a dormitory where he had addressed 50 students. About 25 demonstrators threw themselves under McNamara's auto and delayed his departure. As McNamara left the car, fist fights broke out between SDS supporters and students who backed U.S. policy in Vietnam. Police led McNamara away from the scene.

■ Anti-war students at Brown University (Providence, R.I.) clashed with police Nov. 15 after disrupting a speech by Gen. Earle Wheeler, chairman of the Joint Chiefs of Staff. Wheeler was speaking to a gathering of more than 100 in an auditorium at Pembroke College (an affiliate of Brown) when about 60 students walked out in protest against his defense of U.S. involvement in Vietnam. Some of the students who remained began to shout and heckle the general. At the conclusion of Wheeler's address, about 20 persons stormed the stage, but police and ushers blocked their path, and Wheeler was escorted out of the building. More than 100 students continued the protest outside the building after police had cleared the auditorium; the demonstrators carried signs opposing the war. In his speech, Wheeler had said that the war in Vietnam was an "extension" of Communist worldwide aggression.

■ The Council of Fellows of the American Anthropological Association, meeting in Pittsburgh Nov. 19, adopted a resolution assailing the U.S.' "use of napalm" and the American "heavy bombing of civilian centers" in Vietnam as "harmful to human nature." The resolution, approved by more than 1,000 votes, urged the Johnson Administration to "put an end to their use at once and proceed as rapidly as possible to a peaceful settlement of the war in Vietnam."

■ At a Los Angeles news conference Feb. 8 Ronald E. Ramsey, 27, admitted having produced 9 taped broadcasts used on Hanoi radio to urge U.S. soldiers to "lay down your arms." He said: The "Radio Stateside" tapes had not been solicited or acknowledged by the Hanoi government. They had been undertaken "a few months ago by experienced, sophisticated freedom fighters. We felt there was a need for an escalation of resistance to war—to bring our GIs home alive rather than dead." He explained that U.S. soldiers were told on the broadcasts: "You're committing war crimes unless you resist this war." (Milton Senn, regional director of the Anti-Defamation League of B'nai B'rith, said in Los Angeles Feb. 10 that ADL files indicated that Ramsey had a past history of supporting rightwing causes such as the White Citizens Councils and Americans for America.)

American opponents of Administration policy in Vietnam were criticized in a Freedom House document, *A Crucial Turning Point in Vietnam,* issued in New York Nov. 13. The document, signed by 138 prominent U.S. citizens, chided the critics for failing to make "the distinction between responsible dissent and unfounded attacks upon our society." It urged "men of stature in the intellectual, religious and public service communities" to withdraw their support of the "fantasies" of extreme critics of the Johnson Administration's policies. Among "fantasies" listed by the statement: "This war is Lyndon Johnson's war or McNamara's war"; "the American leaders are committing 'war crimes' or indulging in 'genocide' . . ."; "this is a 'race' war of white versus colored people." Among signers of the statement: ex-Pres. Eisenhower, ex-State Secy. Dean Acheson, Sen. Jacob K. Javits (R., N.Y.) and ex-Postmaster Gen. James J. Farley.

Pres. Johnson had told 121 high school graduates being honored at the White House June 7 as Presidential scholars that "no American, young or old, must ever be denied the right of dissent." But he urged his audience to "know why you protest" and to "try, when you do disagree, to offer a choice for the course you disapprove."

(Deputy White House Press Secy. Robert H. Fleming had said Mar. 9 that Mr. Johnson found a correlation between a decline in support for his Vietnam policy, as determined by public opinion polls, and "any relaxation" of U.S. military pressure in Vietnam. A Gallup Poll published Mar. 9 indicated that 50% of those interviewed approved the way Mr. Johnson was handling the Vietnam situation and 33% disapproved; a Harris Poll released Feb. 28 reported that approval of the President's policy had declined from 63% to 49%. Fleming said the decline represented no increase of the "dove" group [opponents of Vietnamese war escalation], which, he said, remained at about 10%, but an expression of dissatisfaction from the "hawks"—proponents of greater U.S. military commitment in Vietnam.)

DOMESTIC TURMOIL IN SOUTH VIETNAM

Buddhists Oppose Military Junta

South Vietnam's cities were scenes of repeated demonstrations and violance during 1966 as Buddhist opponents of the ruling military junta took to the streets to demand the ouster of Premier Nguyen Cao Ky's regime and the election of a civilian government. Some Roman Catholics also supported the anti-Ky movement. In many cases, the demonstrations took a strongly anti-American tone. Many foes of the junta asserted that the unpopular Ky regime would collapse quickly without U.S. support.

Ky Jan. 15 pledged a popular referendum in October on a new constitution for South Vietnam. The new charter, if approved, would pave the way for "real democratic elections in 1967" of a civilian government to replace the military regime, Ky said. In the face of an upsurge of protests against the regime, Ky announced 2 months later, in a Mar. 25 speech, that a convention would be held to draw up a new constitution within 2 months, rather than in October. But Ky warned that "we must be very careful not to allow Viet Cong or corrupt elements to sit in the next national assembly." Earlier Mar.

25 the ruling National Leadership Committee had yielded to Buddhist demands by announcing that elections for a civilian government would be held in 1966, one year ahead of schedule. The Buddhists also were promised that the group to be appointed to draw up a new constitution would be politically representative. The Buddhists, however, were said to have demanded that the proposed constitutional advisory body be elected and that it serve as a provisional legislature.

In a nationwide broadcast Mar. 26, Ky again assured the South Vietnamese people of his intentions to bring a civilian government into existence quickly. Despite these assurances hundreds of students gathered in Saigon's central market place later in the day to denounce the Ky regime and to demand a civilian government, and South Vietnam's Catholics for the first time joined in the attack against the goverment. The Rev. Hoang Quynh, chairman of the Catholic Greater Unity Force, called Ky's government "worse than the dictatorial government of Ngo Dinh Diem," which had been overthrown in 1963. He insisted that it be replaced by a civilian regime.

Ky Ousts Lt. Gen. Thi

Lt. Gen. Nguyen Chanh Thi, 43, generally considered to be a potential rival of Premier Ky, was ousted Mar. 10 from South Vietnam's ruling 10-man National Leadership Committee. The 9 other members of the Committee, all military leaders, unanimously voted to dismiss Thi and to relieve him of the command of the I Corps area, comprising South Vietnam's 5 northernmost provinces, on charges of insubordination. Thi, a leading Buddhist, was said to have warned that the people of the I Corps area would consider themselves independent if Ky did not crack down on government corruption. Maj. Gen. Nguyen Van Chuan replaced Thi as commander of the I Corps. The U.S. embassy was reported to have praised Thi's ouster as a "step toward political stability" and a "defeat for warlordism." The committee's official announcement said Thi had requested and received a leave of absence for health reasons. But the committee was known to have accused Thi of acting as a "war lord," ignoring committee orders, refusing to prevent anti-government activities in the I Corps area and reshuffling province and district chiefs on his own.

The first public reaction to Thi's dismissal occurred Mar. 11 when thousands of Buddhists demonstrated in Danang. Thi supporters in Hué and Hoian demonstrated Mar. 12. Buddhists in Danang Mar. 12 issued a manifesto denouncing the government and reiterating their demands for Thi's restoration to office and the replacement of the military junta with a civilian government. Strikes and student protests disrupted Hué and Danang Mar. 13-15. Vietnamese civilians employed at the huge U.S. military base at Danang failed to report to work. Buddhist demonstrations spread to Saigon Mar. 16 for the first time. More than 10,000 persons attended a rally sponsored by the Unified Buddhist Church's Institute of Secular Affairs. The protests marked the start of a violent Buddhist campaign to oust the Ky government.

Thich Tri Quang, 43, secretary general of the Unified Buddhist Church's Institute of Religious Affairs and leader of the militant Buddhist faction, said Mar. 15 that his group opposed Premier Ky's military government because "power struggles and purges have been going on right from its birth" and "the present government is rotten."

At the behest of Premier Ky, Gen. Thi toured the northern cities Mar. 16-18 to appeal to his supporters to end their agitation. Thi spoke at rallies in Danang and Hué, calling for calm and national unity. Buddhist speakers at these gatherings continued to denounce the regime. Buddhist delegations met with Ky Mar. 16 and with South Vietnam's chief of state, Maj. Gen. Nguyen Van Thieu, Mar. 17. A government spokesman said the talks were merely "exploratory sessions," not negotiations.

Buddhist demonstrations spread Mar. 16 to Saigon, where more than 10,000 persons attended a rally sponsored by the Unified Buddhist Church's Institute of Secular Affairs. A crowd of about 5,000 persons, including several hundred government soldiers, demonstrated in Danang Mar. 18. Buddhist speakers demanded Thi's restoration, the dissolution of the military junta and a return to civilian rule. The rally was held in defiance of a proclamation, issued earlier Mar. 18 by Maj. Gen. Nguyen Van Chuan, the new I Corps commander, urging an end to the public protests, school boycotts and work stoppages.

Ky and his military junta decided at a meeting Mar. 18 not to consider Buddhist demands while the sect was conducting a campaign of agitation. A communiqué issued after the meeting said the generals were determined to pursue the policy of defeating the Communist military forces, of constructing a democratic form of government, of continuing social reform and of improving "the people's living conditions." Ky reiterated his government's adamant stand in a speech at the resort town of Dalat later Mar. 18. He said: "The armed forces and the administration will not yield to unjustified claims which are contrary to the interests of the nation and people"; "this is a warning to those who by reason of personal resentment and dissent are scheming to betray and sell out the nation." (A Unified Buddhist Church statement Mar. 21 deplored Ky's speech as "hasty and unconstructive." The statement said the Buddhist church "insists on reiterating that its policy is one of moderation, nonviolence and constant patience . . . and it hopes that no one will misunderstand the attitude of the church.")

A conciliatory statement was delivered Mar. 19 by Thich Tam Chau, chairman of the Unified Buddhist Church's Institute of Secular Affairs and the more moderate of the Buddhist Church's 2 major leaders. Addressing more than 10,000 followers in Saigon, Tam Chau said: "We have no essential differences with the present junta. Some people think we want to force the generals out of office. This is not true. We are very grateful to the generals. Ky brought about some stability in the last 8 months, and his government has made a tremendous effort to bring religions together." The Buddhists' Mar. 12 manifesto constituted "observations," not demands. At the Mar. 16-17 meetings, Ky and Chief-of-State Thieu had promised him and other Buddhist officials that they would "carry out the people's aspirations."

A statement issued by the Buddhist church and circulated at the Saigon rally Mar. 19 explained that the Mar. 12 manifesto "was not especially aimed at putting any pressure on the present government. In a spirit of constructiveness, the church . . . will continue to be patient, with the hope that the people's aspirations will eventually be realized."

Thich Tam Chau urged his followers in a broadcast Mar. 27 to halt violence and to wait peacefully for the government "to carry out its promises."

A statement issued by the Catholic hierarchy Mar. 29 denounced the Buddhist-inspired disorders but conceded the right of "orderly struggles" to achieve "righteous" goals. The Catholic statement expressed hope that the Ky regime would fulfill its pledge of democratic reforms.

A communiqué issued by the National Leadership Committee Mar. 30 announced plans for the formation of a council to draft a constitution. Interior Min. Tran Minh Tiet said the council would have 96 members, including 48 representing city and provincial councils; the remaining 48 would be drawn from the law, other professions and religious groups. The committee also voted to "take all appropriate measures against military personnel and civil servants . . . who have taken part in any activities that are harmful to the nation's security." (Hué was the scene of a huge anti-government demonstration Apr. 2. 3,000 government troops, 1,000 national policemen and 1,000 civil servants marched in the demonstration, and speakers demanded the resignation of the government's entire military leadership.)

Tam Chau had said at a rally of 6,000 followers in Saigon Apr. 5: "The church feels it is necessary once more to reaffirm its basic stand, which is to wish for the authorities to enforce democracy by organizing elections for a constituent assembly in 3 months"; if the government acceded to this request, the "situation will return to normal immediately."

Demonstrators Oppose U.S.

The first manifestation of anti-U.S. sentiment had appeared in demonstrations in Danang and Hué Mar. 23. A protester in Danang carried a banner reading: "Down With the American Conspiracy of Hindering the Summoning of a Constitutional Parliament. To Hinder the Summoning of Parliament Is to Intervene in Vietnam's Own Affairs." Demonstrators in Hué and Danang seized the government radio stations to broadcast anti-government statements. Authorities did not intervene.

Saigon was swept by riots Apr. 4 as 1,500 students clashed with police 3 times. One demonstration was quelled by a tear gas attack. In an anti-American outburst, one mob overturned and burned a U.S. jeep and stoned a building housing a U.S. military intelligence team. U.S. and South Vietnamese soldiers were ordered off Saigon's streets at 9 p.m.

In Dalat (140 miles northeast of Saigon), 3,000 students Apr. 4 seized a government radio station; they burned it when troops moved in to disperse the demonstration. The demonstrators also seized a Vietnamese-American police station. The rioters demanded the overthrow of the Ky government and an end to the use of Dalat as a recreation center for U.S. troops.

In Hué, 5,000 persons marched Apr. 4 on the U.S. consulate and submitted a message blaming the U.S.' "policy of interfering with the domestic affairs" of South Vietnam as "the cause of all the crises in South Vietnam."

Testifying Apr. 4 before the U.S. Senate Foreign Relations Committee in Washington, State Secy. Dean Rusk attributed the anti-American aspects of some of the rioting to the fact that "there are those who want the government to do some things that the government is not prepared to do—and some of the South Vietnamese have held us responsible for that." After Rusk's comments, Committee Chrmn. J. W. Fulbright said: "I think we are . . . intervening in a civil war, and our announced objectives are not attainable."

Danang Showdown Delayed

Premier Ky sent 4,000 marines to the Danang airbase Apr. 4 for possible use in the nearby city of Danang, center of the violent anti-government demonstrations that had erupted with the ouster of Lt. Gen. Nguyen Chanh Thi from the military junta.

After an emergency conference in Danang Apr. 5 with Maj. Gen. Nguyen Van Chuan, Ky decided against military action. Ky, accompanied by Deputy Premier Nguyen Huu Co, reached a compromise with Chuan, who was a close friend of Thi's, and thus at least delayed a possible clash between government troops and demonstrators supported by soldiers under Chuan's command.

After the meeting, Ky said he had been mistaken when he had charged Apr. 3 that Danang was in the hands of Communists. Chuan later asserted that Ky had acknowledged this "misunderstanding." Chuan said he supported the "people's aspirations." He added: he would "explain to the people that the government and the people have the same goal, a democratic government, but there are some differences in manner and timing." Chuan said Ky told him that the Viet Cong had infiltrated the agitation movement in Danang and that it was therefore necessary to station more security troops at the Danang airbase.

Brig. Gen. Pham Xuan Nhuan, commander of the First Division at Hué (another center of Buddhist agitation), declared in a Hué broadcast Apr. 5 that his troops would fight central government forces if they were sent to the city to assert Saigon's control.

Ky also conferred Apr. 5 with Thich Tri Quang, the Buddhist church's principal opponent of the Ky regime. Tri Quang assured Ky that the demonstrations in Danang and Hué were not engineered by the Viet Cong. Tri Quang did not demand Ky's resignation, but he insisted on the installation of a "properly balanced" central government that would include all of the country's provinces and political elements.

Ky's decision to send troops to Danang had been made Apr. 3. He had declared then that Danang was "already controlled by the Communists" and that he would send troops to "liberate" the city. The alleged "Communists" referred to by Ky were the leaders of the anti-government organization known as the Struggle Committee. Ky said "Communists will be shot," including Danang Mayor Nguyen Van Man. Ky criticized soldiers who had participated in the anti-government demonstrations but said punitive measures would not be taken against them "if they stop now."

Dr. Man, 38, an appointee of Gen. Thi, denied that Danang was Communist-controlled. He defied Ky's threat to shoot him and expressed sympathy with the Buddhists' anti-government demonstrations. Man assailed Ky's military government as "too weak and too corrupt to rule."

(Gen. Wallace M. Greene Jr., U.S. Marine Corps commandant, contradicted Ky's charge that Danang was in a state of revolt. Speaking Apr. 3 on ABC-TV's "Issues & Answers" program, Greene said the situation in Danang was "calm" and the demonstrations there were "well-ordered and semi-religious.")

As the government troops were flown to the Danang airbase Apr. 4, troops under Chuan's command had set up machinegun roadblocks across roads leading to the city of Danang to prevent an invasion of the city. A U.S. military spokesman in Saigon disclosed Apr. 5 that the Vietnamese government troops had been flown to the north in 6 U.S. Air Force C-130 transports, piloted by Americans. He said the planes had been requested by the South Vietnamese government.

(The decision to fulfill the Saigon regime's request for the 6 planes was reported Apr. 5 to have been approved by U.S. Amb. Henry Cabot Lodge with the U.S. government's later concurrence. The use of the American planes was regarded as politically risky because it was felt it would heighten anti-U.S. feelings. But U.S. State Department spokesman W. Marshall Wright explained Apr. 5: "The United States cooperates with the South Vietnamese government. One of the fields is transportation. For reasons sufficient to the South Vietnamese government they asked us to provide the planes." A U.S. official in Saigon said: "We are committed to the support of the South Vietnamese government, whether this one or that one, and we move Vietnamese troops almost every day of the week.")

(The U.S.' role in the crisis was attacked Apr. 12 in a telegram sent to Amb. Lodge by the Buddhist-controlled "struggle movement" in Danang and Hué. The statement asserted that the Vietnamese people "strongly protests the long-standing United States policy in Vietnam, whose consequences are likely to bring about a civil war. . . ." The statement assailed the U.S. for having "supported and patronized dictatorial [South Vietnamese] governments, such as the 9-year Ngo Dinh Diem regime and . . . other regimes." The statement accused Washington of "directly protecting" Premier Ky and Chief-of-State Thieu and "giving them means and advice to suppress and wipe out the Vietnamese people.")

Chuan Dismissed as I Corps Chief

Premier Ky Apr. 8 dismissed Maj. Gen. Chuan as I Corps commander. Chuan was replaced by Lt. Gen. Ton Thant Dinh, a former commander of the I Corps' First and 2d Divisions. Dinh had been prominent in the coup that had overthrown Pres. Ngo Dinh Diem in 1963. Chuan had flown to Saigon Apr. 8, reportedly to request the withdrawal of government marines from the Danang airbase.

Dinh assumed his command in Danang Apr. 9 and immediately conferred with Buddhist leaders there and in Hué. The Buddhist leaders in Danang were said to have warned that Buddhists would resist any invasion of Danang by pro-Ky soldiers.

Buddhist Drive for Ky Ouster

The anti-government Buddhist leadership Apr. 9 announced an all-out campaign to topple Ky's military regime. The government Apr. 7 had disavowed a Buddhist claim that the Buddhists and the junta had reached an agreement that day on resolving the political crisis. The Buddhists later boycotted a government-sponsored National Political Congress that opened in Saigon Apr. 12 to prepare for the convening of the constitutional convention.

The new anti-government drive was announced in a statement issued Apr. 9 by the Unified Buddhist Church's Institute of Secular Affairs. It said a central leadership committee had been formed to coordinate the campaign against the military junta. Heretofore, the Buddhist church had disowned the violent anti-government demonstrations by Buddhists. The statement said the Buddhist church had decided "personally to lead its faithful." It said the chances of getting an elected constitutional convention, as demanded by the Buddhists, "have become slimmer." Thich Tam Chau, chairman of the Secular Affairs Institute and one of the 4 signers of the Buddhist communiqué, charged later that the government had not provided sufficient guarantees that Ky's pledge of a constitutional convention in 6 months would be honored. The other signers of the Buddhist statement were Thich Tri Quang, chairman of the church's Institute of Religious Affairs, and

Thich Thien Minh and Thich Ho Giac, co-chairmen of the leadership committee.

A statement issued by the leadership committee Apr. 10 charged that Ky had broken his promise to quickly arrange for the accession of a civilian government. The statement, read by Ho Giac, said: "A civil war that will take tens of thousands of lives and cause the total collapse of national unity may very well take place because of the short-sightedness, irascibility and irresponsibility of the present government. All of our letters asking them [the government] to reaffirm the minimum of things they had promised have been unanswered. We have been brutally betrayed."

The claimed agreement reached by the Buddhists and the government following 4 weeks of private talks had been announced in a communiqué issued Apr. 7 by the Unified Buddhist Church. Its principle points: (a) Civil servants and soldiers who had taken part in demonstrations in the I Corps area and elsewhere would not be punished; (b) persons arrested for demonstrating would be released; (c) the marines Ky had sent to Danang Apr. 4 to reassert government authority there would be withdrawn; (d) Chief-of-State Nguyen Van Thieu would publish a decree pledging the convening of a constitutional convention as soon as possible.

The Buddhist communiqué said the church's Secular Affairs Institute had called on the government to "reassert [the aforementioned points] in official documents." The communiqué urged Buddhists to "temporarily stop all forms of struggle in a spirit of vigilance and discipline" and to "close our ranks while waiting for what the government has promised."

Ky was reported Apr. 8 to have said at a meeting of the junta that he had agreed to only one Buddhist condition: elections in 4-6 months to choose a constitutional convention. Ky was said to have insisted that he had not agreed to the other points cited in the Buddhists' Apr. 7 communiqué.

Plans for a transitional civilian regime were said to have been discussed Apr. 6 by Ky and a delegation of about 20 persons representing Catholics, Protestants and other religious sects and heads of labor unions and professional groups. The Buddhists boycotted the talks. The conferees were said to have agreed on the holding of the national political congress.

The intensity of the public violence, meanwhile, began to abate. Only 2 outbreaks were reported in Saigon Apr. 6 and 7. In the first, students gathered at the Unified Buddhist Church pagoda, which had been ordered closed earlier in the day by Thich Tam Chau to discourage students from congregating there. The youths then marched to Saigon's central market-place, shouting anti-government and anti-American slogans. They attacked the offices of a newspaper that had criticized the student demonstrations and burned 2 motorbicycles dragged from the building. Police dispersed the 200 demonstrators with clubs and tear gas. A mob of 300 youths marched through Saigon's streets Apr. 7 and burned a U.S. military jeep and a motorcycle owned by an American.

Constitutional Assembly Elections Set

The Ky government Apr. 14 approved the holding of national elections for a constituent assembly within 3 to 5 months. The assembly would have the power to transform itself into a legislative body.

The balloting for a constituent assembly was one of 10 recommendations adopted at the conclusion of the National Political Congress Apr. 14. The recommendations constituted an indorsement of Buddhist demands. Chief-of-State Thieu signed a decree scheduling the assembly elections, and in speeches to the congress Apr. 14, Ky and Thieu pledged to respect all its proposals.

The congress' 9 other recommendations: (1) Ky's government should pledge to resign as soon as the constituent assembly was elected; (2) the government should convene within 10 days a body to draft an election law and hold elections; (3) the government should prevent the constituent assembly from being infiltrated by Communists and neutralists; (4) freedom of the press should be established; (5) the government should encourage the growth and development of minor parties; (6) the government should pledge not to punish anti-regime demonstrators and should use political not military solutions to end rebellious conditions in such areas as Danang and Hué; (7) the government should promote the education of the people in democracy and elections; (8) all religious groups and parties should halt anti-government demonstrations; (9) all factions in the country should work for national unity.

Only 92 of the 170 delegates invited had shown up at the start of the 3-day meeting. Among those attending were 20 delegates representing the Roman Catholics, the Hoa Hao and Cao Dai religious sects and Mekong delta Buddhists (who opposed the Unified Buddhist Church), and chairmen of 39 elected provincial and city councils, including the Saigon City Council; 9 other chairmen boycotted the congress. In a speech opening the meeting, Thieu declared that his military government was anxious to relinquish power to a civilian regime "as soon as possible."

The Unified Buddhist Church, which had refused to attend the congress, ended the boycott Apr. 14 when Prof. Tran Quang Thuan, an aide of Buddhist church leader Thich Tri Quang, entered the assembly hall to read a letter from the church leadership. The message said the Buddhists regarded their presence as unnecessary since the congress had adopted all their demands.

Thuan returned to the meeting later in the day and demanded that Ky resign because he allegedly had broken pledges to the Buddhists. Speaking in what he called an unofficial capacity, Thuan warned: If Ky and his government remained in office, "the people will nurture misgivings, fear and suspicions," which "might compel them to continue their protest campaign. If such is the case, either the government would have to repress them or they would succeed in overthrowing it. . . . It would be better, then, that the government give absolutely clear evidence of its goodwill by resigning."

In a speech to the congress, Ky offered to resign if the delegates expressed such a desire. But the delegates opposed Ky's resignation, contending that it could lead to turmoil that the Communists would exploit.

The Unified Buddhist Church Apr. 15 promised to halt anti-government agitation if the Ky regime kept its promise to conduct constituent assembly elections in 3-5 months. According to the statement: "The church deems it unnecessary for the faithful to waste their energy worrying about a government that is only going to last 3-5 months." The statement was issued after a 5-hour meeting of the Buddhist leadership. It was signed by Thich Tam Chau, chairman of the church's Institute of Secular Affairs, and was formally handed to Ky by Dr. Phan Kuang Dan. Dan said after meeting Ky that they had informally agreed to convene a joint committee within 10 days to draw up procedures and rules for elections. The committee's composition: 4 government representatives and 25 representatives of religious groups, political organizations and provincial and urban councils.

Ky was denounced Apr. 15 by Danang Mayor Nguyen Van Man and Lt. Gen. Nguyen Chanh Thi, who had been ousted as I Corps commander. Thi called for continued demonstrations until Ky resigned. Buddhists in Danang and Hué Apr. 16 assailed, as deceptive, the government's pledge to hold elections. 2,000 persons marched in Danang and burned a copy of Thieu's election decree. Student leaders in Hué called the decree "a devious plot by Thieu and Ky to deceive the people" and to enable the junta to "eventually turn the tide against the revolutionary government." More anti-government demonstrations swept Danang and Hué Apr. 17. The protesters denounced the government's election pledge and promised to continue to agitate until Ky and his junta quit.

Thousands of Roman Catholics staged a protest march Apr. 17 in Bienhoa, 15 miles north of Saigon. They called on the government to quell Buddhist rioters. Speakers at the rally opposed a coalition government that would include Communists or a national assembly including Communist or pro-Communist elements.

Thich Tri Quang toured the northern provinces Apr. 18 to urge the Buddhists there to cease their agitation and to accept the junta's pledge to hold elections. Tri Quang addressed huge gatherings in Danang, Hué and Hoian. He warned that Buddhist "disturbances in Saigon or elsewhere" would encourage Thieu to cancel his election decree and to charge a "plot." Tri Quang suggested that the Buddhists' tactic should be not to "protest against Thieu and Ky and force them to withdraw" but "to maintain them in such a way that they cannot take advantage of their positions of power to trouble the national assembly by creating chaos . . . in order to break their promise of convening a national assembly." Tri Quang assailed U.S. policy in South Vietnam. He said: "Any nation, when coming into another nation to help or rule it—through its aid —the first thing and the last thing it will try to do is to annihilate the right of the local people to control their government." South Vietnam was "oppressed by 2 pressures—the Communists and the Americans. In the face of such monopolization and control, we must regain our right of self-determination, the right of electing a national assembly."

(The Johnson Administration Apr. 8 had openly expressed preference for Buddhist leader Thich Tam Chau over his rival Tri Quang. The U.S. government's position was stated by Asst. State Secy. [for Far Eastern affairs] William P. Bundy on the NBC-TV program "Today," and his statement was distributed later by the State Department. Bundy said: "One [group] is, perhaps the more moderate one, which wants to get ahead with the constitution and the rest; that's Tam Chau. The other [group], which is associated and, I think led by Tri Quang, wants to accelerate the timetable very, very much indeed, and wants to see procedures established for a constitution and elections that would be dominated by them." Bundy called the anti-U.S. demonstrations in South Vietnam "understandable and, indeed, healthy," because the South Vietnamese "need to and should stand on their own feet."

(State Undersecy. George W. Ball said on the CBS-TV "Face the Nation" program Apr. 10 that the South Vietnamese government crisis was "not a conflict between those who want to give up and turn the country over to the Viet Cong and the Communists. It is simply a conflict as to the form of government which is best for the South Vietnamese people in order that they may continue the fight and resist the aggression from the north." Declining to indorse Premier Ky, Ball asserted that the U.S. supported "the people of South Vietnam, whatever form of government they happen to choose." Ball insisted that the U.S. was "not trying to dictate who should be in charge of that government." He denied that Pres. Johnson's meeting with Ky in Honolulu constituted strong personal support for the South Vietnamese leader.

"What the United States did in Honolulu," Ball said, "was to give its support to the government of South Vietnam, which is at the moment a government in which Prime Min. Ky is the head.")

An NLF broadcast denounced the National Political Congress as "the beginning of the farce of holding dishonest general elections to maintain the dictatorial and country-selling regime." A statement issued Apr. 23 by the NLF's Saigon district committee urged capital residents to "resolutely unmask and smash all political maneuvers of the enemy."

The Rev. Hoang Quynh, leader of South Vietnam's Roman Catholics, warned in an interview in Saigon May 3 against premature elections. Estimating that the Ky government controlled only 10% of the country's territory, Quynh predicted that if an election were held "too soon," the government could not expect to win most of the votes in those areas. Quynh said: "We Catholics have never asked for elections because we know they would be dangerous for anti-Communist elements. We have asked for return to civilian government but with the help of the generals and not through premature elections." Charging that "the Buddhists already control the government," Quynh said the Ky government had made so many concessions to the Unified Buddhist Church that it must "now give us [non-Buddhist groups] a chance to express our aspirations, too."

Election Law Drafting Starts

A 32-member committee created to draft a South Vietnamese election law started meeting in Saigon May 5, and the Buddhist delegation almost immediately extracted concessions from the Ky regime. The committee's task was to draft procedures for nationwide balloting for the constituent assembly. The committee's election draft law was to be submitted to a 100-delegation commission. The commission's composition was to be similar to the election committee's—provincial and municipal council officials, representatives of the Buddhist, Roman Catholic, Hoa Hao and Cao Dai religious sects, jurists and politicians.

As the committee meeting opened, a Buddhist delegate, **Prof. Tran Quang Thuan,** supported by other delegates, demanded that the government (a) issue a decree granting the committee official legal status and delineating its powers and responsibilities, (b) accept in advance the election rules drawn up by the committee and the commission and (c) make public the names of the committee's members. Thuan (an aide of Thich Tri Quang) and other committee members threatened to walk out of the meeting unless their demands were met. Interior Min. Tran Minh Tiet, who represented the government at the meeting, insisted that the committee was merely an "advisory board" and that the government did not feel bound to indorse all its decisions. The committee then adjourned to give Tiet time to consult the government.

The government acceded to most of the committee's demands. At the next meeting, May 6, Tiet read a decree, signed by Ky, formally granting the committee official status, assigning to it "the task of preparing the draft of a decree law governing the election of a constituent assembly" and listing the names of the committee members. Ky, however, rejected the demand that his regime agree to promulgate as law any electoral rules drawn up by the committee or the commission.

Ky declared May 7 that he had no intention of resigning following the election of the constituent assembly. Speaking at a news conference at the Binthuy Air Base, Ky said he "expect[ed] to stay in power for at least another year, perhaps until the middle of next year." According to Ky's conception of the steps that would be required to bring about a civilian regime, the election of the assembly (which he said would take place in September or October) would be followed by balloting for a legislative assembly, and the latter body would appoint the new government. The legislative assembly election, Ky said, would not be conducted until the middle of 1967, and his government would remain in office until then. When asked whether the Buddhists and others would accept the continuance of the military government until 1967, Ky said the political dissidents had "asked to have an organization to draft the constitution, that's all. And we satisfy all these just demands." Ky warned that he and the army would fight any "neutralist or Communist" government that emerged from the election. But he expressed confidence "that the majority of Vietnamese are anti-Communist. I am sure that no such government will be elected."

Thich Thien Minh, co-chairman of the leadership committee of the Unified Buddhist Church's Institute of Religious Affairs, warned in Danang May 8 that Buddhists would launch a strong protest movement if the government did not hold elections in the fall as promised. Thien Minh had accused the government May 5 of acting in bad faith.

Ky's Troops Seize Danang

Danang, in a state of virtual rebellion since Ky's ouster of Gen. Thi, was seized by 1,500 government troops May 15 after an all-day battle with I Corps soldiers who sided with dissident Buddhists. At least 10 persons were killed and 12 wounded, including some civilians. The government explained that the troops had been sent to Danang to help "the armed forces and the population" in an alleged uprising against the Buddhist movement. Chief-of-State Nguyen Van Thieu said in a Saigon broadcast that the marines had been sent to Danang "to bring about security and stability" necessary for national elections. Thieu charged that Communists had infiltrated "several groups and movements" in Danang.

The surprise takeover was begun when Premier Ky ordered 1,000 marines flown to the Danang airbase from Saigon. The marines, later reinforced by 500 paratroopers and rangers, moved into the city and seized I Corps headquarters, civilian and military police stations, the radio station and other key installations. Rebel resistance collapsed after sporadic fighting. But some rebel troops of the South Vietnamese First Army Division took refuge in and around the city's 3 Buddhist pagodas and refused to surrender. Ky dismissed Lt. Gen. Ton That Dinh as I Corps commander and replaced him with Maj. Gen. Huynh Van Cao. (Dinh, whose loyalty to the Ky regime had been in doubt, was granted asylum in the home of Lt. Gen. Lewis W. Walt, commander of the U.S. 3d Marine Amphibious Force, quartered in Danang.)

(U.S. military authorities were said to have been taken completely by surprise by the government operation. American military advisers had flown with the government troops to Danang and were told the planes were on their way to a mission in the north. When the Americans, on arriving at Danang, learned the truth, they detached themselves temporarily from the Vietnamese force and reported to the U.S. base at Danang. American troops in the base were restricted to quarters.)

The Unified Buddhist Church, in a communiqué issued in Saigon May 15, denounced Ky's action in Danang as an "act of treachery" that would "surely lead to civil war." Recalling that the Buddhists had "shown goodwill" by agreeing with Ky in April to call off anti-government demonstrations, the church communiqué charged that "plots to sabotage the [proposed] constituent assembly have been carried out with a view to sowing division among the population."

Danang Buddhists warned May 16 that 3 monks would burn themselves to death if pro-Ky troops who surrounded their pagoda attacked it. Facilities were set up in the pagoda's courtyard to prepare for the suicides. Thich Minh Chieu, 35, senior Buddhist monk in Danang, said: "In the end the responsibility for this is with the Americans because the government used all the American aid and American weapons to attack the people."

Heavy fighting broke out again in Danang May 20 as government troops began tightening the ring around remaining rebel troops. 75 rebel soldiers and 40 Buddhist civilians were captured when the Tan Ninh pagoda fell May 21. Rebel troops in other parts of the city gradually retreated into the Tinh Hoi pagoda and its compound under the pressure of tank-aided pro-Ky troops. The rebels, surrounded in the pagoda by government troops and armor, yielded to a surrender ultimatum May 23. The main rebel force of about 300 soldiers filed out of the pagoda and surrendered almost 1,000 weapons. U.S. forces accepted the surrender of 200 rebel troops who had taken over an ammunition dump outside Danang and threatened to blow it up if attacked. Another 200 rebels were taken prisoner at the Pho Da pagoda. Among them was Danang Mayor Nguyen Van Man. More than 75 persons had been killed and 500 wounded, many of them civilians and noncombatants, before the fighting ended. (Man had been replaced as mayor May 22 by Lt. Col. Le Chi Cuong, 36, a Saigon headquarters commander.) 2 rebel leaders escaped: Thich Minh Chieu and Maj. Tran Huu Trai, the Tinh Hoi military commander. Lt. Col. Dam Quang Yeu and Maj. Ton That Tuong surrendered May 25. Yeu, former commander of the Quangnam Special Sector at Hoian, had attempted the previous week to send a relief force to the rebels holding out in the 3 pagodas in Danang. Tuong, an ordinance officer, had played a prominent role in the unsuccessful defense of Danang"s Tinh Hoi pagoda and had been the main organizer of anti-government demonstrations and strikes in Danang.

(Maj. Gen. Hoang Xuan Lam, ex-2d Division commander, was installed in Danang May 31 as I Corps commander.)

At a meeting of a National People's & Armed Forces Political Congress in Saigon May 24, Chief-of-State Thieu explained that the army had acted because "moderate solutions no longer work. It is unacceptable to have an army within an army, a government within a government and a state within a state." Thieu said he favored expanding the military directorate by ⅓ with civilian members. Ky approved the idea. The congress had been called by the junta and was attended by several hundred army officers and representatives of the Roman Catholics, Mekong delta Buddhists and other factions. U.S. Amb. Lodge also was present.

U.S. officials in Saigon had sought to mediate between the government and the Buddhists. A State Department statement May 15 said American representatives in Saigon had been instructed by the Johnson Administration "to make every effort to bring the South Vietnamese leaders together to resolve their differences." U.S. Deputy Amb. William J. Porter conferred in Saigon with Ky, Thieu and at least 2 prominent Buddhist leaders. In his talks with Ky May 16, Porter was said to have cautioned the premier to "burn no bridges" to the Buddhists and to do nothing to hinder the forthcoming elections.

The U.S. was reported to have tried to arrange a meeting between Ky and Gen. Thi; at that time both refused to meet. Ky and Thi finally met in Chulai May 27. After the meeting, Thi said in an interview that he hoped to reach agreement with Ky's regime. Thi indicated that he no longer entertained any hope of overthrowing the military junta. Ky said after the meeting: "Thi told me he is still my best friend. He told me he is not against me."

Buddhist leaders and South Vietnamese government officials conferred in Saigon May 31 in an attempt to resolve the 2½-month-old crisis. Each delegation was made up of 6 representatives. Among those attending the 2-hour meeting were Ky, Thieu, Thich Tam Chau and Thich Thien Minh, leader of the Buddhist youth movement. In an address to about 600 Buddhist followers after the meeting, Thien Minh said that his group had stressed "that the only solution . . . is that Generals Nguyen Van Thieu and Nguyen Cao Ky resign." Thien Minh said he had rejected suggestions that the ruling military directorate and government be reorganized. Thien Minh insisted that the elections be held for a constituent assembly. Despite the meeting, Thien Minh said, "everything is still hanging in the air." Tam Chau said the meeting had been held at the Buddhists' request.

Buddhists Renew Immolations

At least 10 Buddhists committed suicide by fire May 29-June 17 in protest against the continuation of the Ky government in power and against U.S. refusal to support the Buddhists. Similar suicides by fire had taken place in 1963 during the Buddhist campaign against the late Ngo Dinh Diem.

The wave of self-immolations began May 29 with the deaths of 2 women. One of the victims—Ho Thi Thieu, 58—doused herself with gasoline and set herself afire on the grounds of the Unified Buddhist Church headquarters in Saigon. She had informed the Buddhist Council May 29 that she would make the sacrifice. The 2d suicide was that of a nun, Thanh Quang, 55, who set herself afire in front of a pagoda in Hué. 2 more Buddhist immolations occurred May 30: a monk, Thich Quang Thien, 30, burned himself to death in the resort town of Dalat; a girl committed suicide by fire outside the headquarters of the Buddhist Church's Institute of Secular Affairs in Saigon. Another Buddhist girl, Nguyen

Thi Van, 17, set herself ablaze on a street in Hué May 31. She died several hours later. The bodies of the 2 Saigon suicides were placed in a chapel. A banner nearby read: "Sacrifice and sacrifice much more in order to warn the irresponsible and heartless people about the crimes of the Americans and the Thieu-Ky lackeys."

A communiqué issued May 31 by Thich Tam Chau appealed to all Buddhists "to stop immediately their intentions to immolate themselves by fire or to indulge in self-destruction." Tam Chau insisted that Ky and Chief-of-State Nguyen Van Thieu hand over power to an interim government. He warned that "if our aspirations are not satisfied it would be very difficult to avoid all forms of struggle in a spirit of non-violence."

Despite the church appeal for an end to immolations, 4 Buddhists burned themselves to death June 3-4. The victims were 3 nuns—one in Danang June 3 and 2 others in Saigon and Nhatrang June 4—and a novice monk 14 or 15 years old who died June 4 in Quangtri, 47 miles northwest of Hué. Dao Thi Tuyet, 18, a Buddhist girl, burned herself to death in Saigon June 17.

Saigon & Hué Demonstrators Denounce Ky

Saigon police and troops used bayonets and tear gas in breaking up demonstrations by thousands of Buddhists May 20-23. The demonstrators denounced the seizure of Danang and demanded an immediate return to civilian rule. A sit-down hunger strike was staged in the Buddhists' main pagoda (Vien Hoa Dao) compounds in Saigon May 21. Thousands of Buddhist monks and nuns and their followers took part in the one-day demonstration.

Troops used tear gas to disperse about 2,000 Buddhist monks, nuns and youths who attempted to stage anti-U.S. and anti-government demonstrations in Saigon May 25. Rioting anti-American Buddhist students in Hué sacked and burned the U.S. cultural center and library in the city May 26 and the U.S. consulate June 1. Both buildings were empty at the time. Student leaders explained they had marched on the U.S. cultural center in protest against American support of Ky and because of Pres. Johnson's failure to respond to a protest letter sent to him by the students May 25.

Following the burning of the consulate, Lt. Col. Phan Van Khoa, mayor of Hué, ordered troops into the city to restore order. He acted with the approval of Gen. Thi, deposed I Corps commander. Criticizing Thich Tri Quang's leadership of the anti-government campaign, Thi said the monk "should go back to Saigon if he cannot control the students as it now seems." Buddhist students yielded to Khoa's demands that they relinquish control of the Hué radio station.

Government troops had hurled tear-gas grenades to disperse about 2,000 Buddhist monks, nuns and youths who attempted to stage anti-U.S. and anti-government demonstrations in Saigon May 25. Thich Thien Minh had called for the demonstration to "liberate" the Unified Buddhist Church's compound, ringed by barbed wire barricades and troops for the previous 2 days. A statement issued by Thich Phap Tri, vice chairman of the Secular Affairs Institute, charged the U.S. with "plotting with Generals Thieu and Ky to bring this beloved country to total collapse." Ky ordered the removal of the barriers around the compound and thus made possible a rally of 6,000-8,000 persons there May 27. Addressing the crowd, Thich Man Giac, a professor at the Van Hanh Buddhist University, claimed that more than 600 Buddhists had been killed and 1,000 wounded in the fighting in Danang. Thich Man Giac criticized the U.S. position in the crisis by asserting: "Those who shoot the people are responsible, but those who supply the guns must bear much more responsibility." After the rally, about 2,000-3,000 demonstrators attempted to march through the streets of Saigon but were prevented by a battalion of Vietnamese marines that hurled tear-gas grenades and fired into the air.

At a news conference in Hué May 29, Thich Tri Quang charged that Pres. Johnson was to blame for the slaying of Buddhists by Vietnamese troops. He appealed to the President to support the Buddhists in their campaign to oust Ky. Tri Quang warned there would be Buddhist suicides if Mr. Johnson did not extend such support. Tri Quang claimed he spoke for a majority of the South Vietnamese people. He appealed to Buddhists and Americans to concentrate the struggle against the Viet Cong under a democratically elected government.

Ky Sends Troops to Hué

A South Vietnamese First Division force of 650 soldiers and tanks moved into Hué June 2, ostensibly to reassert central government control of the Buddhist stronghold. However, the troops, whose loyalty to the Saigon regime had been questionable, made no effort to crack down on the Hué dissidents. By June 6 the number of South Vietnamese troops in Hué totaled 4,000 men. Ky June 1 had ordered the mayor, Lt. Col. Khoa, to use force to repress Buddhist-led anti-government violence in the city. In the directive Ky warned that if national guardsmen and militiamen in the area would not be used, then First Division troops in neighboring Quangtri Province would be brought in. In a calculated act of anti-government defiance, Buddhists placed hundreds of makeshift altars in the streets of Hué June 5 and 6, blocking traffic. Similar tactics in protest against the Ky government were employed by militant Buddhists in Quinhon and Danang. Troops made no move to clear the streets of the altars.

Thich Tri Quang warned at a news conference in Hué June 3 that his militant followers would not participate in the scheduled Sept. 11 constituent assembly elections if they were conducted by the Ky regime. Buddhists, Tri Quang asserted, would never accept elections organized "by the bloody hand of those who have killed people in Danang." Reiterating his anti-U.S. position, Tri Quang said he "hate[d] the Americans who have supported Thieu and Ky in doing all that killing." Thieu and Ky "must resign," he declared.

Junta Enlarged to Include Civilians

South Vietnam's ruling military National Leadership Committee of 10 generals was expanded June 6 to include 10 civilians. The plan for enlargement of the junta had been worked out in negotiations May 31-June 1 with the Unified Buddhist Church. But the church remained unsatisfied because its basic demand remained unfulfilled—the immediate resignations of Premier Ky and Chief-of-State Thieu. Church officials had refused to serve on the committee despite the negotiations. The body's civilian representatives included 2 nominal lay Buddhists, 2 members each of the Cao Dai and Hoa Hao sects and a Roman Catholic.

Among the new appointees: Foreign Min. Tran Van Do; Pham Huu Chuong (a Buddhist), a former member of the civilian advisory High National Council, dissolved in 1964; Phan Khoang, a member of the anti-Buddhist Vietnamese Kuomingtang (nationalist party); Nguyen Luu Vien, deputy premier in the regime of Premier Tran Van Huong (overthrown in 1964).

The negotiations had been carried out by Ky and Thieu for the junta and Thich Tam Chau for the Buddhists. Tam Chau, in a statement made June 2, had asserted that Ky and Thieu had promised to step down after the junta's expansion. Tam Chau, who called on all Buddhists to suspend their demonstrations for 4 days in view of the accord, came under attack from Buddhist militants for his settlement with the Ky group. In a move to place the Buddhists' anti-government drive under moderate influence, Tam Chau announced June 7 the dissolution of the Struggle Leadership Committee, which had been headed by Thich Thien Minh. The body was replaced by the Committee for the Defense of Buddhism and was to be under Tam Chau's control. Tam Chau appealed for an end to Buddhist suicides and street demonstrations. He again demanded the immediate resignation of Ky and Thieu. Tam Chau warned that if the 2 leaders did not step down he would order a "noncooperation campaign" against the government. Tam Chau emphasized that as a Buddhist he was strongly anti-Communist. He said that leaders of any interim government that replaced Ky "must be strongly anti-Viet Cong."

Thieu June 16 signed a decree creating a People's Armed Forces Council. The council, to consist of 60 civilians and 20 military men, would advise the government on "political, economic, cultural and social matters." The body could be dissolved or any of its members dismissed by the National Leadership Committee.

Troops Quell Saigon Riots

Government troops put down anti-government riots in Saigon June 15. In one part of the city police turned off electricity in the area around the Buddhists' Secular Affairs Institute in an effort to disperse thousands of demonstrators who had gathered there. Several U.S. and British correspondents and news photographers were beaten and mauled by police while covering the day's incidents.

About 3,000 demonstrators, led by Buddhist monks, had rioted in Saigon June 14. The mobs burned a U.S. military jeep and 2 other vehicles and escaped with 2 U.S. submachine-guns. Police and troops, using tear gas, drove the demonstrators back to the Secular Affairs Institute and virtually laid siege to the building. In line with a government directive issued June 4, many of the youthful demonstrators were rounded up and drafted into army service.

In another crackdown on anti-government practices, troops began to remove Buddhist altars from Saigon's streets June 16. Nguyen Ngoc Dai, 22, a Buddhist nun, reportedly was shot and seriously wounded June 16 in Cholon, a Saigon suburb, by police who were removing altars from the street in front of her nunnery. The altars had been set up at the orders of Thich Tri Quang, who remained in Hué.

Thich Tam Chau June 17 reiterated his opposition to Buddhist street demonstrations. In a letter to the Secular Affairs Institute's governing council, Tam Chau assailed the street riots as contrary to the Buddhist "spirit of compromise and non-violence." Asserting that Buddhist leaders should countermand Tri Quang's orders to place altars in the streets, Tam Chau said he was "not for bringing Buddha into the streets." While Tam Chau continued to plead for moderation, other Buddhist leaders June 17 issued an appeal for a 3-day nationwide general strike against the junta.

A policeman was shot and killed with his own gun following an attack by a mob of 150 persons in Saigon June 18. Another policeman was beaten and dragged into the Secular Affairs Institute compound. Police immediately imposed a blockade around the building, sealing off the entrances and placing barbed wire around the structure. An estimated 500-600 persons, including monks and nuns, were in the compound, along with 200 children in a Buddhist orphanage. In negotiations June 19 with Lt. Col. Nguyen Van Luan, Saigon police chief, the Buddhists were told that the blockade would be lifted if the alleged killer of the policeman were turned over to authorities. The monks refused, and the blockade continued.

Premier Ky called on Tam Chau June 21 to "stop all actions against the government." In a letter to the Buddhist leader broadcast over Saigon radio, Ky explained that the junta's military seizure of the Buddhist stronghold of Danang in May had not been "aim[ed] at any objective other than coping with a minority of undisciplined military men and civil servants . . . who were taking part in subversive activities in Danang." The government's actions, Ky insisted, had not been aimed "at repressing Buddhism." Ky promised government compensation to families of persons killed in the Danang fighting and payment for damaged pagodas in the city.

In reply to Ky, Tam Chau said the government could bring about a reconciliation with the Buddhists if it: (a) assured the safety of all Buddhist leaders, including Tri Quang; (b) lifted the blockade of the Secular Affairs Institute; (c) released all persons arrested since March (the start of the current crisis) on political charges; (d) compensated victims of the Danang fighting and repaired damaged pagodas.

A South Vietnamese force of 70 Rangers and 100 policemen stormed into the Secular Affairs Institute building without opposition June 23 and seized Ngo Van Bay, 19, the alleged slayer of the policeman. About 100 monks and nuns and 30-40 of the 150 laymen in the pagoda were detained but later released. Those who remained in custody included youths who had participated in street violence the previous week.

About 15,000 Roman Catholics had staged a rally in Saigon June 12 in support of the government. A declaration read by the Rev. Tran Du, secretary general of the Catholic Citizens Bloc, a political action group, called Buddhist leaders Communist "stooges." Du described the Buddhist-inspired unrest as the "riots and disorders produced intentionally or unintentionally by a violent minority duped and ensnared by the Communists during some past months."

Hué Resistance Crushed

Troops and combat police put down all anti-government resistance in Buddhist-held Hué by June 19. Militant Buddhist leader Tri Quang, seized in a Hué hospital, where he had been taken after beginning a fast June 8, was placed under virtual arrest June 20 and later flown to Saigon. Premier Ky remarked confidently June 18 that his campaign to end the country's internal unrest was "all over. We are over the hump."

A battalion of 500 paratroopers had arrived in Hué June 16 to reinforce 450 combat police sent there June 10. In their first action, the soldiers and police removed from the streets the hundreds of Buddhist altars that had tied up traffic for days. The troops and police then began a methodical sweep of the city, driving before them armed dissidents, who offered little resistance. 500 more paratroopers were sent to Hué June 17, and the city was declared under martial law. The government force, increased to about 3,000 men, achieved complete control of Hué June 19, when it took possession of the old walled section of the city, known as the Citadel. About 500-600 dissident First Division troops who reportedly had been hiding there apparently had fled. (Brig. Gen. Pham Xuan Nhuan, a pro-Buddhist, was dismissed June 19 as commander of the First Division and replaced by Col. Ngo Quang Truong, the division's deputy commander.)

Ky visited Hué June 25 and received a pledge of loyalty from the I Corps commander and his men. Pleading for unity, Ky said that "after 2 months of turmoil, I ask everybody to forgive one another and forget the misunderstandings of the past."

The only remaining anti-government Buddhist stronghold in northern South Vietnam—Quangtri—had been taken over June 22 by about 300 pro-government marines, paratroopers and policemen. The force had been airlifted from Hué, where it had been employed in the "pacification" of dissidents during the previous 10 days. The troops removed Buddhist altars from Quangtri's streets, and the province chief and the police director were dismissed for failing to take sterner measures against the dissidents.

Election Date Set

Premier Ky June 20 signed a decree setting Sept. 11 as the date for the election of the constituent assembly—to be known as the National Assembly. The decree, made public June 24, provided that the charter could be written and approved by a simple assembly majority. The draft constitution was subject to further action by the ruling 20-member civilian-military National Leadership Committee (which had met for the first time June 8 since its expansion June 6). If the committee rejected the draft or any part of it, the assembly could override the veto by a ⅔ majority vote. The assembly would be dissolved when the committee promulgated the constitution, *i.e.*, within 30 days after presentation of the final draft. The committee then would establish the machinery of government within 3-6 months as stipulated by the charter. One of the provisions called for the election of a legislative assembly, which would appoint a civilian regime to replace Ky's military government. The current timetable would permit Ky to remain in power until the middle of 1967.

The original election plan, submitted to the junta June 5 by the civilian electoral commission, which had been deliberating since May 5, had provided for granting legislative powers to the National Assembly. But the junta rejected this scheme as one means of preventing the dissident Unified Buddhist Church from using the National Assembly to oust the Ky government.

An organization opposing the assembly elections—the All-Religions Citizens' Group—was created in Saigon July 7. The organization was formed by Roman Catholic and Buddhist elements and followers of the Cao Dai and Hoa Hao religious sects. Its chairman was the Rev. Hoang Quynh, a Catholic priest who had been at odds with the Roman Catholic hierarchy. The group's vice chairman was Thich Phap Tri, vice chairman of the Unified Buddhist Church's political arm, the Secular Affairs Institute. Other prominent members of the group included ex-Interior Min. Nguyen Hoa Hiep and Vietnamese Socialist Party Chrmn. Phan Ba Cam.

The Citizens' Group said in a policy statement that it would boycott the Sept. 11 elections because the electoral laws were "unfair" and "anti-democratic." The statement assailed the Ky regime for establishing "a dictatorial rule . . . favoring nepotism, bringing about inflation . . . impoverishing the people."

The NLF also called for a boycott of the elections. In an appeal broadcast over its clandestine Liberation Radio, the NLF urged the South Vietnamese people to "thoroughly boy-cott the election trick of the United States and the Thieu-Ky henchmen." The NLF charged that the Ky government had planned the election to "cheat public opinion at home and abroad." The proposed constituent assembly, the broadcast asserted, was "a tool to promote the aggression and country-selling policy of the U.S. imperialists and their running dogs."

Ky No Presidential Candidate

In an interview in Saigon July 31, Premier Ky said he would not be a candidate for president in elections for a civilian government, which, he suggested, would be held in Feb. 1967. Ky who still retained command of the South Vietnamese air force, said he wished to "be in the front lines again instead of the rear lines." Ky said Aug. 2 that he would resign from politics to devote all his time to military affairs after a civilian government was established in Saigon. Ky's office announced that this would be in Nov. 1967.

Buddhists Suspend Protests

Leading monks of the Unified Buddhist Church an-nounced in a communiqué after a meeting in Saigon July 3 that their campaign against the Ky government was "being suspended for 2 weeks to permit the government to show goodwill toward our religion." In apparent reference to the division within the Buddhist movement, the statement called for a "welding of the ranks" of the church.

Thich Tam Chau took a 2-month sick leave July 13 as chairman of the church's Secular Affairs Institute. Tam Chau was said to have received an ultimatum from the Buddhist High Council earlier in the week demanding that he "take a positive stand" or resign his post. The council July 23 appointed

Thich Thien Hoa, a militant monk, as acting chairman of the Secular Affairs Institute. In his first communiqué as acting chairman, Thien Hoa barred any more human-torch suicides. In an interview July 28, Thien Hoa conceded that the "dictatorial" Ky regime's "tremendously strong measures" had "shattered" the Buddhist struggle movement. But he insisted that his followers would continue to oppose the Saigon government. Thien Hoa assailed the forthcoming constituent assembly elections as a plot by the Ky regime to continue in power. The Buddhist leader contended that the U.S.' "mistaken policy" had benefited only Vietnamese "individuals and cliques," not the people.

(Thien Hoa Aug. 6 had appealed for international aid to halt what he called religious persecution of the South Vietnamese people by Ky's government. Thien Hoa's plea was addressed to UN Secy. Gen. U Thant, the UN Human Rights Commission, Buddhist headquarters in Ceylon and Thailand and to all foreign ambassadors in Saigon. The statement blamed the U.S. for South Vietnam's internal problems. In a later interview, Thien Hoa said the proposed constituent assembly would result in a dictatorship and the body would be dominated by the U.S.)

Dissident Generals Convicted

A Saigon military tribunal convicted 5 generals July 9 on charges of participating in the Buddhist-led campaign against the government. The military court was made up of 20 generals, including Premier Ky and Chief-of-State Thieu. All 5 generals were dismissed from the army and sentenced to 60 days' detention. 4 were placed under house arrest; the other 2 —Lt. Gen. Nguyen Chanh Thi and Lt. Gen. Ton That Dinh —were originally ordered to serve their detention terms in prison. The 3 other generals disciplined were Brig. Gen. Nguyen Van Chuan, Maj. Gen. Huynh Van Cao and Brig. Gen. Phan Xuan Nhuan. All of the generals, with the exception of Dinh, were permitted to retire with full pensions. Dinh, 37, received a dishonorable discharge. Thi's prison sentence was revoked July 31, and he was permitted to leave for the U.S. to visit his 2 sons at school in Lynchburg, Va. and to get medical treatment.

Constitutional Assembly Elected

South Vietnam's voters went to the polls Sept. 11 and elected a 117-member Constituent Assembly that was to draft a new constitution and pave the way for a restoration of civilian government in 1967. Government officials reported Sept. 12 that 80.8% of the 5,289,652 registered voters had cast ballots. About 2½ million potential voters did not vote because they lived in Viet Cong-controlled areas.

The Viet Cong had sought to disrupt the elections by terrorist attacks against civilians and government installations. Guerrilla bands killed and wounded scores of persons, attacked polling places and blew up bridges and railroad tracks and trains. Communist terrorists killed 19 soldiers and civilians and wounded 120 others in attacks on election day alone.

The 117 assembly seats were contested by 568 candidates. 735 had filed in June, but their number was reduced by withdrawals and by the government's screening committee. 59 candidates had been disqualified.

(The new assembly convened its first session in Saigon Sept. 27.)

The Unified Buddhist Church had urged its followers Aug. 16 to boycott the elections. A communiqué signed by Thich Thien Hoa charged that the balloting was a pretext to enable Premier Ky's government "to form a dictatorial regime to serve foreign interests." The church statement instead called for a new transitional government to establish new election rules. Thien Hoa had issued an appeal to Buddhist followers Sept. 6 to start a 3-day hunger strike Sept. 8 in protest against "these unpopular and manipulated elections." Asserting that the U.S. had done more harm than good in South Vietnam, Thien Hoa said South Vietnam was in the grip of "economic collapse" and "general moral decadence."

The Viet Cong terror drive was centered largely in and around Saigon. The attacks were preceded by a Viet Cong broadcast warning that guerrilla forces were "determined to frustrate" the elections. Another Viet Cong broadcast had said: "The so-called candidates must withdraw immediately. Those who deliberately assist the U.S.-Thieu-Ky clique will not be insured as far as their lives are concerned." The launching of the terrorist attacks coincided with the start of the election campaign Aug. 26. The worst incident that day occurred in Vinhlong Province (62 miles southwest of Saigon), where a guerrilla mine blew up a bus. 15 persons were killed and 10 wounded. 10 of the dead and 9 of the wounded were South Vietnamese army recruits; the others were civilians. Among other incidents Aug. 26: Guerrillas broke into a hamlet near Hué and killed a civilian and 2 officials—a pro-government village chief and a village council representative; 3 South Vietnamese national policemen were slain by Viet Cong fire (reportedly from a speeding car carrying 6 terrorists) in the Saigon suburb of Cholon; 3 South Vietnamese marines and 3 civilians were wounded. A force of about 30 guerrillas killed a policeman and 2 civilians in a 15-minute gun battle near Saigon Aug. 27. 3 civilians and 2 policemen were wounded. A South Vietnamese government spokesman said several persons were killed and wounded Aug. 27 when a jeep struck a mine about 66 miles southwest of Saigon. A series of Viet Cong mine explosions and hand grenade attacks in and around Saigon Aug. 31 and Sept. 2 claimed the lives of at least 15 persons. 12 of the victims—8 civilians and 4 government militiamen—were killed Sept. 2 when a bus ran over a mine about 24 miles east of Saigon. 6 civilians and 4 militiamen were wounded. U.S. and South Vietnamese authorities reported Sept. 8 that 13 persons had been killed and 34 wounded in 6 Viet Cong terror acts in the previous 24 hours. The town of Binhchanh, 14 miles south of Saigon, was shelled by Viet Cong mortars Sept. 10; 2 persons were killed. On election day Sept. 11, 19 soldiers and civilians were killed and 120 wounded in widespread terrorist attacks.

Moderate and Militant Buddhists Split

A meeting of officials of the Unified Buddhist Church in Saigon Oct. 21–22 emphasized the split between the church's moderate and militant factions. The meeting had been called by moderate Thich Tam Chau, who had resumed his position as head of the church's Institute of Secular Affairs. In convening the session, Tam Chau sought to reassert his control over the institute, which had been challenged by the militants.

Thich Tri Quang and Thich Thien Hoa boycotted the talks but
sent militant supporters to oppose Tam Chau. The militants
accused Tam Chau of "treason" in his handling of the Buddhists' anti-government campaign during the spring.

About 100 militant Buddhists held a meeting of their own
in the An Quang Pagoda Oct. 23 and elected Thien Hoa as
head of the Institute of Secular Affairs. Thien Hoa and Tam
Chau each insisted Oct. 24 that he was the legal head of the
institute. Thien Hoa asserted that Tam Chau was "protected
by government security agents." He called the Buddhist
church split "irreparable." Thien Hoa scored U.S. support of
the Ky government and assailed the American bombing of
"innocent people" as helping the Communists.

Assembly Drafts Articles of Constitution

The Constituent Assembly met Nov. 30–Dec. 22 and drew
up a series of draft articles for a new constitution.

Among major proposals acted on:

Nov. 30—The assembly, by 75–8 vote, adopted a resolution prohibit-
ing soldiers on active duty from holding public office or belonging to
political parties.

Dec. 15—The assembly approved, by 107–0 vote (5 abstentions), a
proposal for the future civil regime to be headed by a popularly elected
president. The assembly later approved a proposal empowering the
president, rather than the legislature, to appoint a premier. Under the
plan, the legislature would have the authority to remove cabinet members by majority vote and premiers by ⅔ vote.

Dec. 20—The assembly approved the election of all local officials in
hamlets and villages but rejected the proposed election of province
chiefs and mayors of South Vietnam's 6 major cities: Saigon, Hué,
Danang, Camranh, Dalat and Vungtau. Currently only chiefs of hamlets were elected. The central government appointed village chiefs,
mayors and province chiefs.

Dec. 21—The assembly approved by 87–14 vote the establishment
of a bicameral legislature—a senate and house of representatives.

Dec. 22—The assembly approved in principle the creation of an
independent judiciary.

(Ex-Chief-of-State Phan Khac Suu, 66, had been elected
president of the assembly Oct. 26. He received 66 votes to 44
for his rival, Tran Dien.)

A message from Chief-of-State Thieu, read to the assembly Dec. 27, rejected deputies' demands for the abolition of
government veto power over assembly decisions. (Article 20,

under which the assembly operated, permitted the deputies to override a government veto by ⅔ vote.) The message also opposed an assembly request that the Ky government resign after the promulgation of the constitution and that the assembly be permitted to oversee the 1967 general elections.

Political Concessions to Montagnards

The South Vietnamese government was reported Oct. 8 to have tentatively agreed to the political demands of dissident *montagnard* tribesmen in the Central Highlands. As a result of Saigon's concessions, 500 *montagnard* troops had rejoined government forces earlier in October in the war against the Viet Cong. Another 250 *montagnard* troops pledged allegiance to the government in ceremonies held in Pleiku Oct. 17. Among those attending the rites were U.S. Amb. Lodge, Premier Ky and Chief-of-State Thieu.

The government had "agreed in principle" to *montagnard* demands in August following negotiations with the United Front for the Struggle for Oppressed Races (Fulro), the *montagnards'* political organization. Paul Nur, 41, a Bahnar tribesman who was the government's special commissioner for *montagnard* affairs, said the agreement had not yet been implemented. But he said he expected further negotiations with Fulro leaders in November. The government had agreed to grant the *montagnards:* (a) improved educational opportunities; (b) the right to own land; (c) greater opportunities in civil service; (d) the right to fly a special *montagnard* pennant along with the national flag; (e) a separate force to be used in military operations against the Viet Cong; (f) traditional tribal law courts.

The special commission for *montagnard* affairs had been established by the government in February in response to a Fulro demand.

U.S. Aid Reported Diverted

A *N.Y. Times* report from Saigon Nov. 12 said that about 40% of the U.S. economic and military assistance dispatched to South Vietnam had failed to reach its proper destination because of theft, bribery, black marketeering, currency manipulation and waste. The report said the matter had reached

such serious proportions that Pres. Johnson and U.S. aid officials had discussed the situation with Premier Ky and Chief-
of-State Thieu at their meeting in Manila Oct. 24–25. The
newspaper reported that estimates of the total U.S. aid loss in
Vietnam ranged from $500 million to $1 billion. Aid officials
in Saigon rejected the *Times'* figures Nov. 17 and said that only
$35 to $40 million worth of the $686 million in aid budgeted
for 1966 would be lost through theft and corruption.

The *Times* report had said that at least 400 U.S. servicemen and civilians faced charges of corruption and black
market activities. One of them, Navy Capt. Archie C. Kuntze,
was found guilty Nov. 14 by a general court-martial in Trea-
sure Island, Calif. of a charge of conduct "unbecoming of an
officer and gentleman" while stationed in Saigon. Kuntze, 45,
had become known as "the American mayor of Saigon" for his
social activities when he commanded the Navy Headquarters
Supply Activity, Saigon from June 1964 to May 1966. He was
found guilty of allowing Jennie Suen, 27, to "reside openly and
notoriously in his official quarters," of allowing her to use
his official vehicle and giving her illegally imported cloth.

According to the *Times,* U.S. officials had made these other
points: The U.S. Agency for International Development
(AID) program in South Vietnam had succeeded, at least
temporarily, in halting inflation there; surveillance of Saigon
docks and Vietnamese warehouses had prevented any substantial diversion of heavy equipment and had limited to about
1% the loss of commodity import and Food-for-Peace shipments, which were purchased with U.S. funds for the Vietnamese commercial market; about 13% of the $8 million
worth of imported U.S. goods that the current budget earmarked for the Vietnamese pacification program (items included cement, rice and sheet metal) would never reach their
proper destinations because of theft or diversion by Vietnamese officials or civilians.

The White House announced Dec. 16 the appointment of
ex-U.S. Atomic Energy Commission Chrmn. David E. Lilienthal to head the American section of a joint U.S.-South Vietnamese effort to map long-range plans for South Vietnam's
economy. The program included plans for converting military

installations after the war ended. The White House announcement said that the U.S. economic experts would come from the privately-owned Development & Resources Corp., of which Lilienthal was chairman. The U.S. group would operate under contract with AID and would work in conjunction with a panel of South Vietnamese experts. (Pres. Johnson Mar. 22 had named Robert W. Komer as his special $30,000-a-year assistant "for peaceful reconstruction in Vietnam.")

U.S. Agriculture Secy. Orville L. Freeman had inspected farms and villages throughout South Vietnam Feb. 10–14 and listened to the requests of farmers for additional U.S. aid. 10 U.S. farm experts made independent tours at the same time. At a Saigon news conference Feb. 14 Freeman spoke of social and economic development as "the 2d front of this war." As he left Saigon Feb. 15 Freeman added that the war in Vietnam "can't be won without an expanding and healthy agriculture program." At a press conference Feb. 16, Freeman said he had found the state of South Vietnam's agriculture to be "much better than reasonably could have been expected" in view of wartime conditions. He said he had recommended to the President increased U.S. assistance in the provision of fertilizer and feed grains, as well as agricultural specialists and administrators.

A report critical of the U.S.' and South Vietnam's social and political efforts in Vietnam was presented to the Senate Mar. 4 by Sen. Edward M. Kennedy (D., Mass.) as chairman of a Senate Judiciary subcommittee that had held 7 months of hearings on the problem. Kennedy said there was "little evidence to suggest" that either government had "moved significantly beyond a back-stopping position" in regard to persons dislocated because of the war. He recommended: appointment of a U.S. refugee official "responsible only to the ambassador and the President"; creation of a "civilian counter-insurgency establishment" to complement the military effort against communism; more "humanitarian" concern for the war refugees and stress on cottage industries, vocational training and education to promote "active allegiance" of the refugees to the South Vietnamese government.

A 17-member U.S. health and education task force, headed

by Health, Education & Welfare (HEW) Secy. John W. Gardner, toured South Vietnam Mar. 14–18 at the President's direction. In announcing the mission Mar. 6, Mr. Johnson had said: "This can only be the beginning of what must be a continuing effort on the part of both governments to give new promise and new purpose to the lives of the Vietnamese people." The group included Douglass Cater, a special Presidential assistant, Asst. HEW Secy. Francis Keppel and Surgeon Gen. William H. Stewart. At a news conference in Saigon Mar. 17, Gardner said the U.S. effort was "going to have to go more slowly than we had hoped." He said that "things are tough" and that inspection had impressed them with "the urgency of the problem."

COMMUNIST AID TO HANOI

Sino-Soviet Dispute

Communist China Jan. 16 denied what it described as Moscow-supported rumors that Peking was impeding the transshipment through China of Soviet military equipment to North Vietnam. The news agency Hsinhua said that the USSR had first asked Peking Feb. 25, 1965 for permission to use Chinese territory to funnel the matériel to Hanoi. The news agency insisted that China had complied with the Soviet requests and that China had provided trains to transport Soviet "military aid supplies and technical personnel" from the Sino-Soviet border to the Sino-North Vietnamese frontier. This was the first public confirmation by an official Communist source that Soviet experts were accompanying the USSR arms shipments to North Vietnam. Chinese officials had foregone the collection of transit charges to facilitate the shipments, Hsinhua said. Hsinhua said the Chinese government, in a memo delivered earlier in January to the Soviet embassy in Peking and to the Soviet Foreign Ministry in Moscow, had insisted that China had cooperated in the transshipments. But the news agency said that the Soviet officials had rejected the memo. The memo accused the USSR of attempting to disrupt Sino-North Vietnamese relations to "serve United States imperialism."

A 5-man Soviet mission led by Communist Party Secy.

Aleksandr N. Shelepin had visited Hanoi Jan. 7-12 and paved the way for a Soviet pledge of increased military aid to North Vietnam. The military assistance pledge was made in a communiqué issued in Moscow Jan. 14, one day after Shelepin had returned to the Soviet capital. The amount and type of the military aid was not disclosed.

Communist China charged Feb. 10 that the purpose of Soviet aid to North Vietnam was "to get more of a say" for the USSR "on the Vietnam questions, to sow dissension in Sino-Vietnamese relations and to help the United States to realize its peace talks plot." The statement appeared in *Hung Chi,* the ideological journal of the Chinese Communist Party's Central Committee. "The new leaders of the Soviet Union," the magazine charged, were allied with the U.S. against China and were out "to enable the U.S. to occupy South Vietnam permanently and to strike a political deal with it." *Hung Chi* reiterated Peking's opposition to Moscow's pleas for a united Communist policy to counter U.S. actions in Vietnam.

It was reported in Hong Kong Mar. 19 that Communist China had resumed the harassment of Soviet supply shipments to Hanoi through Chinese territory. The report told of Soviet complaints of Peking's hindrance of Soviet railroad transit shipments from Manchouli on the Siberian border to the North Vietnamese frontier. China also was said to have rejected Soviet requests for air landing rights in Yunan and Sinkiang Provinces for the transshipment of supplies to North Vietnam.

Speaking at a meeting of North Vietnam's National Assembly, held Apr. 16-22, North Vietnamese Premier Pham Van Dong praised Communist countries for providing North Vietnam with economic and military aid. He particularly thanked Communist China for its "great and effective assistance" and "its devoted help in the transit of aid from the Soviet Union and other fraternal Eastern European countries according to schedule."

Hanoi radio announced Aug. 30 that Deputy Premier Le Thanh Nghi, currently in Peking, had signed an agreement for Communist China to provide "economic and technical nonrefundable aid to Vietnam." Fresh assurances of support to North Vietnam were made Sept. 2 in a message signed by Chinese Communist Party Chrmn. Mao Tse-tung, Chief of State Liu Shao-chi, Chrmn. Chu Teh of the National People's Congress Standing Committee and Premier Chou En-lai. The message was sent to Ho Chi Minh on the occasion of North Vietnam's national day. The message reaffirmed that Communist China "is the reliable rear area of the Vietnamese people."

The USSR assured North Vietnam Sept. 1 that Soviet aid to Hanoi was being geared to "the new phase of war." The statement was made in a message of greeting sent to Ho by Soviet CP General Secy. Leonid I. Brezhnev, Premier Aleksei Kosygin and Pres. Nikolai V. Podgorny. Brezhnev and Kosygin were reported Aug. 26 to have met secretly the previous week at a Black Sea resort with North Vietnamese Premier Dong and Defense Min. Vo Nguyen Giap. The visit of Dong and Giap was not publicly acknowledged. An agreement to provide North Vietnam with an undisclosed amount of Soviet economic and military assistance was announced by Soviet Deputy Premier Vladimir N. Novikov Oct. 3 in Moscow. Novikov had negotiated the pact with North Vietnamese Deputy Premier Nghi, who had been in the USSR for the previous 12 days. (Nghi reportedly negotiated aid pacts with 10 other Asian & European Communist governments during his trip.) The accords included a 1967 trade agreement. A Soviet report on foreign trade made public Sept. 25 said that Soviet industrial and military exports to North Vietnam had increased greatly since the start of U.S. bombing raids on North Vietnam in 1965. The report said Soviet exports to Hanoi in 1965 had totaled 67.4 million rubles ($74.8 million), compared with 42.9 million rubles in 1964.

The Warsaw Treaty Political Consultative Committee—the alliance's supreme body—met at the summit level in Bucharest July 4-6 and issued a declaration (published July 7) offering to send "volunteers" to North Vietnam if Hanoi requested them.

Articles appearing in 3 Soviet newspapers Aug. 28 said that North Vietnamese fighter pilots were being trained at an undisclosed Soviet air base to fly supersonic interceptors against U.S. aircraft. The newspapers carried photographs showing Vietnamese pilots beside MiG-21 jet fighters. The articles appeared in *Pravda, Krasnaya Zvezda* (the Defense Ministry organ) and *Komsomolskaya Pravda* (the Communist Youth League newspaper). U.S. intelligence sources were reported Dec. 23 to have confirmed that 25 to 30 North Korean pilots were in North Vietnam, presumably to train North Vietnamese flyers. The presence of North Koreans in North Vietnam had been reported in the Dec. 22 edition of the *N.Y. Times.* A *Times* report Dec. 12 had quoted intelligence sources as saying the Soviet Union in recent weeks had given North Vietnam 100 new MiGs, increasing Hanoi's MiG force to about 200. The new planes were said to be MiG-17, MiG-19, and MiG-21 types.

The Soviet Defense Ministry newspaper *Krasnaya Zvezda* reported Oct. 2 that Russian military experts training North Vietnamese in the use of Soviet-made anti-aircraft missiles had come under attack during U.S. raids against North Vietnamese missile sites. The report made no mention of Soviet casualties. It was the first public acknowledgment that Soviet military men had trained North Vietnamese missile crews and observed them in action. The Soviet team had completed its training mission and returned to the USSR, the report said. *Krasnaya Zvezda* emphasized that in repelling U.S. air raids, the Soviet missiles were fired by North Vietnamese while the Soviet military men stood by as advisers. (It was reported in Washington Oct. 3 that State and Defense Department officials had evidence that Soviet military advisers on occasions had actually operated North Vietnamese missile-control systems. The evidence was said to be based on monitoring of North Vietnamese military radio networks. U.S. officials were said to have been aware for months of the presence of Soviet technicians at the North Vietnamese missile sites and of the probable killing or wounding of some of them during attacks on the installations.)

1967

The intensification of the fighting in Vietnam continued during 1967 although Hanoi appeared to be dropping hints that it might be willing to start peace talks. Both sides clarified their terms: North Vietnam insisted on a U.S. halt in bombings and other acts of war as its condition for negotiations; the U.S. refused to stop bombing without military "reciprocity" on Hanoi's part, and it stepped up the bombing by hitting at previously untouched targets. A major move in the bombing increase was a shift of the B-52 bomber force from distant Guam to nearby Thailand. U.S./ South Vietnamese ground forces invaded the southern part of the demilitarized zone to break up the Communist build-up in the area and to keep the area from being used as a North Vietnamese infiltration route into South Vietnam. Allied troops and planes were accused by Cambodia of repeated border attacks. U.S./South Vietnamese spokesmen charged that Communist forces used Cambodia as a sanctuary from which to attack in South Vietnam. Opposition to U.S. policy in Vietnam grew in the U.S. and was expressed in increasingly violent fashion. Nguyen Van Thieu was elected president of South Vietnam in September, and Nguyen Cao Ky was elected vice president.

PEACE EFFORTS CONTINUE

'Feelers' from Hanoi?

Although most official statements from Hanoi during 1967 expressed defiance of the U.S. and certainty of eventual victory, several remarks by North Vietnamese leaders during the year appeared to indicate a growing desire to begin negotiating peace terms. U.S. officials repeated their charges, however, that every American effort to get peace talks started had met with a rebuff from North Vietnam. No solution was found to the problem of how the Viet Cong and its political arm, the NLF (National Liberation Front), would be represented at the peace table. The U.S. seemed to display an increasing willingness to find some way of including the NLF in peace talks, but the South Vietnamese regime held to its stand that the NLF was nothing but a "stooge" of North Vietnam and that North Vietnam, as the true enemy, should be the sole Communist negotiator.

Remarks made by North Vietnamese Premier Pham Van Dong Jan. 3 raised international speculation as to whether Hanoi was modifying its conditions for ending the war in Vietnam. The speculation first arose when Dong told Harrison Salisbury, an assistant managing editor of the *N.Y. Times*, that North Vietnam's 4-point plan for resolving the conflict "constitutes the basis for a settlement" but "should not be considered 'conditions.' They are merely truths." Dong added: "The most simple thing is to recognize our sovereignty and our independence. It involves only recognizing the points in the Geneva agreements. The ruling circles of the United States do not like to accept our 4 points, and particularly the 3d point. That means that they are still clinging to South Vietnam. . . . We must come to a solution on the basis of the 4 points." Dong emphasized that another point Hanoi insisted on was the "demand that the United States put, unconditionally and for good, an end to the bombing and all hostile activity against the North."

When asked by Salisbury later in the Hanoi interview to clarify his statement on the 4 points, Dong replied: "It is wrong to say that we are putting some conditions. What I have told you are not our 'conditions' but conditions for valid settlement. The question is how to reach a settlement which can be enforced."

Among other statements made by Dong in his Jan. 3 interview with Salisbury: "The moment the United States puts an end to the war, we will respect each other and settle every question." "If we do not agree today we will agree tomorrow" or "the day after tomorrow." North Vietnam was "determined to fight on [for 10–20 years] until our sacred rights are recognized." North Vietnam was prepared to request foreign volunteers to assist it in its "sacred war." "Volunteers are not lacking—volunteers for the armed forces. . . ."

A statement by another North Vietnamese official Jan. 5 increased speculation as to whether Hanoi was softening its position on negotiations. Speaking to newsmen in Paris, Mai Van Bo, who headed North Vietnam's diplomatic office in the French capital, said: "If the United States comes to halting the bombardment definitively and without conditions, this fact will be examined and studied by the [Hanoi] government. If after the definitive and unconditional cessation of the bombardments, the American government proposes to enter into contact with the [North Vietnamese] government, I believe that this proposal will be examined and studied, too." Bo scored recent U.S. and British peace proposals and UN Secy. Gen. U Thant's current efforts to get a truce. Hanoi, Bo said, "rejects all intervention by the United Nations in the Vietnam affair for the good reason that this intervention would be contrary to the [1954] Geneva agreements." Bo held that the U.S. "must first recognize" the NLF as "the only authentic representative of the South Vietnamese people, to negotiate with them and settle all the questions of South Vietnam."

The U.S. government's reaction to Bo's call for a halt to U.S. air strikes elicited this statement from U.S. State Department spokesman Robert J. McCloskey Jan. 5: "We are prepared to have talks with North Vietnam without any preconditions at any time. We are prepared to order a cessation of bombing of North Vietnam the moment we are assured, privately or otherwise," that Hanoi would reply with "a corresponding and appropriate de-escalation."

U Thant said in New York Jan. 10 that there was nothing new in Dong's and Bo's statements.

A West German newspaper correspondent, Egon Lutz of the *Nuernberger Nachrichten,* reported from Hanoi Jan. 10 that North Vietnamese Pres. Ho Chi Minh had told him and 2 visiting German prelates earlier in the week that Hanoi's 4 points "can be reduced to one: The United States should quit Vietnam." Lutz quoted Ho as having said in the interview: "If the United States is ready to give up its policy of aggression and to withdraw its troops from Vietnam, then we will gladly invite them to tea. . . . When the Americans withdraw from South Vietnam, the war is over. . . ." Lutz said Ho had "emphasized several times that the Americans must unconditionally stop the bombing of North Vietnam."

Communists Reject British Plan

Proposals by Britain for an international peace conference to end the war in Vietnam were rejected by North Vietnam Jan. 4 and by the NLF Jan. 5. The North Vietnamese Foreign Ministry Jan. 4 called the British plan—proposed Dec. 30, 1966 by Foreign Secy. George Brown—"an impermissible vicious act." Assailing the plan's failure to include the NLF in proposed negotiations, the statement said: "It is absolutely impossible to end the war in South Vietnam without talking" with the NLF.

The British government Jan. 4 expressed hope that Hanoi would reconsider its rejection. A Foreign Office statement said: NLF representation at future talks "has never been a real problem. . . . The problem has been to get the governments most immediately concerned to negotiate." Brown declared Jan. 7 that Hanoi remained the "key to peace" in Vietnam. He urged North Vietnam to "match the Americans' readiness to talk." "Wars can be stopped by negotiation, but only if both sides wish to negotiate," he said.

The British plan had been indorsed Jan. 2 by the South Vietnamese government. Foreign Min. Tran Van Do said his government had informed London that day that Saigon "agrees in principle to the proposal because we want to show our goodwill for peace in Vietnam." South Vietnamese Chief of State Nguyen Van Thieu, in a statement of his own, said

South Vietnam always had been prepared "to talk in any place," but the problem "is whether the other side [Hanoi] is really sincere." Vatican sources reported Jan. 2 that Pope Paul VI, in reply to a letter he had received Jan. 1 from British Prime Min. Harold Wilson, welcomed London's peace proposal.

NLF Claims Independence

An official of the National Liberation Front, insisting on the NLF's right to a place at peace talks, declared Jan. 4 that the NLF was a military and political force independent of North Vietnam. The statement was made by Nguyen Van Tien, a member of the NLF's Central Committee, in an interview with Harrison Salisbury in Hanoi. Tien, the NLF's permanent representative in Hanoi, said "the North cannot speak for the South. Anyone who has to discuss South Vietnam must speak with the Front." The "direction of the struggle" in South Vietnam, Tien insisted, "is run by the South, not the North." Any aid the Viet Cong received was not funneled through North Vietnam, he said. Such assistance was specifically earmarked for the South and had to be arranged directly with the Front. (Tien also said: The U.S. must accept the NLF's predominant position in the South, even after peace was restored. The question of reunification of Vietnam must be discussed by the NLF and the North on a basis of equality; the NLF would have the decisive say in matters in the South relating to reunification. The majority of the NLF's leadership supported an independent reunified Vietnam that would pursue a foreign policy of nonalignment. Other factions of the NLF's Central Committee opposed neutrality, preferring a Communist or Socialist-oriented regime. The differences of opinion were a result of the diversity of the committee's composition. In addition to Communists, the committee represented intellectuals, religious sects and other parties.)

U.S. State Secy. Dean Rusk, in a TV interview made public Feb. 1, questioned the NLF's claim to independence. Speaking with 5 British journalists, Rusk said: The U.S. had informed the Communists that it was prepared to discuss the inclusion of the NLF as a "full negotiating party" in future peace talks; if the Viet Cong "were to lay down their arms, ways could be found to permit them" to participate in the South Vietnamese governmental processes; "the leadership of the Viet Cong in the South is made up of North Vietnamese generals . . . , so we're not very much impressed with this alleged difference between the Liberation Front and Hanoi." (Rusk also assessed the effects Communist China's unrest might have on prospects for ending the Vietnamese war. He told the 5 Britons: "It may be that the events in China may give Hanoi somewhat more freedom of action than they might have felt they had a little earlier." Therefore "we're exploring the possibilities here to find out whether or not that is possibly the case, but we just don't know yet.")

Thant Vs. U.S. Policy

UN Secy. Gen. Thant disclosed at a press conference Jan. 10 that he had 3 basic differences with U.S. policy on Vietnam. Thant, who, at the U.S.'s request, was using his good offices to seek a cessation of hostilities, said: (1) He rejected the view that the NLF was a "stooge" of North Vietnam. Although the NLF "received very substantial help from the North," the front was "an independent entity." (2) He disagreed with the so-called domino theory that if South Vietnam "falls, then Country X, then Country Z will follow. . . . What is true of Country X is not necessarily true of Country Y or Country Z." Every nation's future was determined "by its own peculiar circumstances, its national background, its own political philosophy." (3) South Vietnam was not "strategically vital to Western interests and Western security." Vietnam's leaders were "very independent . . ., obsessed with the principle of nonalignment. . . . If Vietnam is independent and militarily nonaligned, . . . then I do not see how this could pose a threat to international peace or security or how Vietnam could be strategically vital to the interests and security of the West."

Thant stressed one point of his 3-point peace formula for Vietnam—an unconditional halt to the U.S. bombing of North Vietnam. "There will be no moves toward peace," Thant warned, "so long as the bombing of North Vietnam is going on."

U.S. State Secy. Dean Rusk Jan. 11 took issue with

Thant's statement that Vietnam was not vital to Western interests. Rusk said: "4 [U.S.] Presidents have not taken that view, and the United States does not agree with it." In discussing the U.S. air raids on North Vietnam, State Secy. Rusk had said at a news conference Jan. 1 that Thant had received "publicly as well as privately a commitment by us that we are prepared to stop the bombing as a step towards peace." Rusk expressed hope that Thant, "with very wide authority as far as we are concerned, will be able to probe the other side to find out what the effect would be if we stopped the bombing." (Soviet Communist Party Gen. Secy. Leonid I. Brezhnev charged Jan. 13 that U.S. bombing in the Hanoi area presented a further hindrance to halting the war. Scoffing at U.S. peace overtures in the face of the raids, Brezhnev asked: "Who will believe the calls for peace if these calls are accompanied by provocative actions that aggravate the situation and create new obstacles on the way to settlement of the conflict?")

Thant's views were reportedly challenged Jan. 13 at a closed-door meeting with delegates of 7 Asian nations, Laos, the Philippines, South Korea, Nationalist China, Japan, Thailand and Malaysia, who had asked for the meeting to seek further clarification of the views Thant had expressed Jan. 10. Thant had discussed his disagreement with U.S. policy with Thai Foreign Min. Thanat Khoman Jan. 11.

Ho Bars Surrender

North Vietnamese Pres. Ho Chi Minh said Jan. 12 that "we cherish peace but never will surrender our independence and freedom for the sake of peace in our country." In an interview in Hanoi with *Miami News* editor William C. Baggs, Ho asserted that "peace is peace only if you have independence and freedom. . . . We have battled too long for independence and freedom" to give up. Baggs said reports that Ho was in failing health "appeared unfounded." Baggs called Ho "keen in conversation and vigorous in his arguments." Baggs quoted Ho as saying: Americans were "intelligent, and they love peace and democracy." But U.S. soldiers were "sent here to kill and get killed," and "this is a shameful thing." "Most of them have an education. . . . If they came here to help, as technicians, then we would welcome them as friends, as brothers." Ho "grieved not only when the Vietnamese people are killed" but "also when American soldiers are killed."

(Commenting on Ho's remarks, U.S. State Secy. Rusk said Jan. 17: "We're not talking about the independence of North Vietnam. What we're talking about is the attempt to seize South Vietnam by force.")

3 of 4 American women who had visited North Vietnam Dec. 23, 1966-Jan. 2 reported their findings at a news conference in New York Jan. 10. They were Mrs. Joe Griffith, 32, of Ithaca, N.Y., Mrs. Grace M. Newman, 42, of New York (sister of U.S. Army Pvt. Dennis Mora, who was serving a 3-year Army prison sentence for refusing to fight in Vietnam) and Barbara Deming, 49, of Wellfleet, Mass. (The 4th member of the group, Mrs. Diane Bevel, 24, of Chicago, did not attend the news conference.) The women, who said they had been guests of the Women's Union of North Vietnam, said Ho Chi Minh had told them that North Vietnam was determined to fight the war indefinitely rather than accept U.S. peace terms, which he regarded as capitulation.

3 clergymen who had toured North Vietnam Jan. 11–12 reported in a joint statement in London Jan. 23 that Ho Chi Minh had invited Pres. Johnson to Hanoi to discuss peace with him. But one of the clergymen, Rabbi Abraham L. Feinberg, 67, of Toronto, said Ho's invitation was largely symbolic. "It was Ho's picturesque way of saying that when the United States abandoned its attempt to impose a solution by force peace could be negotiated," Feinberg said. The 2 other clerics were the Right Rev. Ambrose Reeves, 67, of Britain and the Rev. A. J. Muste, 82, of New York. Their joint statement was based on talks they had held Jan. 16 with Ho, Premier Pham Van Dong and other North Vietnamese officials. It expressed "serious doubts of the possibility of an early cessation of hostilities." "We have every reason to think that the government and people of North Vietnam" were determined "to fight for their independence and the eventual reunification of their country," the statement said.

Ethiopian Peace Plan

Endalkachew Makonnen, chief Ethiopian delegate to the UN, proposed Jan. 19 a "committee of conciliation," composed of nonaligned countries, that would seek to bring the principal parties in the Vietnamese war to a peace conference. Makonnen's plan called for a halt to U.S. air raids on North Vietnam and for a cessation of ground fighting while the committee engaged in peace moves. The committee's first task, Makonnen said, would be to confer with Pres. Johnson. Makonnen suggested that UN Secy. Gen. Thant should supplement his peace efforts by conferring with leaders of the countries involved in the war or "alternatively should select a representative conciliation committee composed of 3 or 4 nonaligned members to go and talk" with the combatants.

Makonnen said his plan had the endorsement of the more moderate members of the 38-nation African bloc and was meant to reinforce Thant's mediation. The proposal was a follow-up to Ethiopian Emperor Haile Selassie's appeal of Dec. 21, 1966. Selassie had urged that moves be undertaken during the Christmas and New Year's holidays to bring "all the parties concerned to the negotiating table."

U.S. Amb. Arthur J. Goldberg expressed American support of the Ethiopian peace suggestions in a meeting with Makonnen Jan. 20. Goldberg said Selassie's "statements will receive our careful consideration."

U.S.-NLF Contacts

The N.Y. Times reported Jan. 26 that U.S. diplomatic officials had held a series of unsuccessful meetings with NLF representatives in 1966. Most of the meetings were said to have been held in Cairo (where the NLF had a political office headed since Oct. 1966 by Le Guang Chanh, a member of the Central Committee) and to have dealt largely with U.S. prisoners of war held by the Viet Cong in South Vietnam. The contacts were said to have been established in the spring or summer of 1966 and to have continued at least through the fall. (U.S. officials were also reported to have conferred with North Vietnamese representatives in Burma in Jan. 1966.)

The U.S. State Department refused to comment on the report. But an unidentified U.S. official in Washington Jan. 26 acknowledged its veracity. He was quoted as saying: The U.S. government was "naturally concerned for the welfare of individual Americans held captive in South Vietnam, and [we] have been willing to discuss this subject through any appropriate channel with representatives of the National Liberation Front. Any authorized contact has been confined to this subject."

Reported political contacts between U.S. and North Vietnamese officials were confirmed Feb. 4 by Presidential Asst. Walt W. Rostow. Rostow said officials of both countries were involved in "what is or might turn out to be a negotiating process" toward settling the war in Vietnam. Speaking in Washington Feb. 4 at the College Editor's Conference of the U.S. Student Press Association, Rostow said: "This is an extremely interesting and delicate phase in what is or might turn out to be a negotiating process. Nothing has yet happened that would justify us as saying we have a serious offer to negotiate." Rostow's disclosure was in answer to a question about a report that had appeared in the *Washington Post* Feb. 4 that North Vietnam had agreed in Dec. 1966 to hold peace talks with the U.S. but that the Communists withdrew the offer after U.S. planes carried out raids close to Hanoi. Declining to be more specific on the report, Rostow explained that it would be "a bad time to discuss any particular negotiating track."

(The U.S.' position on Vietnam was criticized by another guest of the student panel, Richard N. Goodwin, who had been a speech writer for Pres. John F. Kennedy and Pres. Johnson. Goodwin accused the Johnson Administration of not being forceful enough in pursuing a policy to end the war. He said the Administration should seek out "vigorously and brilliantly" every opportunity for a peace conference and stop bombing North Vietnam because the "reasons for the bombing have disappeared." Goodwin denied that it had been Kennedy's decision to make the Vietnamese conflict "an American war." Asserting that Kennedy regarded it as "a Vietnamese war," Goodwin said Pres. Johnson had decided in 1965 "to make it an American war.")

According to the *Washington Post's* Feb. 4 account of the abortive U.S.-Hanoi peace talks: U.S. Amb-to-South Vietnam Henry Cabot Lodge had first discussed the idea in Saigon

Dec. 2-3, 1966 with Janusz Lewandowski, Polish representative on the International Control Commission. Lodge asked Lewandowski to inform Hanoi of the U.S.'s willingness to meet with North Vietnamese officials. Polish Foreign Min. Adam Rapacki disclosed on or about Dec. 4 that Hanoi had accepted the proposal to participate in talks on an ambassadorial level. Hanoi had not repeated its usual demand that a cessation of U.S. raids on the North remained North Vietnam's condition for entering discussions. Warsaw was designated as the site for the proposed talks, but North Vietnam refused to attend after U.S. planes carried out raids in the Hanoi area Dec. 13-14. Hanoi regarded the attacks as an act of "bad faith."

A Hanoi radio statement Feb. 8 denied the reports of secret U.S.-North Vietnamese contacts as "sheer fabrication" by Washington to develop favorable "public opinion while continuing to bomb North Vietnam."

U.S. Explains 14-Point Plan

U.S. conditions for a peaceful settlement in Vietnam had been incorporated in a 14-point list based on statements made by U.S. Administration officials on different occasions. The list had first been made public by Vice Pres. Humphrey Jan. 3, 1966. The State Department release of a fuller explanation was approved by State Secy. Rusk Jan. 27, 1967. The text of the 14 points and of the State Department elaboration (in italics):

1. The Geneva Agreements of 1954 and 1962 are an adequate basis for peace in Southeast Asia.

2. We would welcome a conference on Southeast Asia or any part thereof:

We are ready to negotiate a settlement based on a strict observance of the 1954 and 1962 Geneva Agreements, which observance was called for in the declaration on Vietnam of the meeting of the Warsaw Pact countries in Bucharest on July 6, 1966. And we will support a reconvening of the Geneva Conference, or an Asian conference, or any other generally acceptable forum.

3. We would welcome "negotiations without preconditions" as called for by 17 nonalined nations in an appeal delivered to Secy. Rusk on Apr. 1, 1965.

4. We would welcome "unconditional discussions" as called for by Pres. Johnson on Apr. 7, 1965:

If the other side will not come to a conference, we are prepared to engage in direct discussions or discussions through an intermediary.

5. A cessation of hostilities could be the first order of business at a conference or could be the subject of preliminary discussions:

We have attempted, many times, to engage the other side in a discussion of a mutual de-escalation of the level of violence, and we remain prepared to engage in such a mutual de-escalation.

We stand ready to cooperate fully in getting discussions which could lead to a cessation of hostilities started promptly and brought to a successful completion.

6. Hanoi's 4 points could be discussed along with other points which others may wish to propose:

We would be prepared to accept preliminary discussions to reach agreement on a set of points as a basis for negotiations.

7. We want no U.S. bases in Southeast Asia:

We are prepared to assist in the conversion of these bases for peaceful uses that will benefit the peoples of the entire area.

8. We do not desire to retain U.S. troops in South Vietnam after peace is assured:

We seek no permanent military bases, no permanent establishment of troops, no permanent alliances, no permanent American "presence" of any kind in South Vietnam.

We have pledged in the [Oct. 25, 1966] Manila [Conference] communiqué that "Allied forces are in the Republic of Vietnam because that country is the object of aggression and its government requested support in the resistance of its people to aggression. They shall be withdrawn, after close consultation, as the other side withdraws its forces to the North, ceases infiltration, and the level of violence thus subsides. Those forces will be withdrawn as soon as possible and not later than six months after the above conditions have been fulfilled."

9. We support free elections in South Vietnam to give the South Vietnamese a government of their own choice:

We support the development of broadly based democratic institutions in South Vietnam.

We do not seek to exclude any segment of the South Vietnamese people from peaceful participation in their country's future.

10. The question of reunification of Vietnam should be determined by the Vietnamese through their own free decision:

It should not be decided by the use of force.

We are fully prepared to support the decision of the Vietnamese people.

11. The countries of Southeast Asia can be nonalined or neutral if that be their option:

We do not seek to impose a policy of alinement on South Vietnam.

We support the neutrality policy of the Royal Government of Laos, and we support the neutrality and territorial integrity of Cambodia.

12. We would much prefer to use our resources for the economic reconstruction of Southeast Asia than in war. If there is peace, North Vietnam could participate in a regional effort to which we would be prepared to contribute at least one billion dollars:

We support the growing efforts by the nations of the area to cooperate in the achievement of their economic and social goals.

13. The President has said: "The Viet Cong would have no difficulty in being represented and having their views presented if Hanoi for a moment decides she wants to cease aggression. And I would not think that would be an insurmountable problem at all."

14. We have said publicly and privately that we could stop the bombing of North Vietnam as a step toward peace although there has not been the slightest hint or suggestion from the other side as to what they would do if the bombing stopped:

We are prepared to order a cessation of all bombing of North Vietnam the moment we are assured—privately or otherwise—that this step will be answered promptly by a corresponding and appropriate de-escalation of the other side.

We do not seek the unconditional surrender of North Vietnam; what we do seek is to assure for the people of South Vietnam the right to decide their own political destiny, free of force.

LBJ Discounts Hanoi 'Feeler'

North Vietnamese Foreign Min. Nguyen Duy Trinh said in an interview with Australian Communist journalist Wilfred Burchett Jan. 28 that "it is only after the unconditional ending of the bombing and the other acts of war being carried out by the United States against North Vietnam that there can be talks between the 2 countries."

But Pres. Johnson, asked at his press conference Feb. 2 about Trinh's remarks, discounted reports that they constituted peace "feelers." "As of this moment," Mr. Johnson declared, "I cannot report that there are any serious indications that the other side is ready to stop the war." The President said he had heard frequent speculation on peace moves, "but I do not interpret any action that I have observed as being a serious effort to either go to a conference table or to bring the war to an end." The President repeated that the U.S. would halt air raids on North Vietnam if Hanoi carried out "just almost any step" in reciprocation; "they haven't taken any yet."

In his interview, Trinh had restated Hanoi's view that North Vietnam's 4-point peace plan remained a basis for settlement of the war.

Trinh's statement was backed by Huyn Tan Phat, deputy chairman of the NLF's Standing Committee, in a statement published by Hanoi newspapers Jan. 31. Phat described

Trinh's call for a halt to the bombing "a just position." But he had made no mention of the suggestion for peace talks with the U.S. Phat said that Hanoi's 4-point plan and the NLF's 5-point program for peace constituted "the sole correct basis for settling the Vietnam problem."

The Soviet news agency Tass Feb. 4 assailed Pres. Johnson's Feb. 2 statement that he saw no "serious [North Vietnamese] effort" to begin peace talks or to end the war. The President's remarks, Tass charged, constituted a rejection of Trinh's proposal, which the news agency called "a new manifestation of goodwill" by North Vietnam. Tass said U.S. refusal to stop the bombing "can only be regarded as a refusal to meet around the conference table and as a sign of their determination to further escalate the aggressive war in Vietnam."

Pres. Johnson's negative response to Trinh's statement was assailed by North Vietnam Feb. 5. The Communist Party newspaper *Nhan Dan* said it was Pres. Johnson's aim to "oppose the urgent and legitimate demand of broad masses of the world's people and the American people" to unconditionally end the bombing of North Vietnam.

U.S. Amb.-to-UN Arthur J. Goldberg appealed to North Vietnam Feb. 10 to clarify what he called the "ambiguity" of its peace proposals. Speaking at Howard University in Washington, Goldberg said Hanoi's vague conditions for participating in negotiations impeded the holding of talks. Citing Hanoi's position that its 4-point plan should be the basis of future peace meetings, Goldberg asked: "Do these statements mean that Hanoi is willing to enter negotiations only if there is an assurance in advance that the outcome will be on their terms and will, in effect, simply ratify the goals they have already stated?" Goldberg insisted that the U.S.' "approach to negotiations is flexible," that "we and our allies do not ask our adversaries to accept as a precondition to discussion or negotiations, any point of ours to which they may have objections." The U.S. would be willing to discuss any subject at peace talks and was "prepared today to go to the conference table as soon as and wherever our adversaries are prepared to join us," Goldberg said. (Goldberg visited Japan, South Korea,

Nationalist China, South Vietnam and the Philippines Feb. 25–March 5 on a fact-finding mission for Pres. Johnson and reported on returning to New York Mar. 6 that prospects for peace were not bright. He said: The principal problem remained the desire to end the conflict. "We have that will. And when that will is matched on the other side, then the promise of peace will be more promising." Goldberg had visited Tokyo Feb. 25-27, and Japanese Premier Eisaku Sato was reported to have told him that it was "most important that the United States carry out its commitment" to the South Vietnamese government. At a meeting with South Korean Premier Chung Il Kwon in Seoul Feb. 28, the ROK leader cautioned the U.S. not to enter premature negotiations on Vietnam. In a Saigon airport address Mar. 1, Goldberg said he was in South Vietnam at Pres. Johnson's request to "reaffirm our commitment of support to the Vietnamese people to be left alone to determine their own political destiny under conditions of freedom without external interference." After 3 days of discussions with South Vietnamese leaders, Goldberg said Mar. 6 that at meetings with Premier Nguyen Cao Ky, Chief of State Nguyen Van Thieu and Foreign Min. Tran Van Do, he had welcomed South Vietnamese reaffirmation of the "Program of National Reconciliation." The program called for the Saigon regime to grant amnesty to Viet Cong leaders. In his talks, Goldberg was said to have expressed U.S. impatience with the Saigon government's failure to implement its pledge to encourage high-ranking Viet Cong officers to defect to the government side by promises of fair treatment and employment in posts equivalent to their previous rank. Goldberg said at a news conference that the reconciliation program was "the core of the pacification program.")

Nhan Dan charged Feb. 16 that the U.S. had hardened its position after Trinh had stated that U.S.-North Vietnamese negotiations could be held if the U.S. unconditionally halted its "acts of war." *Nhan Dan* accused the Johnson Administration of attempting to "make world public opinion believe that the United States wished to stop its war in Vietnam and settle the Vietnam problem peacefully through negotiations." But as soon as Trinh had "declared that the 2 sides could have a

talk after the United States had stopped for good and unconditionally its bombing of North Vietnam, it [the U.S.]
immediately changed its language," *Nhan Dan* asserted.

Mai Van Bo, Hanoi's representative in Paris, repeated
Feb. 22 the North Vietnamese assertion that a permanent
cessation of the bombing would make negotiations possible.
Bo insisted that this position was basically different from
earlier North Vietnamese assertions that if the raids were
stopped Hanoi would study any U.S. requests for negotiations. Bo stressed that unless the U.S. guaranteed that the
bombing halt was "permanent and unconditional," a cessation
of raids would not be considered a satisfactory precondition
because "the threat" of renewed bombing would not be ended.

Nhan Dan Mar. 1 quoted Defense Secy. Robert S. McNamara as having said that the U.S. would halt the bombing if it
received the "slightest signal" from Hanoi. "Yet when . . .
Trinh expressed the goodwill of his government and stated it
was ready to engage in conversations if bombings stopped,"
Nhan Dan charged, "the Johnson clique immediately changed
its language and expressed the demand for reciprocal
de-escalation."

North Vietnamese Premier Pham Van Dong said Mar. 1
that peace talks were unlikely "because the United States
aggressors are continuing their escalations, thus defying public
opinion and the universal conscience of the peoples." Dong
made the statement in an interview in Hanoi with Jacques
Maolic, a correspondent for Agence France-Presse.

Soviet Pres. Nikolai V. Podgorny Feb. 27 had voiced
strong support for Trinh's Jan. 28 statement. Speaking at a
state dinner for visiting Ethiopian Emperor Haile Selassie,
Podgorny deplored U.S. rejection of the proposal. He also
assailed U.S. naval and ground shelling of North Vietnam
and the mining of North Vietnamese rivers.

Tet Truce Halts Fighting Briefly

During the discussions of the reported peace "feelers,"
the U.S. suspended bombing attacks on North Vietnam Feb.
8-12 for a truce in observance of *Tet,* the lunar new year, and
for 2 days beyond the expiration of the truce. The truce halted
heavy fighting then under way throughout Vietnam, but both

the ground fighting and the air attacks were resumed following the cease-fire. The temporary halt in air attacks on North Vietnam was ordered personally by Pres. Johnson. In explaining his decision to resume the bombings, Johnson said in a statement issued Feb. 13: "It had been our hope that the truce periods connected with Christmas, New Year's and *Tet* might lead to some abatement of hostilities and to moves toward peace. Unfortunately, the only response we have had from the Hanoi goverment was to use the periods for major resupply efforts of their troops in South Vietnam. . . . Under these circumstances, in fairness to our troops and those of our allies, we had no alternative but to resume full-scale hostilities after the cease-fire period." Mr. Johnson asserted that "the door [to peace negotiations] is open and will remain open, and we are prepared at any time to go more than halfway to meet any equitable overture from the other side." Appeals for extension of the *Tet* truce had been made by Pope Paul VI, UN Secy. Gen. Thant and other world leaders. (The U.S. State Department Feb. 10 had expressed concern over what it called the Communist build-up in South Vietnam during the truce. Military officials said North Vietnam had sent more equipment into South Vietnam by overland routes Feb. 7-8 than "during the whole month of January." A U.S. State Department official confirmed Feb. 11 that the U.S. also had continued to supply its forces in South Vietnam during the truce.)

Pope Paul's appeals were sent Feb. 7 (made public Feb. 8) to Pres. Johnson, Ho Chi Minh and South Vietnamese Chief of State Nguyen Van Thieu. In his message to Mr. Johnson, the pope expressed the hope that the truce "may open finally the way to negotiations for a just and stable peace, putting an end to the great sacrifices brought on by a war protracted now for years." The pope urged the President "to increase even more your noble effort in these days of truce," "a constant search for a way to peace." Paul's messages to Ho and Thieu were essentially the same as his appeal to Mr. Johnson. The note to Ho included the hope that neither side would violate the truce. The pope asked Ho "to do all that is in his power to hasten the so much desired solution to the conflict." In reply to the pope, Pres. Johnson assured the pontiff Feb. 8

that the U.S., South Vietnam and their allies were "devoting intensive efforts" to extending the truce in the hope that an extension "may open the way for negotiations for a just and stable peace." But the President added: "I know you would not expect us to reduce military action unless the other side is willing to do likewise. We are prepared to discuss the balanced reduction in military activity, the cessation of hostilities or any practical arrangements which could lead to these results." Ho's reply to the pope Feb. 13 called on the pontiff "to use his high influence to urge that the U.S. government respect the national rights of the Vietnamese people, namely peace, independence, sovereignty, unity and territorial integrity as recognized by the 1954 Geneva agreements." Ho reiterated Hanoi's conditions for ending the war: The U.S. "must put an end to their aggression in Vietnam, end unconditionally and definitively the bombing and all other acts of war against" North Vietnam, "withdraw from South Vietnam all American and satellite troops, recognize the . . . National Liberation Front and let the Vietnamese people settle themselves their own affairs."

Wilson & Kosygin Seek Settlement

The Vietnamese war was a major topic of discussion in meetings held by Soviet Premier Aleksei N. Kosygin and British Prime Min. Harold Wilson in London Feb. 8-13. But an undisclosed peace plan they drafted failed to produce any results.

On arriving in London Feb. 8, Kosygin had expressed support for Trinh's Jan. 28 remarks. Speaking at a luncheon at Guildhall, Kosygin said: "It is only after the unconditional cessation of United States bombing and all other acts of war against" North Vietnam "that there could be talks" between the U.S. and North Vietnam. Kosygin said the Soviet Union "welcomes [Trinh's] statement and regards it as an important and constructive proposal for ending the war." Kosygin also appealed to Britain to join the Soviet Union and "other countries" "to make her contribution to the settlement of the Vietnam question on the basis of the Geneva agreements, which must be observed by the United States."

But in their talks with Kosygin, Wilson and other British

leaders were said to have strongly supported the American
position that North Vietnam should slow down its military
activities in South Vietnam in return for a halt in the U.S.
bombing. A joint British-Soviet statement issued at the conclusion of the Wilson-Kosygin talks Feb. 13 contained a brief
reference to Vietnam. The 2 nations pledged to "make every
possible effort" to achieve peace and agreed to "maintain contact to this end."

During his stay in London, Kosygin was reported to have
cabled Hanoi a request that it reduce its military activities in
South Vietnam in return for a halt in the U.S. air strikes.
North Vietnam was said to have rejected Kosygin's plea. The
reputed exchange was reported Feb. 14 by Michel Gordey,
London correspondent of *France-Soir,* a Paris newspaper, and
by Ian Aitken of the *Manchester Guardian.* Aitken wrote that
a phone call from Wilson to Pres. Johnson "appears to have
elicited a brief but heavily qualified postponement of the
resumption of the American bombing [after the *Tet* truce] to
enable Kosygin to make further approaches to Hanoi." Aitken
added: "No response came, and by the time Wilson appeared
in the Commons [Feb. 13] to deliver a statement on his talks
with Kosygin, it was evident that it was not coming at all.
By 6 p.m. Wilson had received the dismal news of the resumption of the American bombing, and the joint efforts of the 2
prime ministers had failed." (In its announcement of the
resumption of the bombing, the U.S. Defense Department
said Feb. 13 that the air-raid suspension "was continued
beyond the end of *Tet* for a short additional time in order to
avoid any possibility that earlier resumption would be miscon-
strued to Mr. Kosygin's visit to London.")

Wilson said in a TV broadcast Feb. 14 that a peaceful
solution "was almost within our grasp" the previous weekend.
"One single, simple act of trust could have achieved it," he
said. But Wilson expressed confidence that the resumption
of U.S. bombing of North Vietnam Feb. 13 and the renewal of
fighting in South Vietnam following the *Tet* truce had not
"ended the possibilities of peace." In his address to the House
of Commons earlier Feb. 14, Wilson had indicated that he and
Kosygin had drawn up a peace plan during their talks. Wilson

said: "One small move would have activated the whole proposal and continued the *Tet* truce until the parties were around the conference table." The plan (whose details he refused to disclose) "could bring peace tomorrow and requires a very, very small movement to activate all the complicated machinery which would bring us to peace negotiations," Wilson said. Wilson conceded that both sides were sincere in claiming to want to settle the conflict at the conference table. Wilson, however, supported the U.S. view that it was difficult to believe that North Vietnamese leaders "wished to use the [*Tet*] truce for an effort to peace rather than for a further effort in war." Wilson cited "the massive southward movement of troops and supplies in the North, on a scale far greater than . . . in any other previous cease-fire." He asserted that this took place at a time when "one gesture by North Vietnam —which would have cost them nothing in terms of security or even face—could have set in motion events which could have led to peace."

Kosygin assailed the U.S. Mar. 6 for spurning what he regarded as North Vietnamese peace overtures. Speaking at an election rally in Moscow, Kosygin referred to Trinh's remarks as "an extremely important peace initiative." Kosygin added: The U.S., however, "did not avail itself of this opportunity. On the contrary, trying to camouflage its aggressive intentions, it hastened to set forth ultimatums that were absolutely unacceptable to the Vietnamese people." Assailing increased U.S. military moves against North Vietnam, Kosygin warned that such escalation would only lead to greater Communist aid to North Vietnam. Kosygin also condemned Communist China for having criticized Trinh's peace proposal. Peking's leaders had, in effect, sided "with the position of the imperialist circles of the United States," Kosygin said.

RFK Denies Hanoi 'Signal'

Sen. Robert F. Kennedy (D., N.Y.) reported to Pres. Johnson Feb. 6 on informal discussions he had held on Vietnam with West European leaders Jan. 28-Feb. 4. After his meeting with the President, Kennedy denied a report appearing in *Newsweek* magazine (Feb. 13 issue) that he had received a North Vietnamese proposal for ending the war. Hanoi's alleged message, *Newsweek* said, had been given to Kennedy during his meeting with French leaders in Paris Jan. 29-31. Kennedy said: "I did not bring home any peace feelers. I never received the impression in any of the conversations" during his European tour "that I was the recipient of any peace feelers."

A *Newsweek* spokesman Feb. 6 insisted on the veracity of the magazine's report, which, he claimed, came from Washington, not European sources. According to the *Newsweek* report: Mai Van Bo, North Vietnam's chief diplomatic representative in Paris, had handed Hanoi's proposal to the French Foreign Ministry. The ministry's Asian affairs director in turn relayed the "peace signal" to Kennedy for transmission to Washington. The North Vietnamese plan called for 3-stage U.S.-North Vietnamese discussions: (1) a bilateral conference on U.S.-North Vietnamese relations; (2) a discussion on the U.S.' future role in Vietnam; (3) "negotiations aimed at an overall settlement in Vietnam." "In transmitting the message to Kennedy, the French officials explained that the 3-stage plan would enable Hanoi to retreat from its '4 points' without loss of face, at least in the first 2 stages."

The French Foreign Ministry and Bo's office Feb. 6 issued separate statements denying that the ministry had given Kennedy a North Vietnamese proposal for Washington.

(*Highlights of Kennedy's European tour:* On arriving in Britain Jan. 28, Kennedy addressed about 1,000 members of the Oxford Union debating society in Oxford and expressed support for Pres. Johnson's policies on Vietnam. Kennedy said the Johnson Administration favored a solution that would permit the Vietnamese people "to choose any kind of government they want. If the people of South Vietnam want the Commies, Pres. Johnson has said he would abide by the result." Kennedy was quoted as saying that secret talks to end the war were in progress and that the following 3-4 weeks would be "critical and crucial." On arriving in Paris Jan. 29 Kennedy denied having said secret talks were going on. Kennedy explained that he was referring to meetings that were known to the public: Soviet Premier Aleksei N. Kosygin's forthcoming visit to Britain, U.S.-Viet Cong contacts on prisoners of war and peace contacts by 3d parties. As a result of these discussions, Kennedy said, "the next few weeks will be crucial and critical." Kennedy met with Pres. Charles de Gaulle Jan. 31. Kennedy said after the meeting: "France and Gen. de Gaulle are going to play an important role in any successful effort we undertake to find a solution to the trouble in Vietnam. If that's not recognized in Washington, we are in great trouble." Kennedy returned to the U.S. Feb. 5. In an airport statement in New York, Kennedy said American participation in the Vietnamese war had resulted in an "undermining of United States prestige" in Europe. Kennedy said that as a result of the war, plus de Gaulle's attempts to undercut U.S. influence in Europe, the relations of European nations "to each other and the United States are quite different than they were 3 years ago. . . . Our influence is diminishing.")

Both the White House and Kennedy denied a report in the Mar. 17 issue of *Time* magazine that his meeting with the President was marked by profanity. *Time* said the President had told Kennedy: "If you keep talking like this, you won't have a political future in this country within 6 months"; "in 6 months, all you 'doves' will be destroyed"; "the blood of American boys will be on your hands"; "I never want to hear your views on Vietnam again"; "I never want to see you again." According to the article, Kennedy "is said to have called the President an s.o.b." White House Press Secy. George Christian said Mar. 14 that he had talked with 3 of the 4 people "who were there" and that, "according to their recollections, nothing like that [the exchange reported in *Time*] took place." (The other 2 persons present: State Undersecy. Nicholas deB. Katzenbach, Presidential aide Walt W. Rostow.) Kennedy Mar. 14 called the *Time* report "wholly inaccurate." He denied to a newsman that the President or he had used swear words, that the President had accused him of upsetting peace negotiations because of the peace-"signal" reports or that Mr. Johnson had said he never wanted to talk to him again. Asked if Mr. Johnson had said he had no political future because of his Vietnam stand, Kennedy said: "I don't want to talk about that." Asked if Mr. Johnson had said that the blood of American boys would be on his hands if peace talks were upset,

Kennedy said: "Not in that context, but I don't want to talk about that."

U.S. Demands 'Reciprocity'

State Secy. Rusk Feb. 9 restated the Johnson Administration position that the U.S. would maintain its bombing offensive against North Vietnam until Hanoi displayed a willingness to de-escalate its military activity in South Vietnam. Rusk spoke in Washington at a news conference, which, the State Department said, had been arranged to "put into perspective" the recent speculation about possible peace talks to end the war in Vietnam. Rusk insisted that "some elementary reciprocity is required, and common fairness would require that if there is an interest toward peace that both sides help move toward it because you can't stop this war simply by stopping half of it." Rusk said the U.S.' conditions for entering peace talks had not changed. He accused the "Communist side" of "a systematic campaign" to get the U.S. to permanently halt the air raids "without any corresponding military action on their side." The Communists, by demanding "an unconditional and permanent cessation" of the raids, rather than a pause in the bombing, "put this matter into a somewhat different context," Rusk said.

A Hanoi statement Feb. 8 had assailed the American insistence that North Vietnam reciprocate for a halt in the bombings. Hanoi radio said: "They have no right to demand any reciprocal measure. The more the United States imperialists are obdurate and perfidious, the more they will be unmasked and isolated and the more ignominious their failure." The Associated Press quoted Hanoi radio Feb. 14 as saying there was no possibility of negotiating Hanoi's demand that "the bombing of North Vietnam be halted unconditionally and for good." North Vietnam's refusal to enter negotiations while the U.S. continued the bombing was reiterated by the North Vietnamese Foreign Ministry Feb. 15. Commenting on the resumption of the raids, the ministry said North Vietnam would never agree to talks under duress: "The Vietnamese people will never accept this. The Americans can never cow the Vietnamese people."

Articles in the Soviet government newspaper *Izvestia* Feb. 11 and Communist Party newspaper *Pravda* Feb. 12 criticized American refusal to accept North Vietnam's conditions for ending the bombing. *Izvestia* said a halt in U.S. raids "would give the signal for the reverse process—the limiting of the scope of military operations and, finally, their complete cessation." Assailing Rusk's demand for North Vietnamese reciprocity, *Izvestia* asserted: "This is not the first time that Washington has swallowed its own words about its yearning for peace in Vietnam as soon as talks turn to the necessity of concrete deeds to back up its widely publicized declaration." *Pravda* also scored Rusk's call for a reciprocal military move by North Vietnam. It said: "How long now have the Washington orators shouted that they were willing to go to the ends of the earth to obtain negotiations? But now Mr. Rusk is turning his nose from a dialogue. What does he want?"

Pres. Johnson Feb. 20 reiterated the U.S. demand for North Vietnamese reciprocity. Presidential Press Secy. George Christian said Mr. Johnson had told visiting farm leaders that for the U.S. to halt the aerial strikes without a reciprocal North Vietnamese military move would be similar to "unloading your gun" and asking the enemy to fire. One of the farmers attending the conference quoted Mr. Johnson as saying: He had not seen "one single indication that the government of North Vietnam was willing to negotiate or talk peace"; "we've reached a point where all the king's horses and all the king's men are not going to move us out of our position." Christian said he had not heard the President say "all the king's men."

In a speech to the Tennessee General Assembly in Nashville Mar. 15, Pres. Johnson said: "Reciprocity must be the fundamental principle of any reduction in hostilities. The United States cannot and will not reduce its activities unless and until there is some reduction on the other side. We will negotiate a reduction of the bombing whenever the government of North Vietnam is ready. . . . To this date and this hour there has been no sign of that readiness. It takes 2 to negotiate." "They [the North Vietnamese] have 3 times rejected a bombing pause as a means to open the way to ending the war and going to the negotiating table."

U Thant conferred with 3 North Vietnamese representatives in Rangoon Mar. 1 and then said in New York Mar. 5 that he believed that the differing U.S. and North Vietnamese views on reciprocity formed the major barrier to peace. Thant explained: To the North Vietnamese, reciprocity "means the United States is bombing North Vietnam and North Vietnam is bombing the United States. Since the United States is bombing North Vietnam and North Vietnam is not bombing the United States, the United States, in their view, should not bomb North Vietnam." Thant had arrived in his native Burma Feb. 22 for vacation, and his meeting with the Hanoi envoys was said to have been unplanned. The North Vietnamese were Consul Gen. Le Tung Son, Col. Ha Van Lau and Nguyen Tu Nguyen; the latter 2 had arrived in Burma Feb. 25 on a routine inspection tour. Reporting on the talks Mar. 5, Thant said that as a result of his exchange of views with the North Vietnamese, he was convinced that "peace is not yet in sight." He foresaw a "prolonged and bloody" conflict unless the U.S. halted its raids on North Vietnam. "The cessation of bombing of North Vietnam alone will bring about useful and meaningful talks," Thant said. He pointed out, however, that he had long held this view and that it was "not necessarily based on recent talks."

Rusk, speaking Mar. 12 on the ABC-TV program "Issues and Answers," denied that the U.S. was "trying to postpone" peace talks in order to improve its bargaining position. Rusk disclosed that in its peace moves, Washington had suggested restricting the U.S. build-up in South Vietnam in exchange for a halt in North Vietnamese infiltration. But Hanoi had expressed no interest, Rusk asserted. He indicated that the U.S. sought at least one specific gesture from North Vietnam in response to a halt in U.S. air raids. Referring to 3 North Vietnamese divisions operating in the vicinity of the demilitarized zone, Rusk said "we are interested, if we stop the bombing, in knowing whether these 3 divisions are going to attack our Marines who are only 3-6 miles away."

Communist China had asserted Feb. 20 that a halt in the U.S. raids was not sufficient to bring about peace talks. The Communist Party newspaper *Jenmin Jih Pao* said Peking's principal condition for the holding of negotiations was the withdrawal of U.S. troops from South Vietnam. The newspaper accused the U.S. and the Soviet Union of exerting military and political pressure on North Vietnam to abandon South Vietnam in exchange for a halt in the raids on the North. "If South Vietnam is lost, North Vietnam will be lost, too, sooner or later," *Jenmin Jih Pao* said. Under Washington's principle of reciprocity, the newspaper warned, the U.S. "can cut Vietnam into 2 and keep it permanently divided while 31 million Vietnamese are not allowed to reunify their fatherland." The CP journal expressed confidence that if Viet Cong and North Vietnamese troops could continue to tie down several thousand U.S. troops in South Vietnam they could win the conflict "by a protracted war."

Kennedy Proposes Peace Plan

In a speech on the Senate floor Mar. 2 Sen. Robert Kennedy proposed suspending the U.S. bombing of North Vietnam as part of a 3-point plan to help end the war in Vietnam. Kennedy's proposals were immediately rejected by the Administration in statements made by State Secy. Dean Rusk and Pres. Johnson. Kennedy's 3-point plan: (1) The U.S. should "test the sincerity of the statements of [Soviet] Premier Kosygin and others asserting that if the bombardment of the North is halted, negotiations would begin—by halting the bombardment and saying we are ready to negotiate within the week."

(2) If negotiations were held, the conferees should seek "an agreement that neither side will substantially increase the size of the war in South Vietnam by infiltration or reinforcement." The agreement would be policed by "an international group" such as the UN or the International Control Commission. The international observers would "inspect the borders and ports of the country" and "report on any further escalation." The U.S. must emphasize that the negotiations "cannot continue for a prolonged period" "while casualties mount and the war gets bigger."

(3) U.S. and North Vietnamese troops would be withdrawn from South Vietnam "over a period of time" and be replaced by an international force. Both sides in the negotia-

tions should work out a definitive agreement that would permit all political factions in South Vietnam, Communist as well as non-Communist, to prepare for national elections to select a civilian regime.

Kennedy said that if the Communists used the negotiations "as a pretext to enlarge the conflict in the South" and bargained in bad faith, then the U.S. could resume the bombing of the North or carry out any other military measures, including "the possible erection of a physical barrier to block infiltration" from North to South Vietnam. In calling for a halt to the bombing, Kennedy alluded to the 37-day U.S. raid suspension that had followed the 1965 Christmas truce. He said: "We were willing to do this a year ago, even without the evidence we now have that an end to the bombing attacks on the North may well bring negotiations. A year ago it was our adversaries who publicly laid down conditions for negotiations—acceptance of [North Vietnam's] 4 points or withdrawal of American troops." Now the Soviet leaders "have said negotiations can begin on terms we clearly would have accepted then. Why then do we not try again in this far more hopeful moment?"

Kennedy conceded that "for years, Pres. Johnson has dedicated his energies to achieve an honorable peace." But the Senator said the U.S. was "now at a critical turning point in pursuit of our stated limited objectives—balanced between the rising prospects of peace and surely rising war." The U.S. military effort in Vietnam was "mounting in intensity," he declared, "just as the evidence mounts that a new and more hopeful moment of opportunity for settlement has been at hand."

After his speech Kennedy asserted during an exchange with Sen. Frank Lausche (D., O.) that North Vietnam had come "all the way around and said we'll talk if you'll stop the bombing." Lausche had said he questioned the feasibility of Kennedy's proposal for a bombing pause in view of the fact that previous American raid halts had not brought Hanoi to the conference table.

Rusk's statement, issued immediately after Kennedy's address, also pointed out that "proposals substantially similar to those put forward by Sen. Kennedy were explored prior, during and since the [Feb. 8-12] *Tet* truce—all without result." All U.S. raid suspensions evoked "only hostile actions" by Hanoi, Rusk said. "There is, therefore, no reason to believe that Hanoi is interested in proposals for mutual de-escalation such as those put forward by Sen. Kennedy."

Pres. Johnson reiterated his policy on the bombing of North Vietnam. In a letter sent to Sen. Henry Jackson (D., Wash.) Mar. 1 and released by Jackson Mar. 2, Mr. Johnson said the U.S. had decided to bomb North Vietnam because Hanoi had violated the 1954 and 1962 Geneva agreements. In 1954, the President said, North Vietnam had pledged not to permit its territory to be "used for the resumption of hostilities or to further an aggressive policy." In 1962, Hanoi had agreed "to withdraw all its military forces from Laos, to refrain from introducing such forces and not to use . . . Laos to interfere in the internal affairs of other countries," Mr. Johnson said. Mr. Johnson said the U.S. had never believed that the air attacks on North Vietnam would end the war. The bombings, however, had accomplished these 3 "important objectives," Pres. Johonson said: (1) They had supported U.S. and allied troops fighting in South Vietnam by "demonstrating that the aggressor could not illegally bring hostile arms and men to bear against them from a security of a sanctuary"; (2) they had "impose[d] on North Vietnam a cost for violating its international agreements"; (3) they had "limit[ed] or raise[d] the cost of bringing men and supplies to bear against the South."

Rusk reiterated Mar. 3 that U.S. bombing halts, similar to the one proposed by Sen. Kennedy, had been tried without reciprocal action from North Vietnam. Hanoi had insisted that a "permanent and unconditional" halt in U.S. air raids on North Vietnam remained one of its conditions for peace talks, Rusk said. It was North Vietnam, Rusk insisted, not Soviet Premier Kosygin, that was the stumbling block to peace.

Kennedy Mar. 4 disagreed with Rusk's contention that Kennedy's plan for a halt to the bombings was not new. "This has not been tried before because we have so far refused to accept the offer of Kosygin and [North Vietnamese Premier]

Pham Van Dong to go to the negotiating table if we stopped the bombing" of North Vietnam, Kennedy said. North Vietnam, Kennedy repeated, had changed its position by stating that it would enter negotiations if the U.S. stopped the bombing. During his talks with British Prime Min. Harold Wilson in London Feb. 6-13, Kosygin had offered to help bring about peace talks, Kennedy declared. He added: "That's a vitally important ingredient. I'm not saying let's do what we've done before. The situation has changed dramatically. They [the Communists] made the offer and I suggested we accept."

Ho Rejects LBJ Proposal of Talks

The North Vietnamese press agency reported Mar. 21 that in a hitherto unpublicized exchange of notes with U.S. Pres. Johnson in February, Ho Chi Minh had rejected a proposal by Mr. Johnson for direct U.S.-North Vietnamese talks on ending the war in Vietnam. The U.S. State Department confirmed the exchange of letters and released them later Mar. 21. Pres. Johnson declared in a statement Mar. 21 that Ho's rejection of his suggestion was "a regrettable rebuff to a genuine effort to move toward peace." Mr. Johnson added: "This has been the consistent attitude of Hanoi to many efforts by us, by other governments, by groups of governments and by leading personalities. Nevertheless, we shall persevere in our efforts to find an honorable peace. Until that is achieved, we shall continue to do our duty in Vietnam."

Pres. Johnson's letter to Ho, dated Feb. 2 and delivered to a North Vietnamese representative in Moscow Feb. 8, said: "I am prepared to order a cessation of bombing against your country and the stopping of further augmentation of United States forces in Vietnam as soon as I am assured that infiltration into South Vietnam by land and by sea has stopped." This reciprocal de-escalation of military activities, the President said, would "make it possible for us to conduct serious and private discussions leading toward an early peace." In suggesting direct U.S.-North Vietnamese discussions, Mr. Johnson said that previous indirect contacts between the 2 countries "may have been distorted or misinterpreted as they passed through these various channels." The President said that the talks could be held in Moscow, Burma or any other country.

Referring to the *Tet* truce, which later halted ground fighting in South Vietnam Feb. 8-12, Mr. Johnson told Ho that his proposal "would be greatly strengthened if your military authorities and those of . . . South Vietnam could promptly negotiate an extension" of the truce. The President said that the U.S. could not accept an unconditional and permanent halt in the bombing of North Vietnam and a cessation of other military activity as demanded by Hanoi. To do so, Mr. Johnson said, (1) "would inevitably produce worldwide speculation that discussions were under way and would impair the privacy and secrecy of those discussions" and (2) would raise U.S. government doubts about whether North Vietnam "would make use of such action by us to improve its military position."

Ho's reply, sent to Pres. Johnson Mar. 10 and received Mar. 15, reiterated the demands incorporated in North Vietnam's 4-point peace plan that the U.S. "must stop definitely and unconditionally its bombing raids and all other acts of war against" North Vietnam, "withdraw from South Vietnam all U.S. and satellite troops and let the Vietnamese people settle themselves their own affairs." North Vietnam would hold direct negotiations with the U.S. "only after the unconditional cessation of the U.S. bombing raids and all other acts of war against" North Vietnam, Ho said. He accused the U.S. of having "unleashed and intensified the war of aggression in South Vietnam with a view to prolonging the partition of Vietnam and turning South Vietnam into a neocolony and a military base of the United States." He said "broad sections of the American people" gave "strong sympathy and support" to the Viet Cong-North Vietnamese cause.

U.S. Administration officials asserted that Pres. Johnson's letter did not constitute a hardening of the American position, although previously Washington had insisted only on de-escalation by both sides rather than on hard and fast evidence that North Vietnam had stopped infiltration of South Vietnam. U.S. State Department spokesman Robert McCloskey said Pres. Johnson's letter had "reaffirmed earlier proposals made on 4 occasions by the U.S. government to Hanoi through representatives in Moscow, commencing in early June [1966]."

The State Department expressed regret that Hanoi had divulged the Johnson-Ho exchange since the secret letters were meant to be a serious diplomatic attempt to end the conflict. Hanoi Mar. 23 defended its disclosure of the notes as "legitimate and necessary" in order "to demonstrate once again the correct stand and the fair and responsible attitude" of North Vietnam. The North Vietnamese news agency charged that the State Department had used Mr. Johnson's letter to give the erroneous impression that private U.S.-North Vietnamese contacts were in progress. The State Department had expressed regret, the agency asserted, because Hanoi's "legitimate disclosure" of the letters had bared the State Department's "odious nature."

Sen. Robert Kennedy Mar. 21 called Pres. Johnson's letter to Ho a stiffening of American conditions for ending the war. Kennedy said: Previously, Mr. Johnson and State Secy. Rusk had stated that the U.S. "require[d] a military de-escalation in return for a cessation of bombing"; Pres. Johnson's letter to Ho "adds to that the further condition that we have evidence that Hanoi has already ceased infiltration before we stop the bombing"; Mr. Johnson's letter "speaks of an unconditional and permanent end to the bombing as his interpretation of the North Vietnamese condition for negotiations," whereas Ho's answer "refers only to an unconditional halt in relation to negotiations and does not use the word 'permanent' in connection with the beginning of negotiations."

New U Thant Peace Plan

UN Secy. Gen. U Thant disclosed Mar. 28 that he had proposed a new 3-point plan to end the war in Vietnam. Thant said that in notes sent to the principals in the dispute Mar. 14 he had suggested (a) "a general standstill truce" in the fighting; (b) "preliminary talks" between the U.S. and North Vietnam to seek agreement on (c) the "reconvening of the Geneva conference" to bring about a permanent settlement. The U.S. and South Vietnam accepted Thant's plan, with qualifications; North Vietnam rejected it.

Thant suggested that Britain and the Soviet Union (as co-chairmen of the Geneva convention), the International Control Commission or all 3 parties could participate in the preliminary discussions. Thant asserted that as belligerents, the South Vietnamese government and the National Liberation Front must take part in "a future formal conference."

Thant said his new proposal was not meant as a substitute for his previous 3-point peace plan, which had failed to get general acceptance. His new plan, Thant declared, "is an adaptation of my 3-point proposal to suit the existing circumstances and the prevailing moods of the parties principally concerned." Thant's previous plan had called for a halt in the U.S. bombing of North Vietnam, a de-escalation of the fighting by both sides and a political conference of the belligerents. Thant, is answer to a question, insisted that his previous call for "the cessation of the bombing of North Vietnam is the first prerequisite for the next move, and I am more convinced than ever that if the bombing of North Vietnam ceases, in a few weeks there will be talks."

A preliminary U.S. reply to Thant's plan Mar. 15 had called it "positive and constructive." A more definitive U.S. response, made in a note handed to Thant Mar. 18 by U.S. Amb. Arthur J. Goldberg, approved the plan. But the U.S. note said "it would be desirable and contributory to serious negotiations if an effective cessation of hostilities, as the first element in the 3-point proposal, could be promptly negotiated."

The first public announcement of U.S. acceptance of Thant's plan was made by Pres. Johnson Mar. 28. Mr. Johnson expressed regret that North Vietnam had spurned the proposal. Mr. Johnson said that he "respectfully disagree[d]" with Hanoi's Mar. 19 contention that the UN had no right to intervene in the dispute.

State Secy. Rusk said at a news conference Mar. 28 that Hanoi's opposition to Thant's proposals had blocked UN efforts to bring about a "standstill truce" in Vietnam as a preliminary to negotiations. Rusk urged North Vietnam to accept "some machinery somewhere that can lead to negotiations." He warned Hanoi that if it refused, the U.S. would continue to "meet its commitment in Vietnam." According to Rusk's interpretation of Thant's plan, it differed from his previous one in that it "does place emphasis upon a mutual stop of the military action on both sides as an important first step."

South Vietnam's qualified acceptance of Thant's proposals had been sent to the Secretary General Mar. 19 by Foreign Min. Tran Van Do and made public in a Foreign Ministry communiqué Mar. 29. Do called for a direct meeting of North and South Vietnamese military command representatives to discuss details of a military truce. The communiqué agreed with Thant's suggestion that after a truce had been arranged an international conference should be held to discuss a "permanent political solution to the Vietnamese problem." But the communiqué said such a parley should include "all interested governments." This reflected Do's statement that Saigon was opposed to including the Viet Cong's National Liberation Front as a separate delegation at such a parley. In a Mar. 31 note, Saigon asserted that "a military truce cannot be effective without prior agreement on details and controls." The note, made public by Nguyen Duy Lien, head of South Vietnam's observer mission at the UN, suggested that "details of the truce" be discussed by North and South Vietnamese armed forces representatives at any place "the Hanoi government may choose."

North Vietnamese rejection of Thant's plan had been made public by Hanoi Mar. 27. A Foreign Ministry statement said: "To call on both sides to cease fire and hold unconditional negotiations while the United States is committing aggression . . . is to make no distinction between the aggressors and the victim of aggression, to depart from reality and to demand that the Vietnamese people accept the conditions of the aggressors." The Hanoi statement quoted Thant as having said: "Hanoi views the hostilities as a civil war in South Vietnam, with Hanoi helping one side and the United States the other. Hanoi held that, if the United States was willing to withdraw support for Saigon, there might be a possibility of reciprocity." Asserting that this assessment of the situation did "not tally with the reality in Vietnam" and was "contrary" to North Vietnam's position, the Foreign Ministry stated that since the U.S. was "committing aggression against Vietnam, the correct way to settle the Vietnam problem is that the U.S. aggression must stop."

North Vietnam's opposition to a UN role in peace negotiations had been reiterated by the Foreign Ministry Mar. 19. The ministry accused the U.S. of attempting to "use the United Nations to interfere in the Vietnamese question." But the UN "has nothing to do with the Vietnam problem and . . . has no competence to deal" with it, the statement declared.

Thant's plan was rejected by the Viet Cong Apr. 6. A Viet Cong broadcast stated that since Thant had not proposed a halt in the U.S. bombing of North Vietnam, as he had in his previous plan submitted in Mar. 1966, his latest suggestion was "basically similar" to the U.S. demand for a reciprocal reduction of military activity in Vietnam. The broadcast also took issue with Thant's failure to include the Viet Cong in proposed preliminary talks.

Thant Urges U.S. to Stop Fighting

UN Secy. Gen. Thant suggested Apr. 1 that U.S. forces in Vietnam should unilaterally stop fighting and "thereafter . . . fire only if fired upon." Thant said that the U.S., "with power and wealth unprecedented in human history, is in a position to take this initiative" as "a first step" of "the standstill truce" he had proposed. Thant expressed hope that the Viet Cong and North Vietnamese forces would follow the U.S.' moves and also cease military operations. Thant based his new appeal on a similar plea that had been voiced Mar. 31 by U.S. Sen. Joseph S. Clark (D., Pa.). Thant said he agreed with Clark's opinion that the U.S. "can afford" to stop the fighting voluntarily "even though there is an admitted, but, in my opinion, limited risk for the United States in doing so." "This impasse can be broken . . .," Thant asserted, "only if one side or the other shows the wisdom and the courage and the compassion for humanity to take the initiative on a first step" toward stopping the fighting.

In a speech to the national convention of Americans for Democratic Action in Washington Mar. 31, Clark had suggested that "the best way" to achieve Thant's proposed standstill truce would be for the U.S. "to make the first move" by halting military operations Apr. 15. Under Clark's plan: The U.S. and its allies would then seek to have North Vietnam and the Viet Cong "follow suit"; if the Communists agreed, "we are on our way to peace"; if the Communists refused, the U.S., in any case, should halt the bombing, cease ground operations and "shore ourselves up in easily defensible positions," hitting back only to protect the defense perimeter.

Thant explained Apr. 1 that by a standstill truce he meant "a cessation of bombing and all other hostilities, with all forces remaining in position." Such a truce, Thant said, must not be conditioned on supervision or control. He conceded that an unsupervised cease-fire was bound to be violated. But if the belligerents were sincerely interested in peace, he declared, negotiations would not founder on breaches of the truce.

The only official U.S. response to Thant's suggestion came Apr. 1 from Amb.-to-UN Goldberg, who said he did not regard Thant's statement as either a proposal or an appeal. Goldberg added: "We have already responded to the Secretary General's latest proposal . . . of Mar. 14, and we stand by that response."

Thant toured Asia in April to discuss the Vietnamese situation with government leaders in Ceylon, India, Nepal, Pakistan and Afghanistan. On his return to New York Apr. 21, Thant said in an airport statement that it was "open knowledge" that "private negotiations" were in progress to end the war. En route to Asia, however, Thant had said during a stopover in Geneva Apr. 5 that peace prospects were "as distant today as they were a year ago." He repeated his previous warnings that "because of the increasing intensification of the war, there are more prospects of the war widening and spilling over the frontiers." Recalling North Vietnam's opposition to UN mediation, Thant said "it is impossible for anyone to perform any function [involving the Vietnamese war] as Secretary General."

(Ceylonese Foreign Ministry sources had reported Mar. 30 that North Vietnam had rejected a peace proposal advanced earlier in March in Hanoi by Ceylonese Amb.-to-Communist China Robert Gunawardena. The plan had called for truce talks by Viet Cong and North and South Vietnamese representatives and a guarantee of Vietnam's territorial integrity by neighboring countries and the UN Security Council. Hanoi replied that it would not consider any peace proposal as long as the U.S. continued to bomb North Vietnam. Following Thant's visit to Ceylon Apr. 8-9, the Ceylonese Foreign Ministry Apr. 10 issued a statement repeating its peace proposals.)

U.S. Proposes Widening DMZ

The U.S. proposed Apr. 19 that the 6-mile-wide demilitarized zone dividing North and South Vietnam be extended 10 miles on each side and that Communist and allied troops be withdrawn behind the widened buffer area. But North Vietnam rejected the U.S. proposal Apr. 21. The American plan was first outlined Apr. 19 at a closed meeting of the Southeast Asia Treaty Organization in Washington and was later made public by the U.S. State Department. The U.S. statement said the plan "offers considerable promise for de-escalation . . . and for moving toward an over-all settlement."

The American plan had been proposed in response to a Canadian peace plan submitted to the belligerents Apr. 11. The Canadian proposal had been rejected by Hanoi Apr. 16 but accepted by South Vietnam Apr. 18. Under the American proposal, the International Control Commission would supervise the pull-back of allied and Communist forces. The ICC would be permitted to inspect the southern part of the widened buffer zone provided North Vietnam allowed the commission access to the territory on its side of the demilitarized area.

A North Vietnamese Foreign Ministry statement Apr. 21 rejected the U.S. plan on the ground that it did not include Hanoi's principal condition for peace talks—an end to U.S. air attacks on North Vietnam. The ministry said the U.S. proposal was "a maneuver aimed at masking the whole of its policy of aggression and the creation of a broad 'no man's land' designed to divide Vietnam for a long time." The North Vietnamese statement accused the U.S. of having violated the neutral status of the demilitarized zone by conducting military operations in the area and by evacuating civilians from the zone and from territory just south of it.

The Canadian peace plan disclosed Apr. 11 by External Affairs Min. Paul Martin called for: (1) "Some degree of physical disengagement" by the military forces of both sides;

for example, the restoration of the "demilitarized character of the zone on either side of the 17th Parallel by the withdrawal of all military forces, supplies and equipment from that zone." (2) The freezing of military activities in Vietnam at their "present level." (3) Cessation of all ground, air and sea operations. (4) A "return to the cease-fire provisions of the Geneva settlement."

North Vietnam's rejection of the Canadian plan, published Apr. 16 by the Communist Party newspaper *Nhan Dan,* asserted that it was "in essence a crafty scheme of the United States imperialists on 'mutual de-escalation' or 'reciprocity' that does not make a clear-cut distinction between the aggressor and those who oppose aggression."

Hanoi Rejected 28 Peace Plans

State Secy. Dean Rusk charged May 1 that North Vietnam's disinterest in negotiations was evidenced by Hanoi's rejection of at least 28 peace proposals that had been forwarded by the U.S. or other nations. Speaking at the annual meeting of the U.S. Chamber of Commerce in Washington, Rusk asserted that American acceptance of these proposals and their rejection by North Vietnam "throw a light . . . upon the question of who is interested in peace and who is trying to absorb a neighbor by force." American "yeses" and North Vietnam's "noes" to suggestions for peace, Rusk asserted, were "relevant to the moral judgments which one might wish to make about the situation in Southeast Asia." The 28 proposals to which, according to Rusk, Hanoi said "no":

"—A reconvening of the Geneva conference of 1954—and a return to the agreements of 1954;

"—A reconvening of the Geneva conference of 1962 on Laos—and a return to the agreements of 1962;

"—A conference on Cambodia;

"—An all-Asian peace conference;

"—A special effort by the 2 (Geneva) co-chairmen;

"—A special effort by the ICC [International Control Commission];

"—A role for the United Nations Security Council—or the General Assembly—or the Secretary General;

"—Talks through intermediaries—single or group;

"—Direct talks—with the United States or with South Vietnam;

"—Exchange of prisoners of war;

"—Supervision of treatment of prisoners by International Red Cross;
"—Demilitarize the DMZ [Demilitarized Zone];
"—Widen and demilitarize the DMZ;
"—Interposition of international forces between combatants;
"—Mutual withdrawal of foreign forces, including North Vietnamese forces;
"—Assistance to Cambodia to assure its neutrality and territory;
"—Cessation of bombing and reciprocal de-escalation;
"—Cessation of bombing, infiltration and augmentation of United States forces;
"—3 suspensions of bombings to permit serious talks;
"—Discussion of Hanoi's 4 points along with points of others, such as Saigon's 4 points and our 14 points;
"—Discussion of an agreed 4 points as basis for negotiation;
"—Willingness to find means to have the views of the Liberation Front heard in peace discussions;
"—Negotiations without conditions, negotiations about conditions or discussion of a final settlement;
"—Peace and the inclusion of North Vietnam in large development program for Southeast Asia;
"—Government of South Vietnam to be determined by free elections;
"—Questions of reunification to be determined by free elections;
"—Reconciliation with Viet Cong and readmission to the body politic of South Vietnam;
"—South Vietnam can be neutral if it so chooses."

In a further discussion of peace prospects, Rusk said May 4 that the U.S. was "not contemplating any nuclear ultimatum" to bring Hanoi to the conference table. Rusk's statement was in response to a proposal by Rep. Paul Findley (R., Ill.) at a hearing of the House Foreign Affairs Committee. Findley suggested that the U.S. warn North Vietnam through UN Secy. Gen. Thant that it must be ready to start peace talks at a fixed date and that if it refused the U.S. would be prepared to escalate the war and use nuclear weapons, if necessary. Rusk said the U.S. was prepared to participate in negotiations "without any such ultimatum, implied or otherwise." The U.S. would agree to Hanoi's demands to "unconditionally" halt air raids on North Vietnam if North Vietnam in turn would agree to reduce "their half of the war," Rusk said. He added: "We will lay a schedule for our withdrawal on the table any time if they will lay a schedule of withdrawal on the table."

Thant Fears World War III

UN Secy. Gen. Thant May 11 expressed fears that "we are witnessing today the initial phase of World War III" in Vietnam. Speaking at a luncheon of the UN Correspondents Association in New York, Thant warned that "if the present trend continues, I am afraid direct confrontation, first of all between Washington and Peking, is inevitable." "We are witnessing today similar conditions" to those that had led to World Wars I and II, Thant said. He asserted that he "must say in this context that the mutual defense pact between Moscow and Peking [signed Feb. 15, 1950] is still in force."

Deploring the intensification of the ground fighting in South Vietnam and the U.S.' "new escalation of the air war against North Vietnam," Thant declared that these developments "jeopardized" a "lasting settlement in Southeast Asia" and threatened "the *détente* between the larger powers who carry the major load of responsibility for the maintenance of world peace." Thant expressed regret that "neither side has fully and unconditionally accepted" his Mar. 14 proposals "for a general standstill truce." Thant said he was "convinced that now, as ever before, the first obstacle to talks remains the continued air bombardment of North Vietnam." He recalled that Hanoi had "repeated [since Jan. 28] that if the bombardment were to cease there could be talks. It may be assumed that such a diplomatic stand has been taken by North Vietnam with full knowledge of the positions of its allies, and I regard this as a very important development."

In a statement issued later May 11, U.S. Amb.-to-UN Arthur J. Goldberg said the U.S. disagreed with Thant's "current assessment of the situation." Denying that the U.S. had rejected Thant's Mar. 14 peace proposals, Goldberg said Washington's reply had been "forthcoming and affirmative" whereas North Vietnam's "response was negative and constituted a rejection of the . . . proposal." Goldberg said: The U.S. shared Thant's anxieties about "the intensification of the war . . . [and] the increasing casualties on all sides." For this reason the U.S. had called repeatedly for "a mutual de-escalation of the conflict and a diminution and stoppage of violence on all sides." American policy remained unchanged from Goldberg's pledge before the UN General Assembly Sept. 22, 1966 that the U.S. would cease "all bombing of North Vietnam the moment we are assured privately or otherwise that this step will be answered promptly by a corresponding and appropriate de-escalation on the other side."

Goldberg called on Hanoi May 12 to clarify its position on a U.S. cessation of the bombing of North Vietnam. Speaking at a regional foreign policy conference in Chicago, Goldberg said Hanoi had implied "without quite saying so" that it "would be willing to talk" if the U.S. raids were halted permanently and unconditionally. If the U.S. were to "proceed along these lines," Goldberg said, North Vietnam must answer these 5 questions: "(1) What would we talk about and how soon? (2) Would the talks embrace our proposals as well as those of Hanoi? (3) Would the purpose of the talks be an honorable negotiated settlement and not a mere surrender of our side? (4) How would Hanoi reciprocate militarily to our action in ceasing the bombing? (5) What assurances would there be that neither side would derive any military advantage from the other's de-escalation?"

LBJ Urges Talks, Meets Kosygin

In a Memorial Day proclamation issued May 22, Pres. Johnson appealed to Hanoi to accept a negotiated settlement of the war. The President urged "the leaders of those whom we fight" in Vietnam to join with him to "end this tragic waste." "Let us sit down together to chart the simple course to peace," he said, and "let us together lead our people out of this bloody impasse." Speaking at the launching of the aircraft carrier *John F. Kennedy* at Newport News, Va. May 27, Johnson said: "It has often been our strength and our resolve which have tipped the scales of conflict against aggressors, or would-be aggressors. That role has never been easy."

Pres. Johnson met with Soviet Premier Aleksei Kosygin at 2 separate meetings in the college town of Glassboro, N.J. June 23 and 25. Kosygin was in the U.S. to represent his country at an emergency UN General Assembly session called to deal with the Middle East crisis. The 2 leaders, meeting for the first time, discussed the Middle East, Vietnam and other world problems. Although the meeting was apparently cordial, no significant agreements or understandings were revealed.

LBJ Accused of Wrecking Peace Effort

Writer-journalist Harry Ashmore, who had contacted North Vietnamese officials in Hanoi Jan. 6-14 on behalf of the Johnson Administration, charged in an article published Sept. 17 that the President had "effectively and brutally canceled" Ashmore's private peace mission by sending an uncompromising letter to Ho Chi Minh. Ashmore's article, "The Public Relations of Peace," appeared in *Center Magazine,* a publication of the Center for the Study of Democratic Institutions (Santa Barbara, Calif.), of which he was executive vice president. Ashmore, accompanied by *Miami News* editor William C. Baggs, had gone to Hanoi ostensibly to seek North Vietnam's participation in the Pacem in Terris II convocation in Geneva in May. After discussions with Ho Jan. 12, Ashmore and Baggs returned to Washington and reported their findings to the State Department Jan. 18.

Ashmore wrote that Ho had insisted on a cessation of American raids on North Vietnam as a requisite for peace talks. Ho also indicated that the U.S. must halt the build-up of its forces in South Vietnam. "Ho had understood that we would report our conversation to the State Department and expected some response, since he had made arrangements to have any further message sent directly to him," Ashmore reported. He said he had drafted a letter of reply to Ho in collaboration with Asst. State Secy. (for East Asian affairs) William P. Bundy and had sent it to Hanoi Feb. 5 through Cambodian channels. Ashmore added in a phone interview with the *N.Y. Times* Sept. 17 that the decision to send the letter to Ho had been disclosed to him and Baggs at a meeting Feb. 4 with Bundy, State Undersecy. Nicholas deB. Katzenbach, Amb.-at-Large W. Averell Harriman and Sen. J. W. Fulbright. In his article Ashmore said that his letter seemed to modify the U.S.' previous conditions for "reciprocal restraint" on the part of Hanoi in exchange for a halt to the U.S. bombings.

Ashmore charged that a letter sent by Pres. Johnson to Ho, dated Feb. 2, had nullified the effect of the Ashmore message of Feb. 5 in several respects. (The Johnson letter had been delivered to a North Vietnamese representative in Moscow Feb. 8 and received by Ho Feb. 10.) Ashmore contended that Mr. Johnson's message had not mentioned the Geneva accords as a basis for peace talks, as the Ashmore letter had done. Ashmore recalled that Mr. Johnson had offered to halt the American bombings and military build-up if North Vietnam ceased infiltration of the South. But the President placed a "time squeeze" on Hanoi by insisting that his proposal go into effect at the end of the scheduled *Tet* truce Feb. 12. Ashmore noted that in the drafting of his letter to Ho, Bundy "had insisted that it would be a mistake to tie any proposal to the *Tet* bombing pause, since this would be interpreted by Ho as an effort to force his hand without adequate opportunity to consult with his people" and the NLF.

Ho answered Pres. Johnson Feb. 15, and Ashmore said that the President "got the sharp negative reply from Ho Chi Minh he must have expected." Ashmore added: "Ours came a little later, the simple unexceptional statement that there didn't seem to be any point in Messrs. Ashmore and Baggs coming back to Hanoi at any time."

Ashmore said in the phone interview that at first he had decided not to publicize the incident because "we thought that as long as we might be a useful channel we didn't want to jeopardize it." But the recent escalation of the war indicated that "whatever kind of channel we had is no use now," Ashmore declared, and there was no longer any purpose in concealing the U.S.-North Vietnamese exchanges.

In reply to Ashmore, Bundy Sept. 18 denied the charge that Pres. Johnson's letter to Ho had contradicted the one sent by Ashmore. Bundy also pointed out that prior to Ashmore's report to the State Department Jan. 18, the U.S. already "had established a direct channel for communication with North Vietnamese representatives in Moscow," which took precedence over Ashmore's contacts. But despite the existence of the Moscow channel (of which Ashmore and Baggs were unaware), Bundy said the State Department had believed that "it would be useful to send a more general message [to Ho] through Messrs. Baggs and Ashmore, which would be consistent with the important messages being exchanged in Moscow." Bundy added: "Mr. Ashmore yields to an understandable feeling that his own channel was the center of the stage. It was not; it was a very, very small part of the total picture."

Bundy said the American contact with Hanoi officials in Moscow and the discussions on Vietnam in London Feb. 7 between British Prime Min. Wilson and Soviet Premier Kosygin had led to Pres. Johnson's message to Pres. Ho. Contending that "there was no basic change whatever" between the President's and Ashmore's letters, Bundy explained: "Hanoi had not responded in any useful way to the variety of suggestions conveyed in the Moscow channel. Its sole and apparently final response was reflected on Feb. 13, in a letter by Pres. Ho to Pope Paul VI. This letter, in the words of one press account today, 'coupled an unconditional end to the bombing with the withdrawal of American forces and the recognition of the National Liberation Front.' "

Bundy said that the President's message to Ho had been sent Feb. 8 and that Ashmore was mistaken in saying it had been sent Feb. 2.

In answer to Bundy's statement, Ashmore Sept. 18 reiterated the view that his letter to Ho and the one sent by the President were "inconsistent in tone and content. . . . The tone of ours is quite conciliatory. The tone of the President's is quite harsh." Ashmore asked: If the American contacts with the North Vietnamese representatives in Moscow were so vital, "why did they send our letter?"

Sen. Fulbright said Sept. 18 that the incident indicated that the U.S. could have entered into peace talks with Hanoi if it had been willing to consider "anything short of surrender" by North Vietnam.

U.S. Seeks UN Role?

U.S. Amb.-to-UN Goldberg was reported Sept. 6 to have proposed a 5-point peace plan for Vietnam to be advanced through the UN Security Council. Goldberg was said to have been discussing the plan with 6 Council members: Britain, France, Japan, Argentina, Brazil and Denmark. But the U.S.' UN mission denied that the U.S. had current plans to promote a Vietnam peace plan in the Security Council. The mission said Goldberg was participating only in "pre-Assembly discussion in which Vietnam certainly is a subject."

Goldberg said Sept. 7 that the U.S. "has under continuous review the possibility of a United Nations role in helping to bring about an honorable peace in Vietnam." Although conceding that he had discussed Vietnam with other UN delegations, Goldberg said it was "premature and does not contribute to the cause of peace to detail such informal consultations."

According to the report, Goldberg had proposed that the Council request an international peace conference based on the 1954 and 1962 Geneva conferences on Indochina. His 5-point plan was said to have called for: (1) a truce and disengagement of military forces in North and South Vietnam; (2) a withdrawal of military forces other than those under the control of North and South Vietnam and the dismantling of foreign-controlled military bases; (3) respect for the frontiers of nations bordering North and South Vietnam and the demilitarized zone dividing North and South Vietnam; (4) reunification of North and South Vietnam through the efforts of leaders of both areas without foreign interference; (5) international supervision of peace agreements.

A proposal to put the issue before the UN had been made in the Senate Aug. 28 by Senate Democratic leader Mike Mansfield (Mont.) and indorsed by these 10 Senators: J. W. Fulbright (D., Ark.), Wayne Morse (D., Ore.), John J. Sparkman (D., Ala.), John O. Pastore (D., R.I.), George D. Aiken (R., Vt.), John Sherman Cooper (R., Ky.), Gordon Allott (R., Colo.), Frank Carlson (R., Kan.), Frank Church (D., Ida.) and Philip A. Hart (D., Mich.). Mansfield told newsmen he thought the Administration was "very interested" in his proposal but admitted that the UN was not. Mansfield said Sept. 1 that his proposal had Pres. Johnson's full support and cooperation. By that time the number of Senators supporting it had risen to 26.

Addressing the UN General Assembly in New York Sept. 21, Goldberg reiterated the U.S. view that the UN had a "right and duty to concern itself" with the Vietnam problem. Commenting on recently expressed opinions that a cessation of

U.S. bombing of North Vietnam would lead to peace talks, Goldberg noted that not even those governments closest to North Vietnam had "conveyed to us any authoritative message from Hanoi that there would in fact be negotiations if the bombing were stopped. We have sought such a message directly from Hanoi without success." Goldberg posed this question: "Does North Vietnam conceive that the cessation of bombing would or should lead to any other results than meaningful negotiations or discussions under circumstances which would not disadvantage either side?" Goldberg asked Hanoi's supporters: If the U.S. ordered a cessation of the bombing, "what would they [Hanoi's backers] then do or refrain from doing, and how would they then use their influence and power, in order to move the Vietnam conflict promptly toward a peaceful resolution?"

Soviet Foreign Min. Andrei A. Gromyko told the Assembly Sept. 22 that the most serious threat to peace in the world was the U.S.' "aggression" in Vietnam, because "at any moment the fighting can overrun new areas and draw new states into its orbit." Gromyko said that Goldberg's speech contained "nothing new" and that "backstage meetings" and talks in the UN had "nothing to do with the solution to the Vietnam problem." He asked what the U.S. reply was to the Jan. 28 statement of North Vietnam "about readiness to begin negotiations on a settlement of the Vietnam problem after the cessation" of U.S. bombings. Gromyko answered the reply had been "barbarous bombings" of cities, dams, irrigation projects and hospitals. Gromyko asserted that "peace can be brought about in Vietnam only as a result of the withdrawal of the aggressors [the U.S.]."

UN Secy. Gen. Thant had said Sept. 16 that he had temporarily abandoned efforts to mediate the Vietnamese conflict. He considered a suspension of bombing the most important prerequisite for peace talks, Thant explained, and since the bombing had not been halted, "I don't see how I can usefully pursue my efforts toward finding a peaceful solution." But Thant called again for an unconditional halt in the U.S. air attacks. Conceding that "there was a limited risk" in such a suspension, Thant said he was "convinced" that a bombing halt would lead to "meaningful talks between Hanoi and Washington" in 3-4 weeks. But Thant said he was certain, on the basis of information he had received, that "if Hanoi is asked to do something, take some reciprocal action as a price for the cessation of bombing, Hanoi will not pay that price." Citing examples of reciprocity, Thant pointed out that "if Hanoi is asked to withdraw its 50,000 regulars from the South, I am afraid Hanoi will not comply with this. Or if Hanoi is asked to cut off its supplies and reinforcements to its men in the South, I don't think Hanoi will leave its men in South Vietnam to their fate."

New Hanoi 'Feelers' Reported

According to 2 separate news reports Sept. 14, Hanoi had dropped fresh hints of interest in peace talks. One report, an Agence France-Presse dispatch from Hanoi, quoted "reliable sources" as saying that U.S.-North Vietnamese peace talks "could begin" 3-4 weeks after the cessation of American bombing attacks on North Vietnam. The 2d report was one in which Canadian External Affairs Min. Paul Martin had said that North Vietnamese officials in Hanoi had indicated to a Canadian diplomat, O. W. Dyer, that they were interested in opening discussions to end the war.

Commenting on these 2 dispatches, U.S. State Secy. Rusk said at his press conference Sept. 15: "I have read these reports. I would be interested in learning what lies behind them, if anything. So far as I know, the situation has not changed since my last press conference" (Sept. 8).

The Agence France-Presse report said that its sources had referred to a speech by North Vietnamese Premier Pham Van Dong Aug. 30 to support the suggestion that Hanoi looked favorably on the prospects of holding peace talks. Dong had said: "If the American side really desires conversations, it should first cease unconditionally the bombing and every other act of war" against North Vietnam. North Vietnam's interpretation of the term unconditional, according to the sources quoted by the French news agency, meant that there should be no specific time limit to the bombing pause and that the U.S should not announce prior to the halt in the raids that it would send reconnaissance planes over North Vietnam.

U.S. State Department officials Sept. 14 said they doubted whether the Agence France-Presse report indicated a shift in North Vietnam's position on peace talks. The officials said that even if the report represented an authoritative reaction from Hanoi, which the officials doubted, it still did not comply with American conditions for a reciprocal North Vietnamese action to balance an American cessation of bombing.

Agence France-Presse Sept. 26 quoted Hanoi sources as saying that North Vietnam was prepared to enter into "serious" and "significant" talks with the U.S. 3-4 weeks after an unconditional halt to the bombing of North Vietnam and a cessation of all "other acts of war." Other views as expressed by Hanoi sources: North Vietnam would regard a U.S. announcement of a suspension of bombing "for a certain period" as conditional, and therefore no talks could start under these circumstances; but if the U.S. ceased unconditionally all acts of war, negotiations would take place.

(North Vietnamese Premier Phan Van Dong Sept. 1 had reiterated his government's stand that an unconditional halt in the U.S. air raids on the North was Hanoi's prerequisite to peace negotiations. In a statement made on the 22d anniversary of the founding of North Vietnam as a nation, Dong said: "So long as the United States pursues its aggression we will continue to fight. If the American side really wants to talk, it must first stop unconditionally the bombing of North Vietnam and all other acts of war against . . . North Vietnam. The United States has no right to demand any reciprocity whatsoever. . . . We know quite well that the United States does not want to negotiate a settlement of the Vietnam problem, because U.S. imperialism is aggressive and warlike by nature. All it wants is war, and it is stepping up its aggressive war." In an interview published July 24 in the Polish Communist newspaper *Trybuna Ludu,* Dong had rejected the U.S.' view that North Vietnam "put greater trust in the movement of opposition against the war" in the U.S. "than in our own efforts.")

LBJ's San Antonio Statement

U.S. terms for a halt in the air and naval bombardment of North Vietnam were restated by Pres. Johnson Sept. 29 in a televised address to the National Legislative Conference, meeting in San Antonio, Tex. The President said that many Americans, sincerely troubled over the course of the war, had asked why negotiations had not been begun toward peace in Vietnam. He replied:

"The answer is that we and our South Vietnamese allies are wholly prepared to negotiate tonight. I am ready to talk with Ho Chi Minh and other chiefs of state concerned tomorrow. I am ready to have Secretary Rusk meet with their foreign minister tomorrow. I am ready to send a trusted representative of America to any spot on this earth to talk in public or private with a spokesman of Hanoi. We have twice sought to have the issue of Vietnam dealt with by the United Nations—and twice Hanoi has refused." "As we have told Hanoi time and time and time again, the heart of the matter is really this: the United States is willing to stop all aerial and naval bombardment of North Vietnam when this will lead promptly to productive discussion. We, of course, assume that while discussions proceed, North Vietnam would not take advantage of the bombing cessation or limitation."

Mr. Johnson blamed North Vietnam for the continuation of the war. He said that it was "by Hanoi's choice, and not ours, and not the rest of the world, that the war continues." "Why," he asked, "in the face of military and political progress in the South, and the burden of the bombing in the North, do they insist and persist with the war?" "From many sources the answer is the same: they still hope that the people of the United States will not see this struggle through to the very end."

The President declared that there were overwhelming reasons why the U.S. would not shirk its obligations in Vietnam. Primary among them, he said, was the belief, backed by 3 Presidents and the Senate, that a Communist victory in Vietnam would menace Southeast Asia and create tensions that could result in a 3d World War. Mr. Johnson asserted that the U.S. had met similar threats in the past and had overcome them because "brave men were willing to risk their lives for their nation's security." The President declared that 2 things were necessary to deal with the Vietnam crisis: "First, we must not mislead the enemy. Let him not think that debate and dissent will produce wavering and withdrawal, for I can assure you they won't. Let him not think that protest will produce surrender, because it won't. Let him not think that he will wait us out, for he won't. 2d, we will provide all that our brave men require to do the job that must be done, and that job's going to be done."

The Johnson terms for negotiations were rejected by North Vietnam Oct. 3. A statement published in the Hanoi newspaper *Nhan Dan* declared that the U.S. had committed aggression in Vietnam and had no right to pose conditions for talks.

At his press conference in Washington Oct. 12, Rusk cited Pres. Johnson's Sept. 29 offer to "stop all aerial and naval bombardment" of North Vietnam if this would lead "promptly to productive discussions" and if North Vietnam would not take advantage of the lull by reinforcing its military position. Rusk also said that Mr. Johnson was ready to meet with North Vietnamese Pres. Ho Chi Minh and other interested leaders "tomorrow" and that Rusk was prepared to leave "today" to meet with North Vietnamese officials to discuss peace.

Nhan Dan commented in an editorial broadcast by Hanoi radio Oct. 19: Rusk "wondered why these proposals had been rejected. The reason is simple. Having realized that the root of the war in Vietnam is U.S. aggression, the world's people, including the Americans, have urged that the root be pulled out," that is, U.S. troops quit South Vietnam. "The American people's movement against the war continues to make headway, as shown in the nationwide struggle to end U.S. aggression in Vietnam." The expanding anti-war movement of "the world's people, including the Americans," was "driving the Johnson Administration into increasing isolation and embarrassment."

U.S. Would Accept NLF at Talks

U.S. Amb.-to-UN Goldberg said Nov. 2 that the Johnson Administration favored participation of the NLF in UN Security Council discussion of Vietnam or in a reconvened Geneva conference on ending the war. Goldberg reported on the Administration's position in testimony before the Senate Foreign Relations Committee in Washington. Goldberg also made public the text of a revised resolution that the U.S. had been circulating at the UN in a new effort to have the Security Council take up the Vietnam issue. The resolution called for "the convening of an international conference for the purpose of establishing a permanent peace in Southeast Asia based upon the principle of the Geneva agreements." Goldberg explained that the resolution referred only in general terms to an "international conference" because the Communists had indicated that they would be interested in something other than a Geneva-type parley.

Heretofore, the U.S. Administration had never stated publicly whether it would agree to NLF representation as a separate delegation or as part of the North Vietnamese delegation at peace talks. The American view, as first stated by Pres. Johnson in July 1965, was that the NLF "would have no difficulty in being represented and having their views presented if Hanoi for a moment decides she wants to cease aggression." Goldberg said that the U.S. would "not stand in the way" of the NLF's being invited to UN Security Council discussions on Vietnam and that the U.S.' "vote would be available if necessary" to approve such an invitation.

Soviet Premier Kosygin had rejected proposals for the reconvening of the Geneva conference. His rejection, in a letter appearing Oct. 30 in the Soviet government newspaper *Izvestia,* was in reply to a proposal forwarded by Dr. Ales Bebler, a former Yugoslav diplomat who was chairman of the World Federation of United Nations Associations. Bebler had suggested that as co-chairmen of the 1954 Geneva conference on Vietnam, Britain and the Soviet Union meet with the 3 members of the International Control Commission—Canada, Poland and India—to seek a formula for peace. Kosygin replied to Bebler that "it stands to reason that an international conference within the framework of the Geneva conference is unrealistic for the additional reason that the United States, which is carrying out armed intervention in Vietnam, has grossly violated the Geneva agreement and refuses to stop interference in the affairs of the Vietnamese people." British

Prime Min. Wilson in September had expressed approval of Bebler's proposal.

LBJ Suggests Meeting on Ship

Pres. Johnson suggested Nov. 11 that peace talks might be held on a ship at sea. During a tour of U.S. military bases, Mr. Johnson, while aboard the aircraft carrier *Enterprise* about 23 miles out of San Diego, reasserted his desire to find peace and suggested that "a neutral ship on a neutral sea would be as good a meeting place as any" for peace negotiators. "Our statesmen will press the search for peace to the corners of the earth," he declared. "That meeting ground could even be the sea . . . so long as both met halfway, so long as one did not insist that the other walk on water and work a miracle alone." He urged Hanoi to "hear this: You force us to fight. But you have only to say the word for our quarrel to be buried beneath the waves."

North Vietnam Nov. 14 in effect spurned Pres. Johnson's suggestion. *Nhan Dan* said "there is no need to go a thousand miles to search for peace." "Peace will be restored," the newspaper said, when the U.S. accepted Hanoi's 4-point peace formula.

Speaking at a Foreign Policy Association dinner in New York Nov. 14, State Secy. Rusk renewed his offer to negotiate "without condition" with North Vietnam to end the war. Rusk said: "Those who would 'negotiate now' should know that if a representative of Hanoi would make himself available anywhere to discuss peace I would be there." "We will negotiate today without condition or about conditions. . . . All the violence could end within hours with minimum cooperation from the authorities in Hanoi. . . . We have tried over and over again, through diplomacy and by practical actions on the ground, to start the process of de-escalation—only to face a categorical rejection from the other side."

NLF Seeks U.S. & UN Contacts

It was reported in press dispatches that the NLF had sought to establish contacts with U.S. officials in Saigon and with the UN in New York. In each instance the NLF reportedly was blocked in its efforts to make contacts. But the NLF

Dec. 9 denied, as "sheer fabrication," the repeated reports that it had sought to send representatives to the UN.

A Dec. 1 report from Saigon had said that South Vietnamese police had arrested a Viet Cong representative while he was on his way to meet with U.S. embassy officials. The seized Viet Cong representative was identified Dec. 2 as Nguyen Van Huan and was described as a "middle-level" NLF official. One report of the the alleged incident said Huan was intercepted after the U.S.' CIA had arranged a meeting between him and U.S. Amb. Ellsworth Bunker. South Vietnamese House of Representatives Deputy Phan Xuan Huy told the House that the CIA had sought to establish other U.S.-NLF contacts without the knowledge of the Saigon regime. Huy charged that the incident represented "a flagrant act of American interference in the internal affairs of South Vietnam."

An AP dispatch Dec. 1 also said that a meeting between Huan and Bunker had been "thwarted" but that soundings between NLF and high-ranking American officials had been made in November. A U.S. embassy spokesman Dec. 1 called the AP report "false." The embassy "would not, of course, undertake any such contacts without the knowledge of the South Vietnamese government," the U.S. statement said.

South Vietnamese Police Chief Nguyen Ngoc Loan, who had ordered the arrest of the Viet Cong emissary, had resigned the previous week, ostensibly for reasons of health. But Loan said he had quit after rejecting U.S. demands that he release Huan. Loan's resignation was rejected Nov. 30 and he returned to his post Dec. 1.

A Washington report Dec. 1 conceded that U.S. and South Vietnamese officials had been in touch with NLF representatives in previous months. But the report said the contacts had dealt with prisoners and similar matters and not with peace negotiations.

The U.S. Dec. 6 conceded for the first time that a Viet Cong representative had been blocked in an effort to meet with U.S. officials in Saigon. A State Department statement said South Vietnamese Premier Nguyen Van Loc had confirmed that the South Vietnamese police had reported to him that "they had picked up a Viet Cong cadre who claimed that he was trying to contact U.S. embassy officials."

The *Washington Post* reported from UN headquarters in New York Dec. 1 that the NLF had sought to send representatives to the UN in October to discuss the Vietnamese conflict with UN General Assembly delegates. The report said the U.S. had opposed the move on the ground that such a matter should be taken up by the UN Security Council. The NLF reportedly had contacted UN Secy. Gen. Thant, who, in turn, relayed the request of U.S. officials.

A Dec. 2 U.S. State Department statement, commenting on the reported NLF-UN contact, said the U.S.' "attitude on this matter" had been expressed by U.S. Amb. Goldberg when he said in testimony before the Senate Foreign Relations Committee Nov. 2: "With respect to groups such as the NLF, Rule 39 of the Security Council is the applicable rule and the United States would not stand in the way of groups, including the NLF, being invited under that rule." Goldberg denied Dec. 7 that the U.S. had sought to prevent the NLF from presenting its case at the UN. He disclosed that the NLF had inquired of the UN Secretariat in September about sending 2 or 3 representatives to New York. Goldberg added: The U.S. requested more information before issuing the visas to the Communist delegates. An NLF reply said the front officials would travel on North Vietnamese passports, would stay in the U.S. for a year and would want assurances that the visas could be extended for another year. A U.S. answer said Washington would grant visas "in connection with any United Nations business as required by and in conformity with" the UN Headquarters Agreement. Goldberg said the NLF had then dropped its effort to send delegates to the U.S. He insisted that the NLF representatives did not seek "status with or at the United Nations" and that they had not raised the point of gaining access to the General Assembly.

The South Vietnamese Foreign Ministry had said Dec. 5 that Saigon would oppose the presence of the NLF in any discussions at the UN on the ground that the front was a "tool of the army of North Vietnam." Foreign Min. Tran Van Do stated: South Vietnam had "never recognized the NLF as a political party. Our position toward peace talks is that one should talk to the aggressors, that is the North Vietnamese, not the Viet Cong." The U.S. assured South Vietnam Dec. 8 that it would not alter its position on the Viet Cong without consulting the Saigon regime or its other allies. The State Department statement sought to allay reported South Vietnamese doubt about U.S. contacts with the Viet Cong and NLF peace probes at the UN. The statement said American policy remained unchanged: The U.S. was "prepared to discuss peace" with North Vietnam "or any other government at any time." The NLF "would have no difficulty being represented and having its views represented." As for NLF moves to be heard at the UN, the U.S. statement said: The U.S. would not be opposed to NLF delegates "presenting their views . . . when they are officially invited for official business. The question of the National Liberation Front coming to the United Nations under an official invitation is, of course, totally different from any question of their entering the United States for propaganda purposes. We do oppose their coming merely to mount a propaganda campaign."

UN Gets NLF Program

The NLF outlined its future political plans in a detailed document circulated among UN delegations in New York Dec. 14. A highlight of the plans was a call for the establishment, after a Viet Cong military victory, of a coalition "national union democratic government" in South Vietnam. The document also stressed the need for economic and agrarian reform and for reunification of North and South Vietnam. The program had been formulated at an extraordinary NLF congress in August and was first made public Sept. 1.

The NLF document called for the abolition of South Vietnam's "disguised colonial regime established by United States imperialists" and of the constitution and of "all anti-democratic laws enacted by the United States imperialists and the puppet administration." The front proposed "free general elections" to choose a new National Assembly, which would have "the highest authority" in the country. This assembly was to "work out a democratic constitution. . . ." The front's document envisaged the establishment of "a national union democratic government including the most representative persons among the various social strata, nationalities, religious communities, patriotic personalities and forces which have contributed to the cause of national liberation." It advocated freedom of speech, press, assembly and the right to form political parties. It vowed severe punishment to South Vietnam's "die-hard cruel agents" of the U.S.

In order "to improve the people's living conditions," the NLF demanded the elimination of "the policy of economic enslavement and monopoly of the United States imperialists." The document said: Private ownership rights would be respected, and "the state will encourage the capitalists in industry and trade" to develop their operations; the new government would "confiscate the lands of the U.S. imperialists and the die-hard cruel landlords" and "allot those lands to landless or land-poor peasants"; "the state will negotiate the purchase of land from landlords who possess" too much land and turn it over to landless peasants.

The document also said: South and North Vietnam would negotiate reunification "without either side using pressure against the other and without foreign interference." Pending reunification, North and South would "make joint efforts to defend the fatherland" and "expand economic and cultural exchanges." The new government would pursue "a foreign policy of peace and neutrality, a foreign policy which guarantees independence, sovereignty, unity and territorial integrity of the country and helps safeguard world peace." Diplomatic relations would be established "with all countries regardless of their social and political system."

U.S. Amb. Goldberg said Dec. 14 that he had been "reliably informed" that the NLF document did not alter the NLF's and North Vietnam's policy of not recognizing the competency of the UN to deal with the Vietnam situation.

The U.S. State Department said Dec. 15 that the NLF "program reflects no significant change in the position of the NLF or of Hanoi, whose '4 points,' which it maintains must be the basis for peace, refer to the NLF's program." The department said an analysis of the NLF program and of captured Viet Cong documents "make clear that the objective in

any coalition structure would be for the National Liberation
Front to secure at once the levers of power and, in effect, control the resulting government both at the local and central
levels."

According to U.S. officials, one of the captured Viet Cong
documents was a translation of notes on a guerrilla training
program conducted at the NLF's central office in September
and dealt largely with the front's views on a future coalition
government in South Vietnam. The document, captured Oct.
10, acknowledged the concern of some Viet Cong leaders when
the NLF first broached the possibility of a coalition government in its Sept. 1 policy statement. But it dismissed these
worries, confidently expressing the belief that "our party will
exercise overall control over" any coalition government. The
captured document reportedly said: "We are not strong
enough to deal a lethal blow. A coalition government could be
advantageous to our revolutionary goals. . . . To all appear-
ances, it will be a coalition government, but the real powers
will be in our hands. The coalition government may include a
non-revolutionary as president, but basically it must follow
the [NLF] line of action."

LBJ Visits Southeast Asia & Vatican

In connection with a trip to Australia to attend memorial
rites for the late Prime Min. Harold Holt (drowned while
swimming Dec. 17), Pres. Johnson conferred with the U.S.'
Vietnam allies and made brief visits to Vietnam, Thailand and
the Vatican Dec. 20-24.

The most important of the President's talks were those
held with Pres. Thieu of South Vietnam in Canberra Dec. 21
on the question of eventual political negotiations with the
National Liberation Front. Mr. Johnson, in a taped TV interview broadcast in the U.S. Dec. 19, had credited Thieu with a
"statesmanlike position" by saying "that he is prepared for
informal talks with members of the NLF, and these could
bring good results." Mr. Johnson continued: "I hope the other
side will respond. . . . I have said that I think the war can be
stopped in a matter of days if Pres. Thieu's suggestions that
he informally talk with members of the NLF are carried out
and if they would agree to what they have already agreed to

in the 1954 accords and the 1962 accords and . . . other points
. . . , like one man, one vote under the present constitutional
government."

Thieu, however, had told reporters Dec. 20 as he was leaving Saigon for Australia: "We would accept any representative of the front who came back to us a returnee [defector
from the Viet Cong]. We will never recognize the front as a
government or even as a legitimate political party." At a refueling stop in Singapore, he said: "Our policy is very clear.
We never recognize the National Liberation Front as a government or anything else, but if any of them wish to come
over to our side we are willing to talk to them on an individual basis but not as front representatives."

After meeting Dec. 21 for 2 hours, Mr. Johnson and Thieu
issued a joint communiqué affirming that Thieu was ready "to
discuss relevant matters with any individuals now associated"
with the NLF but that the front would not be recognized as
an independent organization by the Saigon government. It
said useful talks could not be conducted "with any elements
. . . committed to violent methods to obtain their political
ends," but "full rights of citizenship" would be granted to
any former enemies ready "to live at peace" under the constitutional processes of the elected Saigon government. The
2 Presidents "agreed that the basic principle involved was the
right of the South Vietnamese people to determine their own
future through democratic and constitutional process noted
in the principle of one man, one vote."

On his return to Saigon Dec. 24, Thieu said he and Mr.
Johnson had "found that there had been no change" in either
the Saigon or U.S. "position *vis-à-vis* negotiations with the
NLF." He said he would "listen" to anyone from the enemy
side and afterwards, if that person "wants to go back to the
jungle, we will let him go."

(Vice Pres. Humphrey had said Dec. 7 that the Saigon
government "has contact with individual members of the
NLF." He added that a possible "split" within the NLF could
lead to the front's non-Communist elements entering into a
South Vietnamese coalition government. Speaking on the
CBS-TV program "Classroom USA," Humphrey said: "It

may be that at some future date that some of the non-Communist members of the NLF may very well want to be brought into a government and may very well be the very ones we have to negotiate with." The NLF "is not all Communist. I think it is Communist dominated . . . , but I also know that there are people in it that are not Communist.")

Flying to the Korat air base in Thailand Dec. 23, Pres. Johnson told U.S. fighter pilots the U.S. and its allies were "defeating this aggression," and "the use we are making of air power in all its forms is a major reason the plans of the enemy are doomed to fail." "Your cause is a just one," he declared. "Let no man in any land misread the spirit of our land. The spirit of America is not to be read on placards and posters. It is a spirit manifest in the steadfastness and resolve of a nation holding firmly and faithfully to its course. From our course we shall not turn."

At Camranh Bay in South Vietnam later Dec. 23, the President told U.S. combat troops that the enemy "knows that he has met his master in the field." "We're not going to yield and we're not going to shimmy," he said.

Arriving in Italy later Dec. 23, Mr. Johnson flew to Rome and the Vatican. His meeting with Pope Paul VI, with only interpreters attending, lasted 1¼ hours. After the meeting, Mr. Johnson issued a statement saying: "We are ready at any moment to substitute the word and the vote for the knife and the grenade in bringing an honorable peace to Vietnam." "We agree with His Holiness that 'an honorable settlement of the painful and threatening dispute is still possible.' We shall keep closely in touch with His Holiness . . . as we shall with others who are seeking to lift the scourge of war from Vietnam and Southeast Asia."

A Vatican statement on the meeting said the pope had advanced proposals toward attaining peace. The President was reported to have told the pope that the U.S. was prepared to stop bombing North Vietnam if the Viet Cong and North Vietnam would offer "some [acceptable] guarantee" toward negotiations. Mr. Johnson also reportedly cited "the plight" of U.S. prisoners held by North Vietnam and proposed that the Vatican try to get direct information about prisoners in both North and South Vietnam.

(Appeals for peace in Vietnam were voiced by Pope Paul in 3 statements issued before Christmas. In a message sent to heads of government and churches of all denominations and made public Dec. 15, the pope suggested worldwide celebration of Jan. 1, 1968 and every future New Year's day as a "Day of Peace." In an address to the College of Cardinals in Rome Dec. 22, Paul called for a halt to the bombing of North Vietnam and indicated that he would lend his good offices to help achieve peace. The pontiff expressed hope that the belligerents in Vietnam would not seek "victory which oppresses, but security, peace and liberty for all." Paul deplored the fact that "every disinterested offer of mediation has been rendered vain, every honest and peaceful negotiation repulsed, while there still seems possible an honorable settlement of the dolorous and menacing affairs." A Christmas message delivered by the pope Dec. 23 stressed that "external peace derives from and depends upon interior peace. Peace must be in men's hearts before it can be made real. . . .")

Fresh Hanoi 'Feeler'?

North Vietnamese Foreign Min. Nguyen Duy Trinh said Dec. 29 (in a statement broadcast by Hanoi radio Jan. 1, 1968) that his government would start talks if the U.S. unconditionally halted attacks against North Vietnam. His declaration stirred international speculation that Hanoi might have eased its conditions for peace negotiations. Speaking at a reception for a delegation to Hanoi from Mongolia Trinh said: "The American government never stops repeating that it wants talks with Hanoi but that Hanoi does not react by any sign. If the American government really wants conversations, as clearly stated in our declaration of Jan. 28, 1967, it must first unconditionally cease bombing and all other acts of war against the Democratic Republic of Vietnam [the DRV, or North Vietnam]. After the cessation of bombing and all other acts of war against the Democratic Republic of Vietnam, the DRV will start conversations with the United States on relevant problems."

Heretofore, North Vietnam had insisted that talks could, rather than "will," be held after the U.S. ended hostilities. In his address, Trinh reiterated Hanoi's previously stated position that North Vietnam's "4 points" remained "the basis for the settlement of the Vietnamese question" and that North Vietnam opposed UN Security Council consideration of the Vietnamese situation on the ground that the UN had no jurisdiction. Trinh assailed the U.S. for threatening "to extend the war to Cambodia and Laos."

MILITARY ACTION

Fighting & Build-Up Continue

During 1967 there was both a continued intensification of the fighting in Vietnam and a continued build-up of the forces on both sides. The number of uniformed Americans in Vietnam rose from about 380,000 at the beginning of the year to approximately 500,000 by the end of 1967. (By comparison, U.S. peak strength in Korea during the Korean war was 472,-800.) If Americans serving in Thailand and aboard 7th Fleet ships off the Vietnamese coast were included, the total approximated 600,000. South Vietnam's forces numbered about 700,000, and an estimated 242,000 Viet Cong/North Vietnamese troops were engaged in the struggle by the year's end.

American casualties during 1967 exceeded those of all the previous years of war combined. U.S. dead numbered 9,353, compared to 5,008 in 1966. Total U.S. dead since 1961 numbered 15,997. American wounded in 1967 numbered 99,742. The other casualties in 1967 included: 11,135 South Vietnamese armed forces fatalities; 189 other allied troop fatalities; an estimated 90,401 enemy deaths; and some 25,000 civilian fatalities. In the air war over North Vietnam, the total number of planes lost since the bombings began in Feb. 1965 reached 779—328 of them downed during 1967. The U.S. had lost about 225 planes over South Vietnam since 1961. More than 500 helicopters had been lost in combat, and some 1,000 other planes and 'copters had been lost in accidents, in ground attacks on airfields and in other ways.

According to the U.S. mission in Saigon the Viet Cong killed 3,820 South Vietnamese civilians in 1967; they had killed 1,618 in 1966. 5,368 civilians were reported kidnaped by the Viet Cong in 1967, compared with 3,507 in 1966.

New Year's Truce

A New Year's truce in Vietnam ended at 7 a.m. Jan. 2, and the U.S. announced the immediate resumption of "normal operations." The cease-fire, agreed to by U.S., allied and Communist forces, had gone into effect at 7 a.m. Dec. 31, 1966.

U.S. military authorities reported Jan. 2 that Viet Cong and North Vietnamese forces had violated the truce 178 times; 38 incidents were listed as significant. In one of the more serious clashes, U.S. Navy patrol boats fought for 4 hours Jan. 1-2 with 2 Viet Cong trawlers off the southernmost tip of South Vietnam. One trawler was sunk, the other driven aground.

Hanoi radio charged Jan. 1 that U.S. planes and warships had bombed North Vietnamese residential and industrial targets Dec. 30. The Hanoi broadcast said the U.S. planes had attacked Vinhlin, Hatianh, Nghean, Thanhhoa and Namha and that U.S. warships had shelled residential areas in the Quangbinh Province town of Quangtrac.

An additional 5,000 soldiers of the U.S. 9th Infantry Division arrived Jan. 1 in Vungtau (40 miles southeast of Saigon). They increased American troop strength in South Vietnam to 380,000. A U.S. spokesman said the arrival of the reinforcements was not a violation of the New Year's truce because the landing was an administrative movement, not a hostile action.

U.S. air activity intensified over North Vietnam Jan. 2, immediately after the truce ended. In what a U.S. spokesman described as "the largest air battle of the war," Air Force planes shot down 7 Communist MiG-21s 30-40 miles north-northwest of Hanoi. All the MiGs, believed to have taken off from the Phucyen airfield 12 miles northwest of Hanoi, were downed by F-4 Phantom jets flying cover for F-105 Thunderchiefs raiding surface-to-air missile sites in the Red River delta.

Mekong & 'Triangle' Drives

U.S. and South Vietnamese troops launched separate drives against 2 major Viet Cong strongholds in South Vietnam—in the Mekong River delta Jan. 6 and in the so-called "Iron Triangle," about 25 miles northwest of Saigon, Jan. 8.

The target of the delta offensive was a 60-square-mile area of the Thanhphong district of Kienhoa Province, about 55 miles south of Saigon. In the first direct commitment of U.S. troops to combat in the delta region, a 4,000-man force of U.S. Marines and South Vietnamese troops landed Jan. 6-7 in helicopters and amphibious tanks; they met no resistance. Previous U.S. presence in the delta had been limited to the attachment of American advisers to South Vietnamese units operating there. The offensive, called Operation Deckhouse V, was officially ended Jan. 16 with only 21 Viet Cong reported killed, 14 captured. The delta target area, called the Thanhphu Secret Zone by the guerrillas, had been under almost complete guerrilla control for nearly 20 years. U.S. intelligence sources had reported that the zone contained ammunition factories, ordnance and engineering workshops, hospitals and indoctrination centers. In a news conference aboard the aircraft carrier *Iwo Jima,* from which part of the assault had been launched, Gen. William C. Westmoreland, commander of U.S. forces in Vietnam, had said Jan. 7 that Operation Deckhouse V would continue for at least 10 days. The drive's principal purpose, he said, was to smash a Viet Cong rear-area sanctuary and infiltration route to the Saigon area.

(South Vietnamese troops Jan. 16 came across the bodies of 41 South Vietnamese at a Viet Cong prison camp in the delta 110 miles south of Saigon. The Vietnamese were believed to have been prisoners shot to death by the Viet Cong Jan. 15. 7 other prisoners at the camp were wounded.)

(In a continued effort to wrest control of the Mekong delta from the Viet Cong, a permanent U.S. combat team, a 1,000-man battalion of the 9th Infantry Division, moved Jan. 25 into a fortified camp near Mytho, 40 miles southwest of Saigon. U.S. plans called for permanently deploying at least 30,000 American troops in the delta.)

The drive against the Iron Triangle, Operation Cedar Falls, lasted until Jan. 27 and turned out to be the largest allied offensive of the war so far. 16,000 U.S. and about 14,000 South Vietnamese troops were committed. The allied troops captured 550 guerrilla weapons and 3,700 tons of Viet Cong rice and destroyed more than 500 buildings, bunkers and tunnels. The ground operation was aided by heavy artillery barrages and widespread air strikes by B-52s and other American planes, which flew 1,229 bombing sorties.

The Iron Triangle was a 60-square-mile area of jungle that included the Thanhdien Forest Reserve, one of the principle objectives of the offensive. The zone, a guerrilla stronghold for nearly 20 years, contained base camps and supply dumps. U.S. military authorities suspected that the triangle was the location of the headquarters of the 4th Military Region, which directed Viet Cong military activity in the Saigon area. At least 10,000 civilians, suspected of being pro-Viet Cong, lived in the area. Nearly 6,000 of them were moved to a re-settlement camp 20 miles to the south. Bensuc, one of the 4 villages in the area, was regarded as "hostile" and was leveled after its 3,800 inhabitants were removed. A unit of the First Infantry Division, the dominant U.S. outfit in Operation Cedar Falls, was accidentally hit by division artillery Jan. 13. 8 American soldiers were killed and 34 wounded. The U.S. command reported that 711 Viet Cong had been killed and 488 captured in the campaign; 722 civilians were detained as suspected Viet Cong. The Viet Cong's National Liberation Front (NLF) Jan. 29 claimed that guerrilla troops had killed more than 2,500 U.S. soldiers in Operation Cedar Falls through Jan. 21.

Among other military developments reported in January and early February:

■ 2 Viet Cong companies in Kienhoa Province Jan. 8 sought to shield their advance behind a screen of Vietnamese civilian hostages. In an ensuing exchange of gunfire with a South Vietnamese Ranger company, 10 civilians, all children, were killed. 25 other civilians were wounded.
■ The Viet Cong carried out widespread attacks on allied shipping in the Saigon area Jan. 9. A U.S. construction dredge, the *Jamaica Bay,* sank in the Mekong River about 40 miles southwest of Saigon after being damaged by a Viet Cong mine. Viet Cong recoilless rifle fire hit an 18,000-ton British-registered oil tanker and 2 South Vietnamese minesweepers 13 miles south of Saigon.

■ U.S. planes flew a record 549 single mission attacks over South Vietnam Jan. 13. 82 of the raids were in support of Operation Cedar Falls.

■ U.S. troops Feb. 2 launched a major drive, Operation Gadsden, against the Communists' War Zone C stronghold, about 70 miles northwest of Saigon. The American force, consisting of 6,000-8,000 troops of the 4th and 25th Infantry Division, had started moving into the area in helicopters and armored cars. Another U.S. drive against War Zone D, a Communist stronghold near the Cambodian border, was also under way. U.S. B-52s had carried out heavy fire raids against War Zone D Jan. 18 and War Zone C Jan. 28. Waves of the bombers had dropped magnesium incendiary bombs in an effort to defoliate the areas.

Bombings & Controversy

It was reported from Washington Jan. 10 that the Johnson Administration had ordered a temporary halt to the bombing of the Yenvien railroad yards, 5 miles northeast of Hanoi. The target, struck by U.S. planes Dec. 4, 13 and 14, 1966, was to have been hit a 4th time. But public controversy over the Dec. 13-14 raids was said to have prompted the Administration to issue an order about Christmas time rescinding permission for renewal of the attacks on Yenvien. North Vietnam had claimed that a workers' section in metropolitan Hanoi had been hit in the Dec. 13-14 raids and that 100 persons had been killed or wounded. European sources generally accepted Hanoi's accusations as valid. (The Air Force currently required Joint Chiefs of Staff approval to bomb areas within 10 miles of Hanoi.)

Gen. Earle G. Wheeler, chairman of the Joint Chiefs, announced Jan. 13 that for the time being U.S. planes would not bomb North Vietnam's 4 major airfields in the Hanoi-Haiphong area at Gialam, Phucyen, Kep and Catbi. It was reported in Washington Jan. 25 that an order issued by the Joint Chiefs the previous week had barred American pilots from bombing within a 5-mile radius of the center of Hanoi. U.S. planes were permitted to penetrate the zone only to chase attacking enemy aircraft. The directive reportedly had been issued because of the controversy over civilian bombing casualties.

Gen. William C. Westmoreland, commander of U.S. forces in Vietnam, had said Jan. 10 that "many" U.S. and allied troops were "alive today because of the air campaign against military targets" in North Vietnam. Westmoreland said that "if it had not been for the effectiveness" of the American air strikes "the North Vietnamese and Viet Cong troops in the South would have been better supplied with weapons and ammunition than was the case."

U.S. planes resumed air strikes against the Hanoi area Jan. 15-16. The raids, on targets 14½-15 miles from the North Vietnamese capital, were the first air attacks in the region since Dec. 1966. In the Jan. 15 raids, North Vietnamese surface-to-air missile sites were pounded 15 miles from Hanoi. The attack was part of a 37-plane mission in which railroads, highways and bridges in the Red River valley were hit. The Jan. 16 raids were directed against the Hagia petroleum, oil and lubricants depots, 14½ miles northwest of Hanoi.

An American correspondent, *Miami News* editor William C. Baggs, wrote a series of articles from North Vietnam in January in which he described widespread destruction of civilian structures in such cities as Hanoi, Namdinh and Phuly. Baggs had spent 8 days in North Vietnam as a representative of the Center for the Study of Democratic Institutions. He reported Jan. 14 that a street ½ mile northeast of downtown Hanoi had been bombed Dec. 13, 1966. The bombing destroyed 52 homes and killed several civilians. Baggs said that another U.S. raid that day had centered on a school complex 3 miles south of Hanoi and that one of the 2 buildings had been destroyed. Writing from Phuly Jan. 17, Baggs estimated that at least ⅘ of the city had been destroyed by U.S. bombings Oct. 1, 2 and 9, 1966. (He said U.S. government sources had told him Phuly was bombed because it had become a rallying ground for troops and war supplies being sent into South Vietnam.) Widespread damage to Namdinh was reported by Baggs in a dispatch written Jan. 15 and released in Miami Jan. 19. Baggs said that in his visit to Namdinh (population 90,000 before the U.S. raids had started in 1966) he had found it "pretty much an evacuated city" with its civilian sections hard hit. Baggs said that "the complaint of the people in Namdinh that many civilian neighborhoods with no military function have been bombed appears to be a valid complaint." In a dispatch released Jan. 20 on a 2-day

visit to Namha Province (80 miles south of Hanoi), Baggs
said North Vietnamese peasants he had interviewed accused
U.S. pilots of "trying to bomb their dikes and destroy the
water control system."

Baggs had been accompanied on his trip to North Vietnam by Harry Ashmore, ex-editor of the *Arkansas Gazette,* and
by ex-Mexican Amb.-to-U.S. Luis Quintanilla. Quintanilla
said in Mexico City Jan. 19 that his observations had confirmed civilian destruction that had been reported earlier by
Harrison Salisbury, a managing editor of the *N.Y. Times.*
Ashmore said in Los Angeles Jan. 20 that the damage inflicted
by the U.S. raids was "offset by the unifying influence" on
the North Vietnamese people.

U.S. intelligence sources in Washington were quoted Jan.
21 as saying that aerial photos had shown that North Vietnamese civilian structures as well as military targets had been
heavily damaged. U.S. sources attributed some of the destruction to North Vietnamese antiaircraft fire and accidental
bombings by U.S. planes.

Red Build-Up Curbed

Defense Secy. McNamara reported at a Senate hearing
Jan. 23 that U.S. ground operations, coastal surveillance and
air attacks on North Vietnam had "succeeded in limiting the
build-up" of North Vietnamese and Viet Cong forces in South
Vietnam. McNamara said "confirmed" estimates of Communist military strength in South Vietnam at the end of 1966
had placed the enemy force at 275,000 men: 45,000 North Vietnamese regulars; 62,000 "main force" Viet Cong; 110,000 local
and district Viet Cong guerrillas; 58,000 Viet Cong political
and administrative cadres and support troops. The 1966 Communist totals, McNamara said, represented a 25,000-man
increase over the 1965 estimate. North Vietnamese troop
strength was more than double the total it had been in Dec.
1965 (26,000), while the Viet Cong's force had risen only 3%
during the one-year period (224,000 at the end of 1965),
McNamara said. "These trends," McNamara said, "bear out
the assumption we made last year that the number of North
Vietnamese would increase substantially while the supply of
indigenous military manpower would be further limited."

McNamara warned, however, that North Vietnam had a substantial manpower pool available. McNamara said he believed
monthly North Vietnamese infiltration had decreased from
about 5,300 during Jan.-Sept. 1966 to 2,100 Oct.-Dec. 1966.
McNamara said he doubted whether "any amount of bombing, within practical limits, of North Vietnam would have
reduced whatever the actual infiltration was." McNamara
conceded that the raids limited North Vietnam's ability to
infiltrate the South. But he added: "It is not clear that the
limit that results is below the level that the North Vietnamese
planned on, and, in any event, it is not below the level necessary to support the force in the South at present." McNamara
said the U.S. would be willing to halt the raids on North Vietnam, but Hanoi must first display "some general indication of
how they would act" in return. A Defense Department statement explained later that McNamara's phrase "general
indication" meant a reciprocal military de-escalation.

McNamara said Feb. 15 that although the bombing of
North Vietnam would not "by itself" force Hanoi to end its
military activities in South Vietnam, the raids on military
targets in the North were accomplishing their objectives.
Speaking at a news conference, McNamara emphasized that
"the implication that I consider the bombing ineffective is
incorrect." As a result of the air strikes, McNamara said, the
Communist build-up in the South had "leveled off" in the
previous 6 months and North Vietnam had been forced to
divert 300,000 persons to repair bridges, railroads and supply
centers damaged by the air attacks. McNamara said the raids
had also raised morale in South Vietnam.

At a press conference Feb. 24, McNamara denied that he
and State Secy. Dean Rusk disagreed on the bombing of North
Vietnam. McNamara said he had called the news conference
to refute "press reports of an apparent difference of opinion"
between him and Rusk. "I can't recall a single instance when
the Secretary of State and the Secretary of Defense have
differed on bombing policy," McNamara declared, "and not a
single instance when their recommendations have differed on
particular bombing targets." McNamara said the U.S. might
have to expand bombing targets in North Vietnam "in the

future as the value of specific targets shifts." This observation was in response to a speech, delivered earlier Feb. 24, in which Sen. Henry Jackson (D., Wash.) had called for "some carefully selected additional military targets" in North Vietnam. Expansion of the U.S. bombing, Jackson said, "would further limit North Vietnamese infiltration capabilities." (When queried on McNamara's statement, Rusk said he and the Defense Secretary "have been together at all times in the many efforts to find peace.")

Rusk and McNamara appeared with newsmen Mar. 1 to reiterate that they agreed on Vietnam policy. They explained that U.S. ground and naval shelling of North Vietnam and the dropping of mines into North Vietnamese rivers had been prompted by North Vietnam's "increased supply activity" and the hampering of air attacks by poor weather. McNamara reported that the foul weather had reduced the number of U.S. plane sorties over North Vietnam from 12,000 in Sept. 1966 to about 6,800 in January. Increased fighting in South Vietnam in the previous 3 months, McNamara said, had raised the Communist combat death toll 40%-50%.

Pres. Johnson, at his press conference Feb. 27, had lauded the McNamara-Rusk working relationship. Mr. Johnson said: "I have never observed 2 men who I thought could represent the State and Defense Departments more successfully and also the national interest more cooperatively."

(In an article in the March issue of the *Atlantic*, Douglas Kiker quoted a "liberal columnist" as saying: McNamara was "the biggest dove in the higher echelons of the Johnson Administration. He resisted the bombing of North Vietnam to the very end. He was the chief advocate of the 1965 bombing pause. And he's been arguing ever since that the bombing is not doing what it is supposed to be doing.")

Tet Truce

Heavy fighting in South Vietnam was largely suspended Feb. 8-12 by a truce in observance of *Tet*, the lunar new year. U.S. military authorities in Saigon reported Feb. 13 that during the 96-hour cease-fire 18 U.S. soldiers had been killed and 158 wounded in 89 "significant" incidents initiated by Communist forces. The U.S. officials said 112 Communist troops had been killed and 65 persons had been detained as suspected guerrillas. A South Vietnamese spokesman said 23 South Vietnamese troops had been killed and 30 wounded. The North Vietnamese Communist Party newspaper *Nhan Dan* had charged Feb. 12 that U.S. troops had committed 62 truce violations.

The cease-fire, proposed Nov. 30, 1966 by South Vietnam and agreed to by the U.S. and other allies, started at 7 a.m. Feb. 8 and ended at 7 a.m. Feb. 12. As the truce ended, allied ground and air forces immediately resumed operations in South Vietnam. U.S. air strikes on North Vietnam, however, were not resumed until Feb. 13. Hanoi radio reported Feb. 12 that 2 U.S. planes had been shot down that day over North Vietnam—one in a suburb of Haiphong and the other in Namha Province south of Hanoi.

The Viet Cong Jan. 1 had proposed the extension of the Tet truce to Feb. 15. A South Vietnamese Foreign Ministry communiqué Jan. 17 suggested that North and South Vietnamese officials meet and announced that South Vietnam was prepared to discuss a truce of 7 days "or even longer." The suggested conference with North Vietnamese officials rather than with NLF representatives was in line with Saigon's policy of refusing to have any contacts with the NLF. The Communists Jan. 18 rejected Saigon's proposal to discuss a truce extension. A Hanoi broadcast charged that the South Vietnamese ruling military junta "opposes the 7-day truce upon orders from its American master." An NLF broadcast denounced South Vietnam's proposal as a "dishonest move" because it failed to include the Viet Cong. The front said: "If negotiations are held they should be held with us, since the North has little to do with the war here."

On the expiration of the truce Feb. 12, 16 separate U.S. and South Vietnamese operations were launched in the South. One of several new drives started was Operation Lam Son 67, in support of a South Vietnamese pacification campaign 13 miles south of Saigon. Several battalions of the U.S. First Infantry Division were involved in the offensive, whose purpose was to clear guerrillas from villages in the area.

Operation Thayer II, which had started Oct. 25, 1966 in

Binhdinh Province, was reported ended Feb. 13. U.S. and allied troops were reported to have killed 1,744 Communist soldiers during that period.

Among other events following the truce:

■ 13 U.S. helicopters were downed by Communist ground fire in South Vietnam Feb. 16; this was a record number for a single day. 9 of the aircraft were hit while ferrying South Vietnamese troops during an operation in the Mekong delta, 110 miles south of Saigon. One helicopter—on a medical evacuation mission—was shot down in the same operation. 2 other helicopters were shot down by Viet Cong ground fire in the Central Highlands near the Cambodian border. U.S. authorities said 4 Americans had been killed and 8 wounded in the downing of the 13 helicopters, all but one of which were repairable.

■ Dr. Bernard B. Fall, 40, writer and historian of the Vietnamese war, was killed Feb. 21 by a Viet Cong mine while accompanying a U.S. Marine patrol about 14 miles northwest of Hué. A U.S. Marine photographer also was killed by the Viet Cong mine. Fall, a Vienna-born French citizen, was professor of international relations at Howard University (Washington, D.C.). He had gone to Vietnam to gather material for his 8th book on Vietnam.

■ The U.S. airbase at Danag was shelled by the Viet Cong Feb. 27. 12 Americans and 35 South Vietnamese civilians were killed; 32 Americans and 70 Vietnamese were wounded. The civilian casualties were due to fires, caused by the shelling, that swept the adjacent village of Apdo. More than 150 buildings were destroyed. Some planes and buildings were damaged on the base. The U.S. military command confirmed Feb. 28 that the Viet Cong had carried out the attack with Soviet-made long-range rockets, used for the first time. The rockets were believed to have been fired 6 miles away from the Danang base.

U.S. Artillery Shells North

The U.S. stepped up its pressure on Communist forces late in February by pounding North Vietnamese targets with ground and naval artillery and by air-dropping mines into North Vietnamese rivers. The 3 measures were aimed at curtailing the infiltration of men and supplies into South Vietnam.

The U.S. land-based artillery attacks on North Vietnam were the first of the war. The U.S. military command in Saigon reported Feb. 24 that 175-mm. guns based near U.S. Camp Carroll (10 miles south of the demilitarized zone) had fired 63 shells of 150 pounds each Feb. 22 at North Vietnamese antiaircraft positions in the zone and beyond the zone in

North Vietnamese territory. The shelling was resumed Feb. 25 and then continued on a regular round-the-clock basis. In reporting the Feb. 22 attack, the U.S. command said the American artillery had opened fire after a U.S. spotter plane had been shot at by North Vietnamese antiaircraft guns just north of the buffer zone. Asserting that the artillery shelling "represented no escalation of the war," the U.S. command explained that it was "designed to supplement air strikes against military targets in the demilitarized zone area, particularly at night and in bad weather."

The U.S. military command reported Feb. 26 that U.S. cruisers and destroyers of the 7th Fleet had started that day to shell North Vietnamese supply routes along a 250-mile stretch between the demilitarized zone and Thanhhoa on a continuing basis. The targets reported struck by 5 warships were rail yards, rail lines and an ammunition depot. The ships were ordered to ignore the 3-mile offshore limit and to move within several hundred yards of the coast if necessary. U.S. warships had been shelling the North Vietnamese coast during the previous 5 months, but the strikes were in response to initial attacks by Communist shore batteries. The Feb. 26 shelling was the first aimed at North Vietnamese logistic targets.

The U.S. command disclosed Feb. 27 that U.S. planes (some from 7th Fleet ships) had dropped "a limited number of . . . non-floating" mines in rivers of southern North Vietnam earlier Feb. 27 "to counter" stepped-up North Vietnamese "use of waterborne logistic craft to infiltrate men and supplies into South Vietnam." "This action," the command said, "poses no danger to deep-water maritime traffic." An American military spokesman said the U.S. had no plans to mine rivers or harbors near major deepwater ports such as Haiphong.

Defoliation in DMZ

South Vietnamese and allied forces Feb. 5 began the defoliation of jungle growth in the southern part of the demilitarized zone (DMZ). In a note informing the International Control Commission of the action, the South Vietnamese government protested the "flagrant violation" of the buffer area by North Vietnamese troops. The note also criticized the ICC for failing to maintain the neutrality of the zone. The note added: South Vietnam, "assuming the heavy burden of protecting the integrity of its territory and of protecting the lives and the goods of its population living south of the 17th Parallel, sees itself obligated to use means of self-defense and to start a defoliation operation" in the buffer zone. A U.S. embassy spokesman in Saigon was asked whether the defoliation of the DMZ was a violation of the Geneva accords. He replied: "The U.S. fully supports South Vietnam in this matter."

Operation Junction City

A force of more than 25,000 U.S. and South Vietnamese troops was committed Feb. 22 to the largest offensive of the war so far. The offensive, Operation Junction City, took place about 70 miles north of Saigon. Its purpose was to smash the Viet Cong's War Zone C stronghold near the Cambodian border and thus ease the guerrilla threat to Saigon. 34 U.S. and 2 South Vietnamese battalions participated.

The drive, in Tayninh Province, opened with the landing of more than 5,200 U.S. troops by 250 helicopters near the Cambodian border. 13 of the 'copters were hit by ground fire, and 2 were destroyed. More than 12 landing zones had first been bombed by 4 strikes of B-52s. One of the drop zones, at Katum, about 5 miles from the border, had been secured earlier by 700 U.S. paratroopers who had landed in the area in the first paratroop jump of the war. The paratroopers, of the 503d Airborne Infantry Regiment, encountered little ground resistance; a few were killed or injured in the jump. The first day's operation was supported by 575 U.S. plane sorties, a record number to be flown in South Vietnam for a single day.

In a clash Mar. 1, a company of U.S. First Infantry Division troops, supported by artillery and air strikes, killed 150 enemy troops. The U.S. company's casualties were listed as "heavy," meaning that it was no longer effective as a fighting force. Another U.S. company—150 men of the 173d Airborne Brigade —also suffered "heavy" losses Mar. 4 after being ambushed near the Cambodian border. The U.S. unit was first stopped by a Viet Cong mine and then came under heavy guerrilla fire. The American force, assisted by artillery and air strikes, fought back for 2 hours and killed 39 Viet Cong.

In one of the heaviest battles of Operation Junction City, U.S. First Infantry Division troops killed 210 North Vietnamese soldiers Mar. 11. The North Vietnamese, numbering about 500 men, had opened the attack with a heavy mortar assault and then advanced on the American unit. The U.S. troops repelled the attack with the support of armed helicopters, fighter-bombers and artillery. In what Gen. Westmoreland described as "one of the most successful single actions of the year," U.S. forces killed 606 Viet Cong in War Zone C Mar. 21. U.S. and Viet Cong 9th Division troops fought one of the bloodiest battles of Operation Junction City 70 miles northwest of Saigon Mar. 31-Apr. 1. U.S. sources said 591 Viet Cong were slain. American losses totaled 10 killed and 64 wounded. The Communist attack opened with a 4-hour engagement Mar. 31 and was followed Apr. 1 by a major Viet Cong mortar barrage on a 900-man U.S. infantry detachment. This was the 3d major Communist attack on American troops participating in Operation Junction City in 2 weeks. In repelling the Communist onslaught, involving an estimated 2,500 Viet Cong troops, the U.S. ground forces were assisted by almost incessant air and artillery strikes. 170 fighter-bombers dropped tons of high-explosive and fragmentation bombs and napalm on Communist positions. A U.S. officer estimated that 80% of the Viet Cong fatalities resulted from the air and artillery strikes. The North Vietnamese news agency reported Apr. 2 a Viet Cong claim that 864 U.S. soldiers had been killed or wounded in the Mar. 31-Apr. 1 fighting; the Viet Cong also claimed the downing of 22 U.S. planes, including a B-52 bomber, during the 2-day battle.

Hanoi Generals in South?

The U.S. military command in Saigon Mar. 18 made public photographs of 3 men described as North Vietnamese generals said to be in South Vietnam leading Viet Cong troops. The photos, of Gens. Nguyen Chi Thanh, Tran Van Tra and Tra Do, had been captured with other related information by U.S. troops in War Zone C. The U.S. command said the presence of the generals was "further evidence of Hanoi's direct control over the so-called 'National Liberation Front for the Liberation of South Vietnam.'" The command said it believed the pictures were taken in South Vietnam.

The U.S. authorities described Gen. Thanh as commander-in-chief and senior political officer of the Viet Cong's "liberation army." "Ultimate political control" of the NLF was "exercised by Hanoi through" Thanh as a member of the North Vietnamese "Politburo" in South Vietnam, American officials said. Tra was identified as a lieutenant general in the North Vietnamese army and a deputy chief of staff. Do, described as a major general, was said to be one of 5 deputy commanders of the army in South Vietnam.

Thainguyen Plant Bombed

U.S. planes raided North Vietnam Mar. 10-12 and bombed an industrial target that had never been hit before. U.S. sources in Saigon conceded that the raids constituted an escalation of the war. North Vietnam claimed Hanoi was bombed Mar. 12. The target bombed for the first time Mar. 10 was the huge Thainguyen iron and steel complex, 38 miles north of Hanoi. 14 flights of U.S. Air Force F-105 Thunderchiefs and F-4C Phantoms from bases in Thailand dropped 750-pound bombs on the plant.

In announcing the strikes, the U.S. military command held that they were related to the American effort to curb North Vietnamese infiltration into the South. It noted that the Thainguyen plant manufactured "bridge sections, cargo barges and petroleum drums." Other U.S. sources, however, in supporting the contention that the attack represented an escalation of the war, said it was the first time American planes had bombed a North Vietnamese target not directly connected with the infiltration of men and supplies into South Vietnam. (Construction had begun on the Thainguyen complex in 1959 with the aid of Communist China and was still under way. U.S. intelligence sources estimated that as of June 1966 the plant had been capable of producing 200,000 tons of cast iron a year.) The Thainguyen plant was bombed again Mar. 11 by Thailand-based Thunderchief and Phantom jets.

(The use of Thailand bases for U.S. air attacks on North

Vietnam had been publicly acknowledged by Thailand for the first time Mar. 9. A spokesman for Thailand Foreign Min. Thanat Khoman said Thailand was permitting the use of its territory for the air strikes as "a contribution . . . toward bringing the war to a speedier end.")

In a speech to the Tennessee General Assembly in Nashville Mar. 15, Pres. Johnson strongly defended his policy of continuing the bombing of North Vietnam. Mr. Johnson assailed the "moral double bookkeeping" of people who criticized the U.S. air raids but ignored the fact that "tens of thousands of innocent Vietnamese civilians have been killed and tortured and kidnapped by the Viet Cong." Mr. Johnson said the bombing of North Vietnam served 3 purposes: "to back our fighting men by denying our enemy a sanctuary; to exact a penalty against North Vietnam for her flagrant violations of the Geneva accords of 1954 and 1962; to limit the flow or to substantially increase the cost of infiltration of men and material from North Vietnam." The President said U.S. intelligence had confirmed success in attaining these objectives. Pres. Johnson expressed regret at the Vietnamese civilian casualties resulting from the bombing. But he said: The U.S. was "making an effort that's unprecedented in the history of warfare" to avoid civilian targets. "We have never deliberately bombed cities nor attacked any target with the purpose of inflicting civilian casualties." "Any civilian casualties that result from our operations are inadvertent in stark contrast to the calculated Viet Cong policy of systematic terror."

Guam Conference

Pres. Johnson and major Administration officials held a top-level meeting with South Vietnamese leaders in Guam Mar. 20-21. A joint communiqué issued at the conclusion of the talks Mar. 21 said the conferees had discussed the military and political aspects of the war, South Vietnam's pacification program and Saigon's progress toward establishing a civilian government.

The conference was attended by: *For the U.S.*—State Secy. Rusk, Defense Secy. McNamara, CIA Director Richard M. Helms, Gen. Earle G. Wheeler (chairman of the Joint Chiefs of Staff), Amb. Henry Cabot Lodge, Gen. William C.

Westmoreland (commander of U.S. forces in South Vietnam) and Adm. U. S. Grant Sharp (commander of U.S. forces, Pacific). *For South Vietnam*—Premier Nguyen Cao Ky, Chief of State Nguyen Van Thieu, Foreign Min. Tran Van Do and Gen. Cao Van Vien, defense minister and chief of the Joint General Staff.

Pres. Johnson introduced at the meeting 3 new top American civilian aides in Saigon, whose appointments he had announced Mar. 15. They were: Amb.-at-large Ellsworth Bunker, to replace Lodge as ambassador to South Vietnam; Amb.-to-Pakistan Eugene M. Locke, to replace William J. Porter as deputy ambassador to South Vietnam; Presidential Asst. Robert W. Komer, to head the pacification and economic assistance programs in Vietnam.

Addressing the conferees at the conference's opening session Mar. 20, Ky said, "The enemy has shown no sign of ending the aggression. . . . Despite terrific losses, despite disruption of the supply lines in North Vietnam, they persist in this struggle, all the while rebuffing all offers of discussion or negotiation." Ky asked: "How long can Hanoi enjoy the advantage of restricted bombing of military targets? How long can the Viet Cong be permitted to take sanctuary in Cambodia . . . ? How long can supply trails through Laos be permitted to operate? How long can war matériel be permitted to come into Haiphong harbor? How long can the North be permitted to infiltrate soldiers and weapons across the demarcation line?" (The *N.Y. Times* reported Mar. 20 that Ky had brought to the conference a plan for halting the infiltration from North Vietnam into South Vietnam. The plan called for a 100-mile defensive zone extending from Savannakhet, Laos on the Laos-Thailand border to South Vietnam's South China Sea coast. The fortified line would be defended by at least 5 allied divisions, which would be moved into southeastern Laos, and by the U.S. 3d Marine Division, currently operating just south of the demilitarized zone that divided North and South Vietnam.)

At a news conference prior to leaving Guam Mar. 21, Mr. Johnson insisted that "there were no military decisions taken of any nature" at the talks. He said great emphasis was placed on South Vietnam's political and economic development.

(A call for continued U.S. and allied military pressure in South Vietnam had been sounded Mar. 8 by the U.S. Chiefs of Mission of the East Asian and Pacific area. The conference, representing U.S. diplomats from 14 Asian capitals and Hong Kong, issued a communiqué at the close of a meeting in Baguio, the Philippines declaring that "any slackening of the collective military effort or of the policies and programs in non-military fields" would slow down the drive to achieve a "stable and honorable peace." The Baguio conference was attended by Gen. Westmoreland, who reported on the progress of the war in Vietnam.

(The Vietnamese war was the principal topic of discussion at the Southeast Asia Treaty Organization's annual ministerial meeting in Washington Apr. 18-20. A communiqué issued at the conclusion of the conference: condemned North Vietnam for "its aggression by means of armed attack" on South Vietnam; charged that "Communist military operations in South Vietnam have long been directed and controlled by North Vietnam"; reaffirmed "that the defeat of this aggression is essential to the security of Southeast Asia"; expressed "disappointment that Hanoi had rejected all the opportunities open to it for negotiations on a reasonable basis"; voiced the view that "reciprocity is an essential element of any acceptable proposal for reduction in the fighting." Speaking at the conference's opening session April 18, Thailand Foreign Min. Thanat Khoman assailed France and Pakistan for not joining other SEATO members [the U.S., Australia, New Zealand, Thailand and the Philippines] in sending military forces to fight in Vietnam.

(After the conclusion of the SEATO conference Apr. 20, representatives of the U.S., Australia, New Zealand, Thailand, the Philippines, South Vietnam and South Korea held a closed-door strategy meeting on Vietnam. South Vietnamese Foreign Min. Tran Van Do said at the meeting that his country's 2 northernmost provinces—Quangtri and Thuatien —"are presently under terrible pressure of North Vietnamese regular units which have openly crossed the demarcation line." South Korean Vice Foreign Min. Kim Yung Chu advised the allies to wait for "the right opportunity for negotiations" rather than to enter peace talks prematurely. Kim urged the allies to "further intensify and strengthen our war effort" to achieve peace.)

Westmoreland Addresses Congress

The U.S. commander in Vietnam, Gen. Westmoreland, returned to the U.S. late in April amid growing public concern over the course of the war and reports that he was planning to ask for expansion of the U.S. forces from 440,000 to 600,000 men. (Pres. Johnson said at his news conference May 3 that there were no immediate plans to act on Westmoreland's request for a substantial increase in American forces in Vietnam. He said that an Administration decision [announced May 2] to withdraw 35,000 U.S. troops from West Germany in 1968 was not related to the Vietnamese situation.)

Westmoreland delivered an unusual address to a joint session of Congress Apr. 28. He evoked a standing ovation by declaring that: "Backed at home by resolve, confidence, patience, determination and continued support we will prevail in Vietnam over the Communist aggressor." Long applause greeted his statement that the Communists could not win military victory in Vietnam. Westmoreland warned, however, that the enemy in Vietnam was "far from quitting" and could be defeated only by "unrelenting but discriminating military, political and psychological pressure on his whole structure and at all levels." He stressed that, in evaluating the enemy strategy, "it is evident to me that he believes our Achilles heel is our resolve." "Your continued strong support is vital to the success of our mission," he declared.

Westmoreland described the current U.S. policy in Vietnam as "the proper one." It "is producing results," he reported. He asserted that "in 3 years of close study and daily observation, I have seen no evidence that this [conflict in Vietnam] is an internal insurrection. I have seen much evidence . . . , documented by the enemy himself, that it is aggression from the North."

Westmoreland reported: "Nearly half" of the "enemy combat battalions in the South . . . are now North Vietnamese." In the past 22 months "overall enemy strength has nearly doubled, in spite of large combat losses. . . . The enemy's logistic system is primitive in many ways. Forced to transport most of his supplies down through southeastern Laos, he uses . . . trucks, bicycles, men and animals . . . with surprising effectiveness. . . . Many of the caches we have found and destroyed have been stocked with enough supplies and equipment to support months of future operations. The enemy emphasizes what he calls strategic mobility. . . . His operational planning is meticulous. He gathers intelligence, makes careful plans, assigns specific objectives in detail and then rehearses the plan of attack until he believes it cannot fail. Local peasants are forced to provide food, shelter and porters to carry supplies and equipment for combat units and to evacuate the dead and wounded from the battlefield. When all is ready he [the enemy] moves his large military formations covertly from concealed bases into the operational area. His intent is to launch a surprise attack designed to achieve quick victory by shock action. This tactic has failed because of our courageous men, our firepower and our spoiling attacks. . . . The enemy also uses terror—murder, mutilation, abduction and the deliberate shelling of innocent men, women and children—to exercise control through fear. . . . A typical day in Vietnam was last Sunday. Terrorists, near Saigon, assassinated a 39-year-old village chief. The same day in the delta they kidnapped 26 civilians assisting in arranging for local elections. The next day the Viet Cong attacked . . . revolutionary development workers, killing one and wounding 12 with grenades and machinegun fire in one area, and in another they opened fire on a small civilian bus and killed 3 and wounded 4 of its passengers. These are cases of calculated enemy attack on civilians to extend by fear that which they cannot gain by persuasion. One hears little of this brutality here at home. . . . For years the enemy has been blowing up bridges, interrupting traffic, cutting roads, sabotaging power stations, blocking canals and attacking airfields in the South . . . and he continues to do so. Bombing in the North has been centered on precisely these same kind of targets and for the same military purposes—to reduce the supply, interdict the movement and impair the effectiveness of enemy military forces. Within his capabilities the enemy in Vietnam is waging total war all day—every day—everywhere. . . . To us a cease-fire means cease-fire. Our observance of past truces has been open and subject to public scrutiny. The enemy permits no such observation in the North or the South. He traditionally has exploited cease-fire periods when the bombing has been suspended to increase his resupply and infiltration activity."

(In a speech before the South Carolina General Assembly in Columbia Apr. 26, Westmoreland paid tribute to Negroes serving in Vietnam as "particularly inspirational to me." "They have served with distinction," he said.)

Communists Attack in North

A major increase in Communist offensive action in South Vietnam's northern provinces began in early April. A force of about 2,500 Viet Cong/North Vietnamese troops Apr. 6 carried out 4 closely coordinated attacks on the city of Quangtri, 15 miles south of the demilitarized zone (DMZ). The Communist force also attacked the neighboring towns of Lavang and Hailang to the south. U.S. sources said 125 South Vietnamese troops were killed and 180 wounded in Quangtri. 4 U.S. Marines attached to the defending South Vietnamese First Infantry Division were killed and 27 wounded. The Communist raiders also freed 250 guerrilla prisoners in a jail on the bank of the Tachlan River. An estimated 77-115 Communists were slain.

South Vietnam charged that the Communist raiders had infiltrated from the DMZ. Making their way into Quangtri, the invaders attacked the city hall, the South Vietnamese military headquarters, the U.S. advisory headquarters, the civilian prison and the headquarters of a government artillery platoon. A South Vietnamese source attributed the success of the Quangtri raid to aid given to the North Vietnamese and Viet Cong troops by disloyal South Vietnamese soldiers. Some government troops were said to have led the raiders through barbed wire and minefields that surrounded the South Vietnamese military camp that was attacked.

South Vietnamese Premier Nguyen Cao Ky flew to Quangtri Apr. 7 to inspect the damage.

While the Viet Cong and North Vietnamese were attacking Quangtri Apr. 6, a North Vietnamese force that day carried out the first attack of the war across the bridge spanning the Benhai River at the 17th Parallel. Outnumbered South Vietnamese national police guarding the south side of the river fled. The North Vietnamese withdrew after South Vietnamese and U.S. artillery fired at the bridge. The span was said to be usable despite artillery damage. South Vietnamese Chief of State Nguyen Van Thieu warned Apr. 6 that South Vietnam might bomb Hanoi or invade North Vietnam in retaliation for the Benhai River bridge attack. If Saigon retaliated, Thieu said, "it would only be a natural act of self-defense." A South Vietnamese protest to the International Control Commission said that because of the attack on the Benhai River span, Saigon "reserve[d] the right to undertake all necessary actions in the context of legitimate defense, to protect the life and property of its citizens."

The intensification of Communist operations took place in all 5 of South Vietnam's northern provinces—Quangtri, Thuathien, Quangnam, Quangtin and Quangngai.

Communist forces Apr. 12 mounted a mortar attack on the U.S. Marine airbase at Chulai. One American was killed and 27 wounded, but damage to aircraft and equipment was reported light.

2 bridges between Danang and Quangtri were blown up by Communist forces Apr. 13. The bridges, on North-South Highway 2, were part of a major supply route to U.S. forces along the DMZ. 2 of 5 steel spans of the 750-foot-long Cade River highway and railroad bridge 6 miles north of Danang were blown up when about 300 pounds of Viet Cong explosives were detonated against a masonry pier. The bridge was rendered unusable as the 2 spans collapsed in the water. Engineers started a temporary pontoon bridge pending repair of the permanent span. The Cade River bridge was attacked at about the same time that Viet Cong explosives caused heavy damage to a highway bridge near Quangtri, 60 miles to the north. The blast occurred as other Communist troops carried

out the 2d mortar attack against the city of Quangtri in a week.

U.S. Troops Shifted North

2 U.S. Army units totaling 7,500 men were shifted to South Vietnam's 5 northernmost provinces to help U.S. Marines and South Vietnamese troops already there to cope with the increasing Communist military activity in the area. The U.S. reinforcements were reported by U.S. Army authorities Apr. 14 and 17. In a further move to strengthen allied defenses in the 5 provinces, South Vietnamese Premier Nguyen Cao Ky announced Apr. 15 the start of construction of a fortified barrier just south of the demilitarized zone (DMZ) to halt infiltration from North Vietnam.

The U.S. reinforcements included 3,000 men of the First Cavalry Division's 2d Brigade, who started moving north into Quangngai Province from neighboring Binhdinh Province Apr. 8. The 2d American unit, 4,500 troops of the 196th Light Infantry Brigade, was airlifted starting Apr. 9 from its Thayninh Province camp base (45 miles northwest of Saigon) to the U.S. First Marine Division base at Chulai in Quangtin Province. The brigade, led by Brig. Gen. Richard T. Knowles and placed under the over-all command of the First Marine Division commander, Lt. Gen. Lewis W. Walt, was assigned to protect South Vietnamese pacification workers in Quangtin and Quangngai Provinces.

The U.S. military command in Saigon announced Apr. 22 that a 15,000-man U.S. task force (Oregon), under the command of Gen. William B. Rosson, had been established in the 5-province area. The new troops were assigned to Quangtri and Thautien Provinces, and the U.S. Marines there were thus enabled to take up positions near the DMZ. An undisclosed number of Marines landed by ships and helicopters Apr. 22 in an area 21 miles southeast of the DMZ. U.S. officials estimated that 40,000 North Vietnamese troops were massed in Quangtri Province and in or near the buffer zone.

The South Vietnamese-requested barrier was being built less than 2 miles below the southern section of the DMZ. U.S. Marines and South Vietnamese soldiers were using bulldozers to clear a 200-yard-wide, 6-mile-long stretch of land from the

China Sea inland of heavy jungle growth, vegetation and rice paddies. Brig. Gen. Michael P. Ryan, assistant commander of the U.S. 3d Marine Division, said Apr. 16 that the barrier was not meant to be a fortified line, that its actual purpose was to improve observation, surveillance and maneuverability to cope better with Communist infiltration through the demilitarized zone. Other U.S. sources had expressed skepticism about the effectiveness of the barrier in halting the movement of Communist men and matériel to the South. American officers pointed out that the principal Communist infiltration routes were located in rugged mountains to the west of the barrier, near the Laotian border.

In announcing work on the barrier, Premier Ky had indicated Apr. 15 that it eventually would be lengthened to 15 miles. Ky said 20,000 civilians living within 3 miles of the DMZ would be evacuated as a safety measure.

Northern Troops Defeated at Khesanh

U.S. Marines defeated North Vietnamese troops in a fierce battle Apr. 24-May 5 for 3 hills overlooking an American garrison and airstrip at Khesanh, in Quangtin Province, just south of the demilitarized zone and less than 10 miles from the Laotian border. 764 North Vietnamese deaths were listed in the 12-day battle. U.S. casualties totaled 160 killed and 746 wounded. The American losses represented ½ the combat strength of the 2 battalions of the 3d Marine Regiment engaged in the operation.

The fighting had started Apr. 24 when a Marine patrol was battered heavily by the North Vietnamese in an encounter on one of the 3 elevations, Hill 861. The Americans launched an all-out drive against the entrenched Communist troops Apr. 25 after flying in the 2 Marine battalions to reinforce the Khesanh military base, which was manned by one infantry company, one reconnaissance company and a battery of 6 howitzers. The Americans captured Hill 861 by Apr. 29, encountering little opposition. The Marines then attacked Hill 881 South (4 miles northwest of the Khesanh base) Apr. 30, scaled the summit but were repelled by Communist troops with a loss of 50 killed and 150 wounded. A Marine counterthrust the following 2 days led to the recapture of the hill May

2, but the North Vietnamese had fled. The remainder of the battle for the approaches to Khesanh centered on Hill 881 North, a mile away. The Marines fought their way to the top May 3 but were thrown back by the North Vietnamese, who penetrated the Americans' defense perimeter.

In a diversionary action, a North Vietnamese force of about 300 men moved down from the hills May 4 and attacked a U.S. Special Forces camp at Langvei, 3 miles west of Khesanh. The camp was garrisoned by 200 *montagnard* tribesmen and 8 U.S. Army advisers. In the ensuing 2-hour battle, the Communist troops, attacking with mortars, killed 39 irregulars and the American commander and his executive officer. 37 irregulars and 2 South Vietnamese soldiers were wounded; 38 irregulars were listed as missing. Langvei's village chief and 3 local militiamen were kidnaped. At least 5 North Vietnamese were killed.

U.S. Marines resumed the assault on Hill 881 North May 4 and captured it May 5. During most of the 12-day battle, the North Vietnamese, deeply entrenched in complex bunkers, were heavily pounded by U.S. artillery and air strikes.

In a visit to the Khesanh battlefront May 5, Gen. Westmoreland said the North Vietnamese units involved, the 18th and 95th Regiments of the 325th Division, had definitely moved in from Laos.

U.S. B-52s Based in Thailand

North Vietnam and Communist China had warned Thailand Jan. 10 and 19 against military intervention in the Vietnamese war. Both warnings threatened stern measures if Thailand permitted the U.S. to base B-52 jet bombers on its territory for strikes against Communist forces in Vietnam. Currently, the huge 8-engine craft flew Vietnam missions from Guam. But U.S. officials had announced Jan. 9 that Bangkok and Washington would soon discuss arrangements to permit the stationing of B-52s in Thailand. (U.S. Amb.-to-Thailand Graham A. Martin had disclosed Jan. 18 that U.S. forces in Thailand totaled 35,300 men, 8,000 of whom were assigned to construction projects.)

Thailand had accused Communist China Jan. 24 of directing terrorist bands in northeast Thailand. The Bangkok announcement charged that the guerrillas included North Vietnamese and pro-Communist Pathet Lao soldiers from Laos. A unit of 25 U.S. Air Force helicopters was reported Mar. 13 to have been withdrawn from Thailand after the completion of the training of Thai pilots in airlifting Thai soldiers to northeastern Thailand to fight pro-Communist guerrillas. But several U.S. helicopters remained in Thailand for rescue work in connection with U.S. aerial strikes against infiltration routes in North Vietnam and Laos.

U.S. officials in Washington announced Mar. 22 that Thailand had agreed to the stationing of U.S. B-52s on its territory for bombing raids against Communist targets in North and South Vietnam. The first B-52s to be shifted to Thailand under the agreement landed at U Taphao airbase in Thailand Apr. 10. The 3 B-52s had arrived from Guam and had dropped bombs on a Communist base camp and storage center 30 miles northwest of Saigon before landing in Thailand. The shift reduced the flying distance on bombing runs from 2,500 miles to a few hundred miles.

The first Thai combat troops sent to South Vietnam—1,200—arrived Sept. 21. The troops, members of the Royal Thai Army's Queen's Cobra Regiment, commanded by Col. Sanan Yuttasaphrasit, were greeted by Gen. Westmoreland as they disembarked from a ship in Saigon. 1,300 more troops of the same regiment arrived Sept. 22. The arrival of the Thai ground forces brought to 6 the number of allied countries that had sent troops to Vietnam. According to U.S. Defense Department figures cited Oct. 5 by U.S. Sen. Strom Thurmond (R., S.C.), allied forces in South Vietnam as of Oct. 1 totaled: South Vietnam—730,000 (about 327,000 regulars); South Korea —45,000; Australia—6,300; Thailand—2,500; Philippines— 2,000; New Zealand—400. U.S. forces totaled about 465,000 troops.

Thailand reported Dec. 2 that it had received U.S. ground-to-air missiles to protect it against possible retaliation for permitting its territory to be used for the launching of U.S. air strikes against North Vietnam. It had been confirmed in Bangkok Nov. 10 that the U.S. had agreed to give Thailand the missiles in exchange for the dispatch of 10,000 more Thai combat troops to South Vietnam. The Thailand Foreign Ministry's Dec. 2 statement assailed 4 American news publications for linking receipt of the American missiles with a deal to send Thai mercenary troops to Vietnam. The ministry said reports to this effect, appearing in the *Washington Post* and *Washington Star,* served to drag Thailand into the "dirt of American politics." A ministry spokesman later accused the *N.Y. Times* and *The Nation* magazine of publishing similar "malicious and scandalous" articles about Thailand in respect to the U.S.-Thai agreement.

Haiphong & Hanoi Targets Bombed

North Vietnam took increasing punishment from U.S. bombers during April and May as the American planes struck at targets that previously had been left untouched.

U.S. planes, for the first time, bombed Haiphong Apr. 20 and 2 MiG bases north of Hanoi Apr. 24. These targets had hitherto been immune from attack. The American pilots bombing Haiphong avoided the port area and attacked 2 power plants inside the city. The raids were carried out by 86 planes from the aircraft carriers *Kitty Hawk* and *Ticonderoga.* The first U.S. announcement of the bombing claimed that the targets were 1.1 mile northwest of Haiphong. But American authorities later said the power plants were within the city limits. One was in the center of Haiphong, the other was northeast of the downtown section. Returning pilots reported 80% of both plants destroyed. Reconnaissance photos, according to U.S. authorities, showed little significant damage to surrounding civilian areas. But North Vietnamese officials reported heavy destruction and civilian casualties.

U.S. Asst. Defense Secy. Phil Goulding denied Apr. 20 that the raid on Haiphong was an escalation of the war. "We have bombed power plants before, and the bombing of these power plants contributes to our objective of limiting their [the Communists'] ability to carry on the war and makes them pay a price for their aggression," Goulding said. Goulding reported that in addition to the 2 Haiphong power plants, 8 other North Vietnamese power installations had been attacked since the start of U.S. raids on the North in Feb. 1965. These 10 of the country's 12 plants produced about 90% of North

Vietnam's electricity. Goulding said that some of the 10 plants were put out of operation by the attacks.

State Secy. Rusk said Apr. 21 that Haiphong's 2 power plants were regarded by Johnson Administration officials as "essential military targets." "We do regret civilian casualties that may result," he declared.

North Vietnamese Public Health Min. Pham Ngoc Thach reported Apr. 22 that 44 civilians had been killed and 110 wounded in the U.S. raid on Haiphong. Thach denied any "shortage of electricity" in the city. Rejecting American claims that the raid was directed largely against the power plants, a Haiphong official said Apr. 22 that the U.S. planes had "in fact . . . launched concentrated attacks on industrial installations in the town's populated districts." According to the Haiphong official's account of the raid: 30% of the civilian casualties had occurred in "Haiphong proper"; 7 workers were killed and 25 wounded in a raid on an enamel tableware factory in the eastern Ngonguyen district, near one of the 2 power plants; 14 persons were killed and 44 houses were destroyed in the bombing of a cement factory in the western Hongbang district of Haiphong; at least 12 villages and suburbs around Haiphong also were pounded by U.S. planes; in one of these villages, Lamdong, north of Haiphong, 13 persons were killed and 35 wounded by 4 bombs and other missiles dropped by the American planes.

The 2 North Vietnamese MiG bases attacked by U.S. planes Apr. 24 were at Hoalac, 19 miles west of Hanoi, and at Kep, 37 miles northeast of Hanoi. Hoalac was bombed by about 15 Thailand-based planes. Kep was bombed twice by about an equal number of U.S. Navy A-4 Skyhawks and A-6 Intruders from the *Kitty Hawk.* U.S. officials described the raids on Hoalac and Kep as a "limited response to increased MiG activity in the last few days."

Speaking at a news conference Apr. 3, Defense Secy. McNamara had said U.S. planes would not bomb North Vietnam's MiG bases "under present circumstances." Resisting some Congressional demands for such attacks, McNamara had warned that bombing of the Communist airfields would result in higher American casualties. Sen. John Tower (R., Tex.)

and Rep. L. Mendel Rivers (D., S.C.) Apr. 24 lauded the attack on the MiG bases as a helpful move in bringing Hanoi to the conference table. Senate majority leader Mike Mansfield (D., Mont.) called the raids "a further escalation of the conflict" that, he predicted, "will make it more difficult to get negotiations under way." Mansfield warned that the attack on the North Vietnamese airbases could result in the shifting of bases to South China, "and a difficult situation will be made more delicate and dangerous."

In a new raid on Haiphong Apr. 25, U.S. Navy jets from the carriers *Kitty Hawk* and *Bon Homme Richard* attacked a cement plant a mile from the center of the city, an oil depot and an ammunition dump. Thailand-based U.S. Air Force planes the same day hit a railroad repair yard and an electrical transformer station $2\frac{1}{4}$ miles and 7 miles, respectively, from the center of Hanoi.

(North Vietnam reported Apr. 26 that the 2,739-ton British freighter *Dartford* had been hit by bullets in the Apr. 25 raid on Haiphong. 6 British seamen were reported by Hanoi to have been wounded. In Hong Kong, a spokesman for the agents for the *Dartford* said Apr. 27 that 6 Hong Kong Chinese crewmen had been wounded. In British House of Commons debate Apr. 26, leftwing Laborites assailed the U.S. for attacking the *Dartford* and urged Foreign Secy. George Brown to protest to Washington. Brown rejected the request and recalled that when a British ship was almost sunk by a Viet Cong mine in Saigon harbor earlier in the week, "no one in the House asked me a question about that." Brown said the *Dartford* was operated on charter by Chinese Communist interests. The U.S. State Department disclosed May 5 that a report sent to Britain had denied that American planes were responsible for damage inflicted on the *Dartford*. The U.S. said damage to the *Dartford* was "most likely caused by [North Vietnamese] antiaircraft missile debris." This version was substantiated May 10 by a British seaman who said he had witnessed the incident from another ship, but *Dartford* crewmen insisted May 10 that their ship had been strafed by American planes. The seaman who backed the American version, Barney Giles, 2d mate of the freighter *Ardrossmore,* said May 11 that an armed Chinese Communist merchant ship had fired at American planes during the Apr. 26 raid on Haiphong.)

Returning to Hanoi Apr. 26, U.S. planes from Thailand attacked a 5-span concrete-and-steel bridge that carried railroad tracks and Highway 1A over the Canal des Rapides, 4 miles north of the center of the city. The purpose of the raid was to sever North Vietnam's rail links with Communist China. As part of the same mission, other U.S. planes dropped bombs on rail yards at Hongai, 27 miles from Hanoi. The electrical transformer station 7 miles north of Hanoi was attacked for the 2d time, and U.S. carrier-based aircraft bombed an oil storage area 2 miles southwest of Haiphong.

U.S. jets returned to the Hanoi area Apr. 28 for one of the heaviest attacks of the war. Waves of U.S. planes dropped hundreds of bombs near the Danphuong highway causeway 12 miles west of the capital and on the Gialam railway repair yards. The city's main power station in the northern outskirts of Hanoi was heavily pounded. The attackers encountered heavy antiaircraft fire and Communist MiG interceptors.

U.S. planes Apr. 29 concentrated on Chinese-North Vietnamese rail links; they attacked, for the 2d time, the Canal des Rapides bridge and railroad yards 43 and 51 miles northeast of Hanoi. The North Vietnamese MiG base at Hoalac, 24 miles west of Hanoi, also was hit for the 2d time.

U.S. planes Apr. 30 bombed railroad yards at Hagia, Viettri and Vuchu, all within 42 miles of Hanoi. Other U.S. planes, assisting ground artillery and U.S. naval ships, hit a surface-to-air missile site 10 miles north of the demilitarized zone.

The Communist MiG bases at Kep and Hoalac were bombed for the 3d time May 2. Pilots reported heavy damage.

U.S. jets bombed the center of Hanoi May 19 for the first time. The target of the air strike was a 32,000-kilowatt power plant (the largest in North Vietnam) 1.1 miles from the downtown section of the city. A U.S. spokesman said the plant provided North Vietnam with about 20% of its electricity. The attacking planes were launched from the carrier *Bon Homme Richard*. Hanoi claimed the downing of 10 American planes during the day's raids and said 5 U.S. pilots were captured. Hanoi reported that the captives had been brought before a news conference.

An Agence France-Presse report from Haiphong Apr. 27 had said the entire western section of the city along the main road to Hanoi had been devastated by the U.S. air strikes. The Czech press agency reported Apr. 29 that non-essential residents had been ordered evacuated from Haiphong. The agency's Haiphong correspondent said only defense units and people vital to the operations of the city would remain.

China's Terms Vs. Intervening?

A French correspondent had reported in the Jan. 15 issue of *U.S. News & World Report* that Communist China had set 3 conditions for staying out of the Vietnamese war and that the U.S. was observing them. French and U.S. officials Jan. 16 denied the veracity of the report. The correspondent, René Dabernat, foreign editor of the magazine *Paris-Match,* said Peking's price for non-intervention was that the U.S. (1) not invade Communist China, (2) not invade North Vietnam and (3) not bomb the Red River dikes in North Vietnam. Dabernat said China's conditions had been transmitted to Washington in the spring of 1966 by a Chinese Communist embassy diplomat in Paris through the French Foreign Ministry. According to Dabernat, Pres. Johnson and other U.S. officials quickly "gave the necessary signals to Peking in various public speeches to show that they agreed to these conditions." Dabernat said that after the Oct. 1966 Manila conference Communist China had been "informed through diplomatic channels that Pres. Johnson wanted to bring about a process of stabilization and peace in the Pacific, if only Red China did not try to use force to extend its influence in Asia."

A French Foreign Ministry spokesman said Jan. 16 that "there is not a word of truth" in Dabernat's report. In denying Dabernat's report, U.S. officials in Washington acknowledged Jan. 16 a tacit understanding between the U.S. and China that Peking would not enter the Vietnamese war if the U.S. refrained from invading China or North Vietnam. But the officials said there was no truth to the report that France had acted as an intermediary in transmitting China's alleged conditions to Washington. The officials also said they were not aware of the 3d condition mentioned by Dabernat—the ban on the bombing of North Vietnam's dikes.

According to an article in the *Chicago Daily News* May 14, Communist China had threatened to send troops into North Vietnam if U.S. troops invaded North Vietnam. The threat was reported to have been made by Premier Chou En-lai and 4 other Chinese officials during interviews Mar. 27-29 with Simon Malley, 41, Cairo-born naturalized U.S. correspondent for *Jeune Afrique*, a French-language magazine published in Paris. Peking denied May 16, however, that the interview had taken place. Malley quoted Chou as saying during a 2½-hour meeting: China was "ready, tomorrow if need be," to send a volunteer army into North Vietnam if Hanoi made such a request; "Americans won't be allowed to approach our borders, our security would be at stake"; a "sell-out peace" in Vietnam would lead to Chinese military intervention. "Inevitable" war between Communist China and the U.S. was foreseen by Chou, according to an installment of the Malley interviews that appeared in the *Chicago Daily News* May 16. Chou was quoted as saying: "Sooner or later the United States will find itself in a situation where the realization of its imperialist objectives will require the violation of our sovereignty and territorial integrity. And that day a military showdown will have become inevitable."

In denying Malley's interview with Chou, the Chinese Foreign Ministry said May 16 that the report was an "out-and-out fabrication put up with ulterior motives." The ministry said that during his stay in Peking Malley had met neither Chou "nor any other Chinese leaders." Malley insisted May 16 that he had seen Chou while in Peking.

Peking radio reported May 23 that Foreign Min. Chen Yi May 22 had repeated Peking's warning that China would intervene in the war if such aid were requested by North Vietnam. At a meeting in Peking with North Vietnamese Chargé d'Affaires Le Chung Thuy, Chen was said to have stated that China was "paying serious attention" to the U.S.-South Vietnamese invasion of the southeastern sector of the Vietnamese demilitarized zone.

An unnamed State Department official warned May 23 that the U.S. would attack the Chinese mainland if Peking's forces intervened in the Vietnamese war on a massive scale. The American official, briefing a group of newspaper editors and broadcasters, first said U.S. forces would respond with conventional weapons. He later said Chinese intervention would elicit retaliation by the U.S. with everything it had. Department officials explained that this did not mean that the U.S. would employ nuclear weapons in countering a Chinese military thrust. The department spokesman also made the first public acknowledgment that American air intrusions had occurred over Communist China during the recently intensified air strikes against North Vietnam. The spokesman said the U.S. planes had not penetrated deeply into Chinese territory. China had accused the U.S. of 4 violations of its airspace since Apr. 24.

Various other incidents of U.S. planes intruding in China's airspace were reported during 1967. Among them:

■ Peking charged Feb. 9 that U.S. planes had flown over China's Kwangtung Province Feb. 7 and that another U.S. aircraft had violated the province's airspace Feb. 8. The Chinese announcement said U.S. planes also had flown over Yulin, Hainan Feb. 7-8.

■ The U.S. Defense Department conceded Feb. 9 that a U.S. Navy plane from an aircraft carrier in the Gulf of Tonkin had "inadvertently" flown over Communist China's Hainan Island that day because of "a navigational error." A Peking statement Feb. 11 called the U.S. State Department's explanation an "out-and-out lie." The armed forces newspaper *Chiehfang Chun Pao* claimed that U.S. planes had intruded over Chinese territory 5 times Feb. 8-9. The newspaper said American aircraft had intruded 4 times over Chinese airspace Feb. 10 after Peking had issued a "serious warning."

■ Communist China charged Feb. 22 that 2 U.S. planes had strafed Chinese fishing boats in the Gulf of Tonkin Feb. 20. The Peking broadcast claimed that one fisherman was killed, 3 fishermen wounded and 2 boats damaged. The broadcast charged that prior to the alleged attack other U.S. planes had carried out 20 sorties over Hainan Island. Peking claimed U.S. planes had intruded over the same area Feb. 21.

■ Peking radio asserted Apr. 25 that 2 U.S. F-4 Phantom jets had been shot down by Chinese fighter planes Apr. 24 after flying over the Kwangsi Chuang Autonomous Region, which bordered on North Vietnam. The Peking report charged that the American aircraft "intruded into China's air space for the purpose of creating a war provocation."

■ Communist China charged May 3 that 4 U.S. jets May 2 had bombed the southern Chinese town of Ningming, about 20 miles north of the

North Vietnamese border. One house was said to have been destroyed. The Chinese Foreign Ministry said the planes, F-105 jets, had fled after Chinese air force planes attacked them. The U.S. Defense Department May 2 denied the incident.

■ The U.S. Defense Department had reported May 15 that a U.S. F-105 Thunderchief might have crashed in Communist China or near its border that day. The craft had been struck by North Vietnamese antiaircraft fire during a raid on the Kep area.

■ A U.S. Defense Department announcement said May 26 that a U.S. Navy plane might have inadvertently strayed into Communist China before returning from an attack on the North Vietnamese MiG base at Kep, about 27 miles north of Hanoi. The announcement did not say when the incident had occurred.

■ Hsinhua claimed June 12 that Chinese armed forces had shot down a pilotless U.S. reconnaissance plane over the southern part of the Kwangsi Chuang Autonomous Region.

■ The U.S. Defense Department announced June 26 that an unarmed U.S. F-4 Phantom jet, being ferried from the Philippines to Danang, had strayed off course and was shot down that day by Chinese planes near or directly over Hainan Island. The 2 crewmen parachuted from the plane and were rescued unhurt from the China Sea by a U.S. Navy helicopter.

■ Communist China claimed July 12 that its planes had forced 4 U.S. jets that day to flee after they had attacked a Chinese frontier post near Tunghing, in the Kwangsi Chuang Autonomous Region. The Peking report said the U.S. planes had fired 2 guided missiles, injuring 4 soldiers and damaging a house.

■ Communist China charged Aug. 6 that a U.S. plane that day had flown over the Hsi-sha Islands, in the South China Sea.

The stationing of 32 North Vietnamese MiG-15 and MiG-17 jet fighters and 2 Ilyushin-28 twin-jet bombers in southern China had been reported by U.S. intelligence sources in Washington Mar. 13. According to the intelligence report, the North Vietnamese planes were at the Chinese bases for training purposes and were not using the fields to attack U.S. planes. One of the bases was said to be at Mengtzu in Yunnan Province, about 40 miles north of the Vietnamese-Chinese border.

The N.Y. Times reported Aug. 27 that Communist Chinese territory was being used by North Vietnamese MiGs as a "sanctuary" to escape air clashes with American planes bombing North Vietnam. The report said the North Vietnamese planes also were using Chinese territory to prepare for later attacks on U.S. jets. It was believed the Chinese-based MiGs first made a refueling stop in North Vietnam before taking off again to intercept raiding American planes. Because of this belief, it was said, American military commanders had appealed for permission to bomb all MiG bases in North Vietnam; Defense Secy. McNamara rejected the request. McNamara had estimated Aug. 25 that about 20 North Vietnamese MiGs were based in North Vietnam. Other Defense Department officials said this meant that the remainder of North Vietnam's 75-MiG force was based in China.

Westmoreland Heads Pacification

The civilian-operated pacification program in South Vietnam was turned over to the American military command May 11. Ellsworth Bunker, who had succeeded Henry Cabot Lodge as U.S. ambassador to South Vietnam Apr. 25, announced in Saigon May 11 that the project, aimed at re-establishing South Vietnamese government control over thousands of rural villages and hamlets, would be headed by Gen. Westmoreland. The change resulted from Washington's dissatisfaction with progress of the program. Under Westmoreland's supervision, Gen. Creighton W. Abrams Jr. would handle the program's military aspects, and Robert W. Komer, a Presidential assistant, would be in charge of the civilian side. Previously, the pacification program had been headed by ex-U.S. Deputy Amb. William J. Porter.

Allies Invade DMZ

A force of 5,500 U.S. and South Vietnamese troops May 18 invaded the southeastern section of the demilitarized zone that divided North and South Vietnam. The operation was aimed at smashing an alleged North Vietnamese and Viet Cong build-up in the area and at denying the zone's use as a Communist infiltration route into South Vietnam. It was reported May 23 that the first phase of the allied drive had ended and most of the allied troops had been withdrawn to a defensive position just south of the buffer area. One U.S. Marine battalion remained in the western end of the 17-mile eastern sector of the zone. U.S. authorities reported May 24 that 663 North Vietnamese and 96 Americans were killed in the operation and 595 Americans wounded.

South Vietnamese civilians in the part of the zone affected were evacuated by U.S. troops; at least 6,000 of the area's 12,000 residents were removed by May 23 to a resettlement camp at Camlo, several miles south of the DMZ. The evacuation of the civilians made the southeastern sector "a free-fire zone," permitting allied troops to fire at any moving target, according to Brig. Gen. Bruno Hochmuth, 3d Marine Division commander and head of the operation. Hochmuth said a major cache of Communist arms and ammunition found in bunkers in the battle area made "it obvious to the world that they [the Communists] have been using the zone for military purposes and it is not a demilitarized zone."

The drive against the estimated 2,500 North Vietnamese troops in the sector was carried out by a 3-pronged allied assault. One U.S. Marine battalion of more than 1,000 men was airlifted from 7th Fleet ships to an area north of the town of Thuyban on the southern bank of the Benhai River, which divided the 6-mile-wide zone. Encountering heavy resistance, the Marines, aided by off-shore naval fire, pushed west to link up with other U.S. and South Vietnamese troops in an effort to trap the North Vietnamese units. 2 Marine battalions moved north into the zone from the American outpost at Conthien, a mile south of the buffer zone. 5 South Vietnamese First Division battalions drove into the zone up Route 1. An additional 3 U.S. Marine battalions from Conthien advanced into the zone May 21, raising the total allied force there to more than 10,000 men.

The allied invasion of the zone followed almost 2 weeks of fierce North Vietnamese attacks against American positions just south of the buffer area. The base camp at Conthien had come under heavy assault May 8. The Communists' 3-hour attack, backed by mortars, was repulsed. 179 North Vietnamese and 44 U.S. Marines were killed and 124 Americans were wounded. During the assault on Conthien, other North Vietnamese mortar teams carried out attacks on nearby Marine camps at Dongha, Giolinh and Camp Carroll. Fighting broke out at the western end of the area below the DMZ May 9 when a North Vietnamese force attacked a 3d Marine Regiment unit 9 miles northwest of Khesanh; in the ensuing 5-

hour clash, the Marines, aided by reinforcements and air strikes, killed 31 North Vietnamese; 24 Marines were killed and 19 wounded. U.S. positions near Conthien and Giolinh were hit again May 13 by North Vietnamese howitzers, and U.S. artillery responded against suspected North Vietnamese gun emplacements across the Benhai River. Marine positions between Dongha and Conthien were pounded May 15 by North Vietnamese artillery as heavy fighting raged along the DMZ. More than 100 Americans were killed or wounded in the day's clashes. The Conthien base came under intermittent shelling. Reinforcements were rushed to Conthien May 17-18 (raising the total force there to 2,500 men) as the base came under continued North Vietnamese attack. Conthien, along with Dongha, Giolinh, Camlo and Camp Carroll, were shelled May 17. Dongha was shelled again May 18, and 11 Marines at the base were killed and 41 wounded. The 3 other bases struck the previous day were hit again by North Vietnamese shells. North Vietnamese artillery positions in and below the demilitarized zone were attacked by U.S. planes May 16-17. Marine pilots May 17 dropped bombs on 2 surface-to-air missile sites in the demilitarized zone; the announcement of the attack was the first indication that the North Vietnamese had positioned these weapons in the DMZ.

A State Department statement May 19 said the allied offensive in the DMZ was a "purely defensive measure" against a "considerable build-up" of North Vietnamese troops. The statement said: "There is no question about the legal right of allied forces to move into the southern portion of the demilitarized zone to protect the territory of South Vietnam against this intrusion from the North. Although it is demilitarized—or supposed to be demilitarized—it is South Vietnamese territory which is being used by North Vietnamese forces."

A North Vietnamese government statement May 21 charged that the invasion of the zone was "a brazen provocation" that "abolished the buffer character" of the DMZ as provided by the Geneva agreements.

Speaking on ABC-TV's "Issues and Answers" program, Gen. Earle G. Wheeler Jr., chairman of the Joint Chiefs of

Staff, said May 21 that the U.S. had "no intention of invading North Vietnam." Gen. Westmoreland "is not going across the Benhai River" into North Vietnam, Wheeler said. Westmoreland's "mandate is to fight the war in South Vietnam, not elsewhere."

Fighting broke out again in the southeastern section of the DMZ May 25 when 2 U.S. Marine battalions of about 1,200 men assaulted a North Vietnamese force dug in on Hill 117, about 3 miles west of the base at Conthien. The clash erupted when one of the 2 Marine battalions maneuvering just south of the buffer area was fired on by Communist forces inside the DMZ. 14 Marines were killed and 102 wounded. Marines moved into the zone and stormed Hill 117, capturing it May 27. They withdrew the same day after blowing up enemy bunkers. 41 North Vietnamese troops were reported killed in the operation.

Truce Fails to Halt Fighting

The intensity of combat abated but did not halt completely during a 24-hour truce May 23-24 in honor of Buddha's birthday. South Vietnam had proposed the cease-fire Apr. 8. The National Liberation Front accepted the offer Apr. 27 but suggested a 48-hour truce starting May 22. The U.S.-allied forces recognized only the May 23-24 truce. The U.S. command reported May 24, following the resumption of fighting, that the truce had been marred by 71 clashes in which 12 Americans were killed and 60 wounded. 51 Communist soldiers were reported slain.

U.S. air raids over the North were suspended during the May 23-24 truce but were resumed immediately on the expiration of the one-day cease-fire with attacks on 2 rail lines north of Hanoi that carried supplies from Communist China to the North Vietnamese capital. Tracks at both points were reported cut by the bombings. One strike was located 40 miles south of the Chinese border. The other rail point hit was at the Thainguey steel and power complex, 40 miles north of Hanoi.

M-16 Rifle Debate

Public controversy over the M-16, the basic combat rifle in Vietnam, began in May after Rep. James J. Howard (D.,

N.J.) read to the U.S. House of Representatives a letter in which a Marine in Vietnam, writing to his parents, attributed deaths in battle to M-16 malfunction. The rifle, a lightweight automatic firearm, was defended May 26 by Gen. Wallace M. Greene Jr., Marine Corps commandant. The Defense Department Aug. 28 acknowledged that there had been "a serious increase in frequency of malfunctions" in the M-16 and reported that a re-evaluation of the situation was under way. But a $25,871,701 contract to Colt Industries for 242,716 more M-16s was announced Sept. 1. A House Armed Services subcommittee investigated the controversy and reported Oct. 18 that the M-16 had malfunctioned "seriously and excessively" in the field, that jamming was the most serious malfunction, that the major cause of this was the type of powder used, that corrective action was unnecessarily delayed and there was no proof that further Army-proposed modifications would correct the situation.

DMZ Battles Near Conthien

U.S. and North Vietnamese troops suffered heavy casualties in several fierce battles fought July 2-7 near the Marine base at Conthien, just south of the western end of the DMZ.

The first clash erupted July 2, about 1½ miles northeast of Conthien, when 500 troops of the 90th Regiment of North Vietnam's 324B Division ambushed the U.S. 9th Marine Regiment's 3d platoon, which was conducting a sweep of the area. 35 Marines were killed in the surprise attack. Both sides rushed reinforcements to the scene and the fighting increased in intensity. Lt. Gen. Robert E. Cushman, who had taken command of the Marine force in Vietnam in June, said July 6 that the bodies of 250 North Vietnamese had been counted at the scene of the battle and that the bodies of 100 other Communist troops had been spotted by observation pilots. Cushman said U.S. Marine casualties totaled 96 killed and 211 wounded.

The U.S. command reported July 5 that North Vietnamese mortars, rockets and artillery had fired 300 rounds in 8 separate attacks at American positions at Conthien and Dongha in the previous 24 hours. The report said 15 Marines had been killed and 51 wounded. Marine positions near Conthien came under North Vietnamese artillery attack again July 6. 12 Marines were killed and 25 wounded. One of the artillery shells scored a direct hit on a Marine post, killing 9 men and wounding 21.

U.S. Admits Hitting Soviet Ship

The U.S. apologized to the Soviet Union June 20 for what it called an inadvertent American air attack on the Soviet ship *Turkestan* June 2 off the North Vietnamese port of Campha. The American apology was followed by a new Soviet charge that a Russian merchant ship had been hit by U.S. planes raiding Haiphong harbor June 29. The U.S. at first had denied the *Turkestan* attack. But the Defense Department said June 15 that further investigation of the raid on Campha June 2 had shown that a flight of U.S. aircraft not previously reported had been in action in the area. The department said it appeared that there had been "suppressive fire against a North Vietnamese anti-aircraft site at Campha by aircraft of [this] flight and that some of this fire may have struck the *Turkestan.*"

In a protest delivered to the U.S. embassy in Moscow June 30 on the 2d ship incident, the Soviet government charged the Russian merchant vessel *Mikhail Frunze* had been bombed by American planes in Haiphong harbor June 29.

The North Vietnamese news agency reported June 30 that in addition to the *Mikhail Frunze,* 2 other foreign merchant ships had been struck by American planes in Haiphong harbor. The vessels were identified as the British ship *Kingford* and the Chinese Communist ship *Hongqi No. 157.* The agency reported one crewman on the *Hongqi No. 157* was injured.

The East German news agency ADN reported June 30 that the Italian merchant ship *Bertani* had been hit by American planes in Haiphong harbor.

(ADN reported July 24 that Communist-bloc cargo ships continued to reach the North Vietnamese port to unload goods. It was reported in Washington July 29 that according to U.S. intelligence sources, the number of non-Communist ships that had called at North Vietnamese ports had increased from 20 during July-Dec. 1966 to 39 during Jan.-June 1967.

The total figure for 1966 was listed at 74, a decrease from 402 in 1964 and 256 in 1965.)

U.S. Unit Destroyed Near Dakto

A 130-man company of the 173d U.S. Airborne Brigade was virtually wiped out by a North Vietnamese ambush June 22 near Dakto in Kontum Province, about 280 miles northeast of Saigon. 80 Americans were killed and 34 were wounded. 106 North Vietnamese were killed. Gen. Westmoreland arrived at the Dakto headquarters of the brigade June 25 to visit survivors of the battle. He told the paratroopers that they had won "one of the toughest battles Americans have fought in the history of Vietnam."

The Dakto battle was one of a series of heavy engagements fought by American forces against Viet Cong and North Vietnamese troops throughout the country June 2-22. During that period U.S. planes continued to carry out intensive air strikes against targets in North Vietnam. The raids centered on power plants, jet fighter bases and the China-North Vietnam rail line.

In the ground fighting, troops of the U.S. 5th Marine Regiment were reported to have killed 540 North Vietnamese soldiers in a battle June 2-3 near Tamky, 30 miles southwest of Danang. Marine losses were said to have totaled 73 killed and 139 wounded. The fighting erupted when a Marine battalion, on patrol in the Hiepduc Valley, came under heavy fire from a 2,900-man North Vietnamese regiment dug in along a trench line.

The Central Highlands city of Pleiku was struck by 2 separate Communist mortar attacks June 10. Most of the shells were directed against a pacification school for *montagnard* tribesmen. 27 were killed. 60 *montagnards* and 37 U.S. servicemen were wounded. 2 American soldiers were killed and 3 were wounded in the 2d mortar attack, on a maintenance and transportation area 3 miles northwest of the first target.

A South Vietnamese force of about 1,000 men, assisted by armed U.S. helicopters, overwhelmed a 450-man Viet Cong battalion in an all-day battle fought June 14 in the Mekong delta 10 miles southwest of Cantho. 211 Communist troops were reported killed and 17 captured. South Vietnamese casualties totaled 5 killed and 60 wounded. The Viet Cong had started the battle by attacking 2 South Vietnamese militia companies. 900 other South Vietnamese soldiers were nearby and quickly sent in to relieve the government units.

Troops of the U.S. First Infantry Division launched a drive June 12 in the War Zone D area 50 miles north of Saigon in an effort to trap 3 Viet Cong battalions believed operating there. In the first significant contact, made June 13, the Americans killed 60 guerrillas in a 4-hour clash. In another engagement in the same area the U.S. troops June 17 killed at least 196 soldiers of the Viet Cong's 271st Infantry Regiment. The 3-hour battle was precipitated by a Viet Cong ambush of 2 U.S. division battalions in which 31 Americans were killed and 113 wounded. The American units came under attack as they were moving from one helicopter landing zone to another.

Another major clash took place June 19-20, 19 miles south of Saigon on the Rach-hui River. About 800 men of the U.S. 9th Infantry Division and U.S. Navy river assault boats killed 169 Viet Cong. American losses totaled 28 killed and 126 wounded.

McNamara Mission to War Zone

Defense Secy. McNamara reviewed the course of the war with U.S. commanders on his 9th fact-finding mission to South Vietnam July 7-11. Major interest in McNamara's mission centered on requests made July 7 by Gen. Westmoreland for a substantial increase in American reinforcements beyond the rise currently authorized. The publicly-known plan called for raising the existing 450,000-460,000-man force in Vietnam to 480,000 in 3 months. Westmoreland reportedly had asked for an additional 100,000 to 200,000 soldiers.

McNamara reported his findings to Pres. Johnson at the White House on his return to Washington July 12. The Defense Secretary said at a news conference after the meeting that "some more" troops would be needed in Vietnam, but the reinforcements would not necessitate the calling-up of reserves in the U.S. McNamara also said: U.S. and allied troops were making progress toward defeating the North Vietnamese and Viet Cong forces, and—in the words of the U.S. and allied

commanders he had spoken to—the reports of a military stalemate were "the most ridiculous statements they ever heard";
the "most dramatic" development in the conflict was the
opening up of large sections of major roads, hitherto under
Communist control, to military and civilian traffic; all-
weather air strikes had become possible against Communist
targets with "significantly reduced" plane losses due to improved technology, and they were becoming more effective;
although more cooperation between civilians and military men
was apparent, the pacification program was still making slow
progress.

In requesting a greater increase in American reinforcements, Westmoreland told McNamara at their initial Saigon
meeting July 7 that "we are winning slowly but steadily.
North Vietnam is paying a tremendous price with nothing to
show for it in return." Westmoreland's statement was made
during a 10-hour briefing given McNamara at the U.S. Army's
headquarters at Tansonnhut airbase. U.S. Amb.-to-South
Vietnam Ellsworth Bunker opened the briefing with a statement reviewing the pacification program. Only "some mo-
mentum" had been achieved in the program, he reported.
Bunker added: "We have had a good measure of success and
I believe we are gradually achieving our aims in Vietnam. If
we stick with it long enough—and this is not a short-term
proposition—I am confident that we will have some reasonable
success in achieving our long-term objectives."

Pres. Johnson disclosed at his press conference July 13
that the U.S. had decided on a relatively modest increase in
the build-up of American forces in Vietnam beyond the currently authorized maximum. The decision was publicly indorsed at the news conference by Westmoreland, McNamara
and Gen. Earle G. Wheeler, chairman of the Joint Chiefs of Staff.
Westmoreland, who had returned to the U.S. July 12 to attend
the funeral of his mother, had discussed the troop issue with
Mr. Johnson July 12 and 13. The President's announcement
was made amid renewed reports that Administration officials
were in disagreement with Westmoreland and other U.S. commanders in Vietnam who had requested a substantial increase
in American reinforcements. The President said at his news

conference that "we have reached a meeting of minds. The troops that Gen. Westmoreland needs and requests, as we feel it necessary, will be supplied."

Forrestal Fire Kills 134

A fire July 29 swept the 76,000-ton aircraft carrier *Forrestal* in the Gulf of Tonkin off the coast of North Vietnam. The blaze, described as the worst U.S. naval disaster in a combat zone since World War II, killed 134 crewmen and injured 62. The ship's commanding officer, Capt. John K. Beling, said that of the carrier's 80 planes, 21 were destroyed and 42 damaged. Beling said the vessel was "in good shape except for the after section," which was a charred and twisted wreck.

Rear Adm. Harvey P. Lanham, commander of Carrier Division II, who made the *Forrestal* his flagship, said July 31 that the blaze had broken out after an A-4 Skyhawk fuel tank "punctured and ignited." The flames quickly spread across the flight deck and ignited bomb-laden aircraft and shells stored on the deck. The fire broke out 7 minutes before the *Forrestal's* planes were to take off on a bombing mission. 2 other U.S. warships in the area—the destroyers *Rupertus* and *Henry W. Tucker*—sped to the side of the stricken vessel and poured water onto the carrier's deck. The carriers *Oriskany* and *Bon Homme Richard,* on station with the *Forrestal* off the North Vietnamese coast, sent doctors by helicopters and removed casualties. The *Forrestal's* crewmen brought the blaze under control one hour after it had broken out. Smaller fires, however, continued to smolder, but they were extinguished by the time the *Forrestal* docked July 31 at the U.S. naval base at Subic Bay, the Philippines. The loss of the carrier's services curtailed U.S. naval air attacks over North Vietnam July 29-30. The carrier *Intrepid* replaced the *Forrestal* in the Gulf of Tonkin.

Taylor-Clifford Mission to Allies

Gen. Maxwell D. Taylor, a consultant to Pres. Johnson, and Clark Clifford, a Presidential adviser and chairman of the Foreign Intelligence Advisory Board, toured South Vietnam, Thailand, Australia, New Zealand and South Korea July 24-Aug. 3. The 2 officials, who had left Washington July 22, were sent by Pres. Johnson to sound out allied opinion on the possibility of another summit conference of the Vietnam allies and reportedly to seek more allied troops for the war.

Taylor and Clifford reported to Pres. Johnson on their return to Washington August 5. Prior to meeting with the President, the 2 men had discussed the results of their mission in general terms with newsmen at Anderson Air Force Base, Md., where they had landed. Taylor said he and Clifford had found no major disagreement on any aspect of the war in their talks with allied leaders. Clifford said "there was unanimous agreement among all the allies that the [U.S.] bombing [of North Vietnam] should be carried on at its present level, or possibly at an increased level." Clifford and Taylor denied that they had discussed the question of more allied troops for Vietnam or the possibility of new peace proposals in their visits to the 5 allied capitals.

U.S. Expands Air War

U.S. planes launched an intensified air offensive against North Vietnam Aug. 11. They bombed targets in the Hanoi-Haiphong area and other objectives in the northeastern part of the country that previously had been declared off-limits by the Johnson Administration. The lifting of these restrictions permitted American pilots to attack objectives within 10 miles of the Chinese Communist border. Heretofore U.S. planes had been under orders to stay at least 25 miles away from the frontier. During one of the strikes, 2 U.S. Navy A-6A Intruder jet bombers from the carrier *Constellation,* pursued Aug. 21 by North Vietnamese MiG jets, strayed over the border and were shot down over Communist China. (Peking said its air force had downed the 2 U.S. planes over the Kwangsi Chuang Autonomous Region bordering North Vietnam). The raids continued with mounting intensity, and at least 16 U.S. aircraft were reported to have been lost over North Vietnam in the period Aug. 20-26.

Pres. Johnson was reported August 12 to have authorized the lifting of the restrictions in a directive issued Aug. 8 to Adm. U. S. Grant Sharp, U.S. commander-in-chief in the Pacific. The new target list included transportation and industrial installations in the Hanoi-Haiphong area and rail lines linking

Hanoi with Communist China. Mr. Johnson was said to have ordered a step-up in the air offensive against North Vietnam in response to Congressional pressure for removal of the target curbs.

Reporting on the Aug. 11 incident, the Defense Department said that 2 Navy A-6 Intruder jets had strayed off course after encountering heavy anti-aircraft fire during the bombing of the Ducnoi rail yard, 7 miles north of Hanoi and about 75 miles from the Chinese border. White House Press Secy. George Christian said Aug. 21 that "with all precautions, you are going to have incidents like this one." He added, however, that "we are confident Peking is aware that the United States does not seek involvement of Red China" in the war.

The first air strikes carried out under the expanded bombing orders were directed Aug. 11 against the Paul Doumer (Longbien) Bridge, which spanned the Red River in the northeast part of Hanoi. The raids reportedly cut a span of the bridge, Hanoi's only rail and road connection with Haiphong and with the Chinese border. U.S. pilots Aug. 12 bombed rail and highway bridges crossing the Canal des Rapides, 5 miles northeast of Hanoi. Other targets hit Aug. 12 included fuel and ammunition depots at the Kienan MiG airbase, 5 miles southwest of Haiphong, military barracks 33 miles south of Hanoi and 35 miles northwest of the capital, and surface-to-air missile sites 11 miles southeast of Hanoi.

U.S. planes Aug. 13 bombed the 360-foot Langson rail and highway bridge spanning the Kikung River, 10 miles from the Chinese border. It was the closest target to China ever hit by U.S. planes. (The closest previous strike was on the Caonung railroad yard, 30 miles from the Chinese frontier.) Langson was at the northern end of the northeast rail connection between Hanoi and China. The bridge's entire center span was reported to have caved into the river. American pilots also bombed rail yards at Langgai and at Langdang, 19 and 26 miles from the Chinese border. U.S. Navy pilots returned to the Langson Bridge Aug. 14 and claimed to have knocked out another span, described as "a by-pass bridge" a mile to the east of the center span.

U.S. B-52s maintained heavy pressure against the southern part of North Vietnam in raids carried out Aug. 13, 15 and 18. The bombings were directed against North Vietnamese troops and installations in the DMZ (demilitarized zone) and in the sector just north of the buffer area. The purpose of the mission was to knock out Communist guns threatening Marine positions just below the DMZ.

With bad weather forcing a suspension of raids against northeastern North Vietnam, U.S. planes concentrated on targets in the southern part of the country Aug. 18 and 19, carrying out a record 209 missions the 2d day. The raids were directed at coastal shipping and infiltration traffic.

(U.S. planes Aug. 3 had flown 197 missions, the highest total for a single day since Oct. 14, 1966. They hit at targets ranging from the Hanoi-Haiphong sector to the DMZ.)

16 U.S. planes were downed over North Vietnam Aug. 20-26 in the stepped-up air offensive. This was a record for planes lost over the North in one week.

North Vietnam declared Aug. 29 that Communist military activity in South Vietnam had been intensified as a direct response to the increased American air war against North Vietnam and that the Communist side would match each phase of American military escalation. An article appearing in the North Vietnamese army newspaper *Quang Doi Nhan Dan,* reputedly written by Defense Min. Vo Nguyen Giap, said that American policy in carrying out heavy air raids on the North "to bring pressure in the South" was "backwards logic" and that Pres. Johnson had "erred in his calculations." Pointing up what it labeled the futility of bombing the capital city, the article said that a year had passed since Hanoi had first been bombed but that U.S. troops had become bogged down in the South whereas North Vietnam had increased its defensive and economic powers. The Viet Cong had not "returned to guerrilla warfare" and had increased its strength with the use of long-range artillery, the article said. The article rejected what it said was a recent suggestion by U.S. State Secy. Rusk that the U.S. would consider a cessation of the raids on the North if North Vietnamese military forces halted their attacks on U.S. Marine positions along the demilitarized zone. "Let us answer Mr. Rusk right away," the article said, "that in this land of Vietnam there are no sanctuaries for Americans and no categories that can enjoy privileges of not receiving retaliatory blows struck by the Vietnamese people." (U.S. officials in Washington denied Aug. 29 that Rusk had made a new offer to halt the bombings in exchange for a cessation of North Vietnamese hostilities along the DMZ. Rusk, however, had often said that he would regard a stop to military activity near the buffer zone an example of the Communist reciprocity that was necessary if the U.S. was to end the bombing of the North.)

North Vietnam Aug. 25 had announced plans for the further evacuation of all non-essential civilians from Hanoi in view of the increased U.S. air attacks. The city's Administrative Committee ordered all workers in light industry and all craftsmen and their families to leave Hanoi; only persons vital to the city's defense and production were to remain. Diplomatic sources in Saigon estimated August 25 that following a previous evacuation order issued in June 1966, half of Hanoi's 1,200,000 inhabitants had left the city.

The authorization of air attacks near the Chinese border was deplored Aug. 14 by Congressional critics of Johnson Administration policy in Vietnam. Senate Democratic leader Mike Mansfield (Mont.) called it "a very dangerous extension of the war" that "brings us that much closer to the brink of a possible confrontation with China which could be made probable through a miscalculation, an error or otherwise." Senate Foreign Relations Committee Chrmn. J. W. Fulbright (D., Ark.) called the extension "dangerous and stupid." Sen. Charles H. Percy (R., Ill.) questioned what the U.S. reaction would be "if the Chinese bombed Mexico within 10 miles of the Rio Grande." But ex-Pres. Dwight D. Eisenhower indorsed the attacks on new targets Aug. 14. He said military targets should be bombed. Asked by newsmen if he thought the expanded bombing enlarged the risk of China's entrance into the war, he said no.

In testimony before the U.S. Senate Preparedness Investigations Subcommittee Aug. 9, Adm. U. S. Grant Sharp had said that "the enemy is hurting" from increased U.S. pressure, especially in the last 2 or 3 months, and that "we should increase our pressures." North Vietnam, he said, faced "mounting logistic, management and morale problems" because of the air attacks. Gen. Earle G. Wheeler, Joint Chiefs of Staff chairman, told the subcommittee Aug. 16 he did not "foresee any shortage of worthwhile military targets" in North Vietnam. He added that previous targets could not "be crossed off the list and forgotten" because of North Vietnam's "marked ability to recuperate from and accommodate to our air attacks." Wheeler urged that the port of Haiphong and rail lines from China to Hanoi be blocked as a means of shortening the war.

Gen. John P. McConnell, Air Force chief of staff, said in Aug. 22 testimony that when the bombing of the North had been authorized in 1965, the Joint Chiefs had recommended "a very severe application of air power"—a plan to destroy 94 targets in 16 days. Instead of this "sharp, sudden blow," he said, the Administration had adopted a plan of "applying pressure gradually." "I believe," he said, "that if we had gone in 1965 and really pounded them when they didn't have any defenses, that we would have been better off today." Asked if "we probably would have suffered fewer casualties in the South if the air campaign against the North had not been burdened with restrictions and prohibited targets," McConnell said: "In my opinion, that is correct."

In Aug. 23 testimony, Adm. Thomas H. Moorer, chief of naval operations, supported McConnell's views. Moorer said the U.S. would be in "a better situation" if the Joint Chiefs' original bombing plan had been adopted.

Defense Secy. McNamara said in Aug. 25 testimony that he did not think the bombing of North Vietnam "has in any significant way affected their war-making capability." He said: There was no "direct relationship between the level of bombing in the North and the United States forces required in the South." "There are many who believe, and there is much evidence to support the conclusion, that the flow of men and matériel into the South is not determined by the air campaign in the North but by the ability of the Viet Cong and the North Vietnamese, operating, by the way, without for all practical purposes, a single wheeled vehicle in all of South Vietnam, to accept the men and matériel from the North. In other words, the bottleneck is not on the lines of communication in North Vietnam but . . . the lines . . . through Laos and . . . in South Vietnam." McNamara testified, however, that he would be against any reduction in the bombing unless "we got something substantial in return for it." He said the bombing was the "price" North Vietnam was paying for its aggression in South Vietnam. "On balance," he said, "we believe it [the bombing of the North] helps us." McNamara testified against bombing or mining the port of Haiphong on the ground that such action would cause no "significant reduction" in supplies to the enemy. He reported that "recent prisoner interrogations suggest that 10%-20%" of the troops North Vietnam sent to the South "never reach the battle area—about 2% are casualties caused by air attacks." He said aerial forces "destroyed in transit" "a much higher percentage of the supplies sent South to support the DRV fighting forces."

Major Summer Ground Battles

The fiercest battles fought by U.S. and allied troops with Communist forces throughout South Vietnam in July and August centered around the demilitarized zone, the Mekong delta, the Central Highlands and around Saigon. Among major actions reported in July-September:

■ Outnumbered South Vietnamese troops repelled an attack July 10 by 2 battalions of the 141st North Vietnamese Regiment on a South Vietnamese military camp 5 miles east of Anloc (60 miles north of Saigon). The Communist forces had managed to penetrate the camp's outer defenses and capture ⅓ of the base camp before they were thrown back with the assistance of U.S. and South Vietnamese air and artillery strikes.

■ U.S. forces suffered heavy casualties in 2 separate battles fought in the Central Highlands July 10 and 11. In the first action, about 400 men of the 173d Airborne Brigade came under heavy North Vietnamese machinegun and mortar fire during a sweep of the Dakto area, near Kontum. 26 Americans were killed and 49 wounded. A U.S. spokesman reported that 6 North Vietnamese bodies were found in the area after the battle. In the 2d Highlands clash July 11, 35 soldiers of the U.S. 4th Infantry Division were killed and 31 were wounded 5 miles south of Ducco.

■ U.S. 4th Infantry Division troops July 23 virtually wiped out a North Vietnamese company in a 5-hour battle 4 miles south of Ducco in the Central Highlands. At least 148 men of the 400-man Communist force were killed after they had crossed into South Vietnam from Cambodia, 5 miles away. 22 U.S. soldiers were slain and 39 were wounded.

■ The U.S. airbase at Danang was struck by 50 rounds of Communist rocket fire July 15. The U.S. high command reported 12 U.S. servicemen killed and 40 wounded in the 45-minute attack; 6-8 planes were destroyed and 10 damaged.

■ A battalion of U.S. Marines penetrated the southern part of the DMZ July 29 and was ambushed by a North Vietnamese force on its way out. An official U.S. report July 30 said 23 Marines had been killed and 119 wounded. An unofficial source placed American losses in the ambush at 50 dead and 351 wounded.

■ Viet Cong gunfire Aug. 7 shot down 5 U.S. helicopters along the banks of the Saigon River within 4 miles of the capital. The 'copters were taking part in an air-ground search for a suspected guerrilla force in the area. 5 more helicopters were lost to enemy gunfire during the landing of U.S. First Cavalry Division troops Aug. 9 on a North Vietnamese fortified position in the Songre Valley, 25 miles west of Ducpho, a coastal village south of Danang.

■ The U.S. command disclosed Aug. 10 that 40 South Vietnamese civilians had been killed and 36 wounded Aug. 2 when 2 U.S. Army helicopters returned fire against a group of Viet Cong in a Mekong delta village near Phuvinh, 60 miles south of Saigon. The spokesman said the Vietnamese province chief had given the Americans permission to carry out the air strike.

■ Viet Cong units Aug. 27 killed an estimated 355 persons, mostly civilians, in a series of coordinated attacks ranging from the northern provinces to the Mekong delta. The heaviest attack was directed against the delta city of Cantho. 46 civilians were killed in a 10-minute mortar and rocket barrage. 222 persons, including 5 U.S. soldiers, were wounded. At least 60 Vietnamese civilians were killed or wounded when a Viet Cong battalion, aided by mortar fire, smashed into Hoian, 30 miles south of Hué. Other targets that came under Viet Cong fire that day were Pleiku, Hué, Dienban and Banmethout.

■ U.S. and North Vietnamese troops fought a fierce 4-day battle in the Queson Valley 25 miles south of Danang Sept. 4-7. 114 men of the U.S. 5th Marine Regiment and 376 North Vietnamese were killed. The fighting came at a time when many U.S. and allied troops were involved in providing security during South Vietnam's national elections.

■ 134 Marines were killed and 397 wounded in fighting just south of the DMZ Sept. 4-7. 479 North Vietnamese troops were killed in the same period, according to a U.S. spokesman.

■ In the Mekong delta, more than 200 Viet Cong were killed in a U.S. offensive (Operation Coronado 5) Sept. 13-16. Most of them were slain Sept. 13 when U.S. 9th Infantry Division troops, flanked by South Vietnamese forces, killed 134 Viet Cong in a 12-hour sweep 47 miles southwest of Saigon. The greatest part of the Communist losses were attributed to 39 U.S. Air Force jet strikes and supporting artillery fire. 9 U.S. troops were killed and 21 wounded in the day's fighting.

Fighting in the same area flared anew Sept. 15 when a flotilla of the U.S. Navy's River Assault Task Force in the delta came under heavy Viet Cong attack as it moved through the Rachba River, 16 miles west of the provincial capital of Mytho. The troops aboard the ships promptly rushed ashore to pursue the Viet Cong attackers in the rain-swept rice paddies. Artillery and air strikes assisted the naval gunboats in firing on the enemy positions. By the time the fighting tapered off Sept. 16, 69 Viet Cong had been killed. American casualties totaled 21 killed and 101 wounded. Most of the losses were suffered in the initial guerrilla attack on the naval task force.

U.S. Plans DMZ Barrier

U.S. Defense Secy. McNamara Sept. 7 announced plans to build a fortified barrier just south of the eastern end of the demilitarized zone to curb the flow of arms and troops from North Vietnam into the South. The barrier was expected to extend westward and further fortify a 15-mile-long 600-yard-wide strip that had been cleared below the DMZ since April by U.S. and South Vietnamese engineers. The old barrier consisted of barbed wire and mine fields. McNamara said the new barrier's "objectives will be consistent with those of our present air campaign against lines of communication." He said that "highly sophisticated" devices would be installed and that they would not be put into operation until "late this year or early next year." McNamara refused to discuss the type of equipment that would be used on the ground that advanced knowledge of it would enable the Communists to "defeat the system once it is installed." McNamara conceded that "no obstacle can stop the infiltration of men or supplies from North to South." The new barrier, he emphasized, would only "impede" that movement.

It was reported in Saigon Sept. 8 that the projected barrier, dubbed the McNamara Line, was opposed by Gen. Westmoreland and by Marine commanders in Quangtri Province, which bordered on the DMZ. The Marine officers contended that their tactic of making stabbing attacks inside the demilitarized zone to throw the North Vietnamese off balance was more effective than a static defense based on a permanently fortified line. Other U.S. military men were said to have argued that Communist troops could nullify the effectiveness of the barrier by sending troops around it through Laos, by setting off the barrier's alarm devices to draw wasted fire and by shelling it with long-range artillery.

Senate majority leader Mike Mansfield (D., Mont.) indorsed McNamara's proposal Sept. 7. Speaking at a Missouri Bar Association meeting in Kansas City, Mansfield said: "I have advocated that a defensive barrier be built across Vietnam just south of the demilitarized zone and extended across Laos to Thailand as an alternative to an extension of the war in Asia in consequence of ever-expanding aerial bombardment."

Laotian Premier Souvanna Phouma Sept. 26 expressed opposition to any extension of the barrier into Laos. To permit this, Souvanna said, would "enlarge the Vietnam conflict at a time when we are all trying to limit and contain it." Extension of the barrier also would constitute "foreign intervention" in Laotian affairs, and his government "cannot accept intervention no matter where it comes from," Souvanna asserted. (Souvanna said his government was not worried about the pro-Communist Pathet Lao rebels in Laos. He said it was more concerned by the North Vietnamese, "who have 40,000 troops in Laos.")

Chinese Nationalist Embassy Bombed

The Chinese Nationalist embassy in Saigon was heavily damaged by a bomb explosion Sept. 19. 27 persons, most of them outside the building, were injured. A South Vietnamese civilian employed by the embassy was shot to death by a sniper. A 19-year-old Chinese of Vietnamese nationality was captured by police after an exchange of gunfire during which a Vietnamese passerby was shot to death. Police said the youth, reputedly a member of the Viet Cong, admitted planting the bomb.

Police investigated 3 other shootings, 2 of them fatal, to determine whether they were connected with the embassy incident: An embassy attaché, Col. Chung Tao, was shot twice and wounded at his home by a 20-year-old woman one hour after the blast; his assailant was captured by police. The 2 other persons were shot to death at their homes in Cholon, the Chinese section of Saigon; Hang Hing, an instructor at the Brotherhood School, had been slain Sept. 18; and Chu Kin

Chen, an executive of a textile mill near Saigon, was killed Sept. 19.

According to a South Vietnamese intelligence report Sept. 20, the attack on the Chinese Nationalist embassy might have been linked to a Viet Cong raid Aug. 30 on the U.S. Marine helicopter base at Phubai, about 5 miles south of Hué. The report said that a principal target of that raid had been a secret radio station manned by Chinese Nationalist communications experts who monitored North Vietnamese and Chinese Communist transmissions. After the blast, an investigation carried out by Col. Chung uncovered the presence of Chinese Communist agents in the Nationalist military mission in Saigon, the South Vietnamese sources said. The radio station was closed and its staff returned to Formosa. The initial U.S. military communiqué describing the attack on Phubai had not mentioned the raid on the radio station. It had reported only that 2 men had been killed, 17 men wounded and 13 helicopters damaged. But U.S. sources Sept. 20 conceded that 10 persons had been killed and 30 wounded in the attack on the radio station. They refused to identify the nationality of the operators. (South Vietnamese military sources disclosed that 18 American helicopters had been damaged, 55 South Vietnamese troops killed and 61 South Vietnamese troops wounded in the Viet Cong raid on the U.S.' Phubai base.)

A South Vietnamese military spokesman said that a Hanoi broadcast Sept. 7 had reported that the Viet Cong had hit an "intelligence technique center" at Phubai and had wiped "out 150 United States and puppet intelligence personnel."

Reds Pound Conthien Base

North Vietnamese artillery and mortars inside the demilitarized zone pounded the U.S. Marine base at Conthien (5 miles below the DMZ) almost incessantly in September and were not silenced until Oct. 4. The shellings, increasing in intensity since Sept. 1, brought the Marine casualty toll at Conthien and nearby areas to 63 dead and 987 wounded in the 26-day period through Sept. 26. The firing was from North Vietnamese guns in the South Vietnamese sector of the demilitarized zone. The adjacent U.S. bases of Dongha, Camp Carroll and Camlo also came under Communist artillery attack during that period. The heavy shelling of the U.S. strong-holds continued despite repeated raids by B-52 bombers and other U.S. planes on North Vietnamese installations in the DMZ and in North Vietnamese territory just above it. A U.S. military spokesman said the B-52s had attacked 83 times along the DMZ since Aug. 13. U.S. artillery and aircraft finally ended the North Vietnamese pounding of Conthien Oct. 4.

U.S. Troops Bolster North

The U.S. command announced Oct. 9 that about 4,000 troops of the U.S. First Cavalry Division (Airmobile), 3d Brigade, had been flown Oct. 4 to 2 of South Vietnam's northernmost provinces—Quangtin and Quangngai—to relieve pressure on Marine units fighting North Vietnamese troops in the 3 other provinces closest to the demilitarized zone—Quangtri, Thauthien and Quangnam. The move, in effect, placed Quangtin and Quangngai under Army responsibility and could free more Marines in that area to shift to positions farther north, along the DMZ. About 300 Marines had been killed and 3,000 wounded in the DMZ area operation in the previous 2 months.

More than 500 North Vietnamese troops Oct. 14 resumed their assault against Marine positions near Conthien just below the DMZ. Following a 130-round mortar barrage, the Communist troops attempted to penetrate the Marines' de-fenses. But they were thrown back in fierce hand-to-hand fighting by the Marines, who were assisted by heavy fire from U.S. helicopters, artillery and planes. 21 Marines were killed and 20 seriously wounded before the North Vietnamese broke off their assault. Conthien and the nearby base at Giolinh had come under heavy North Vietnamese shelling Oct. 13; the bases were pounded by 364 rounds of artillery and recoil-less fire. During the Oct. 13 operations, a U.S. plane acci-dentally dropped 2 500-pound bombs on the perimeter of the Conthien base, killing 2 Marines and wounding 2. 3 more Marines were killed and 9 wounded in a similar mishap Oct. 15 when a 250-pound bomb dropped by a Marine jet in a bombing run fell short and struck a position 2 miles southwest of Conthien.

Air Activity

U.S. planes flew heavy strikes against the Hanoi-Hai-phong area and the sector close to the Chinese border. Among air raids reported:

■ U.S. planes Sept. 10 bombed the North Vietnamese port of Campha for the first time. The raid was the first against the dock area of a major Communist port. A U.S. military communiqué said heavy damage had been inflicted on Campha, 46 miles northeast of Haiphong.

■ U.S. jets Sept. 11 carried out heavy raids on Haiphong and its suburbs in a major effort to isolate the port area from the rest of the country. Planes from 2 U.S. Navy aircraft carriers heavily damaged 13 warehouses and 4 support buildings just west of the city limits and dropped bombs on a railroad yard that extended more than a mile westward from the city limits. The jets also pounded a canal bridge near the center of Haiphong and bombed another railroad and highway bridge over a canal in the southwestern section of the city. The raids were reported to have blocked all rail traffic from the port and to have halted all road movement from Haiphong with the exception of one highway bridge 3 miles to the southwest. A U.S. spokesman said that 3 foreign ships in Haiphong harbor had been damaged during the raids, apparently by shrapnel from North Vietnamese missile fire. One ship was identified as Polish, another as Italian.

■ U.S. planes Sept. 17 bombed the Thatkhe highway bridge, 7 miles from the Chinese Communist border. This was the closest that U.S. bombing had come to Communist China's frontiers.

■ U.S. aircraft bombed the Haiphong area Sept. 17 in raids directed against a railroad and highway bridge one mile from the center of the city and against a warehouse area 1.3 miles from the middle of Haiphong. The U.S. Navy jet pilots were said to have avoided Haiphong's dock area. Other U.S. planes attacked a surface-to-air missile site 9 miles from Hanoi and a rail siding 17 miles northwest of the capital.

■ U.S. Navy planes Sept. 18 again bombed rail and highway bridges within Haiphong's city limits. The city's warehouse section and rail yards were pounded for the 2d successive day.

■ U.S. Navy planes returned to Haiphong Sept. 21, and a spokesman reported the destruction of the last previously intact bridge leading from the port of Haiphong, the Kienan highway span, 1½ miles southwest of the city. Other jets Sept. 21 bombed the Haiphong railroad and highway bridge one mile from the center of the city.

■ Navy fighter-bombers from 2 aircraft carriers Sept. 26 bombed 2 key bridges one mile and 1.7 miles from the center of Haiphong. Air Force pilots pounded the Thanhmoi railroad yard, 64 miles northeast of Hanoi and 22 miles from the Chinese frontier.

■ Navy pilots from the *Coral Sea* Sept. 28 knocked down part of the Haiphong railroad and highway bridge, which carried the only rail line and a major road out of the city. The span had been the last intact bridge in Haiphong. The raid had been preceded by a strike by A-4 Skyhawk jets at antiaircraft and surface-to-air missile installations ringing Haiphong. Thus far 4 bridges in Haiphong had been destroyed since U.S. planes had launched a concerted drive Sept. 11 to cut off the port area from the rest of the country. The air offensive was reported to have restricted the movement of supplies from the Haiphong port to coastal barges and to some minor roads.

■ Navy planes Sept. 30 bombed the Loidong transshipment point on the Cua Cam estuary 4 miles northwest of Haiphong; 2 surface-to-air missile sites in the area were reported destroyed. Other planes that day pounded the Kienan MiG base, the Kepha army barracks 40 miles north of Haiphong and the Phucloi petroleum storage area near Vinh.

■ American raids Oct. 3 centered on key bridges that were part of the North Vietnam-Communist China supply link. The spans that came under attack were at Locbinh and at Caobang, respectively 10 and 15 miles south of the Chinese border. In a strike 14 miles from the Chinese frontier, Air Force jets bombed a railroad yard.

■ American planes Oct. 4 again attacked targets close to the Chinese border—Langson railroad bridge and the Chienchiang highway bridge, 10 and 15 miles from the frontier.

■ U.S. planes Oct. 5 struck the Kep, Kienan and Hoalac MiG bases, pounded a petroleum storage area 2 miles northwest of the center of Haiphong and a highway bridge ½ mile northwest of the center of the city. 3 anti-aircraft sites in the area were also hit.

■ The Chienchiang and the Langson bridges near the Chinese border were struck again Oct. 6. In other attacks that day, American planes destroyed a bridge 39 miles northeast of Hanoi, heavily damaged the nearby Motrang railroad yard and destroyed 2 antiaircraft sites south of Donghoi. Navy pilots, flying 34 missions, attacked the Namdinh power plant 45 miles southwest of Haiphong, a railroad and highway bridge 24 miles southeast of Hanoi and 8 buildings in the Yenbac military storage area 27 miles northeast of Thanhhoa.

■ North Vietnamese Education Min. Nguyen Van Huyen charged Oct. 5 that an American raid on a North Vietnamese school Sept. 20 had killed 33 children and wounded 28. Huyen said that anti-personnel bombs dropped by the planes had sprayed hundreds of tiny steel balls.

■ The highlight of far-ranging U.S. air attacks on North Vietnamese targets Oct. 7 was a strike on Soviet-built helicopters on the ground 30 miles west of Hanoi. 6 of the aircraft were destroyed. 2 were large twin-turbine MI-6s, each capable of carrying 120 men, and 4 were the smaller MI-4s, which could each carry 14. A U.S. military spokesman said it was the first time in the war that Soviet helicopters had been bombed and destroyed. The 'copters had been spotted by reconnaissance photos.

■ The North Vietnamese MiG airbase at Catbi, 4 miles southeast of Haiphong, was bombed for the first time Oct. 8 by U.S. Navy jets. Pilots returning to aircraft carriers in the Gulf of Tonkin reported several secondary explosions, indicating that fuel and ammunition had been destroyed. Aerial photos showed that the base's runway had been heavily damaged. U.S. planes Oct. 8 also bombed Kienan, a highway bridge at Caobang, 15 miles south of the Chinese Communist border, and a rail bridge at Langlu, 36 miles north of Hanoi.

Navy planes bombed the Catbi airbase again Oct. 9.

■ Haiphong's shipyards were raided Oct. 12 by Navy jets, and American officials reported heavy damage. Direct hits were reported on drydocks and on surrounding support structures at one yard, 1.6 miles northwest of the center of the city; the other yard was 1.2 miles west of the center of Haiphong. A dispatch filed by Australian Communist correspondent Wilfred Burchett from Haiphong Oct. 14 noted American communiqués that U.S. planes had scored direct hits on the city's shipyards and on the military barracks area Oct. 12. But he quoted North Vietnamese authorities as saying that the U.S. claims "bear no resemblance to the facts." Burchett said that according to his personal observation, the attacks were directed against a large hospital complex, which was almost completely destroyed and in which 3 persons were killed. In 2 other raids on Haiphong that day, Burchett said, bombs fell on the Lachtray River, about 3 miles southwest of the city, and on a ferry station more than one mile from the shipyards cited by the American communiqué. Burchett said he had visited the port area after the raid, had found no evidence of air damage and had seen 2 Chinese, one Soviet and one Polish freighter unloading. Burchett quoted Haiphong Mayor Le Duc Thinh as saying that ⅓ of the city's residential areas had been destroyed, principally in the heavy raids that had started Sept. 1.

■ U.S. jets Oct. 14 bombed several targets in the Hanoi-Haiphong area that hitherto had been spared. In one raid, the planes pounded a barge building and repair yards 1½ miles west of the center of Haiphong on the banks of the Trambac River. It consisted of drydocks and covered shipways that reportedly accounted for 10% of North Vietnam's annual construction of barges. The early warning radar station at Kienan, 8 miles south of Haiphong, was bombed as were a warehouse complex and vehicle maintenance yard 1.3 miles to the south and smaller boat yards at Xomtrai and Hoaloan, 30 miles northwest of Hanoi.

■ The U.S. command reported that 2 Navy jets had sunk 4 of 6 North Vietnamese patrol boats in the Gulf of Tonkin Oct. 21. The Communist craft were attacked a mile offshore, east of the mouth of the Thannhoa River, 90 miles south of Hanoi.

■ U.S. Navy jets Oct. 22, for the first time, bombed the North Vietnamese naval base at Nuidong, 7 miles northeast of Haiphong. Reporting heavy destruction, the pilots said they had destroyed at least one torpedo boat and struck the base's rail yards, a drydock, an oil dump and antiaircraft sites.

■ U.S. jets carried out sustained attacks on the Hanoi-Haiphong area Oct. 23-30 and bombed many targets that previously had not been touched. The U.S. command acknowledged the loss of 13 American planes during this period and claimed the downing or destroying on the ground of at least 27 North Vietnamese MiGs. Hanoi said at least 35 American planes were shot down.

A major North Vietnamese center struck for the first time Oct. 24 was the huge Phucyen airfield, 18 miles northwest of Hanoi. The field was the only one of the 5 MiG bases in North Vietnam that so far had not been bombed. It was believed to be the largest MiG base in North Vietnam. More than 65 Air Force, Navy and Marine fighter-bombers from ground bases in South Vietnam and Thailand and from aircraft carriers pounded the field all day. Returning pilots said they had flown through heavy anti-aircraft fire and surface-to-air missiles to reach the target, one of the most heavily defended in North Vietnam. (A U.S. Defense Department spokesman said Oct. 24 that a "significant recent increase" in MiG fighter activity had prompted the Pentagon and the White House to remove Phucyen from the restricted target list. A department statement reported that there had been 7 engagements between U.S. jets and MiGs in July, 7 in August, 14 in September and 10 between Oct. 1 and 15. The department said that in anticipation of further American strikes on North Vietnamese airfields, the North Vietnamese in August had moved many of their planes to the Peitun-Yunnan airbase in southwest China. Among these were the 6 Soviet-made IL-28 medium-range bombers previously based at Phucyen. About 50-70 MiG 17s and MiG-21s and 8 IL-28s were believed stationed at the Peitun-Yunnan base. U.S. jets Oct. 25 bombed Phucyen for the 2d consecutive day.

American jets Oct. 25 bombed the Longbien Bridge, Hanoi's only rail and road link with the port of Haiphong and the Chinese border. Pilots reported that 2 spans of the bridge had fallen into the Red River. An Agence-France Presse report from Hanoi confirmed the damage.

U.S. Navy planes Oct. 26 bombed a 32,000-kilowatt thermal power plant, about a mile north of the center of Hanoi. The complex, the largest electrical plant in North Vietnam, had first been attacked June 10, hit twice in July and pounded again Aug. 21.

A military barracks and storage area 3 miles south of the center of Hanoi was hit for the first time Oct. 27 by U.S. Air Force planes from Thailand. 19 barracks and 11 warehouses in the area were reported set afire.

Among targets hit by U.S. bombers Oct. 28 were 2 bridges carrying rail and road traffic to the city—the Longbien Bridge and a span over the Canal des Rapides, 5 miles northeast of Hanoi. Also bombed was the Phapco barge yard, 13 miles north-northwest of Haiphong, where 10 storage buildings were reported destroyed.

In the 6th and 7th successive day of raids on the Hanoi-Haiphong area Oct. 29-30, U.S. planes pounded the Kienan, Kep and Hoalac MiG bases, the Yenbai airfield (65 miles northwest of Hanoi), a rail bridge in the same area and an army barracks 40 miles north of Haiphong.

(Hanoi radio reported Oct. 29 that the North Vietnamese had brought down a U.S. Air Force B-52 in the southern part of the demilitarized zone. This was the 3d B-52 claimed by North Vietnam. None of the B-52 claims had been confirmed by the U.S.)

U.S. State and Defense Department officials had claimed Oct. 2 that the increased U.S. aerial offensive that had started against North Vietnam Aug. 11 had slowed the flow of war supplies from Communist China to Hanoi. The U.S. bombing of bridges had halted the movement of Chinese and Soviet military matériel on the key rail line from Dongdang, near the Chinese border, to Hanoi, according to the American officials. Prior to the start of the bombing offensive, 10-12 trains monthly had reached Hanoi from China on this rail route. The American officials conceded that Communist military equipment was reaching Hanoi by other means of transportation—trucks, cars, bicycles or ferryboats. The principal rail span into the North Vietnamese capital, the Longbien Bridge (formerly the Paul Doumer Bridge) over the Red River at Hanoi, had been closed since Aug. 11, when it had been heavily damaged in an American air raid.

Hanoi appealed to all governments Oct. 31 to help stop the U.S. bombing of North Vietnam. The statement claimed that American planes had started "continuous bombing of the capital city of Hanoi" and that the "furious attacks" on the area in recent days had "killed or wounded 200 civilians and destroyed or set fire to more than 150 homes." North Vietnam said Hanoi's center and suburbs had been hit by bombs, missiles and fragmentation bombs.

Giap Rejects Compromise

Gen. Vo Nguyen Giap, the North Vietnamese defense minister, said Oct. 21 that Hanoi would not compromise with the U.S. and that Communist forces would pay "any price" to win the war. In an article in the Soviet Defense Ministry's newspaper *Krasnaya Zvezda,* Giap insisted that the U.S.' intense air offensive against North Vietnam would never force Hanoi to the conference table. Giap said: The Communist forces were not only fighting to "liberate" South Vietnam but were defending North Vietnam as the "advance post of the

Socialist camp in Southeast Asia." Communist military strategy in the war was "changing from guerrilla actions" to operations "employing large forces, forces that are growing daily." "The American imperialists not only have not achieved a single strategic goal but also have suffered heavy losses." In the 1966-7 dry season the Viet Cong had "annihilated" 175,000 allied troops, including 70,000 Americans.

Communist military successes had been cited by Giap in an analysis of the war appearing in the Sept. 14-16 issues of North Vietnam's armed forces newspaper *Quang Doi Nhan Dan*. Giap said: The allied pacification program for winning control of the South Vietnamese countryside had failed because U.S. troops, required to make the program effective, had to be shifted to the area below the demilitarized zone to reinforce U.S. Marines under heavy attack there by North Vietnamese forces. The U.S. faced a stalemate on all fronts and was confronted with 2 alternatives: (1) expand the ground war by invading North Vietnam or (2) continue slowly increasing military pressure with a limited number of troops. Giap warned: If U.S. forces invaded the North, "the war would become more complex because . . . they would be attacking the mainland of a member country of the Socialist camp." "Attacking the North means opening another large battlefield. The United States imperialists' forces would become more scattered and would be annihilated more easily." "Even if they increase their troops by another 50,000, 100,000 or more, they cannot extricate themselves from their comprehensive stalemate in the southern part of our country." Giap called opposition to the war in the U.S. a "valuable mark of sympathy." But he said the most important element favoring the Communists "is our efforts to turn the balance of forces more and more in our favor on the Vietnam battlefield."

Locninh & Dakto Battles

U.S. and South Vietnamese troops were reported to have killed more than 900 Viet Cong soldiers Oct. 29-Nov. 3 at the district capital of Locninh, 72 miles north of Saigon near the Cambodian border. 11 U.S. and 20 South Vietnamese troops died in the fighting. Most of the town's 5,000 civilians fled during the height of the battle. The fighting had started when the Viet Cong's 273d Regiment attacked a U.S. Special Forces camp at Locninh and a nearby South Vietnamese militia camp and compound. The defenders were quickly reinforced by 2 battalions of the U.S. First Infantry Division, about 1,400 men. In the initial assault, prior to the arrival of the allied reinforcements, the Viet Cong had stormed into Locninh, overrun the district headquarters and local militia position and raised a Viet Cong flag over the headquarters. The Viet Cong also attacked the Special Forces camp with mortar, antitank and small-arms fire but were thrown back from the perimeter of the camp by defending Vietnamese irregulars and U.S. advisers. The reinforced allies fought the Viet Cong through the streets from house to house and finally drove them from Locninh. 117 Viet Cong were said to have been killed in the first day's fighting. At least 100 more Viet Cong were slain around Locninh Oct. 30. A reinforced Viet Cong unit of 2,000 men mounted another assault against the town Oct. 31 and was repelled with heavy losses. After scattered clashes Nov. 1 and 2, the Viet Cong broke off the battle Nov. 3. In the last major clash at least 43 guerrillas were killed Nov. 2 when about 1,500 Viet Cong charged a U.S. infantry battalion position west of Locninh and the district headquarters inside the town.

One of the bloodiest and most sustained battles of the war was fought Nov. 3-22 by U.S. and North Vietnamese troops in the Central Highlands around Dakto near the Cambodian border, about 280 miles north of Saigon. In 19 days of action, 285 U.S. soldiers were killed, 985 wounded and 18 reported missing. North Vietnamese fatalities were estimated at 1,455. Dakto was the site of a big U.S. military complex. It included an airfield, an ammunition dump, a South Vietnamese militia camp headed by U.S. Army Special Forces advisers and a brigade headquarters for the U.S. 4th Infantry Division's forward base camp. Before the battle started, 3,500-4,500 troops of the U.S. 4th Division and the 173d Airborne Brigade had been flown in to reinforce about 1,000 American troops already in the Dakto area. They faced 4 Communist regiments of an estimated 6,000 troops who had infiltrated the area in recent weeks. Gen. Westmoreland, visiting the camp Nov. 8, said: "The enemy is here in strength. He wants to dominate this valley. . . . I think it's all part of a scheme to capture the headlines after the [South Vietnamese] presidential inauguration." The climax of the operation came in a savage battle Nov. 19-22 for Hill 875, a 2,870-foot peak 12 miles southwest of Dakto and 4 miles east of the Cambodian border. The hill was one of several fought for in the 3-week battle. The 173d Brigade, assisted by heavy air and artillery strikes, forced the North Vietnamese to abandon their last defense line on the ridge of Hill 875. But the 173d Brigade lost 158 men killed and 402 wounded. 30 of the fatalities resulted from an accidental American air strike on U.S. positions Nov. 19. Another strategic height, Hill 1416, 6 miles northeast of Dakto, was captured by South Vietnamese troops Nov. 19 in a battle that had started Nov. 16. In heavy fighting against North Vietnamese troops, 50 South Vietnamese were killed and 150 wounded. 2 battalions of South Vietnamese paratroopers, numbering about 1,000 men, had been flown in Nov. 17 to support government infantrymen locked in heavy combat on the ridges of the hill. In another major action, North Vietnamese mortars, in 3 separate barrages Nov. 15, had pounded the Dakto base itself, killing 20 Americans and wounding 22. The airfield was blasted, 2 C-130 transports were destroyed, a 3d was damaged and an ammunition dump was blown up. A nearby military camp was forced to evacuate.

Gen. Hochmuth Killed

Maj. Gen. Bruno A. Hochmuth, 56, commander of the U.S. 3d Marine Division, was killed Nov. 14 when a helicopter in which he was flying crashed near Hué. 5 other persons in the aircraft—3 crewmen and 2 members of Hochmuth's personal staff—were also killed. The U.S. command in Saigon announced Nov. 15 that the helicopter crash had been caused by groundfire.

Maj. Gen. Ravthon M. Tompkins replaced Hochmuth Nov. 14 as commander of the 3d Marine Division.

Hochmuth was the first American general to be killed in combat in Vietnam itself. Maj. Gen. William J. Crumm, commander of the Strategic Air Command's 3d Air Division on Guam, had been killed July 7 when 2 B-52s, flying to a combat mission in Vietnam, collided and crashed into the South China Sea off the Mekong delta.

Air Raids Intensive

American jets continued to carry out heavy raids on North Vietnam. Among major attacks reported during November:

■ Air Force fighter-bombers from Korat Air Base in Thailand Nov. 6 bombed the Giathuong storage complex, 3 miles from the center of Hanoi. The target, hitherto on the U.S. Defense Department's restricted list, was the largest military storage complex in North Vietnam, consisting of 91 buildings.

■ U.S. planes Nov. 7 bombed rail facilities 21 miles from the Chinese Communist border. This was the deepest penetration of North Vietnamese air space in 2 weeks. Other planes struck the Anninhgoai shipyard and repair facilities 12 miles west of Haiphong. A U.S. spokesman expressed belief that it was the first time this target had been bombed.

■ North Vietnamese officials reported Nov. 17 that 4 U.S. air-to-ground strike missiles exploded in Hanoi during a U.S. raid on Hanoi that day. The announcement said 2 damaged the Soviet military attaché's residence and killed an Indian soldier of the International Control Commission.

■ The Chinese Communist Foreign Ministry charged Dec. 2 that U.S. planes had "divebombed" a Chinese freighter in the North Vietnamese port of Hongay Nov. 25. 8 crewmen were wounded and the ship damaged in "more than 20 places," Peking said. The ship was identified as the *Hongqi No. 154*.

LBJ Gets Optimistic Reports

Firsthand reports on the military and political situation in Vietnam were given to Pres. Johnson Nov. 13-16 by Gen. Westmoreland, Amb.-to-South Vietnam Bunker and Deputy Amb. Robert W. Komer, head of the pacification program.

Bunker told newsmen after conferring with Mr. Johnson Nov. 13 that "steady progress" had been made on the military and political fronts in Vietnam. "There is every prospect, too, that the progress will accelerate," he asserted. He predicted the pacification of 1,500-2,000 South Vietnamese hamlets in 1968, compared to about 1,000 in 1967. (According to White House figures, as of August, the South Vietnamese government was in control of 5,188 hamlets, the Viet Cong controlled 4,038, and 2,723 were contested.) Bunker cited these developments as indicating a turn for the better: "the reinstitution of local government," the holding of 5 elections in the past 14 months, Saigon government moves against corruption, an improvement in the fighting capacity of the South Vietnamese army, a 50% decline in Viet Cong recruitment in the past year, Viet Cong alienation of the Vietnamese under their control because of their demands for higher taxes and the interdiction of guerrilla food supplies. Bunker said that, as a result of Viet Cong difficulties, "more and more of the war effort has been taken over by the North Vietnamese."

Westmoreland briefed Pres. Johnson and the House and Senate Armed Services Committees Nov. 16. The chairman of the Senate Armed Services Committee, Sen. Richard B. Russell (D., Ga.), said Westmoreland had expressed "cautious optimism" but that he "does not see an early termination of the war." Westmoreland and Bunker made a joint appearance Nov. 19 on the NBC-TV program "Meet the Press." Westmoreland said: U.S. and South Vietnamese troops were "winning a war of attrition." It was "conceivable that within 2 years or less the enemy will be so weakened that the Vietnamese will be able to cope with a greater share of the war burden. We will be able to phase down the level of our military effort, withdraw some troops. . . ." Westmoreland reiterated his case for the continued bombing of North Vietnam, which, he said "has hurt the enemy very much." He said: The aerial strikes had tied down about 175,000 men to North Vietnam's air defenses and another 500,000 to maintain the transportation system. The raids had "retarded infiltration of men, equipment and supplies, and it has destroyed a great deal of ammunition that would otherwise be used against our troops." The Communist forces in the South had "very serious manpower problems," were unable to recruit new guerrillas and were, therefore, forced to bring men down from North Vietnam, which had its own manpower problems. Westmoreland repeated U.S. accusations that enemy troops were operating from Cambodia: "The enemy has taken advantage of this sanctuary, with or without the consent of the Cambodian authorities."

Speaking at the National Press Club Nov. 21, Westmoreland said: "I am absolutely certain that whereas in 1965 the enemy was winning, today he is certainly losing"; the "enemy has not won a major battle in more than a year"; the Viet

Cong/North Vietnamese force had declined from 285,000 men in 1966's 3d quarter to 242,000 in 1967's 3d quarter. Westmoreland said a U.S./South Vietnamese plan to win the war "involved 4 distinct phases," 2 of which had already been completed. He explained: In Phase I, the U.S. "came to the aid of South Vietnam, prevented its collapse under the massive Communist thrust, built up our bases and began to deploy our forces" and completed this by the middle of 1966. Phase II continued the pattern of Phase I and, in addition, "drove the enemy divisions back to the sanctuary or into hiding places" and improved the capability of the South Vietnamese armed forces. Phase III, in 1968, envisioned a reduction of American advisers in Vietnamese training centers and "other places where the professional competence of Vietnamese officers makes this possible" and continued "pressure on the North to prevent rebuilding and to make infiltration more costly." The final phase, Phase IV, "will see the conclusion of our plan to weaken the enemy and strengthen our friends until we become progressively superfluous. The object will be to show the world that guerrilla warfare and invasion do not pay as a new means of Communist aggression." Westmoreland said: Since the U.S. had not invaded North Vietnam, "it is difficult to conceive of a surrender" by Hanoi. "But it is not inconceivable that the enemy will realize that he is not in a position where he can win. This is what is happening. But apparently the enemy hasn't realized it yet."

In a briefing at the Pentagon Nov. 22, Westmoreland said that the battle around Dakto was "the beginning of a great defeat for the enemy." Westmoreland disclosed that a document removed from the body of a dead North Vietnamese soldier Nov. 6 had revealed that the Dakto battle was to be the start of a winter/spring offensive by the B-3 Front, the North Vietnamese corps-level command in the western Central Highlands. According to the document, the principal aims of the North Vietnamese drive at Dakto were to (1) destroy "a major United States unit," (2) destroy "a large part of the South Vietnamese army," (3) force the Americans to deploy their forces to the highlands and weaken their positions elsewhere and (4) seize more Central Highlands territory to expand the North Vietnamese base there.

At his televised press conference Nov. 17, Mr. Johnson had said: Westmoreland "anticipates no increase" in troops above the previously authorized level. The American people "in a contest of any kind" "want it decided and decided quickly and get in or get out, and they like for that curve to rise like this [gesture of sharp upturn], and they like for the opposition to go down like this [sharp downturn]. Now that's not the kind of war we're fighting in Vietnam. . . . It's a new kind of war for us, so it doesn't move that fast. . . . We're moving more like this [gradual ascent], and I think they're moving more like this [gradual descent]. . . . We are making progress. . . . We are inflicting greater losses than we're taking. . . . We have a lot to do yet. A great many mistakes have been made. We take 2 steps forward and we slip back one. . . ."

Cambodia Called Red Sanctuary

Reports about a Viet Cong base in Cambodia were filed from Pnompenh Nov. 19 and 20 by AP correspondents George McArthur and Horst Faas. They had visited the alleged Communist camp with UPI correspondents and had photographed the site. According to their dispatches: An abandoned Viet Cong camp site was found 4 miles inside Cambodia on the South Vietnamese border opposite War Zone C, about 70 miles northwest of Saigon. Military records written in Vietnamese indicated that the camp had been used for several months since February by possibly several hundred men and that it had been evacuated several days before the AP correspondents got there. A heavily traveled road from the camp led to the Vietnamese border and crossed it 9 miles from Locninh, where allied and North Vietnamese forces had fought Oct. 29-Nov. 3. Cambodian Premier Son Sann said his government would investigate. He said: "It is impossible that the camp was used for any long period of time. It was not a sanctuary." Son Sann conceded that some Communist troops had crossed into Cambodia, but he said his government had always insisted that they leave as soon as the intrusions were discovered.

The Cambodian government asserted Nov. 21 that the reports of a "new military complex constructed by the Viet

Cong" in Cambodia were "grotesque and a challenge to good sense." The statement denied that there were North Vietnamese or Viet Cong in Cambodia. Cambodian Chief of State Norodom Sihanouk declared Nov. 22 that if there were Viet Cong soldiers in Cambodia, "it is the fault of the Americans."

A *N.Y. Times* report from Washington Nov. 23 said U.S. military authorities in Saigon and Washington had expressed concern about reports that large ammunition shipments were reaching Viet Cong and North Vietnamese forces in South Vietnam through Cambodia. The ammunition reportedly arrived at the Cambodian port of Sihanoukville, on the Gulf of Siam, was transshipped from there to Pnompenh and then moved into South Vietnam. According to U.S. intelligence reports, large rice shipments bought in Pnompenh for the Vietnamese Communists were moved toward the Vietnamese border by Cambodian army trucks, possibly without government authorization, by corrupt Cambodian officers. The U.S. naval command was ordered to undertake a study of the feasibility of quarantining the Cambodian coast to interdict strategic supplies for Communist forces. A U.S. State Department official said Nov. 29, however, that "we do not contemplate initiating any quarantine of the Cambodian coastline."

Cambodia Nov. 29 denied that Sihanoukville was used to funnel supplies for the Communists. The statement said: Cambodia remained neutral; if the U.S. wanted "to stop the sending of arms and equipment to the Vietnamese patriots, it would be logical that military reprisals be made against powers and countries which furnish them, that is Russia, China and all the Socialist countries."

In retaliation for the U.S. press reports, Sihanouk had said Nov. 24 that "from now on the door of Cambodia is hermetically sealed to all American journalists."

The U.S. State Department disclosed Dec. 26 that Washington Dec. 4 had sent Cambodia a note reassuring the Pnompenh regime that it had "no hostile intentions toward Cambodia or Cambodian territory." The note was aimed at countering speculation that the Johnson Administration was considering extending the war into Cambodia to hunt Viet Cong or North Vietnamese forces seeking sanctuary there.

The U.S. had decided to make public the note after Cambodia had broadcast the text of its reply. Asserting that its territory was not being used as a base for Communist forces involved in Vietnam, Cambodia stated that the U.S. was seeking to justify military action against it by raising "groundless" charges of a Viet Cong/North Vietnamese presence in Cambodia. Cambodia charged that U.S. and South Vietnamese forces committed "flagrant violations" of international law through "daily incursions" into Cambodian territory for "purposes of sabotage and assassination." Cambodia warned the U.S. Dec. 21 and 26 that it would fight if American forces invaded Cambodia. The Dec. 26 statement said Cambodia would enlist the support of friendly nations to help it resist any incursion on its territory.

The U.S. Dec. 27 again disavowed intentions of expanding the Vietnamese war and reiterated its concern over alleged military pressures by Communist forces in neighboring Cambodia, Thailand and Laos. A State Department statement said pro-Communist Pathet Lao and North Vietnamese forces in Laos had started a drive that appeared to be more intense than the usual annual dry-season foraging activities. Communist military activity along Thailand's border with Laos, "in a measured way, seems greater than in the past," the statement said. The department, at the same time, released the note it had sent to Cambodia Dec. 4 on alleged Communist use of Cambodian territory as a sanctuary and Cambodia's reply of Dec. 24. "The root cause of incidents affecting Cambodian territory," the U.S. note said, "is the Viet Cong and North Vietnamese presence in the frontier region and their use of Cambodian territory in violation of the neutrality of Cambodia."

Sihanouk warned Dec. 27 that if U.S. troops invaded Cambodia in search of North Vietnamese and Viet Cong forces, his government would "ask [Communist] China, Russia and other anti-imperialistic powers for new military aid." "In the event we are unable to contain the successive waves of the aggressor, we will call on 'volunteers' from certain friendly nations, in the first place China, North Korea and Cuba," Sihanouk said. In an interview appearing in the *Washington*

Post Dec. 29, Sihanouk said that "if limited combat breaks out between American and Vietnam forces" in uninhabited areas of Cambodia, "it goes without saying that we woud not intervene militarily." Sihanouk explained that Cambodia would shun retaliation in this instance because "on the one hand we lack sufficient and rapid means of transport and on the other hand because this would constitute a double violation of our territorial integrity and our neutrality. In that case we would protest to both parties involved."

South Vietnamese officials had said they favored "hot pursuit" of Communist forces into Cambodia if necessary. Foreign Min. Tran Van Do said in Paris Dec. 26: "We would be obliged to do so if the enemy troops use Cambodian territory as a sanctuary and cross the frontier to attack our troops. But we have no intention of invading Cambodia. . . . For our defense we are obliged to follow the enemy if he crosses the frontier." Pres. Nguyen Van Thieu had said Dec. 2 that he "advocate[d] for the South Vietnamese forces the power to pursue and attack inside Cambodia during battles with the Viet Cong."

North Vietnamese Fight in Laos

Laotian military authorities had reported Sept. 28 that government troops had killed 70 North Vietnamese soldiers in an ambush 50 miles north of Luang Prabang, the royal capital. According to the report, the North Vietnamese were on their way to reinforce other Communist units fighting Laotian government troops at Nam Bac. Government forces were said to have suffered a severe setback at Nam Bac Aug. 16 when Communist-led Pathet Lao soldiers drove them from a hilltop outpost. The Laotian government Oct. 13 displayed 19 captured North Vietnamese soldiers at a news conference in Vientiane, the administrative capital, to support charges that Hanoi was interfering militarily in Laos. The prisoners were said to have belonged to the North Vietnamese 325th and 316th Divisions. One prisoner said he had gone from Laokay in North Vietnam to Communist China, then to the northernmost Laotian Province of Phongsaly to work as a military adviser to the Pathet Lao.

Laotian Premier Souvanna Phouma reported in a communiqué Dec. 26 that North Vietnamese troops had started a "general offensive" against government forces in southern Laos. Diplomatic sources in Vientiane, the Laotian capital, conceded that at least one battle was being waged near Phalane, 50 miles east of the southern city of Savannakhet, but said Laotian troops appeared to be in control of the situation. 2 other battles were said to have prompted the government to express the fear of a Communist offensive. A Laotian government army headquarters at Nam Bac, 40 miles north of Luang Prabang, was shelled by mortars Dec. 24; 3 soldiers were killed and 7 wounded. About 300 Pathet Lao soldiers Dec. 12 had invaded the southern Laotian town of Lao Ngam, killed 26 government troops and escaped with rice and ammunition. Laotian government reports in previous weeks had charged that North Vietnamese troops, defeated by allied forces at Dakto near the Laotian border in November, had moved into Laos and occupied several villages near Savane.

North Vietnam denied Dec. 29 that its forces had begun a drive in Laos. Describing the Laotian claims as "entirely groundless," Hanoi asserted that the reports were aimed at "serving the U.S. scheme to dispatch American troops to Laos and expand the war."

McNamara Resigns

Robert S. McNamara's resignation as U.S. Defense Secretary, effective at an undetermined date, was announced Nov. 29. McNamara was nominated by Pres. Johnson to be president of the International Bank for Reconstruction & Development (World Bank), but the President said he had agreed to remain in the Defense post until the completion of the fiscal 1969 defense budget. Mr. Johnson said that McNamara's departure from his cabinet would not affect Administration policy in Vietnam. "The course of our participation in the war in Vietnam is firmly set," the President declared. "Major defense policies are clearly defined."

Fighting Spreads in Mekong Delta

A combined U.S.-South Vietnamese force Dec. 4 killed 235 men of a 300-member Viet Cong battalion along a canal near the Mytho River in the Mekong delta. The fighting started when the U.S. 9th Infantry Division's riverine force, led by about 400 South Vietnamese in armored troop carriers on shore, came under Viet Cong rifle and automatic weapons fire from the bank of the Rach Ruong Canal. The American troops went ashore and, in a coordinated action with the South Vietnamese force, surrounded and attacked the Viet Cong battalion. The assault was assisted by a helicopter airdrop of another 9th Division battalion. The guerrilla unit was later identified as the 502d Viet Cong battalion.

A South Vietnamese force of regiment size trapped 2 Viet Cong battalions Dec. 8 near Vithanh, 100 miles southwest of Saigon. The battle was described as the biggest fought in the delta. The South Vietnamese force of 2,000 men claimed to have killed 365 Communist troops. The offensive was assisted by heavy American air and artillery strikes. The initial assault against the guerrillas was carried out by 3 South Vietnamese infantry battalions. 3 South Vietnamese Ranger battalions were later rushed in to reinforce the government units. Sporadic fighting resumed in the Vithanh area Dec. 10 when survivors of the 2 battered Viet Cong battalions pinned down a 400-man South Vietnamese battalion with mortar and machinegun fire. The attack was suppressed as 2 South Vietnamese battalions were flown in. South Vietnamese casualties in the fighting Dec. 8 were listed as 60 men killed and 102 wounded. U.S. officers questioned the high enemy casualty toll claimed by the South Vietnamese. In one sector of the battlefield, only 15 Viet Cong bodies had been counted.

Outside the delta, U.S. and South Vietnamese troops killed 252 NorthVietnamese soldiers in fierce fighting Dec. 6-8 near Bongson, 140 miles south of Danang. U.S. losses totaled 16 killed and 90 wounded. The Communist force, heavily entrenched in bunkers, was identified as the 22d Regiment of the North Vietnamese 3d Division and 2 of its battalions, totaling about 1,000 men. The regiment was one of the 3 in the division that had been fighting U.S. First Cavalry Division (Airmobile) troops on the Bongson plain for the past 2 years. The latest fighting occurred 5 miles from the division's forward headquarters at Bongson.

A renewed clash in the Bongson area Dec. 15-16 resulted

in the killing of 104 Communist troops. In another action 15 miles south of Bongson, 115 Communist troops were slain during the same 2-day period, U.S. authorities reported. In the first operation, 22 Americans had been killed and 52 wounded.

A North Vietnamese/Viet Cong attack Dec. 10 against a U.S. artillery base camp 50 miles north of Saigon was repelled with the loss of 124 Communist troops and one U.S. First Infantry Division soldier killed. The attacking unit was identified as the 165th North Vietnamese Battalion, of about 400 men, which had been battered in fighting at Locninh, 17 miles to the north, in October.

U.S. ground, sea and air forces launched a drive Dec. 21 against Communist positions in and around the demilitarized zone to thwart plans for what Hanoi called "the winter/spring offensive." U.S. intelligence estimated that the North Vietnamese had a force of 35,000-45,000 men poised in or just above the DMZ. About 1,000 U.S. Marines landed by boat and helicopter along the coast of Quangngai Province, which adjoined the buffer area. 4 Marines were killed and 9 wounded in an exchange of fire with some entrenched Communist troops. U.S. B-52s Dec. 22 carried out heavy raids on artillery positions and suspected Communist troop concentrations inside the zone. The raids were directed 7 miles northwest of the U.S. Marine base at Conthien. Other U.S. planes bombed surface-to-air missile sites 25 miles north of the DMZ and a North Vietnamese artillery base 10 miles northwest of Giolinh. Guns of an American cruiser were reported to have destroyed a Communist bunker 5 miles east of Giolinh.

Air Curbs Lifted Further

It was reported Dec. 19 that the U.S. government had granted American pilots permission to fly through 2 hitherto restricted target areas in North Vietnam—the 25-mile-wide buffer strip along the Chinese Communist border and the outer 20-mile circle around Hanoi. White House permission would still be required to bomb targets in both sectors. The lifting of restrictions was accompanied by stepped-up air attacks in North Vietnam's northern Tonkin delta sector, particularly in the Hanoi-Haiphong area. Whereas previously the bombings were designed mainly to interdict supplies flowing to Communist forces in South Vietnam, the latest attacks were said to be aimed directly at breaking the will of North Vietnam and forcing it to the negotiating table.

A new aerial onslaught against the Hanoi-Haiphong area was mounted Dec. 14-19. The American raids in the Hanoi area Dec. 16 were directed largely against the rail yards at Yenvien, 6 miles east of the city. Tracks at both ends of the yard reportedly were cut, and 50 boxcars were said to have been destroyed. A North Vietnamese report on the Dec. 16 raids claimed that homes in the northeastern section of Hanoi had been destroyed.

Hanoi radio claimed that North Vietnamese surface-to-air missiles Dec. 21 had shot down 2 U.S. B-52 bombers. U.S. authorities in Saigon denied the loss of any B-52s. The U.S. command, however, said that North Vietnamese surface-to-air missiles, 13 miles north of the demilitarized zone, had fired 3 times Dec. 20 at B-52s during an air strike on North Vietnamese targets inside the DMZ. The missile site was then attacked and knocked out by other American planes from Korat, Thailand and Danang, the command reported.

Christmas & New Year's Truces

Ground action in South Vietnam was largely suspended and air operations over North Vietnam were halted (except for reconnaissance flights) by a Dec. 24-25 Christmas truce agreed to by the allies. The Viet Cong observed a 3-day truce that started 1 a.m. Dec. 24 and ended 1 a.m. Dec. 27. U.S. authorities reported that 118 enemy-initiated incidents during the 24-hour cease-fire had resulted in the death of 2 American soldiers and the wounding of 24. 5 South Vietnamese and 33 Communist troops were killed during the same period, according to American officials. North Vietnam charged that U.S. forces had violated the truce Dec. 25 by carrying out air strikes against at least 8 targets in North Vietnam and by shelling the northern part of the demilitarized zone and the North Vietnamese district of Vinhlinh.

The South Vietnamese Foreign Ministry Dec. 30 announced the extension of a proposed New Year's truce 12 hours beyond the 24 hours originally planned. South Vietnamese and allied troops, the ministry said, would observe a cease-fire from 6 p.m. Dec. 31 to 6 a.m. Jan. 2, 1968. The fighting pause was to have ended at 6 p.m. Jan. 1. The Saigon government announcement said the decision to extend the truce was made in response to Pope Paul's Dec. 15 appeal urging all nations to celebrate Jan. 1, 1968 as a worldwide Day of Peace.

A Viet Cong cease-fire went into effect 1 a.m. Dec. 30 and was to expire 1 a.m. Jan. 2, 1968. Sporadic but sharp allied-Communist clashes, however, occurred during the cease-fire period through midnight Dec. 31 and beyond.

U.S. air action had been resumed on the expiration of the Christmas truce at 6 p.m. Dec. 25 with strikes against North Vietnam's southern panhandle. One of the targets struck was a 7-mile convoy of about 150 trucks near Thanhhoa, 90 miles south of Hanoi. 23 trucks were reported destroyed and 8 damaged. In other air action that marked the end of the truce, U.S. B-52s bombed a Communist assembly area near Hoian, 15 miles south of Danang.

In the first major ground fighting to follow the Christmas truce, South Vietnamese troops, backed by American artillery and air strikes, killed 203 troops of the Viet Cong's 416th Battalion Dec. 26-27 about 9 miles northeast of the city of Quangtri, 15 miles south of the DMZ. The battle erupted along the South China Sea coast when a 400-man battalion of government troops encountered the Viet Cong force during a search-and-destroy operation aimed at providing security for pacification teams in Quangtri Province. The U.S. command reported Dec. 30 that 48 U.S. Marines had been killed and 81 wounded in a battle with North Vietnamese troops Dec. 27 in the coastal village of Thonthamkhe on the boundaries of Quangtri and Thuathien Provinces.

Ho Urges Greater Efforts

It was reported Dec. 26 that Ho Chi Minh had appealed to the Vietnamese people to intensify their efforts to defeat U.S. forces. Ho made his plea at a meeting in observance of the 23d anniversary of the founding of the Vietnamese People's Army and the 21st anniversary of the start of Vietnamese resistance against French colonial rule. It was Ho's first public appearance since Aug. 31 and followed foreign press reports that he was seriously ill. Ho Dec. 30 extended New Year's greetings to Americans opposed to U.S. policy in Vietnam. Expressing thanks "for your support for the Vietnamese people," Ho said: "We shall win and so will you. . . . No Vietnamese has ever come to make trouble in the United States. Yet half a million United States troops have been sent to South Vietnam who, together with over 700,000 puppet and satellite troops, are daily massacring Vietnamese people and burning down Vietnamese towns and villages."

Toll High in Mistaken Attacks

Attacks made in error by allied forces took a high toll of civilians and allied military personnel during 1967. Among incidents reported:

■ U.S. helicopters and patrol boats accidentally killed 31 Vietnamese civilians and wounded 38 in the Phongdinh Province village of Phuhuu (80 miles southwest of Saigon) during an operation against the Viet Cong in the Mekong River delta Jan. 28-29. The civilians, apparently mistaken for Viet Cong, were attacked as they were crossing the Bassac River in 200 sampans at 11:45 p.m. Jan. 28 in violation of an 11 p.m.-5 a.m. curfew. A U.S. spokesman said the American helicopters bombed the sampans after they were fired on from the vessels and the river bank. Patrol boats later fired on the sampans with rockets and machine-guns. The attack was called off after the first civilian casualties were brought to a nearby Vietnamese army post. Interrogated civilians indicated they had sought to reach the army post to escape being caught in Viet Cong-allied crossfire.

■ A South Vietnamese hamlet 12 miles southwest of Danang was accidentally hit Feb. 1 by U.S. Marine artillery and planes. 8 South Vietnamese civilians were killed and 18 wounded. The Marines had been engaged in heavy fighting in the area for several days.

■ 4 Australian soldiers were killed and 13 wounded Feb. 6 when their positions near Datdo were accidentally shelled by New Zealand artillery.

■ 7 soldiers of the U.S. First Cavalry (Airmobile) Division were killed and 4 were wounded Feb. 13 when a U.S. artillery shell accidentally struck their positions near the coastal lowlands about 300 miles northeast of Saigon.

■ 5 South Vietnamese civilians were killed and 24 were wounded Mar. 1 when the Mekong delta village of Trungluong was accidentally hit by 11 shells of a U.S. 105-mm. gun. 24 houses were destroyed. The U.S. artillery piece was positioned in Trungluong.

■ More than 80 South Vietnamese civilians were killed Mar. 2 in an accidental air attack on the village of Langvei, 15 miles south of the demilitarized zone and one mile from the Laotian border. The raid was carried out by 2 U.S. F-4C Phantom jets. According to American sources, 83 of the village's 2,000 civilians had been killed and 176 wounded. South Vietnamese authorities reported 95 killed.

■ 41 South Vietnamese troops were killed and at least 50 reported seriously injured Apr. 15 when a South Vietnamese army battalion position 23 miles northwest of the coastal city of Quinhon was hit by bombs dropped off target by 2 U.S. Air Force F-100 Supersabre jets.

■ 14 South Vietnamese civilians were killed and 25 wounded Apr. 16 when a U.S. jet struck a village housing Viet Cong defectors near Trucgiang, southwest of Saigon.

■ U.S. planes supporting South Vietnamese troops Dec. 28 accidentally killed 4 government soldiers and wounded 34 in Binthuan Province about 125 miles northeast of Saigon. The government unit—mostly *montagnard* tribesmen—broke off the fighting against Viet Cong soldiers immediately after being strafed by 2 B-57 Canberra jets.

Fewer Refugees in 1967

U.S. sources in Saigon estimated Dec. 28 that the number of South Vietnamese who became war refugees in 1967 totaled 430,000-450,000, less than half the 1966 figure of 983,000. The refugee figure for November had shown a drop of 2,000; 11,000 had entered refugee camps, while 13,000 had returned to their former homes or were relocated in the 662 hamlets established for persons displaced by the fighting. According to the U.S. sources, 309,000 South Vietnamese were currently living in 402 refugee camps; this was a decrease of 40,000 since Jan. 1, 1967. An additional 475,000 persons were classified as refugees but were living with friends or relatives.

South Vietnamese official figures placed the number of classified war refugees since 1964 at 2.1 million. 641,000 had been returned to their villages, and 669,000 had been resettled elsewhere, according to the Saigon regime.

PRISONERS OF WAR

Viet Cong Threatens U.S. PWs

The Viet Cong's National Liberation Front (NLF) radio warned June 16 that the guerrillas would execute captured Americans "should the U.S. aggressors and their Saigon stooges execute 3 Vietnamese patriots sentenced to death by a so-called special military tribunal in Saigon May 29." The tribunal referred to by the broadcast had convicted and sentenced to death Bui Van Chieu, 37, a confessed Viet Cong member, for leading a guerrilla raid in the bombing of national police headquarters and the Metropole Hotel, site of a U.S. officers' billet, in Saigon. (2 other suspected Viet Cong agents, both women, had been sentenced to 5 years' imprisonment by the same court for a "breach of public security." 2 other Viet Cong terrorists, Le Minh Chau and Truong Thanh Danh, had been sentenced to death June 5 for throwing grenades at policemen and Americans.)

(The U.S. State Department had listed 21 Americans as Viet Cong prisoners as of May 31. Another 128 Americans were listed as missing and believed captured.)

Commenting on the Viet Cong threat, a U.S. State Department statement June 16 said the U.S. was "taking every appropriate step to protect the rights of prisoners of war in Vietnam."

Reds Display U.S. Pilots

3 U.S. pilots, reported by North Vietnam to have been shot down and captured during a raid over Hanoi May 5, had been paraded through the streets of Hanoi and then briefly displayed to newsmen in the city May 6. The U.S. May 8 protested the action as a violation of the Geneva convention on prisoners of war. The North Vietnamese said the 3 American pilots had been based in Thailand. They were identified as Lt. Cols. James Lindberg Hughes and Gordon Albert Larson, both 39, and Lt. James Richard Shively, 25. Hughes was said to have been injured; Larson appeared to be suffering from shock. The Soviet news agency Tass reported May 6 that the 3 American airmen had been captured by workers, militiamen and soldiers and then led through shouting crowds in the streets of Hanoi to newsmen at the International Press Club. Reporting on the raid, Hanoi radio claimed May 6 that American planes had bombed "heavily populated districts and industrial installations in the very heart" of the city. The North Vietnamese press agency said that 3 factories had been hit.

Reds Bar Data on PWs

Cambodian Chief of State Norodom Sihanouk reported in a letter to an American woman Aug. 31 that North Vietnamese and NLF officials refused to release information on American and other prisoners of war "since they [the Communists] cannot expect reciprocity." Sihanouk's letter was sent to Mrs. Gustav C. Hertz of Leesburg, Va., whose husband, a U.S. aid official, had been kidnaped outside Saigon Feb. 2, 1965. Mrs. Hertz had appealed to Sihanouk to seek information on the condition of her husband. Sihanouk July 19 had received from NLF Pres. Nguyen Huu Tho a letter informing him that Hertz and Douglas Ramsey, a U.S. aid official who had been kidnaped Jan. 17, 1966, were alive and well. In a later message to Sihanouk, Tho had accused Hertz and Ramsey of having taken part in the evacuation of South Vietnamese villages suspected of harboring Viet Cong. (Sihanouk reported in a letter to Mrs. Hertz Nov. 6 that her husband had died Sept. 24 of malaria.)

U.S. State Department officials Sept. 2 expressed surprise at Sihanouk's statement on captives. The officials pointed out that all Communist troops captured by Americans had been turned over to South Vietnam and that information on the 6,000 Communist captives in 6 South Vietnamese prison camps was registered with the International Committee of the Red Cross (ICRC) and transmitted to North Vietnamese authorities.

U.S. State Department spokesman Robert J. McCloskey had reported Apr. 26 that the Soviet Union had rejected Washington's request of Apr. 11 to use its good offices with Hanoi to let International Red Cross observers enter North Vietnam to "look into the fate" of U.S. prisoners of war. The Soviet government was said to have advised the Johnson Administration to make direct contact with Hanoi.

U.S. officials reported May 11 that American efforts to gain North Vietnamese agreement to exchange an estimated 169 Americans held captive by Hanoi had met with no response. South Vietnam June 12 released 39 sick and wounded North Vietnamese prisoners. The freed captives crossed the Benhai River bridge between South and North Vietnam. And in separate ceremonies June 12 Premier Nguyen Cao Ky released 4 Viet Cong prisoners at Binhdinh Province headquarters in Quinhon.

Viet Cong Frees 3 Americans

3 U.S. Army prisoners were released by the Viet Cong Nov. 11 in ceremonies held in Pnompenh, Cambodia. The men

were returned to the U.S. Nov. 13. American authorities in Saigon said they had been "brainwashed," but the U.S. State Department denied this Nov. 17. The released soldiers, all staff sergeants, were: Edward R. Johnson of Seaside, Calif., a former adviser to a South Vietnamese battalion, captured in Rachgia Province July 21, 1964; Daniel Lee Pitzer Jr. of Spring Lake, N.C., a medical aide who had served as an adviser to South Vietnamese forces, captured in Camau Province Oct. 29, 1963; James A. Jackson Jr. of Talcott, W. Va., a medical corpsman, captured in Camau Province in 1965.

The 3 said they had been freed by the Viet Cong Oct. 31. The men were turned over by a Viet Cong representative to Thomas Emmett Hayden, 27, of Newark, N.J., a "New Left" activist and member of a U.S. committee formed to help the 3 Americans. Other members of the committee were the Rev. Dr. Martin Luther King Jr. and Dr. Benjamin Spock. Hayden said arrangements for the release of the 3 had been broached to him and others by Viet Cong representatives in Bratislava, Czechoslovakia in September.

The Viet Cong member who turned the men over to Hayden, Nguyen Van Hieu, said the guerrillas had freed them in response to opposition to the war in the U.S. and also to express support for the "courageous struggle" of the Negroes in the U.S. Johnson and Jackson were Negroes. Jackson confirmed that the Viet Cong had told him he was being set free "in solidarity with the people's movement in the United States" and "in response to the cause of American Negroes' search for peace."

Plans to free the 3 had first been disclosed in a Viet Cong broadcast Nov. 2. The statement said the release was a display of "solidarity and support for the just struggle of the United States Negroes in claiming their basic national rights. ..."

The report on the alleged brainwashing of the soldiers was made public by U.S. officials in Saigon Nov. 11. The document, written by Donald Rochlen, a psychological adviser to the South Vietnamese government, said a Viet Cong defector named Phung Van Tuong had confessed that he had taken part in the brainwashing of the 3 Americans. Tuong, 25, was quoted as saying he had instructed 2 of the sergeants in "the facts of war—how the Americans caused it"—and in "how much suffering the Americans have caused the Vietnamese people." The report said the Viet Cong captors had sought to persuade the prisoners that they "should try to convince many others of the wrongness of the American cause in Vietnam." (Tuong told *N.Y. Times* correspondent Bernard Weinraub Nov. 13 that he had interrogated Pitzer and Johnson for 2 years but was "unsure" as to whether they had been successfully brainwashed.)

A U.S. State Department statement Nov. 17 said that discussions with Johnson, Jackson and Pitzer Nov. 12 had made it "quite clear that they have not been brainwashed." This also had been confirmed by Amb.-at-Large W. Averell Harriman in a meeting with Hayden Nov. 15, Hayden said Nov. 17.

U.S. POLICY & DISSENT

Dispute over the war in Vietnam caused a cleavage among Americans that continued to deepen during 1967.

Johnson Administration policy in Vietnam was attacked both by "hawks," who called for escalation of the allied military effort, and by "doves," who in some cases approached violence in their demands that the U.S. curtail the fighting and try harder to make peace. Public opinion surveys indicated that while a majority of Americans probably still thought the U.S. should continue to fight in Vietnam, the number of those who favored getting out was growing.

Opposition to U.S. policy was expressed during 1967 in even more violent demonstrations than had taken place in previous years. Targets of the protests included the White House, the Pentagon, draft boards, recruiters for the military services and the Dow Chemical Co., which manufactured napalm used in Vietnam. The issue was debated at length in both houses of Congress and especially in the Senate, where leading figures in the Democratic Party bitterly denounced the Vietnam policy of the Democratic Administration.

Pres. Johnson continued to insist that he was doing his best to make an honorable peace but that he would not abandon American commitments or desert the South Vietnamese to almost certain conquest by Communist invaders from the North.

LBJ Foresees Long & Costly Fight

In his annual State-of-the-Union message to Congress Jan. 10, Pres. Johnson warned that the U.S. faced a long struggle in Vietnam and must be prepared to make sacrifices to support the cost of the war. He asked specifically for enactment of a 6% surcharge on personal and corporate income taxes for 2 years "or for so long as the unusual expenditures associated with our efforts in Vietnam continue." In a televised evening appearance before a joint session of Congress, the President asked "Congress and this nation to resolve" the issue of "whether we have the staying power to fight a very costly war when the objective is limited and the danger to us is seemingly remote."

The President said that the U.S. would support peace initiatives by the UN or others and would "continue to take every possible initiative ourselves to constantly probe for peace." But, he continued, "until such efforts succeed, or until the infiltration [in South Vietnam] ceases, or until the conflict subsides, I think the course of wisdom for this country is that we just must firmly pursue our present course. We will stand firm in Vietnam." He added: "I wish I could report to you that the conflict is almost over. This I cannot do. We face more cost, more loss and more agony." "Whether we can fight a war of limited objectives over a period of time and keep alive the hope of independence and stability for people other than ourselves; whether we can continue to act with restraint when the temptation to get it over with is inviting, but dangerous; whether we can accept the necessity of choosing a great evil in order to ward off a greater one. Whether we can do these without arousing the hatreds and the passions that are ordinarily loosed in time of war—on all these questions, so much turns. . . . But we have lived with danger for a long time before, and we shall live with it for a long time yet to come. . . . Let us remember that those who expect to reap the blessings of freedom, must, like men, undergo the fatigues of supporting it."

Fulbright's Peace Plan

Chrmn. J. W. Fulbright (D., Ark.) of the Senate Foreign Relations Committee proposed an 8-point plan for ending the war in Vietnam. The proposal was detailed in a book, *The Arrogance of Power,* published Jan. 23. Fulbright's plan, appearing in a chapter entitled "An Alternative for Vietnam," suggested that:

(1) The South Vietnamese government seek a peace conference with the Viet Cong's National Liberation Front (NLF).

(2) The U.S. and South Vietnam jointly propose talks to arrange a cease-fire among the 4 principal belligerents: the U.S., South Vietnam, North Vietnam and the NLF.

(3) The U.S. cease air attacks on North Vietnam and decrease its military actions "to the maximum extent consistent with the security of American forces" pending peace efforts.

(4) The U.S. vow eventual military withdrawal from Vietnam.

(5) The U.S., South Vietnam, North Vietnam and the NLF negotiate a truce and plans for self-determination in South Vietnam.

(6) The agreements reached by the 4-party conference be guaranteed by an international parley of all interested parties that would also draw up plans for a referendum on the reunification of North and South Vietnam.

(7) The international parley neutralize Vietnam and negotiate multilateral treaties for the neutralization of the rest of Southeast Asia.

(8) If the proposed conferences fail to produce agreement, the U.S. should consolidate its military forces in defensible areas of South Vietnam and maintain them there indefinitely.

Fulbright's book, based on lectures he had delivered in the summer of 1966 at Johns Hopkins University, said the Vietnamese war both threatened world peace and impeded U.S. efforts at a *rapprochement* with Communist states of Eastern Europe.

(In an NBC-TV interview, Fulbright suggested Jan. 22 that South Vietnamese Premier Nguyen Cao Ky be replaced if he refused to negotiate with the NLF. Ky was "there only because we put him in," Fulbright said.)

Ex-Sen. Barry Goldwater (R., Ariz.), who had returned Jan. 20 from a 4-day tour of South Vietnam, derided Fulbright's 8-point plan Jan. 23 as "foolishness." Speaking at an informal gathering of the New York chapter of the Air Force Association, Goldwater said: "There's no chance" of negotiations; "we're not far enough along the military road . . . to be able to bring the enemy to the conference table." Goldwater called for an expansion of U.S. air attacks on North Vietnam. Referring to the controversy over civilian bombing casualties, Goldwater said: "You've got to forget about this civilian stuff. Whenever you drop bombs you're going to hit civilians; it's foolish to pretend you're not."

Views similar to Goldwater's had been expressed by 2 Southern Senators: Sen. Russell B. Long (D., La.) suggested Jan. 15 in a CBS-TV interview that the U.S. "bear down on this bombing [of North Vietnam] and hit them a lot harder than you're hitting and quit worrying whether the Communists like it or not." Sen. John Stennis (D., Miss.) proposed in a speech delivered in Philadelphia Jan. 19 that the U.S. step up the air war over North Vietnam and provide a "substantial increase" of U.S. troops in Vietnam, "even if this should require mobilization." Stennis foresaw the need of 500,000 U.S. troops in Vietnam by the end of 1967. Stennis called North Vietnamese civilian bombing casualties "regrettable and unfortunate." But he said: "We must not be panicked into making the tragic mistake of letting pressure, either domestic or foreign, or the worldwide propaganda offensive which Hanoi has mounted, force us to halt the bombing."

Policy Criticized at Senate Hearings

The Senate Foreign Relations Committee began hearings Jan. 30 on what Chrmn. Fulbright described as "the responsibilities of the United States as a great power." Fulbright said the hearings would be "primarily educational in character" as part of an attempt to find a "rationale" for the U.S. role as leader of the non-Communist world. Many—but not all— witnesses told the committee that the U.S. should stop bombing North Vietnamese targets without insisting on reciprocal de-escalation. Among developments during the hearings:

Jan. 30—Ex-Amb.-to-USSR George F. Kennan of the Institute for Advanced Study (Princeton, N.J.) testified that "we stand today at something of a parting of the ways with respect to our approach to the Communist world." "The unity of the Communist bloc is a matter of the past and it will not be restored," he declared. The "naive world revolutionary force of Lenin's day" and "the grim monolith of Communist power" of Stalin's day were gone, he said, and if the U.S. did not respond to "encouraging elements" in the Communist situation it might be "neglecting" an "only chance" to avoid a world war. Kennan advocated a flexible policy of standing firm on important issues where Soviet policy seemed "adverse" to U.S. interests and of "holding the door open" on smaller issues. Kennan called the U.S. involvement in Vietnam "unfortunate" but backed the Administration "in its unwillingness to get out of Vietnam in an ignominious way." As for the bombing of North Vietnam, he said he would be "more comfortable if we stopped it whether or not there were reciprocity."

Jan. 31—Ex-Amb.-to-Japan Edwin O. Reischauer called the bombing a "psychological blunder" in a mistaken belief that it would force Hanoi to negotiate. He advocated "prudent de-escalation" of the bombing no matter how "gloomy" the prospect of negotiations might appear. As an alternative to bombing and as a way of "simmering down" the war he suggested a massive border blockade at the 17th parallel. He said he was "a supporter of the Administration's objective in Vietnam which, as I understand it, is to bring the war to as speedy an end as possible, without resorting to either of the dangerous alternatives of withdrawal or major escalation." Reischauer said: "The threat of unitary world communism sweeping Asia has largely faded and the menace of Chinese domination . . . is growing weaker"; "we have tended to overestimate [Communist China's] strength and its immediate menace to our interests and to its neighbors." Reischauer proposed, as a basis for a long-range Asian policy, that the U.S.: (1) "minimize" military involvement; (2) avoid formal alliances; (3) shun sponsorship of political, social or economic change, because such sponsorship leads to "responsibility for the existence or nature of a regime"; (4) not attempt the role of "leader in Asia, rallying allies to our policies."

Feb. 2—Assistant managing editor Harrison E. Salisbury of the *N.Y. Times,* who had recently visited North Vietnam and reported on the effects of the U.S. bombing, said: The bombing had slowed the southward flow of supplies, but enough supplies were still being shipped, and the bombing had unified the North Vietnamese behind the war effort. In reply to a question, he said: "If the question is, do we stop bombing right out of the blue, with nothing from them, I'd say no." Salisbury said he felt that Hanoi was "ready to begin to talk business" about peace but preferred direct and secret negotiations.

Feb. 20—Historian Henry Steele Commager said: The U.S. had "greatly overextended" its power abroad because of a "moralistic obsession" to stop communism; "it is not our duty to keep peace throughout the globe, to put down aggression wherever it starts up, to stop the advance of communism or other isms which we may not approve of"; "we do not have the resources—material, intellectual, or moral—to be at once an American power, a European power, and an Asian power." Commager considered the U.S.' Vietnamese involvement a "misguided venture" and advocated an end to the bombing without insistence on reciprocal action.

Feb. 21—Retired Lt. Gen. James M. Gavin called for an immediate end to the bombing of North Vietnam "without any stipulation" for reciprocal de-escalation. He denounced the bombing as "militarily as well as morally wrong."

Congressional Declaration on War

A bill declaring Congress' intention of supporting U.S. armed forces in Vietnam, of supporting efforts to end the war honorably and of preventing its expansion was passed by both houses Mar. 8 and was signed by the President Mar. 16. The declaration, written by Senate Democratic leader Mike Mansfield to forestall a harsher statement, was attached to an authorization of $4½ billion in supplemental funds for the war.

Text of the declaration: "The Congress hereby declares: (1) its firm intentions to provide all necessary support for members of the armed forces of the United States fighting in Vietnam; (2) its support of efforts being made by the President of the United States and other men of good will throughout the world to prevent an expansion of the war in Vietnam and to bring that conflict to an end through a negotiated settlement which will preserve the honor of the United States, protect the vital interests of this country, and allow the people of South Vietnam to determine the affairs of that nation in their own way; and (3) its support for the convening of the nations that participated in the Geneva Conferences or any other meeting of nations similarly involved and interested as soon as possible for the purpose of pursuing the general principles of the Geneva accords of 1954 and 1962 and for formulating plans for bringing the conflict to an honorable conclusion."

Senate Group for Escalation

In a report released Mar. 27, the U.S. Senate Preparedness Investigating Subcommittee recommended, in effect, that the U.S. escalate the air war against North Vietnam by lifting restrictions on bombing targets. The report, based on a subcommittee staff investigation in Vietnam in Oct. 1966, contended that the policy of curbing the raids had resulted in a loss that had been "heavy for the limited gains we have achieved." The report explained: "In the time that meaningful military targets in North Vietnam have been protected by immunity from possible strikes, the North Vietnamese have been able to place formidable networks of air defensive weapons around them, and these have taken their toll when the immunity was lifted"; this policy "can only result in increased aircraft losses from resources that have already become very seriously strained; until Oct. 1966, the worldwide inventory of Air Force tactical aircraft was dwindling as a result of attrition in Southeast Asia."

The subcommittee urged an "affirmative response to some recommendations of responsible commanders to strike more meaningful targets in North Vietnam." The report agreed with an incorporated Defense Department statement that the air strikes against North Vietnamese targets had saved the lives of American soldiers fighting in South Vietnam by curbing "large-scale attacks" by Communist forces there. The subcommittee lauded American air attacks on North Vietnam's Thainguyen iron and steel complex as suggesting "some relaxation of prior restrictions."

Sen. Stuart Symington (D., Mo.) had expressed regret in a report released Mar. 26 that the Johnson Administration had not used American air and sea power to greater effect against "the more meaningful targets in North Vietnam." Symington, who had toured Asia in Dec. 1966 and Jan. 1967, said a U.S. fighter pilot in Thailand had told him that MiG fighter pilots over North Vietnam were "becoming more aggressive and pressing their attacks with a sophistication they haven't shown before." Symington said that the U.S. pilots were anxious to destroy the MiGs on the ground by attacking the airfields around Hanoi but that these targets were on the Defense Department's restrictive list. Symington's suggestions were made in a report, based on his Asian visit, that he had filed Feb. 3 with the Senate Armed Services and Foreign Relations committees and with the Defense Department. (The MiG bases were all removed from the restricted list and attacked by U.S. aircraft later during the year.)

ADA Assails Johnson Policy

A resolution expressing "disenchantment and dismay" with the Administration's policy on Vietnam was approved by Americans for Democratic Action (ADA) Apr. 2 at the concluding session of the 3-day ADA national convention in Washington. The convention Apr. 2 also approved a proposal for a unilateral "stand-still truce" in Vietnam beginning Apr. 15, as suggested by Sen. Joseph S. Clark (D., Pa.) in an address to the convention Mar. 31. The convention Apr. 1 had rejected a preamble that would have lauded the Johnson Administration's efforts to find peace and would have blamed both the Communists and the U.S. for having failed to reach agreement. Economist John Kenneth Galbraith of Harvard, in accepting the ADA's national chairmanship, called Apr. 2 for a suspension of bombing in North Vietnam and for intensified efforts at a compromise settlement. He charged that the Administration was seeking a "military solution" in Vietnam. Referring to "generals or high State Department officials" who "speak rather briskly of a 5- or 10-year war," Galbraith warned that a prolonged conflict in Vietnam could "mean the death and burial of the Democratic Party."

The ADA national board Sept. 24 adopted a position against the Administration's war policy in Vietnam and charged that in Vietnam the U.S. was "in league with a corrupt and illiberal government supported by a minority of the people." The board pledged support to whichever 1968 Presidential candidate "gives the best prospect for a settlement of the Vietnam conflict, for a liberal and civilized foreign policy elsewhere in the world and a strong and effective attack on the urgent domestic problems of our own country." But the board Sept. 23 had rejected, 73-12, a statement opposing Pres. Johnson's renomination. Daniel P. Moynihan, director of the Joint Center for Urban Studies of MIT and Harvard University and a member of the ADA board, had told his liberal ADA colleagues Sept. 23: "The war is Vietnam was thought up and is being managed by the men John K. Kennedy brought to Washington to conduct American foreign and defense policy. Most of us in this room know some at least of these men. Many here know them all. And we know them to be persons of immutable conviction on almost all matters we would regard as central to liberal belief, and further to be men of personal honor and the highest intellectual attainment. Knowing that, there are not a few of us present who did not contribute something considerable to persuade the American public that we were entirely right to be setting out on that course that has led us to the present point. . . . It is this knowledge, this complicity if you will, that requires of many of us a restraint in a situation that gives to others the utmost play to the powers of invective and contempt, the plain fact being that if these men got us into the present situation, who are *we* to say we would have done better?"

Republican Views Vary

The Administration's policy in Vietnam was supported by Sen. Edward W. Brooke (R., Mass.) in his first formal Senate speech Mar. 23. In the past a critic of the Vietnam war policy, Brooke reversed his stand following a 2-week fact-finding tour, beginning Mar. 4, of Japan, Taiwan, South Vietnam, Cambodia, Thailand and Laos. Brooke recalled that he had previously contended that the U.S. "ought to take the first step toward creating a better climate for negotiations." He had favored a bombing pause or some other "military deescalation which might have persuaded Hanoi to enter serious negotiations," Brooke said. But "everything I learned" from the trip "has now convinced me that the enemy is not disposed to participate in any meaningful negotiations at this time." He said the "burden of responsibility had shifted" from the U.S. to Hanoi, and "continuation of the war is based upon the influence of those in Hanoi who believe" that the U.S. "will falter in its commitment." Brooke said he was against "escalation of our military commitment" and for "containment of the war within its present limited framework." He advised "patience until the enemy has finally concluded that negotiated peace is the best and only solution." At a news conference Mar. 24, Brooke said: "Cessation of the bombing is not the key to a negotiated peace at this time. Either you're in the war or not in the war. I believe in a limited war and would not want to do anything to bring Red China in." On the CBS-TV "Face the Nation" program Mar. 26, Brooke said: "Ho Chi Minh was now listening to the hawks" in North Vietnam who contended that the U.S. "is seriously divided at the present time" on war policy. "If we show strength, I believe he will come to the peace table sooner."

The Administration's military policy on Vietnam was praised Apr. 9 by ex-GOP Presidential candidate Barry M. Goldwater. Appearing on the ABC-TV "Issues and Answers" program, Goldwater said: "I think the President is now determined to win this war and end it, and all of us are behind him on it"; "I have been convinced for the last 2 weeks that Pres. Johnson has finally disregarded the words of Bobby Kennedy and Bill Fulbright and others who would pull out at any cost, recognizing that Hanoi will not come to the bargaining table." Goldwater advocated bombing Haiphong and MiG bases in North Vietnam, and he opposed the planned cease-fire on the anniversary of Buddha's birthday May 23.

Sen. Charles H. Percy (R., Ill.), in a speech before the American Society of Newspaper Editors in Washington Apr. 22, assailed a policy that would "allow our men to die at the rate of 150 to 250 a month, for an interminable number of years, in search of a total victory which cannot, in my judgment, really be achieved." Percy denounced as "unrealistic" proposals (a) for negotiations "without inviting the Viet Cong to fully participate" and (b) for Hanoi "to end the supply and reinforcement of its forces in the South" before the U.S. would end its bombing of the North. Percy proposed a peace settlement that would let the Viet Cong eventually become "a legal political party competing peacefully at the polls and shunning violence."

Henry Cabot Lodge, who had resigned as U.S. ambassador to South Vietnam, was one of the more prominent Republicans who supported the Johnson policy. On returning to the U.S. Apr. 26 to assume his new duties as ambassador at large, Lodge assailed domestic critics of U.S. policy in Vietnam. He declared: "Disunity in America prolongs the war"; Americans demonstrating against the war "make Hanoi think all they have to do is hang on and we'll fall apart"; a unilateral U.S. cease-fire would be impractical because "the Viet Cong can go on with their terrorism, kidnaping and torture while our side is precluded from trying to prevent them."

Romney's Positions

Gov. George W. Romney (R., Mich.) Apr. 7 outlined a position on the war in Vietnam that was construed by the White House as a "strong endorsement of the fundamentals of the Administration's position." Romney presented his views, his first major statement on the war, in an address in Hartford, Conn. Romney had largely avoided discussing Vietnam publicly prior to Apr. 7 but had been studying the issue with the aid of advisers, including such GOP leaders as New York Gov. Nelson A. Rockefeller and Sens. Jacob K. Javits (N.Y.), Hugh Scott (Pa.) and Edward W. Brooke (Mass.). Romney said: "It is unthinkable that the United States withdraw from Vietnam. We must not oversimplify this conflict by talking only in terms of bombing or withdrawing. The failure to induce negotiations at this time should not result in massive military escalation. We should continue to seek meaningful negotiations. . . . We must give our gallant fighting men our full support. We must use military force as necessary to reduce or cut off the flow of men and supplies from North Vietnam, to knock out enemy main forces, to provide a military shield for the south and to establish military dominance. . . . At the point of achieving military dominance, we should encourage the government of South Vietnam to achieve 'peace with amnesty' to avoid a very long and brutal 'other war.' The Hanoi leaders may be holding out in the desperate hope that America will tire of the struggle, that our purpose will falter, that disillusionment and discord here at home will somehow induce us to abandon our friends and dishonor our commitments by pulling back or pulling out. That is a false hope— and I for one will not contribute to it. . . . I have even heard that the leaders in Hanoi think a Republican Administration might come into power that would settle on their terms. For what it is worth, I would like to tell them right now that here is one Republican I can speak for who will not settle on their terms under any circumstances."

Romney July 11 criticized the Administration's "over-reaction in military terms" in Vietnam and said that this had been accompanied by an "unfortunate growth of feeling among the American people that a purely military solution in Vietnam is possible." He said he favored curtailment of the bombing of North Vietnam by concentration on targets "directly related to the infiltration of men and supplies." Romney conceded, however, that an increase in U.S. manpower in Vietnam "may be helpful in providing a military security shield for the pacification program."

Romney charged in a TV interview broadcast in Detroit Sept. 4 that he had undergone a "brainwashing" during his visit to Vietnam in 1965. The charge evoked considerable political criticism and speculation that it might have impaired Romney's Presidential prospects. Romney said: "I just had the greatest brainwashing that anyone can get when you go over to Vietnam, not only by the generals, but also by the diplomatic corps over there, and they do a very thorough job." Romney had come back from his 1965 trip expressing the conviction that the U.S. involvement in Vietnam was morally right and necessary. But he said Sept. 4: " I have changed my mind, in that particularly I no longer believe that it was necessary for us to get involved in South Vietnam to stop Communist aggression in Southeast Asia and to prevent Chinese Communist domination of Southeast Asia." But "we're there, we are involved, we have created the conflict that now exists between communism and freedom there, and this is the complexity and difficulty of the situation. And furthermore, we have involved other nations in Southeast Asia, and we have to deal with it on the basis of current circumstances rather than what might have been if there hadn't been an overreaction." The U.S. should tell South Vietnam that unless it fought harder against the Viet Cong, it "can't just count on continuing [U.S.] supplies of men and material without limit."

Gov. Philip H. Hoff (D., Vt.), one of 9 other governors who went on the 1965 Vietnam tour with Romney, said Sept. 6 that Romney's "brainwashing" statement "tends to be almost incredible." All of the other governors on the trip (except one who was on vacation and unavailable for comment) said Sept. 6 that they disagreed with Romney over the brainwashing issue.

Romney told reporters Sept. 9 that he had not been talking about "Russian-type brainwashing but LBJ-type brainwashing" and that this was "the same thing you mean when you write about the credibility gap, snow jobs and manipulation of the news." He said the Administration, by "a systematic continuation of inaccurate reports, predictions and withholding of information, . . . has kept the American people from knowing the facts about the Vietnam war and its full impact on our domestic and foreign affairs."

Romney, appearing on NBC-TV's "Today" program Nov. 20, said that it would be unwise to halt bombing without assurance of worthwhile results.

Nixon's Views

Ex-Vice Pres. Richard M. Nixon said Apr. 14 that "Democratic critics" of Administration policy in Vietnam should "see that the way to get peace is to have a moratorium on the kind of criticism that gives aid and comfort to the enemy." While conceding that there was "some division" in Republican ranks on war policy, he said it was "not as great" as the division among Democrats. He asserted that "this apparent division at home" was "the major factor that is prolonging the war." Nixon made the comments while in Saigon on a private tour. He told newsmen in Saigon Apr. 17 that Sens. Mike Mansfield (Mont.) and Robert F. Kennedy (N.Y.) were 2 Democratic critics who were "raising false hopes for peace" in the U.S. "and prolonging the war."

Nixon in Boston Aug. 21 spoke against the Administration policy, as he put it, of "gradual escalation," which, he said, could lead to World War III. He favored use of "massive pressure" but ruled out the use of nuclear weapons in the conflict.

Nixon warned in Chicago Oct. 27 that the alternative to a "successful" conclusion to the war in Vietnam might be a 3d world war. Nixon called the war "the costliest . . . in American history" in terms of "lives and dollars" and "the deep division" within the U.S. The only way to "justify these costs," he said, was to bring home to the people that "this war is about the United States, about peace and freedom in the world," that the U.S.' "vital stategic interests" were involved.

Religious Pressure

Religious leaders and organized religious groups called with mounting urgency during 1967 for greater efforts to end the fighting. Many of them attacked Administration policy and demanded unilateral U.S. de-escalation. Among developments involving clergymen and religious organizations:

■ The Rev. Dr. Reinhold Niebuhr, retired vice president of the Union Theological Seminary in New York, suggested Jan. 18, in an address to a seminary audience, that the universities, the church and the communications media "press for a solution that guarantees an American presence in Southeast Asia, while saving face for the United States and China." Niebuhr called the war a "fantastic adventure of United States imperialism in an Asian war. . . ." He said he did not oppose a U.S. presence in Southeast Asia, "but it might be better to have that presence in perhaps Thailand."

■ About 2,000 members of the New York-based National Committee of Clergy & Laymen Concerned About Vietnam marched in front of the White House in Washington Jan. 31. They demanded that Pres. Johnson order a halt in the bombing of North Vietnam and a de-escalation of the ground war in South Vietnam to pave the way for peace talks. The organization's demand was in the form of a note handed to William Jorden, an assistant to Presidential Asst. Walt W. Rostow. The message also urged the acceptance of the National Liberation Front at future peace talks and a greater peace role for the UN and the International Control Commission. The demonstration took place during the 2d day of a 3-day "Peace Mobilization" held by the committee in Washington. (A counter-demonstration was staged across the street by the American Council of Christian Churches, a fundamentalist Protestant group; about 200 persons carried signs supporting American policy in Vietnam.) Committee representatives held separate meetings Feb. 1 with Rostow and Defense Secy. McNamara. Rostow reported that the Johnson Administration was under "terrific pressure from people who want to go militarily further" to win the war. At the closing session of the meeting, the committee decided to sponsor a 3-day "Fast for Peace" by Christians and Jews throughout the U.S. as "an act of penitence" for the war in Vietnam. The fast was held Feb. 8-10. A national coordinator of the fast, the Rev. Carl S. Dudley, 34, pastor of the Berea Presbyterian Church in St. Louis, estimated Feb. 11 that more than "800 groups in more than 412 cities in 37 states" had participated in "the fast in some form."

■ The Rev. Dr. Eugene Carson Blake, general secretary of the World Council of Churches, called on the U.S. Apr. 26 to stop the bombing of North Vietnam and "agree with our allies in Asia and Europe that we will accept any peace that they will develop and agree to with us." Speaking in Norwalk, Conn., at a public meeting sponsored by several clergymen's groups in the city, Blake asserted that U.S. policy on Vietnam posed "the greatest danger to human survival, with the single exception of the present policy and action" of Communist China.

■ The Most Rev. Fulton J. Sheen, bishop of the Roman Catholic Diocese of Rochester, N.Y., appealed to Pres. Johnson July 30 to "withdraw our forces immediately from South Vietnam" "for the sake of reconciliation."

■ A Vietnam study group of the National Council of Churches recommended at a conference in Detroit Oct. 26 that the council call for a one-day nationwide strike if the U.S. escalated the war in Vietnam. The group's statement said it would regard any one of these 4 actions as escalation of the war: the use of nuclear weapons; a land invasion of North Vietnam; "intentional direct military offensive action" against Communist China; U.S. air attacks on the major Red River dikes of North Vietnam.

■ Pres. Johnson, attending Episcopal services Nov. 12 at the Bruton Parish Church in Williamsburg, Va., heard the Rev. Cotesworth Pinckney Lewis say in a sermon questioning U.S. policy in Vietnam: "Since there is a rather general consensus that something is wrong in Vietnam —a conviction voiced by leaders of nations traditionally our friends, leading military experts and the rank and file of American citizens— we wonder if some logical, straightforward explanation might be given without endangering whatever military or political advantages we now enjoy. . . .We are appalled that apparently this is the only war in our history which has had 3 times as many civilian as military casualties. It is particularly regrettable that to most nations of the world the struggle's purpose appears as neocolonialism." "While pledging our loyalty, we ask humbly: 'Why?' "

New York & San Francisco Marches

Massive parades were held in New York and San Francisco Apr. 15 in protest against U.S. policy in Vietnam. The demonstrations were sponsored by the Spring Mobilization Committee to End the War in Vietnam.

In New York, demonstrators from all parts of the U.S. marched from Central Park to UN headquarters (about 1½ miles away), where they heard speeches by the Rev. Dr. Martin Luther King Jr., Floyd McKissick, Stokely Carmichael and Dr. Benjamin Spock. According to police estimates, 100,000-125,000 persons marched in the parade. King estimated that 300,000-400,000 participated. The New York parade was orderly despite some jeering and heckling by counter-demonstrators. Prior to the march, youths burned nearly 200 draft cards in Central Park. King, who led the march along with Spock and singer Harry Belafonte, called on the U.S. to "honor its word" and "stop the bombing of North Vietnam." He urged "students from all over the nation to use this summer and coming summers educating and organizing communities across the nation against war." Prior to his address, King and a 5-man delegation submitted a note to UN Undersecy. (for special affairs) Ralph Bunche in the UN building. The message affirmed the rally's "support of the principles of peace, universality, equal rights and self-determination of peoples embodied in the [UN] Charter and acclaimed by mankind, but violated by the United States." Among statements by other speakers at the New York rally: Carmichael—The U.S. was playing a "brutal and racist" role in Vietnam; he opposed "drafting young men, particularly black Americans." The Rev. James L. Bevel, national director of Spring Mobilization—Pres. Johnson would be given "one month to stop murdering those folks in Vietnam. That's all we give him, one month to pull those guns out. If he doesn't, we'll close down New York City."

The San Francisco march was led by a score of Black Nationalists, but most of the marchers were whites—largely teenagers and youths in their early 20s. The climax of the march was a protest rally at Kezar Stadium. Police estimated that there were 20,000 people in the line of march and 50,000 at the stadium. Speakers included Mrs. Coretta King, wife of Martin Luther King Jr., Georgia state legislator Julian Bond and E. M. Keating and Robert Scheer of *Ramparts* magazine.

Commenting on the demonstrations, State Secy. Rusk said Apr. 16 on the NBC-TV program "Meet the Press" that the "Communist apparatus" was behind the peace movement "all over the world and in our own country." But he denied "mean[ing] to say . . . that all those who have objections to the war in Vietnam are Communists."

The House Committee on Un-American Activities had charged in a report issued Mar. 31 that the 2 Apr. 15 antiwar demonstrations had been proposed by Communists and that many of the organizations involved were infiltrated by or dominated by Communists. The Spring Mobilization Committee to End the War in Vietnam had been formed in Cleveland, O. Nov. 26, 1966, and the HUAC report said many Communist leaders, including Arnold Johnson, Bettina Aptheker (Kurzweil) and Alberta J. Lima, were sponsors. The report conceded that many other sponsors and the committee's top officers were not Communists, and it implied that this represented a success for the "Communist united front strategy." The HUAC report was assailed the day it was issued at a rally in Washington aimed at encouraging persons in the Washington area to attend the Apr. 15 demonstration. The Rev. Bevel, freed from his duties with the Southern Christian Leadership Conference to permit him to direct the mobilization committee staff, charged that HUAC and its chairman, Rep. Edwin E. Willis (D., La.), were "liars" and "spreaders of trash." (The HUAC report had noted that Bevel had cooperated with the pro-Communist DuBois Clubs and that Bevel's wife, Diane Nash Bevel, had "recently made an unauthorized trip to Hanoi.")

(Parades in support of U.S. troops in Vietnam were held in New York Apr. 29 [Loyalty Day] and May 13. The 2 Loyalty Day parades—in Manhattan and Brooklyn—were sponsored by the Veterans of Foreign Wars. The May 13 parade, with an estimated 70,000 participants, was organized by N.Y. Fire Department Capt. Raymond W. Gimmler to counter anti-war demonstrations.)

King Links Rights & Peace Efforts

The presence of Negro leaders King, McKissick and Carmichael at the New York anti-war demonstration was the outgrowth of efforts to link (although apparently not "merge") the civil rights and peace movements. King, head of the Southern Christian Leadership Conference (SCLC), had indicated Apr. 4 that such a link was forming. Speaking at a press conference in New York, King described the U.S. government as the "greatest purveyor of violence in the world" and urged Negro and white youths to declare themselves conscientious objectors to military service. He said Negroes were "dying in disproportionate numbers in Vietnam. Twice as many Negroes as whites are in combat," and this was a "reflection of the Negro's position in America."

Without mentioning King by name, a resolution approved in New York Apr. 10 by the directors of the NAACP rejected as "a serious tactical mistake" the suggestion that the civil rights and peace movements in the U.S. amalgamate.

UN Undersecy. Ralph Bunche Apr. 12 took issue with what he called King's suggestions that the U.S. civil rights and peace movements merge. Bunche, a Negro, said: King "should positively give up one role or another. The 2 efforts have little in common." King "should realize" that his opposition to the American role in Vietnam "is bound to alienate many friends and supporters of the civil rights movement and greatly weaken it." Bunche, a director of the NAACP, disclosed that he had persuaded the NAACP board to adopt tougher language in its Apr. 10 resolution criticizing King's civil rights-peace position. At a news conference in Los Angeles later Apr. 12, King denied that he advocated a merger of civil rights and peace drives. "But we equally believe that no one can pretend that the existence of the war is not profoundly affecting the destiny of civil rights progress," King asserted. King challenged the NAACP to assume a "forthright stand on the rightness or wrongness" of the war in Vietnam. King said he was determined to pursue the goals of civil rights and at the same time "to speak out positively and forthrightly on the war in Vietnam."

(Stokely Carmichael returned to the U.S. Dec. 11 after a 4-month tour that included visits to Tanzania, Egypt, Algiers, Sweden, Spain, Cuba, England, France, North Vietnam, Guinea and Czechoslovakia. He had violated prohibitions on unauthorized travel to Cuba and North Vietnam. In a broadcast monitored in Tokyo Aug. 30, Hanoi radio had quoted Carmichael as pledging the support of American Negroes for North Vietnam in the Vietnamese war. In an Aug. 17 broadcast over Havana radio, he had called on U.S. Negroes to arm for "total revolution.")

King had led a march of 5,000 white and Negro anti-war demonstrators in Chicago Mar. 25. The march ended at the

Coliseum, where King declared in an address that the Vietnamese war was "a blasphemy against all that America stands for." He charged that American forces in Vietnam were "committing atrocities equal to any perpetrated by the Viet Cong" "in a war that seeks to . . . perpetuate white colonialism."

King, interviewed in Louisville, Ky., Mar. 30 by *N.Y. Times* correspondent John Hebers, warned that if the U.S. "insists on escalating the war, and if we don't see any changes, it may be necessary to engage in civil disobedience [in the U.S.] to further arouse the conscience of the nation and make it clear that this is hurting our country." King said Mar. 30 that there were "at least 3 reasons why I felt compelled to take a stronger stand against the war in Vietnam": (1) The conflict was "playing havoc with our domestic destinies," making it "more difficult to implement the programs that will deal with the economic and social problems" of Negroes and "poor people generally"; (2) escalation of the war could "lead to a grand war with China and to a kind of full world war that could mean the annihilation of the human race"; (3) as an advocate of the nonviolent movement in the U.S., "it is very consistent for me to follow a nonviolence approach to international affairs." (The SCLC's 60–70-member board of directors in Louisville Mar. 30 adopted a resolution assailing American military intervention in Vietnam as a "morally and politically unjust" action that "drowned the Negro's cry for equal rights.")

Speaking Apr. 4 at Riverside Church in New York, at a meeting sponsored by Clergy & Laymen Concerned About Vietnam, King said he suggested the avoidance of military service "to all those who find the American course in Vietnam a dishonorable and unjust one." He said: The Vietnamese peasants "watch as we poison their water, as we kill a million acres of their crops. . . . They wander into hospitals, with at least 20 casualties from American firepower for one Viet Cong-inflicted injury. So far, we may have killed a million of them —mostly children." King compared the employment of new U.S. weapons on Vietnamese peasants to the Nazis' testing in World War II of "new medicine and new tortures in the concentration camps of Europe." King proposed that the U.S.

undertake these moves on its own to end the war "in order to atone for our sins and errors in Vietnam": (a) stop all bombing of South and North Vietnam; (b) declare a unilateral truce in the hope that it would lead to peace talks; (c) set a date for withdrawal of U.S. and other foreign troops from Vietnam; (d) recognize the fact that the NLF had substantial support in South Vietnam and, therefore, must be given an important role in negotiations and in a future South Vietnamese government.

The launching of another nationwide peace drive, Vietnam Summer, was supported by King with an address at Christ Church Parish House in Cambridge, Mass. Apr. 23. King urged an "escalation of our opposition to the war in Vietnam," which, he said, had "increased the possibilities of nuclear war to destroy mankind." The Vietnamese conflict, King asserted, "is poisoning the soul of our nation and has isolated our nation morally and politically." (Vietnam Summer had been organized by Harvard faculty members, students and residents of Cambridge. The acting director of the group, Chester Hartman of the Harvard faculty, said its purpose was to create a political force strong enough to end the war. He said 100,000 volunteers could conduct a nationwide canvass to organize the drive.)

The formation of Negotiation Now, a U.S. group urging an end to the war in Vietnam, was announced in New York Apr. 24 by King and others. One of the group's leaders, Joseph L. Rauh Jr., vice chairman of Americans for Democratic Action, said Negotiation Now would seek a million signers for a petition to Pres. Johnson. The appeal called for: (1) A halt in U.S. bombing raids on North Vietnam "now and without conditions"; (2) further U.S. steps that would lead to a stand-still truce; (3) acceptance by North and South Vietnam and the National Liberation Front of any U.S. initiative for peace and their participation in a cease-fire. Others who had helped form the peace group: Rabbi Maurice Eisendrath, president of the Union of American Hebrew Congregations; Gerhard Elston, Vietnam affairs director for the National Council of Churches; William J. Butler, general counsel of the Committee for a Sane Nuclear Policy (SANE).

McGovern Leads Senate Attack

An attack on Pres. Johnson's policy in Vietnam was mounted in the Senate Apr. 25, a day after U.S. jets bombed airbases in North Vietnam and the day after Gen. William Westmoreland said U.S. critics of the war fostered belief by the enemy that "he can win politically" what he could not win "militarily." The major speech attacking Administration policy was delivered by Sen. George McGovern (D., S.D.). Sens. Robert Kennedy, Fulbright, Frank Church (D., Ida.) and Ernest Gruening (D., Alaska) also joined in the attack. Sens. Spessard L. Holland (D., Fla.), Russell B. Long (D., La.) and Frank J. Lausche (D., O.) defended the Administration.

McGovern said: "In trying to imply that it is American dissent which is causing the Vietnamese to continue the war, the Administration is only confessing the weakness of its own case by trying to silence its critics and confuse the American people." "The new level of escalation marked by our bombing of the North Vietnamese airfields has brought us one step closer to World War III involving the limitless legions of China backed by the enormous firepower of Soviet Russia."

McGovern made several "indictments of our Vietnam policy." Among them: "Our Vietnam policymakers have distorted history to justify our intervention in a civil conflict supposedly to defend a free nation against external aggression; actually we are backing a dictatorial group in Saigon against a competing group backed by a dictatorial regime in the North"; "while orally calling for negotiations, we are practicing military escalation and diplomatic rigidity in such a fashion as to foreclose negotiations"; "we are weakening America's moral position and beclouding American idealism"; "we are creating at home a climate of intimidation designed to silence dissent and meaningful discussion of policy."

As an alternative policy, McGovern recommended: (a) ending the bombing, confining military action to "a defensive holding action in the South"; (b) a clear statement of "our willingness to negotiate directly with the Viet Cong with some recognition that they will play a significant role in any provisional government"; (c) encouragement of "a more broadly based civilian government in Saigon, a government willing to start discussions with the other side looking toward arrangements to end the war"; (d) advocacy of "an international presence to police a cease-fire, supervise elections, provide an umbrella for the resettlement of Vietnamese concerned about their safety, and arrange for the withdrawal of all outside forces and the conversion of military bases to peacetime uses."

Kennedy warned against accepting escalation as inevitable: "Is it not really inevitable that after the events of last week our adversaries in that part of the world will have to take other steps themselves? . . . The Soviet Union, Communist China and North Vietnam will have to react to what we have done by acting themselves." Kennedy opposed a policy of trying "to bring about a peace through military action, which is really going to bring about destruction of Vietnam and the people."

Fulbright said: The Administration was mounting "a final drive for a vastly enlarged manpower and a great drive for a military victory." In such a drive there would be increasing pressure against dissent. Dissent would lead to charges of disloyalty, to charges of "muddle-headedness and then to treason."

Church contended that the expansion of the fighting had not achieved its avowed purpose of interdicting the enemy's troop supplies and of forcing a peace conference. Gruening said he agreed with McGovern that "we are not weakening communism; we are aiding it" and "weakening ourselves" since neither the Russians nor the Chinese "have to date committed a single soldier to combat" whereas Americans were being killed in Vietnam.

Holland rejected any charge that critics would be accused of "disloyalty or treason." Long declared that a Communist victory and subsequent "expansion elsewhere would be a much greater disaster than a bloodier war in Vietnam. . . . What a defeat in Vietnam would mean is a much greater price to pay for victory than our present sacrifice." Lausche said: "It is one thing for the President to say that we cannot pull out of Vietnam; it is another thing for others to say that we should pull out. The President is being plagued and hit from every side." "The following out of his honest judgment on Vietnam has made him politically weak."

The Garden City, N.Y. newspaper *Newsday* May 4 quoted Fulbright as saying he "no longer believes statements on Vietnam by Pres. Johnson, Secy. Rusk and Secy. McNamara." The report said Fulbright had expressed concern about the influence of the "military-industrial complex on policy in Vietnam and had mentioned Sens. Richard B. Russell [D., Ga.] and Henry M. Jackson [D., Wash.] and Rep. L. Mendel Rivers [D., S.C.] as coming from areas with large defense industries." Russell and Rivers were chairmen of their chambers' armed services committees. The report quoted Fulbright as saying businessmen and some government officials considered the war "a nice little war—not too much killing but a big help to the economy." *Newsday's* publisher, Bill Moyers, was former press secretary to Pres. Johnson. Fulbright apologized May 4 for "any embarrassment" the article may have caused members of Congress. He said that he was quoted out of context and from an off-the-record interview and that "this may be an effort to discredit me because I am critical of Administration policy in Vietnam."

Westmoreland Vs. Dissenters

Gen. William Westmoreland visited the U.S. in April and aroused controversy with an Apr. 24 statement that the enemy in Vietnam had "gained support" in the U.S. and abroad that "gives him hope that he can win politically that which he cannot accomplish militarily." He made the statement in a speech at an AP luncheon in New York. Westmoreland added that the GI in Vietnam was "dismayed, and so am I, by recent unpatriotic acts here at home."

Westmoreland's remarks were criticized Apr. 25 in a Senate debate on Vietnam policy. Sen. Thruston B. Morton (R., Ky.) said in a Senate speech Apr. 27: "Those who would decry 'unpatriotic acts' at home during a period of bloody conflict abroad, without differentiating between flag burners, draft-card burners, peaceful demonstrators and United States Senators exercising their responsible rights of dissent, only add fuel to the fires of irresponsible opposition that continue to plague present Administration policies." Morton described

Westmoreland's appearance before Congress as part of an Administration attempt to spread "an epidemic of verbal over-kill that, far from instilling sanity and moderation in the discussion of issues, engenders a dangerous and irresponsible over-reaction."

Westmoreland visited ex-Pres. Dwight D. Eisenhower in Palm Springs, Calif. Apr. 29. Eisenhower said later: "I hope America will wake up to the fact that our soldiers are dying for something we believe in. We will not abandon people who want to live in dignity. America doesn't have to apologize for her part in the war. She can be proud of it."

On his way back to Vietnam Apr. 30, Westmoreland said in Honolulu that "the attitude of the American people" toward the war was "wholesome." "Based on what I heard and saw," he said, "95% of the people are behind the United States effort in Vietnam. I am gratified to see this measure of support."

LBJ Defends Right to Dissent

Pres. Johnson May 1 defended both the right to dissent and the right to answer dissent. He said: "Freedom of speech is a 2-way street. We must guard every man's right to speak, but we must defend every man's right to answer." He made these remarks in an address to the 1967 White House Fellows, who were to start, in September, a one-year tour of government service.

American domestic opposition to U.S. policy in Vietnam was the subject of several questions directed to Pres. Johnson at his May 3 news conference. Queried as to whether "the general level of dissent" had "reached a particularly critical point," the President replied: "Whenever you have men dying and men sacrificing, . . . you have dissent. It occupies a stage of discussion in our lives every day." On the question of whether the peace movement in the U.S. was Communist-influenced, the President answered: "There is a Communist position which you can judge from the Communist propaganda which comes out of Peking, North Vietnam and the Soviet Union every day. One can judge their position on this general Vietnam question." The President said he saw no "hopeful prospects at the moment" for a peaceful settlement of the war, but "we are pursuing . . . every road that could lead in that peaceful direction."

Republicans Divide on Issue

The division among leading Republicans over U.S. policy in Vietnam became more evident May 2-3 as they reacted to a white paper on Vietnam released May 1 by the staff of the Senate Republican Policy Committee. Among other things, the staff paper said: "Before making any further decisions to support or differ with the President, Republicans might agree to seek hard, realistic answers to 2 basic questions—what precisely is our national interest in Thailand, Cambodia, Vietnam and Laos and to what further lengths are we prepared to go in support of this interest?" "Does the Republican Party serve America best by saying that politics stops at the water's edge? That we must rally behind the President? Does bipartisanship mean that Democratic mistakes are Republican responsibilities?"

Senate Republican leader Everett M. Dirksen (Ill.) left Walter Reed Army Hospital May 2, although he was recuperating from pneumonia, to attend a Senate GOP conference, at which he declared that "we reaffirm our position standing 4-square behind . . . [the President] and our field, air and sea commanders in Southeast Asia." GOP Policy Committee Chrmn. Bourke B. Hickenlooper (Ia.) added that Dirksen spoke for "the general consensus of Republicans."

In the Senate May 2 Sen. George D. Aiken (R., Vt.) declared, however, that the Administration "cannot achieve an honorable peace in Vietnam." He said the 1968 GOP Presidential nominee should "promise a new look" at U.S. policy in Asia. Sen. Mark O. Hatfield (R., Ore.) agreed that "this Administration does not have the capacity to conduct negotiations." He said the staff paper "strongly" supported his belief that Republicans should develop "alternatives to Administration policies which have been unable to bring either victory or solution" in Vietnam. A statement calling for "greater efforts" toward negotiations and warning against "initiating actions . . . likely" to bring Communist China into the war was issued by Republican Sens. Charles H. Percy (Ill.), Jacob K. Javits

(N.Y.) and Hugh D. Scott (Pa.). Javits, who reportedly had suggested the staff report, said May 3 that the report was very fair and "very accurate." Percy described it May 4 as "a very good factual analysis."

In a letter to Chrmn. Hickenlooper, Sen. John G. Tower (R., Tex.) protested May 3 that the release of the report "may well be misinterpreted by Hanoi as evidence that one of the major parties is on the verge of withdrawing support to the President in the war." At a news conference May 4, Tower said the release of the document was "a classic political mistake" in that it could be interpreted as a "hint we are trying to make political capital out of the war." He said the "mood of the country is hawkish" and "the Republican platform and the Republican nominee in 1968 will reflect the majority viewpoint of Republicans everywhere, as I have enunciated it." The Administration attempt "to win a military victory" was correct, he said, for "what is there to talk about" with the Communists at this point? Tower's position was disputed May 4 by Javits and Sen. John Sherman Cooper (R., Ky.). Javits said "relatively few Senators . . . feel the way he [Tower] does" Cooper indorsed the staff report's "implication that we should not accept as final all that was done in the past, that we should keep our minds open, voice our opinions and continue to seek a solution or settlement of the war other than on the field of arms."

In the Senate May 9, Senate Republican whip Thomas H. Kuchel (Calif.) said "the nation is committed today in Vietnam" and urged Republicans not to "abandon our clear and long-standing support of a system of collective security against Communist expansion in Asia in any effort to gain possession of the White House in 1968."

House Republican leader Gerald R. Ford (Mich.) had told newsmen May 3 that the President's determination to fight Communist aggression in Vietnam had the "overwhelming" support of House Republicans. "Pres. Johnson is commander-in-chief," he said. "I did not elect him. I tried to defeat him. I will try to defeat him again in 1968. But on the issue of our country meeting the challenge, we had better, as a nation, continue doing just that."

Senate Critics Caution Hanoi

16 Senate critics of Administration policy on Vietnam warned Hanoi in a statement issued May 17 that dissent on the war was a minority view in the U.S. and that "there are many more who either give their full endorsement to our government's policy in Vietnam, or who press for even greater military action there." The statement said that while the 16 Senators would press for "a negotiated peace," they "remain steadfastly opposed to any unilateral withdrawal of American troops from South Vietnam." A negotiated peace, they said, was "the last and only remaining alternative to a prolonged and intensified war."

The statement originated with Sen. Frank Church (D., Ida.), who had cleared it with State Secy. Rusk. In a separate statement on his personal views, Church said it was "vital" that "the purpose of the debate in the Senate . . . be understood by all, particularly by the Hanoi government. Our objective is the settlement of the war at the conference table, not the repudiation of American commitments already made to South Vietnam, or the unilateral withdrawal of American forces from that embattled country."

In addition to Church, the signers of the principal statement were Sens. John Sherman Cooper (R., Ky.), George McGovern (D., S.D.), J. W. Fulbright (D., Ark.), Frank E. Moss (D., Utah), E. L. Bartlett (D., Alaska), Lee Metcalf (D., Mont.), Vance Hartke (D., Ind.), Gaylord Nelson (D., Wis.), Quentin Burdick (D., N.D.), Joseph S. Clark (D., Pa.), Stephen M. Young (D., O.), Robert F. Kennedy (D., N.Y.), Mark O. Hatfield (R., Ore.), Wayne Morse (D., Ore.) and Claiborne Pell (D., R.I.).

Support for the statement was expressed May 17 by Vice Pres. Humphrey.

GOP Plan for Ending Bombing

A 5-stage plan to end the bombing of North Vietnam in return for de-escalation by Hanoi was proposed July 10 by 8 liberal Republican Congressmen. The plan called for 60-day suspensions of bombing, first above the 21st parallel, then above the 20th parallel, and in 3 further steps down to North Vietnam's 17th parallel border with South Vietnam.

The first suspension would be initiated by the U.S., but the others would be contingent on reciprocal de-escalation by North Vietnam, such as cessation of military shipments between depots in southern North Vietnam and along specified parts of the Ho Chi Minh Trail, a halt in terrorist attacks in specified areas of South Vietnam, release of U.S. prisoners of war.

The plan was proposed by Reps. F. Bradford Morse (Mass.), John R. Dellenback (Ore.), Marvin L. Esch (Mich.), Frank Horton (N.Y.), Charles McC. Mathias Jr. (Md.), Charles A. Mosher (O.), Richard S. Schweiker (Pa.) and Robert T. Stafford (Vt.).

Mansfield Vs. Escalation

Senate Democratic leader Mike Mansfield (Mont.) warned in the Senate July 11 against further escalation of the war. His remarks were based on the reported progress toward winning the war. Such reports, Mansfield said, apparently had been presented to Defense Secy. McNamara during his recent tour of Vietnam. "It must be said," Mansfield continued, "that these generalizations of progress would be more reassuring if they had not been heard from American leaders in Vietnam at many other times, stretching years into the past." He said the American people must ask themselves (a) what "indiscriminate bombing in North Vietnam may have in common with any objectives of the United States anywhere in Vietnam or Southeast Asia" and (b) at what point the conflict "becomes wholly an American war against all Vietnam, becomes a war in Korea, becomes a war in the Formosa Straits, becomes a war with China." "Who will say," he asked, "that a 3d World War is not already incubating in the ever-deepening and expanding struggle in Southeast Asia?"

As an alternative to expansion of the war, Mansfield urged (a) putting the entire question before the UN and (b) containing the conflict by building a defensive barrier south of the demilitarized zone separating North and South Vietnam. The latter proposal was criticized July 11 by Sen. Stuart Symington (D., Mo.), who said that U.S. military leaders considered such a barrier "ineffective to the point of being plain silly." Symington, commenting on reports that the Administration would seek more help from the South Vietnamese and other Asian allies, said: "Why not face it? From here [on] out it is the American forces that must do a steadily increasing amount of the fighting if the present South Vietnamese government is to survive."

Mansfield's speech was supported July 11 by Sen. George D. Aiken (R., Vt.), who suggested that the Administration give more attention to its Senate leader than to "certain military leaders who have far more knowledge of weapons than they have of people." Aiken said it would probably require one million U.S. soldiers in Vietnam "to control the situation and restore a semblance of order."

Newsmen asked Senate Republican leader Dirksen July 11 if he favored an increase in U.S. troops in Vietnam. Dirksen replied: "If Gen. Westmoreland says we need them, yes, sir."

Tonkin Gulf Resolution Debate

The Johnson Administration's broad interpretation of the 1964 Gulf of Tonkin resolution came under fire at U.S. Senate Foreign Relations Committee hearings Aug. 16-23 on the extent of the U.S.' foreign commitments. The Administration's position was that the resolution was Congress' authorization of the measures being taken by the U.S. in Vietnam.

Committee Chrmn. Fulbright Aug. 17 informed State Undersecy. Nicholas deB. Katzenbach, who was testifying, that the Administration had not sought and did not have a declaration of war for the Vietnamese conflict. Katzenbach replied: "Didn't that [Tonkin Gulf] resolution authorize the President to use the armed forces of the United States in whatever way was necessary? Didn't it? What could a declaration of war have done that would have given the President more authority and a clearer voice of the Congress than that did?" He said that because of the U.S.' limited objectives in Vietnam, a war declaration would have been "outmoded phraseology." Katzenbach also pointed out that the Constitution made it a function of Congress to declare war but not to "wage" or "conduct" war.

Fulbright asserted that in explaining the Tonkin Gulf resolution to the Senate during the 1964 debate, "I misinterpreted it" because "it wasn't clear to me." "I did make statements that I thought this did not entail nor contemplate any change in the then existing policy," Fulbright said, "and of course there has been great change in it." The confusion, he said, was in the "distinction . . . between repelling of an attack and the waging of war as a broad policy."

Katzenbach retorted that "the President didn't need such a broad authorization to repel an attack upon American ships in the Tonkin Bay" and that "that isn't what the resolution says." "That was not the way you [Fulbright] presented it" to the Senate, Katzenbach insisted. "It was not the way the Administration presented it, it was not the way the Congress understood it, and it wasn't what it [the resolution] said."

Fulbright replied: "I think in all fairness the circumstances were we were responding to an attack. As you have said, the President didn't need this authority to respond to an attack. And I agree with that. . . . But we did resolve, we did act, and, I have said many times, I think wrongly, precipitously, without due consideration to giving authority far beyond that particular attack. . . . This was a mistake."

Sen. Albert Gore (D., Tenn.), a committee member, asked whether Katzenbach's interpretation was "that this resolution authorized a war with China." Katzenbach replied that "in the course of that authorization, . . . there can be risks taken. Other people could be involved. You could have that situation arise." Gore said he "did not vote for the resolution with any understanding that it was tantamount to a declaration of war" and did not intend that the authorization should be construed as sanctioning "the commitment of ground troops." He asked Katzenbach whether the President should not seek Congressional authorization for bombing targets "within seconds" of Red China. Katzenbach replied that the President should not do so. After approving the Tonkin resolution, Katzenbach declared, Congress could not "then proceed to tell the President what he shall bomb, what he shall not bomb, where he dispose his troops, where he shall not."

Katzenbach said Congressional approval of the SEATO treaty in 1955 and of the Tonkin Gulf resolution "fully fulfills the obligations of the Executive in a situation of this kind to participate with the Congress, to give the Congress a full and effective voice, the functional equivalent . . . of the constitutional obligation, with respect to declaring war."

At his news conference Aug. 18, Pres. Johnson was asked about the issue. He replied: "We're well within the rights of what the Congress said in its resolution," but Congress could rescind the resolution if it thought "we have acted unwisely or improperly." "We stated then, and we repeat now, we did not think the resolution was necessary to do what we did and what we're doing. But we thought it was desirable, and we thought if we were going to ask them to stay the whole route and if we expected them to be there on the landing, we ought to ask them to be there on the takeoff." (Asked about the expanded bombing to within 10 miles of China, Mr. Johnson said: "These air strikes are not intended as any threat to Communist China and they do not, in fact, pose any threat to that country. We believe that Peking knows that the United States does not seek to widen the war in Vietnam." The new targets were "directly related to the enemy's capacity to move material into South Vietnam to kill American boys." The expanded air strikes "were made by the most highly trained pilots that we had," and "every human and every technical precaution" was employed "to insure that the ordnance fell on target, and it did.")

Reagan Urges Victory

Gov. Ronald Reagan (R., Calif.) Aug. 18 advocated U.S. disengagement from the Vietnamese problem but specified that "my idea of honorable disengagement is that you win the war." "I can't say technically how you'd do it," he conceded, "but some experts have said too many qualified targets have been put off limits to bombing." Reagan said at a news conference in Des Moines Oct. 25 that consideration should be given to "an outright declaration of war and possible revision of the rules regarding aid and comfort to the enemy." "If we weren't technically in an undeclared war, most of the recent riots would have been covered by the laws against treason and aiding the enemy," he said. "I don't see how the American people can continue to buy their sons being asked to fight and die when the same government is defending the right of the dissenter to take his dissent actually into aiding the enemy that is trying to kill their sons."

Senators Urge Intensified Bombing

The U.S. Senate Preparedness Investigating Subcommittee called unanimously Aug. 31 for an intensification of bombing attacks against North Vietnam and a closing of the port of Haiphong. The port closing and the bombing—"striking all meaningful targets with a military significance"—should be ordered, the subcommittee said, or "we cannot, in good conscience, ask our ground forces to continue their fight in South Vietnam." The panel made the recommendations in a report issued after 8 days of closed hearings on the air war.

In the report, the subcommittee said: Defense Secy. McNamara and his military commanders held "diametrically opposed" views on the use of air power in Vietnam. The current policy of "a carefully controlled, restricted and graduated buildup of bombing pressure" "has not done the job and . . . has been contrary to the best military judgment." "What is needed now is the hard decision to do whatever is necessary, take the risks that have to be taken and apply the force that is required to see the job through." The subcommittee agreed with the Joint Chiefs of Staff that to fight effectively required "isolating" Haiphong "from the rest of the country" and "increasing the interdiction of the lines of communication from Red China." As to the risk that intensified bombing might trigger a "reaction by Communist China and the USSR": "When the decision was made to commit American fighting forces to South Vietnam, certain risks became inevitable."

Defense Secy. McNamara had told the subcommittee Aug. 25 that intensified air attacks would "not materially shorten the war" and that there was no indication that North Vietnam "can be bombed to the negotiating table." McNamara told newsmen that the differences between him and the military chiefs on the bombing issue were "very narrow" differences and did not involve fundamental strategy. The "final decision" in the war, he said, "will not come until we and our allies prove to North Vietnam she cannot win in the South." The prospect of replacing the conflict in the South "with some new kind of air campaign against the North," "however tempting," was "completely illusory," he said, and "would not only be futile but would involve risks to our personnel and to our nation that I am unable to recommend." Testifying Aug. 28, Gen. Harold K. Johnson, Army chief of staff, and Gen. Wallace M. Greene, Marine Corps commandant, advocated a "stronger air campaign" against North Vietnam. (Gen. Johnson had told newsmen Aug. 12, after reporting to Pres. Johnson on an 11-day tour of Vietnam, that "we're winning the war," that he expected by the end of the year to see "very real evidence of progress" on the economic and social fronts of the Vietnamese conflict and that, if no more Communist countries interceded and if the bombing continued, the latest 45,000-man troop increase would be the last one necessary to "see us through to a solution in Vietnam." Johnson affirmed in a speech at Fort McNair, Va. Aug. 28 that, given the current rate of progress, the U.S. would be able to consider within 18 months a scaling down of U.S. troops in Vietnam.)

(Senate Democratic leader Mansfield told the Senate Aug. 31 that McNamara had held that to expand the bombing "much further would be meaningless except in the context of the barbarism of total war on the entire civilian population— a bombing back into the Stone Age, so to speak—or in a context which, while it would not bring significantly close the end of the war, would raise sharply the likelihood of expanded war with the participation of China, and perhaps the Soviet Union.")

Policy Questioned in Congress

Calls for a halt in the bombing of North Vietnam were issued by Kentucky's 2 Republican Senators, Thruston B. Morton and John Sherman Cooper.

Morton, on a TV program Aug. 13, called for a "complete change" of policy to achieve an "honorable disengagement" of U.S. forces from Vietnam. He wanted "a de-escalation of this thing," he said, "a disinvolvement." He reversed his stand on bombing, which he had favored previously. "I think we've got to admit, and be big enough to admit, that we're on a bad wicket and should try something else," he said. Morton charged Sept. 27 that Pres. Johnson had been "brainwashed" by the "military-industrial complex" into believing a military victory could be achieved in Vietnam. "I believe he has been mistakenly committed to a military solution in Vietnam for the past 5 years," Morton said, "with only a brief pause during the election campaign of 1964 to brainwash the American people with the statement that 'the war in Vietnam ought to be fought by Asian boys.' " "If the President has been mistaken, so have I," Morton declared. "In early 1965, when the President began to escalate the war, I supported the increased American military involvement. I was wrong." "I am convinced that further military escalation and an additional United States military commitment will not obtain our objectives of peace in Vietnam," he said. "I am convinced that unless we gradually and, if necessary, unilaterally reduce the scope of our military involvement, we may well destroy the very society we sought to save." Morton called for an indefinite halt in the bombing of North Vietnam and an end to "search-and-destroy" missions by the U.S. forces in South Vietnam. Morton made these remarks before a group of business executives forming Business Executives Move for Vietnam Peace. The executives signed an open letter to the President calling for an end to the bombing, reduced U.S. military activities and negotiations with all parties involved, including the National Liberation Front.

Cooper, in a speech on the Senate floor Oct. 2, urged that the U.S. take the "first step" toward negotiations with an "unconditional cessation" of the bombing of North Vietnam. This "first step," Cooper said, "lies in the choice and control of our country." Regardless of the result of the bombing halt, he said, the U.S. should restrict its military role to "reverse the dangerous expansion of the war." Sen. Gale W. McGee (D., Wyo.), defending Administration policy, said the stake was not only Vietnam but all the nations in Southeast Asia. Cooper responded that "my own judgment is that these countries are going to settle their own destiny, and sometimes they settle it better if we are not there."

Senate Republican whip Thomas H. Kuchel warned in the Senate Oct. 3 that a unilateral halt in bombing would be of "enormous value to the North Vietnamese" by permitting them to supply their forces in South Vietnam.

Sen. Stuart Symington (D., Mo.) proposed Oct. 3 that Hanoi's intentions toward negotiations be tested. He suggested that the U.S. stop all military action, including troop reinforcement, and that at the same time the South Vietnamese government announce it would "negotiate with anybody," including the NLF, and offer amnesty to members of the Viet Cong. If North Vietnam did not respond to these moves and maintained hostilities, Symington said, then the U.S. would "feel free to pursue this war in any manner of its own choosing" and intensify its military effort. (Symington made clear later that he did not mean nuclear military force.)

Sen. Charles H. Percy (R., Ill.) Oct. 5 introduced—with the bipartisan support of 22 other Senators—a resolution urging Pres. Johnson to intensify efforts to have the free nations of Asia make a greater contribution of economic and military aid to the South Vietnamese cause. The U.S., it said, "should not continue to bear an ever-increasing proportion of the fighting in Vietnam." The resolution was opposed by Senate Republican leader Dirksen, who characterized it as "full of mischief." Percy indicated that he did not intend to seek enactment of his resolution but was content that about ⅕ of the Senate membership agreed with it.

House Speaker John W. McCormack (D., Mass.), in a rare appearance in the well of the House, defended Administration policy Oct. 11. He declared: "If I was one of those [whose dissent heartened the enemy], my conscience would disturb me the rest of my life." "Nobody argues with the right to dissent," he said, "but if I had an opinion I thought would be adverse to the interests of my country, I would withhold it."

The President's policy was supported in a Senate speech Oct. 9 by Sen. Hugh Scott (Pa.), former GOP national chairman. Scott warned Republicans that "the war in Vietnam is not, and must not become, a political issue." He said: "It would be unwise to seek political gain from involvement of American servicemen in this far-off land" and "wrong" for his party "to become a 'peace-at-any-price' party." While there was "room for dissent," criticism should not be pursued to the extent that it would "undermine the stature of the Presidency."

"Frustration and dissatisfaction" with the war were not "valid justification for attacks upon the President, especially in the light of absence of alternative courses of action based on anything more substantial than a desire to get it over with and the hope that the other side will behave like good fellows."

In the Senate Oct. 19, Sen. Henry M. Jackson cautioned against the "negative" tone of the anti-Administration criticism. Saying he was speaking out because of a "fear that our frustrations are showing," Jackson warned that the war cannot be ended "by attacking each other here at home" but "can" and "will" be lost "if we destroy our confidence in each other." Jackson defended the Administration's policy goal "to create a balance of forces in Asia such as we were able to create in Europe."

Rep. Morris K. Udall (D., Ariz.) said in a speech in Tucson, Ariz. Oct. 22 that the U.S. was on "a mistaken and dangerous road" in Vietnam and should stop further escalation and "start bringing American boys home and start turning this war back to the Vietnamese." Udall said he had made a "mistake" when, previously, he had supported Administration policy in Vietnam. Current U.S. policy, he warned, would require the deployment of "several hundred thousand more American troops" in Vietnam, the expenditure of $40-$50 billion a year "or more" and would result in "a wider war." (Udall told a questioner that his brother, Interior Secy. Stewart L. Udall, had tried to persuade him not to make the speech.)

In a Senate speech Oct. 24, Sen. Albert Gore (D., Tenn.) proposed that the U.S. "honorably extricate" itself from Vietnam by accepting neutralization of Southeast Asia. He said: "We have stumbled into a morass in Vietnam," and neutralization was "the best we can hope to achieve under present circumstances." "We should be willing to accept less than what is and has been our real objective in Southeast Asia in return for a cessation of the conflict." The war was raising "the danger" that the USSR and Red China "will be dragged into the quagmire with us and cause a wider war, perhaps the war which will be the final holocaust."

Senate Democratic leader Mansfield and 54 co-sponsors

introduced in the Senate Oct. 25 a resolution urging a Presidential initiative to have the UN Security Council take up a U.S. proposal to discuss the conflict in Vietnam.

Administration Views

Pres. Johnson declared at the White House Sept. 22, in a speech before about 200 visiting leaders of fraternal and ethnic groups, that it was "worth paying the price" to keep South Vietnam from falling to the Communists. He warned that "the price of Communist conquest in Southeast Asia, of risking a 3d World War by our failure to stand in Vietnam now, is a far heavier price to pay."

Mr. Johnson said Sept. 28 that "we recognize and always have recognized that there can be no military solution to the problems of Southeast Asia. But we have also had to face the hard reality that only military power can bar aggression and make a political solution possible." He pledged to continue the Vietnam effort "until there is a response that might lead to a just political settlement."

At a Democratic fund-raising event in Washington Oct. 7, Pres. Johnson referred to his current low standing in popularity polls and said he was getting much advice on how to recoup his standing "cheaply and fast." He said he knew he could temporarily regain popularity "by renouncing the struggle in Vietnam or escalating it to the red line of danger." But he would do neither, he declared. He said: He would hold firm in Vietnam because that "road does lead to a free Asia and a more secure America"; "I believe the American people will follow its course, not blithely, not cheerfully, for they lament the waste of war, but with a firm determination to see it through."

Vice Pres. Hubert H. Humphrey, speaking at the National Shrine of Our Lady of Czestochowa in Doylestown, Pa. Oct. 15, asserted that the U.S. was in Vietnam because the U.S. "has a stake in freedom and because our own national security is best protected when the enemies of freedom are denied victory." He said: "Imagine what kind of a world we would be living in if the sweep of Asian communism should include all of Southeast Asia. . . . The entire power structure of the world would be destroyed and drastically changed." "The threat to our security is in Asia, and we are fighting there not only for the Vietnamese but for ourselves and the future of our country." "The hope of victory for the enemy is not in his power but in our division, our weariness, our uncertainty. The road to peace that you want and that I want is not in our words but in our unity, our steadfastness and having the enemy know it."

Humphrey, addressing 2,500 business executives in Washington Oct. 23, said: Non-Communist Southeast Asian leaders believed that if the U.S. failed in Vietnam, "they would be under unbearable pressure from a nuclear-armed Communist China." "If our policy of mutual security and containment of Communist power in Europe has been right, the same logic and compelling reasons require the application of such a policy in Asia." "We do not seek to make mainland China our enemy. We do not seek to encircle or crush her. What we seek to do is to help the independent nations of Asia strengthen themselves against subversion and aggression so that a new generation of mainland Chinese leaders may, in time, see the futility of subversion, wars of liberation and militancy—and that peaceful coexistence may be possible." While dissent in the U.S. was "useful" and "interesting," "it has not offered realistic alternative courses for action today."

State Secy. Rusk had told reporters Oct. 12 that Congressional proposals for peace initiatives—a bombing halt or limitation, UN action or a new Geneva conference—were futile because of Hanoi's opposition. As for unilateral halting of the bombing, without the pressure of the bombing of North Vietnam, "where would be the incentive for peace?" He would "be glad to hear from any . . . foreign ministers what their governments will do if we stop the bombing, and there is no response from Hanoi." Rusk denied a report (published Oct. 11 in the syndicated column of Rowland Evans and Robert Novak) that he had assailed "pseudo-intellectual" critics of the U.S. war policy and that he had charged that the antiwar protest movement was controlled by Communists. Sen. Fulbright, in Hot Springs, Ark. Oct. 14, accused Rusk of a "McCarthy-type crusade" against war critics. "One thing you're not supposed to do is oppose the war, according to the

Secretary of State and some others," he said. He rejected what he called a constant refrain heard in Washington that "if you oppose the war you're aiding the enemy."

In a speech at the University of Kansas in Lawrence Oct. 17, State Undersecy. Eugene V. Rostow said dissent in the U.S. was "rousing" a new isolationist spirit in the U.S. "Stirring these nostalgic yearnings for the past constitutes a real and present danger," he said. He and State Undersecy. Nicholas deB. Katzenbach, who spoke Oct. 17 at Fairfield (Conn.) University, cited the Korean war. "Pres. Truman's firmness and restraint in Korea achieved nearly 12 years of relative peace," Rostow said. Katzenbach said the U.S. "commitments to South Vietnam are far better grounded than were those to South Korea at the time of the aggression there," while the criticism of both wars was "almost interchangeable" —that the Koreans or South Vietnamese were "not doing enough for themselves" and that their governments were "not really representative." Katzenbach said: It would be "a grievous and dangerous delusion to believe all our problems would be solved if we withdrew from Vietnam, or from Asia, or from anywhere else. On this shrinking planet, the strongest nation in the world cannot so easily escape its responsibilities."

'Yellow Peril'?

State Secy. Rusk asserted at his press conference Oct. 12 that the U.S. was fighting for its own security in Vietnam and that Communist China threatened the world. Sen. Eugene J. McCarthy (D., Minn.) charged in the Senate Oct. 16 that Rusk had raised the "specter" of the "yellow peril."

Rusk had said in his Oct. 12 new conference: "If any who would be our adversary should suppose that our treaties are a bluff, or will be abandoned if the going gets tough, the result could be catastrophe for all mankind." ". . . Those who would place in question the credibility of the pledged word of the United States under our mutual security treaties would subject this nation to mortal danger." "Within the next decade or 2 there will be a billion Chinese on the mainland armed with nuclear weapons. . . . The free nations of Asia will make up at least a billion people. They don't want China to overrun them on the basis of a doctrine of the world revolution." "From the strategic point of view it is not very attractive to think of the world cut in 2 by Asian communism, reaching out through Southeast Asia and Indonesia . . . and that these . . . people in the free nations . . . should be under the deadly and constant pressure of the authorities in Peking, so that their future is circumscribed by fear." The Administration was "not picking out Peking as some sort of special enemy. Peking has nominated itself by proclaiming a militant doctrine of the world revolution, and doing something about it."

McCarthy, accusing Rusk Oct. 16 of raising "yellow peril" fears, said: This could only "obscure the issue upon which judgment should be made and cause further frustration and division within the country as well as between the Congress and the Executive Branch"; "if this is the specter that is haunting Asia, it is difficult to see how we will rid Asia of it even though we achieve an unpredictable and total victory in South Vietnam."

A State Department statement later Oct. 16 said Rusk "wholly repudiates the effort to put into his mouth or into his mind the notion of a 'yellow peril.' " The concerns of the free nations of Asia over the militancy of Red China, the statement said, "have much to do with their security, with our security and with the peace of the world. They have nothing to do with race."

Pres. Johnson commented Oct. 25 on the injection of the "yellow peril" issue into the debate over U.S. policy in Vietnam. "Let me take just a moment to point out the absurdity of this charge," Johnson said. "We have utterly repudiated the racist nonsense of an earlier era." "We fought side by side with Asians at Bataan and Corregidor, in Korea, and now in Vietnam," the President noted.

March on Pentagon

Thousands of Americans participated in a massive demonstration in Washington Oct. 21 in protest against U.S. policy in Vietnam. Demonstrators first attended a rally at Lincoln Memorial, and then many of them marched to the Pentagon in nearby Arlington, Va., where they held another rally and a vigil that continued through the early hours of

Oct. 23. Many demonstrators at the Pentagon were arrested after clashing with U.S. Army troops and federal marshals who had been called out to prevent the Defense Department's headquarters from being stormed. The demonstrators included a wide variety of participants, among them liberals, radicals, costumed black nationalists, hippies and students. The Washington demonstration, organized by the National Mobilization Committee to End the War in Vietnam,* was the culmination of nationwide anti-draft protests that had started Oct. 16. U.S. Army and police authorities estimated that 55,000 persons had taken part in the Lincoln Memorial rally. But David Dellinger, chairman of the National Mobilization Committee, said the true figure was 150,000. The crowd in front of the Pentagon was reported to number 35,000. According to military authorities, 686 persons were arrested, most of them in the Pentagon area, during the 2-day demonstration. 13 U.S. marshals, 10 soldiers and 24 demonstrators were reported injured in the clashes, which saw the paraders circle the Pentagon and throng its main steps. At the height of the demonstration, 2,500 U.S. Army troops were deployed to keep order, and 2,500 were held in reserve.

(The Justice Department disclosed Nov. 13 that 580 of those arrested had been convicted of federal law violations. 51 of those convicted had served or were serving 35-day jail terms. Convicted demonstrators paid a total of $7,944 in fines.

* Plans for the demonstration had been announced by the National Mobilization Committee in New York Aug. 28. A committee statement, read by the Rev. Thomas Lee Hayes, executive director of the Episcopal Peace Fellowship, one of the sponsoring peace groups, called on "all Americans who oppose the government's aggression in Vietnam" to march on Washington "for a direct, personal and collective confrontation with the warmakers." The aim, the statement said, would be to "shut down the Pentagon. We will fill the hallways and block the entrances. Thousands of people will disrupt the center of the American war machine." The committee had formerly been known as the Spring Mobilization to End the War in Vietnam. Supporters of the demonstration who participated in the Aug. 28 announcement included SNCC Chrmn. H. Rap Brown, comedian Dick Gregory, Prof. Robert Greenblatt of Cornell University, ex-Co-Chrmn. Jerry Rubin of the Vietnam Day Committee of Berkeley, Calif. and Msgr. Charles Owen Rice of Pittsburgh. The Rev. James Bevel was the committee's national director.

The Defense Department had reported Oct. 25 that the Pentagon protest had cost the government $1,078,500, including $641,000 to transport troops to protect the Pentagon.)

Among those arrested Oct. 21 were Dellinger, novelist Norman Mailer, Mrs. Dagmar Wilson, head of the Women Strike for Peace, the Rev. John Boyles, an assistant Episcopal chaplain at Yale University, and MIT Prof. N. A. Chomsky. Dellinger was fined $50 and sentenced to 30 days in prison. Mrs. Wilson was fined $25 and given a 30-day suspended sentence. Mailer was fined $50 and given a 30-day jail term, with 25 days suspended.

In an address at the Lincoln Memorial rally Oct. 21, Dr. Benjamin Spock said: "We are convinced that this war which Lyndon Johnson is waging is disastrous to our country in every way and that we, the protesters, are the ones who may help save our country if we can persuade enough of our fellow citizens to think and vote as we do." The enemy, "we believe in all sincerity, is Lyndon Johnson, whom we elected as a peace candidate in 1964 and who betrayed us within 3 months, who has stubbornly led us deeper and deeper into a bloody quagmire in which uncounted hundreds of thousands of Vietnamese men, women and children have died, and 13,000 young Americans, too."

Following the Lincoln Memorial rally, 30,000-35,000 of the demonstrators marched 2 miles, across the Arlington Memorial Bridge over the Potomac River, to the Pentagon. They were restricted by a government permit to a huge parking lot on the north side of the Pentagon and to a 20-acre grass triangle below the mall entrance, one of the 2 main entrances to the building. The building itself was surrounded by troops, as were the mall entrance and the area near the parking lot. Less than 2 hours after their arrival, about 2,000 demonstrators, crossing the lines authorized by the permit, pushed up the steps and clashed with marshals backed by troops. At this point, troops carrying tear-gas grenades emerged from the Pentagon building to reinforce the guard. About an hour later another crowd of 3,000 dashed to another entrance of the building. 30 demonstrators managed to get into the Pentagon but were quickly ejected by troops and club-wielding marshals.

Several tear-gas canisters exploded outside the building during the day's mêlées. The Defense Department said the troops had not used the tear gas and claimed that the demonstrators had. Demonstration leaders charged that Defense Department officials "lied." Many demonstrators taunted the troops with shouted obscenities. Some bottles and eggs were thrown. Shortly before the demonstrators surged toward the Pentagon, David Dellinger announced that some marchers would commit civil disobedience by crossing into the off-limits area. He and Norman Mailer were the first to do so and were arrested.

After the clashes subsided and most of the marchers left, several hundred war protesters remained for a sit-down near the main entrance to the Pentagon. 206 of them were arrested shortly after midnight Oct. 22 for refusing to disperse as the 2-day permit for the demonstration expired.

Dellinger announced after a meeting of the National Mobilization Committee in Washington Oct. 22 that the group had decided to change its tactics from peaceful parades to "confrontations" with the government by sit-ins and other acts of civil disobedience. Dellinger said: "We have been calling for a step-up to a new phase in the movement. We were gratified and enthused that so many people came in from all over the country ready for this."

(Demonstrations supporting U.S. fighting men in Vietnam were held in the New York area and other parts of the U.S. Oct. 21-22. The demonstrations were organized by the National Committee for Responsible Patriotism. A 31-hour vigil by almost 1,000 persons was staged in Manhattan's Battery Park Oct. 21-22 in support of Americans in Vietnam.)

The Washington anti-war protest was paralleled by demonstrations in the major cities of Western Europe and Japan Oct. 21-22. Many were anti-U.S. rather than anti-war in tone. In London, police clashed with more than 3,000 demonstrators who attempted to storm the U.S. embassy. In Copenhagen, fighting broke out between police and 15,000 demonstrators who marched on the U.S. embassy. Demonstrators threw stones through embassy windows. Molotov cocktails were tossed at the building, but did not explode.

'Ike' & Truman in Group Backing U.S. Policy

A new committee, including in its membership ex-Presidents Harry S. Truman and Dwight D. Eisenhower, was formed Oct. 25 to speak for those "who have consistently opposed rewarding international aggressors from Adolf Hitler to Mao Tse-tung." The new group, named the Citizens Committee for Peace with Freedom in Vietnam, issued a statement expressing strong support for the current U.S. policy in Vietnam and opposing "surrender, however camouflaged." The statement said: "America cannot afford to let naked aggression or the suppression of freedom go unchallenged"; "our objective in Vietnam is to make the price too high and the risk too great for the aggressor." But the statement opposed "unnecessarily risking a general war in Asia or a nuclear war in the world." A committee co-chairman, ex-Sen. Paul H. Douglas (D., Ill.), said the group was backing "the office of the President" but was "not committed to support [Pres.] Lyndon Johnson." The other co-chairman: Gen. of the Army Omar N. Bradley, ex-chairman of the Joint Chiefs of Staff.

Eisenhower, appearing on CBS-TV Nov. 28, advocated a limited U.S. invasion of North Vietnam to eliminate the "menace" of enemy artillery positions near the demilitarized zone separating North and South Vietnam. He added that "it wouldn't bother me" if U.S. forces pursued retreating enemy forces into Cambodia or Laos. "I'd go at them as long as they'd come in there in the first place," he said. "And . . . if an airplane attacked me and we wanted to chase him, I'd go in wherever his base was." Eisenhower said he would favor hot pursuit even over Communist China. Eisenhower made the statements in an interview taped Nov. 24 with Gen. Bradley. Bradley concurred that the U.S. could make limited ground or sea attacks on North Vietnam and had the right to "hot pursuit" into Laos and Cambodia. (Ex-Vice Pres. Richard M. Nixon said Nov. 29 that the diplomatic risks of "hot pursuit" into neighboring countries appeared to "outweigh" the military advantages. He said the U.S. "should be very cautious about taking any action that could be interpreted as widening the war.")

Eisenhower Dec. 22 urged continued public support for the war effort and said world peace and the fate of Southeast Asia was at stake in the conflict. Interviewed in Indio, Calif., Eisenhower said: "It's as simple as this. Some 13,000 Americans have given up their lives to keep South Vietnam free and independent and to stem the tide of Communist aggression across Southeast Asia. . . . To pull out now under whatever guise would mean the end ultimately of all the free and independent countries of that area. You pull out our armed forces from South Vietnam and it will only be a question of time before every country up to the borders of India fall under the Communist heel. That includes Laos and Cambodia—as well as Thailand and Burma, and I'm not too sure about India either, once they have got that far." "We can win this war if the American people are willing to see it through."

Anti-Draft Movement

Protests against U.S. policy in Vietnam were often coupled with attacks on the Selective Service system and recruiting for the armed forces.

The leaders of 15 student organizations of diverse political affiliation signed a resolution in Washington Feb. 5 calling for the end of the draft. The document urged establishment of a voluntary national service system to eliminate "such social ills as ignorance, poverty, racial discrimination and war." The statement was issued at the end of a 2-day conference on voluntary national service sponsored by *Moderator* magazine. It reportedly was the first time that leaders of such diverse groups as the leftwing Students for a Democratic Society, the rightwing Young Americans for Freedom and the moderate Youth & College Division of the National Association for the Advancement of Colored People had taken a common stand on a controversial political question.

The formation of a movement to help youths resist the draft was disclosed Sept. 27. A group of 320 professors, writers, ministers and other professionals signed an advertisement appearing in the *New Republic* and the *N.Y. Review of Books* for funds for the drive. Many signers were said to have pledged acts of disobedience to challenge the government. The statement, "A Call to Resist Illegitimate Authority," asserted that the Vietnamese war outraged the "deepest moral and religious sense" of young Americans. It urged "all men of goodwill to join us in this confrontation with immoral authority," which was perpetrating "agression in Vietnam." Among the signers: Dr. Linus Pauling, Nobel Prize winner; poet Robert Lowell; anthropologist Ashley Montagu; the Right Rev. James A. Pike, resigned bishop of the Episcopal Diocese of California; the Rev. William Sloan Coffin Jr., chaplain at Yale University; Dr. Benjamin Spock; writers Edgar Snow and Susan Sontag.

Demonstrations against the draft were held throughout the U.S. Oct. 16-21 by opponents of U.S. policy in Vietnam. Major incidents occurred in Oakland, Calif. Oct. 16-17 and 20. While 400-500 persons picketed Oct. 16 in front of the Northern California Draft Induction Center, about 40 demonstrators sat down in front of 3 entrances to the building to prevent inductees from entering. 125 pickets were arrested, including folk singer Joan Baez. Miss Baez and the others received 10-day prison sentences in Oakland Municipal Court Oct. 17. About 3,000 anti-war demonstrators showed up at the Oakland induction center Oct. 17 in another effort to bar entrance to inductees. A force of 400 police and highway patrolmen routed the demonstrators with clubs and chemical sprays. 20 persons were arrested in the 10-minute mêlée. About 6,500 persons staged a silent demonstration Oct. 20 near the Oakland center but were dispersed by police.

Other anti-draft protests were staged the same week in Los Angeles, Boston (where 67 youths publicly burned their draft cards), New York, Chicago and smaller cities. 1,000 students fought police Oct. 19 at Brooklyn (N.Y.) College when they attempted to disperse demonstrators protesting the presence of U.S. Navy recruiters at the school. (The college was virtually closed Oct. 20 by a student strike protesting alleged police brutality during the clashes.)

An anti-draft statement issued in New York Oct. 3 by representatives of 320 signers of "A Call to Resist Illegitimate Authority" pledged to make "synagogues and churches across the country sanctuaries for conscientious objectors." Coffin of Yale said the "arrests of those who refuse to answer the draft will have to be made in a synagogue or church. Any man who asks asylum in a church will be given it." Civil disobedience, Coffin said, was "an act of religious conscience." The signers of the petition, including 35 clergymen, had organized the anti-draft protests held throughout the U.S. Oct. 16-21.

In a statement issued in Detroit Oct. 25, the Clergy & Laymen Concerned About Vietnam pledged "to aid and abet" American youths in resisting the military draft and "to be prepared to pay whatever price may be exacted to defend the right of conscience our government refuses to honor." The statement, signed by 18 Protestant, Catholic and Jewish clergymen and supported by about 50 delegates to the U.S. Conference on Church & Society, was circulated among the 700 participants at the organization's conference in Detroit. Expressing determination to "keep faith with those who refuse to surrender their consciences to the state," the statement proposed that churches and synagogues establish counseling centers to advise youths on how to avoid military service. Signers included Coffin of Yale, Methodist Bishop Charles F. Golden of Nashville, Episcopal Bishop William Gordon Jr. of Alaska, Episcopal Bishop C. Kilmer Meyers of California, ex-Episcopal Bishop James A. Pike and Rabbi Abraham Heschel, a Jewish philosopher.

Selective Service director Lewis B. Hershey confirmed Nov. 2 a policy decision to require the early induction of draft-eligible persons interfering with draft procedures and the prosecution of culprits not subject to the draft. Hershey, in a letter dated Oct. 26, had urged local draft boards to draft as soon as possible any registrants violating draft laws or interfering with recruiting or the laws' operations. Hershey said he had "talked with somebody" at the White House before issuing the letter. Hershey came under considerable academic and Senatorial attack for his proposal. In a joint statement issued Dec. 9, Hershey and Atty. Gen. Ramsey Clark stressed that lawful protesters were still under protection of the law but that violators of the Selective Service Act faced early induction or legal action. (The U.S. Court of Appeals for the 2d Circuit had ruled unanimously in N.Y.

City Jan. 30 that local draft boards could not punish registrants who publicly protested the Vietnamese war and the draft by reclassifying them into 1-A status. The court said that local draft boards had acted without jurisdiction and had threatened the First Amendment's rights of free speech and assembly by reclassifying 2 University of Michigan students after their arrest at an anti-war demonstration.)

A coalition of about 40 anti-war organizations staged "Stop the Draft Week" demonstrations throughout the U.S. Dec. 4-8. Among organizations that comprised the Stop the Draft Week Committee, sponsors of the demonstrations, were the War Resisters League, Women Strike for Peace, the Women's International League for Peace & Freedom, the U.S. Communist Party, the Resistance, the W. E. B. DuBois Clubs, the Workshop in Nonviolence and the Student Christian Movement. The marchers sought to disrupt U.S. armed forces induction centers.

The largest and most violent of the demonstrations took place in New York, where thousands of persons, largely youths of draft age, attempted unsuccessfully to close down the induction center on Whitehall St. The demonstrations spread to other parts of the city, and police and demonstrators clashed repeatedly. Police arrested 585 persons Dec. 5-8. Among those seized were Dr. Benjamin Spock, poet Allen Ginsberg and Conor Cruise O'Brien, an NYU professor, who had headed a UN mission to Katanga during the 1961 Congo crisis. Spock and Ginsberg were arrested after they took part in a symbolic sit-down on the steps of the Whitehall building. After attempting unsuccessfully to block inductees from entering the induction center Dec. 6, about 2,500 demonstrators marched uptown and disrupted traffic. In one incident, police prevented demonstrators from picketing the UN building.

Oakland police Dec. 18 arrested 218 of about 750 anti-war demonstrators who tried to block the armed forces induction center in the city. Nearly 50 persons were arrested in a 2d day of demonstrations in front of the induction center Dec. 19. Among those arrested was Joan Baez. She received a 45-day jail term and started serving the sentence Dec. 20.

Similar protests took place at induction centers in Cincinnati, O., Madison, Wis., New Haven, Conn. and other cities near major university campuses.

The Administrative Office of the U.S. Courts reported Dec. 12 that convictions for draft law violations had increased from a total of 372 in fiscal 1966 to 748 in fiscal 1967 (the 12 months ended June 30). In fiscal 1965 the average prison sentence was 21 months, in fiscal 1966 26.4 months and in fiscal 1967 32.1 months.

Demonstrators Vs. Dow

There were demonstrations in various parts of the country during 1967 in efforts to block employe recruiting by the Dow Chemical Co., which manufactured napalm used in Vietnam. The protests reached their peak in October.

Hundreds of students at the University of Wisconsin (Madison) had demonstrated Feb. 22 in protest against the presence of Dow representatives on the campus. 21 students were arrested. The student Senate Mar. 2, by 19-11 vote, barred the Students for a Democratic Society from using campus facilities because of SDS' involvement in the demonstrations.

About 20 University of Minnesota students engaged in an anti-Dow sleep-in the night of Oct. 24-25. They said they believed the university was "for human development, not human destruction." About 300 persons picketed the University of Illinois chemistry building Oct. 25 and participated in a sit-down outside a room used by Dow job recruiters; 7 of the demonstrators were expelled Nov. 22. 200 Harvard students participated Oct. 25 in a sit-down in front of a conference room occupied by a Dow recruiter. Harvard officials announced Oct. 31 that 74 of the demonstrators had been put on probation for their "forcible obstruction" of the Dow recruiter. A sit-down by about 125 persons at the University of Connecticut Oct. 31 prevented Dow representatives from carrying out scheduled job interviews.

About 2,000 San Jose (Calif.) State College students demonstrating Nov. 20 against Dow were attacked by police after they refused to disperse. About 50 policemen charged into the crowd and threw 5 tear-gas grenades. Defying Gov. Ronald Reagan's warning against further demonstrations, San

Jose students Nov. 21 again staged an anti-Dow demonstration. About 500 students marched through an auditorium meeting of students and faculty and picketed the college administration building.

200 NYU students and faculty members invaded an NYU office Nov. 29 and prevented a Dow representative from interviewing job applicants.

Dow spokesmen had said in New York Oct. 26 that the university protests had not affected their recruitment program. Dow said that the firm's job recruiters generally carried a statement explaining the company's position on napalm. It said in part: "Our company has made the decision to continue to produce napalm B and other materials as long as they are needed by our government"; "as long as we are involved" in Vietnam "we believe we are fulfilling our responsibility to this national commitment of a democratic society." Dow Dec. 8 released a letter in which Defense Secy. McNamara lauded the firm "for the contributions" it was "making to our commitment in Vietnam." McNamara said the protests against Dow job recruiters were misdirected because "those are matters of military and foreign policy over which private industry has no control." Denying that American forces were employing napalm indiscriminately in Vietnam, McNamara said it was being employed with precautions that were "as painstaking as we can make them without hamstringing our military operations."

Dissent in Uniform

There were a number of cases of members of the armed forces involved in actions opposing U.S. policy in Vietnam:

■ An Army court-martial in Fort Benning, Ga. Feb. 23 sentenced Sp/4 J. Harry Muir, 22, of Goldsboro, N.C. to 2 years at hard labor for having refused to serve in Vietnam. Muir also was convicted of going absent without leave to present his case to newspapers. Muir pleaded guilty to all charges.

■ Air Force Capt. Dale E. Noyd, 33, sued in Federal District Court in Denver Mar. 27 to be reclassified as a conscientious objector to the Vietnamese war. Noyd filed the suit after authorities at the Air Force Academy in Denver, where he was stationed as a psychology instructor, ordered him transferred to the 27th Tactical Fighter Wing at Cannon Air Force Base, N.M. Noyd's suit requested that the Air Force be required to accept his resignation or to assign him to non-combat duties.

Noyd, a career officer pilot, objected to his reassignment on the ground that Cannon Air Force Base was a replacement training center for "assignees to Southeast Asia, and specifically to combat in Vietnam." Noyd had stated previously that the war in Vietnam was "unjust and immoral, and if ordered to do so, I shall refuse to fight in that war." The Supreme Court ruled June 2 that the Air Force had the right to assign Noyd to combat duty in Vietnam.

■ An Army court-martial at Fort Sill, Okla. July 31 dismissed charges against Pvt. Andrew Stapp, 23, of Merion, Pa., who had been accused of leaving his base in violation of a detention order to address an anti-war rally at the University of Oklahoma in Norman. Stapp, who called himself a Communist and said he would not fight if sent to Vietnam, had been convicted by a court-martial June 1 and restricted to the base for disobeying an officer's order to open his foot locker. The foot locker contained Communist and leftwing literature.

■ The U.S. Court of Military Appeals in Washington Aug. 4 upheld the 1965 Army court-martial of 2d Lt. Henry H. Howe Jr., 25, of Boulder, Colo. Howe had been sentenced to dismissal from service and a year at hard labor for participating in an anti-war demonstration in 1965 outside Ft. Bliss, Tex. In rejecting his plea, the Military Appeals tribunal held that Howe's involvement in the demonstration was illegal because his presence represented "a danger to discipline within our armed forces."

■ Army Pvt. Ronald Lockman, 23, of Philadelphia was jailed in Oakland, Calif. Sept. 15 when he refused to board a troop plane for Vietnam. An Army court-martial in San Francisco Nov. 13 convicted Pvt. Lockman of refusing to obey orders sending him to Vietnam. He was sentenced to 2½ years at hard labor and a dishonorable discharge.

■ The U.S. Court of Military Appeals in Washington Sept. 26 upheld the court-martial convictions of 3 Army privates who had refused to go to Vietnam. The 3—Dennis Mora and James A. Johnson of New York and David A. Samas—were serving 3-year sentences.

■ Chief Federal District Judge Richard E. Robinson in Omaha Sept. 29 rejected a plea by Airman 3/C Richard A. Saunders, 21, to be discharged from the Air Force because he had become a conscientious objector. Saunders, stationed at Offutt Air Force Base near Omaha, had filed his suit to prevent the Air Force from sending him to Vietnam.

■ A Japanese pacifist group in Tokyo said Nov. 13 that 4 U.S. Navy enlisted men opposed to the war in Vietnam had deserted by refusing to return to the aircraft carrier Intrepid when it left Japan Oct. 24 after a recreational visit. The ship had been conducting air operations against North Vietnam. The 4 deserters were identified by the Japanese as Airman John Michael Barilla, 20, of Catonsville, Md., Airman Richard D. Bailey, 19, of Jacksonville, Fla., Airman Apprentice Michael Anthony Lindner, 19, of Mount Pocono, Pa. and Airman Apprentice Craig William Anderson, 20, of San Jose, Calif.

The deserters arrived in Stockholm, Sweden via Moscow Dec. 29 and were given temporary asylum.

■ Capt. Howard Brett Levy, 30, a dermatologist from Brooklyn, was convicted by a general court-martial in Fort Jackson, S.C. June 2 of willfully disobeying orders and making disloyal statements about the U.S.' policy in Vietnam. He was sentenced June 3 to dismissal from the Army, forfeiture of all pay and allowances and confinement at hard labor for 3 years. The Supreme Court May 22 had rejected an appeal to stay the court-martial proceedings, and the high court Nov. 13 rejected an appeal to review a lower court's refusal to bar the military trial. Levy had been charged under provisions of the Uniform Code of Military Justice with: (1) refusing to give Special Forces (Green Beret) medics elementary instruction in skin disease; (2) trying to promote "disloyalty and disaffection among the troops" by making statements "disloyal to the U.S. and prejudicial to good order and discipline"; (3) making "intemperate, defamatory, contemptuous and disrespectful statements" to enlisted men; (4) conduct unbecoming an officer, specifically for sending to a sergeant in Okinawa a letter in which he described U.S. foreign policy as a "diabolical evil"; (5) intending to impair loyalty, morale and discipline of the armed forces by suggesting to another sergeant in a letter that he return to the U.S. and work for the cause of suppressed Negroes and poor whites.

Levy had refused to instruct the Green Berets on the ground that they would use medicine as "another tool of political persuasion" and that this would be "a complete prostitution of what medicine stands for." He charged that the Green Beret medics were "cross-trained"—taught to fight as well as heal—and were "liars, thieves and killers of peasants" and "murderers of women and children."

Levy's attorney, Charles Morgan Jr., Southern regional director of the American Civil Liberties Union, had filed suit in Federal District Court in Washington, D.C. Apr. 17 against Defense Secy. Robert S. McNamara and 14 other officials and military officers. Requesting a preliminary injunction to bar the court-martial, Morgan contended that military regulations under which Levy was being tried were vague, overly broad and violated Levy's constitutional right of free speech. The injunction was denied.

In the course of the court-martial, which opened May 10, the court's chief officer, Col. Earl V. Brown, ruled that Levy's attorneys could introduce evidence in an effort to prove that the Green Berets were guilty of war crimes and crimes against humanity as defined by the Nuremberg war crimes tribunal. To make a *prima facie* case of war crimes, the defense would have to prove that the atrocities were part of a general policy or general practice and not isolated incidents. Morgan conceded May 23 that Levy had "never accused this nation of war crimes, crimes against humanity or genocide." Although Levy disagreed with U.S. policy in Vietnam, Morgan said, he had only accused the Green Berets of atrocities. Although defense witnesses said Special Forces personnel tolerated atrocities by Vietnamese troops, none said they had seen Special Forces men themselves commit any. Brown ruled May 25 that the defense had failed to support its charges that Green Berets were guilty of calculated atrocities in Vietnam.

Gavin Restates Criticism

Lt. Gen. James N. Gavin, a critic of U.S. policy in Vietnam, visited South Vietnam Nov. 1-7 as a guest of Gen. Westmoreland. Gavin toured the battle areas, was briefed by American officers, visited villages and conferred with South Vietnamese Pres. Nguyen Van Thieu. Before leaving Saigon Nov. 7, Gavin made clear that his critical views of U.S. involvement in Vietnam remained unaltered. In a fuller assessment of his trip, Gavin said on the NBC-TV program "Meet the Press" Nov. 12 that under current U.S. policy, American troops would have to stay in Vietnam 5-10 years, with or without a military victory. He criticized American officials for not publicly acknowledging this. Gavin took issue with the U.S.' demand for North Vietnamese reciprocity as the price for halting American bombing of the North. He said: "They don't bomb us, so they can't talk about 'we don't bomb you if you don't bomb us.' We will continue to supply our troops to the front [during a suspension of the raids], so they will continue to supply theirs. Yet we expect them not to, I presume, as a reciprocal act."

Gavin called for: (1) an unconditional halt in the "immoral and militarily unproductive" bombing; (2) a freeze of U.S. military strength in Vietnam; (3) a greater U.S. effort to start peace talks; (4) the right of the South Vietnamese to organize "as a political entity—be it partly neutralist, or whatever it is." Advocating "a buffer country between ourselves and Red China," Gavin warned that if the American military effort continued "at this rate," Ho Chi Minh "will be absolutely in the arms of Peking and will be unable to act on his own." Gavin also indicated support of the National Liberation Front as a nationalist movement independent of North Vietnam; he said U.S. policy was pushing the NLF "into the arms of Hanoi."

N.Y. Protest Vs. Rusk

Hundreds of anti-war demonstrators clashed with police in New York Nov. 14 during a rally in protest against State Secy. Rusk, who was attending a dinner of the Foreign Policy

Association. 40 marchers were arrested and many persons were injured, including 5 policemen. More than 3,000 persons participated in the demonstration, sponsored jointly by the 5th Avenue Vietnam Peace Parade Committee and Students for a Democratic Society (SDS).

Demonstrators carrying anti-war placards had gathered in front of the New York Hilton Hotel, which Rusk had entered to address the diners. Violence erupted when a police guard of about 1,000 men prevented more marchers from gathering in the vicinity of the hotel by blocking off side streets. In ensuing incidents ranging to the Times Square area, 12 blocks to the south, a minority of more militant demonstrators stopped traffic, hurled plastic bags of cattle blood, stones, bottles and bricks at police, cars and buildings and taunted police and passersby. SDS staff member Robert Gottlieb said Nov. 16 that the demonstration was part of new tactics in which persons involved in foreign policy decisions may be pursued wherever they go.

The 5th Avenue group's director, Eric Weinberger, had conceded Nov. 15 that plans had been made to permit some "resistance activities." "We were in agreement that demonstrations must be conducted on all levels, that just peaceful demonstrations are not effective," he reported. "Provo-type actions are necessary to obstruct the functioning of the war machine." But the police, in severely restricting picketing activities at the hotel, in contravention of a police-peace group agreement, had provoked more civil disobedience than had been planned, Weinberger asserted.

300 pickets marched Dec. 6 outside the Waldorf-Astoria Hotel while Rusk was addressing a luncheon of the National Association of Manufacturers. Alluding to the pickets, Rusk said: "I gather there's a welcoming committee . . . outside. I didn't see a representative of Hanoi prepared to talk to me about peace. I haven't seen a group produced anywhere in the world with a representative of Hanoi ready to talk. If they are ready, I at least would be there."

LBJ on Dissenters

Pres. Johnson said Nov. 1 that he did not think the anti-war demonstrators had "made any great contribution to solving the problem that we all are so earnestly seeking to solve." If they were aware of enemy propaganda based on dissent in the U.S., he said, he thought the protesters "would agree with me that all their private proposals and statements have not contributed a great deal to the solution that we so eagerly seek." The President made these remarks at his news conference.

(Hanoi radio had reported Oct. 17 that the NLF Oct. 16 had formed a new organization designed to spur anti-war sentiment in the U.S. This new South Vietnam People's Committee for Solidarity with the American People sought to encourage American desertions by aiding U.S. servicemen or civilians in Vietnam "who wish to return to their country or go to another place," the broadcast said. According to other Hanoi broadcasts, the committee was appealing to Americans "to step up the struggle to demand an end to U.S. aggression in South Vietnam." The committee had lauded the National Mobilization Committee to End the War in Vietnam. In a message to this U.S. group, the NLF committee had wished it "brilliant success" in its Oct. 16-21 nationwide protests. The NLF message added: "We warmly hail your drive of struggle" to put pressure on the U.S. government to end "its war in Vietnam. We highly value the American people's movement against the U.S. war in Vietnam.")

In a televised press conference Nov. 17 Mr. Johnson said: Hanoi's negative response to U.S. peace offers was "very clear" and had "never changed"; "so all these hopes and dreams and idealistic people [advocating a bombing pause] that go around just mislead and confuse and . . . weaken our position." ". . . I don't think it's unusual for a President to be criticized. . . . The important thing for every man who occupies this place is to search as best he can . . . to find out what's right and then do it without regard to polls or criticism."

Pres. Johnson Nov. 17 assailed the tactics of some critics of his policy on Vietnam. He said at his press conference that "there's a great deal of difference [between] . . . responsible dissent, . . . which we insist on and . . . protect, and storm-trooper bullying or throwing yourself down on the road and smashing windows, and rowdyism, and every time a person attempts to speak, to try to drown him out." "We believe very strongly in preserving the right to differ in this country and the right to dissent," he continued, "and if I have done a good job of anything since I've been President, it's to insure that there are plenty of dissenters. . . . But if I by chance should say, 'now I'm not sure that you saw all the cables on this,' and . . . 'let me explain the other side of it,' I would hope that you wouldn't say I'm lambasting my critics. . . . What I'm trying to do is preserve my right to give the other side. . . . Let's realize that there are 500,000 of our boys out there that are giving their life to win that war. . . . If you think that you can . . . make a contribution to helping them by expressing your opinion and dissenting, then do it. . . . But there's a great deal of difference between responsible dissent and some of the things that are taking place in this country which I consider to be extremely dangerous to our national interest. . . ." The President's remarks were in answer to a question on accusations that he was "trying to label all criticism" of his Vietnam policy "as unpatriotic." He denied the charge. "I haven't called anyone unpatriotic," he declared. ". . . I do think that some people are irresponsible and make untrue statements and ought to be cautious . . . when they're dealing with a problem involving their men at the front." He said: While he did not question the "motives" of dissenters, "I do question their judgment. I can't say that this dissent has contributed much to any victories we have had. . . . We've never said they're unpatriotic, although they say some pretty ugly things about us. . . ."

(Pres. Johnson Nov. 12 had canceled plans to attend the Nov. 13 annual meeting of the National Grange in Syracuse, N.Y. Grange Master Herschel D. Newsom said Nov. 13 that Mr. Johnson had decided not to come to avoid a threatened anti-war demonstration by 2,000 students.)

RFK Calls 'Moral Position' Changed

Sen. Robert F. Kennedy, appearing Nov. 26 on CBS-TV's "Face the Nation," asserted that America's "moral position" in Vietnam had been altered by the Johnson Administration.

Kennedy said: During his brother's Administration "we were making the effort there [in Vietnam] so that people would have their own right to decide their own future, and could select their own form of government. . . . Now we turned, when we found that the South Vietnamese haven't given the support and are not making the effort." "Now, we've changed and we've switched—maybe they [the South Vietnamese] don't want it, but we want it." "We're killing South Vietnamese, we're killing women, we're killing innocent people because we don't want to have the war fought on American soil. . . ." "Do we have that right here in the United States to perform these acts because we want to protect ourselves?" "Now we're saying we're going to fight there so that we don't have to fight in Thailand, so that we don't have to fight on the West Coast of the United States, so that they won't move across the Rockies. Our whole moral position, it seems to me, changes tremendously."

Interviewed on NBC-TV's "Meet the Press" later Nov. 26, Vice Pres. Humphrey, referring to Kennedy's criticism of the South Vietnamese war effort, said that "some of the most courageous fighting of this war has been by some of the units of the South Vietnamese Army." (Speaking in Minneapolis Nov. 17, Humphrey had warned that a "new isolationism" was arising in the U.S. and had alarmed "our friends around the world." "Were we to abandon our role in Asia," he said, Asian leaders "would be under immediate pressure to come to terms with the militant, aggressive Asian communism which they have resisted for 20 years.")

McCarthy Challenges LBJ in Primaries

Sen. Eugene J. McCarthy (Minn.), 51, announced at a press conference in Washington Nov. 30 that he would enter 5 or 6 Democratic Presidential primaries in 1968 to further the campaign for a negotiated settlement of the war in Vietnam. If his effort did not bring about a policy change in this direction by the Administration, he warned, "I think this challenge would have to go all the way to a challenge for the nomination for the Presidency." "I am concerned that the Administration seems to have set no limit to the price which it's willing to pay for a military victory," McCarthy said.

McCarthy had declared Nov. 9 that the time had come for the U.S. to consider "the ultimate question" of whether the war in Vietnam was "morally defensible." Speaking at Macalester College in St. Paul, Minn., McCarthy said "an escalation of objectives—our war aims—has gone along with the escalation of means." "We must raise the essential moral question," he said, "as to whether or not there is a proper balance in what we may gain in what is projected as victory, in contrast with the loss of life, the loss of material goods, the loss of moral integrity and moral energy which goes with the effort. The answer, I think, is that it is not."

Addressing a Boston convention of the College Young Democratic Clubs of America Nov. 11, McCarthy asserted that leading Democrats who opposed Administration policy on Vietnam or other issues "have an obligation to speak out, and party unity is not a sufficient excuse for their silence." He urged the group to guard its right to dissent and "to maintain a continuing moral watch on the policies and programs of the senior party." (The College Young Democrats Nov. 12 approved a resolution condemning the Administration's Vietnam policy as "unsound." However, a move to permit indorsement of Presidential candidates other than Pres. Johnson was defeated. Delegates to the convention of the Young Democratic Clubs of America in Hollywood, Fla. Nov. 18 adopted by voice vote a resolution backing Pres. Johnson's policies in Vietnam but urging consideration of a bombing pause, land reform and negotiation with the Viet Cong.)

McCarthy, speaking in Chicago Nov. 12 before the Assembly for Peace, repeated his contention that "the war is no longer justifiable." (The assembly was made up of 523 union leaders from 38 states; all were in disagreement with the AFL-CIO leadership's support for Administration policy in Vietnam. The assembly called for "an immediate and unconditional end to the bombing of North Vietnam" and "a clear and unambiguous statement" by the U.S. of its "intention to negotiate a settlement of the war with the parties directly involved in the conflict, including the National Liberation Front.")

McCarthy told reporters Dec. 6 that "some kind of coalition government" in Vietnam with the National Liberation Front would result from "an honorable settlement" of the war. "Part of the price you have to be willing to pay," he said, "is a government that is not particularly friendly to us. It doesn't have to be a Communist government, but there'd be Communist influence in it, no question."

McCarthy said Dec. 10 that the U.S. "ought to begin to vacate or not try to control all of South Vietnam." Appearing on the CBS "Face the Nation" program, McCarthy said Administration conditions for negotiation of the war were unrealistic. "Let's open up some areas and see what happens and then press for negotiations," he said. "You let the Viet Cong come in, you see what happens and during that time you try to negotiate."

Senate Resolutions

The Senate Foreign Relations Committee Nov. 16 approved by 14-0 votes a resolution to curb the commitment of U.S. armed forces and a resolution urging the President to take the initiative to have the Vietnamese conflict brought before the UN Security Council. The latter resolution, originally introduced by Senate Democratic leader Mike Mansfield (Mont.), was indorsed by the Administration and was adopted by 80-2 Senate vote Nov. 30.

The "commitments" resolution, introduced by Chrmn. J. W. Fulbright (D., Ark.), was not supported by the Administration. As reported by the committee, the resolution, amended from the original Fulbright version, would apply to future circumstances where the U.S. was "not already involved." It would express the sense of the Senate that in such circumstances "the commitment of the armed forces of the United States to hostilities on foreign territory for any purpose other than to repel an attack on the United States or to protect United States citizens or property properly will result from a decision made in accordance with constitutional processes, which, in addition to appropriate executive action, require affirmative action by Congress specifically intended to give rise to such commitment."

Fulbright's committee said in a report on the "commitments" resolution Nov. 21: While the Constitution vested war power "almost exclusively" in Congress, this authority had been "substantially negated" until the "process of constitutional erosion" reached an "extreme point" in the Tonkin resolution. Although Congress, in approving the Tonkin resolution, had "acquiesced" in the flow of war power from Congress to the President, "the prevailing attitude was not so much that Congress was granting or acknowledging the executive's authority to take certain actions but that it was expressing unity and support for the President in a moment of national crisis and, therefore, that the exact words in which it expressed those sentiments were not of primary importance."

Wheeler Sees Reds Counting on Dissent

In previously secret testimony given Feb. 20 and released by the House Appropriations Committee Mar. 13, Gen. Earle G. Wheeler, chairman of the Joint Chiefs of Staff, had said that the North Vietnamese "don't expect to win a military victory in South Vietnam" but "expect to win a victory in this war right here in Washington, D.C."

In a speech to the Economic Club of Detroit, Wheeler suggested Dec. 18 that American war critics were responsible for preventing an early conclusion of the war. Americans had a right to express opposition to the conflict, Wheeler conceded, "but they also have a responsibility to recognize and acknowledge what their dissent means. The single most important factor prolonging the war is Hanoi's calculation that there is a reasonable possibility of a change in United States policy, before the ultimate collapse of the Viet Cong." (Wheeler asserted that the U.S. was ready to enter into peace talks with the Communists, "but we are not ready to negotiate our defeat or a face-saving withdrawal." Wheeler added: The Communists in Vietnam "can end this war anytime they want to. All they have to do is to knock it off. If negotiations could make it easier for them to cease their aggression, we would be happy to oblige." Wheeler reiterated the Administration stand that the U.S. "is prepared to stop the bombing of North Vietnam, but we must have some assurance that such a stoppage would be promptly followed by productive talks whose objective is peace.")

Sen. George S. McGovern (D., S.D.) Dec. 19 criticized

Wheeler for "blaming Hanoi's refusal to surrender on American critics of United States Vietnam policy." Describing Wheeler's statement as "both irresponsible and irrelevant," McGovern asserted that "the Pentagon and State Department are running out of excuses, so now they are blaming the failure of their policy on those who warned all along that it wouldn't work."

Fulbright Blames Administration for Disorder

Sen. Fulbright, in a Senate speech Dec. 8, blamed the Administration, in part at least, for the increasing disorder in some of the dissent against U.S. policy in Vietnam. The President's critics "dissent . . . because they wish to bring about changes in their government's policies," he said. But pleas for order and responsibility in dissent "are unlikely to be persuasive as long as it is apparent that, no matter what the dissenters say, or how they say it, their views will be ignored. In making the distinction between orderly dissent . . . and disorderly dissent, . . . the Administration seems unable to understand that it is the futility of the one that has given rise to the other." Fulbright criticized State Secy. Rusk for refusing to testify on the war before his committee. "The unwillingness of the Administration to participate in such a dialogue [questioning by committee members] is almost certainly a factor in the angry demonstrations which are taking place with increasing frequency," Fulbright declared.

Fulbright said: Even if the U.S. won in Vietnam, "we would still have fought an immoral and unnecessary war" and "would still be the sole military and economic support of a weak Saigon regime at a cost of perhaps $10 billion or $15 billion a year." "Far from demonstrating America's willingness and ability to save beleaguered governments from Communist insurgencies, all that we are demonstrating in Vietnam is America's willingness to use its B-52s, its napalm and all other ingenious weapons of 'counterinsurgency' to turn a small country into a charnel house"; "far from demonstrating America's readiness to discharge all of its prodigal commitments around the world, the extravagance and cost of Vietnam are more likely to suggest to the world that the American people will be hesitant indeed before permitting their government to plunge into another such costly adventure."

Shoup Vs. U.S. Policy

Gen. David M. Shoup, 63, retired U.S. Marine Corps commandant, asserted Dec. 18 that it was "pure unadulterated poppycock" to believe that an American military presence was necessary in South Vietnam to prevent a Communist invasion of the U.S. In a taped interview with Rep. William F. Ryan (D., N.Y.) over New York radio station WNYC, Shoup held that the war in Vietnam was a civil conflict between "those crooks in Saigon" and Vietnamese nationalists striving for a better life.

In response to Ryan's question as to whether he believed "the vital interests of the United States are at stake in Vietnam," Shoup replied: "I do not." Shoup derided Johnson Administration efforts "to keep the people worried about the Communists crawling up the banks of Pearl Harbor, or crawling up the Palisades or crawling up the beaches of Los Angeles, which of course is a bunch of pure, unadulterated poppycock." The Communists, Shoup asserted, "won't have enough ships in the next X years, or not enough planes to get over" the Pacific to confront the U.S. "I don't know what they're going to get here with," he said.

Shoup urged that Pres. Johnson (a) announce that American military operations would cease when peace talks started and (b) ask Ho Chi Minh to set the time and place for negotiations. The U.S. could achieve a military victory over North Vietnam but only by committing "genocide on that poor little country," Shoup said. The war could only be won through peace talks, he said.

Asian Experts Warn Vs. China

A report issued Dec. 19 by 14 U.S. scholars of Asian affairs said it was necessary for the U.S. to "deter, restrain and counterbalance" Communist China's power in Asia to prevent a major war in the Asian-Pacific region. But, along with "a firm and explicit set of deterrents to extremism," the scholars urged, "we must establish an elaborate structure of inducements to moderation," such as proposals for "exchange, discussion and interaction." The report said limited experimental steps should be taken to de-escalate the war to indicate that "there is no inevitable progression upwards."

The report was prepared at a conference sponsored in Tuxedo, N.Y. by the Freedom House Public Affairs Institute, a nonpartisan, educational organization. Participants included Prof. Robert A. Scalapino of the University of California at Berkeley; Prof. A. Doak Barnett of Columbia University; Executive Director Leo Cherne of the Research Institute of America; Chancellor Harry D. Gideonese of the New School for Social Research; Harvard Prof. Oscar Handlin; Princeton Prof. William W. Lockwood; University of Michigan Prof. Richard L. Park; Guy J. Pauker of the Rand Corp.; Prof. Lucian Pye of the Massachusetts Institute of Technology; Harvard Prof. Edwin O. Reischauer; Brandeis University Prof. I. Milton Sacks; Berkeley Prof. Paul Seabury; University of Wisconsin Prof. Fred Von Der Mehden; Michigan Prof. Robert E. Ward.

Medical Aid to Hanoi

Some opponents of U.S. policy showed their dissent by sending medical aid to North Vietnam.

A private U.S. yacht, the *Phoenix*, carrying 8 American pacifists (6 of them Quakers), arrived in Haiphong, North Vietnam Mar. 28 with $10,000 worth of medical supplies for North Vietnam. The supplies were bought in Hiroshima, Japan. The *Phoenix*' trip was financed by a Quaker group in Philadelphia. The boat was captained by anthropologist Earle L. Reynolds, 56, a Quaker, who lived in Japan and who had participated in demonstrations against nuclear weapons. The trip to North Vietnam was made in defiance of a U.S. rule that banned the travel of Americans to North Vietnam. Dr. Reynolds had said Feb. 24 that Quakers had sent medical aid to South Vietnam. He said that his group had sought to send similar aid to North Vietnam through regular channels but that the U.S. State Department had denied permission.

The Very Rev. Edward E. Swanstrom, auxiliary Roman Catholic bishop of New York and head of Catholic Relief Services, disclosed that the overseas relief agency of the Roman Catholic Church in the U.S. had provided funds for sending medical supplies and hospital equipment to North Vietnam. Writing in the Dec. 2 issue (published Nov. 25) of *Ave Maria,* a national Catholic weekly magazine, Swanstrom said that the contributions had been funneled through Caritas Internationalis, a Vatican relief agency. Swanstrom's statement refuted *Ave Maria* editorials asserting that CRS had refused to cooperate with Caritas in work done in North Vietnam. (A statement issued by Caritas in Rome Dec. 2 denied that it had a direct financial aid program in North Vietnam. Caritas said that the relief it provided was channeled to commercial sources and was distributed by the North Vietnam Red Cross.)

Other Developments

Among other developments involving domestic U.S. opposition to policy in Vietnam:

■ An advertisement in the *N.Y. Times* Mar. 12, signed by 6,766 college and public school teachers, called on the U.S. to end the bombing, declare a cease-fire and act to implement the 1954 Geneva accords. The appeal, sponsored by the Inter-University Committee for Debate on Foreign Policy of Ithaca, N.Y. and the Teachers Committee for Peace in Vietnam (based in N.Y. City), charged that the war continued in Vietnam "because vital facts about its origin and development have been deliberately glossed over, distorted and withheld from the American people."

■ U.S. policy in Vietnam was assailed in a nationwide "teach-in" staged simultaneously May 10 at more than 80 colleges. Harvard economist John Kenneth Galbraith, in a taped message heard on a radio-telephone network at 20 colleges in the East and South, said there were so many Americans opposed to the war that there was "very little chance of shutting them up." Other participants in the program, called "a national day of inquiry," included Prof. Hans Morgenthau at the University of Chicago and Prof. Henry Steele Commager at Amherst College. The teach-in was sponsored by the National Association of Student Presidents & Editors, which had been organized in April.

■ In a major editorial shift, *Life* magazine called in its Oct. 30 issue for a pause in the bombing to create a better climate for peace, "to recapture domestic political and intellectual respect" for the U.S.' Vietnam policy "and to rally more diplomatic and moral support abroad." A *Time* magazine (Dec. 22 issue) editorial said the U.S. should seek a "diplomatic compromise" in Vietnam rather than a "military victory." Negotiations, the editorial said, "could lead to an acceptable end to the war" that could result in these compromises: "a cease-fire policed by a greatly expanded International Control Commission; a withdrawal of North Vietnamese troops in return for recognition of the Viet Cong as a political party; the guarantee of Vietnam as an independent country for 5 or more years, during which time the U.S. would be permitted to keep troops in the country—much fewer than at present but still a substantial force."

■ In a referendum in Cambridge, Mass. Nov. 5, voters defeated a proposal calling for the "prompt return home" of U.S. forces in Vietnam. The results: 57% against, 37% for, 6% of ballots blank.

'War Crimes Tribunal' Condemns U.S.

An "International Tribunal on War Crimes"—created by opponents of U.S. policy in Vietnam — opened sessions in Stockholm May 2 and "convicted" the American armed forces May 10 of atrocities in the Vietnam conflict. British philosopher Bertrand Russell, 94, who had organized the "trial," said in a statement sent from his home in Britain May 2 that the court convened "at an alarming time—the United States is beginning an enormous new onslaught on the people of Vietnam." French philosopher Jean-Paul Sartre served as the court's executive president. The co-chairmen of the tribunal were Yugoslav writer Vladimir Dedijer, Laurent Schwartz, a French mathematician, and British historian Isaac Deutscher. U.S. members were David Dellinger, Carl Oglesby and Cortland Cox (representing Stokely Carmichael). The tribunal, which heard evidence from Europeans who had witnessed U.S. air attacks on non-military targets, handed down a decision accusing the U.S. of aggression and "widespread, deliberate and systematic" bombing of civilian objectives in Vietnam. The court specifically cited the U.S.' alleged use of cluster bombs, whose only purpose, the tribunal claimed, was "to strike civilian populations as hard as possible and which must be regarded as weapons prohibited by laws and customs of war." (During a tribunal hearing in Tokyo Aug. 28-30, the Japanese government was singled out for its involvement in the war. The hearing, sponsored by the leftist Japan Committee for Investigation of U.S. Crimes in Vietnam, charged that the Japanese government "and monopolistic capitalists were guilty of aiding the United States in its war efforts in Vietnam." Dr. Hiroshi Suekawa, president of Ritsumeikan University, presided at the Tokyo hearings.)

The tribunal met again Nov. 20-Dec. 1 in Roskilde, Denmark. After hearing several more witnesses, it handed down

a verdict accusing the U.S. of genocide, of employing forbidden weapons and of mistreating and killing prisoners of
war. The court's finding also held the U.S. responsible for
aggression against Laos and Cambodia and charged that
Japan, Thailand and the Philippines were aiding the U.S. in
its aggression.

SOUTH VIETNAMESE POLITICAL SCENE

The major development in the domestic affairs of war-
torn South Vietnam during 1967 was the September election
victory of Chief of State Nguyen Van Thieu, 44, as president
of the republic and of Premier Nguyen Cao Ky, 37, as vice
president. The elections, held under a new constitution, were
seen as a test of the nation's progress toward responsible
government. Semi-official American election observers reported that South Vietnam had met this test; opposition
candidates and some American newsmen contradicted this
view. Similar differences of opinion surrounded elections for
the Senate (Sept. 3) and the House of Representatives (Oct.
22). Candidates who were openly neutralist or allegedly pro-
Communist were not permitted to run.

Ky on Tour

Premier Ky visited Australia and New Zealand Jan. 18-26
to thank the leaders of both countries for their troop aid in
the war. The tour was marked by violent anti-war demonstrations. The demonstrators were particularly angered at a 1966
statement in which Ky allegedly had expressed admiration for
Hitler.

During his first stop-over, in Sydney, Australia Jan. 18,
the opposition Labor Party staged a protest march and a rally
outside Parliament House and another demonstration in front
of a hotel where Ky was holding a news conference. At the
first event, Labor Party leader Arthur A. Calwell recalled
that he had referred to Ky as a fascist in Dec. 1966. "I repeat
it," Calwell said. "He is a murderer, a little miserable butcher,
a gangster Quisling," a Hitler-lover. At the news conference,
Ky denied that he was pro-Hitler. "I quoted people like
Hitler, like Mustapha Kemal [founder of modern Turkey],
like Sir Winston Churchill. . . . I condemned the policy and
actions of Hitler."

Following a tour of the countryside Jan. 20, the South Vietnamese leader was greeted outside his hotel in Brisbane by a crowd of 700 pro-Ky and anti-Ky demonstrators. The 2 factions fought each other. At a news conference in Sydney Jan. 22, Ky pledged a new constitution soon and free elections.

Ky arrived in Wellington, New Zealand Jan. 23. He encountered a crowd of 350 hooting demonstrators as he received an official welcome. At a news conference later Jan. 23, Ky said: "Only the Vietnamese have the right to decide the destiny of Vietnam. We are not the puppet of the American or any other government." His remark was in response to a Jan. 22 statement in which U.S. Sen. J. W. Fulbright (D., Ark.) had called for Ky's ouster if he refused to negotiate with the Viet Cong.

The worst outbreak of the visit occurred Jan. 24 when Ky arrived at the Auckland airport. Anti-war demonstrators there splattered the official motorcade with eggs and pounded the cars with their fists. The attack occurred after several of the 300 demonstrators had halted the motorcade by throwing themselves in its path. Several rioters were arrested, and the motorcade made its way into downtown Auckland, where Ky was met with a further outbreak. As he stepped from his car to enter his hotel, members of a crowd of about 200 hurled ink at police, booed Ky and shouted, *"Sieg heil,"* the former Nazi cry.

Constitution Adopted, Elections Scheduled

The South Vietnamese Constituent Assembly Mar. 18 unanimously adopted the draft of a new constitution that provided for a democratically elected civilian government. The ruling National Leadership Committee, headed by Chief of State Thieu and Premier Ky, unanimously approved the charter without change Mar. 19. The charter provided for the election of a president and vice president and for a bicameral legislature—a Senate and House of Representatives. Balloting originally was to stretch over an 18-month period, and this would delay the full establishment of a civilian government until late 1968. But it was agreed "in principle" at the Mar. 19 meeting of the cabinet and National Leadership Committee that elections would be held for the presidency and the

Senate at the beginning of September and for the House of Representatives one month later.

The military leaders' approval of the constitution without change had followed a junta warning to the Assembly Mar. 17 that it would have to modify 7 key articles or face the prospect of junta vetoes of some of the charter's provisions. The warning, in a letter from Thieu, declared that if the Assembly overrode junta vetoes by the required ⅔ vote, the military rulers would take more drastic action to prevent "detrimental influences on the stabilization of the situation." Articles opposed by the junta dealt with such items as the dismissal of future cabinets by ¾ Assembly vote, the extension of the Assembly's life after promulgation of the constitution and the election of village chiefs. The final draft of the constitution was said to have represented concessions to the junta. The reported concessions were mainly the provisions dealing with the transition from military rule to elected government.

The new constitution went into effect Apr. 1 after Thieu signed the document.

Local village elections, as provided for in the constitution, started Apr. 2 and continued during the following 4 Sundays. Balloting for legislative Peoples Councils was held in 984 villages with a total population of 5 million, and 2,511,455 South Vietnamese voted. (South Vietnam's 6 autonomous cities, including Saigon, were not involved in the local balloting.) The councils were made up of 6-12 members each. The candidate that received the largest number of votes in each council was automatically made his council's chairman. The council then elected the village chief. (Direct popular balloting for local chiefs in 4,487 hamlets was held May 14-June 11.) U.S. sources reported that the Viet Cong had launched terrorist attacks to disrupt the local elections. The terrorist activity was marked by the killing or abduction of several candidates.

Ky Forced to Back Thieu's Candidacy

Rival claims to the presidency by Ky and Thieu were resolved in favor of Thieu June 30 when the Armed Forces Council forced Ky to accept 2d place on the ticket. Ky had announced May 11 that he would run for president. Speaking at a news conference in Dalat, Ky said he wanted to head the civilian regime in order to carry out the policies of the military leadership. But Ky was reported to have been forced to withdraw as a presidential candidate because of allegations that he had abused his current office to promote his candidacy. Ky had circulated posters and had used broadcasts and newspapers to laud his regime, to campaign widely and to censor a June 14 statement formally announcing Thieu's candidacy for president.

Civilian Candidates Charge Fraud & Pressure

The opening of the election campaign was marked by opposition charges that the military slate headed by Thieu and Ky was deliberately impeding campaign efforts of the 10 civilian presidential candidates and was using fraud and intimidation to promote its own candidacy.

The 10 civilian candidates and the Thieu-Ky slate had been certified for the ballot July 19 by the Constituent Assembly. 7 tickets had been denied approval, among them one headed by retired Gen. Duong Van Minh, potentially the major rival to the Thieu-Ky slate, and one headed by Au Truong Thanh, former economy minister in Ky's cabinet. Gen. Minh, 51, had been forbidden by the Ky government June 28 to return from exile in Bangkok, Thailand on the ground that he was "a security risk." (Minh had headed a military junta after he led the coup that overthrew the late Ngo Dinh Diem in 1963. Minh, overthrown in turn Jan. 30, 1964 by Gen. Nguyen Khanh, was sent abroad and took up residence in Bangkok after the Saigon regime barred his return in May 1965.)

The civilians' charges of harassment erupted Aug. 6 at the start of a scheduled 22-day government-sponsored provincial tour by the civilian nominees. 2 transport planes carrying 18 presidential and vice presidential candidates landed at the Quangtri Province town of Dongha instead of at the city of Quangtri (7 miles to the south), where a crowd of 1,000 persons was awaiting an election rally. The candidates refused a U.S. Army offer of truck transportation to Quangtri. Thieu appealed to the civilian candidates Aug. 8 to resume their campaign. Speaking at a news conference, Thieu said the government had no intention of thwarting the Quangtri rally. He attributed the mix-up at Dongha to "an inadvertent technical error." Thieu offered to arrange another campaign tour. 7 of the civilian presidential candidates declared at a Saigon meeting Aug. 10 that they would not resume their campaign until the government "put an end to harassment." They resumed their campaign Aug. 16, in Bienhoa, after announcing in a statement Aug. 12 that they would renew their election drive if the government provided travel and security arrangements.

Among other campaign statements and related developments:

■ Phan Quang Dan, vice presidential candidate on a slate headed by Phan Khac Suu, Constituent Assembly speaker, had said Aug. 3, the opening day of the presidential campaign, that he favored negotiations to end the war "at all levels, including the Viet Cong." Suu, in apparent disagreement with Dan, said he opposed talks with the Viet Cong but would be ready to "deal with Hanoi."

■ Thieu said Aug. 11 that if he were elected he would seek to arrange a one-week pause in the bombing of North Vietnam in an effort to open peace talks with Hanoi.

■ Presidential candidate Truong Dinh Dzu charged Aug. 14 that Ky had told all regional and provincial military and security chiefs and civil police chiefs, at a gathering in Dalat July 16, "to use all means in their power to bring pressure on the voters." Ky promised "that if they were successful" they would be rewarded, Dzu said.

■ Tran Van Huong said Aug. 18 that many members of the NLF "are true nationalists." Speaking near Saigon, Huong said they were "eagerly awaiting the establishment of a clean and effective government in Saigon to make the life-and-death decision to break away" from the Communist-dominated NLF.

■ Addressing 2,000 union members in Danang Aug. 18, Ky appealed to them to vote for his "policy for the poor" on election day. He denied that he had "committed any act of dishonesty, or corruption." Ky also denied that he had threatened in a statement May 13 to stage a coup if the presidential election results were not to his liking. Ky explained: "I said if it turns out that some bad men get in, then I'm sure the whole people will stand against them. I said it applies to our ticket as well."

■ Thieu Aug. 19 also sought to dispel any idea that the military would oppose the accession of a civilian regime. Thieu said: "The army has no right to plan a coup to disturb a freely and fairly elected civilian president. I don't want the army to interfere in political affairs." Thieu promised to "go back to the army" and serve under a civilian regime if the Thieu-Ky slate were defeated in the presidential elections.

■ Civilian presidential candidate Ha Thuc Ky charged Aug. 21 that 19 of his Dai Viet party members had been arrested by government police during a rally at Thuathien Province Aug. 7.

■ The militant Buddhist faction Aug. 24 accused Thieu of a "Machiavellian" policy to destroy the Buddhist religion. The statement was issued by Thich Lieu Minh, a spokesman for militant Buddhist leader Thich Tri Quang, following a meeting of 53 regional militant delegates. Thich Lieu Minh called for repeal of a new Buddhist church charter under which the government, in July, had recognized Vien Hoa Dao, the rival moderate Buddhist faction, as South Vietnam's national church.

■ In his first appearance with other candidates since the election campaign had started Aug. 3, Thieu Aug. 26 denied opposition charges that he and Ky sought to rig the elections. Speaking to an audience in Mytho in the Mekong delta, Thieu said: "Even if someone tells you to vote for Thieu-Ky, and if you don't like Thieu-Ky, you can vote for anyone you like by secret ballot." Thieu reiterated his peace plan to "stop the bombing [of North Vietnam] for one week as a goodwill gesture" if he were elected. "But if Hanoi does not show its will for peace," Thieu said, "we will prosecute the war."

■ Thieu said in Saigon Aug. 27 that his military government was "ready to meet any [NLF] representatives" if they wanted "to discuss some problem." But he said "we will not invite them."

■ Speaking at his final news conference in Saigon Aug. 29, Tran Van Huong conceded that there had been a reduction in the campaign of "intimidations" against his staff in the previous 2 weeks.

■ Truong Dinh Dzu emphasized his peace plank in a statement issued Aug. 31. Asserting that it was his "duty to end this war and lead this country," Dzu said that if elected he would seek a cessation of the U.S. bombing of North Vietnam. "After that I would propose to Hanoi to stop all infiltration into South Vietnam, and then I would have our government sit down at the conference table."

■ Phan Khac Suu declared Aug. 29 that the major issue of the campaign was whether the South Vietnamese government should continue to be led by military men. "After 20 years of war," he said, "we are afraid of the military and military dictatorship. We need a civilian."

■ In a statement Sept. 2 to election observers of 24 nations, Thieu promised that he would abide by the results of the national elections "no matter what it will be." Thieu said: "During the . . . campaign everyone could see that there was complete freedom of speech and complete freedom for the press to report . . . the statements and sometimes harsh criticisms made by the candidates against the government." (The government later Sept. 2 announced the suppression of 2 Saigon newspapers.) Observers addressed by Thieu included Americans, Australians and Nationalist Chinese appointed by their governments to observe the voting. Other observers invited by the Saigon regime included journalists and public figures from France, Belgium, the Netherlands and other European and Asian nations.

Thieu Elected President

Chief of State Thieu was elected to a 4-year term as president of South Vietnam in the national balloting Sept. 3. Thieu and Premier Ky, his vice presidential running mate, received 1,638,902 votes (35% of the total cast), according to final unofficial results released Sept. 4. Total votes received by the other presidential and vice presidential candidates: Truong Dinh Dzu-Tran Van Chieu 800,285 (17%); Phan Khac Suu-Phan Quang Dan 502,732 (11%); Tran Van Huong-Mai Tho Thuyen 464,638 (10%); Ha Thuc Ky-Nguyen Van Dinh 346,573 (7%); Nguyen Dinh Quat-Tran Cuu Chan 315,329 (7%); Nguyen Van Hiep-Nguyen The Truyen 158,498 (3%); Vu Hong Khanh-Duong Trung Dong 148,652 (3%); Hoang Co Binh-Lieu Quang Khinh 129,429 (3%); Pham Huy Co-Ly Quoc Sinh 106,388 (2%); Tran Van Ly-Huynh Cong Duong 91,887 (2%).

Elections were held simultaneously for a 60-member Senate. Voters chose 6 of 48 slates of 10 candidates each. According to final unofficial results announced by South Vietnam's Supreme Court Sept. 6, 3 slates supported by the Roman Catholic Church won a combined majority of the vote and about 35 seats. The Farmers-Workers-Soldiers ticket, headed by retired Maj. Gen. Tran Van Don, a leader of the coup in which Pres. Ngo Dinh Diem had been assassinated, received the highest number of votes for a single slate—978,137. The votes received by the 3 Catholic groupings: The Lily—599,596; the Bright Star—598,768; the Vietnamese Sun—568,512. The rightwing Revolutionary Dai Viet party received 551,446 votes. A coalition of the Hoa Hao-Cao Dai Buddhist splinter sects got 550,157 votes. (The Central Election Committee had ruled off the ballot 2 Senatorial tickets entered by the rival militant Buddhist group led by Thich Tri Quang.) The Lily party was composed of southern Catholic laymen and headed by Saigon lawyer Nguyen Van Huyen, 53. The Bright Star had the support largely of 600,000 Catholic refugees from North Vietnam and was led by Nguyen Gia Hien, head of the Catholic Greater Union Force, a neo-Fascist youth group. The Vietnamese Sun ticket was led by retired Gen. Huynh Van

Cao, a conservative, who had commanded the IV Corps under Pres. Diem.

Ballots were reportedly cast by 4,868,262 persons. They were 51% of the 8½ million persons of voting age and 83% of the 5,853,384 registered voters. About 2,650,000 persons of voting age did not register, mainly because they lived in Viet Cong-controlled or contested areas. The Viet Cong had launched widespread attacks against civilians and allied military positions in Saigon and elsewhere in South Vietnam in an effort to disrupt the elections. More than 200 civilians were reported killed during the election campaign and on the day of balloting.

Election Frauds Charged

Opposition candidates charged Sept. 4 and 5 that the elections had been rigged in favor of the Thieu-Ky military slate. Phan Khac Suu, a candidate and Constituent Assembly speaker, said Sept. 4 that 7 of the 10 civilian candidates had filed protests on the results of the balloting, which, he claimed, was "fraudulent." Suu, who had carried the cities of Hué and Danang and Thuanthien Province, all in the northern part of the country, charged that in the Thanbinh district just outside Saigon, the district chief had dropped a large number of Thieu-Ky ballots into ballot boxes at the last minute to give the military slate a higher number of votes.

Tran Van Huong's vice presidential running mate, Mai Tho Thuyen, charged Sept. 4 that the government had committed vote irregularities in Saigon in a move to reduce Huong's majority over Thieu. Final returns had shown 129,678 Huong votes in Saigon to 126,456 for Thieu. Truong Dinh Dzu announced Sept. 5 that he would seek to have the Constituent Assembly annul the election results. Dzu charged that ⅔ of Thieu's votes "were obtained by fraud. Without cheating he would have 10% of the vote."

A favorable impression of the election in South Vietnam was reported by 22 prominent Americans who visited Vietnam as election observers at the invitation of Pres. Johnson. Among the 22 were 3 Senators (Edmund Muskie of Maine, Bourke B. Hickenlooper of Iowa, George Murphy of California), several governors and business, religious, press and television officials. The group, which had been in Vietnam Aug. 30-Sept. 4, met with Pres. Johnson at the White House Sept. 6 for a round-table conference at which they generally hailed the elections as fair and democratic. Nearly all of the observers were supporters of Administration policy in Vietnam. Asst. State Secy. William P. Bundy Aug. 11 had presented this "factual information" on 4 controversial points of the campaign: (1) On reports that Ky was threatening a coup if the election results went against the junta, Bundy said Ky had pledged publicly that "if civilian candidates win, we will uphold them." (2) On the flight of the civilian candidates, intended for Quangtri but diverted to Dongha, where there were no crowds and no transportation, Bundy said the diversion was caused by an unfavorable crosswind and there was "no evidence that the difficulties were caused by deliberate action on the part of the government." (3) On reports that the junta planned to set up a committee to rule behind the scenes after the election, Bundy said the U.S. embassy had no information to substantiate the reports. (4) On the disqualification of 2 presidential candidates and 2 slates of senatorial candidates, Bundy said the disqualifications had been effected by the Constituent Assembly under the South Vietnamese constitution. "As things turned out," Bundy said, "there are 11 presidential candidates and 480 senatorial candidates, representing a very broad spectrum of Vietnamese opinion, so that the voters have a wide choice." (Clark Clifford, who had visited Vietnam with Gen. Maxwell D. Taylor on a mission for the President, said Aug. 13 that in "a personal message" they had taken, Mr. Johnson had informed the South Vietnamese leaders "that if there was any one act on their part which would be calculated to alienate the American people, it would be to have a rigged election in South Vietnam." Clifford disclosed this during an appearance with Taylor on the CBS TV-radio program "Face the Nation." Taylor said "all the evidence Mr. Clifford and I saw indicates that the [Saigon] government is insistent on an honest election.")

Demonstrations against the election of Thieu and Ky were held in Saigon, Danang and Hué Sept. 24. The demonstrators, supported by the militant Buddhist faction, charged that the elections had been rigged. They demanded that the Constituent Assembly cancel the results and that the elections for the lower House of Representatives, scheduled for Oct. 22, be postponed. The Saigon demonstration was coupled with an anti-government news conference conducted at the An Quang pagoda by militant Buddhist leader Thich Tri Quang. Tri Quang said his followers had not organized the street protests, "but we support them fully." A statement issued at the conference again assailed Thieu for signing, in July, the decree recognizing the moderate Buddhist faction as the official Buddhist Church and stripping Tri Quang's group of legal status. The statement also assailed the newly-elected 60-member Senate, which included 29 Roman Catholics. The military government, it said, "did not even bother to conceal irregularities and produced a Senate grasped by the ill-famed Can Lao." (Can Lao was the political party of Pres. Ngo Dinh Diem, who had been assassinated in 1963.)

The South Vietnamese Constituent Assembly Oct. 3, by 58-43 vote (1 abstention, 4 irregular ballots), validated the results of the national elections. Assembly Speaker Suu refrained from voting and refused to announce the results. He said: "I am absolutely unwilling to accept the verdict." The Assembly had been in session since Sept. 30 debating whether to legalize the election results. A 19-man subcommittee earlier that day had voted 16-2 (one abstention) to recommend that the Assembly overturn the election on the ground that it was fraudulent and that it order a new one. (Saigon police earlier Oct. 3 had forcibly blocked hundreds of students, representing 5 universities, from marching in protest against the elections. The police had broken up a similar demonstration of 2,000 students outside the Assembly Sept. 30.) In its findings, released Oct. 3, the Assembly conceded 2,724 cases of irregularities affecting 1,444,647 of the 5,853,251 votes cast. But in discarding votes in precincts where these discrepancies had occurred, the Assembly said, Thieu's margin over his nearest rival, Truong Dinh Dzu, has increased (from 832,441 to 988,081) rather than decreased. Among the alleged irregularities cited by the Assembly: illegal removal of ballot boxes from polling places; illegal erasures on district tally sheets; intentional errors in adding election returns.

Defeated Candidate Jailed

The Saigon military regime took punitive action Sept. 15 and 22 against defeated candidate Truong Dinh Dzu and ex-Economy Min. Au Truong Thanh, who had been barred from running for the presidency. The Saigon Criminal Court Sept. 15 convicted Dzu of issuing a bad check and of illegally transferring $11,500 to a bank in the U.S. Dzu was sentenced to terms of 3 and 6 months for the 2 offenses, but he remained free pending appeal. He was also fined $27,711. The charges dated from 1962 and 1966, but court action had been held in abeyance pending the presidential election. Dzu, who did not appear in court, asserted that the conviction "shows that justice is not independent in Vietnam and that the judges received their orders from the government."

Thanh was arrested Sept. 22 on undisclosed charges but was released Sept. 23 after U.S. embassy intervention.

Thieu Sworn in as President

Thieu was inaugurated Oct. 31 as first president of South Vietnam's 2d republic. Premier Ky was sworn in as vice president. Thieu appointed Nguyen Van Loc, 45, president of the Army People's Council and a close associate of Ky, as premier. The inauguration was attended by Vice Pres. Humphrey.* Thieu said his government would be guided by 3

---

* Humphrey visited South Vietnam Oct. 29-Nov. 1, principally to represent the U.S. at the inauguration. In a statement at Saigon airport on his arrival Oct. 29, Humphrey reaffirmed American support for the South Vietnamese government. Addressing Vice Pres.-elect Ky and a welcoming unit of troops, Humphrey said: "I came as witness for those millions of Americans who trust in the steady progress being made in Vietnam as symbolized by this inauguration." After attending the inaugural ceremonies Oct. 31, Humphrey conferred separately with Thieu and Ky. A U.S. embassy briefing on the talks said Humphrey had advised Thieu to press for legislation in the Constituent Assembly during his first month in office. Humphrey toured combat areas Nov. 1, flying to the northern provinces just below the demilitarized zone. He landed at 3 bases, including Danang. Humphrey said in an interview in Washington Nov. 10 that he had informed Pres. Johnson at a Nov. 8 conference that the new South Vietnamese government's biggest problem was to establish control over the commanders of the 4 corps areas. These corps commanders, Humphrey said, were "now like war lords" because they appointed lower officials who were responsible for most of the corruption that existed in South Vietnam.

principles: "democracy building, peace restoration and social improvement." The South Vietnamese people, he said, were determined "to defeat 3 enemies—totalitarianism, war and injustice." Thieu added: "Again I confirm that I will make a direct proposal to the North Vietnamese government to sit down at the conference table in order that the governments of the South and the North can directly seek together ways and means to end the war." Appealing for a more austere standard of living, Thieu urged "all those who are living in well-being and prosperity not to forget our war-torn country, to restrain their luxurious lives and contribute to the relief of the suffering of the people."

During an inauguration reception later Oct. 31 in Saigon's Independence Palace, 3 Viet Cong mortar shells exploded on the lawns of the building. 3 people on the grounds were injured, but none of the 2,000 in the building were hurt.

Thieu Nov. 1 addressed the inaugural session of the new 137-member lower House of Representatives, which had been elected Oct. 22. (4,275,000 persons, 73% of the registered voters, had balloted.) The legislative body included 30 officers and soldiers, 25 civil servants, 12 followers of Thich Tri Quang, militant Buddhist leader, 15 Roman Catholics and about 20 members of the Constituent Assembly, who had been appointed to the house. The newly-elected Senate had convened Oct. 11, and its inaugural session was addressed by Thieu.

Thieu Nov. 9 announced the formation of a new 19-member cabinet. With the exception of 2 new officials, the cabinet was composed entirely of ministers who had served in the previous government. U.S. officials in Saigon expressed disappointment that Thieu had failed to form a government of national unity that would include at least some of the civilian candidates defeated by Thieu in the elections. The new cabinet had 4 military officers, compared with 9 in the previous administration. 3 of them held key posts: Lt. Gen. Linh Quang Vien, who retained the position of interior minister, Lt. Gen. Nguyen Bao Tri, pacification minister (shifted from the post of information minister), and Lt. Gen. Nguyen Van Vy, who was transferred to the position of defense minister from chief of staff.

Buddhist Rebels Convicted

South Vietnam's III Corps Military Field Court announced Dec. 22 that it had convicted and sentenced to 10 years in prison the former mayor of Danang and 3 military officers for participating in the anti-government Buddhist revolt in May 1966. 23 other officers were acquitted of the same charges. The 4 men convicted were Nguyen Van Man, who had been ousted as mayor of Danang shortly after the uprising was suppressed, Col. Dam Quang Yeu, Col. Tran Van Mo and Maj. Tran Huu Trai.

U.S. Aid Rises to $700 Million

An agreement was signed in Saigon Mar. 18 for an additional $150 million worth of U.S. economic aid to South Vietnam. According to Administration officials, this raised the total amount of American assistance to Saigon in 1967 to a record $700 million (1966 total: $550 million). The new aid pact provided South Vietnam with, among other things, a large supply of rice to offset shortages and rising prices. Plans called for sending 750,000 tons of rice in 1967, compared with 400,000 shipped in 1966.

An Agency for International Development (AID) report submitted to Pres. Johnson Jan. 9 had asserted that, despite charges of widespread thievery and corruption, "no more than 5-6% of all economic assistance commodities delivered to Vietnam were stolen or otherwise diverted" in 1966. Citing American measures to prevent the loss of U.S. aid materials, the report said "heightened security efforts are reflected in the fact that port area arrests for improper documentation, trespassing, theft and other offenses rose from a rate of 150 a month in early 1966 to 500 a month by the end of 1966, while reports of major crimes dropped sharply." Despite the diversion of some of the American assistance, the report assured Pres. Johnson that the "vast majority of United States aid commodities provided to bolster South Vietnam's economy and improve its social structure are being put to their intended use."

COMMUNIST AID TO HANOI

Sino-Soviet Pact

U.S. officials in Washington reported Apr. 11 that the Soviet Union and Communist China had reached agreement "in the last 6 weeks" on speeding the shipment of Soviet military supplies to North Vietnam across Chinese territory. The accord was believed to have ended a long-standing dispute in which Moscow had accused Peking of harassing and impeding the flow of Soviet supplies carried to North Vietnam on Chinese railroads. The report said one of the compromise solutions provided for North Vietnam to take title to Soviet military shipments as they reached the Sino-Soviet border. Despite the reported Sino-Soviet agreement on aid to North Vietnam, Communist China declared Apr. 30 that "under no circumstances" would it align itself with Moscow to "take any united action" on the Vietnamese war. A statement appearing in the Chinese Communist Party newspaper *Jenmin Jih Pao* described Soviet leaders as "a pack of rank traitors to the Vietnamese revolution, shameless scabs serving as advisers to U.S. imperialism and No. 1 accomplices to the U.S. gangsters in their efforts to stamp out the flames of the Vietnamese revolutionary war."

USSR & China Continue Aid

It was reported in Moscow May 4 that under an agreement signed in Moscow in March the Soviet Union had agreed to give North Vietnam "hundreds of millions of rubles" worth of Soviet military and economic aid in 1968. Food shipments also were included. Signing for North Vietnam was Premier Pham Van Dong who headed a delegation that included Gen. Vo Nguyen Giap, defense minister. (According to the July issue of the UN Monthly Bulletin of Statistics, the value of Soviet non-military exports to North Vietnam had dropped from $74 million in 1965 to about $67 million in 1966. The value of North Vietnamese exports to the Soviet Union had declined from about $31 million in 1965 to about $25 million in 1966.)

The North Vietnamese Communist Party newspaper *Nhan Dan* reported Aug. 7 that Communist China had signed an agreement to give Hanoi an undisclosed amount of aid in the form of an outright grant. The pact had been signed in Peking by Vice Premier Le Thanh Nghi.

Continued Soviet military and economic assistance to North Vietnam in 1968 was pledged under an agreement signed in Moscow Sept. 23. According to a communiqué on the pact, signed by Deputy Premiers Vladimir N. Novikov of the Soviet Union and Le Thanh Ghi of North Vietnam, the USSR would send Hanoi "aircraft, anti-aircraft and rocket equipment [including ground-to-air missiles, as announced later by Tass], artillery and small arms, ammunition and other military equipment and also auxiliary equipment." The non-military aid would include "means of transportation, oil products, ferrous and nonferrous metals, foodstuffs, chemicals, fertilizer [and] medicines." The communiqué declared that the agreement "reaffirmed the readiness of the Soviet Union, which is true to its internationalist duty, to render all-round assistance" to North Vietnam. The pact provided for outright grants to North Vietnam, for new credit and for trade. The agreement was worked out in about a month of negotiations by the Soviet and North Vietnamese delegations.

Thant Reports Air Aid Pledge

UN Secy. Gen. U Thant Sept. 16 disclosed unconfirmed reports that North Vietnam had been promised foreign air force and other military personnel. According to these reports, he said, "an agreement had been reached between Hanoi and its sympathizers regarding the provision to Hanoi of volunteer technicians, particularly air crews, such as pilots, gunners and engineers." Thant said he was in no position to identify the nation, but diplomatic sources at the UN speculated that Communist China was the nation most likely involved. Thant also said "there were indications that Hanoi is receiving increasing aid, both military and economic, from countries friendly to Hanoi." According to earlier reports from Eastern European missions at the UN, Soviet and Chinese military missions had conferred in Kunming, China on stepping up military assistance to Hanoi.

A U.S. State Department spokesman said Sept. 16 that Washington had known that volunteer North Korean pilots and Chinese Communist engineers were in North Vietnam.

INDEX

Note: This index follows the Western usage in regard to most Vietnamese names. A Vietnamese individual, therefore, would be listed not under his family name but under the last section of his full name. *E.g.,* Pham Van Back would be indexed thus: BACK, Pham Van (not PHAM Van Back). Exceptions are usually the cases of monks or others (*e.g.* Ho Chi Minh) who use adopted names; such persons are generally listed under the first sections of their names (HO Chi Minh, not MINH, Ho Chi).

AMERICAN Anthropological Association—209
AMERICAN Baptist Association —See BAPTISTS
AMERICAN Bar Association— 182
AMERICAN Broadcasting Co. (ABC)—160, 163, 180, 216, 274, 345, 398
AMERICAN Civil Liberties Union (ACLU)—197, 440
AMERICAN Council of Christian Churches—402
AMERICAN Federation of Labor & Congress of Industrial Organizations (AFL-CIO)—446
AMERICAN Friends Service Committee—See QUAKERS
AMERICAN Institute of Public Opinion (Gallup Poll)—210
AMERICAN Jewish Congress (AJC)—198
AMERICAN Legion—191
AMERICAN Newspaper Publishers Association—191
AMERICAN Patriots for Freedom—201
AMERICAN Rabbis, Central Conference of—197
AMERICAN Samoa—See SAMOA, American
AMERICANS for America—209
AMERICANS for Democratic Action (ADA)—185-186, 283, 396-397
AMERICAN Society of Newspaper Editors—398
AMERICANS Want to Know— 125
AMERICAN Writers Against the Vietnam War—200
AMHERST (Mass.) College—206
ANDERSON, Airman Apprentice Craig William—439

ANLAO Valley (South Vietnam) —131
ANLONG Trach (Cambodia)— 123
ANTI-Defamation League—See B'NAI B'rith
ANTI-War Demonstrations (non-U.S.): Australia—65, 454-455. Canada—208. Communist China —109. Denmark—431. Europe— 431. Great Britain—98, 431. India —99. Japan—431. Malaysia—67. New Zealand—455. South Vietnam—202, 214-215, 220, 223, 230-231
ANTI-War Demonstrations (U.S.) —See UNITED States Domestic Controversy; also specific city, state or college
ANTON, Anatole Ben—196
APTHEKER (Kurzweil), Bettina —405
APTHEKER, Dr. Herbert—18
ARDROSSMORE (British freighter)—337
ARENDS, Rep. Leslie C. (R., Ill.)—25
ARGENTINA—36, 292
ARMED Forces (U.S.)—See specific branch of service; 'Armed Forces dissent' under UNITED States Domestic Controversy; subheads under UNITED States Military Involvement
ARMY (U.S.): Court martials— 438-440. Negro casualties—76. Pentagon demonstrations—429. For fighting, see UNITED States Military Involvement
ARROGANCE of Power, The (book)—391
ASHAU Camp (South Vietnam) —131
ASHMORE, Harry—290-292, 315
ASHWORTH, Brig. Gen. Robert L.—141